Shamanic Secrets
for
Spiritual Mastery

SPEAKS OF MANY TRUTHS
AND REVEALS THE MYSTERIES THROUGH
ROBERT SHAPIRO

EXPLORER **RACE**
SHAMANIC SECRETS
SERIES

Other Books by Robert Shapiro

Shamanic Secrets for Spiritual Mastery

Speaks of Many Truths and
Reveals the Mysteries through
Robert Shapiro

**Light Technology
Publishing**

ISBN 1-891824-58-9

Published by

800-450-0985
www.lighttechnology.com

Printed by

PO Box 3540
Flagstaff, AZ 86003

Foreward

Spiritual mastery is almost entirely about heart, and the other books in the *Shamanic Secrets* series are more about functional application. If you understand that spiritual mastery is about heart, then it becomes the easier to accomplish rather than the more difficult, precise—as one approaches it on the basis of fine-tuning. The forms shown in *Shamanic Secrets for Material Mastery* and *Shamanic Secrets for Physical Mastery* require a degree of fine-tuning by each individual. One particular position is not going to be identical for all individuals. That's why individuals need to access the warmth in their own bodies, so when they get their hands or their body positioned in just so a position that appears to come close to matching the photograph, if they do not have the warmth in their body while at the same time putting their hands and body and so on in that particular position, they haven't got it just right.

—Isis through Robert Shapiro
January 17, 2003

Preface

Speaks of Many Truths is an after-death title I was given by my people. I used another name during life. Once I was given this and other titles for others by my people, the boundaries of living and afterlife were affected. When I use this title, I am able to speak to you in your time while remaining in my time, so as to acquire new wisdom in the context of my old life here. It is also this same mechanism that allows me to acquire new wisdom from other beings to pass on to you and through you to people in your time.

In your time this is less understood, though it is still done—such as people who earn and use such titles as doctor or counselor or healer. These titles also change the person and allow him or her to be more of that title, but they do not affect the afterlife. When titles are granted by acknowledging the truth that all people know after death, then that title or those titles affect the memories of those left behind. When that takes place, the combination, to a lesser degree of that and a greater degree of who and what you became after death, is what causes you to become that title.

This is why I often pause before writing Speaks of Many Truths, as it is a title granted to me. I am moved in a loving way, and the feeling is humility.

—Speaks of Many Truths through Robert Shapiro

Contents

Part 1: How to Awaken to Your Natural Self and Live a Benevolent Life

Part 3: The Beauty of Life

THE LIFE OF A CHANNEL

Originally printed in the Sedona Journal of Emergence!, *May 2001.*

I was working in a dead-end job in a large health-maintenance organization in Los Angeles, when I started reading some spiritual material. And you know, when you start reading that, it's not just spiritual; it's also philosophical by its very nature. It makes you question your life, and you start thinking that maybe things can be better, which is good. I think that's the purpose of philosophy. So I was discussing this with people, and of course, everybody I knew was working this same kind of a dead-end job. So I decided that my sister, being an insightful person, would be a good person to ask about this.

The First Catalyst

I flew to her home for a visit, and we went for a walk. On that walk, I told her what was going on for me. I wanted to know, "Is this all there is? Am I just going to work for this outfit for the rest of my life and look forward to my pension?" She, I might add, is an entrepreneur and has her own business. This is how she answered the question, which is typical for her sometimes. She answered obliquely, saying, "I was on a plane the other day, and I was in one of those planes that is a commuter special. It stops here; it picks people up; it drops people off. I got on the plane, and you know how I like conversation and I like to chat with whoever is sitting next to me. I sat down, and the person sitting next to me was reading, so I knew I couldn't have my airplane chat. So I waited quietly and did what I needed to do. At the next stop, he got off, looking very happy, and he handed me the book he was reading, saying, 'Here, I hope you get as much out of this as I did.'" My sister told me that she had read about seventy pages of the book by the time she had to get off and decided that it was interesting but it really wasn't for her. And she said, "Maybe that book is for you." That was her answer to my question.

So she gave me the book. It was an introductory overview as to how Jane Roberts had first made contact with Seth. I was really fascinated by it, but it was a little too clinical for me. Being a sequential type of person who likes to do things one step after another, I found the first book in the series, and I read the Seth material. It was profoundly helpful to me. I mean, no one had ever told me that I could create my own reality. It may seem like an obvious thing to us all now, but no one had told me that before then. So it was a stroke; it was a light bulb. I read those books for quite a while, getting more involved in different spiritual practices, not the least of which—and perhaps the most helpful after that first step—was what I learned at the Body, Mind and Spirit Festival.

I was living in the Los Angeles area at the time, and the Body, Mind and Spirit Festival rolled through town. Well, it was near there, but you know how it is in LA; it seems like it's in town, but you have to drive fifty miles. Anyway, I went to it, and I walked all around and everything looked interesting but nothing really grabbed me until I saw this lady in a very remote location. There was hardly anybody hanging around her, so I asked her what she did. She described the Inner Guide Meditation, which would allow a person to have an inner dialogue with a being within himself. She said that this being would be your guide, and the guide would never lie to you as long as you were introduced to the proper guide in the proper way.

I thought, "Well, this is great. This is just what I need." When I had first started reading the Seth books, I had thought, "Man, I'd love to be able to do something like this," but without any sensation of ever being able to possibly do it, because Jane Roberts described it by saying, "I **was** walking down the street one day and *bam!*" meaning there was no setup. It was like it just happened.

Anyway, I had let that go completely. So here's a lady telling me that I can have a conversation in my mind through a creative visualization process with a being like this. I thought, "This is awesome." So I went for it, and it was very helpful. It was my first interaction with such a creative visualization process. That step was the second most important step, because it led to something else. That lady also believed that it was then useful to interact with that guide and reach out to your most recent spiritual past life, which I did. And this was the third most important step, because it set up within me the realization that I had a spiritual past life and now, using this creative visualization process, I could actually communicate with that life. That life gave me a lot of teaching. Eventually, over the years—because it all didn't happen overnight—that being, my past life, introduced me to his teacher. And that teacher is Speaks of Many Truths.

Meeting Bear Claw, a Past Life

My name in the past life was Bear Claw, whom I have, on rare occasions, channeled for the public. But in those days, with that process, it wasn't really channeling. It was using this other system called the Inner Guide Meditation, which was put together by a guy named Edwin Steinbrecher—who, by the way, does not believe in channeling whatsoever. That's okay; I don't require that he does. It was still helpful. Someone may not believe in peanut butter sandwiches but can make excellent bread.

In the beginning, when I first was able to channel in some way—meaning practicing—the practicing really got started by these communications with the Inner Guide Meditations, which were all supposed to happen. You'd visualize it; you'd hear the conversation. Then after the visualization, you'd write down everything you could remember. So I was working with a friend. At that time, I was going to hear another man channel and I met some people there, Sara and Sherman, who were very helpful to me. I did know that Sara was a schoolteacher, but what I didn't know at the time and what Sara didn't tell me was that she had worked with a lot of channels. So she knew what she was doing, and she really was a huge help to me.

Sara told me that the Inner Guide Meditation was useful to me, but now that I was communicating with Bear Claw, it would be better for me to ask my questions to Bear Claw out loud on tape instead of writing the question down, then connecting in my mind to Bear Claw and repeating what he was saying onto the tape. It's pretty smart if you think about it, because what she was doing was helping me to condition myself to speaking out loud that which was coming from the spirit world.

There's a visual picture that goes with this. I'm trying to put what happened into words, which are a poor substitute. When I would have these conversations in the beginning, I'd ask the question and then I'd have to really focus absolutely on what Bear Claw was saying, paying more attention to what he was saying than what I might normally give so that I could hear him talk and speak what he was saying shortly after he said it. If you've ever done that as an exercise in communication, for instance, just try to have somebody talk to you, saying something reasonable (not shocking), and while they are talking to you, repeat in your language—not translation—exactly what they are saying. It's not easy. Anyway, it required a lot of concentration, but that was good. In the beginning, one of the most important things a channel can do is to learn how to develop absolute focus and just focus on one thing.

So what would happen in the beginning is that I would be speaking, repeating what Bear Claw was saying, and gradually instead of waiting to hear him say the words to the end of the sentence, I would be speaking what he was saying within a word or two after his saying it. And eventually, over quite a bit of time, I'd be speaking when he was actually saying it, which is a form of channeling, but I didn't know it at the time. However,

I was given evidence, physical evidence, that it was a form of channeling: Once I got to the point where I could speak what I was hearing in my mind onto the tape, I could no longer shift gears to ask questions mentally because I had shifted into that altered state and place. I've never actually been able to explain this before, so this is important.

The Next Catalyst

That step was really useful. I would have to go into that state every time to receive an answer and then come back out of it so I could ask another question. This was about the time I realized I needed assistance; I needed somebody else to ask questions. And fortunately, either Sara or Sherman would sometimes be available to ask questions that were not challenging. Then right around that time, the channel I was going to for these classes in channeling started doing public channeling. He was doing an amazing thing to get our attention in class on ETs and UFOs, whom I admire him for channeling even to this day.

The focus toward ETs and UFOs was very helpful to me, because after Bear Claw, a lot of the beings I was attracted to channeling were ETs. My experience with the Inner Guide Meditation and learning the form of channeling that Sara helped me to do was useful, but the next big thing was taking these channeling classes with this guy. It wasn't so much what he was channeling, but at one point, he had different people come up and sit next to him, and he'd tell them to try to channel. Of course, you'd be in front of all these people, and it would be like sweating bullets—you could hardly do it. But then he did something with me and a couple of other people.

I was sitting on his right, or more importantly, he was on my left—that kind of stuff comes in on the left. So here I am sitting next to him, embarrassed and nervous. Everybody in the group knew I was practicing channeling, and they were wondering why I couldn't do it. And so he reaches over, and the being says through him, "It's all right," as he puts two fingers and a thumb on my hand. Suddenly, from one split second to another, I was boiling hot and sweating profusely. It was the energy. Even though it was just a few words, I was able to channel at a deeper level than I had been channeling before. The progress I made in my channeling after that experience really accelerated. And this is a neat thing, because people have had this experience from my channeling too, but this is my experience of it in the early days.

Even so, I knew that my channeling wasn't 100 percent accurate, and I'd get regular readings with this guy in order to find out when I could count on it being 100 percent accurate. But in the interim, while I was learning, I was experimenting with channeling every day. I was working a job at the health-maintenance organization, but every day, usually late at night, 2 A.M. in the morning, I was doing channeling practice—I was totally devoted. This went on for years.

Even at that point, it didn't occur to me that I was going to do this professionally. I just thought this was something I wanted to do, and it was fascinating. Anybody who begins to channel or anybody who has ever channeled out there, when you look back at that material years later, it kind of makes you laugh. If you feel good about yourself, it makes you laugh in a sort of loving, amused way, because you remember how excited you were, and you look back at it and say, "Well, so what?" But it is exciting in the beginning.

The Importance of Practicing

What happens is that the first bulk of the material brought through just sounds like stuff you've read, and you don't feel that you're really doing it. But it's like running water through a pipe that you've just laid to drain water from a house. You run the water through the pipe in order to clear the pipe out before you start running whatever it is you actually want to run through the pipe. It's like you're clearing out the channel.

I was listening to the tapes. I was told to tape everything, and I do recommend that channels, when they are first starting, tape everything and keep the tapes. Don't tape over the tapes. Keep everything. If you use a tape for a session and you have half a tape left, don't use the tape over again, use a fresh tape; otherwise, you lose sessions. What happens is, you get in deeper and you channel deeper and deeper. If you come out and flip the tape over, you'll forget and tape right over something else.

Anyway, as I was doing this deeper and deeper, I began to get more confident, and the way you get confident is that you listen back to the tape and hear yourself channeling something that you have no knowledge of whatsoever, and when you listen to it, you say, "That's entirely new! That's awesome! I didn't know anything about that!" And this is so exciting while at the same time being uplifting! It gives you confidence that what you are doing is actually relevant and you're not just parroting something back that you read or heard. Those steps are vital in terms of learning how to trance channel. I grant that the trance process is different. I feel that it is a little easier to learn how to conscious channel. But trance channeling, in my experience, allows a person to go deeper.

The difference is that conscious channeling, to me, is a step on the way toward learning how to trance channel. In trance channeling, you have to not only allow an energy to come through but also the personality of the beings. And the physical difference is that you step out of your body and somebody else steps in. So you gain more confidence in doing this kind of channeling; it's a process of one day at a time. If I hadn't been working at a full-time job, I might have been able to do it quicker.

Watching for UFOs

I was then getting interested in ETs, and there were a couple of guys in the channeling class who were also interested in them. I could no longer ask questions on my own, as I was making a better connection and couldn't jump in and out of trance. I was moving past a point of being able to consciously, mentally, ask a question and then get an answer, since I had already moved past the point of conscious channeling.

These two guys and I knew of a spot where we could go out and watch for UFOs, and we went out there all the time. These guys were both independent at that time, so they could go out any time, and they would sometimes do that, but I could only go out on the weekends. We'd go out every weekend without fail, and we'd go to a particular spot out in the desert around 11:00 at night. We'd bring all our supplies. It wasn't too far from places where people lived, but the particular spot was remote. And we'd be there from about 11:00 at night till about 3:00 in the morning. Of course, in the beginning, we were there for much longer, but that's when we saw as much UFO activity as we did. When we'd get the feeling that UFOs were around or we'd see something, I'd start to channel. One guy brought all the equipment and would record everything. Another thing we did that channels can do is that if you find there's a place where you feel better about channeling, do your channeling there.

Vital Steps to Build Trust

When you first start, when people ask questions, tell them not to ask personal questions. That's not okay in the beginning when you are first learning how to channel because you go through and you're still there somewhat, and if somebody asks some gut-busting question—which is what I used to call it—you go through flip-flops. You're desperately worried as a human being that you might say something to that person that would be wrong, while at the same time you know that the being who is channeling through you is trying to gently get you out of the way.

It takes time to develop confidence in the connection with whatever being you are channeling to learn to trust that (1) they will treat your body right, (2) they'll take the questions that people ask seriously, (3) they will answer the question to the best of their knowledge, wisdom and ability, (4) it's okay with the other person hearing that, and (5) if you have personal integrity, which I feel I do, you can get out of the way and it's all right. These are all important steps. They are vital steps, and I haven't spoken about this before. So it's coming up now, and I'm assuming it's important.

My Communications with Bear Claw

As for Bear Claw, my past life, he's existing in another time, space or dimension; he's in existence. Normally, when people die, they go on and do other things, but certain individuals for various reasons might choose to remain accessible, meaning that they still have a connection with who they were in that life. In the cases of Bear Claw and Speaks of Many Truths, I might add, they were both shamans in those lives. And when those lives were over, they wanted to be able to communicate on a spiritual level from the focus of what they had learned in their culture because they felt that this was an important part of their being.

So when Bear Claw would talk to me, he would always be talking to me from his life, meaning about four hundred and some years ago. And he'd speak to me with the wisdom of his Earth experience while being able to access spiritual wisdom to some extent. Speaks of Many Truths does that in a more flexible way, meaning he could do more along those lines, but he still chooses to speak to me from that point of view. Even though in spirit form, outside of the context of each of their respective lives, they could communicate beyond that from their greater selves, they prefer to communicate in this way. So I'm drawing a fine point here, because in my experience channeling beings, they will sometimes choose to communicate from a particular state of their being, which we can say is another dimension, another life. But I feel this whole thing about past lives is more of a focus of personality rather than an actual rigid happening.

I'm going to have to take up the issue of whether one soul was in Bear Claw and me outside of the context of soul. Soul is a religious term, and the reader might take it that way. Zoosh refers to the soul as the immortal personality, which I like. So my personality, which had gone as far as it had and done as much as it had before as Bear Claw, was there. Since then I've done other things and I've been other places, and now I'm here.

I don't really channel Bear Claw anymore; that was kind of like a training phenomenon, but I can still connect with him. He gave me roughly three hundred hours of material on tape, not counting what I wrote down before that—and that was pads and pads and pads of paper. Anyway, he gave me all of this material, much of it teachings that he had received in his lifetime through Speaks of Many Truths and other teachers he had. And he was just talking about different things he knew and understood, sometimes in response to a question I might have.

So I'd have to say, from this perspective, that given the process by which I was introduced to this being as my most recent spiritual past life, I believe, yes, that that was me there. However, I do not feel a sense of personal—as who I am now—identification with Bear Claw as an individual. I don't feel a sense of personal ownership in that sense. Not that you don't own a life, but I don't feel a sense of owning that experience—how you might remember how you learned to ride a bicycle as a kid and other experiences you had. Bear Claw doesn't feel like that to me. Learning to ride a bicycle is an experience you could own and say that's something you did. I don't have that same feeling about Bear Claw's experiences.

Lessons in Personal Growth

In my experience, these connections to past lives can be wonderful if they have something to offer to you in a way that is helpful. For me, Bear Claw had a lot to offer since he is a trained shaman and has a great deal of cultural and spiritual wisdom to pass on. You cannot do spiritual practice like this and learn how to become a channel without immediately engaging in personal growth; you just can't help it. Now, I grant that you don't have to be conscious or spiritual or channeling or all this kind of stuff to be involved in growth. I mean, we're all involved in it here on Earth, no matter what we think or what we hold dear. However, once you engage in a process like this, in my experience, you really grab on to personal growth and start working on it consciously. At least for me, it was that way because I was trying to achieve something that required me to become more of a being to do it. So I had to grow.

I think once you do that, you open up a lot of avenues. For one, you start asking questions you've never asked before, some of which have ready answers and others that I'm now just asking spirit beings whom I'm channeling myself. But still at that time, I was going to others who were doing channeling and having them channel things to me or talking it over with other friends who had knowledge or wisdom in general. In short, I was acquiring knowledge and wisdom to apply to my life where it fit and learning how, with discernment, to let go of what didn't fit in my life without judging what I wasn't letting go of.

Regardless of how so-called spiritual you are or if you are just living a regular life, it is very easy to hear something that doesn't feel right to you at all. And your natural response might be, "Wrong," because it doesn't fit into your life. This doesn't mean it's wrong; it just means that it's not for you. Now, it took me awhile to realize that. And that's another one of the lessons involved in personal growth. I think we all go through that or many of us go through that in life; just because something isn't right for me, the fact that I haven't chosen certain paths in this life, doesn't mean it isn't right for other people. This is the way I see it these days—with a little humor. Somebody might tell me that she is doing something and be very enthusiastic about it. If she is a friend, I might say to her, "Well, I'm glad you're doing this, and I'm glad you like it so much because then I don't have to."

Channeling Zoosh

I can describe Zoosh in one word, and that is *more*. Zoosh is more. I think the reason I'm describing him that way is because Zoosh has bent over backward over the years since he's been channeling through me to avoid being deified. Zoosh used to like to say (and would say all the time when people would ask him who he was), "I am exactly what you are, but I remember who I am." And I used to like when he would say that because it would shock people. Of course, they had been listening to Zoosh for a while, and they thought he was the greatest thing since sliced bread. But he would say that, and it would rock them back on their heels. They might think less of Zoosh for a short time, but the whole purpose of it was that they might think more of themselves.

I think it's necessary to have an editorial policy as a channel—not that you censor what beings are saying through you but that you're interested in certain kinds of things. My policy is—and it's very broad—that I'm interested in having beings channel things through me that will make our lives easier, more simple, and allow us all to have better lives here on Earth in some way. That's my general editorial policy. So if you look at it broadly, you could say that that covers just about everything, but it does actually exclude a few things.

I haven't ever really gotten into any channeling that I would describe as negative. I do know other channels who have gotten into that, and it's not because they are bad; it's because they don't have the discernment or they don't have the knowledge that they can have the hand on the lever (I always see it like a lever on a steam shovel). If it doesn't feel good as it's passing through you, if it feels uncomfortable physically—even if you are in a completely altered state, you do have some awareness if your physical body is uncomfortable—then you can move the lever and say, "Thank you very much," to that entity and go on to the next one.

I think this is something I learned early on in my spiritual studies. I'm pretty sure this was a lesson in discernment, which I can relate right back to childhood, of learning who is a good friend for you and who is not. Someone might be a good friend to somebody else but not the right friend for you. I also credit the Inner Guide Meditation, which would teach discernment so you would know how to find your guide and the difference between your guide and a false guide. Those lessons were all very helpful, and I would use those same lessons to discern which being to channel through me. That was very important in the early days, because I learned how to channel by channeling a variety of beings, unlike some channels who learn how to channel by channeling only specific beings or sometimes only one being. I learned on the multiple level from the get-go, which is probably why to this day I am able to channel anyone or anything with whom I feel compatible.

I'd say that Zoosh is an immortal personality who has been with us, the Explorer Race, since before we became the Explorer Race. He's seen the creation of this universe, and he's existed before that. He has vast knowledge and wisdom, and has the ability to deliver communications through me to others in a knowledgeable, interesting and sometimes, when called for, humorous way that many people find intriguing, interesting, occasionally amusing and often stimulating (so they tell me). I like Zoosh; I think he's a lot of fun. But he's not always easy to channel because Zoosh is vigorous, a stimulating being, and I have to be reasonably refreshed to channel him. Some beings, as other trance channels know, are easier to channel than others. It's a little harder for me to channel Zoosh because I need to be more personally physically refreshed or have more energy physically, whereas other beings are gentler on my body and easier to channel. However, I've been willing to make the personal investment physically to channel Zoosh because of the profound nature of the wisdom he's chosen to pass through. So you have to recognize that there's a cost; there's a price in trance channeling that I haven't noticed with my friends who are conscious channels.

Conscious versus Trance Channeling

For instance, I know a conscious channel, Gwen Ellen Nordquist, who has done a lot of travel globally. We were out of touch until recently, but we used to talk a lot. She used to tell me that she could channel for hours and hours at a time, and I've talked to other conscious channels who say the same thing. I've noticed that even in the early days when I had a lot more physical energy and was obviously younger and more vital and so on, that at the very most, I was able to channel for four hours. I know other trance channels who are able to channel much longer, but I've never been able to channel for more than that. In recent years, I can't even channel that long. When Melody Swanson [the publisher of the *Sedona Journal of Emergence!* and Light Technology Publishing] and I do a book session now, it's usually an hour to an hour and a half. We used to do book sessions that would go as long as two hours, occasionally a little longer, but that is a rare thing these days. It's not because the connection isn't any good; it's because I don't have as much physical energy anymore.

Conscious channeling does not drain your own personal physical energy very much, whereas trance channeling utilizes your personal physical energy somewhat. I'll give you an example: When I used to go in the early days to hear that other fellow channel, there would be thirty people in the room, and everybody who was the least bit receptive would be blasted by the energy. We'd all really feel it. And the guy was able to allow the maximum personality of this being to come through, so he would look physically different. He would allow that being to make gestures, allow that being to be in his body and use his body while he was elsewhere.

When he would come out of that channeling, he'd be very quiet. We were told that we weren't supposed to talk to him right away because he needed to ease back in, and it would take him awhile to do so. And then after that, he would need to do something that would allow him to become more physical. He didn't put it to us that way, but I realize now, as a result of becoming a channel like that, what was necessary for him to do; I also used to do this in the beginning years. He would gradually, slowly and in the same way every time pack up his recording equipment, which allowed him to do something physical and repetitive to ease back into physical life. The very next thing he needed to do—and I went with him a couple times when he did this—was to get in his car and drive down to the Bob's Big Boy as fast as he could get there legally and eat two big hamburgers. It was the only thing he could consume that would not only give him the energy he needed to replenish his strength—and meat will do that for you—but also ground him very quickly so that he would then have a physical life. This guy, I might add, was one of the skinniest guys I had ever met!

Now, I won't say his name, although he's an outstanding channel—and he may have changed his position on this—because years ago he was shy about my publicizing his work. I don't know why, but he was. I'd love to give him publicity. I used to talk about him, but this is for the public record. I'll just say that he's an outstanding channel.

People ask me if I remember what was channeled. Fortunately, I've had an opportunity to try on different answers to that question over the years, and it took me awhile to get the best answer that would help. And this is what it's like: If you've ever stood in a stream that's running (or for that matter, been in the shower and the water's running on your body, but it's different when you stand in a stream that's running), you are conscious of the water as it touches your feet and ankles as it runs by. But you're conscious of it as a constant. You're not conscious of individual portions of the water touching your feet and legs, and then aware of those portions as they go by. So I'd say it's like a constant that you are aware of. It's being in a stream while something is flowing by that you are neither directing nor controlling. You are aware of the flow, but you are not controlling it, nor are you attached to the outcome or attempting to regulate it. It's a lot like that.

Where Do I Go?

People also ask if I am consciously hearing the words or if I have gone somewhere else when I'm channeling. People used to ask me this all the time: "Where do you go?" And I have to say that as a channel, it is very easy to be intimidated by the most reasonable and innocent questions. In the early days, these questions all intimidated me because I didn't know what to say. I wasn't in contact with other channels very much. Once I started doing it on my own, I didn't know anybody else who was channeling, and I couldn't communicate, for various reasons, with that guy I'd been going to hear channel. I tried to establish a social relationship with other channels, but I wasn't able to do it. So I didn't have anybody to advise me. That's part of the reason why when other channels ask me to help them these days, I usually try to help, because I know what it's like.

When people would ask those kinds of questions, I didn't know what to say. And very often, the people who were asking the questions were attached to what I was going to say, and I felt that they were essentially grading me by my response. If I said this, they would react negatively; if I said that, they might react positively. And I may or may not know that, so it was very intimidating. I'm mentioning this because for all of you channels out there who are either starting to trance channel or even conscious channel, try to be yourselves and answer the questions honestly, but know that if you are in even a slightly altered receptive state, it's better to wait. If you've just gotten done channeling, you'll be in an altered receptive state. Somebody can ask you a question and you'll give your answer, whatever it might be. But if their response—which they might give in any conversation they are having with anybody—isn't positive or gentle, it can hurt you; it will feel just like someone punched you in the stomach. I have to warn you of these things because there are prices to pay.

This is why some channels have "buffers," people who pass questions between the audience and the channel. Buffers know that when they are asking these kinds of questions of the channel after he comes out, the channel needs to be talked to in a very gentle, soothing manner because he is wide open. You can't channel like this without being wide open. And when you come out and you communicate with people again, you tend to still be rather wide open and vulnerable. While those answers might be very clear because you've just gotten done channeling and still have a foot in both worlds, you are also profoundly susceptible to the response of the other beings. So I just want to say to those of you who have talked to channels after they've come out, try to be gentle and don't expect them to answer right away.

Now, where do I go when I channel? I give this long roundabout answer because in the beginning I would have a sensation of going somewhere and I could describe that. I might see scenery, almost as if I were flying somewhere, and I'd describe it a little bit. But then after a while, I didn't have that to report. I felt intimidated by the question, and I didn't know how to respond. By the time I'd gone professional years later, a neat thing happened. So now when people ask me that question, I respond with this story, which is the response of an eyewitness. It's a lovely story, and I'm going to repeat it here.

When I was living for a while in Durango, Colorado (one of my favorite places), once a month I used to drive up through Red Mountain Pass to Grand Junction and do a monthly session there for some people who had been organized by one person in particular, whose name is Zandrion. He organized this session, and I'd go there and do it. I was doing a session at this lady's store one night after it closed. A young woman, among others, came to the session, and she brought her little boy with her. Occasionally, people would do that because they couldn't get anybody to take care of their kids. Usually, it was never a problem. I mean, if they were little kids, they would play or do something quietly. They were always well-behaved. Very often, they would go to sleep because the energy would affect them. It would nurture them to sleep, and they would just snooze through the whole thing. I don't know what happened in this session, but I'm pretty sure this little guy didn't go to sleep. He was maybe eight or nine years old—that was my best guess. And of course, this being a small town, he wasn't like a hip eight- or nine-year-old. He was a small-town eight- or nine-year-old kid.

We were all sitting in a circle, and when the session was over, I came out of the trance. When people felt like it was okay to get up and say or do anything, half the people got up and went over to this little boy (he was still sitting next to his mom) and asked, "What did you see?" I had no idea he could see anything other than what everybody else saw. But this is what he said in his little kid voice: "Well, first the one man was talking," meaning me—I was talking to people before I did the channeling. And he said, "Then his lightbody got up and took two steps to the right and one step back. Then the purple man appeared. And the purple man sat down in the man's body and he talked for a while. When the purple man was done, he got up and took one step to the left and disappeared. Then the man's lightbody got back in."

Now, this was a little boy, and it turned out that he could see—he was born with the ability to see. And his mom was enlightened. Her attitude was, "Well, if he can see, that's great." She never discouraged him, never told him it was his imagination and that he could disregard it. So he was able to see and describe these things. Now, I don't know if he still can. I don't even know his name. But I've told this story many times, because when people ask me where I go, I can give them this eyewitness report.

Avoiding Outside Influences

I don't read other channeled material, because I'm trying to avoid being affected. This is so important. I know other channels, even trance channels, even people whom I feel are really making a profound contribution, who read other channeling and do this kind of stuff, and I have seen how they are affected. Although it's not a terrible effect, my goal is to bring through new material. I grant that it isn't always new, I'm sure. But if it's new for our time and presented in a profound, enlightening and useful way, that's what I want to do. So it's not only that I avoid reading other people's channeling, I'll also avoid reading things that I know I'm going to be asked about.

Before I got into channeling as a regular thing, one of the things I really liked doing when I was reading spiritual books was reading about UFO and ET contactees and their experiences. I've had experiences myself, so I found it fascinating to read about that stuff. I remember a few years ago, I had a few extra bucks at the time and thought, "Well, I know what I want to do." I was in touch with Wendelle Stevens—I think we had given a presentation at the same time at the same place, and it reminded me that I wanted to get all his books and read them. I thought, "I can do it now. I've got the money. I'm going to buy all his books." So I bought all of Wendelle's books, the whole set of everything that was in print at that time. And when I went to look at those books, I realized, "I can't read these books; this is the kind of stuff I'm channeling about." I hadn't even channeled the first book in the *Ultimate UFO* series at that time. My first feeling was disappointment. Then I burst out laughing, thinking, "This is a desire based on something I used to want to do, but I have to let it go." I did give myself a gift, though. I went through the books, and I looked at all the pictures. Then I passed the books on to somebody else.

I've been trying to record these memories. My publisher wanted me to do an autobiography, so I've been putting on tape as many of the stories and events of my life as I can remember. Let me finish on this note. Channeling is a calling; yes, it's a service too, but it's a calling for me. Some of you as you read this—and perhaps having read some of my work—might feel the way I did when I first read Jane Roberts' experience of meeting Seth. And that's that. Know that if you have that feeling, you've already begun and you'll find your way in your own time. And even if that's not a goal for you, I hope you enjoyed my recollections. Good life to you all.

Overview

Loving Magic from Creator

Speaks of Many Truths
September 8, 2000

[From a public session in Hawaii.]

All right, this is Speaks of Many Truths. I am a Native American mystical man alive in my own time, about 420 years ago from your time. Let me describe to you where I am, so you can get a picture of it. I am embodied, though in fact, as you can tell, I am in spirit. But I choose to speak to you from the time when I was alive. I'll tell you why: It is in the nature of spirit, when they speak to you, to have to make an effort to make it relevant. You have all heard, from time to time, spirits speak who say wonderful things and give wonderful energy, but who do not always have the means to ground what they're saying understandably.

So it is my intention to speak to you in a way that allows my connection with the human being. This way I hope to not ask you to do something that is not realistic. Do not take this as a criticism, but if any of you out there are channeling or perhaps have just started, whoever you channel, also try to channel, for practice, trees, plants, rocks. I'm not speaking to you professionals out there, but to those of you who have just started, and there are a few. Try to connect also with earth spirits, even if you have them connected to your regular spirits. This can be nurturing, and I will explain why in detail later.

Now, all human beings know that there are times when it is safe to be in your heart and there are other times when it does not feel safe. One sometimes is in spirit at these times; other times one simply withdraws and uses a shield of some sort to protect yourself. I understand that very well. But what I feel is of value is to have another means to offer you protection that can do no harm to others and that can nurture and support you as well. That is why tonight I want to talk about and show at least some of you a very simple exercise that can literally change your life. Some people might say it's a mystical or a shamanic thing to do, but I like to think of it as something that is practical, useful and, most of all, simple.

It's Your Body's Job to Teach Your Mind

In ancient times, all people on Earth did this because they had been instructed how to live. In your modern times, where there are so many distractions—some pleasant, some not so pleasant—this has been, sometimes for some people, forgotten. And because the threads of ancient civilizations are not as entrenched in the modern times in which you live, much wisdom and knowledge has been lost. So tonight let's do something that is ancient in its nature, that is practical. The animals do it, the plants do it, Mother Earth does it, and since you are made up at least partly of Mother Earth's body, it won't be hard for you to do it either. Don't feel funny if you cannot do it tonight; practice, and you will be able to do it someday.

I'd like you to take your hands and put your fingertips together—feet flat on the ground and no crossing of your legs or arms. I assure you, you will be safe; I am not going to thrust anything upon you that would be anything else. Now, very gently rub the tips of your fingers together—do that for a moment. Do you notice when you do that how it brings your physical attention to that area? Your fingertips are very sensitive.

This tells you that this thing we're going to do is not particularly mental; it is only spiritual insofar as you're being guided to do it, although once you achieve it, it is profoundly spiritual. It also intends to create a wedding or a bond that is the ultimate purpose of you being here on Earth, which is to be able to constantly, easily, in a practical fashion, unite spirit with the Earth human. Of course, you are always united with spirit, but this is intended to give you that union in the physical sense and to provide you with that wonderful physical thing for which you were set up by Creator to look for in order to be able to appreciate the value of something.

Many things are of value that can be appreciated in other ways, but you were intended to look for physical evidence in order to be able to feel the value of something as well. You've all been told for some time now that this is a feminine-energy time, and yet what we're doing tonight will bond the feminine with the masculine, spirit and Earth, feelings and ultimately (though that is not the objective) . . . ultimately thoughts will be involved, in time.

It is your body's job to teach your mind, not the other way around. Your body is made up of Mother Earth, and she is a spiritual master, a physical master, a teaching master, a dimensional master, and she is also a master of consequences. You are made up in large part of Mother Earth's body; you are here to learn about all those things, to bring them together, so that someday when you all join to become a creator in your own right, you will know about these things. Earth, even though sometimes you cannot picture it this way, is really a creator school—"Creator Training 101." Because of its capacity to constantly show you your responsibility by presenting to you consequences of what you do (sometimes good, sometimes not so good) and also consequences of what others do [chuckles] (sometimes good, sometimes not so good), you come here to learn. Creators must know that everything they do—everything—will have consequences, and they must have the capacity to benevolently work with those consequences forever.

Feeling the Heat

So now we've warmed up the fingertips for quite a while, haven't we? I want you to understand that what you're going to be doing now may or may not involve your fingertips, but you've all become aware of this physical feeling. Now, what I'd like you to do is to relax your hands for a moment. Then I'd like you to bring that same physical feeling down inside your chest. It can be on the right side or on the left side or in the center—anywhere across your chest. Or it could be in your abdomen, right down here, below your chest—that's fine too. I'd like you to be inside there, to become aware of your body inside those places. And remember, it is physical awareness; this is not a mental thing.

Now, I want you to hold your hands up—got those fingertips all warmed up? I'd like you to either generate or see if you can notice a physical heat that you can feel. You can move your hands around if you want to, either away from your body or closer to your body—just work on that for a moment. Focus inside your body. Later I'm going to build on this, and I'm going to tell you what it's all about.

Now, if you feel the heat . . . it is a physical heat. If you feel it, go into it and feel it more; don't try to move it around. Some of you might feel it one place, some another place, some here, some there. Wherever you feel it, go into it and feel it more. On some other occasion, it might be in some other place—never try to move it around. If it expands, that's fine. If it doesn't, then just feel it where it is. If you don't feel the heat, don't worry. If you practice it, you'll feel it in time.

The Heat Is the Physical Evidence of Loving Yourself

Now, relax. I want to tell you more about what this is. This heat is the physical evidence of loving yourself. You know, very often you will send light to other people, and that's good. But this is something that functions on a different level. This is something that is the foundation of your instinctual self. It is also the marriage between you and Earth, who supports you. It is also the ring or the symbol of connection between you and Creator on the physical level.

These connections are valuable for you individually (first I'm going to talk about the individual). For those of you who felt the heat, I want to encourage you to practice feeling it at least once a day for the next two weeks and then as often as you can. But I don't want to disrupt your lives; you have other things to do. Don't do it while you're driving obviously—that's too distracting. But someday, if you practice it well, you may be able to do it while you're shopping, while you're washing the dishes or changing a diaper or something like that—though one does have to watch out when one changes diapers as well [chuckles].

Now, this heat is the physical evidence of loving yourself. Creator has designed you to be able to feel this heat. Animals feel it, plants feel it, Mother Earth feels it, and many of you will feel it now too. The heat naturally radiates, you know, as heat does, and love also naturally radiates. So this thing is not intended for you to send to others. Oh, you can tell them about it if they want to know, if they ask about it. Don't tell them about it because you've got a way of life for them—not like that. That's competition.

But, on the other hand, if they want to know why you're more cheerful, why your life seems to be working better or, in short, what's new and what's working for you, you can share it with them. Tell them, "Oh, I'm doing this thing," or "I feel heat in my chest, sometimes I feel it down in my belly, but it just makes my life so much better." "Oh, why is that?" they say. And you say, "Well, I've noticed something amazing about this heat. It feels good, and when I do it, it makes me feel better. It tends to push things out of my body that are causing me pain or discomfort. It tends to put a field of protection around me as well." "How does that work?" says your friend. "Well, I don't really know, but it works pretty well."

Physical Feelings Are the Creator's Gift

How does it work? Let's talk about that for a moment. It works because all life is sanctified with love—and by sanctified, I do not mean religiously. I mean that it is in Creator's nature to provide love that supports life, always. As a result, Creator has the opportunity to observe the effects of that love, while at the same time wanting you, Creator's children, to do the same thing that all parents want everywhere: Creator wants you to be more than Creator Itself.

How is that possible? Creator has purposely given you certain gifts when you came here. These are gifts in responsibility training. These gifts have to do with things that don't always seem like gifts. On other planets, when you have other lives, you know many, many things that you don't know here. You have knowledge and wisdom that your culture gives to you and helps you with so that you are not ignorant. But here, once you learn the culture of the people you are born to, you have to give up that knowledge.

Oh, babies have it when they're born, but they soon discover that those beings around them usually need them to speak their language, act in ways that are right for their culture. Babies protest this sometimes—sometimes you see a child, a baby, getting angry for no apparent reason. There is plenty of food, there are no pins poking them, diapers are okay, everything else seems to be okay: "What's the baby upset about?" At least half the time, sometimes more than that, it's because the baby's having a hard time adjusting to the fact [chuckles] that he's been born into a world that does not understand emulated feelings, which are interpreted by the receiver in his or her language.

Part of the reason your culture, even today, has been having such difficulty in mastering mental telepathy, is that telepathy is not mental, it is physical and on the feeling level. Emotions are the mind's word for physical feelings. Physical feelings are the Creator's gift for material-mastery training. This tells you that the mind doesn't seem to understand something pretty important [chuckles], and that's that the physical has a great deal to teach.

Fortunately, Creator knew that this would be the case and made sure that you in this time of consciousness expansion would find your immortal personalities (also known as souls) encased—at least while you're awake and not asleep—in the vehicle of the human body, which is provided by this profound master, Mother Earth, who loves you no matter what and who, by the way, sees no separation (*none*) between her body as you know it to be and your bodies. She sees no separation between them. She sees no separation between her body and trees or animals—why should she single you out? You are just portions of her body walking around or moving around on your own, or in the case of the animals, lying around or swimming around. She doesn't create any separation. That's important to know for later; I'll get to that.

You have the opportunity here to become more than Creator, but Creator has not limited Itself. When you are living a benevolent life on other planets—an easy life compared to what you live here—you will have so much knowledge, but you don't have to learn anything to survive, nothing. Here, a baby has to learn all the time. Sometimes the baby protests, sometimes not so much. When you learn the culture as a baby, as you all did, you let go of all other knowledge gained on other planets. Babies . . . and you've seen this, you've looked into the eyes of babies before, when they are present. Sometimes you see amazing things. Sometimes it is pure joy; sometimes you feel like you're looking into the eyes of a profound sage or teacher, because at that point in babies' lives, they still remember. It's very inspiring to be around children like that; lots of you have noticed children like that these days. So don't despair of generations who are coming—they'll be all right.

You Have the Capacity to Be More

Now, Creator wants you to be more—how can you be more? Creator scratches Its head [chuckles], though It doesn't really have a head, but for the sake of our talk: "How can I make them more? I can only make them what I am. If I want them to become a creator, how can I make them more?" Then Creator gets the light bulb: "Oh! I can make them more by giving them less so they have to find their own way! But I must give them a means to know that they've found the right way. How? I will allow them to forget the natural love-heat that other beings have all around them, but I will surround them with animals and plants, and make sure they are on a planet that has this natural love-heat present so that even if they forget it, they will joyfully discover it at some point. Plus, I will encourage various beings to remind them, and I will make sure that the threads of this reminder go back in ancient bloodlines on the planet so that when they feel this heat, they will know it is something of value. It will feel good to them, it will feel loving to them, and it will feel like they've found something of value."

Creator has this conversation with Itself and other creators. One of the other creators says, "Well, how is that going to allow them to become more? Even if they have ignorance and they have the means to discover truth using this love-heat, how can they discover anything other than the truths you have provided?" And Creator says—and this is the true sign of a creator—"I don't know." Now, that may be hard for you to imagine, that Creator would ever say, "I don't know." But in order to understand why Creator said that, you have to understand Creator's objective.

This Creator always wanted to find out if there was more beyond what It knew—that's quite something for a creator. A being that can make a universe, and yet with all that's going on in that universe . . . "Is there more? Could there be more?" Creator decided that there could be more and that Creator did not have to know what more that is, but that at some point, Creator would give birth to some souls, and the source of those souls would have been from another universe—thus allowing something new and unknown, though fully loved and supported by Creator, to come into this universe.

So Creator invited that, and the seeds of your souls came. That's why you're called the Explorer Race, because you came from very far away, traveling at a rate of speed that can only be measured in light. And that travel still took you—though time is not a factor; I'm just trying to give you a measurement—millions of years to get to this universe. That's how excited you were about being involved with this. You all came from another universe, in the seed of your being. I'm not saying that this makes you bad or good or better or worse; what it does make you, however, is more.

You have the capacity to be more, and because Creator knows that you have this capacity, Creator sent you on a vast journey throughout this creation. Some of you chose to have lives in that journey—some had more, some had less—but you've all been here since almost the beginning of this universe in one way or another. So don't let anybody ever tell you you're a young soul; you might be a young soul in terms of how many lives you've lived, but there's nothing young about any of you.

Finding Wisdom That Works

Now, Creator wanted you to have opportunities to learn how to become a creator, and you've had almost all of those opportunities so far, up to this point, on other planets, in other places. Creator asked for a planet to volunteer to give you material-mastery lessons. Why? Many of you would like spiritual-mastery lessons. But every person associated with your seed group—and every person, for that matter, who has ever lived on Earth, but let's just stay with your group, the Explorer Race—everyone has been required to have at least one life . . . not just an existence outside of lives, but at least one life of spiritual mastery before you came here to live on Earth now. Some of you had more than one life of spiritual mastery. But regardless of that, you were required to forget that knowledge when you came here so that you could find your way to truth on the basis of physical evidence in your body that you could honestly say and believe is true.

In short, it is the intention to find wisdom that *works* and that can be shared with others on the basis of that total feeling of, "*It works!*" It's not just the belief, which is of the mind and *can* be of the body, but the physical evidence, which must be recognized by the mind because, "There's the physical evidence." So Creator has given you the thread to find your way to becoming more by giving you the means to find your way in truth, which can be acknowledged by your physical self. How? Extra-credit homework [chuckles].

For those of you out there who can do this heat or find a way to do it, after you've practiced it for a couple of weeks . . . for those of you for whom it is new, I'd like you to fully integrate it into your lives. How? I'll tell you how. Your body knows what it needs to eat; your body knows who it needs to be with; your body knows what clothes are best for you to wear that day. In short, your body can give you evidence of what's the best decision to make in that moment. You do not need to exclude other evidence—there might be demands on you, there might be responsibilities or obligations. But it is also good to have the body's instructions.

Now, given that the body can give you instructions, here's your homework. Keep it nice and simple; let's not complicate it. What I want you to do is, after practicing the love-heat for a couple of weeks or if you're already doing it, try this: When you go to your closet in the morning to decide what you're going to wear, pull out a garment. Hold it up close to your body; you don't have to touch your body, just close, maybe eight inches, maybe a foot. You don't need to take the garment off the hanger; just pull it toward you. Notice which garment gives you the most heat— that's the one to wear. Do the same with the tops, the bottoms, all of that. You don't have to do it with your undies, okay? [Chuckles.] Keep it simple. And that's a good start. The one that gives you the most heat, that may be the fabric, the color, the design—any of those, or all of them—that your body needs to have that day.

Using the Wand to Create Real Magic

This is very useful, because you will find that you can use this for everything: what food to eat and so on. Do you see this [points to the left arm]? You think it's your left arm, don't you? [Chuckles.] And you're right! But it's more than that. It is not an accident that one of the most exciting and wonderful things in children's stories is the magic wand. But you know, the magic wand is based on fact; it's not based on wands that others have been able to use to produce magic, or a certain amount. I'm not talking about illusion—say, a rabbit out of a hat. I'm talking about real magic, benevolent magic, creator magic, loving magic.

This is the wand, your left arm. It is the feminine arm. Even if you're left handed, it's still the feminine arm. The right is the masculine arm, all right? For some of you who may be left-handed, it might feel more balanced than that, but we don't want to go into all the details tonight. This is the beginning. Perhaps I'll come back and give you more material-mastery work in the future and explanations if that's desired, but for now, let's do this.

This wand is wonderful. It comes—your fingers, your wrist, your forearm, the rest of your arm—straight into your heart. This right arm also connects to your heart, but not to your physical heart. No, it connects to your feeling heart, which lives over here [points to the right side of the chest]. Your physical heart lives here [points to the left side of the chest]. Your feeling heart is very important. Many is the time you might experience the heat there, and that's wonderful. But your physical heart is about your physical life on a day-to-day, moment-to-moment basis, so we want to use your left arm as the wand.

Now, the wand—how to use that? Suppose you go into your kitchen in the morning. You have an idea of what you're going to eat; maybe you have only so much time, which you often do. Or maybe it's in the evening—whatever. Go up into the cupboards and take your left arm . . . I'll tell you how to hold your hand. Maybe some of you remember the peace symbol, or for some of you, it's the victory symbol, or for some of you, it might even be the Boy Scout thing. But let's do this . . . it's the V mark, all right? Now, make that, and then what you do is this: You relax it, so that your thumb is not quite touching your fingers and your fingers are relaxed. [To see an illustration of the wand, see p. 6.]

Now, when you use the wand for inspiration from spirit, you hold it up with the palm up. But when you're using it to make a practical decision about your daily life, hold it palm down or slightly turned inward. So you go the grocery cabinet, and you aim . . . you don't have to touch the groceries, just aim your fingers, the tip of the wand, toward each grocery, one at a time. Notice which one you get the most heat for—probably that would be a good thing for you to eat, that's what your body wants. If you have the time, see if you can make that and eat it. You may not have to eat a lot of it; maybe you'll need to eat more. You'll know when you're eating it how much. If you're not sure, just make a little bit. Maybe you can make more later.

I'm not saying you have to do all this homework; what I'm suggesting is—and you can see where I'm going with this—that if you're not sure about what to do, what's best for your body in that moment . . . and at different times, it could be entirely different: different clothes, different food. You can use the wand in other ways: "Which bank is the best one for me to have an account in or to get a loan from? Which car is the best one for me to have? Which car wants to come to me?" Maybe you're looking for a used car, a new car—hold your wand out like that. People probably won't think anything of it; don't worry about it. If they ask you what you're doing, just say, "Oh, I'm just kind of getting a feel for it." That's true! You don't have to explain it any further. If that person is a spiritual person, has interests like you, you can explain it if you want to. That's up to you. "Which house?" You're looking at all these houses: "Which one's best for me? Where do I feel the most heat?"

In the case of a house or a car or a product you're going to buy, maybe it will be listed in the paper. How can you avoid calling a lot of places that aren't right for you? You can use the wand. You can go down the columns—maybe you've read the paper, you've circled a bunch of things: "These all look good." You can point with the wand. You don't quite touch the paper, just be near it. Give yourself plenty of time—which ones give you the most heat?

If at any time with any of these things you get discomfort, immediately stop pointing [snaps fingers]. Relax for a moment. Then you know that's definitely not for you: "Wow, I wanted to wear that shirt today! Guess not!" Maybe some other day; maybe not. You haven't worn it in a year, so you can probably give it away. So you go through the newspaper, and you get three or four things that you have pretty good heat for. Those are the cars to call about or the houses to call about or the apartments to look at. The best chance is that you'll get those; the best chance is that you'll like them—maybe not at first, but in the long run, you might discover, "Whoa, this is nice! Good feelings here."

We don't have to cover all this tonight, but I wanted to give you an idea of what the wand can be used for. Maybe you go into a room, and maybe you're not in a relationship and would like to be. If you get good at this, you can just go like this [makes a whooshing sound] with your hand throughout the room. If you get a little heat, you say, "Maybe there's somebody here I can be in a relationship with," or "Maybe there's a new friend," because it will respond that way. It won't always tell you who's your new lover; it might tell you lover or friend. You won't know—you'll find out.

Practice the Love-Heat with a Tree

So what I want to say is that the wand can be used for important things like that, as well as for which shirt feels best today. Now I want to reveal something else to you as well that's very important—profound, if you think about it. Someday it might be useful to have a peace meditation with this heat. I'll tell you why. With everyone doing that heat for themselves, something interesting happens.

I'm going to give you a little extra-extra-credit homework you can do, but I want you to practice this with a tree to start with, because you'll know that you're safe. If anybody happens by you, you can say, "Beautiful tree, isn't it?" You don't have to feel foolish. So once you've got that heat down, you've got that working, go out in the forest somewhere, if you can, or someplace where you can be kind of alone with a tree, where no other human beings are likely to be within ten, fifteen, twenty feet of you. Walk up to that tree, but don't touch it. If it has boughs that come down, no, don't touch those, but the closer you can get to the trunk, the better—within, say, twenty feet. Try to go up to an older tree that's been around for a while, that has probably been exposed to human beings.

First off, say out loud, if you can—you can whisper if there are human beings a ways off—"Good life." That's what trees say to each other. The nice thing about saying "Good life" is, it's a hope and a blessing and a greeting all in one. It's very nice. And the tree will know that you're addressing the tree—not just staring into space as trees know human beings do sometimes. Then go into that heat inside yourself, and just feel it.

Now, if the tree is busy—and trees sometimes are; even though they may not be doing things like human beings, they are busy sometimes—you'll feel the heat the way you normally do. But if the tree can engage with you, you will feel the heat in your body much more significantly than you normally do, and I'll tell you why. The interesting thing about this is that it defies the laws of physics. You all know that one and one equals two, but in this case, one and one equals three.

The tree normally feels that heat almost all the time. And a tree, if it can engage you, if it's not busy, will feel happy: "Oh, a human being who knows how to do this!" And so the tree will feel your heat; you don't have to send it to the tree. Remember, you're the foundation, each person is the foundation—just like Creator is the foundation and Earth is the foundation, you are the foundation too. Don't send the heat out; it naturally radiates, and that's wonderful. And because it is love, it can do no harm. So you're feeling the heat, and the tree feels that. Then if the tree can engage with you, you will also feel the tree's heat. But because the two of you are involved in this, you will both—both you and the tree—feel it like *three* were doing it.

This tells you something very important, that when this work is done by more than one being, it will produce more heat and love than either one of those beings needs for themselves. So after you do this for a while with the tree, you can say, "Good life"—good life is hello *and* goodbye—and then you can nod if you like, a thank you. But "good life" is sufficient. Then walk away from the tree.

This Is the Key to Material Mastery

Now, you can practice with some more trees, but what I'd like you to do is, when you find out that there are human beings you know, your friends maybe, who can do this . . . you don't have to hold hands, you don't have to sit in a circle, you don't even have to be in the same place. You can be on other continents, if there are enough people doing it. But it can be in the same room—you can feel the heat. And when there are other people in that room feeling that heat, it will be very much like the tree: one and one equal three, and so on. I'll tell you what happens.

This is the key to material mastery, and material mastery encompasses spiritual mastery, so you can do it. When enough people are doing this at the same time, what happens is that Earth herself will become involved with that extra love-heat, and she will do it with you too. Plus, she will radiate more love to beings all over the Earth, so the animals, the plants and even people who aren't doing this will feel it in some way: "Oh, what was that?" "Gee, that felt interesting. I've felt that before; it feels pretty good." Some people will say, "Oh, heartburn . . ." [Chuckles.] But most people will say, "Oh, what was that?"

This is something that can do a lot of good for a lot of people, and the more of you who do it, the better. But don't tell people about it unless they want to know. Tell them only as much as they can hear, and it's perfectly all right to couch it in terms that are comfortable to the listener. You might have a friend who's very religious; it's okay to say it's Jesus' love—it is! It's the love of all beings everywhere, including Creator. It's okay to say that it's the love of anything or anyone, but it is also your own. You are a child of Creator; you can never be more or less than that while you're on Earth. But it is Creator's intention that you be more than that when someday you all come together and become a creator of your own, take over this creation so that this Creator can go on and discover the more that this Creator believes there is. We'll talk more about that some other time.

But tonight I want to give you this work because I feel it can improve greatly the quality of your life and have pretty good effects on the quality of the lives of others. Try it—if you like it, spread it around. Now I'll take a few questions.

Mother Earth Is Allowing You to Take Some Discomfort from Her

As you said the word "heartburn," medically speaking, there's one form. But what about if people get the feeling of heartburn but don't think it's acid reflux? Is that the physical trying to give a wake-up call or something?

No, but that's a very interesting question. If you get that feeling and you are quite certain that it is not the medical condition you described, then I'll tell you exactly what it is. Have any of you been having any pains and aches lately? [Chuckles.] And have you noticed that sometimes you will get these pains and aches for no reason? You'll say, "Well, how did I do that? I pulled that muscle and I don't remember doing a thing different." I'll tell you how.

As you know, Mother Earth has been under a great deal of strain. Many of you have been sending light and love to Mother Earth, and she appreciates that. But now because Mother Earth needs to use more of her personal resources . . . remember, I said before that she sees no separation between your bodies and hers. If she has more discomfort than she can handle, she is allowing you [chuckles] to take some of that discomfort for her. She's not punishing you and saying, "Bad!" No. She knows that many of you are involved in religious or spiritual practices that support transformation, and therefore, she believes in your capacity to transform this, and she will generally not give any one individual anything more than something annoying.

Obviously, you get other injuries or discomforts from time to time—she's not doing that. This is something that's going to be an annoyance and will tend to be felt for a brief time, or at most, maybe for a few days. Do whatever helps you to feel better. Don't be shy about using modern medicine, holistic medicine; it's a whole pie—that's a piece of the pie. Or do whatever helps you to feel better and know that when you're doing that, especially when you say, "How did that happen?" you can say, "Oh, this is some service I need to perform for Mother Earth on a practical level; I don't feel that I like that too much."

That's another bonus from that heat that goes into the Earth, because it will be your job to replenish Mother Earth. When you do that heat, it causes that response from her, but it replenishes you—even when you do that with the tree. Initially you feel the heat more strongly. The first thing that happens is that both you and the tree are completely replenished in that moment, and then the excess goes off to help others, whoever.

So thank you for your question, and understand that it is because Mother Earth trusts and has faith in your capacity that she's doing this now. And this also tells you something important—this tells you that you must . . . say you, "I must be making progress!" It's true, for you would not be given this responsibility if Mother Earth and Creator did not have faith in you that would allow you to do that. It won't happen all the time; it will be shared, spread around from time to time. But don't always look at every discomfort as, "What am I doing wrong? What do I need to correct?" Obviously sometimes it is about that, but these days, not always.

Women Are Naturally Spiritual Instruments

A couple of years ago, there was a release from the medical department in Washington D.C. about how there have been eighty-six thousand unnecessary hysterectomies of women and their uteruses. The atrocities to women . . . it seems as though that's continuing.

So you wish to know about Mother as it relates to the human mother?

Not the human mother, but the Divine Mother, and how it relates to women's uteruses and the womb.

All human beings—male or female, makes no difference—must be born through the mother, the female being, in order not only to live on Earth, but to experience life initially as something of nurturance. Water, as you know, is the feminine element on Earth; water encases the baby. This is not an accident. Those of you who have been fortunate to have children in this life have experienced—granted, not always in a fun way—the gift and the responsibility of initiation.

The first spiritual and physical—meaning spiritual on Earth—initiation you all receive when you pass from spirit into form is this initiation: passing through mother. And when you do that, it is intended that you—all human beings—remember that mother, when she is . . . from the moment the sperm and the egg find each other . . . think about it: millions of sperm finding that egg. It is not random as science might suggest or has suggested in the past. It is always intended, from the moment that takes place, that mother become an instrument of initiation.

Now, you all know—or many of you do—that the spirit who's going to occupy that baby body is not always present. In some rare occasions, from the moment of conception, spirit is present, but that's almost unheard of. Spirit wants to get in, get out, get in, get out, and sometimes mother does not go to term because that spirit, that soul, does not . . . "No, no, no; not physical life yet, but I'd like to try and see what it's about, just a little bit." So guides and teachers and angels who are talking to you before you're in the body say, "Well, on Earth it is possible; you can go and be in the instrument of initiation."

Think back on all the ceremonies you know, how there is almost always an instrument of initiation. But ancient cultures know that the first instrument of initiation is the mother's body—always. In ancient times, there were objects, ceremonial objects: the woman who was with child, or if no one in your tribe was that way, then you would bring in any woman who had had a child, or if for some reason that was not available (which was very unlikely), as a last resort you might bring in a young girl. It wasn't because she wasn't pure that she was the last resort, but because she hadn't been the instrument. In short, she hadn't been the initiation.

I'm not trying to make men feel bad, but I must say that all women are born naturally as instruments of initiation, from Creator . . . love . . . spirit—three things, but united. Always. Don't ever feel, women, that you have to achieve something beyond your nature in order to take the first step toward spirituality. By being a woman, you've taken that step. I'm not trying to say you're "better than"; I'm just saying that you are performing a valuable service just by being.

Men come here to learn. Now, understand, all men who have had lives before have always had at least one life of being a feminine being, and the same can be said for women—they have always had at least one life of being a masculine being. If that isn't the case—and it's always the case on Earth—if that wasn't the case at some time, then a person would be born here and feel like he or she had been born on an alien planet. No, no; you have to have depth, just like you've had to have at least one life of spiritual mastery so you'll have the depth to know how to survive certain things here, which may not be mentally solvable but for which you have the depth beyond your physical self to tap into, if needed.

So what I am saying is this: Woman is naturally a spiritual instrument. Does this mean the wand of God or the wand of Creator? Yes. When you take the form of a man, man is here to learn from woman, and man is initially, even if he doesn't want to learn from woman . . . which is not true, of course, in spirit. Men must learn, because the doorway to physical life is through a woman. That's how you're going to be living here. I grant that someday you'll be doing cloning—that's a whole other story we can talk about some other night—but for the purposes of discussion tonight, your lives here exist because of woman. Science can tell you that one man with one ejaculation could theoretically populate a nation, if you could preserve those sperm.

Of course, it wouldn't be much fun, to say nothing of the fact that the sperm that don't unite with the egg are doing the same thing exactly (there's a purpose for everything) as that spirit who wanted to experience just a little bit of physical life but not enough to be born as a baby. You know, sometimes you have miscarriages, and this is usually what that's about. For a sperm, it's the same thing—for millions. All, everything has life. Whatever that sperm is, it has its own being, its own soul, its own immortal personality—the tiniest particle has that. It's not just big things. If it were that way, then the elephant or the whale would have more soul than you, but that's not true. It's the same amount for everybody. And those sperms that don't unite with that egg—just like those eggs that don't unite with a sperm—they wanted to experience just that much of physical life, but they weren't prepared to make a long-term commitment. [Chuckles.]

So for our purposes of talking tonight, because it is a very long subject, Mother is the instrument of initiation for all human beings on Earth. Of course, it's the same for animals—no different. Animals are not here to learn a thing; they're all volunteers, down the last individual, regardless of their species. Like you, they are from other planets in their origin, but unlike you, they do not have to learn anything. Oh, of course, when they are born, they need to know where the food bowl is eventually, or how to find water—practical things. But they are not here to learn anything in terms of how to become more, to achieve more, to accomplish more. But they are available to teach, and we'll talk more about that some other night. One more question?

Healing Light and Mother Earth

I have a question about when we give healing light to another human. What is the effect on Mother Earth when we do that? What happens at that time?

When you pass healing light through you to another being, remember that you might be doing something. One of the main things you are doing, of course, is that you are the vehicle so that the light will know that it is intended for something that applies to a human. It is in the nature of the personality of light to have an acquaintance with all beings everywhere, to know how to adapt to all beings everywhere and to their needs, so that when you are acting as a vehicle, what you are doing essentially is you are focusing that light.

Say you're sending the light to your dog—okay, then you're focusing it intentionally toward your dog. However, that is best done by another dog. So if you're ever working on a dog or a horse or something, try to have at least one other dog or horse who's in good shape around, because you cannot focus the light for a dog, but if there's another dog or horse around, it will naturally do that. Maybe you didn't know that.

Now, the effect on Mother Earth: It is just—how can we say?—that she participates no more or less than is necessary. Healing light is really something that does not heal in its own right, but it triggers the effect . . . no, let's be specific. It triggers a benevolent effect in the recipient. Now, sometimes the practitioner—not the recipient, but the practitioner—is confused, because even in the long term there is no apparent alleviation of symptoms, whatever they may be. But you have to remember, healing light does not feel attached in any way to prompting the person to feel better symptomatically; rather it will go beyond the symptoms to the source.

When that healing light goes to that person, it will go to the source—meaning, what was it that prompted that discomfort? Maybe it would have been an old attachment to something; maybe you had some problems in the past with someone or something or some event. It will go straight to that, while remaining connected to the intended recipient, and it will work on that. And it might take this form, it might take a direct form, it might manage to resolve it, but more likely it will prompt the guides and teachers and angels of that person. It will prompt, either through those beings or through the subconscious thought process of the being, the resolution of the problem.

The subconscious is not something awful, and you understand, it's not called the subconscious in spirit, but I'm utilizing it as a readily recognized intellectual term. The subconscious is that which links feelings and the mind. If it weren't for that, your mind would never know what was going on anytime with your body, or often (which is worse in your modern civilization) with the bodies of others in your neighborhood, in your family, in your culture, in your church, whatever the organization. So the subconscious, then, is the divine part of the mind; it is an initiator, it is a link, because it can interact well with feelings and well with the mental. It's very important. So, subconscious, thank you very much.

Now, the function of the light is to prompt resolution. So if you do not see, as a practitioner, immediate relief in symptoms, you do not have to continue to do the practice. The first time you do it, it will prompt that action. Every time after that won't necessarily alleviate symptoms, and it will not have to prompt that action through resolution. But what you can do, if you want, if the person has not been able to consciously become

xxx ◇ Shamanic Secrets for Spiritual Mastery

aware of the source, the original source, that through various avenues . . . you understand, if the body has not heard from its subtle messages, which it gives you all the time, it will continue to amp those up, as you say, or expand them to more dramatic messages until you hear it. Eventually, you'll hear it—meaning, feel it.

What you can do—this is for practitioners—is help that person. He knows where his pain is; you might even be able to tell what in his body is causing his pain, especially if you understand meridians and so on. But if you don't have that knowledge or you don't need that knowledge to do your function, then what you can do is use your intuition or your sources to help that person become aware of how that part of his body where he's feeling his pain, wherever it may be, relates to some place inside Earth. Earth's body on the inside functions exactly the same way yours does, which is why she is, in a sense, your mother. In some ways, from my point of view, she is.

Mother Earth has liquids that run around inside of her, and she breathes. Any of you who've ever gone into a cave have heard the wind whistling in there; sometimes you can go way, way down, and that wind is whistling around. She's breathing. She even has a heart that beats, but because it's not like this [snaps fingers in regular rhythm], like your own heartbeat, you don't always hear it, because her heart beats in a constant. Some of you can hear that. Have you ever been at a mountain or near a mountain and there's a sense of a sound, or have you done meditation with a mountain and there's a sound [makes a "mmmmm" humming sound]? That's the sound, like many M's. That is the sound of Mother Earth's heartbeat.

So what you can do is, use your intuition. Relate it to the part of that person's body that hurts, whatever that might be. Relate it to some part of Mother Earth's body that will be stronger. Tell him that as Mother Earth's child and as Creator's child and as the child of all life, that he might be able to help Mother Earth and all life by requesting something, which I will say in a moment, to be united with that part of Mother Earth's body for which you are feeling pain. It may not be the part that has problems, but it's where you're feeling the pain.

This is how to tell that person to ask, and it's the foundation of another kind of work, called disentanglement. This is the beginning of that. Suggest that this person say this, practitioners. Have him say, "I am asking that gold lightbeings"—I'll explain why "gold lightbeings" in a moment—"that Earth gold lightbeings, that gold lightbeings from all times, places and dimensions, and that lightbeings who can work through gold lightbeings or radiate to them, disentangle me from all my discomforts."

Now, I grant that this is part of disentanglement, but tell this person that this will work not only for him, but it will help Mother Earth and all life. Now, why gold lightbeings? Gold light has within it all the colors of other light. It is the Earth-mastery color. As you know, mastery is not mastery over things; it is rather the learning of how all works in harmony and

> DISENTANGLEMENT: A GIFT FROM THE EXPLORER RACE MENTORS
>
> # THE
> # DISENTANGLEMENT
> ## BASIC PROCESS
>
> ### Ssjoooo
>
> Lie on a flat surface on your back, hands by your side, palms down and slightly away from your body—preferably three hours after eating and before you go to sleep, but it works anywhere, anytime. Remove any metal buckles and take coins or metal keys out of your pockets. Do not cross your legs or feet. This position allows you to get used to being open in your most receptive area.
>
> Say out loud (if possible): *"I am asking gold lightbeings, Earth gold lightbeings, lightbeings who can work through gold lightbeings and lightbeings who can radiate or emanate to gold lightbeings, to disentangle me from my discomforts and their causes."*
>
> Squeeze your eyelids shut and then focus on the light patterns—don't think. If you catch yourself thinking, gently bring your attention back to the light patterns and continue.
>
> Do this for twenty or thirty minutes or for as long as you feel you need to do it or until you fall asleep. This can be done twice a day.
>
> After a few weeks, make a list of every person and event in your life that makes you feel uncomfortable. Say the above statement and add: *"I am asking to be disentangled from the discomfort and pain of _____,"* reading one or two names or events from the list. Do each name for two to three days or until you feel clear with the person.
>
> **SPEAKS OF MANY TRUTHS ADDS:**
> "You may notice that if you say those specific words or names during the course of your day, after you've done disentanglement on them three to five times, that you no longer feel physically as uncomfortable about them as you once did.
>
> "This means the disentanglement is working. The objective is to feel physically calm. Keep saying those specific words or names in your disentanglement process until you feel physically calm. When you do, move on to other words or names, never more than one or two at a time."
>
> See our website for this process in Hungarian, Japanese, Portuguese, Norwegian, German, Italian and French. Learn more at our website: www.sedonajournal.com.

being able to very nicely connect with that. That's mastery, whatever form it takes. So if you want to say that to this person, that's fine; if he finds that too complicated, then ask him to say, "I am asking that beings of loving light"—always attach loving to light; I'll explain why in a moment—"come and remove the causes of my discomfort." That's okay too.

Now, why loving light? Why not just light? White light, which is a primary foundation of the bond that connects one particle to another, because it is unconditional love, is unconditional, and because it is unconditional, it might tend to attract that which is uncomfortable but is looking to be feeling better! So those of you exclusively using white light and who feel good about that, try to say "loving light." That will help you and anyone you are working on. And if you want to say "gold light," it will encompass that.

I don't want to give you too much work in one night, and we've already kind of gone past that point. But I want to congratulate you all. You are living in a time and in a place that requires much of you. Remember that you are known and loved, appreciated throughout all time and observed even by beings from other planets who now have been informed of what you are really doing here—which is why they're not preaching at you so much anymore. Now that they know what you're doing, it's "Oh!" [Chuckles.] I want to congratulate you for volunteering to be here in these times. They are exciting times, stimulating. You'll have lots of stories to swap with your buddies once you move past here on your natural cycle, and you'll also, just by being, make a contribution—some of you more, some of you less. Thank you for being. Good life!

Nurturing and Welcoming: Foundation Blocks for Spiritual Mastery

Isis
August 1, 2001

This is Isis.

Welcome.

I want to talk about something today. In your world, people are learning, ever so suddenly for some and slowly for others—sometimes painstaking slowly, as others might judge—that nurturing works and that control doesn't. The people in Sicily, where the volcano is erupting . . . the older ones, they know that you have to let the mountain do what it's going to do. And when it's done doing it, then you pick up and go on with your life. But if you try to fight her, she will fight back. And she will always win. The old ones over in Sicily, they all know this, but the young ones have yet to learn. It's not about this that I wish to speak today, though.

I wish to speak to the idea that nurturing does not work very well when it is prompted or done as a homework assignment. Zoosh, Speaks of Many Truths and myself from time to time give homework that is intended to clear out or expand your spiritual being within yourselves so that you can live more benevolent lives for yourselves and others, as you know. And yet the nurturing homework is hard for people to do because it seems like an act. Nurturing might be, "Be kind to yourself; be gentle with yourself; don't rush yourself; slow down," but when a person feels rushed or feels that he or she *needs* to do something and that sense of urgency is overwhelming for whatever reason—it may be based upon the actual thing the person has to do, or very often it is based on something else entirely—then what you have is a circumstance where the homework cannot be done properly.

Nurturing as a Means to Resolve

So I want to talk about the function of homework only a little bit, but I want to talk about nurturing as a means to resolve. I'm using Mount Etna as an example, because Mount Etna is an example of Mother Earth giving birth in her own way to parts of her body that, when they get older, you don't necessarily recognize. Here now you personally in this room find yourself in a highly volcanic area [in Hawaii]. You can look out the window and see a volcano, an old volcano, right there directly in your line of sight. Yet most people with a casual glance would not think of it as a volcano; it just looks like it's a hill where there are some houses and so on. And the land, of course, since it is an old volcano, is covered—granted, now with soil, but underneath that soil, there is lava.

Of course, the Hawaiian Islands are a tribute to Mother Earth's capacity to give birth, to let the stone cool, to send out a welcoming invitation for plants and animals. That welcoming invitation, which is also understood by the old ones on the Hawaiian Islands, is what people feel when they go to parts of the islands that are not excessively constructed by humans. It is that welcoming energy without any qualifications.

Most of you have known that energy very few times in your life. It is usually felt by you initially when your mother picks you up or the nurse puts you in your mother's hands and she holds you for the first time outside of her body. You feel that love and that welcoming, which is unfettered with demands and requirements and any of that. After all, what mother feels a sense of demand when she picks up her baby for the first time? Does she think, "What are you lying around for? Get up and take out the trash!"? [Laughs.] Obviously not. She's just happy that the birth is complete and that she can welcome her child into the world.

That's usually the first time you feel that kind of nurturing once you've entered the physical world—without qualification, pure welcoming. You have perhaps, if you are fortunate, an opportunity to feel that again, maybe from human beings, as a child. Children can be welcomed sometimes, especially if you are raised in a loving, nurturing family. But the key to understanding nurturing is to understand completely—not just mentally, but to understand and apply physically on the physical and on the feeling level—that *real* nurturing that affects you or others in the most benevolent way is *only* nurturing, never anything else. It's not, "Okay, five minutes for nurturing" [laughs]. So it is tricky, that.

The Feminine Energy Is Rising

What about Mount Etna? It is a lost art, but some of the old ones over in that part the world know that there were people—some of them even remember some of their skills—who could go to Mount Etna and give her that nurturing love, either by standing near her slopes or, when she is quiet, by walking up near the top and feeling that pure nurturing love of welcoming. And in the old days in that part of the world, when most people had their training—and of course, it was passed on from generation to generation to the youngsters (not just passed on in families, but passed on to the youngsters who showed that they had the gift or the ability to nurture and love that way)—the people would go to the volcano. And whether it was quiet or perhaps steaming very slightly—not so much as to create a problem, but steaming just slightly—they would go in numbers (three, four, five, maybe a few more), and they would stand there. Maybe sometimes they'd stand in different places on her body, or they'd all stand together and move around, climb around in various parts of her body or on her slopes, and they'd be that feeling of nurturing. By being that feeling of nurturing all together in the same moment, that nurturing would be compounded—it would become more.

This is just as Speaks of Many Truths has spoken about when doing the love-heat/heart-warmth/physical-warmth experience [see Overview]. One does it with another, and you experience a greater volume. It is the same thing when this nurturing is done this way. One, two, three, four, five people do it, and they feel a greater volume. And then when they include and really are gifting Mother Earth, in the form of this volcano, with that nurturing, she responds—not with the volcano's lava explosions, but rather she responds with *her* love. The people feel her love and nurturing, and she feels their love and nurturing, and then she is calmed. She is reminded that there are people there, because Earth does not think the way you do. She needs to be reminded.

Nurturing and love are not intended to be given once: "Here it is, 'I love you'—remember it for the rest of your life" [laughs]. It's not like that. They are intended to be given frequently. So I'm bringing this up now and using Mount Etna as an example—not only because it is in the news, but also because it is a well-known volcano—because you need to understand as a world population that what works to create solutions in greater things, big things, is the same energy and feeling and application that will work to create solutions in small things.

As Zoosh used to say, the feminine energy is rising. It is still rising and getting stronger, which tells you that using feminine strength like nurturing becomes not just something you need to get through life or something you need to do for others so that they might become more full human beings. But it becomes a powerful skill, an influential act, and more to the point, it is more influential than, say, something that involves will and force. This isn't to say that will and force aren't still with you, but they become less and less effective to achieve their goal. Whereas nurturing becomes more and more effective to achieve its goal, and it's more pleasant to do, no one has to suffer and everyone gets something benevolent out of the experience.

Homework: Practice Nurturing

Now, to practice nurturing, you have to first tell yourself for perhaps maybe an hour or so: "No rush—nothing to do." If you're a business-person or if you have children or what-have-you, you have to do as much as you can do, so get to the point where you can genuinely say, "Okay, everything seems to be covered at the moment." If you have a mate, please ask him or her to do for you so that you can do this nurturing homework. Perhaps an older child will fill in if he or she is old enough to take on such responsibility. But make some arrangement, perhaps with a sister or brother, someone who will take on the responsibility of your duties while you do this homework, because the homework doesn't take five minutes or ten minutes, all right?

The preparation to the homework might easily take an hour, an hour and a half. Some of you might fall asleep for a little time before you do the homework. Some of you might simply relax and let go, or as Zoosh likes to say, do the letting-go exercise by saying, "I give up," which is the same thing as letting go in its physical effect. You can't just say it; you have to say [sighing], "I give up," like that. Or for those of you who know how to let go, [sighing] "Letting go now." But it is done with an exhale and a relaxation of the body, and it takes time. You can't say, "Okay, five minutes to do the homework" [laughs].

So after you relax, then you go into that feeling of love that you feel in your chest or your solar plexus, something like that. When you have that heat up, then start doing things either with yourself, or if you have a mate, to him or her, but your mate has to prepare also. It's not about lovemak-ing; it's about nurturing. I grant that lovemaking can be nurturing, but it's not about that.

That person has to be old enough and understand the homework enough if he or she is going to do it with you, in which case you nurture each other. Maybe you brush that person's hair gently—no talking going on now, all right? And try not to think. If your thoughts come up, try to become involved in the physical action if you're doing it for someone else: brushing his or her hair, gentle touch, but not massage because that requires thought. Often, even if you are a professional, some thought will come up during the massage or you might pick up things from the per-son's body and your mind will become active.

But let's say that for most of you, to do this homework, you will do it with yourself. So when you get that warmth going, then do something like this—I will describe it. Take your hand and touch the top side of your head; then bring your hand down slowly, over your ear. This is a gesture that when done very lightly will remind some of you of being nurtured, perhaps by a beloved grandfather or grandmother. That's a grandfatherly gesture that when done gently with a child is very nurturing and tender and loving.

So doing it for yourself can be good, either with the left hand or the right hand, very gently and easily. You can do that for a time—you can take either hand and touch your shoulders and very gently stroke downward, down your arms, as if you were petting a beloved family dog or cat or horse. Do this very gently, very calmly. Try to maintain the heat or warmth in your solar plexus or chest, but if it goes away, the main thing is to be relaxed: "No rush; this is what I'm doing. I can take a nap afterward if I want to," like that, that knowledge, not, "It's four o'clock; I have to do this" [laughs]. Then try to proceed with that one hand on the shoulder or arms, and maybe bring a stroke gently down the front of your body.

You can move, say, your right hand, putting your left hand on your right shoulder. Allow your hand to move down in the natural arc it might move, which would move it in a diagonal pattern down, say, to your left hip. And your right hand on your left shoulder very gently crosses the surface of your body over your chest, over the solar plexus, down to your right hip—all the while relaxed, nurturing. It's important to learn how to nurture yourself in this way physically because it affects most benevolently your physical body and your physical body learns that you can speak its language. Ideally you will do this on the skin of your body with no clothing on, but if it is more convenient or necessary, do it on your clothing— that's all right too.

After you have done that a few times, then take one hand and put it on your hip on the same side (right hand, right hip) and make the gesture down on the top of your leg, then down over the top of your knee, down to your ankle and across the top of your foot to your toes. Do this on the one side for a while—gently, slowly, no rush at all—and then with your left hand on your left hip, do the same gesture down over the top of your knee, down the front of your leg and across the top of your foot to your toes.

Harmony, Love and Welcoming:
The Foundation Levels of Material Mastery

This is not the same as mother holding you and kissing you, but one of the things that parents often do with babies is that they gently stroke them, and most adults forget that. You only remember if you are gently stroking your cat or your dog or a baby, perhaps your sister's baby or your friend's baby or your grandchildren. It's not about thumping them; it's not about thumping cats or dogs either. It feels good to be gently stroked because it's welcoming, it's, "Welcome, so happy to have you here." It's not the words; it's the feeling.

Learn to practice that when you are doing this touching for yourself as well. From time to time, say, "Welcome, so glad you are here. I love you," or "Be yourself," things like that. This is said in a nurturing, gentle way without being a demand—not authoritarian, but always very welcoming and gently nurturing. It's not only something that causes you to feel better and helps you to learn how to nurture others in a way that will cause them to feel better and allow to them to feel welcome on Earth—which most people don't, I might add—but it also allows you to exercise your abilities to do this so that it will be easier for you to do it with yourself and others.

This does another thing too: It reminds you of the foundation levels of material mastery. One of the things that all the animals and all the plants now on Earth and Mother Earth herself, of course, know is that the foundation of material mastery is harmony and the foundation of harmony is love. And the first application of that is welcome. No one wants to be someplace where he or she is not welcome. It creates tension. What is the first tension for human beings? The first tension is not feeling welcome, and that tension is built upon. Granted, other tensions are added throughout your lifetime. But the reason your life proceeds in these manners with simple things and simple things built on simple things until they seem to be complex things, is that when you have the review of your life when your life is over, you go back to the very beginning—not only reviewing how you interacted with others, but what physical life is all about. You understand completely, "Oh, that's why that happened," yes, but you understand the basics.

Self-Compression Leads to the Mental

What I'm teaching you today is something that might seem very basic, and yet every one of you, with very few exceptions, forgets to do this basic thing every day. Now, granted, you cannot take three or four hours a day to do this benevolent work for yourself or others. But it is important that when you do this homework, you do take that amount of time. It might not take that much time, but you need to allow yourself three or four hours in case it does and, most importantly, so your physical body will feel safe to have these experiences that you are doing and to give you the gift of its capacity for material mastery.

You need to allow that much time so that your physical body will not feel rushed. Your physical body communicates with its feelings. If your physical body ever feels rushed, the feelings are compressed. When you compress feelings, even the best welcoming love and nurturing will be jammed up with "rush, rush; hurry, hurry," frustration, anxiety and all of that other stuff so that it's completely canceled out.

You may have noticed when you are feeling particularly nurturing or loving or calm that someone comes into your midst—perhaps a child or perhaps a relative, somebody visiting you—and you're relaxed and you've been doing this homework perhaps, and you've learned the value and the power of the influence of nurturing, what it can do, how it benevolently affects you, your spirit, your feelings, your physical self, your life, your career, your acquisitions, everything. Someone blusters in—a friend, a neighbor, a relative—and you shower that person with this affection: "So good to see you! Welcome!" But it doesn't seem to prompt any result. That person is saying, "Oh, this that, this that"; he or she is still experiencing the "rush, rush" of his or her life.

I'm not saying that this person is wrong or that you are doing the technique in a wrong way. This is to give you the example of something you can all identify with, because many of you have welcomed others at various times in your life feeling that welcoming genuinely but knowing that the other person did not experience your welcoming. All that the other person demonstrated was whatever feelings he or she came in with. This is an example of self-compression.

When you compress yourself for whatever externally or internally driven reasons, you not only cancel out your capacity to spiritually grow, but you force yourself—since your spirit is always designed to grow—to grow in the only way your spirit can accommodate when you are self-compressing, which is the mind. That's why in recent years many people have been very interested in reading this and that and this and that in order to expand their mind spiritually. Or they go to church and experience church and take it in mentally—these words or that song. But if you don't take in church on the feeling level, you don't always get what it has to offer: companionship or relationship with God and so on. I'm not try to say, "Go to church"; I'm speaking across the board to those of you who don't necessarily embrace the value of exploring spirituality in the way these books encourage.

Now, if the effect, then, of your welcoming and nurturing on your beloved relative or friend doesn't work, then you have to simply let that be. You've given that person the example—that's all you can do. When your loved one is ready, perhaps he or she will ask. He or she might notice, "You seem very calm; you seem relaxed. Don't you have things to do?" "Oh yes, I have things to do." By this time, you will have learned how to integrate after you do this homework many times. How many times? As many times as you need to do so that you can begin to have these feelings of being loved, nurtured and welcomed by yourself, to say nothing of others, all right?

Demonstrate Your Nurturing Feeling to Others

When you start to have that feeling outside of the boundaries of doing the exercise and the homework, then you'll know that you can keep this up and it will benevolently affect your life. You will also have the capacity to know what is important to do and what may not be important to do. The feelings can decide this. I'm not talking about business things that need to be done, but very often in your private lives, you will think that something needs to be done and you will do lots and lots on that, and then you will discover later that maybe that didn't need to be done at all. So it helps your discernment, all right? I'll give more on that later.

You cannot expect people to be able to respond in the way you can respond with the welcoming homework, à la embracing the relative or friend and there's no reaction. But what you can do is demonstrate. Try to maintain your calm, your loving, your nurturing feeling for yourself around that person. If that person says something, if she gives herself permission to ask questions, then you can share as much or as little with her as you like. The main thing is, this isn't about a messianic movement, where I want you to go out and teach people how to do this. Rather, it is about something you do for yourself. If other people ask you how to do it, then good. If they don't, that's okay too.

The main thing is to begin doing it, not only to have the benefits that come to you and to others as a result of your work, but as more and more people do it, to begin to remind people that this kind of being not only feeds and nurtures and welcomes a citizen, let's say to Earth, but it is also what connects animals to plants and plants to animals, to Mother Earth and, of course, to human beings. Human beings have stepped outside the natural harmony on Earth, and you need to reunite with it. This is one way to do that. It feels good and it's comforting. And there's more.

Use Nurturing to Soothe Earthquake- and Tornado-Prone Areas

There are many souls, beings, humans like yourself on Earth now, who were born with the capacity to learn easily how to do this nurturing work with, say, volcanoes. Or say you go to an earthquake area where you never know when the next big one is coming, and when they come, it's often catastrophic. These individuals, when they learn this homework and a few other things (but even just the nurturing homework, the love-heat homework), doing that, they can go in numbers of five, six, seven. They can walk around an earthquake-stricken area or an earthquake-prone area, either one, and feel that nurturing provide that welcoming for Earth.

That welcoming has this effect on Earth—it literally has a physical effect on Earth. She becomes warm, and the warmth is expressed in the benevolent harmonious way for human beings and plants and animals and the others who are her guests. So you, being made up of a physical body, are actually expressing to her, her natural way of being. It is like, as they say in some careers, you are giving the sign and she gives you the cosign—meaning she provides warmth that is benevolent.

The warmth to her affects her underground in an earthquake area. It might cause the underground areas that are difficult for her to move to be able to move more easily and slowly so that earthquakes in that area are felt in the future as two or one and a half or very slight, meaning that she can move regularly and steadily—not in a jerky way, but just regularly and steadily in a smooth way that doesn't impact her suddenly. It doesn't have to be a quick "Let's get it over with" gesture that creates catastrophe for human beings. This is an example.

Other people might go to tornado areas where they exist—they exist all over the planet, you know, and in the United States—and simply have those feelings and walk around on Earth. And when Earth herself has those feelings, it's less likely that she will produce tornadoes. Yes, she might produce wind, but wind helps to dissipate the unprocessed feelings of human beings in those areas. When she doesn't feel your sign/cosign, or warmth, which is love and nurturing, she will then use tornadoes to dissipate that unresolved human feeling, which is excessive and agitated. In other areas, it's earthquakes; in other areas, it's volcanoes.

So these material-mastery tests are presented to you by Mother Earth in a way that not only allows you to resolve them in a nurturing way for yourself but also, more to the point, allows you to express a means that nurtures you and nurtures Mother Earth and also resolves and heads off potential calamities that might occur. Other areas have hurricanes—you can think of a lot of things. There are some areas that have lots and lots of lightning that's sometimes very dangerous to people. That can all be resolved in a mild way.

When Mother Earth uses her lightning, if she does not have to resolve leftover residual human tensions and anxieties, which are uncomfortable to her body, if she doesn't have to resolve much of that, she can bring her lightning down in totally remote areas. But if it's getting clogged up in an area near a city or a town, for instance, then she needs to have a lightning storm right there in town, striking the ground and being dangerous for human beings.

In the future, in a more benevolent environment—where people are going around nurturing the young ones who have these capacities, learning these skills again of the nurturing feminine influence to create a more benevolent personal and societal and worldwide environment this way—what happens is that a lightning storm comes along that Mother Earth needs to do, and the lightning simply travels across the sky and never touches the ground. Because her atmosphere touches the ground and she doesn't need to resolve your unresolved feelings, simply doing the atmospheric discharge of the lightning is sufficient. I might add that it is not natural on a world that is calm and harmonious for lightning to ever touch the ground.

The fact that lightning touches the ground at all in your time has to do with resolving things for beings—in this case, of course, human beings—who have been unable or forgot or didn't know, didn't have the knowledge, didn't have the permission and so on to resolve them for themselves, or to be taught how to resolve them, or to have other trained loving nurturers who go around and resolve them. On other worlds, often you find empaths doing this. But you can't do empath on Earth in that way because you are all here to learn material-mastery lessons. If you were here to learn spiritual-mastery lessons exclusively without material-mastery lessons, the empath would be fine here. But that is not the case, so you need to learn these things on an individual basis.

Being Nurtured at Birth and in Old Age

I haven't talked today about things that are brand-new to many of you, but I've talked about some things that are brand-new to a lot of you. Know that your feelings are all based on very important facets of material mastery, harmony, spiritual mastery, physical mastery and even levels of mastery that you won't need on Earth but that you will need in future lives on other places. Many levels of mastery and lessons are available here. But the first ones that you need to do and apply involve nurturing.

You all know what happens to children who aren't nurtured. Very often they grow up out of sorts, they might become attracted to something criminal, they certainly will be self-destructive (as Zoosh defines self-destructive, which I agree with completely, where self-destructive means harming yourself or someone else). You've all seen that. Sociologists, anthropologists and behavioral scientists understand this. Psychologists have explained it to you. You know; you're clear. If you don't nurture the child, if you don't love the child . . . it's just a disaster waiting to happen, to say nothing of the child's suffering. But even if you were a child like that, you can learn how to nurture yourself in this way. It might take time, but it's worth the effort. And you can also learn how to nurture Earth.

When you are a child, you need to be nurtured. When you are very old and can no longer care for yourself in the way you once did, you need to be nurtured once again. Mother Earth knows how to display both of those things to you. She knows how to be the child so that she needs you to nurture her, which is good for you to learn, and she will give you the feedback that lets you know that that nurturing is doing something good. You don't want to go in with an agenda that says, "If we nurture her enough, Mount Etna will stop exploding." You need to nurture her for the sheer pleasure of it.

When you love your baby, when the nurse puts your baby into your arms after you've given birth, you don't say to yourself, "If I love baby enough, baby will stop being annoying when he or she grows up." If you love your baby, you're welcoming him, you're happy to see him. Granted, when baby gets a little older, when baby is crying sometimes, you hold and love baby hoping he will stop crying, but that's another story—we'll get to that another day. Still, recognize that you have the opportunity now to use the basic skills that you are presented with when you arrive here in order to serve yourself and others and the planet in a way that will improve the quality of your life and the quality of everybody else's life as well: animals, plants, the planet, everything.

What about when you get old and need to be nurtured? Mother Earth knows how to demonstrate needing to be nurtured when she is old as well. You need to do different things. What do you need to do with the very young and the very old besides loving and welcoming? You need to be patient. You can't be demanding; you recognize that they can't . . . they are literally unable to do things. You don't look at your baby two hours after his birth and say, "Walk! What's wrong with you? Walk now!" [Laughs.] You don't look in your baby's mouth and say, "Teeth, grow now!" [Laughs.] It's just funny to say it, because you wouldn't think of doing that.

On the same level, you wouldn't say to someone old and infirm, "Walk, grow new teeth and become strong and vigorous so I don't need to take care of you anymore." You wouldn't think of that. It's, "Here, Grandmother, how can I help you?" Or, "Grandfather, let me help you down the hall to the bathroom." Or, "Here, let me help you eat. It's my pleasure. Don't worry about that dripping down. It happens to everybody." In short, there is nurturing every step of the way.

This helps people to be welcomed into Earth. It helps people to be loved so that when they are exiting Earth when they are old and infirm, they feel that welcoming, that love (which is exactly the same energy they will feel when they exit), so they can follow that ribbon. And even when they don't exit, when they are asleep or dreaming or their guides are there . . . even if you don't see their guides, they'll see them. They might be talking to those guides and you think they're talking to you. You might get confused sometimes, but they're often talking to spirits who are real—not hallucinations, because hallucinations don't come into it. It's all about loving and nurturing, and the power and influence of loving and nurturing for you now. It's about patience. It's about discovering the power of feminine wisdom and, in the case of nurturing and loving, the power of feminine application and its capacity to transform like magic—and I'm talking about benevolent magic, all that you see, feel and experience around you. Isn't that worth doing?

Spiritual Mastery Can Transform Your Life!

Spiritual mastery has to do with tenderness and nurturing first, and other things are built on that, because that tenderness and nurturing are what welcome you to do the other things. Demands, commands, will, control, force and manipulation have nothing to do with spiritual mastery. This doesn't have anything to do with any level of mastery, but it often shows up in your lives because of the stresses that your civilization and culture have, in some cases unintentionally, but that are very often in other cases intentionally induced into an individual's life, a society's life or planetary cultural life.

All of that needs to be discarded. You need to operate with your strength. This is a picture of your strength: flexing the muscle on your arm, pointing with your finger toward that muscle. If you want to see how that strength relates in a visual to will, force, creation, then flex your little finger. That's the difference. The feminine wisdom and application have the power and capacity in the most benevolent and nurturing way to speedily transform your personal life, your family life, your societal life, your planetary life. Why wait?

Introduction

Attunement through Mother Earth

Reveals the Mysteries
August 31, 2001

This is Speaks of Many Truths' teacher. Now comes the time to begin *Shamanic Secrets for Spiritual Mastery.*

Mother Earth Is a Profound Teacher

The Earth is a much more profound teacher than even my fine students recognize. When I was walking upon it, I established fairly quickly, for one as slow-witted as myself [chuckles], that everything I saw, felt, heard, tasted—in short, everything I sensed and beyond—were all lessons passed through Mother Earth so that these lessons would be able to reach me. When one is born of Earth, one is able to interpret lessons more easily than one can do on almost any other planet. That is because Earth has the resonance and the expertise combined to not only adapt lessons of the universe through her, but the means to adapt them in fine-tuning to all who are made up, at least in part, of her body.

She is capable, yes, but the student must also be capable. That is why the Explorer Race, who are our students, must understand not only your mission but also your inclinations. To be a member of the Explorer Race, one needs to have qualifications, as your Zoosh and others have explained. All of you come here with various purposes, yes, but you all come here with intent. And that intent is universally for you all to grow as immortal personalities, yes, but in the larger sense, to grow as a group in order to achieve the greatest degree of expansion and, more to the point, capability to expand when lessons are stimulated around you that are for you and that are attuned specifically through Earth to reach you for all time.

If you think about this, you will realize that I am not speaking only of your Earth lives. When you go on from here, in time, to re-form together and become a creator, your capacities to achieve creatorship will not only be heightened by the attunement through Mother Earth to expand your abilities to learn, but for your personalities (or as you say, souls), the permanent connection through Earth to function as an interpreter—yes, for universal lessons and, as a creator, universal needs—is firmly planted. But there is more. Because she is attuning you to her capabilities and passing those capabilities on to you, she is not enslaving you to her but rather is granting to you the capacities that she has in all dimensions and in all of her memories.

Earth's memories are an important point here. I'm not just speaking of memories of the future, as Zoosh might say, but I'm speaking of the practical matters of all that you might need to provide for civilizations of beings in great variety. Looking about at the life forms who have lived on Earth and for whom Mother Earth has provided, you are struck almost immediately by the variety—almost infinite, given that she is but one planet. I can assure you that at other dimensions of herself, this variety and the inclination to embrace variety is equally shown: different animals, different people, different life forms on each and every planet, sometimes looking similar, oftentimes quite different.

Mother Earth is the Creator of this universe's direct descendant—not a servant, but a direct descendant. That is why she has so many capabilities of mastery and continues to hone her skills. On the one hand, it is her personal preference to do so; on the other hand, as your teacher and as your atonement . . . no? That's not it, that's religious—please excuse me [chuckles]. As your attunement . . . let's say, as your music teacher. Her job is to attune your souls or immortal personalities, not only to her multiple frequencies, but also to show you why such attunement is beneficial to you. You need to be shown, not because of some external authority, but rather because you have been trained to seek evidence, proof. This is part of your given discernment skill from Creator. Creator chooses to provide you with this tool of discernment so that you can not only convince yourself of validity, but more to the point, convince one another, based upon each of your own methods of validity, of the value of any given thing, lesson or even perception.

Appreciating the Songs of All Beings

Mother Earth is like a lens, and you are like the light rays that pass through the lens. Before you come to the lens, you are free to travel wherever you wish; when you pass through the lens, you experience an effect that not only benefits you but also causes you to enjoy the feeling, to suddenly notice the world around you in new and wonderful ways—a form of noticing that you did not experience before you passed through the lens.

It's almost like learning the Earth's languages of all its peoples and all its animals, and suddenly you understand everything that everyone is saying and the world makes so much more sense. It is like that when you pass through and become attuned to Mother Earth and her methods.

That's why it is so popular to come here, and even a difficult life gives one the opportunity to experience such levels of wisdom in a practical sense. On a creator level or even on some spirit levels, one might have some (not all) of these abilities and feel as if it is natural—not, "So what?" as you say, but feel that it is so natural, it is not something you put your attention or focus on very much. But when you are living a physical life and are addressed by effects, applications or, more to the point in the physical life, consequences of your acts and the acts of others, to have even occasional or (as I hope to do with this book) to have the capacity to utilize these skills with all life on Earth and in time with the voice of Earth herself *through* all life . . . not directly—others do that well—but it is possible to speak not only the voice of all beings on Earth but the voice of Mother Earth through all beings, meaning with their capacities that Mother Earth focuses through. To have such abilities of understanding and depth that all apply to living on Earth as a physical being and a spirit being combined would make it so much easier, not only to instruct others how to live here, but more to the point, it would allow you, as a physical human being, to appreciate the songs of all beings.

In your time the song of man is thought. In my time the song of man—and woman, of course—was feeling. You have embraced thought as a means to understand. We can understand from our spirit place why you would do that in your time, and yet we feel that feeling gives you the ability and, more to the point, the capability to learn and interpret, and as it applies to you, to practice the wisdom taught by all other creatures (plants, animals, microbes, plankton [chuckles], everything), to practice their wisdom on Earth—speaking, yes, of their wisdom of their beingness that they've lived here on Earth and beyond, but also speaking of the attunement of Mother Earth through them. That is why in this book I will be your guide. Speaks of Many Truths may make comments as well, and we will sometimes hear from these individual beings [Reveals the Mysteries often guides Speaks of Many Truth in the channeling process].

Shamanic Secrets for Spiritual Mastery, then, will be a fine-tuned medley of animals, plants and even the spirit of humans that will provide for you the lessons learned by such sources of beings and, after such spoken statements, will provide Mother Earth's voice, focused through their beingness, to pass on the lesson of their songs to you. You sometimes hear these songs by birds or frogs, occasionally sea creatures. You hear their sounds, you think of it as language, but very often it is a song associated with their heart, to broadcast their feelings, and has less to do with a specifically worded language based in thought. In my experience, I have best understood these beings by being focused in feeling. Then the communication is immediate.

Granted, the details of the vast meaning of the communication need to be expanded on to include more than feeling, and that is where you can use your thought to consider what they will say through this channel.

Welcome to *Shamanic Secrets for Spiritual Mastery*! In the future, you can refer to me by an interpretation of my name, which I will give you now. The interpretation is . . . hold a moment. I will translate it into your language. The best interpretation I can receive for you was suggested by Speaks of Many Truths, and that is Reveals the Mysteries. He says, smiling at me, that that is really what I have always done for him, and I hope you will find me a good guide to do so for you as well. May you enjoy the experience.

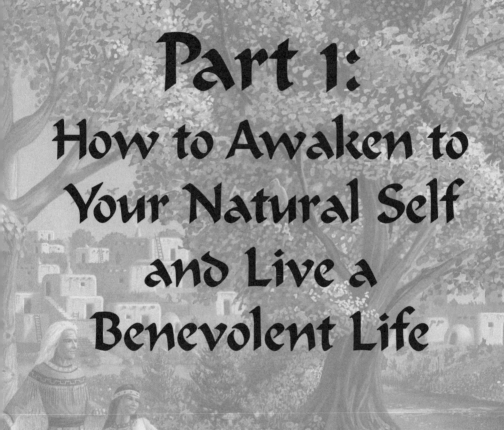

Part 1:
How to Awaken to Your Natural Self and Live a Benevolent Life

Physical Messaging

Speaks of Many Truths
November 26, 2001

All right, this is Speaks of Many Truths. Greetings.

Mystical Trackers: Finding the Feelings in Animal Tracks

In your time the popular myth of Native American guides and trackers is that they look at tracks and they understand what the tracks mean. But in my time—and I don't rule out that there are some trackers in your time who can do this—one not only looked at tracks, but one felt them. Feeling them does not mean putting your hand necessarily in the tracks, though I have seen some people who might put down their hand . . . say this is the indentation of a track [puts his right hand out with fingers up, and then his left hand comes close to it]. So they might put their fingers down inside the track without actually touching it.

But if they were trying to pick up something, they would use their left hand—that's your more receptive hand. And they might put a finger, say, in the animal's track, and then if they were tracking the animal for some reason, they would know, perhaps, whether the animal was wounded, whether it was hungry, whether it was frightened—things like that. They would know, because with animals it is exactly the same as with human beings. Every place you put your foot when you walk, you leave your feelings in that moment there for a time. It isn't just that you leave your physical mark; you leave everything you're feeling in that moment.

Now, it may be true that a human being in any given moment might be feeling a broad spectrum of different feelings, but if there are predominant ones—especially if the track was made, say, thirty minutes ago, or maybe in the case of a tracking that takes place after some time, the track was made yesterday—the predominant feelings then would be present. "Thirsty"—there are physical feelings with that. "Hungry"—there are physical feelings with that. "Frightened"—the fear creates a very distinct feeling that the tracker might put his fingers down on the track or hold his hand over the track and feel.

There have been reports in your historical articles about some Native American trackers who would sometimes hold their hand over the track if others were looking, and if others weren't looking, then they might put their fingers down into the track—not touching the Earth, but they would put their fingers down into the track with the idea of not revealing to anybody outside the mystical profession of tracking (which it is, mystical) the more intimate methods of tracking. So they might in public, as it were, in front of others—the uninitiated, if you would—hold their hand above the track, which doesn't give you as clear a feeling but gives you some feeling. Sometimes this has been mistaken to be that the tracker might be blocking the sun so that there is no light or shadow on the track, so that the light is even over it, but that's not what's going on.

So in my time this was known. The trackers were like other trades, if I might call it that. I was a mystical man, there were medicine women, sometimes medicine men, and there were warrior teachers. For the case of this talk, we're talking about the mystical tracker, whom I will just refer to mostly as the tracker. But it is important to recognize that even if I call them trackers, I'm really saying mystical trackers, because that's their training.

Using Physical Messaging to Track a Kidnapped Man

Feelings, as I've said many times before, are the means of knowing all things, whether they are your feelings, meaning you're getting training, for instance, in understanding feelings—one learns with one's own feelings first. But it goes past that. Once you have an understanding of your feelings (what they mean, what they're prompting you to do and so forth) and you begin to take action on those feelings and can recognize, say, even the applied-feeling techniques that we've talked about before—which have to do with making decisions with your feelings (there's warmth, that's good for you; there's discomfort, that's not good for you)—steps beyond that have to do with feeling . . . in the case of physical messaging, the feelings of others in a given moment.

I will give the story about my kidnapped brother and the tracker who found the hairs my brother had pulled as he was being marched along by those individuals. My brother waited until he was frightened; it wouldn't have done any good to pull them out if he felt calm and comfortable, when he was walking with friends, because initially they approached him as friends—"Oh, greetings," like that, as much as you could communicate with different languages. It was all very cordial: "Oh, eat with us," "Have some food," and so on. In other words, they kind of snuck up on him that way, and it wouldn't have done any good to pull out a couple of hairs to leave a message to say, "Met new people; seemed like fun."

But when they were marching him off and really discarded some of his things, then he pulled a couple of hairs out of his head and put them on a leaf. This was a leaf of a particular bush that had slightly sticky leaves— not exactly sticky with sap, but the leaves were . . . it's hard to describe, but it was sort of like they had thin hairs on them.

And he knew that?

He knew that. He knew that if he casually put the hairs down like that, that it wouldn't be noticed and they wouldn't think anything of it. He waited until he was frightened—genuinely, not fake. When you are frightened, you understand, you have heightened senses: you hear better, you taste better. All of your senses are heightened so you can take in the immediate environment, the details of the people, how they looked, how they smelled, the foreignness of them compared to your people—in short, the heightened sensations of the moment. Then was the time to put down the hairs, leaving them for the tracker who would follow when my brother did not come home.

So when the tracker found those hairs . . . you understand, describing it as "finding the hairs" is a bit confusing. You might say reasonably, "How could the tracker possibly find two hairs in a forest with trees, leaves, fields and so on? How could he find two hairs?" You have to remember that once we found where my brother was initially met by these people, which wasn't too difficult to do because at his campsite . . . you have to understand that what he was doing was, he was going out and looking for certain herbs that the medicine woman asked him to go out to gather, since he was learning some of her skills. So he had picked those up, but he didn't leave them at his site; he left them nearby, next to a tree, where the herbs felt best to be.

If you pick things like that and you're camping, you walk around with them. You want them to do something for you, you want them to remain vital and strong, so you don't put them in a pouch next to where you're camping because it's convenient. You walk them around the general area where you're going to be camping, and if that's not comfortable to those plants—you're feeling them, all right?—then you take them to where it is comfortable. It was comfortable for them to be next to this tree. It was really, in terms of your distance, about a hundred feet from my brother's campsite.

So when the tracker found the campsite, then explored the immediate area and found the herbs over there, that's when he knew. My brother would never leave that; something was wrong. It wasn't too difficult to follow their footprints by that time, but the tracker was paying less attention to the footprints and the general trail of where the people were moving than he was to feeling for my brother's feelings.

Fig. 1-1a. Here is the wand, using the left hand.

Fig. 1-1b. Detail showing position of fingers for the wand.

In short, the tracker had his hand out like this [see Fig. 1-1]. He put it out like this, feeling. And if he lost the sensation of my brother's feelings, how my brother felt—meaning, how the tracker had felt around my brother when feeling his feelings when he had been around him before . . . because the tracker was trained to not only understand his own feelings but to understand the feelings of others. He did not come by this understanding mentally; it was entirely a physical memory within his physical body.

So the tracker was feeling, as it were, for my brother's feelings, anything from my brother's feelings—looking for a drop of sweat, a hair, even a piece of skin, something. And if he at any moment lost the sensation of my brother's feelings, then my job—I was along for part of it—was to think of my brother, since I was his blood relative. Then the tracker would not focus on my feelings, but he would focus somewhere off one of my shoulders and pick up my brother's feelings, because I was a blood relative. He did that once or twice, okay? And in doing that, that's how he found the hairs. Normally finding hairs is like the proverbial needle in a haystack . . . how would you possibly? But this is how it's done—it's all done through feelings.

So he found the hairs; he found them through feeling. He saw them on the leaf, but before he picked the hairs up, first he went around that particular bush and he got all of the feelings from that bush. Then he went to the leaf where the tree and the hairs were, and pointing toward that leaf, he separated out the feelings of the bush from the feelings of the hairs. Then he thanked the bush and pulled the hairs off, and then he felt into the feelings left by the hairs. So that's when he picked up all of the feelings.

We stood back from him, everybody stood back, while he did this. And while he was doing this, he got as connected as possible with the feelings that my brother left for him in those hairs. The more in touch he got with those feelings, the more he began to be able to envision what my brother was actually feeling, sensing, smelling, seeing, hearing—all of those things—in the moment when he pulled the hairs out and put them there in the bush.

So even though the tracker didn't get the kind of description of the faces of the people who took my brother, he got the impression of four or five individuals around my brother and their general appearance, where they were going, this kind of thing. And because he got the heightened sense of the feelings of others through the hairs that my brother had when he was pulling them out, because of that heightened sense, he could actually tell the general direction that they would be walking to get to their camp—or as the tracker said, "Or their village." But he said, "I don't know how far this is."

So the tracker could generally tell all of these things and more: that the people with my brother were all men, roughly how old they were (mostly young men; one older man). And he could even pick up the general sensation of how they smelled—different from our people. This doesn't always have to do only with diet; sometimes it has to do with the minerals and the area: for example, what kind of rock is there. Then the water runs over that rock and the minerals are different. Or it might have to do with the feelings that the people have, or their cultural identity, all these things. But the fact that these differences exist allowed him to differentiate my brother's feelings and sensations from the others he was with.

So this all might take upward of fifteen to twenty minutes at most; it usually doesn't take more than a minute or two. Then from that point on, the tracker could strike off in a general direction without having to read the tracks, because if you're reading tracks, you're moving very slowly. After that he could strike out in a general direction without really having to read the tracks, saying, "This is the way." All this from two hairs.

Feelings Led Us to My Brother

I'm talking about this now because the subtleties of perception in your time have largely been lost; it's a lost art. But so much can be gained by you all from it. Now, it's true that some sensitives and others are performing different types of this practice—not all the same kind of practice, but different types of practice. This is because when healers, as they are called in your time, are interacting with the energy of other people's bodies, sometimes they will pick up the feelings of those people. So this isn't a completely lost art; it's not a foreign thing to your times, is what I'm saying. You can still do it, and it has great advantages.

Now, that was physical messaging, but what about when we were approaching the camp of the people where my brother was? At that point, we didn't have hairs anymore; my brother had been able to leave those hairs that once, but apparently they were watching him after that. He wasn't able to leave anything other than what was in his footprints and his feeling—sometimes the tracker could pick that up. But how would the tracker—who had kept the hairs, by the way; you don't just get that and toss the hairs aside—be able to pick up from a distance where my brother was in that camp, who the people were who guiding him and everything about the camp that we would need to know so that we could sneak in and get my brother out of there without violence? Because the people in the other people's camp, there were lots and lots of them, and there were just a few of our own people.

So the hairs would be used by the tracker. He would take the hairs in his left hand, pinched between his thumb and first finger, and he would aim them toward the camp. Now we're talking about remote physical messaging, using something like an anchor, something physical, something solid.

Almost like dowsing.

He aimed at the camp, feeling that my brother was there. Then the tracker moved from a distance (we were up on a ridge) those two hairs back and forth across the camp, covering every bit of the camp at a distance until the feeling was strongest. And when the feeling was strongest, that was where my brother was—inside a small dwelling. But we wouldn't have known this just by observing, because he was kept in there but it wasn't obvious—they didn't have guards and so on. It wasn't obvious because, unknown to us at that time, my brother was tied to something. So we wouldn't have been able to know. That's remote physical messaging.

So holding the hairs toward the area and moving closer, creeping up silently at night—it takes time, but it's worth doing—the closer we were able to get to that place, the more we could pick up from my brother, even though my brother was asleep at the time. We were able to pick up his body's physical feeling. My brother was, after all, in a place that was foreign. He couldn't sleep well; he was sleeping fitfully. When you sleep fitfully, you fall asleep for ten or twenty minutes perhaps, and then you wake up and you're uncomfortable for a while. Then because you're tired, you fall asleep again. That was the situation for him at that time. So the closer we could get, the tracker holding out the hairs in front of him when he could, the more the tracker could pick up on the level of feeling of what would be found there. And so we were able to get my brother out. We got him out very quietly; no one was injured. It was all very gentle.

The other tribe was stealing him as a potential bridegroom?

That's right. Because there was nobody in their camp, with their people at that time, who felt right to this young woman who was of the age of marriage, you would say, or betrothal. She was at that age, she was ready, and there was no one there who was right. And their people were not the sort of people who would say, "Well, there's no one who's right; you'll just have to take someone." They weren't like that. They were the sort of people who would . . . they didn't thrust someone upon her. So they were very honorable in that way. And out of their desperation, they kidnapped my brother. But as it turns out, there was a resolution.

Wasn't your brother also radiating his feelings while he was in that shack?

But he was exhausted by then. He had walked a great distance over foreign territory, and when he was in that little dwelling, by the time they got there, he was completely exhausted. The only reason he was sleeping at all was because he couldn't stay awake. So he wasn't radiating very much.

And he was nervous and upset; he didn't know what they had planned for him. They had not told him, and there was not a common language, so he was worried, he didn't know what to expect. [Chuckles.]

[Laughs.] He didn't know there was a beautiful woman out there!

Yes. If he had realized it was a beautiful woman, he wouldn't have stayed, but he might have tried to have her come back with him. We laughed about it later, even though later on he came together with a woman from our people. But we had many good laughs about that in later years, especially since we were able to see that it all worked out okay.

With your long vision?

Yes, and of course, then it became a tribal story and everybody laughed about it for years and years. At the time, it was funny.

But you never got into any kind of relationship with those people, though, because you couldn't communicate with them?

That's right, there wasn't a shared spoken language. You can only go so far with hand signs and general gestures to indicate basic needs and basic necessities; it is hard to go into more details, philosophies.

So they just lived a few miles away from you?

Well, not a few.

Did they travel or did you travel a long way?

It was a camp they were in. The camp wasn't permanent. They were moving from place to place. I did not even look to see where the places were where they would stay normally at different times of the year, but they were on the move. So that's why I'm describing it as a camp, not a village. In those days anyway (and my people too), we didn't think of where we lived . . . even if it was peaceful and we lived there for years, we never thought of it as a village. It was a camp, because it might be necessary to leave at some point in time. So we didn't think of it as roots and all of that.

All Sensing Organs Also Leave Something Behind

But I wanted to keep clear about physical messaging. In your time it is possible, when people are walking, given the type of shoes they might have on the bottom of their feet . . . let's say someone walks down a beach. It's obvious—this person's feet sink into the sand and leave a track. But this person might even be walking out in the woods. Even with something over the bottom of her feet—not necessarily rubber or plastic material like you use nowadays, but something more natural like leather—she's going to leave her feeling there. It's not as strong as if a bare foot touched the ground, but this person is going to leave her feeling there.

Remember, your feet, although they perform a different function than your hands, have something similar to your hands. You're conscious of your hands being sensing organs; you not only pick things up and manipulate things and touch things, but you also might reach out and gently touch something, explore. The hand is an exploratory organ, and you're conscious of that. But it's been forgotten that your feet are the same way. It's not always forgotten—you might stick a toe in the water and see if it's warm enough to swim in. So then you're conscious of your foot being a sensing organ.

All sensing organs—that which is receptive that way, like the skin—also leave senses behind. So for people in your times, many of whom might need to find someone—someone's lost and so on—one of the best ways is to check for tracks and physical evidence. Don't just look at physical evidence as if it were a spot of this or a dab of that.

As if it were one-dimensional?

That's right. Most physical evidence like that is saturated with feelings—even within thirty-six hours of being left there. A good sensitive who is either a master tracker or even a mystical person—someone sensitive like that—might be able to put a finger near that evidence, as it were (that air, that drop of sweat), and feel and sense and possibly even see what was going on in that environment in the moment that drop of sweat hit the ground.

You know, a drop of sweat can fall into the dust, and if you look at the dust on the ground, it forms an actual pattern. You can see that a drop of liquid fell there. You've seen that, perhaps, in the dust? On a hot day, you can go out and lean over, and if it's a dusty ground, the ground pattern will change. Trackers are trained not only to feel for the feelings but to notice things.

Decreasing Misunderstanding in Relationships

How would we use this today?

In your times, for example, people have misunderstandings all the time. Whether they're friends or workmates or lovers or relations or even acquaintances, there are often misunderstandings. But physical messaging will greatly decrease that. For instance, say a man and a woman are living together, and they are having a talk about something meaningful to them both. Each relates to the subject on the basis of his or her feelings. They might be able to communicate intellectually about the subject, but that doesn't always help to create a better communication, because the intellectual explanation is often a means to rationalize the inability to communicate in a way so that it can be understood what is being physically felt by the individual who's trying to speak in words about it.

So if there is a miscommunication, a misunderstanding, or if the other person simply doesn't know what you're trying to talk about, it may be necessary, in the case of intimates, to do something like this. You might say to the other person, "Would you mind?" and have him reach over with the left hand and perhaps touch your hair, the hair on your head. The other person has to touch something that's not clothing, all right? That's why I'm using intimates for this example. He might touch the skin in a sensitive spot, say here [touches inside the elbow]. He might touch back here behind the knee, on the skin. Or your hair, especially here [points toward the back of the head]. The very front of your hair isn't always going to message as well.

But when my brother, for instance, pulled out hairs, he reached back here [points toward the back of the head, straight up from the ear, but not around the face]. He reached back here because this part of the head is especially associated . . . and he pulled it out with his left hand, because that's sensitive and more likely to engage feelings, and left it from there. So if you were trying to impart physical messaging to a loved one, you'd want him to reach up with the left hand to the left side of your head. Don't pull any hairs out, but just touch the hairs gently, all right?

Around from the temple toward the back.

That's right. And while your loved one is doing that, you can try to describe how you're feeling—not your rationale to justify your feelings, but how you're feeling about whatever issue it is that the two of you are having a misunderstanding about. It's not a time to be going on, because that will heighten the feelings for that other person. If your loved one is paying attention, he will . . . this is what works: What will happen in his body is that your loved one will temporarily, while he is touching your hair or behind the knee or behind the elbow—and sometimes it works touching here, not exactly the wrist, but a little ways up from the wrist, on the inside of the arm—while he is touching those sensitive spots, he will feel your physical feelings. And when your loved one feels your physical feelings, he will have a much better understanding of how you are feeling.

Then in order to understand how *he* is feeling, wait a few moments, maybe five minutes after that; then do the same with him, while he is attempting to describe his physical feelings. When he is attempting to describe his physical feelings, it's not about saying, "How could you say this to me?" It's not about justifying your feelings; it's not about rationale. What you are trying to do when this process is going on, as the person who's having the side of your head or the inside of your elbow or the inside of your knee touched, when you are doing that, you are trying to say, "I'm feeling something kind of uncomfortable in this part of my body"—for instance, say, the abdomen—or "I have this sort of uncomfortable painful tightness in this part of my chest."

In other words, you are attempting to describe your actual physical feelings in your body to maximize the impact on the other person so that she can experience what you are physically feeling without it simply being a miscommunication, a mental exercise—which as anyone knows who's ever had a miscommunication or a misunderstanding with someone, whether that person be an intimate or not, you know it can almost always with the mental fall into a rationale, which becomes an argument, which becomes an entrenched difference of opinion. But you still don't know why the other person is adamantly pressing his or her case so strongly, because you don't know what that person is feeling. So this is an application in your present times of how you can use physical messaging and how you can train to use physical messaging.

So I'm feeling my partner, and he's saying, "I have a tightness in my chest," and then I can feel that in my body—but then how do I get from that to understanding more about what he's saying about the issue?

At some point, you say, "All right, I'm feeling something, I'm feeling this in my body." You can say that to yourself or you can say that to your partner. Then you do that, and you have those feelings, right? Then the other person does it with you, then he has the feelings. Then you talk again.

So you don't get to know what that means?

It doesn't interpret into a mental description, each thing. Your soul doesn't interpret into a mental description either, you understand? You have these different parts of you: your spirit, your physical, your mental and your feelings. Each one of them stands alone, but they can work together, especially if you make the conscious effort for them to do so. So after you have that sensation, where you now have an understanding physically in your body of how the other person is feeling, then you talk again. Try to sit close to each other. You talk again and you say, "Now, this is how I'm feeling about this." Try to stop communicating strictly on the basis of, "This is what I believe," or "You're wrong; I'm right." Because the point is that your feelings, even if they do not represent something that you're trying to communicate, they physically will, in the case of two lovers, for instance, help the other person to know more about you in terms of your overall feelings.

Therefore, this suggests something to you: Even if you're getting along and communicate well with each other, it's good for lovers to touch the hairs or touch these intimate spots. I consider an intimate spot to be behind the knee or behind the elbow, because these are places that people do not normally touch unless you are intimate with each other. And they are spots that tend to encase and hold things. It's not an accident that the elbow bends this way. If you examine that location, even in a youngster's arm, there will always be little wrinkles there. Things are held there. Usually it's totally interlaced with feelings and experiences—not interlaced with feelings and thoughts, but with feelings and experiences.

A good tracker or a good mystical person can do this; you might see it sometimes. The person will take a thumb, put his or her thumb on the bone part of an elbow and put the first two fingers on the inside of the elbow, the inside of the arm, and be able, given the set of circumstances, to know the feelings of a person and the experiences of a person, what happened. The person says, "I don't remember what happened; I don't remember it. Someone came in and hit me over the head, and then I was out and I didn't wake up until I woke up, and then everything was different." What happened? Well, there was a feeling. Your body still perceives, even if you are unconscious. So it is felt right there, all right? And the sensitive, the tracker, the mystical person, says, "All right, I am seeing this, I am seeing that," and so on.

Become Conscious of Your Pet's Feelings

Now, here's another example: For people who have animals, this comes up all the time, and in your time *many* people have animals: dogs, cats, horses, birds and so on. When the animal is not feeling well . . . animals start not feeling well the same way a human being does. Maybe the animal feels a little off; maybe it has a few pains and aches. In short, it usually eases in exactly the same way it might ease in with a human being, all right?

So in the case of a pet, say a dog or a cat, you're used to touching it regularly. If you can touch your pet in a different way sometimes, just so that you can become conscious of its feelings . . . for instance, in the case of a cat, off the left shoulder, all right? Reach up in a quiet moment; don't just walk over to the cat and grab its fur. But say the cat's in your lap and you've been petting the cat for a while. Then you might be able to reach over, the cat might allow you, and at the fur off the left shoulder—on the side of the body, off the left shoulder, down the side of the body—you might reach over and with your left hand, your thumb and your four fingers, feel the fur, not to feel it as a smooth petting action, but just gently.

This is done when the cat is comfortably relaxed in your lap and you are comfortably relaxed—not when you're talking on the phone or watching television or listening to the radio or reading, but just relaxed, in a relaxed moment with your beloved pet (it could be a dog). So then you're feeling just a few hairs. What you're doing in this relaxed position that you're in—and you're feeling fairly relaxed—is that you are feeling the general feelings of the cat; this is how the cat normally feels when it's relaxed.

You don't necessarily feel all the feelings of the cat, because it's a different species. But very often you get the general feeling. You will get this just by petting the cat, but this tends to heighten it—off the left shoulder, all right? "Off" means not where the left shoulder is but slightly down the side of the body of the cat—in the shoulder area before you get to the leg, the side of the body.

Now, say the cat is acting a little funny, not quite right. Then what you can do is walk over to the cat . . . if the cat will let you touch it, walk over. If it's not feeling comfortable, maybe it's fussy or upset, hold your hand near the left shoulder and see how you feel physically. Use your left hand, or at least hold your fingers in the wand position toward the cat. Notice how you feel. Don't do it for so long that you actually start to feel uncomfortable, but just notice. The cat is feeling perhaps not so well.

This is particularly important with cats who sometimes get wounds that might turn into an abscess—with cats this happens because a wound doesn't heal right, becomes infected. (It can happen with dogs too.) It may not have any outward symptoms that you notice right away, but something is not quite right. Your cat might be upset about something, but it might also be injured or getting sick. Feel the fur, and notice how you feel. If you get an uncomfortable feeling down in your intestines or perhaps a pain in some part of your body, the moment you notice something uncomfortable in your body, release the fur. That's a sign that the cat isn't feeling well. And it might be passing, but in a day or two, if the cat still isn't feeling well or is feeling worse, it's time to have somebody help out.

I mention that because the hairs of the body, whether it be a cat or a dog or a horse . . . or in the case of a bird, the feathers, yes, but the little bits of the feathers that come out. What happens is that the energy (your radiating energy) comes out, and it concentrates in the hairs before it moves out. It doesn't concentrate in the skin; it just passes through the skin and radiates out. But if there are hairs above the skin, then it will concentrate in those.

A person might have hairs on his or her leg and so on, but we're talking about behind the knee and the elbow. The hairs will maintain the general feeling and ambiance of the feeling self for a while, and during that time, you can perceive and pick up physical feelings from those hairs. Now, if a tracker in my time can pick up all of these feelings and sensations—and all of these senses in general—from hairs that have been removed from the head, think how much stronger they would be if they were still part of your body, a vital part growing out of your body, and fully affected by irradiating energies.

Much of Communication Is Nuance

Now, there are other uses in your time. Think about the profound difficulty in communicating: other languages, other people. It is just as big a problem, if not bigger, in your time because of your capacity to travel and communicate at a distance—telephones and all of this—which we certainly didn't have. In my time meeting people who couldn't communicate directly with us was limited by the simple fact of how many people existed in those times, plus how much traveling actually went on and how likely it was that you might actually meet someone other than your own people.

So in your time what you are dealing with is a need to improve not only the *means* of communication—meaning, "I translate my language into yours; you translate your language into mine; we get the general intellectual idea of what each other is saying"—but the nuances. Think of it: Even in your cultures where you speak the same language . . . do teenagers, for example, speak the same language as adults or parents? Certainly not. They might use the same words, but the nuances are entirely different. How do you pick up nuances when you don't even understand the person's language?

In your time I would say—not on a global-crisis level, but on the basis of simply trying to do business, for instance, with people who don't speak the same language and whose culture is completely different or even slightly different—that fully 40 percent (speaking for the sake of the economic level here) of business deals that don't work out are not just because you were impolite in some way you didn't understand, based upon the culture of other people, or because the translations of your languages with these other people missed the mark a few times. But rather they don't work out because of a word that might translate from one language to another and be very precise in the language as to a certain meaning if you say it different ways. So perhaps you say a word or a series of words in a sarcastic way; it might read, say in a translation, one way where the sarcasm would be completely missed. So the nuance is missed.

For example, people in your culture all the time will say something that is a factual statement as it reads, but if it's said sarcastically, it's actually a joke and means the opposite. So you are dealing with things like that on a daily basis in your culture, and when a young country such as the United States, for example . . . you are young in your global approach. I do not think of your country as being more than two hundred years old, and you have not really been global citizens with a desire to pursue global interests for much more than fifty years, so you're very young in that way. As a result, your communications tend to be straightforward on a business level, but you are not looking for nuances, and you are missing them very often. Whereas older cultures are looking for nuances in what you are saying. That's why sometimes the older cultures get the better of you, whether it be in business transactions, personal transactions or even occasionally, yes, in political transactions—maybe sometimes more often than occasionally.

Homework: Improving Communication through Touch

I don't want to digress too much into that area, but I want to bring this up to date so you can see that it's of value in your own times. What you are looking at here, now, in your times, is a means to improve the quality of communication, because so much of communication is nuance. So for homework, I'm going to recommend something that will require . . . I don't want you to go overboard with the homework, but it will require you to interact with a friend. This has to be at the very least a very good friend. It doesn't have to be the opposite sex; it can be, but it doesn't have to be.

Pick a subject for which you have a difference of opinion—not to create a battle. It can be something political, it can be something personal, though not too personal, please. It can be something that is just . . . something that in the past you've disagreed about. Maybe one of you likes stripes, and maybe one of you likes checks. Or maybe the other person likes solid colors and can't understand how you can wear those stripes and checks together—something simple, all right? Talk about it for a while. This is just for fun, but it's training. It won't take more than thirty seconds probably for that conversation to get going to where both of you will have strong feelings about it, not that you will necessarily express them. And I don't mean you need to argue or battle about something—"This baseball team is better than that baseball team"—not necessarily really arguing, but your strong feelings will come up quickly.

This has to be done with a good friend, you understand, because it's going to involve touch. Then since you both know what you're doing— this can't be one person experimenting and not telling the other; both have to go into their homework consciously—then you try the touching of the hair, all right? One person touches the hair of the other person on the left side with your left hand, between your thumb and two forefingers. Feel a few hairs on the left side of the person's head, let's say above the ear but not at the top of the head. So the hairs that grow up higher might actually be extending down the side of the head, but that's okay; it's the general area, all right? And feel them—don't pull them, just feel them. You can move your fingers around. It doesn't have to be one hair or one lock of hair; you can move your fingers around a bit. But don't ruffle the hair. You're not reaching over to rub the head of somebody; this is something where you're . . . it's sensitive, it's sensations, it's sensing—all of those things.

So it's very gentle.

It's gentle, and you're attempting to feel something, and you're also allowing those sensitive tips of your fingers to feel this enough so that you will get a physical feeling in your body. If at any time you get an uncomfortable physical feeling, stop and relax; you've had too much of it. So you're not going to feel the hairs for more than, say, a few minutes, maybe up to three or four minutes, but no more than that. It could be less than that. Then relax . . . both of you relax quietly for at least three or four minutes. Then the other person does that.

But before the other person does that, I want you to resume your talk so that you're disagreeing: "Stripes are better than checks," something simple, all right? It could be, "This baseball team is better than that one," something that doesn't . . . it's not life and death, all right? So then the other person feels, and you stop talking. There's no talking while the person is feeling the hair. The other person feels your hairs, then you relax for a minute—again, for three or four minutes at the most—then you talk again, trying to describe why the stripes make you feel better, trying to engage your physical feelings, describing how you feel physically when you're wearing stripes and how it feels so much better than when you're wearing checks.

Now, I'm using something innocuous like that, but it's actually true that people might actually feel—people who wear stripes, for example—physically better wearing stripes. Remember, this whole thing is about material mastery; these are lessons in material mastery, because material mastery is everything, everything, and how it feels, and how it comes together, on the basis of mutual shared physical feelings. That's material mastery. So this is all about material mastery. I talked to you about feelings and the story about my brother and the tracker, and how trackers can feel the feelings that were imparted in the track, that they can know that the bear was hungry or the bear was thirsty, that the bear was missing its cubs—all of these things. It's all about material mastery.

Using Physical Feeling in Business and Politics

How do we use this with someone from another culture in, as you said, a business or political situation, when we can't be feeling that person's hair?

You train with this technique, all right? You train with people who are intimate or close friends so that when you go into a business discussion like this, you take the same fingers [in the wand position]. You can perhaps be crossing your arms across the body, or you might reasonably, in a business conversation, be able to lay your hand down and have your hand in the wand position, aiming toward the hairs of the person on his or her head. Or you might even be able to quickly, as you move your hand, say, from your side to . . . you might move your hand and touch the side of your face and then move it back down. But if you move it up and at a distance, your hand can briefly aim for the side of the other person's head, to the left and aiming toward his or her hairs. It's not invasive if it's very quick.

I grant that if the person is bald, it's different. If the person is bald, then you might lead toward—if he or she is wearing a short-sleeved shirt—the inside of the elbow, the inside of the arm. But I'm just going to stay with hair for now; even though there are other techniques, we're just going to use hair for now.

So you just aim quickly at the side of the head, which is the person's hair, yes? And you might pick up the feelings that the person's talking about, so you can tell the difference. Think about it: You're in a business conversation, and someone is talking; she might talk for quite a while and then stop, and then the translator translates. Very often this will happen in a different culture. Say, for instance, you as an English-speaking citizen are talking to a Japanese citizen. You can hear the Japanese citizen talking at length, and then the translator translates it into your language and it's very brief, and you know you're missing a lot. This has to do with cultural differences in the language as it is spoken. You might also hear the person who is communicating to you in this other language saying something, and you can tell he's upset about something. You can tell he's having a feeling, but you can also tell, on the basis of what the translator is saying to you, that that feeling isn't coming across to you, and you don't know what it is. Is he feeling excited? Is he feeling sad? Is he feeling agitated? Is he angry? All these things it would help to know.

Think of how this would be helpful to diplomats in negotiating differences in cultures and treaties. It would be vital, because the diplomat you are speaking to would not be able to say more than she would be able to say, but she would, in her feelings, be able to communicate in the unspoken. Diplomats are used to communicating in the unspoken, which is why diplomats and people in these professions have to be highly sensitive so that they can get the best sensation of the nuances or the unspoken. This would help them to be able to sense the unspoken better. I grant that it might be a basic lesson, but it is a good foundation.

So practice with your companions and good friends or lovers. In short, practice with people who are comfortable with you practicing. And then go to places where you cannot touch the other person; in some cases, it might even be dangerous to do this. Maybe, for instance, you have to walk down a street to your home, but someone has broken the street lamp or it has just burned out. You can tell there are people down there. Maybe they are friends, maybe they won't bother you, but maybe they will. But you move the wand in the general direction of their heads, and you get the sensation of what they're feeling. If you get a bad feeling in your body, then maybe they just don't feel well, but on the other hand, maybe they represent a danger.

I am not suggesting that you use this in that circumstance, because there are other techniques to use that are better. What I am saying is that with fine-tuning, with applications of instinct—because what I'm talking about generally here, now, today, has to do with the instinctual body—that all of these things, when taken in an accumulated whole, allow you to know (not just to think) how many mistakes have been made because you *thought* you were right.

This Is Mastery Based on Mutually Shared Experience

We're talking about material mastery; we're talking about spiritual mastery. We're talking about a mastery based upon mutual shared experience, and life is mutual shared experience. All life, whether it be a blade of grass, an ant, a cow, an elephant, a human being, an atom—*all have feelings exactly the same as each other*. Even though bodies are completely different, the function of physical feelings is exactly the same on an interspecies or even other-matter basis. A rock has the same feelings as you. A storm, a bolt of lightning . . . I don't recommend that you feel the feelings of a bolt of lightning for obvious reasons. But if you know that there is a shared language, then the value of learning about and being able to apply this shared language that is felt exactly the same by all forms of existence is vital. As I said, with hand gestures, you might be able to gesture that you need water, you need food, you need to go to the bathroom and so on, but it is limited. You have to have something else.

Can you give me some more advanced processes, just the names of them, that I can ask you a different time when you might not think of them? You said this was very basic.

It's basic because I'm trying to give people a foundation.

But there are more advanced processes in this process, right?

In terms of feeling the feelings of others, there are many different processes. But I'm trying to give you something that is accessible by a great many people, because not everyone has a lover but you might have a cat or a dog or a good friend. That encompasses a great many more people. So I had to start you off with something that is not so esoteric, that you can access, that is accessible. But I will give you more on this, a lot more, or we can talk more about this now if you have further questions.

Using the Wand to Sense Danger

For instance, with the streetlight that was out and people were down the street, you said you wouldn't use this, that you would use another technique. What would you use in that instance?

I would use the wand like this: Say this is the street in front (I'm pointing to the general front). You go like this with the wand if you're covering an area, not just pointing at something. If you're covering an area, you always move the wand, the hand in the wand position, right to left. You never move it from left to right.

Why?

It's not a mental reason; it's a feeling. You are more sensitive and receptive moving to the left. If you attempt to move the wand from the left to the right, you are not protecting the most sensitive area. Where is the most sensitive area in the wand? It is in the palm. So when you're moving from the right to the left, you're protecting that sensitive area.

Take your hand right now and move it like this in the wand position. You will notice, when you stop the motion, that you will have a sense, a physical sense, in the palm. While you're moving it, of course, you have a physical sense on the back of the hand, but when you stop it, the last physical sense you have is in the palm. You're protecting that when you move from the right to the left.

So say you're looking at the street at a distance. Maybe you're in a car or you're walking; maybe you're in a bus and you're not sure whether to get out at this stop. You move your hand up like this [move your hand across, as he said, from the right to the left]. Most people aren't going to think that you're crazy, but if they do, so what? You're getting off the bus, and you move like that. Or if it feels a little uncomfortable, move like that—move your hand like that if you get an uncomfortable feeling. You can't see anybody, there are no people on the streets, but what you don't realize is that there are people standing in the doorways. Maybe they don't mean you any harm, but maybe they are doing something, and if you happen to walk past them, they will be startled, upset, and they might say something. In short, it would be better to get off at the next stop. So get off at the next stop. But you feel.

In the case of the streetlight, you can walk up the street and move your hand wand from the right to the left. How does your physical body feel? Yes, you get the sensations in the wand hand, but how does your physical body feel? Does it feel uncomfortable? Maybe you take a different route home. Do you feel all right? Well, okay. You don't have to know what the people are doing. You walk home, and that's that; you're safe. It's about safety, but ultimately it's about compatibility.

Finding a Sense of Compatibility

Material mastery at its most basic form is about touching. When you have contact between two compatible things, whether they be atoms or cells or ants or hands of human beings, there will be a comfortableness, a desire to come into greater contact or simply a welcoming of that contact—compatibility, touch. But if those two things (atoms, cells, ants, hands) don't feel that sense of compatibility, then they go elsewhere— meaning that, in the case of human beings, your hand is meant to touch the hand of somebody else. Granted, this isn't always the case with relatives and so on, but for the sake of our description, your hand reaches toward someone and doesn't feel quite right.

Say you're a young person at a dance, and you feel attracted or you look at a person and know, "Oh, he's so beautiful; oh, he's so good-looking." You want to go over there. You're walking over with your friends; people are milling around. No one's really decided to dance yet or maybe they have but you haven't. You walk over and you reach your hand out. Maybe you're ten to fifteen feet away, but your hand is aimed toward the hand of the other person, and you get a slightly uncomfortable feeling either in your fingertips or in your body.

Granted, you may not have this experience at a dance when you're feeling nervous, but I'm giving you examples of different cultures and groups of people. So you get that uncomfortable feeling, that this isn't the right person. You move your hand from the right to the left . . . oop! There's a hand you feel comfortable with. It doesn't look quite the way you would normally . . . you understand, maybe this isn't the sort of appearance of a person whom you would normally be attracted to. But you're at a dance and you want to have a good time, and that hand feels more comfortable to touch. If that hand feels more comfortable to touch, it will be more comfortable to dance with that person—or if that person can't dance, to sit down and talk. In short, compatibility, all right?

Robert Uses Compatibility and Compassion to Move Storms

For example, Robert has been trained to move hurricanes. How does he do that? It is all involved with compatibility, compassion, influence.

That is a formula in material mastery. It's not will; will doesn't come into it at all. It's that Robert is compatible and compassionate with Mother Earth, and the storm is part of Mother Earth's body. Robert moves his hand, the wand . . . Robert uses the wand, points at the picture of the storm, moves his hand [he's pointing his wand at it, and he flips his fingers up and moves his fingers aside]. He points to the storm and moves his fingers in different directions. What's he doing?

He's actually moving his fingers in a clockwise direction, usually. He moves to one o'clock, but he doesn't just point to one o'clock. He points toward the storm, then moves his fingers, sliding toward one o'clock, and pulls his hand back, points to the storm, moves his fingers, slides his fingers out in the wand position toward two o'clock, and on around the clock. What's he doing? When he does that, he is noticing how he feels in his physical body. When he gets warm, that is the direction the storm, as part of Mother Earth's body—compatibility and compassion—is prepared to move, will move, will choose to move if he then applies the techniques he's been given in material mastery to move the storm.

The Feeling of Welcome

So what we're talking about here is ultimately . . . when I'm talking about physical messaging, we're talking about another aspect of material mastery. And by discussing it in this detail, we're also engaging spiritual mastery here, because spiritual mastery has a lot to do not only with feelings but with how feelings are integrated from one being to another—and the being could be an atom or a person or an elephant—in order to recognize compatibility. When there is compatibility, there may be shared mutual experience, or there might simply be compatibility on a physical feeling level. That's how atoms come together to form cells and ultimately how these individual atoms know that they're supposed to be a toe in your body when you're growing inside your mother as a baby, or whether they're supposed to be a nose. It's all based on compatibility, compassion and ultimately the influence exerted by welcoming.

Say you're an atom floating around inside of mother, not yet having gone to the child but on the way. You're not thinking, because you're entirely based on feeling, you have feelings. You're going toward the child, maybe in the bloodstream, you're moving around in there, and you know you're there for a reason. But this isn't a mental process; you're just in a heightened state of feeling. You're moving around in the bloodstream of the child, for example, or you're moving around in some portion of the child's body. Are you seeking the nose? You don't even know what a nose is. No. As an atom, using that as an example (it's a good example, though), you are looking for compatibility, and that term can best be described on the feeling level as you are looking for the feeling of being welcome.

Now, you know how it is to feel welcome. It's one thing when a person says to you, "Oh, welcome; welcome to my shop" [said in a flat unemotional tone]. You may not necessarily feel welcome. But if someone says, "Welcome to my house! It's so good to see you! I've missed you!" [said in clearly exuberant tones]—in short, it is genuinely, actually at the physical feeling, the feeling level.

For the atom, it's the same thing. The atom is moving through the body— everything feels all right, maybe this feels a little foreign. But the atom is moving through the body of the child in some way or around the body in that fluid, and all of that stuff is going on inside of the mother's body. How does that atom know where to go? Does it randomly become a toe? No. It's moving around in the child's body or around the outside of the child's body; it becomes part of the body based upon the physical feeling of welcome.

All life experiences feelings in exactly the same mechanical way. If you know that and even if you learn nothing else about material mastery, you will have an insight that will allow you to see that if all life is like that and everything is alive—which it is—then you will know that you have one means for certain of knowing where is the best place for you to be at any given moment, because of compatibility, compassion (welcome), which often has influence associated with it. You feel, as the other atoms already amassed there, another atom coming that you know is supposed to be with you, and you exude a feeling of welcome. The influence of that feeling is that that atom feels welcome in that moment by the atoms it is meant to join. But if it is an atom that is meant to be somewhere else, it doesn't feel that feeling of welcome and it keeps on going. Only the atom that is meant to be there feels that feeling of welcome.

Say you walk into a room, and the person you were looking for . . . maybe you're at the airport, with hundreds and hundreds of other people. You walk into the gate as you say, off the plane, and your friend or loved one says, "Welcome! I'm so happy to see you!" You walk straight to that person. You are the atom going straight to where the welcoming feeling is.

The Mechanics of How to Know How to Be

You see, the mechanics of material mastery are very important. And this is applied material mastery. It's different than the material mastery that we talk about theoretically, or material mastery applied for spiritual purposes in order to engage a connection between you as an individual and a mountain, say, in order to improve the quality of life for all beings on Earth—that is another form of applied material mastery. But here I'm trying to give you the actual physical mechanics of how it works and give you enough examples so that you can learn, expand and grow, and understand to some degree the spiritual underpinnings of material mastery—so that you can grasp as much as possible with words and thought the means of knowing. When I say "knowing," I'm talking about the physical knowing (how you feel) of knowing how to be.

Look at New Age and even philosophical literature; it's all associated ultimately with that statement: *how to be*. How to *know* how to be. Granted, some philosophies are wonderful; they have a great deal to offer. Religions are very often wonderful. Even insightful philosophies and statements are wonderful. But how to *know* . . . how to know, as the atom knows, that, "I feel welcome; that's where I go." How to know? It is physical. How to know to take this street instead of that street when you're driving home. How to know in a room where people are networking, doing business, and you look around and everybody looks pretty much the same, that there are certain people whom you have an idea are interested, whom you can approach—how to know which one to approach? Feeling.

I'm not trying to say that you are prepared, after you read this, to go out and apply this. What I am saying is that there is value in learning these things, because you can not only put this into effect in your personal life, in your intimate, immediate life (of how to know, for instance, whether this apple is good for you to eat that day or whether this orange is good for you to eat that day, on the basis of what feels right to your body when you point at it with the wand), but also how you can improve the quality of your business, your career, your personal life, your health—in short, everything.

The Importance of Feeling Body Messages

Once this happened to another person I knew. It was really not through a pure spirit connection. But this person was living in another part of Earth, and he felt uncomfortable. It was like his body was vibrating on the inside, and he didn't know what it was about. Physical feeling. There was like a shaking on the inside, and he didn't know what it was about. But as he moved around on the Earth and where he lived . . . he lived about the same time I did, and my connection with him was remote, all right?

Long vision.

Long vision is where the connection was. This person told me that he was feeling this shaking, and he didn't know what it meant, but if he moved around on different parts of the Earth where he lived, that it would get better or worse depending on where he lived. And he felt very uncomfortable. He was the local mystical man there, with their people. He didn't know what it was about, there was nothing in their tribal culture to explain it, so he said that he suggested that they move camp to another place, about a half mile from where they were.

There was some resistance, because the place they were in was right next to their water source. If they were a half mile away, someone would have to walk every day to go get water, then walk back and so on. It was inconvenient. But he said he felt strongly, and they believed him, so they moved. Three days after they moved, there was an earthquake right in that spot—meaning that the earthquake was felt by them where they were, but the Earth actually erupted in that spot, and rocks and everything were hurled around and so on, and the Earth shifted its actual position.

If their camp had been there, people would have been hurt or even killed. And the moment after the earthquake, the shaking inside his body stopped. I'm not saying that for everybody who has a shaking inside his or her body, it means there is an earthquake coming; what I am saying is that your body—and this was a highly trained mystical man who had this experience—is trying to communicate to you all the time.

The advantage of getting to understand your own physical feelings and identifying your physical feelings with what's going on in your life—"This happens to me; this is how I feel physically"—meaning . . . say you are a youngster, you are at school, and the other children don't take you in as friends. Maybe the people you want to be friends with don't take you in. This makes you feel physically a certain way. You want to be friends with them, you want to be with their crowd, and physically you feel a certain way. If you describe how you're feeling, "Oh, I feel like they're keeping me away," and so on, you can come up with words, but each person might have physical feelings with that sort of rejection that show up in his or her body in a different way.

You need to identify how you feel that in your body. When you are able to identify that, then you will know. This is particularly common in your time, which is really problematic for you all, and that is that sometimes you have an instantaneous feeling—meaning it doesn't last long—a physical feeling of some discomfort that quickly passes. It may not have anything to do with disease. You'd be surprised how many body messages are interpreted as something coming on, a discomfort or, "I'd better go see the doctor"—not by many people, but by some—when it's actually a body message.

If you know, let's say, how it feels to be rejected . . . maybe you even went up to somebody at a bus stop and you were going to say, "Could I have a cigarette?" or "Would you like a stick of gum?" and that person turned his or her back and moved away from you. It may seem like a small thing, but you get the feeling in your body every time, usually in the same place—a physical feeling that has to do, in that case, with being rejected. If you know that, then sometimes when you get those feelings, you won't have to wonder what they are.

You might get a mixed group of feelings that happen all the time, that are constant for you—your body giving you multiple messages at the same time of physical feeling. The more you can train to know what your physical feelings are and what they are associated with in your life . . . either in the moment, or sometimes if you're having a recollection that you're thinking about, your body might bring up the physical feelings from that time and then you have those physical feelings again to a lesser degree. And if you can identify your physical feelings with actions in the present or in the past, it might be very helpful to know how to move more easily toward circumstances, experiences, and how to find your compatibility.

Sometimes in your world, which is so confusing and so frought with different circumstances and different distractions, a hundred things going on at the same time, you feel overwhelmed—how to know what to do? Use compatibility, compassion, influence. In short, remember the lesson of the attraction the atom felt when it was feeling welcomed by the place it was supposed to be in the child's body. Other atoms were whizzing by, and they didn't feel that welcome; only the atom that was supposed to be there felt that.

There Is an Urgent Need to Improve Communication

It's important to understand that in your time the most urgent need is to improve communication. And you as a people on Earth actually know that, which is why there has been a pell-mell, massive rush toward different means of technical communication—because you are in an intellectual time, in a technical time. You are expressing the need for communication externally by creating more and more complex and very often more useful tools of technology, not recognizing that you are actually being driven to improve communication internally on the material- and spiritual-mastery levels.

But future historians will look back and mark the beginning of that increased feeling of the desire, the mass feeling by all people, to improve communications at the time of the telephone being developed. They'll say, "Earth, this is the beginning, this is when people started to feel the need to improve communications, and they started out externally and then they moved ultimately internally." But that will be their marker. They'll say, "Telephone—that was the beginning." And they will say, "Look. They went through all of these different communications—computer, Internet, fax machine—all of this being a means to communicate and, yes, to improve communications. But all external."

But that makes sense, when you think of it, because in your time, much culturalization takes place externally. Granted, there was external culturalization in my time, but equally there was internal as well. A child would get a name when he or she was born that that child would use, but by the time children were, say, two years old, two and a half at the latest, maybe three (I know of one example that was not until three) . . . by expressing their feelings and moving their bodies, then the elders or those who could understand these things would give them their actual name based upon all of their expressed feelings. In short, this was internal, because the child was told, "This is your name, and it expresses to you the actual physical feelings of you, how you are physically inside and out," giving the child a means to explore herself or himself on the basis of a name that was an actual description of his or her personal character.

So the value of that was immense. Then the child didn't have to look in a hundred other places or possibly a thousand other places—an infinite number—of other people's identities, names, based upon their actual personal identification . . . the child didn't have to look in all the wrong places to find himself or herself. The child started out with the right place, to know how to find himself or herself, and it made the job of finding oneself and ultimately how to be easier.

In your time that is largely missing, but we are talking about these things because we feel that they are valuable for your time as well as for our own. Yes, when you have a child, you can't just call him, "Hey, you!" You have to give your youngster a name; that's fine. Keep giving your children their names. But also, if you can, take notice: "How are they? How do they act?"

Children are different. Don't expect parents to be able to get this. Grandparents, though—not just older people, but people who were younger who had children of their own, raised those children and now there are grandchildren—by that time there's often enough wisdom; you can see. The child is extrovert; he's introvert; he is studious; he is friendly. In short, children have different qualities. They move this way physically or not that way. When someone comes into the room who is familiar, they jump because they are edgy and nervous, or when someone comes into the room and is familiar, they get up, they are friendly. In short, all these different qualities, and many others are different.

Try to give the child a descriptive name that describes him, which he can use to identify with as a personality quality that he can cultivate based upon the way he actually is. Grandparents, I do not expect you to be able to do this immediately, but be thinking about it. Consider it. Some of you have had lots of youngsters, raised families successfully—be thinking about it. Grandparents, you will know that you raised your families successfully, because when you look at your youngsters, you feel comfortable, you feel good looking at them. Yes, you might feel proud, you might feel enthusiastic, you might feel love, but you feel good looking at them. That's how you will know when it's successful.

Now, be thinking so that you can work up a means that will fit into your culture as to how you can describe . . . sometimes this happens with nicknames, but if the nickname is given by other children, it's usually something disparaging—a putdown, as you say. Whereas if a loving grandparent could give a name, it might be different. Think about it: The name used to be something that described qualities that it would benefit the child to explore. This is not a name meant to manipulate the child. Maybe the child is artistic; you don't want to give that child a name that would manipulate her into becoming scientific when she doesn't have an aptitude, and her aptitude and interest lie in being artistic. Do you wish to suppress a Beethoven? Of course not.

So compatibility, compassion, influence . . . whereas in your time, very often influence happens as the result of something else. Different reasons: sometimes good, sometimes not so good. But when compatibility and compassion are involved, influence is much more likely to take place, and it is much more likely to be enduring as well as nurturing and beneficial. Three good things, eh?

So that's what you want. You want to have the atom in the child feeling welcome to be a part of the bellybutton rather than being lost and not knowing where to go and deciding to be an eyelash instead. Maybe that eyelash never quite feels right and falls out pretty soon. All things . . . Creator creates this universe, yes? Creator says to Itself, "In order to create this universe, I know one thing for sure, and that's that in order for things to come together as I wish them to, in my image of beauty, I must at the very least have a shared feeling process amongst all creation, all beings. If they have this shared-feeling process, then the easiest thing to do would be to be able to find your way to that which is compatible." So that is a given. Creator does that absolutely—never even considers doing anything else.

You are in a school—Explorer Race school—on this Earth right now. You do not necessarily know that, it is not necessarily part of your culture, but you are in the school attempting to learn, attempting to cocreate with Creator—consciously sometimes, but most of the time unconsciously. The processes you are learning, being forced to learn, are almost exclusively based on answering questions based upon the unknown.

Feelings Are the First Language for Children

As a child, you are fascinated by things; as you get older, you wonder why. How many parents have heard (well past the point that they want to hear) that famous question from youngsters, which is a word they learn very early on, which is, "Why?" If you think about it, it can be annoying, but on the other hand, the child is not only exploring his or her world— and it's a small world when you're a youngster—but the child is also exploring philosophically his or her world. Even though the child may not understand the words you use, he or she will understand the feelings you are feeling when you explain why.

That is why, when you say to a child, "I haven't got time to explain that to you right now," even though it might be true . . . I'm not casting any blame on you. You might say, "I can't talk to you about that right now; I'll talk to you about it later," and maybe you do talk about it later, maybe you don't. The child will probably not understand, unless the child is old enough, but let's talk about a child two or three years old who knows how to say, "Why?" The child will probably not understand, "I haven't got time to talk to you about it now; I'll talk to you later." He or she may not understand that mentally, but the child will understand absolutely your feelings. So the child might identify "Why?" with discomfort. You were feeling uncomfortable; you were rushed, you had to go somewhere, you had to do something.

I want you to understand this because feelings are the first language for youngsters. This is why, when you have youngsters growing up . . . the child says (and you are the parent, a young parent), looking at snow, "Why?" You may not have an answer for that. This is a perfectly legitimate answer to your child, that young one who looks up to you—you're the world, all right?—you can say, "I don't know." Maybe you don't know why; very often you won't have a good explanation for why. But if your feeling expresses something that you don't know, or it is a question mark, "I don't know," but it's also a loving feeling toward your child—that child is going to come away with that.

Your child might continue to say, "Why?" And you pause, try to stop what you're doing for a moment . . . if you're ironing or cutting some food up, pause for a moment, focus on that and say, "I don't know why." You can also say, "We'll have to read up about that, so I can explain why to you." The child may not understand any of that, but he or she will understand, because the child is open and connected on the feeling level. The child understands his or her world, when he or she is very young like that, entirely on the basis of feelings.

That is how when children grow up sometimes and become adults, in your time perhaps more so than in my time, they will sometimes have, as you call it, inappropriate reactions to certain circumstances or things that might stimulate them. So in the case of this example, say it starts to snow and the child, or in this case the adult, still doesn't know why each crystal of snow looks different, but she knows on the basis of her feeling that it's uncomfortable: "Can't think about that." This is because that person identifies at the root of her being, when she was learning about your culture, that when you say quickly, "Haven't got time to explain that now; I'll explain it later," she will know that feeling of impatience, distraction and annoyance—that that is "Why?"

Now, I realize that sounds overly simplistic, and it's not always the case, because often there are children who will grow past this. But we can't overemphasize in your time that the most important career that exists anywhere in your world right now is being a parent. When you have children, there is, granted, a limit to what you can do. You can read the books that say "Do this; don't do that"—that's good. But try to stay connected with your feelings, what feels good to you, and try to communicate to your child on the basis of what, in that loving warmth, feels relaxed and comfortable. And try to make time, if you can.

When your child says, "Why?" answer why to the best of your ability, even if you have to continue ironing or cutting up food or sawing wood. If you have to do that, answer why to the best of your ability, even if it's, "I don't know." And try to pay attention, if you can, to your feeling when you say that, because you could say, "I don't know," and there's a sense of curiosity on your part. The child then identifies, "Why?" with curiosity, which is healthy. Good night.

Good night.

Other Aspects of Physical Messaging

Speaks of Many Truths
November 27, 2001

his is Speaks of Many Truths. Greetings.

Greetings.

I'm not sure whether we are done with the topic we discussed yesterday, physical messaging—something from the physical self that is imparted in one way or another. But the foundation of physical messaging is as in the story of my brother discussed previously.

Magnetic Imprints on Channeling Tapes

Does energy from the channeled entity during channeling get stored onto magnetic audio- or videotape? Can it be felt by the person who listens to the tape?

The energy that passes through Robert [the channel] that is identified with myself creates a magnetic imprint on the tape or other medium that creates a specific patterning. I do not wish to make it sound so esoteric. Let us simply say that a person could listen to the tape once, and if he was spiritual or sensitive to energies, he could then take the tape—not in a box, but the tape itself in its cassette only—or other media (say it was a disk of some sort), and he could put it somewhere on his body, possibly in a chest pocket, or possibly in the center of the chest or somewhere even above the middle of the bellybutton, or possibly on the back as well if he chose. He could wear it there for a time once he listened to the recording, and the energy in its own right would impart some form that is physical.

Think of a strip of tape. There would be certain technical means to show where the recording is. A recording would appear essentially as little stripes from a distance. But the imprinting also happens on portions of the tape that are not totally engaged in recording sound. Understand that this is an example. This cannot be seen.

It might be possible to measure it with a device that measures magnetic things, but even under a microscope, it would not be visible. Interestingly enough, some of these patterns are not unlike the shapes, for those of you who can see them, of lightbeings. The recording media shown in the case of the tape would be impacted by the energy. However, there are other things that the energy might impact gently and be usable, but only for a short time.

Tape is something that is intended to be specifically reactive to magnetic energy. Some other recording media are like that too. So generally anything that's intended to have that description—"specifically reactive to magnetic energy"—is likely to hold the energy for a while and actually provide some form of usable resonance, meaning that it would continue to exude a certain amount of radiated energy. I might add that even if the tape was reproduced, the energy would be to a lesser degree but still present. Let's say a reproduced tape would still radiate energy for up to ten years.

What percentage of the original?

The loss from the original tape to a duplicated copy, for example, might be about 7 percent. If you were to make a copy of that copy, then the loss might be maybe 16 percent more, but it would still be useful.

If you had a master tape and you made hundreds of copies, what would that be?

It depends. The original tape would have as much energy as it could imprint. It depends on how you make the copies. If the copies that are distributed widely are third-generation tapes, then the loss might be 24 percent. But if any of them are second-generation tapes, then the loss would be 7 percent. But it depends on how much demand there would be. In any event, technology like that is not my strong suit.

I would say that CDs would be more likely to hold the energy longer. The loss from, say, the original . . . I believe only the second generation would be necessary there. The loss from the original to the second generation would be about 4.5 percent.

Your energy is flowing through Robert, so it doesn't deplete him. You have infinite energy, so it doesn't deplete you. So it's a gift.

Yes, and it has heretofore largely been experienced only by those present during the channeling. I grant that being present during the channeling compared to the energy on a tape or compared to the energy on even some other media . . . being present would be two or three times as much in energy. You know, the energy flows sometimes more, sometimes less.

But it's surprising how much energy can be felt by listening to a recording and then just keeping that recording nearby. You don't have to wear it on your person; you could just simply have it. You could sit in a chair, for a person who reads, and every once in a while just glance at it—it's there—maybe reach over and touch it. This can make a difference, because it retains and is receptive to that magnetic energy. So it has to be something like that.

Crystals Breathe Magnetic Energy In and Out

Some crystals are that way, but since crystals are more of a living matter, the way a crystal *breathes* is that it takes in magnetic energy, then it releases magnetic energy. It works very much like a breath, except breath for a human or another lunged creature is more frequent. From crystal to crystal, it would be different, but a crystal might take in whatever it's taking in and then exhale on the basis of who needs what that the crystal can exude, because it has that present, even if the person does not accept it, understand?

I don't want to get too far afield here, but say, for example, that a crystal has taken in, by being exposed to human beings and their activities, or animals, plants . . . wherever it has been, it has taken in and absorbed the energy that is compatible with that crystal from all of those experiences and happenings; it has taken that in. And then since it doesn't need it for itself, when someone or something . . . perhaps a leaf blows by or a human being walks by, a deer, a beagle, something goes by the general area of the crystal (depending on the crystal, that could be up to thirty feet away, or if it's a massive crystal, maybe even three miles away). And the crystal has that experience—a magnetic imprint, if you would—within itself.

If that leaf, beagle, person, what-have-you, needs some of that energy, the crystal will *exhale* that energy toward that person, but not with an attachment to that person receiving it. So it is simply exuded in that person's general direction, and if that person welcomes it, then he or she takes it in and does something with it in some way that might benefit him or her. It might support and sustain one of that person's guides, for instance, who might not know everything, as guides do not. It might prompt the guide to inspire the human being with a message that the guide might not normally consider.

It might, on the other hand, be something more physical. It might be that an organ in the body of the human being always functions in a certain way, but that human being is perhaps getting older or is injured or getting over an injury so that this organ needs to perform in a way it has never performed in that individual human's body—but that organ does have a capacity to perform that way. So in this example, that exuded energy from the crystal—that "exhale," as we're calling it—the organ might feel that.

Let's say it's the pancreas. The pancreas suddenly, without thought, has that needed wisdom or needed energy available for it. Besides performing its valuable function, it will then perform some other function engaged in the recovery of that person, in the case of an injured person. Or in the case of an older person, it might engage in some activity that will either help that person in some way, maybe physically, or in the case of a person who is of advanced age and is really a little bit in both worlds—meaning not dying, but one usually begins to make contact with the world beyond the veil several years before death—the organ might begin to work or function in a way that supports that coming transition.

So this is what I mean by a crystal breathing in and out. And that crystal would be an example of something that might, depending on the individual crystal, be able to absorb the energy we're using here. But it wouldn't be the same as that kind of a tape or disk, because the tape or disk is created by humans—not necessarily in the best way, but it is created by humans. And it will perform a function that has been given to it, even though the materials that make up the tape or disk might wish to be somewhere else doing something else—which is why a tape, for example, deteriorates over time, because it was not asked to be a tape, that wasn't done in a sacred manner. If it was done in a sacred manner, the tape would last forever.

So the reason I am not suggesting using crystals is that crystals are all like people: they are individual, they have their personality, they have their purpose and form and function and so on. You couldn't be certain whether a crystal would hold the energy for even ten minutes much less ten years.

Healing with Crystals

How does a healing practitioner work with crystals?

The crystal must be attuned to the healer's purposes. If the healer is reasonably good, when she acquires crystals, she will feel which one feels right for her. The healer won't take just any one, but only the one that feels right: "That's the one that feels good." It's not just that it feels good on the physical outside, but the healer might pick the crystal up, for instance, and hold it near her body in this position [using the left hand and holding it about six inches over the chest].

If she holds it up that way, then the healer might feel: "Oh, this is good, wonderful warmth here; this is perfect." And a healer wishing to get the best might even ask the question: "Is this the best to work on this client or that client and so on?" Healers will often acquire crystals and not use the same ones on different individuals: "This crystal for this person; this crystal for that person." If the healer is good, she would do all those things.

So the crystal then essentially volunteers to work with the healer, knowing that the crystal will be involved in transmitting or receiving between the healer (the energies that pass to and through the healer) and the patient (the energies that pass to and through the patient). The crystal, depending on the type, might also be able to acquire energy from planets, dimensions, angels and so on—various other resources that the healer or the patient does not have a direct connection with. And the healer will, of course, if she is reasonably good, be able to know that the crystal is doing something on its own to support the process. But she may not necessarily know where that is coming from (nor is that necessary to know). You wouldn't, as they say, look a gift horse in the mouth.

If one is not a healer but has a large collection of crystals, is it possible to get into a meditative state and ask the crystals if there are energies they hold that would be good for you?

It is unnecessary to do that. If the crystal has some energy like that and you are near it, it will automatically exude that energy. You do not need to ask it. This is a confusion on the part of some people. But I do recommend that if you have a collection of crystals, under no circumstances are the crystals to be touching each other unless you feel with the warmth in your body or you've been spiritually inspired to have them touch each other. And then they are to touch each other only in the way that feels exactly right. Move them toward each other, touching just so.

For example, notice the fountain over here that Robert has. The rocks are all set up, every single one of them, in exactly the positions that the stones themselves wish to be put in. This was all done by taking the stone, checking the warmth in the body—in the body of Robert in this case—and moving the stones very carefully around the whole area to see where the stones wanted to be. Some of them wanted to be in the water, and therefore, they are under the water, under the surface. Some wanted to be partially in the water, partially not. In short, Robert asked the stones what position they wanted to be in—up one way, down the other way.

The same thing is to be done with crystals if *they* wish to be touching or if you, in the case of being a healer, might feel the need to have them in contact. And so it is all done though feeling. Feeling is a universal creation magnetic energy that is the foundation for physical mastery, spiritual mastery, teaching mastery, dimensional mastery and, yes, even quantum mastery—although none of you on Earth will become quantum masters in this life on this planet at this time.

Quantum Mastery Is the Mastery of Consequences

Quantum mastery is the mastery of consequences. In time you will *all* on Earth become quantum masters, because quantum mastery is a requirement to become a creator—all the other levels too. But I mention that one because you are exposed to it on Earth since all those levels of mastery that I mentioned are ones that Mother Earth is now. This is how you can come to Earth and learn through not only, as Zoosh likes to call it, the gift of ignorance, but also you can learn because consequences are available here. Mother Earth, being a master of consequences or quantum master, has multiple potential consequences available to any given incident, moment, thought, event or whatever.

So you are exposed to that here in this institute of higher learning on Earth as the Explorer Race because it is intended that you have the opportunity to sample that which you are working toward. You're all spiritual masters; you've been spiritual masters before you came here. You may not all be spiritual masters now, but you have done that. Now you are working on material mastery on this level of Earth. But at some point, you will do that and have a life of spiritual mastery and also have a life of material mastery. And then you will all go on at various different times and places to work on teaching mastery and on to dimensional mastery and on to quantum mastery.

Once you have all completed that—it will take awhile—then you will begin to work as a creator apprentice, in which case by that time many of you will be melded together in one being. But there will be more than one being, because different portions of the Explorer Race coming together, melded together in that way, will need or desire to explore different aspects of creation. Therefore, some of you will learn from the Creator of this universe, and some of you will apprentice to creators of other universes.

Therefore, when you all get together as one creator-apprentice graduate to relieve the Creator of this universe so that this Creator can go on and you can take over, you will have acquired the skills and lessons—not only from the Creator of this universe, but also from creators of other universes—that you will use when you take over the responsibilities of being the creator for this universe. And then you will be able to create it, not only in the image of the original Creator of this universe, but more to the point, in your own image. Of course, as the children of Creator, your own image will be one that will be approved of by this Creator by that time—maybe not right now, but by that time.

This Will All Take Place on Earth

We are privileged to be on this planet. Is there any other school or venue like Earth for us to go to?

To engage these kind of things?

To have the opportunities that we have here.

Nowhere. This is it. This is why you'll work on a given level as the Explorer Race. You work on a given level. Zoosh has mentioned to you that not all of the individual souls in the Explorer Race are here. They're waiting somewhere else. But they are not going to wait indefinitely. At some point, when you move on to teaching mastery, some of those will join you. And when you move on to dimensional mastery, more of those will join you. By the time you move on to quantum mastery, everyone will be engaged in that.

You may question, where will you be? That is a reasonable question. In order to learn these lessons, you will need to be somewhere that has all of those levels of mastery available and still has the capacity to allow you to demonstrate yourself in all of those levels—meaning in spirit, yes, spiritual mastery; meaning in form, yes, material mastery; meaning in personal knowledge, yes, teaching mastery (in some form passing on knowledge); meaning in the multidimensional expression of self, meaning in creation capacity, yes, quantum mastery. So creation capacity is the level before becoming a creator apprentice.

Creation capacity would be the form of quantum mastery. That's why I said that spirit relates to spiritual mastery, form or a body to material mastery and all of the others. So we're clear on that, yes? Now the question is, where would this take place?

What theater is there?

Only one. Right here on Earth, but on other levels of Earth. You have been told before that Earth has multiple levels, and actually Earth has available to her the capacity for multiple levels. Right now, if you were on the ninth level—the ninth dimension, as you might call it; it's a little different, but let's call it the ninth level of Earth—you would feel as if you were in heaven. You will have all of these different dimensions and capacities available to you—the ninth level, the twenty-seventh level and so on, and beyond. You can only learn these things on a planet that has that many faces and that much mastery and, more to the point, that much capacity in and of her own right—Mother Earth, yes?—to be a creator herself.

So is she going to go out and become a creator somewhere else when we're done?

No. She is a teacher. She will remain as a teacher. When you are done and you move on, and when you take over this creation, you will honor her. You will recognize her and you will see Mother Earth as your old teacher pal. And should you have anything that you're not sure about, you will do the same thing I do—you will run home to teacher and say, "What about that?"

[Laughs.] Well, where did she learn all of these things, then?

You will have to ask her.

The Energy Felt by Trackers

Let's consider other aspects of physical messaging. Consider what leaves the body. You have noticed on occasion that animals will sometimes do things that offend human beings—meaning that animals might sniff in areas where other animals have urinated or defecated. Human beings feel uncomfortable about this, and yet master trackers and even trackers—I'm not creating levels intentionally here, but trackers learn from master trackers—all know that anything that passes through the body of someone you're tracking will retain for quite some time not only the obvious . . . whether the animal is a male or a female and whether, in the case of the dog smelling, if the female is in heat, as they say—not just things like that.

But it will also retain a degree of that being's feelings, sometimes a greater degree, when something passes through the intestines where a great many feelings are stored. It will retain that, and therefore, the energy can be felt by a tracker.

Sometimes people who don't understand the ways of trackers, especially master trackers, will not understand when a master tracker leans over and puts his or her hand over a pile of defecation from an animal, but a great deal is understood here. You know what the animal is feeling. For example, if you're tracking for the purpose of hunting, you will be able to know immediately if the animal is tired and whether it will need to sleep soon. Then you will know whether you can catch up.

So I am not saying that you all are to be doing these things. But understand that anything that passes through the body of a human being or an animal or even through a plant . . . although plants are more efficient. Still, plants drop things (usually seeds, sometimes fruits to entice that the seeds be consumed), but let's stick to human beings here. Anything that is emitted . . . hairs fall out of the heads of people, and people sometimes find that annoying or upsetting. Men go bald; sometimes even women lose some hair. But usually the hair imparts something. Every hair that falls out at any time has something to impart. Most of the time, in the case of human beings, these hairs are not going to be felt directly by another human being. I'm talking about hairs that have not been pulled out and left as a message, as in my example of my brother, but simply a hair that falls out as hairs do all the time.

This hair will retain the energy and wisdom and the full experience of that individual human being while he or she existed during the time when that hair was engaged in that person's head. When it falls out, you as a sensitive person could pick up that hair and hold it up—perhaps you'd have to pinch your fingers out—near your chest to feel it. But I don't recommend this unless that person is an intimate. Rather, I would recommend that you do the same thing the tracker does. Hold your hand briefly, maybe even just using the tips of your two fingers, in the wand position [see p. 6] pointed toward the hair from a distance, and see how it feels in your body. If it feels all right, then you can approach that hair.

In the case of a loved one, this can be useful. Say your loved one has gone out to the store and for some reason she hasn't returned, and you're worried. Then go find a hair, go find her hairbrush, point some fingers at the hairbrush and try to get a picture of where she is. She might have been delayed in traffic; perhaps there was a little accident and she had to go with the car to the garage to have it repaired. Maybe it's something simple like that; maybe it's something more than that.

I'm not saying you should do this. What I am saying is that I am putting this out because these books are training, to be read in the order of material mastery, physical mastery and spiritual mastery—intended to be read in that order. For those who have been reading the books and practicing and applying these things, they are maybe ready to hear this. And for others who are shamans in their own right or students who are working with shamans or apprentices or healers, they might also do this. Should the average person do this? I would say no. Do those other things first as recommended. Learn other things first.

Learn how to become receptive; learn how to become discerning to know when to receive. When something doesn't feel good in your body, that's not meant for you to receive. Someone else is meant to receive that—let it go. I won't go into all of that because that's been covered before. But I'm putting this out very clearly because you might point at the hairbrush and get an uncomfortable feeling. Don't assume that this means your loved one is in trouble or frightened or is experiencing some discomfort. I will give more on that in time. But I'm putting out a taste of it right now, because when we do other levels—meaning book two for material mastery or book two for spiritual mastery—then I will perhaps go into more precise detail on what to do with that. I'm just touching on it for now.

A Living Pool of Matter

Now, when hairs fall out from the head, most of them just go into the earth or you throw things (your trash and so on) into these landfills or burn them. I don't approve of burning. I understand why you have to—I completely understand—and I recognize why you do. Why I do not approve of the burning of trash is not a terrible crisis, but generally speaking, it is better to allow things to return to their natural form. But I recognize that you have to do that. I don't particularly approve of landfills either.

But let's talk about hair. Let's say you're walking the street and a hair falls out of your head as happens regularly; maybe you even notice it and brush it off your sleeve, and it goes on to the ground. That hair retains for a period of fifteen days at least all that you are up to the point of when it fell out of your head, including all your wisdom, knowledge, fears, everything. It will also include quite a bit of physiological knowledge about your body, which scientists know. But I'm not going to discuss that, since scientists are exploring that and speaking of that themselves. I want to discuss rather how much of your being is engaged there.

After fifteen days, the hair begins to change form. It transfers, it begins to turn. When that turn happens . . . it doesn't happen immediately, but it gradually begins to turn, and when it just begins to turn, what it does is it releases all that you are in knowledge, wisdom, unresolved things, fears, worries, all of that. It releases that into the earth so that all that you are when it becomes soil then becomes available for other human beings or other life forms to express those traits and qualities that—combined with all the other hairs that have fallen out and everything else that has fallen out of human beings—ultimately create a living pool of matter. This is not just physical matter, but a living pool of retained qualities, abilities, hopes, wishes, dreams, desires—everything that the creation of the physical process can tap from.

Mother becomes pregnant, and she consumes food that was grown in the land. What is the land? It is not only rotted twigs and leaves and grass but also all those who have passed before: humans, animals, everything that has gradually returned to the earth. She eats that food, it passes through her body and some of it goes to form her baby. Portions of the living reservoir of all life that has been on Earth are made available to that child growing in her womb, so that the hopes, dreams and desires of the soul have a physical counterpart that they can pull on from the reservoir of what is possible, what might be experienced, in order to match up the soul's desires with the physical reservoir of what is available here—to anchor the soul's desires in the physical reservoir of the particle consciousness of all beings so that the soul has a means and manner to ground its desires. And when the baby is born, it can express its desires. Because no matter what the soul wants to do, until it has the matter of the physical body to express itself in its multiple ways as a child . . . you must have the physical means to do so.

Nothing that happens on Earth is an accident. But that does not mean that your fate, as you call it, is chipped into stone; rather, there is a multiple possibility. Just think of all that the particles on Earth have done, all they've been involved in. In *Explorer Race: Particle Personalities*, a particle said how it was a mountain lion, but before this it had been something else, and after the mountain lion, it will be something else, and so on and on and on.

It is because of this multiple expression and experience that all the particles find themselves doing things voluntarily—not because they have been forced into it, but because they have been welcomed. They have been welcomed to some place within the body, and they *feel* welcomed. When they have that experience, then they naturally evolve or devolve— not in becoming less than, but they become something, then they fall away from it, go on, exit the body of whatever they're in and are available as a particle at some point to ground the desires of a given soul who comes here to manifest in form.

Residual Energies Left on the Earth

This planet started life in Sirius and was moved here to replace the planet we destroyed. Are we drawing on some of the experience that was generated in Sirius? Is that a possibility?

Not too much. You would have to go down to find residual matter, to actually get to residual matter leftover from Sirius, which is actually altered—this occurred in the transit from one point to another. If you could get a sample from the Sirius level, it would show some qualities that, even scientifically, you would be able to say, "Well, this resembles this matter like a first cousin." You would have to first look in the right place, and second, you would have to really go down into matter that would be difficult for you to obtain, at least forty miles into the Earth. I don't recommend it.

When ETs came here, did they drop hair or body substances?

No, most ETs are profoundly careful not to leave the slightest portion of their matter. That's why when they come here, they might even wear protective garments, not only to retain and keep themselves safe in their own energy, but also to keep them from exuding anything. Some ETs might not wear a garment but will have an energy around them that will hold their energy in and allow nothing of their energy to be left. That is why to find examples left from ETs—whether in the case of a crash and bodies or in the case of technology—is so rare, because they do not do it on purpose.

So then it's safe to say that the first humans who came to this planet after the planet moved here . . . there have been, let's say, eighteen different rise-and-falls of civilizations, so how far back do you have to go? Who were the first beings?

The first humans from my perspective who can be tracked in contemporary times were what would be called native peoples of the Earth. In some cases, the threads from those early days still exist today. I am *not* counting the so-called *Australopithecus* and all of this. I'm not counting beings who walked upright who were humanoids and are considered in the theory of evolution—by the way, evolution doesn't exist. But I am not talking about those beings, because I do not consider those to be human beings. They are beings, they are worthy beings certainly, but they are not human beings

But they were created by various ET races.

Yes, but maybe they chose to immigrate to Earth and live life the way they did. Just because you look at a group of beings and decide or you project on them qualities from the present to the best of your ability as an archaeologist . . . just because you do that and guess what their culture might have been like based upon their skulls and other remains that you might be lucky enough to find, doesn't mean that you are right. Also, you have no idea of their philosophy. So when you refer to them as primitive, that is an error.

A very big error.

They might have been *profoundly* advanced but *chose* to live in certain ways. Another obvious possibility is that they might have been profoundly advanced but found that they *had* to live in certain ways on this planet.

They got stranded, crashed or something like that?

Or maybe they chose to immigrate here, supplies ran out and they had to do the best they could. And that's how things have happened quite a bit. But those beings are not here anymore. As an archaeologist, you could reasonably ask, "Why aren't they here anymore? Why are there only a few remains that are found? Is it just because there were so few who could survive given the conditions of Earth?" There is certainly that. But the reason, in most cases, is that whoever dropped them off in the first place came back to see how they were doing and asked them if they wanted to stay or if they would like to come with them. And in most cases, most of the populations went somewhere other than the surface of the Earth.

A Dinosaur Particle Would Have Nothing to Offer You

I might add that this is the explanation for what happened to many of the animals of Earth as well who are popular with the children nowadays—dinosaurs and so on. Obviously, they wouldn't be so popular if they were living amongst you, but they are popular at the moment. Some of them moved on as well: "Would you like to live somewhere else?"

Suppose you were a dinosaur, and suppose someone came to visit your planet where you were living and spoke to you in your form of communion and said that all this was going to happen in the future with all of these human beings and their technology and machines. And you became partly shocked because you're used to living in this tropical atmosphere. You've discovered what is going to happen to the planet, and the first thing you're going to think about is your loved ones and your family and your extended family of kind: "Where can we go where we can experience a lovely lifestyle even better than we have here?"

And suppose whoever came to give you this message said, "Come with me," or "I will send someone for you." Granted, some of the species would have died or left tracks in this or that or got caught up in volcanic explosions and so on, because that's how Earth transforms itself from time to time. But that does not account for the vast bulk of those creatures. They moved on.

But the point here is what they left.

Just as you will do when you choose to immigrate to other planets someday.

But the reason I'm asking this is, are the particles that these beings left available to humans, then, as possibilities of experience?

Probably not, because the particle might pass through the mother— maybe in the case of this, a particle of a dinosaur. They were here certainly. The particles that had been dinosaurs are everywhere, all over the Earth. You might ask reasonably, "Well, if that is the case, then would a human being who wished to experience, say, all of these possibilities for his or her soul, might that person also have a potential to experience something that could only be experienced as a dinosaur?" No.

Those particles, even though they might be . . . oh, say it is in the broccoli that the mother is eating while you as the baby are forming up inside her womb. That particle might very well pass through your body as it's going through the inside of mother, all right? But in the case of our demonstration particle, let's just say it had only and always been a dinosaur. It would not have the depth and breadth of capacity to offer something to you.

Now, suppose the particle had been, for example, a cat of some sort, a saber-toothed tiger. Suppose it had also been a dinosaur. Suppose it had also been a mythical unicorn. Suppose it had also been a chimpanzee. Suppose it had been *all* of these things, and also suppose it had briefly been a human being.

Why would a particle that had been all these other creatures only have been briefly a human being? Because human beings or souls (to be human beings) come to Earth who sometimes do desire that. They may wish as a soul to have an experience associated with being a chimpanzee or a dinosaur or a saber-toothed tiger. The bulk of their desires have to do with being a human being and so on, but there is some desire to experience something associated with being, say, a saber-toothed tiger. Would you be able to find particles that could do that? This is how it would happen:

Say you have that desire as a soul. Most often your teachers would attempt to dissuade you from doing that, but let's say you stubbornly stamp your foot in the spiritual territory and say, "I want this in whatever way I can have it, even if it's only briefly." Your teachers will warn you that it may be a brief life; it may not even take place outside of mother. And you say, "I want it, I really need it and I'm not attached to it being a long life." Then your teachers say, "All right then."

Now, recognize that this is a rare circumstance. But since I gave that example, I wanted to explain how that would happen. What would happen would be this: In most cases, the child would not go out to term and be born. In most cases, that child would miscarry. Miscarriages do not happen simply because the mother has an accident or for some other reason, but it can be for a soul that desires to have an experience not intended for a human being. What happens if a soul wants to and is adamant? Souls are allowed to make mistakes. Before they come, your teachers talk to you, but your teachers are not attached to changing your intentions. They just want to advise you. But suppose you as a soul decide, even with that advice, that, "I want to have this experience." Those children inside of mother will often miscarry.

Miscarriages Allow Souls to Leave Who Need To

In my time women had miscarriages too, even though once we realized a woman was with child, she was not expected to do as much heavy work and she was nurtured. After no more than three months of your calendar time, the woman would be taken in with the women, the grandmothers, and looked after and trained and allowed to do certain things, of course, but not allowed to do other things and so on. I won't go into all of that at this time.

To protect her with the baby?

Yes, but also to prepare her for being a good mother. But even under those circumstances, which I feel are ideal, there would be miscarriages. And we believed—and I still believe on the basis of everything I've been exposed to after life as well in my physical life—that those miscarriages ALWAYS took place because of either someone just wanting to sample physical life without actually living a life, or because the soul made choices that were inappropriate to be expressed as a human being on Earth at that time.

So miscarriages do not generally happen, even in your time . . . I am speaking now, you understand, to young mothers or even middle-aged mothers: Don't assume that if you have a miscarriage, you have made some mistake. It might very well be an opportunity for a soul to experience a taste of life without intending to become a living child outside of your body, or perhaps the soul made an inappropriate choice.

I don't understand how the souls in the womb can have an experience of a dinosaur or a unicorn. Are you saying that the soul's desire is attracting particles with dinosaur or unicorn experience that would not allow the soul to function and live in a human body?

That's right.

It would be deformed or malformed or found dysfunctional in some way?

It might. But much more likely, if Creator would allow that being to be born, function and live on Earth, it would be constantly distracted. The child would have a difficult time becoming acculturated into any civilization that did not included a direct connection or even an indirect connection (through culture myths, stories and so on) with that particular animal.

Don't assume, young parents, that if your child has a rapturous love of dinosaurs or lions or tigers or bears, that he or she has somehow engaged on the soul level with these creatures. That is not the case—no. Such a child, if allowed to live on Earth even for a few months, would have a very difficult time being human. That's why Creator does not allow it. And teachers will advise souls that they *may* not have a life outside of mother. The teachers are not going to be rigid and say that they won't. There have been cases where a child has been born and lived for a few months.

Mother Earth Is Focusing on You

So why did your ancestors and all of the other native people come here?

We came here in order to help Mother Earth to interact with us so that she would know what human beings who would follow would need. Because Mother Earth is very reactive, she can adapt to what beings need given certain fixed parameters. You could not have a civilization of extraterrestrials come down here. Even if they adapted to the third dimension of Earth—which is extremely unlikely, but say they came down here and created a domed city that had their own environment—Mother Earth would probably reject them. She would not allow that, because you are here and she is focusing on you and the animals and the plants that are here now. She is focusing her creative actions and reactions with you. This is not to say that in some other time extraterrestrials could not come here and be here, but they'll almost always create an underground base that does not interfere with surface creation.

You've discussed before that your people came to make Mother Earth aware and to send her love. We've discussed that before, but we didn't discuss the particles that you were leaving as part of your legacy. But there had to have been particles here from other civilizations before you, right?

Certainly.

Existence in the Many Dimensions of Earth

So this goes back to when Jehovah created bodies for the first human beings?

I'm not prepared to agree with the whole Jehovah story at all. I'm not saying that it isn't true; it's just not my vision of it. There is more than one truth. Picture this: You are throwing an orange in the air. You toss it up in the air, you catch it, you toss it up in the air, you catch it—that's what you see in the third dimension, yes? What do you see in the fifth dimension? What do you see in the ninth dimension? What do you see in the eighteenth dimension? It is entirely different.

That story of Jehovah creating the beings and so on . . . that is all relevant through the fifth, the fourth, the third and, to a degree, the second dimension. But where I function . . . granted, I like to be in my body and sit on a hill and look over where my people are or sometimes focus myself in the times of when I was physical on Earth so that I can speak to you with empathy about being a human being. But where I exist in general is throughout all the dimensions of Earth. So from my perspective, I do not focus only on the idea that a being came from far away and created human beings. Nor do I perceive that that is my truth; it is not what I have seen. May I describe what I have seen?

Please!

This is what I see: I see colors. I see streams of color approaching Earth. Sometimes there are ribbons; sometimes there are single lines. All of these lines are coming toward the Earth. I see these ribbons of color coming toward the Earth. My understanding is that the Earth comes to a point before the ribbons . . . let's go back before the ribbons.

The Earth is ready. She has completed herself here in your universe. She is ready, she has expressed herself in all of the usable and functional dimensions that she needs to be to prepare herself for the arrival of human beings—and for that matter, the arrival of any beings. Before humans came animals; before animals came plants. She's ready with herself.

From Plants to Animals to Humans

Let's go back: I see approaching ribbons of color, because she is prepared to receive plants. Her ribbons will be the colors of the plants: some green, some yellow, some all different colors that plants on the Earth in her original stage would have expressed (turquoise, magenta, lapis). Some of these plants are still around in your time, but many more existed then, because some plants existed in the beginning that were intended strictly to be preparatory.

Some of the plants existed only at the beginning. There are certain plants that would be helpful to creation, helpful to the surface, helpful to create soil, helpful to purify the water, helpful to create oxygen—in short, helpful to generate qualities or to attune Mother Earth's energy to welcome the animals. Those colors come, they permeate, they come from a distance; Mother Earth is ready, yes? I see the colors come in—fields of color. They are attracted to Mother Earth. They come; they go beyond her surface to within. They move inside her body, then they gradually begin to move out to the surface. As they move out to the surface, from beyond come souls, coming from beyond as new souls come.

They come to the Earth as little flecks of light or some other form of lightbeing. These are the animals. They come and merge with the color. The initial creation takes place with a marriage between the color and the sound of existence, including the ambient sound. And the first animals, the first of the species—there may be more than two, maybe four or six or eight—all form up this way: being birthed from the color, the sound and the mass of Earth on their own. As you like to say in your Bible, it is an "immaculate conception," but I do not care for that term. It would suggest that normal conception is somehow dirty. So let's call it a creation that occurs as a result of a phenomenon not known to Earth at this time.

But Earth is pristine then. It is possible for a living soul, when exposed to living matter and those colors and the nutrients and the energies that they contain, to generate an actual physical body, though it does not take the time of the normal gestation in which the animal might give birth. That's how all the animals started. They live there for a time—the animals, the plants—and when the human beings are prepared to come, then the first human beings arrive the same way.

Again there are colors—the colors of all of human beings. These are not only the colors that exist on the surface, on the skin of the human being, but also the colors that exist inside the body of the human being and the colors having to do with the auric and energy fields of the human being. These colors might have to do with lightbeing colors, such as gold and white and pink and green and all of these things.

As a result, the original human beings form up in the same way, arriving with the souls. All the colors come their way. It works just the same as it did with the animals, because animals are beings from other planets, just as your souls are beings from other places. Your souls come and do exactly the same things, and there are different races of human beings that develop that way.

The race you now recognize as the human race developed that way, in all of its varieties that you now know. There were at least fifteen—depending on how you count, maybe sixteen sometimes—other expressions or races of human beings of the sex of male and female that existed initially. I'm not talking about primitive man; I'm talking about actual human beings that you have now. Some of these, those ones who are no longer here, moved off to other places in time, but they existed in the beginning.

Some of the Original Human Races Will Return to Earth

So this tells you something very important: It tells you that there are at least fifteen or possibly sixteen other forms of human beings with slightly different appearance qualities from the different races that you have in existence right now on Earth, that are potentially available to be born on Earth in the future when you are ready for them. They have qualities and abilities that would be of innumerable value to you right now.

Some of them automatically, even as children, can look at someone who has a disease and [snaps fingers] the disease is gone. Some of them can look at a material as children . . . or when they grow up, they can reach out like this with the wand (more likely they would use the right-hand wand), reach out and point it toward some toxic waste, and [snaps fingers] it automatically returns to something benign. In the case of, say, oil, it goes right back to the Earth, inside the Earth, in its pristine condition as it was inside Earth—including all of its beingness when it was inside the Earth before it was taken out. They can do all these and many other things.

They are not with you now because the conditions on Earth are not compatible with them at this time. They will look different; they will not look like you. Oh, their skin color is not going to be an aberration; they're not going to be green or striped.

Some are blue, right?

Most likely you have some blue people with you now; you just don't recognize them. They're in the darker-skinned races, sometimes referred to as blue, because there is a quality in their skin that is blue. But I'm not going to refer to the blue people, though I know who you are talking about. Rather these people will have appearance factors that are a little different: their eyes might be set a little different, their cheekbones might be set a little different. There will be nothing radical—they will obviously be human beings.

I'm mentioning this level of detail because I want physicians in the medical community and midwives to be on alert that in the coming years, in the next fifty to seventy-five years, these races of human beings will begin to show themselves again, but not until a race of human beings has been fully appreciated and welcomed into your society, which you have made considerable progress in doing in recent years. This race of beings is those children who are born who look a little different and are so full of love.

Down Syndrome children?

That race of beings, who are here to express love unconditionally. This has been discussed in previous material. I mention this, because your cultures have begun to welcome these people much more. Even in your scientific literature, there has been encouragement: "Take them out, don't keep them in the houses, and they will live a long and fulfilled life." In short, you are beginning to welcome them, which is why I am now passing on this notification that the new races appear to be here— all right, they are not that new [laughs], they were here initially. They will be coming, and they will have a slightly different appearance, and they will have amazing abilities, all of which you desperately need right now on Earth.

Have they incarnated on other planets?

They lived elsewhere; they incarnated elsewhere. They didn't want to be here in the times gone by. Let's just say that they didn't want to be someplace where they wouldn't be welcomed. You are living in times that are profoundly racist; they don't want to be here if they are going to be rejected out of hand for their purpose of being or for their appearance.

The First Humans Who Formed

So back to the first birth of all the beings.

It is before; it was before. It was in a sequence.

So anything that we've ever heard of would come after this?

Yes.

So those first humans who formed—what kind of life did they have? They didn't have the particles necessary to give them a lot of possibilities, right?

They lived very unusual lives compared to what you know today. Compared to what you know today, their lives were very unusual. They did not eat; they did not breathe. They looked like human beings, but they were different; they were multidimensional. They had capacities that you do not have at this time.

But the fact that they existed that way originally tells you that what they left behind on Earth is a potential for you when you decide to allow such potentials and to get past the desire to make the world you live in to be less than its potential, because its potential frightens you. It will take awhile for you now, because your cultures express their beliefs in religions and philosophies and political expressions that are largely a reaction to the fear of variety, which is really the opposite of what the Creator of this universe intended. But you will get past that.

So in the beginning, they did not do many of the things you do now, but that is because it was up to them to evolve—not in the meaning of the theory of evolution, but to evolve on the basis of social systems, customs, manners and ways of being that would allow potentials for different cultures to express themselves who would come along after. In the beginning, when there were children birthed through women, there was no pain because it was not considered necessary. That came eventually. And when pain arrived as an expression, as a tool, as an experience and so on, then many of the races of human beings decided they did not want that, and they left. So they did not reproduce, all right? But in the beginning, things were quite different.

Are any souls embodied on the planet now that were souls at that time? That were souls in those bodies?

I think there is one. There might be two more coming up very soon.

Are they going to start coming back, then?

Maybe. We'll see.

Linear Time versus Spherical Time

So the coming of pain . . . why did the pain come? Why did women begin to have pain in the birthing process?

Not women only, but everyone: "Why did pain come for anybody?" This was not only in birthing. It came because of an exploration of what might be needed in the future. These original beings lived for thousands of years, I might add . . . roughly years. I can't really express it in your time.

The planet was in a different position then, wasn't it? Isn't that one of the reasons they had such problems?

You can't really express that time in words. If two lines were the same size, the same length, only one line was curved, you could do more in curved time. It does not translate directly.

Was this before the loop of time? Or was this the first time around?

It was way before the loop of time. The beings on Earth then were human beings. You asked originally who came here, and I said original native peoples, some whose strands exist today—not necessarily in soul expression through a human being, but in culture. That's what we're talking about. I'm talking about human beings.

I thought the souls of the original race on Earth evolved to become the Zeta Reticulans.

That may well be true, but it does not bear on what we are discussing now. What you are talking about is the Zeta experience, which relates to, I think, *The Explorer Race* book. Picture it as a sphere, not a line; we're talking about spherical time now. Spherical time goes out in all directions. This means that even though this might be true here [making a small circle with his thumb and first finger] . . . this is the story of Jehovah, the

Zeta Reticulums being the past or your future—it is all of that in this space, the whole story.

The circular space between the forefinger and thumb?

Yes, but *only* the circular, because I'm talking about spherical time, not linear time, all right? I'm talking about the colors coming to Earth to form the plants and the animals and humans and all of that. That's out here [holds his hands out at his shoulders]. The circle is bigger, but it is a sphere.

The circle is the width of the shoulders?

Yes, not necessarily the size, but more to the point, the sphere has expanded. But how do we measure it? It's not a matter of being an unknown quantity like X, the unknown in mathematics. It is more like when you say "apples and oranges"—they cannot be measured as the same quantity because they do not relate. So it's like trying to measure . . . you can measure with geometry and other forms of mathematics a given quantity of space based upon the arc of the circle between these two spaces, but how do you measure, given that that space is not just an arc for that example . . . how do you measure something like the sphere the width of the shoulders?

Now, you could easily as a mathematician measure the volume of the circle or measure the volume of the sphere. But what if the curved line I mentioned previously is a part of a sphere? If a straight line is linear time, spherical time begins, say, at an infinite point on the sphere, meaning you could go in and in and in and in and in and in and in into the larger sphere infinitely, and you could go out and out and out and out of the large sphere infinitely. How do you measure that time using the tools and techniques that are designed to measure a known quantifiable linear amount? It's not possible. That's why when you say or try to say or I feel you wanting to say, "How can we put that within the known calendar?" I really have to say, you can't.

I didn't want to put it within the known calendar, but in the history of the Earth.

I understand. I want to explain it to you, not only because you are the human representative for this conversation, but because others might have similar questions. It is a reasonable question to ask, "Where does this fit into what we now know?"—which is what you were really asking.

Yes, not what the people of Earth know, but what we have learned through you and others about the history of the planet.

That's right. So what I'm saying is that it *doesn't* fit into what you now know as you know it, but it does fit in. Let me give you another example.

Contact with Lightbeings Is a Daily Occurrence

ETs, when they talk to human beings in contacts, often do not have a shared language. They might be able to communicate by adapting their

ET language through some form of universal translator into the conscious mind of a human being. But say these ET races have a completely different experience of their existence, including functioning in a form of time that is totally unlike your form of time. For the most part, such ETs would not come into contact with human beings in your recent past, meaning for the past, say, six or eight hundred years to the present. They would not come into contact at all with you in that type of contact, where they come down in their ships, land, take you on the ships, take you somewhere—not that kind of contact.

But they might come into contact with you on a daily basis in their natural form, which is light. You are always surrounded by light. If you could take a known quantity of light, if you could take your hand and scoop it through the air and catch a quantity of light in it and maintain it, you might have in your hands for a brief amount of time numerous lightbeings as well as space taken up by matter.

Our light is lightbeings? The light we use for illumination?

Sometimes it is. Sometimes it's other things. But the reason I mention this is that even if you are totally dense and unconscious as some people are described—though they might simply be involved in other things and not pursuing spiritual pursuits for any reason—coming into contact with lightbeings is a daily occurrence.

Tracking by Feeling

What about things that fall out of the body, like bits of skin—sometimes you call it dandruff, but most of it is simply pieces of scalp? Every day parts of your skin might fall off. I'm not talking about bumping yourself and losing part of your skin, but just little bits of dead skin that flake off. All of that—just like the hair—has contained within it all that you are, all that you've been up to the point when it is discharged from your body.

Trackers, good trackers and master trackers who teach this, understand this. It is possible to track someone or something, yes, using only the tracks and only the sign, as trackers call it. But to have the means to know what that person is feeling—that makes all the difference in the world if you are trying to find him. You may not be trying to find this person to destroy or to kill him; you might be simply trying to find this person to rescue him.

What about a lost child? You might be able to know, as a tracker, a good tracker, where the child is going on the basis of engaging with the feelings of the footprint. Or the perhaps there is a sign: the child bumped against the bushes out in the woods and got lost and scraped against a bush, and you can see that the bush or twig is bent and there may be a little dab of blood or a little skin on there. You first, as a tracker, like in my brother's time, become conscious of the bush's energy.

You don't remove it from the bush—that's where it landed, so that's where it stays. But once you are familiar with the bush's energy and feelings of the moment, then you can differentiate that from the feelings and energy of the blood and the skin that's on that twig where the child bumped and skinned himself and wandered on looking for mom and dad or a brother or sister or whoever the child is looking for—or perhaps running after the beautiful deer and getting lost.

When you know how to be a tracker like this, you can know what the child is feeling. In that moment that the child left that there, was he cold? Was he hungry? Was he thirsty? Was he tired? Was he ready to give up? All those things are vitally important. Where might he have gone? You engage with his blood and his skin: Where might he have gone? You might initially be able to get the direction at least; that would be of immense help in finding the child.

I'm not trying to say that the trackers in your time do not know what they are doing. I'm saying that there are levels of tracking that can be immensely helpful—in this case, in this example, to rescue someone. There are things to be learned and remembered. That's why I'm speaking of these matters. Because the things to be learned and remembered that I'm speaking of . . . for the most part, I'm not talking about the first beings who came here to Earth, but rather, in this practical sense, this is about things you can use now to improve the quality of your lives.

Which are, in many cases, lost in tradition?

It is information that has gone by the wayside sometimes, or that is not widely known, or that needs to be known and applied more in your time so that your lost companion or your lost child can be found more easily. Or this might be for your lost pet whom you heard was hit by a car and probably forgot temporarily where it lived. Its instinct was injured somehow, and it wandered off into the woods or wandered off into a part of town where it doesn't know anyone and isn't known.

Then you look for a sign. Maybe it is blood; maybe it is hairs. Or maybe, if you are instinctual in nature, you can find your pet on the basis of love, which you feel for it. But as a tracker, you always look for a sign, and you don't always use only the sign's direction to track which way it is going, but also feelings, what it felt. All these things can be learned.

It starts with how you feel in your body in pointing to that sign. Maybe, in the case of the lost child, the child had a cracker and ate a cracker, and then as children do, he dropped the cracker and wandered on and later wished he still had it. But you come across the cracker; maybe the ants have found it and they are eating it. Don't grab it away from the ants. The master tracker knows that you always recognize that those ants who are there eating that cracker—even though they're eating it for their own purposes, bringing it to their young—that some of those ants are coming and going, yes? And some of the ants who are coming will have perhaps made that physical contact with the energy of the child who bit that cracker. So you don't want to discourage the ants from touching that cracker. They might also have within them some of that energy.

So you point your fingers toward the cracker, even if the ants are all over it. If you are unsure which energy is the energy and feeling of the ants, then you go over to a place where the ants are that is well away from that cracker and you point your fingers toward them, and then you see their energy, their feelings. Then you go back and you point them toward the cracker. Some of the cracker might be what wheat, for instance, feels like.

If you are a good tracker, you will have felt into all these things before. What do ants normally feel like as a group? Individual ants will feel differently, but as a group, what do they normally feel like? What does wheat as a plant normally feel like? What does salt feel like, what does water feel like, all these things? As a tracker, you go through to see what they feel like. And how do you know what they feel like? By the way your body reacts. What does my body feel like when I'm pointing to this? If it doesn't feel comfortable, pull your hand back; that's not something you're supposed to feel. If it feels comfortable, leave it there for a while. That's what that type of species feels.

It may not be what each individual in that species feels, but you're just trying to feel as a tracker that general feeling, because each individual in that species—each ant, each stalk of wheat—will have the same range of feelings that you have as a human being: fear, happiness, love, humor, all of these things that are felt as feelings. The range is the same, even though a stalk of wheat may not express as many feelings as a human being might go through, because you as a human being are here to learn a great deal and a stalk of wheat may not have anything to learn. It is more likely here to teach as well as to nurture.

Trackers Can Do a Great Deal

In your time one of the professions that is, as they say, misunderstood, not fully appreciated, which can be of great benefit—since I've been talking about it in the case of physical messaging—is tracking. Trackers can do a great deal. Sometimes children are separated at birth. Maybe you knew you had a brother, but something happened and your brother is living somewhere else. Maybe there are lots of different possibilities—you were separated at birth or separated later on. A good tracker might be able to find your brother. It might take a master tracker, but he or she might be able to find him. Granted, people who have sensitive skills could be helpful. Other information might be helpful that you can use and tap into. But a good tracker might also be helpful.

What could a tracker do if there is no physical evidence of your brother? If you're fortunate, maybe you have something that your brother used to wear. But if you don't have that, if you have nothing, then a good tracker will feel your energy body around you, will tell you to think of your brother. If you remember what your brother looked like, you do that.

If you simply know you have a brother somewhere and don't know what he looks like, then the tracker will say, "Imagine being with your brother." And if your energy body would feel like that . . . maybe while you're in the full energy, the tracker might feel a greater sense of you and your brother being together, in which case the tracker might touch your body, perhaps remove a little sweat, smell it, feel it, even taste it. A good tracker knows all these things and might be able to find your brother that way.

Most people who live in cities no longer have these skills. Are there some people still living on the land who have these skills?

Yes, there are some people who have some of these skills. Now, I'm talking to them, because trackers who live out in the country and so on don't always recognize that there are other levels to tracking, and they don't always recognize what they might be able to do to help people in the cities, if they are prepared to go into cities for a week or two sometime. That's a lot to ask. But some of them might.

But you know also, good trackers usually have a good nose; they can smell pretty good. And instead of sweat, they might use . . . when you're remembering your brother or imagining being with your brother, your body smell changes, has a different odor. The tracker will smell that [sniff, sniff, sniff] and might be able to use that as a portion of the smell of your brother. Yes, people exist out in the countryside and in other countries also who can do tracking. But so much more can be done with it.

Physical Messaging Is Vitally Important in Your Time

That's why I feel physical messaging is so vitally important in your time—not only to improve communications, but to find that which you may feel is lost or to find that which you definitely feel is lost or to find that which may be dangerous in order to put it someplace where it will no longer be dangerous, such as a wounded animal. A bear might be peaceful most of the time, but if it is wounded, it is not so peaceful, nor would you be that way. If you are wounded, you might not be quite so peaceful either.

So a tracker might be able to find a wounded person. Maybe the wound is in the head and it is causing the person to behave in ways the person would not normally act. Perhaps that person is now violent. A good tracker can help find someone like that, not just on the basis of that person's footprints, but on the basis of the feelings the tracker has when connecting with a piece of physical evidence—a footprint, a hair, something like that.

How will the tracker know it is the hair of the person he or she is tracking? Because of the way the tracker feels. The hair would normally not have, say, violence or a sense of being deranged. But this is from a person with, say for example, a brain tumor who has not in the past been violent but because of the tumor is now violent all of a sudden. This is not always the case with brain tumors; it is just one of many symptoms. But as a result, the person has to be found for his own good and for the good of others. The tracker does not normally feel violent in his or her own right but finds a hair, and that hair is a human hair, and that hair has that feeling of being violent or disarranged mentally and on a feeling level.

This is the hair of the person being tracked. There are other qualities, but I'm only mentioning a few. This is the hair of the person the tracker is tracking—this is the way he went, this is what he was feeling. He needs food; he needs water. There is only water here, here and here, so the tracker can go to those places. If that person knows those places, that's where he'll go to get water. If he knows these places for food, that's where he'll go to get food. You can find a person through many means.

What if you've lost something from yourself? What if you've lost a feeling that you used to have and you don't have it much anymore? What if you, when you were younger, had thoughts of curiosity or thoughts of enthusiasm about life, good humor, and you found things funny, and you don't have this anymore? Can you find things like that?

Maybe not physically, with physical messaging, but tomorrow we'll talk about finding things that you've lost that you'd like to regain or experience once again as a portion of yourself that is not involved in soul or recovery—not that. But you'd like to reengage with feelings that you once had that you wished you still had and, since you have had them before, you know you have the potential to have again. And you'd like to simply have them more present within yourself, because when you see things that you know used to make you laugh or used to make you happy, and those same things or those circumstances aren't making you happy, are not causing you to laugh anymore, how can you regain that? We'll talk about that tomorrow. Good night.

Using Physical Messaging in the Physical Body

Speaks of Many Truths
November 28, 2001

ll right, this is Speaks of Many Truths. Greetings.

Finding Your Lost Humor

Let us consider how to find lost humor, how to locate within yourself experiences you once had looking forward to life, possible joyous spontaneity, not just reacting to things—in short, how to attitudinally as well as on the physical level and on the feeling level (which are first cousins), not exactly recapture your youth, since you wouldn't want to live it over again, but reactivate those potentials in yourself. Of course, there have been many contributions in this direction by psychologists and therapists and analysts over the years, but I would like to also add this.

There are places in your body that physically store these things. Also there are points [draws Fig. 3-1]. These points that I'm drawing arrows to may not always be in the same place on the same person. Understand that this is not anatomical, but I'll give you an anatomical frame of reference: the little cir-

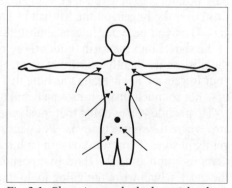

Fig. 3-1. Places in your body that might physically store your humor.

cle in the middle there is the bellybutton. But those points might be places in a person's body that you have something coming from, from the inside.

Picture almost like a circuit, only it is a strand of light; it comes up to the surface of the body there, but it does not extend beyond the body. That might be humor. Maybe you've lost your humor, or perhaps you can't find it: "Where did it go? I used to hear jokes like that and laugh. That's a new one; a joke like that would normally make me laugh. How come I'm not laughing?" I'm not saying there aren't good reasons why you're not laughing, but what I am saying is, how can you stimulate those centers so that you might be able to laugh?

Here's what we're going to do: Take your left hand, palm out. The left hand is open. The fingers are straight out, but the hand can be relaxed, all right? But we want the fingers generally out away from the palm of your hand, generally open. What you do is, you say, "I would like to find, using my warmth in my body"—meaning the love-heat/heart-warmth/physical-warmth exercise [see Overview]—"I would like to find, by moving my hand around the front of my body and my warmth giving me the indication by being the most warm when I come to that point on my body, where my humor is in residence."

Here, in Robert's body, this is where the humor comes up from the inside [his hand is outspread about six inches above his belt on the right-hand side of his body. It's about halfway in from the side, toward the center]. A strand of light comes to the surface and, in his case, continues on out because his humor is still intact. But in the case of some individuals where the humor wouldn't be intact or wasn't present or at least was not present in the way they would like, there might be sort of a dark area here.

So this is what you would do. Locate the place using that warmth. "Oh, it's very warm here," you might say [holds hand over place where humor comes up in Robert's body]. Now, what you do is this: You try to maintain the warmth, and you take your fingers on your left hand like this [in a cupping position]. Then you take your fingers on your right hand and place them over the fingers on the left hand. The thumb is close to the small finger. Then you put your fingers almost like a shovel, like sticking the spade of the shovel into the earth, under those ribs. Here's the point here [under the ribs], so it's slightly below that point, all right? It's below enough so that your fingers are not actually touching that point. And you just push in and up—not so much that it causes pain and discomfort, just in and up.

Then while you're doing that, push your left thumb very gently into the area where the spot actually is. Put your right thumb on top of it, and very gently push as if you were pushing a buzzer, but very gently. What you're doing is stimulating it. Hold that position for maybe a minute or two at the most, which we're not going to do in this case because we do not have to stimulate Robert's humor.

Then you finish off by . . . you have your left hand [fingers outspread, level with the body] and you make little circles above the area. It's not quite circles; it's sort of brushing toward the outside. It's sort of brushing a few inches [about six inches] above the body, and we're spreading it . . . see what we're doing?

Oh, I see. You're using the fingers almost to spread the energy.

It's just as if we were finger painting and there was a blob of paint and we were just spreading it out. As we're spreading it out, we're moving slightly away from the body so that we're spreading it out and welcoming it into the auric field that extends from within the body out away from the body, and we continue doing that. Describe what I'm doing.

You're continually using the fingers as you said, as a paintbrush, farther away now from the body—about eighteen inches into the auric field—continually moving the fingers.

Now, you can continue that as far out as you like, as far out as your arm can reach, or stop wherever you feel you need to stop. All the while you'll probably notice the warmth, but at some point you will notice warmth in the actual area—meaning that wherever you normally feel your warmth to help you to do this, you will start to feel warmth in the actual area, the point where your humor is. You will actually feel that point.

When you feel that warmth, then your humor has been activated. You may not suddenly find yourself rollicking in mirth, but it will have been activated, and over the next day or two or three, you will find it easier to laugh, gradually more so. If the conditions that have suppressed your humor become overpowering again, you can use exactly the same method to reactivate it in exactly the same way. This can be done repeatedly, only don't do it more than once a week.

Finding Your Curiosity

Now, say you have some other issue. Maybe as a youth you had your curiosity, and maybe you're not curious anymore. Maybe there are good reasons; it's not about that. It's about you wanting to become more curious. I'm not saying this is pro or con; I'm saying that maybe you miss your youthful curiosity, where you would want to look at the flower more closely. Or you might want to examine the picture of the bee in the magazine, and then when you go out to places where bees land on flowers and pollinate them, you can get close (not too close; we don't want to frighten the bees) and see how the bees are walking around on the flowers and extracting what they need, and in the process pollinating the flowers in the wonderful way Creator has prompted all life to support one another— that kind of curiosity.

You might find it again. Use exactly the same method, where you use your warmth and move your hand over your body until you find the place where your curiosity resides. Then use exactly the same technique. Now, what happens if your curiosity resides in some place where there is bone, such as in the rib cage or sternum? Or what if it resides in some place where you cannot press your fingers in deeply? Even so, make the gesture and press your fingers in slightly—you will be able to press in slightly because there will be skin and some tissue there. Press in just a little bit, and then again use the thumbs on the exact spot, pressing in just a little bit, all right? That's all there is to it.

That's wonderful.

Finding Qualities You Don't Recall Having

So let's name some more qualities: curiosity, humor, spontaneity, wonder at life, joy.

You're doing pretty good. All those are qualities that someone might miss. What about qualities you don't recall ever having? Perhaps you've always been timid and shy; for whatever reason, as far back as you can remember, you've always been timid and shy. And you'd like to be strong and confident—not necessarily brave, because you're not ready to go swinging from tree to tree on a vine, à la the famous fictional character, but you would like to feel a little more courageous so that you could approach certain things or accomplish certain things or meet people and so on.

So what you do, then, is you use a similar technique. Again, you use your warmth, and instead of saying you want to find the point in your body where something was that you want to *reactivate*, you say, "I am now wanting to locate the point on my body where my strength and endurance"—or courage, or whatever it is that you want to *activate* (you see, this is not reactivation; this is activation)—"is in residence. Where is it?" And you move your hand over your body until you find that location, wherever it might be, and you use exactly the same technique.

Reactivation and activation will work the same way. The only difference is that once you've activated a point like that—again, moving your hand around the surface of your body, roughly about four or five, maybe six inches away from your body, whatever feels good, wherever you get the most warmth, finding that exact location—once you've used that technique to activate it, then you never activate it again. Once it's been activated, you don't activate it again. And I think I will differentiate it. I'm going to add something slightly extra with the activation so that you will be able to remember the difference between activation and reactivation.

So in this case we will say that when you activate it, doing the same thing with your fingers and both hands, press your thumb down on the spot—your left thumb first, then your right thumb. You're going to push gently with your right thumb on top of your left thumb for the count of three: one, two, three. Push gently, then remove your thumb for a moment. Then put it back down and again push for a time, maybe a minute or two. That's it. That's how you're going to know the difference between activation and reactivation. It works fine.

Physical Messaging and Energy Radiation

So in my understanding, there's an energy that emanates from every human body all the time?

Yes.

And that communicates to everyone else we interact with, but we don't control the radiation or we're not conscious of it, right?

Fortunately, yes.

Why fortunately?

Fortunately you don't control it, because when you say "control," you mean mentally control. When you apply words like that, it always has to do with mentally controlling, and the mind is not any form of master. The mind is not a spiritual master. It is an interesting point, isn't it? How is it possible that your mind cannot be a spiritual master? If you were a spiritual master—all people here, at least once before they came here—how is it possible that your mind wasn't part of that?

Because the mind is something we're evolving for the Andromedans; it's not native to who we are.

That's right; it's not your actual mental function. Therefore, to put your mind in control of your functions in your body, which are based . . . your body is based entirely in material mastery and harmony. To put your mind in control of that . . . and how many people's minds try to control their bodies? Think about it—it's like putting the apprentice in charge of the teacher. It doesn't work too well.

And this is not well-known at all.

Not well-known.

The Only Way to Know Is by Physical Feeling

So that's why the only way to know is the feeling, right?

That's right. How do you know when you are exercising control with your mind as compared to experiencing or being physically and on the feeling and spiritual level? You will know because your body will instantaneously message you with some . . . initially it's like discomfiture, and if you ignore it for a considerable length, that discomfiture will become more so. It will not turn into disease, but it might ultimately become chronic. Not always, because there are many stress-inducing circumstances, but much of the chronic discomfort that you usually don't do anything about—say, stiffness in your shoulders or muscles, or lack of flexibility in certain joints (meaning you can turn your head so far one way but not as far the other way)—has to do with physical messaging. Your body is telling you that your mind is exerting unnecessary control on your physical body.

What might be an example of that unnecessary control? I will tell you. This is something that the mind does. In your time it is typical for people to do this and even to feel sometimes that it is not only justified—meaning they justify it—but also that it is valuable because they have learned how to use it in ways that, as they feel, benefit them. What the mind does when it is exercising this control is worry. Worry, as you know, does not change things, although sometimes you have used it to your advantage. By worrying you tend to plan ahead and do things that will cause your mind to worry less: "Okay, I've got that covered and that covered and that covered, so that if those contingencies actually take place, I'm covered." So in that case, you can say, "Well, in this way worry is good."

But what I would say is that it does not require worry to do that; it just requires planning. You can look at a situation, analyze what might occur and then plan and put into place circumstances, events, people, objects and so on that will cover that potential eventuality. It does not require worry. Worry is different. The difference with worry is that even after you've put those things into place, you're still worrying—*that's* worry.

How to Keep from Worrying

So when you're doing things like that, your body will usually message you by stiffening up muscles in some way—usually this is the first thing. This will initially cause a difficulty—not an impossibility, but a difficulty—in range of motion, for example. Your muscles might feel tight; it's not as comfortable moving in that particular way. Granted, you have many good ways to work with this: yoga, stretching or, in extreme cases, something that is analgesic (aspirin or something). Yes, there are other things that cause your muscles to grow stiff, but in order to pay attention to your body, you might do something like this.

People's muscles . . . the shoulders often stiffen up between the shoulder bone and the neck, don't they? You might put your left fingertips on that muscle, especially when you're sitting down and are a little more relaxed. If you put your head back, maybe to one side, then the muscle can relax a little bit more. And you can then use the heat in your chest or solar plexus area, and you can ask the question, "Is my mind controlling . . . ?" Well, let's put it personally: "Is my mind controlling my body and keeping my body from creating my life in a more benevolent way?"

A question like that can be answered with a yes or a no, so if you feel the heat, in this case that is yes. What happens if you feel a little bit of heat? That means, ask the question at another time or rephrase the question. So rephrase the question and try this: "Would it be better for me to concentrate my mind in this moment on something else rather than worry in order to free up my body?" Then comes more warmth.

So how do you do that? The easiest thing to do is to become like the artistic observer. Take the hand that you are not using, hold it right up near your face—within, say, five or six inches—and look at your hand.

Open your eyes and look at your hand. If you're wearing glasses or contacts, that's fine; you can see your hand better. It doesn't make any difference. You don't have to remove them. Look at your hand, and concentrate on the lines. You don't have to analyze what they mean.

Or if you like, you can have something handy, perhaps something soft like a silk handkerchief with many colors. Drape it over the hand that you're not using, and hold it up closer to your eyes—you need to hold it close to your eyes so that other things that you might look at are blocked out. And you can rub the handkerchief between your fingers and thumb in order to get the stimulation of the feeling while you look at the colors. Generally that would be enough to keep you from worrying.

I mention this because most people cannot automatically switch off their worry; they can shove it into a subconscious state, but we don't want to do that. We want the worry to be exposed, conscious, so that when you do this physical stimulation, which also uses your eyes to stimulate you (and so your mind must be involved), then it will take your mind off of the worry. Do this for at least four to five minutes. Then reach over and see how your muscle feels. Probably it will feel a lot softer. This is an example. This is how you will know. The question was, "How do we know whether our mind is controlling our body?" This is a good way to find out.

Your Body Speaks in Physical Language

This gives you something physical that you can do with your body to learn the pleasures of working with your body so that you can recognize your body's language. Your body speaks in physical language, and it will message you hundreds of times every day. The more you become aware of what your body is feeling—slight discomfort, a little tension—then you can begin to touch your body.

You can use whatever hand you like. If it's a small spot, always use this finger, the middle finger. Touch with that. Your left hand will always be more sensitive, but there will be times when you will not be able to reach a place or it will be awkward or uncomfortable to use that finger; then use the middle finger of your right hand. It will work much better with the middle finger of your left hand, in the case of a small place; if it is something larger, then use your fingertips in general, but not your thumb, all right?

Your thumb is intended to take action. Whether you are a man or a woman, it is a masculine digit—it does things. Your fingers are all feminine, whether you are a man or a woman, especially the fingertips—they are very receptive. The foot is not like that. The toes on the foot—the big toe as well as the small toes—are all receptive, all feminine, whether you are a masculine or feminine being. It doesn't make any difference. So this is a very useful technique, eh?

Physical Messaging through Body Language

Do you consider body language in interactions with other people to be physical messaging?

It is a form, is it not? How people sit, they telegraph to others what they might be feeling. That has been written up extensively, and I will not comment on that too much. although I think it might be useful for you to look at some of the famous books of that subject in your library or bookstore.

But more importantly, since this is the budding shaman, if I might say, learning with himself, it is useful to note how you are sitting at times or how you are standing or how you are carrying yourself or what you are doing. We don't want to make you self-conscious; only do this when you are working and practicing and training. But you might notice yourself at some point sitting in a certain way, and how you are sitting might demonstrate what you are feeling.

Removing Tension from the Body

Many men in your time do not know what they are feeling. For men, sometimes they are even self-conscious about crossing their arms. It is perfectly all right to cross your arms if it makes you feel safer or more comfortable or more protected, but some men feel like they cannot demonstrate that.

So what to do in that case is to explore the muscles between the shoulders back along behind the neck. You'll know from the way those muscles feel. Or explore what you're doing with your fingers. You might be doing something . . . you might even be pinching your thumb and fingers together in some way. For people who are shy and for some reason don't want to cross their arms in front of them to feel safer—which there is nothing wrong with that—they might often be found doing that.

You're putting your fingers in a fist, with the thumb against the top.

Not quite a fist. The fist is open; the hands are cupped. The thumb is pressed against the first finger, usually close to the first knuckle of the finger, the first joint down at the base of the finger or between that and the second joint. I am not saying that this is always the case, but for those people, if you see them like that and they are loved ones or friends, you might suggest that they do this just for the fun of it.

So they make a steeple of their hands in front of their body, beneath the chest and pretty close to the belt.

Just do that, using the thumbs and all the fingers together, making this shape, all right? And that will relieve the tension quite a bit. This position with the hands in general gives a feeling of greater protection and balance in the body. The feet, the legs, everything in the body will feel more comfortable doing this. It will not ultimately remove tension, but it will greatly reduce it.

Allow Others to Have Their Thoughts and Create Your Own Benevolence

It's been so widely taught that crossing the arms means the person is defensive or defiant, that many people don't want to assume that position because they might be judged.

That's right. And yet your arms would not be able to do to that were it not acceptable. So just know that if other people are judging you, it is creating a discomfort for them in that moment of judgment, but it does not have to create one for you. The good thing about others judging you is that most often they will say nothing. So one of the big challenges you need to do all the time, for everyone, is to allow other people to have their thoughts. I cannot tell you how many people react to others because of what they think or fear others are thinking about them. Most of the time most people are more concerned about their own issues and their own circumstances, and only occasionally are thinking about others.

There's something I really want to bring up, because I've noticed that people do it, that I do it: We create a situation in our minds that may or may not relate to reality, and then we react to what's in the mind and not to what is.

That is because we are so uncomfortable—meaning human beings (I'll say "we," if that's all right)—with reality and feel so foreign in that reality and don't feel like we are welcome in that reality, that it is easier to create a mental scenario or picture of what might be happening and react to that. This is because that is a creation of your own, as compared to the reality you find yourself in, which given all the other people and circumstances and buildings and structures (maybe it's a place you've never been), is not your own creation, and you feel . . . what? Out of control. But when you're creating something in your mind, even if it's false, and you react to that with others, it creates a sense of security because it's your creation.

Now, how to use that to your advantage rather than in a self-destructive fashion? What people have done over the years and have been learning to do for the past few years is to create a more benevolent scenario. Do this, obviously, only in circumstances where you feel reasonably safe. Assume that people around you are thinking of you in a benevolent way and that the building was built by people in order to serve you—that everything in the building (the machines, the seats, the windows, everything) was built just to please you. This is not just a creative visualization; rather it is an attitudinal shift that you make. What this does is it allows you almost instantaneously to feel welcome. And when you feel welcome, you relax, you are yourself and you are not as reactive in ways that are self-destructive to yourself or harmful to others. It is a small thing but very helpful.

Create your own benevolence—that's great!

You create it. You say, "Well, these people built this building to please me. Maybe they didn't get it exactly the way I would like it, but their intention was to make me happy. And I must admit, I do like looking out the windows; it is interesting to see what's going on outside."

Whatever I'm doing, I am much more relaxed. All this poking and moving my fingers and following your gestures is very good for me.

Well, that's one of the purposes of the book. You are not only the questioner, but you are the reader. This suggests to the readers, were they here, that they might have similar circumstances, and of course, it supports and nurtures them to try some of these things also.

Sometimes people . . . it's not that they create their reality so much to feel secure; they don't even know they're doing it. But it's like they're missing a piece of information and they set up this scenario of worry when it may not even be real. I mean, some people create worry that way, the way you just said to create benevolence. They create worry when they don't have all the facts. They set up a scenario in their head, and then they react to it and live their life that way, and it's not even real, and it's not benevolent.

But that reason is still the same; it is because . . .

Oh, it's the same thing! To control! Even though they're just missing facts?

Even though they're just missing facts. Reacting to it that way, and then building on that and continuing to react to it that way . . . that might feel uncomfortable to them, but it feels more comfortable than having those missing pieces—"missing pieces" meaning things they don't know— because the things they don't know are invariably the creations of others. As a result, that idea of having the creations of others always will relate back to times when they were out of control and frightened. But being in control, your mind controlling your body, is not necessarily always a good thing when your body is the material-mastery teacher and your mind is the apprentice.

Study the Palm of Your Hand to Become Conscious of Your Body

Would you recommend that students at least become acquainted with what is known as body language if they're not familiar with it, so they can understand their own? Or is it really irrelevant to this?

I recommend, generally speaking, that people become conscious of their bodies as a general intention. In your Western culture, most of the consciousness of one's physical body, no matter how beautiful the person might be, is critical. It is a sad thing, then, that the most beautiful men and women only occasionally look at themselves approvingly. With women, perhaps, it is more so because of your culture.

I feel it is therefore valuable to study the palm of your hand. There is less likelihood that with the palm of your hand, which has many lines, intricacies . . . if you look closely, it is less likely that you will find a means to criticize it. It's a good place to begin looking. I recommend that all women and men do this as a beginning place to examine your body when you are adults. Of course, as babies, the first thing you're doing is examining your body and there is no criticism at all then; you're just happy to be there, and everything is wonderful.

Although I feel that palmistry is a valuable art and practice—and for master palmists especially, it can be a profound contribution to society—nevertheless I feel that in this case, it is better to look at your palm as one might look at a leaf or a flower, just examining the infinite lines, because depending on what you do with your palm, it changes the appearance of the lines. And you can look at something like that for a little while and just be fascinated. You do not have to look at complex problems only to be fascinated; you do not have to count the petals of a flower to be fascinated. You can look at the flower and appreciate its beauty and still be fascinated. But most of you have hands, and you can often find one to be handy to look at.

I had heard somewhere that one hand is like the reference beam and the other is like the working beam of a hologram. Do our life decisions and actions reflect more in one hand than the other?

Generally speaking, your left hand is more receptive, and that's whether you're a man or a woman. It's the more feminine hand, and the right hand is more action-oriented. Whether you are left- or right-handed, the right hand is going to be more masculine. Now, I grant that this would be moderated slightly if you happen to be left-handed, but generally it is a fixed situation. But I do not use the hologram idea, because that creates an artificiality in the body and it moves your natural physical beauty in your body into a mathematical or scientific formula. In short, it takes you out of your body into your mind.

Well, let me phrase my question differently. You just said the lines change depending on your life—do those changes show up in both hands equally or in one more than the other?

They might show up more so in your right hand. But you might also find that the lines in your left hand would be more associated with receptivity or the feminine, whereas the changes in your life, learning life skills, doing more, activities, potentials for the future, what you might do, what you could do and so on . . . this will show up in your right hand, which is why palmists often in your time will look at the right hand, because people want to know their future. Whereas a master palmist might look at the left hand to get a better idea of the soul's purpose or the feeling body's intention. But usually this is something done only by master palmists.

Suppose you are needing something, meaning you want something, you are trying to create something—you can work with a palmist on this. You can have the palmist tell you, "Where is my heart line?" or "Where is my head line?" or "Where is my lifeline?" So say the palmist tells you where the head line is, which has to do not only with the health of your head but also has to do mostly with your capacities mentally. (I bring in that thing about the health because it's not always remembered.) Now, your line moves in a certain direction. If you feel or know that you are going to need to expand your mental capacities, even for a short time, what you can do is have the palmist show you which direction the line generally moves in, or where does your lifeline begin, where does it end—in other words, which direction you're going.

Find the point where the lines are stopped . . . either where they stopped going or where they become very small or fine lines, meaning potential lines for the future, but where they haven't moved into that point of being actual lines. Slide your finger along the line that's of interest—the physical or your mental or your heart. Slide it along there, depending upon what you want to expand and have more of for the future—slide it along.

When you get to that point where only small lines exist, you're going to shove not just your . . . in the case of mental capacity, you're going to slide it along, but not to bring the past to the future; it's not that. It's that when you slide your finger, you slide fairly quickly. If you slide it slowly and press in, then you are trying to bring the past to the present or the future. But you're going to slide it quickly—that means it has to do with your learning curve, how much you have learned and how much capacity you have. Bring it over to the point where only the little line extends beyond that, and hold it on there for a moment, maybe wiggle your finger. Notice I'm using the middle finger, which is the sensitive here, all right? You wiggle it a little bit, and then move your finger. You can do that up to three times, but no more.

Now, as the years go by, you can do it again. Say you need to expand your mental capacity for the future and a few years have gone by. Then you can slide it across there up to three times and do that again to expand your mental capacity for the future. What about if you want to expand your heart's capacity or ability? Same thing. You will often find that heart lines and head lines and other lines will intersect, but you can still do it. You slide it along, you get to that point where the lines become small, then slide it quickly and move your finger—that means it expands the capacity or capability, possibily the durability. But very often in this case, with this technique, what you are doing is expanding what your heart can do—not only physiologically, but more to the point, what you can accomplish in terms of your understanding, how you might nurture others, how you might nurture yourself, how you might have more sensitive skills of love.

Say you're having difficulty in feeling the love-heat exercise. You might slide your finger along there and do that in the areas where your heart line just becomes little lines. What you are doing is . . . those little lines are actually happening now, but they're forming up for the future, and as you get older and as time goes on, they'll become more defined. That happens all throughout life. And so you do that gesture, and then perhaps your heart can then expand and do other things—I don't mean expand physically, but expand in its capacities.

The Light of the Night

Speaks of Many Truths
November 28, 2001

t is often a mistaken assumption in your time that the night is dark and that the light of the night is the moonlight or even the starlight, but that the light is absent. This is a mistake. Even though you identify light as illumination . . . it is dark, you light a candle and it illumines an area, you can see that area better. Nevertheless, that which you consider dark, or what I call the light of the night—because that is also light, it's just a different definition of the word; you might even say it is a color—is a most important nutrient to your physical body and to your soul's interaction with your physical body.

Be Nurtured by the Light of the Night

Maybe you want to progress in some way spiritually and it's been slow or difficult. This is what you might try. It's not guaranteed, but it's worth a try. I might add, you don't have to go out in the night stark naked, but if it is a warm night and there are no mosquitoes around or other creatures who might be dangerous to you, then you might, for instance, go out wearing less garments. In the case of a woman, perhaps you might wear a bathing suit, or in the case of a man, you might wear shorts with no shirt—in this way, exposing quite a bit of your skin. You could, if you feel safe and the area is as pitch-dark as it can be, go out without anything on—outside, though—but only if you feel safe. When you don't have any clothes on in your society in your time, you often feel nervous anyway, and we don't want to start you off feeling nervous. So even if you are dressed completely and have a short-sleeved shirt on, that's something.

That light of the night . . . it soothes your soul. Think about it: When you are inside your mother, when your soul is just getting acquainted with your body as it's forming, it is usually dark, right? And so you usually feel very safe inside mother. So you, as a soul *and* as a physical being (forming, granted), immediately in those moments identify the dark with that which nurtures your soul and physical self in the union it is forming to create your physical life.

This is why your soul will feel nurtured in its interaction with your physical body by getting fed with the night light. Now, you don't have to go out when it is only cloudy and there are no stars or moonlight, but if that is the case, that's fine too. If there is moonlight, that's all right, because sometimes in your mother there will be a little light. Especially if your mother is real skinny, there will be some illumination that might come in—not completely, but a little bit. And you will notice it as a baby in there—or more to the point, as a soul. A baby's eyes are usually closed inside mom, but not always, certainly not when you are forming up in the early stages. So I mention this to begin with because there is so much confusion about the light of the night and it is literally food for the soul and body together.

When we talked to the being who had created what we call the void, he said our Creator along with all the others had borrowed some of this to create what we call darkness. So what we're really being nurtured by is the beingness of the being who's the void, right?

Ultimately you're being nurtured by Creator, because Creator, working with all of these wonderful beings, has needed things that Creator did not, in Its own right, bring. So the being who offered it . . . yes, there is that free gift, but ultimately it is an ingredient added by Creator, so it is actually from Creator. Maybe you make cookies for your friend. Say your friend likes nuts in chocolate chip cookies as well. You don't really like that, but you think, "That's what he likes, and he really likes these particular nuts, cashews, so I'm breaking them up, putting in broken pieces of cashews." When he's eating his chocolate chip cookies . . . it is like that. The cashews freely offer themselves, in this case of our scenario. The darkness, as you call it, or the dark light (or what I prefer to call the light of the night) is freely offered, but it is applied lovingly by the chef—in this case, Creator.

That's wonderful.

The Light of the Night Initiates Dreams of Home

So the light of the night provides certain specific energies that are important to all life. Is there more to say about that?

Yes. Consider for a moment the valuable and really essential element of dreams. In your time now, a great deal of research has gone on and continues to go on about the impact and necessity of dreams. It has specifically been shown—initially with military and defense department research in trying to find how to make their soldiers feel better—that if people do not dream, that they become agitated, nervous, upset, and are much more likely to create an accident that injures themselves and possibly others. That was the initial finding, and much work has therefore been prompted there.

But for me, I will say that it is the light of the night that initiates dreams—not just dreams, but more important, dreams of home. You have dreams when you are asleep that you do not remember. Your dream researchers have established that for the most part, when deep sleep takes place . . . and deep sleep is not only rapid eye movement, but deep sleep is also something that goes a little deeper than that. Your sleep researchers have noticed that there is rapid eye movement, and then very often there are only flickers with the eye and they know you are even deeper yet. When you are even deeper yet, that's when—not always, but very often— you are dreaming or interacting, since your soul does not need to sleep . . . that's when you are dreaming of home. It is that light of the night—not the artificial dark room that is created by the sleep researcher to stimulate as best as possible a benevolent environment for sleep, no, but the actual outdoors.

Say you're outdoors and you're sitting in your lawn chair, maybe a relaxing version of the lawn chair, and there are no mosquitoes to worry about and it is a warm night. You are in your yard and safe—somewhere safe, all right? But it is pitch-dark, and there are no lights on in your house and everybody else is asleep, so it's quiet. Or maybe you are camping out somewhere that is safe, quiet and dark. It is that light of the night that nurtures the optimal dream of home. What is the optimal dream of home? The optimal dream is this [draws Fig. 4-1]. Say, in a sleep researcher's lab, your dream of home—[drawing] here you are in your dream of home—might occur just for an instant. That's the dream of home. When you wake up, you don't remember it at all.

But say this is an optimal circumstance where you and your loved ones and maybe even a beloved pet are camping out and it is pitch-dark and you are in your reclining lawn chair and it's completely safe. Maybe you've been there many times before. In short, you feel safe for whatever reasons—it might be that maybe you are on your ranch and you're sleeping under the stars. You might then, if you feel safe, instead of having that kind of dream of home that you don't remember, your dream of home might be like this [draws Fig. 4-2]. The wiggly line in the middle is just to indicate that your dream of home is more massive.

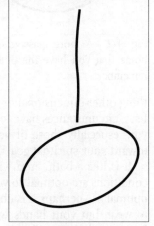

Fig. 4-1. The dream of home you do not remember at all.

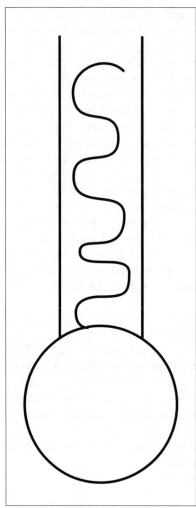

Fig. 4-2. A more massive dream of home that you have the potential to remember.

What happens when you have a dream of home like that is that the potential to remember some fragments of what your actual soul home is, is greatly amplified. However, it may not occur in, say, one experience; you might dream of home several times in a given night's sleep. But after sleeping like that over time, maybe ten nights in a row—meaning an accumulated experience—by the time the tenth night has come around, you are probably beginning to have some recollections of color or place. But even the first night after such a dream episode, you will wake up feeling much safer, more comfortable, refreshed. In short, you will wake up with the feelings that people are inspired to go camping for in the first place, because they will feel refreshed and comfortable and relaxed and often more happy to be alive—given that there are no critters biting you, all right?

But after, say, ten days in a row of sleeping like that, not only on the lawn chair but perhaps on something more comfortable, then the chances of remembering some fragment that is home . . . it is unlikely that you will see Earth things. It is more likely . . . I'll put a percentage on it. The chances of it being something other-dimensional or extraterrestrial is greater than 95 percent. So, as I say, circumstances have to be just right to do this, but I want to encourage you, especially those of you who want to improve the spiritual progress toward your spiritual goals, to try bathing in the night light this way.

It is like a bath. You will have to do what you can to create where the conditions are optimal so you can do that. As I say, if the conditions are not optimal . . . perhaps it is chilly at night. Then you can wear what you need to wear, but your hands will probably be exposed at least, and also your face—surely that will help. But if you are on a tropical island somewhere and you feel completely safe, or maybe you are in a fenced area or whatever it takes for you to feel safe, and it is pitch-dark at night, then try this sometime if you are wanting to make spiritual progress a little more quickly. Because the light of the night will feed not only your soul, not only your body, but it will feed the connection between your soul and your body.

That's how you lived, when you were in a body!

Well, that's right. In my time to be able to sleep in the light of the night was normal. [Chuckles.] In your time, given so many people—and the people have to live somewhere and have comforts—the light of the night is more rare.

Now, what about that? Is there any area where you could go to experience the light of the night that is not artificially created?

Yes. It is not as good, but it is about, oh, three-quarters as good. And that is in a cave. You can sleep in a cave—again, in a way you feel safe, but with some skin exposed. That will also work. Not everyone can do that, but some of you can. Try it.

As long as you're outside. Let's say you have a house on three sides and a wood fence across one side, but it's open to the sky. Does that qualify? Or do you have to actually be on the ground?

Oh, no, you don't have to be on the ground. As I said, you can be sitting in an aluminum lawn chair, if you like. Granted, it would be better in a wooden lawn chair, but I'm picking the chair idea so that you can make yourself comfortable. Bring your blanket and so on. But try to have some of your skin exposed. If it is cold, then by all means wear your sweater or even your sleeping bag, but try to have your hands and face out. Again, if there are mosquitoes present, pick another night. But try it for a while in some place and see what happens. For example, you, Melody, happen to live in an area where there isn't always an excess of light, although there is certainly more now there than there used to be.

So there should be no extraneous light there in my backyard?

Not too much.

Maybe an airplane or something?

Or your neighbors might stay up late.

So to back up a little bit, the sleep research is . . . they call it the four levels of sleep. So are you saying that you have to go into the very deepest delta level?

The very deepest level. And at that level, you are not even working with your teachers; you're uniting with home. Granted, your teachers might be present, but more to the point, you are uniting with home. And it is that union with home, your soul's home, that feeds your soul and allows your soul to endure what happens on Earth in this learning school—which is often very harsh to the soul's delicate energies. So the soul requires being refreshed from the place of home on a daily basis.

So when you say "the place of home" . . . what we learned in the totality book was that all souls come from this place beyond the totality [see Explorer Race: The Totality and Beyond, *coming 2006]. Is it that level? Or is it merging with the immortal personality? Or is it a place?*

It might be all of those. And you might connect with your total being home, to your point of origin—meaning that it will be a ribbon that connects you as a constant. It might be one place or the other. It might go from different places, it might move around, it might even connect you with the home in which your soul is focused through—your star home—to give your life its purpose, intent and goals toward your desired accomplishments.

People say, "I am from the Pleiades," "I am from Orion," all of this— that is where your soul focuses through in order to assist you to accomplish your soul's purpose. And that might be there also. So you might even, should you have a fragment where there seem to be people, if the feeling associated with that fragment is very benevolent and warm and nurturing, it might be a portion of your home perhaps in the stars or planets. If it is color or feeling or perhaps even an undertone, it is probably closer to your point of origin.

Beautiful!

Connecting with the Light of the Night

So that direct contact with the light of night, then, is the most beneficial. Now, when we are in our bedroom with the door shut and the light out, that is not directly connecting to that energy, right?

No, it is not. If, for instance, you have to, for whatever reason, sleep in the daytime, your soul is not refreshed with the light of the night. What do you do if you are, say, a worker and you work the night shift? Recognize that this is something you can do if you are working outdoors, or even if you are working in an office, perhaps you can go outdoors. Even though you might be able to escape all of the light from your place of work, walk out somewhere at a distance if it is safe and just be, all right? You don't have to go out just for a smoke; go out and just be out there, just stand. You can look at the stars, if you like, if you can see them. Do what you can.

If you go out at night, say, but you do not sleep out, you are still . . . you understand, there are other means to connect your soul to your body. This is not the only way; it is just the most profound way. It is the best way, but I am giving this for people who are trying to make spiritual progress and connect their soul more with their physical body. It is not the only way. Your soul is always connected to your physical body, but this is a way of optimizing it.

So we're always connected to our soul—we have to be, to be here, right?

Yes.

What if you're in a bedroom and you leave the windows and the doors open, rather than just having the air conditioning or the heat on and blocking it all out? Does any of that energy come in?

Yes, if you can do that. I grant that it is not always acceptable. At night nocturnal creatures might come in—that is not always acceptable. But it might be possible to open a window even a crack. And by doing that, of course, you'll get some fresh air, but you may allow some of the light of the night to come in. It does not come in as well through windows, but it . . . how can we say? The light of the night, transmitting through a typical glass window . . . if you're out in the light of the night, it would be, say, 100 percent exposure to the light of the night, and in a house with one glass window in the bedroom where you are sleeping, it would be, perhaps, that 1 to 1.5 percent of the light of the night might get through that window.

But if you open the window wide and it comes in . . .

If you open the window, then you might get as much as 10 percent of the light of the night to come in.

What about screens? Do they obstruct?

Yes. If you have a screen, that will cut it down to perhaps 8 percent. But say you have more than one window. Let's say, for example, you have three windows. Then with those windows, you might allow 15 to 20 percent of the light of the night to come in. The screens—those cut it down a few percentage points.

What about a fan? Does that pull it in if you reverse the blades?

No. No. The light of the night comes in because it is welcome. You can move the air, but that is not the light of the night. You could, for example, have a flashlight, and you could blow across the light of the flashlight, but that doesn't make it brighter.

Okay, so what are some other ways? The big question is going to be safety. Very rarely are we concerned these days with mosquitoes or animals—I mean, it's going to be what people perceive as being safe, right?

Depending on where you live, that's true. In some places, you might be concerned.

Oh, yes, yes. But I mean, the biggest percentage is going to be people in cities, right?

That's right, and people in the cities are, of course, struggling with getting the light of the night. Sometimes you can, in the case of some cities, go up on the roof with a few friends and maybe take a nap up on the roof, where there is more light of the night. But even so, there would be a lot of ambient light, so it's not the same. But if you can get away from the city sometime and go camping someplace where you do not have to worry, then you can try this. Even one night . . . even sleeping for, say, two or three hours on a lounge chair like that, where you feel safe. You can't be frightened, so do what it takes to feel safe, all right?

I don't recommend keeping a loaded gun in your lap, because if you do that, you'll probably . . . aside from waking up and hurting yourself or somebody else in reaction, you might safely say that that loaded gun would make you edgy in the first place.

The Light of the Day and the Light of the Night

So how does this work? That energy is always there—that is the energy that is between everything and around everything. Now, in the daylight, obviously the Sun is more powerful. So does that keep you from feeling it?

I'm glad you brought that up. What about the light of the day? What does it do? The light of the day or the sunlight feeds your physical body. Remember, we have the process . . . let's do this as a drawing [draws Fig. 4-3]. I'm drawing this as a graph because it really is that. It's something that connects one thing, then connects another thing. The light of the day, then, feeds your physical body and the physical actions you must take to conduct your life. I'm drawing it that way, in that graphical picture, because I want to demonstrate that one thing feeds the other, and then it continues to be fed. It is like a circuit—one thing progresses to another.

So the energy's still there; the light of the night didn't go anywhere. It's just that the Sun . . . it's like turning a light on—you don't see the dark, right?

That's not quite true. The light of the night goes into your physical body, and then the light of the day also goes into your physical body and supports and nurtures the actions that you take. The light of the night supports and nurtures your soul's connection to your physical body and embraces that. So you have something that supports and nurtures the various portions of you that support, nurture *and* sustain life.

So the light of the night . . . it's there; the void is always there.

It's not a void. The light of the night *is light*. The void is not the light of the night. Void is the absence of light, including the absence of the light of the night.

Well, then, we shouldn't call that being's creation the void.

It's all right to call that being's creation the void if that being calls itself that. That is what the being defines itself as. It means that it does not

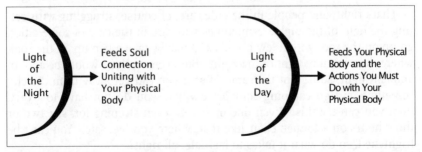

Fig. 4-3. The light of the night feeds your soul's connection with your physical body, whereas the light of the day nurtures the actions that you take.

have the light of the night present.

But my understanding is that the light of the night came from that being's creation.

That may be your understanding, but it may be a misunderstanding. But it could also be that that being offered that, and between that and something Creator added to it—chocolate chips *and* nuts—it became the light of the night. Creator says, "Can you supply me this? I have this, but if you can supply me this, then I can make this thing that we put together. We put this together now, and presto!" [Claps hands. His two hands are clasping.] "We have the light of the night." What was it that was provided? Not just the absence of something. This is what is in the void. It doesn't have the light of the night—what is it? It has receptivity with nothing in it yet. So that tells you, if it's 100 percent receptivity with nothing in it yet, that it is 100 percent pure feminine energy.

What did the Creator add?

Creator added the joy of living and created the light of the night, which is an illumination—meaning that in the philosophical sense, it has an impact that triggers and otherwise stimulates the soul's joy in connecting to the physical body that you have here on Earth now.

That's so powerful.

The Impact of Not Enough Light of the Night

This really explains, then, in this time of machines and cities, why there's so much drug use and so much mentality, because that whole aspect of life is missing.

The soul is always connected to the physical body, yes, but not nurtured as it needs, not refreshed. You know how it feels to be refreshed: a hot bath, comforting sheets that are cold when you first slide into them and then warm up, or a good meal when you're hungry. You can think of a hundred different examples of being refreshed. And yet you know that when you're not refreshed, you can do what you need to do.

But there's no joy.

You can be exhausted, but you can do the work. You can cut the wood, you can type the letters, you can do it, but you're exhausted and drained, and it's a struggle. Your soul can perform the function of being united with your physical body, but it has no capacity to resist the impact of what produces stress. Discomfort, a little thing, triggers a major impact, total collapse, meaning, "Oh, my alarm clock didn't go off! Oh, I just can't face the day! I think I'll stay home." Something like that, which would normally . . . if you were refreshed, you'd say, "Oh, my alarm clock didn't go off; I'll be late. Well, okay, I'll be late."

So as you said in your example, sensitive people who very often need to have that extreme overstimulation in the city softened might be attracted to drugs or alcohol, which will soften the corners, as Zoosh likes to say.

But, of course, that has consequences: If you can't get those drugs or alcohol, your body is not happy. And that is very much an impact of no feeding or not enough feeding from the light of the night.

The Light of the Night Is Essential for Crops

Now, I grant that the light of the day is vitally important; obviously you wouldn't have any crops growing that feed you without the light of the day. But the plants are also fed by the light of the night, as most good farmers know. It's not an accident that farmers use that almanac, which has been lovingly produced by other farmers over the years, because it is understood that the Moon cycles are just as important. It is identified as the Moon; the Moon, granted, illumines, and that is the way to identify, for the sake of the almanac. But it is the light of the night that nurtures the plants, unites them with their home (just like you), helps them to feel welcome, safe, and gives them the strength to face what they ultimately know will occur—that is, harvesting, when they will be cut.

If there isn't enough light of the night, the crop might not work as well sometimes. Granted, it is different with, say, mushrooms and so on, where they need to have the light of the night almost exclusively. But with typical crops, especially ones that haven't been hybridized this way or that way—natural plants—if they are too close to the city or there is too much light on them, they don't get the light of the night. They do not feel so good; they might not grow so well. Some of the rows you have planted and cultivated might not grow so well, because there's too much light.

A good farmer knows this. That is why he or she will try to grow his or her crops as far out in the countryside, as far away from the city, as possible, to create the best optimal natural conditions so that the plants will feel welcome. They will thrive. Not only do they have the light of the day, but they have the light of the night, so they will thrive. That's what it takes. So you farmers who have gardens in the cities, sometimes even with the best of seeds or hybridized seeds, and they still don't grow, it isn't always because you did something wrong. They might need more light of the night than is available where you live.

Is the moonlight a reflection from the Sun, or is something added to it or subtracted from it in the process of reflecting the sunlight?

Well, it is certainly reflected from the Sun, but of course, there is also a degree of starlight that is reflected. It may be minute, but it is certainly there, and I think it could even be quantified by a good mathematician. So yes, it is reflected from various light sources. But because it is where it is, it also, to the other side of the Moon, is always being nurtured by the light of the night.

And out there it is often being nurtured by the purest version of the light of the night, which allows the Moon—since it is performing a function for Earth, the plants, the animals and so on—with that pure light of the night to have . . . what? A greater connection with its soul to its body to perform its purpose, and . . . what? A greater capacity to do it, more endurance, more strength. That's how it can survive such things as impacts. Bang—something hits it, forms a crater. So it can perform that way because it is constantly being exposed to the 100 percent pure light of the night on at least half of its surface.

And it was intended that . . .

Everything that is natural is intended.

I mean, was it intended that it not orbit like all other planets, all other satellites and asteroids and things? I mean, it always shows one face.

Everything that is natural is intended.

All right, we won't get into that.

We can get into it anytime you want, but "Everything that is natural is intended" is an important statement, because it is really . . . everything that I am talking about in all of the *Shamanic Secrets* books, the whole point is to support, nurture and unite. I am interweaving my fingers: It creates union.

How to See the Light of the Night

Do you know that the light of the night, even if there is no moonlight or starlight because it's cloudy, do you know that it shimmers? Oh, scientists might say, "Oh, that's because of the moisture in your eyes," but no, it really shimmers. Sometime if you want to test it, go out into the light of the night and focus, say, on a spot. Just focus on a spot out in front of your eyes, not something in the distance that you can see—just focus. Then you're looking at the actual light of the night. After a while you will see something shimmer.

You might also, by focusing between something . . . see, here are your eyes, and there's enough ambient light at night that you can see a fence off in the distance or maybe the vague shape of a house. Focus your eyes between those two things and fairly close, maybe ten or twenty feet away from your eyes. Just focus there in that space. Granted, you might at some point notice a lightbeing because you will be focusing there, but if you just see a sensation of shimmering, you're seeing the light of the night, because it is filled with life and soul-giving energy, and you can see it.

So how does it work? If there's no Moon and there are no stars, then it's totally the light of the night? When the moonlight comes in, would you consider that this dilutes it or that there's also power and strength in the moonlight, just a different proportion?

It is its own; it does its own thing, as you say. So it adds something to the light of the night. It is . . . what? The baking powder in the cookie analogy, right? It adds something, but it is not the light of the night, so we're going to get off the subject if we talk about the moonlight.

I just really wondered how it worked. If you shine a flashlight into a dark room, you can see what the flashlight illuminates. So is it the same principle, that the moonlight illuminates certain things but the light of the night is still there?

The light of the night is still there, but because the light from the Moon is illuminating it, you don't see only the light of the night and your eye is naturally drawn toward something brighter. So you see the moonlight. But recognize that even though your eye naturally is drawn toward something brighter—as in looking at a picture, as the photographer might say—what you consider to be light (moonlight, starlight, sunlight, flashlight), even though you might consider that all to be light, it's just brighter than the light of the night, which can also be seen if you focus and concentrate on it. It may be brighter, but the light of the night is also light.

The Light of the Night Heightens Your Sensitivity and Awareness

So when you're in a city and you have all of this, what you call artificial illumination, versus the moonlight and the starlight—does that keep you from feeling or seeing or experiencing the light of the night?

Yes, artificial light, yes.

Because it's artificial, then—is that the difference between it and the moonlight?

Moonlight nurtures in its own right; it is not the light of the night, but in its own right, it nurtures. Whereas artificial light does not nurture, but of course, it is practical.

So that's why it's more beneficial to the soul to be in the light of the night in the moonlight than in the light of the night in artificial light?

Yes.

Because it strengthens the soul's connection to the physical body.

And it does something else. It heightens your sensitivity and awareness. That's right; think about it. I originally started this by saying that the light of the night can help you to make spiritual progress toward your spiritual goals—how does it do that? It does that by heightening your sensitivity. You know that if someone drives you out to the countryside in a car, the car is illuminated somewhat by the instrument panel, plus to some degree the headlights—in short, there is some illumination. But you stop, pull over by the side of the road for whatever reason, turn the lights out, get out of the car, and it's pitch-dark. What's the first thing that happens? An intense immediate sensation of alertness.

So, of course, your physical body is at maximum alert because you are in an unknown place where you can't see at all. There's that. But say you're in a place where you feel completely safe in the light of the night where you can't see—you put your hand up and you still can't see it. So what is happening with that light of the night? You are in this place where you can't see your hand in front of your face, meaning that even with your pupil expanded completely, there is minimal capacity to see—you can almost see, but it is pitch-dark. With enough training, you can see somewhat, but still the basic impression is that you cannot see.

Then what occurs is that the sensitivity is present for being alert—meaning that your auric field is energized very powerfully and sensitively out to a distance of fifty feet, and just slightly less spherically out to fifty feet, above and all around you. And then just slightly less to a distance of, say, one hundred fifty feet is still very sensitive, and even well beyond that is very sensitive. Your auric field runs way, way out. Even triggering that and being highly sensitive like that, even not feeling particularly safe, frightened—"Gosh, what's happening? I don't know, can't see anything" . . . in the daytime you'd feel completely safe, probably see everything around you—parking lot, trash receptacle, restroom. In the light of the night, you don't see it.

Granted, your body is alert, but what happens if, in the environment where you're out in the light of the night, you still have that tendency to, at the slightest sound . . . a leaf falls out of a tree or an acorn falls off the tree and hits the ground and makes the tiniest sound. Immediately your heightened awareness clicks into place. So you will go from heightened awareness to protect your body, to keep you safe, to moments of relaxation when the light of the night is fully merging with you and uniting your soul and your body together, to moments when you're at heightened alert—where that light of the night doesn't stop uniting your soul and your body together, but it becomes more fixated. It doesn't interact freely as much.

But going back and forth between those two versions of sensitivity . . . that is the mechanics of why your soul and spiritual growth in your physical self—your soul self, which has grown plenty spiritually, but your interaction into your physical self—going back and forth between those two things, creates mechanically, as we say (breaking it down into how and why it works), the heightened sensitivity that strengthens your spiritual growth muscles in application in your physical body in your life on Earth.

And also, as with when you can't see, you hear better, you smell better—it heightens the senses in those ways too.

That's right. It's good to do that. The people who are exposed to training like this are often in the military services. But it's very good to do this as a person who wants to expand your capacities and become more sensitive in spiritual growth. What do you do after that experience? Then whatever spiritual activities you are pursuing, it will probably become easier; you will get it quicker, or whatever techniques you are applying will work faster. Things will simply be smoother and easier most likely, because you will not only be recently reminded of your sensitivity capacity, but you will have honed your sensitivity capacity in a practical sense in your physical body, interacting with your soul. So in that sense, you simply can do more, be more, because you can switch on [snaps fingers] that experience.

You remember. You can bring up in your recollection having sat out there or slept out there in the night sky, in the night. You can call it forth as a remembered physical experience because it is recent enough that your body calls it forward. "Recent enough"—what does that mean? It means that if you're working on your spiritual growth like this and you notice that when you remember that time when you were out experiencing the light of the night in this kind of sensitizing experience of your soul and your body in order to improve the progress of your spiritual life . . . if you notice that when you remember back on that experience in order to bring that heightened sensitivity up, to practice it, to put it into practice with whatever you are doing in your spiritual life or spiritual-growth technique, you cannot feel it as much anymore in a significant way, then go back out and do it again. Refresh it. That's when it needs to be refreshed.

The Light of the Night Is Always Present

So the light of the night is always there, unlike the sunlight, which comes and goes with the revolution of the planet. It's still there, even though it's overlaid by the sunlight during the day, right? Is that true?

Yes, it is true. Just as in a dark room . . . a flashlight illumines only a certain area, but the rest of the darkness is present.

It's still there; it doesn't go anywhere.

So the light of the night is present, but when other forms of illumination are not present, then you can see the darker illumination—just as when you light a candle in a dark room, the light is quite obvious, but if you flip on the light switch and all the lights come on, the light from the candle is no longer as obvious. The more we remove other forms of illumination, brightness, then the light of the night becomes more obvious, if you look for it.

But the point I'm trying to make is, even if you can't see it, it's still there. It's always there; it's the substrate of reality.

That's right. It's the canvas upon which other light is painted.

Yes. But more than a canvas, isn't it . . . it's total receptivity, right? Can we use it in some other way? Is it available as a resource in some way?

An individual might feel that he or she is not receptive enough. Perhaps you're in a relationship and your husband or wife tells you, "How come you can't hear me?" And you say, "I want to, but I just don't seem to be able to." In this case, you could go out to the light-of-the-night experience. You can experience something that will sharpen up your sensitivity, all right?

And you could ask for that, right?

You don't have to say it mentally; it will do it.

It will do it?

It just does; it will prompt you to be more sensitive.

So there's no need to ask it for anything, then? The light of the night does what it does, and then that's it?

Yes. Your desire to ask it for something is actually restricting it; that makes it less. If you ask it to do something, a specific function, and do that before you go out in the light of the night, what you're doing then is, your mind is trying to control it so that it becomes something mental. That's what's really going on here.

You're controlling your reality again.

That's right. But if you want to ease your mind and help your mind to understand what's going on, talk out loud before you go out and do this. Talk out loud to yourself so that your mind understands: "This is what I'm going to do." You can say, "Mind . . ." Talk to your mind as if it were someone: "Mind, this is what I intend to do, and this is my intention. Please be alert and observe so we can think about it later." This way the mind does not feel rejected; it participates, but it does not control or *narrow the focus*.

Why might you do this? Because otherwise you might feel out of control. That is typical of people, because your life feels out of control enough—meaning things are happening extraneously to you, and there's enough happening that is absolutely and obviously out of your control. So when you focus your mind on something and say, "This is what I want to get," only that happens so that you are not frightened any further.

Claiming Your Natural Mind

That is a typical human experience. But our whole conversations in general here are about helping people to feel safer in a world that they understand with their total physical being—which includes their body, their feelings, their spirit and, to a lesser degree but present, their mind.

When will we get help on that? Is it years? Is it an individual thing? Is it a movement of the planet in frequency when the linear mind is actually pretty much gone?

It will not leave of its own accord. In order for it to leave, you will have to claim your natural mind, which is the whole purpose, also, of the *Shamanic Secrets* books.

How do we do that?

Read the *Shamanic Secrets* books and apply them.

Every step on the path will connect us more and more to our vertical mind, our natural mind?

Your natural mind does not involve thoughts, plans, ideas, control—none of that. Your natural mind is, as your friend Zoosh said, knowing what you need to know when you need to know it, and then when you don't need to know it, it is no longer present to clutter up your consciousness. In short, you do not think, but mental awareness becomes essentially identified *as the observer*. All of your senses interact with your mental process so that you *KNOW* what you need to know when you need to know it.

People are seeking knowledge; they want to know. That's why we're capitalizing the word "know"—that's what occurs. But you do not have past-oriented or future-oriented thought at all—no worry. You are in the present, all of your senses combining to enjoy and to experience the present. But there is no linear thought at all. This Andromedan mind is linear; your natural mind is vertical.

Would you say that you live totally in that vertical mind?

Yes, and I was trained to live in that in my physical life, as we are training Robert [the channel] to live in that now, in his physical life. When he unites with Mother Earth to request that her storm be moved away from people as much as possible, he is in his feeling self. His linear mind is— when he is doing the work—completely not there. It is elsewhere. So in that moment, he is completely in his vertical mind, though the process is not mental at all. It does not even include the vertical mind, but it is present and available if needed.

How many people like that have you got trained?

Not many. That's why Robert is kind of nervous. He wants to pass it on, but it takes the right student. He or she has to be dedicated. And it helps if the person doesn't have a whole lot else that he or she has to do.

Youth Is Where the Unresolved Lives

What happens in your culture, since everyone is doing that, is that people think that the reason they're hanging on to youth is because of beauty and no wrinkles and all of these surface things, when in fact, the real reason they're hanging on to youth is that that's where the unresolved lives, and it is in your soul's nature to never let the unresolved stay that way.

What a revelation! I didn't know that! I hope there's another level ahead that is from maturity to old age . . . there's still something ahead, right?

There is so much ahead that it is not possible to draw a line from here to the end—meaning that your personality is immortal. And regardless of what happens with your physical body . . . Mother Earth will say, "Time to return it!" at some point.

"Give it back!" [Laughs.]

"Give it back!" But you would just keep on going. There is no break in continuity whatsoever—not even for a second. Did you know that?

No, I thought there was a fuzzy time.

When people die, there is not even for a split second a break in continuity; your conscious personality keeps going right on. The only major difference is that you don't sleep; you don't need to—unless, of course, you reincarnate again in a life that requires sleep as you know it. But for the sake of our conversation about the continuity of life here, you essentially go on without that much [snaps fingers]—not even that much. You just keep right on going.

Is that an instantaneous thing? Or do you have time to think?

Oh, well . . . not think, but there will be plenty of time in between in which you can . . .

To reflect?

. . . have fun.

Oh, have fun!

Do you know that what now seems like thinking and struggling and spiritual—"I can't get this," and "I'm just going to ask this one more time"—all of that stuff that's a struggle, that when you depart this physical body, which anchors you to this school that you're in . . . it's awfully easy to forget that this is a school.

Even when you know it.

Even when you know it, it's awfully easy to forget, and you suddenly feel liberated like the bell went off and it's summer vacation! You know that as a child, you don't even think about coming back to school; you just know you're out of school for a few months. It's like that, it's that feeling of liberation—bursting out the front door and the homework and schoolbooks are behind you.

Maximizing the Light of the Night

When the light of the night hits your skin, what is the dynamic? Why your skin? The more skin that the light of the night hits, the better it is for you, right?

Because your skin is the most receptive organ in your body. And it is that which makes contact with the world first, physically speaking. So we want it to touch your skin to maximize the effort, but obviously in some circumstances—certainly cold being one of the obvious ones—you don't want that to take place because you need to keep yourself warm. But if it's not too cold, then you can keep your hands out or even pull your sleeves back a bit for a time. But the whole purpose is not to see how long you can keep your teeth from chattering.

When you breathe outside in the light of the night, is there any element of that that we breathe? Does it come into you with your breath?

Yes, you can breathe the light of the night into your body. It goes in and it actually feeds your physical body. Remember, inside your physical body it is much darker; there's not much illumination in there in terms of lumens . . . light, you understand? So the light of the night is a much more natural light than the inside of your body—your body organs and so on—is used to.

So when you breathe at night and breathe that in [heaves a big sigh], that's how your physical body feels on the inside. It is relief, it is nurturing, it is love, it is . . . what? You're growing inside your mother; it is natural. This doesn't mean that sunlight is unnatural, but it is stimulating, a little different for your organs. So yes, breathing in the light of the night is very helpful. Good night.

The Advantage of the Light of the Night

Speaks of Many Truths
November 30, 2001

This is Speaks of Many Truths. Greetings

Attraction Has to Do with Love

I think that the light of the night is what scientists are looking for as the missing dark matter. Is that correct?

No, because what they are looking for is something out in space. They're trying to figure out how things are attracted to each other. But, of course, you and I know that things are attracted to each other because of the magnetic resonance of compatibility and compassion—in short, the love energy that is not only universal and unconditional but, in order to get two particles to come together, also has to be personal love. Because if these particles are going to come together for a long time, such as with particles coming together to form a planet, there needs to be an actual personal particle-to-particle attraction, since they're going to be together for a time.

Does the light of the night have mass?

It doesn't have atomic mass, no. It is not quantifiable as a substance, but then neither is the energy of your soul quantifiable as a substance. But occasionally it has been either photographed or seen by sensitives. So it exists, and of course, simply by the fact that people exist, you can assume that it exists. But it is not measurable as a physical substance might be.

In the third dimension.

Exactly.

How high do you have to get before it's quantifiable?

Well, your question has a misnomer aspect to it, because by the time you get high enough to where you could measure it, you don't use those systems anyway, so it's pointless. No, it's kind of like: "Well, I needed a shovel to shovel the snow and I didn't have one, so I went to the eighth dimension, and then I didn't care about it. I wanted the snow to be where it was."

[Laughs.] Good analogy. There have been stories—I guess they call them old wives' tales—where women used to close the windows, close the doors, get all panicky because they said the night air was dangerous. Where did that come from?

That isn't about the light of the night; that was when people were afraid of the damp. Even in the desert, the air gets more damp at night—to a lesser degree in the desert, but it gets more damp at night. So that was essentially a fear of the damp when consumption and other lung diseases were terribly threatening.

Pneumonia and tuberculosis.

That's why people used to do that.

I really thought that was the missing dark matter. Then if particles come together because of love, how do you explain gravity? We're held to the Earth by gravity—is that because we love to be here?

That's a very good question, but actually gravity is a physical energy caused pretty much the way science has described it. But one might reasonably ask, "Even if it is caused by that, why does it exist?" This is off the subject, but I would say that it exists simply for the sake of being practical; we can't have you floating about on a planet when you're supposed to be learning things. So [chuckles] I would say that it is not the same, just as it is not the same for you to accelerate a rocket to something that the rocket strikes. You might reasonably ask, "Are not those two things attracted?" No, that would be forcing. So I would say, no, it's not that you're attracted magnetically through love to the planet; it is essentially because it would be awkward to learn things if you had to grab ropes to move about.

Or if they had to use butterfly nets. [Laughs.]

[Laughs.]

How to Deal with Your Fear of the Night

How do you feel about the night?

My body is afraid of the night.

Why do you think that people are often afraid of the night? It is not always for a deep psychological reason or for something traumatic in childhood. You might reasonably say (and this has been experimented with, I might add), "Well, some people are born and nothing frightening happens to them in the nighttime, but they are afraid of the night." And you can even put those people outside in an environment that is benevolent, such as in our times, and they are afraid. This is not common, but it comes up. We had several children in my time who were apparently for no reason—no mental reason, no explanation—frightened of the night. I'll tell you what this means: It usually means, in most cases, if there is no other reason that can be found out, that these beings have never experienced a cycle of day and night.

Not ever having experienced that . . . that probably means that in all other lives they experienced only illumination, an illuminated place—some place that was bright, all right? This means that when they became aware of their personality, it was in some bright place, and when they had lives, that was also in some bright place. But to have a cycle of illumination and then the foundation of the light of the night—that can startle a child.

What you do to ease the child in is that you build a fire, which illuminates it . . . in my time you built a fire that illuminated the night, and you brought the child over—not too close to the fire—so that there was light. And you held the child lovingly and then you gradually stepped away from the fire into the darker space, letting the child look at the fire. If the child got upset, you moved back toward the fire, and then when she calmed down, you moved away. In short, you gradually stepped away until the child got to the point where the fire might be just a tiny little light on the horizon. And eventually you, in short, weaned the child.

This has to be done gradually, lovingly, and it might take several days or several nights, but it's worth doing. In your time, of course, you would perhaps use an electric light. You would have to use it outside, because in order to step away far enough and still have the child be able to see the light in a dark place, maybe when out camping somewhere . . . you'd have to have plenty of space to step away, all the while allowing the child to keep her eyes on the light.

Don't ever force it. The moment the child gets upset, immediately move back toward the light. When he or she relaxes, then you can stop; you don't necessarily have to move all the way to the light, but move to the point where the child relaxes. It is best if you can always allow the child to have her eyes on the light, meaning that when you are walking away from the light, the child is held to you with her head over your shoulder so that her eyes are looking back toward the light. When you turn around, you also turn the child around so that her eyes are toward the light. In short, you don't ever have the child positioned in such a way that she cannot actually see the light—that would just make things last longer.

At what age do you determine this?

You can usually tell within the first week—I mean, once the child's eyes have opened—because the child will cry when it gets dark.

But that means you catch it before it becomes chronic.

You catch it before, as you say, it becomes a constant trauma where the night is coming and becomes frightening.

Because I've heard of kids who have night-lights on all their life, and they never had the advantage, then, of the light of the night.

Weaning Yourself from Night Fears as an Adult

Well, the nice thing here is that you can be a seventy-year-old kid and do this yourself—meaning that you can go out somewhere that is basically dark and bring a lamp of some sort, and you can put it there and you can walk away. But you'll have to walk backward, you'll have to be able to see the light—meaning that you probably ought to have someone walking in front of you, so you're not tripping all over the place. But you can do it yourself as an adult.

Or you could put the headlights on in your car and walk away.

Any form of illumination, as long as the light stays in one place and is fixed. But you don't want the light shining like headlights toward you; then you'll have to walk a long way. You need to have a fixed light, and you back away from it. When you get nervous, you walk back toward the light, and you notice, in this part of your body—in the chest and solar plexus, or the chest and gut—when that part of you relaxes physically. When that part of you relaxes, you take another step maybe or two, and then you stop and wait awhile. You don't rush it; never force it, all right? Weaning doesn't involve forcing; you don't teach people how to swim by throwing them out of the boat when they don't know how. You don't make it a trauma.

You're trying to help people to get more comfortable with physical life, and in order to get more comfortable with physical life, you have to be gentle. So once you are relaxed, then you move back slowly. Try to remember that you need to back away from the light very slowly. Say you have two or three hours to do this at night—you might not accomplish it. But every night, you keep it up—it has to be done one night after another.

Every night that you keep it up, you'll be able to get farther and farther away. At some point, you'll be able to be so far away from the light that it is way off in the distance. But you *never* have anybody turn the light off; you just keep moving farther and farther and farther and farther away from it until you can't see it anymore. This might mean, in a flat area, that you essentially are walking a few miles, from the curvature of the Earth there. But in a hilly area or in an area that's got occasional bushes and trees, then it might be a bush or a tree. But you never have the light off. It's important for your mind to know that you can find your way back, because all you have to do is just start walking forward and you'll find the light again.

This implies that some planets don't have a day-and-night cycle.

No implication intended; it is a fact. When I said that people have light lives where there is only illumination, that means there are planets that have light all the time. It may not always be very bright, or it might be very bright all the time—this includes everything, all the way to the point of where it is just a fairly dim light all the time. There are certain parts of the Earth that are bright like that for months at a time.

Yes, I've been there, in Alaska.

You might have found that comforting without having been weaned. I might add that in order for adults to wean themselves, they must have another person present. You cannot wean yourself alone. You will, from time to time, get frightened, and it will be very beneficial to know that there is another person within a few steps of you. Because if you get frightened, you'll say, "Oh! Where are you?" And the other person can say, "I'm right here." That's very comforting. But if you're all by yourself, you just get frightened and then the whole experience might become a trauma.

What are some other reasons people are afraid of the night?

That's the only one I know of, other than something unsettling happened to them when they were youngsters. That's the one that I know about. You can extrapolate as far as your own experience goes. I will say that given a rough percentage of the people who are afraid of the dark . . . you might ask how many in a percentage are afraid of the dark, not because of a trauma when they were a child in the dark or at night, but strictly because in other lives they had never experienced a life where there was a cycle of night. And I would have to say that starting about a hundred years ago, the percentage of people like that, of the people who are afraid of the night, was about 12 percent. But now, in your now time, it's more like 7 percent. So it's dwindling. This tells you that the people being born today are more likely to have had a broader spectrum of experiences—many lives, different situations. They are born more versatile.

Ah! I would have been totally wrong, because I thought the new Indigo children had not had Earth-type lives.

I am not familiar with this term "Indigo children," but I would say that the children being born today are more likely to have had more experience than to have had less experience.

A Walking Stick Can Help You Feel Safer at Night

Well, I just don't go out at night. I mean, I go out in a car, but I just don't go out walking. Why not?

Because it makes you nervous. You just don't do it for a reason, because it makes you nervous. Do you know what would make you feel better? It might surprise you. If you had a walking stick . . . it could even be metal, like the kind they sell for people who go hiking in the mountains. If you had a walking stick and you could put something down besides your own legs and feet, something you can get a good grip on . . . a vertical grip. This grip has to be like this [his hand is vertical, with the thumb on top— not horizontal]. If you can grab it like that and put your walking stick down—you can even have your thumb on top, if you want to—you will immediately feel 15 to 20 percent safer at night, even without weaning yourself in the way I described.

What that does is, it's almost like having another leg that makes a connection or a contact to the Earth. You might find that metal, especially conductive metal, will work even better than wood. But you can try them both and see which works better for you. Because your body will ground, you understand? Your body grounds through your legs, but your body will also ground through this stick.

It's like having our tail back, eh?

Also in the more deeper parts of your body, you'd know that not only is this a stick that you can lean on and that you can ground, but it gives you a sensation of having something you can push things away with.

For protection?

Yes, for protection. But you wouldn't have the same feeling if you had a rifle or a gun. That's certainly protection, and devastating at that, but it wouldn't help you to feel safer in the night. Whereas a stick, putting a stick on the ground, especially a metal one that's conductive, would immediately give you that 15 to 20 percent better feeling.

Don't Force Yourself into the Night

What about someone who's forced? Maybe a child has had traumatic experiences and the parents don't realize it and think the child is wimpy and force him to go out at night. Does that make it worse, then?

It depends. Some people can learn that way, but sometimes it also, as the psychologists say, sublimates the trauma and it comes up in some other form. I do not recommend that under any circumstances. For those of you who have had the experience, have been forced to go out at night because of some intolerant parent or well-intended individual (sometimes it's done with good intentions), for one thing, it would be good to see a counselor or therapist, but even if you don't do that, you will probably note that you are a nervous person.

It will create . . . it starts out, you understand, as an uncertainty. You're a baby, you are born, and the night comes and this is something entirely unknown and you are frightened. And without the weaning process, if you're simply, as a youngster, sent out into the night, it will make you nervous and you will not be able to trust in the cycle of life on Earth. And so it will not only make you nervous at night, it will make you nervous in the daytime. In short, it's not a good idea.

So don't force yourself. Don't say, "I'm going out in the night no matter what." Do things—bring a flashlight, bring your walking stick, especially a metal one. That will help. But don't force yourself. You might have been forced as a child; don't compound that and force yourself as an adult. In time a metal walking stick and a flashlight might greatly soothe the problem. You will probably always need some kind of a light, but it will perhaps be less of a need as time goes on.

Remember, with the walking stick, that your hand must be vertical.

Your right hand, yes.

Some people might find that the left hand is better, those who are left-handed. Try it in both hands and see which feels better. At times you might actually find that you have to lean on the stick, in which case, if you need to put your hand down on the top, that's all right. But you want to start out with your hand up. That gives you a feeling of greater security, safety.

Your Hands and Feet Are Fed by the Light of the Night

You have said that the light of the night nourishes, that there are specific energies that nourish the body.

Yes.

Are there specific energies you want to talk about?

There are certain organs in the body that are literally fed by the light of the night. But let's talk about things that are on the surface of the body. I will tell you a couple of things right off the mark, parts of your body on the surface that are fed directly and nurtured by the light of the night. One is the space between your fingers, right here [specifically where one finger joins another at the palm, the very point where one finger turns around to become another finger].

It's the same thing with the toes, it's the same position with the toes. This is also a place that is fed by the light of the night. In a child, being fed between the toes by the light of the night will help the child to have better physical balance as he or she grows up. So the light of the night is particularly helpful for children up to the age of four or five years old. It won't help you to have better balance when you're an adult, so sorry about that. As far as the effect on the hands, between the fingers, it will usually help you to manipulate your hands better.

Now, there's something interesting here: For people who have arthritis or some other discomfort that makes it difficult to move your hands, or who are even recovering from a discomfort such as a broken bone or finger problems, if you can, be out in the light of the night and, if possible, spread your fingers. In the case of having a cast or a splint, that may not be possible, but to the best of your ability, let the light of the night be exposed here to where your fingers meet the body at the palm of the hand. Then if you can let that in, it will probably speed your recovery.

The Light of the Night Supports Your Vision and Endocrine System

There are other places on your body that are fed by the light of the night. One of them is right here at the base of the skull. Reach your hand around and feel the soft part behind your skull. Go up right to where you feel the bone, then slide your finger down about half an inch—right there. The light of the night feeds that part of your body.

That's an important part.

Your hair might reasonably cover that, so what you can do is, when you go out into the light of the night to feed that part, you can, if you have long hair, put your fingers back behind your head and part your hair right there. For a woman or a man who has long hair, perhaps you might part your hair and make a couple of temporary plaits or braids on the side of your head, and let that part of your head be exposed to the light of the night.

What that does is it supports and stimulates the body's endocrine system. On a secondary level, it supports your vision, your eyes, how you see. That's particularly important when you are about forty-five years old, because right around that time, people are going through changes in vision, and it's also important for the potential times when it's helpful to have your endocrine system supported.

Another place where the endocrine system can be supported by the light of the night is underneath your arms.

Really?

That's right, in the armpits, as they're called. And the light of the night will also support your vision, your sight. So if it is a warm night, you can wear a sleeveless garment and let the light of the night feed that.

How Long to Stay Out in the Light of the Night

Now, you might reasonably ask, how long might you wish to stay out to get the feeding for all of these situations that I've mentioned? If you can be out in the light of the night for forty-five minutes, that will be sufficient. Obviously, if you can stay out longer in the light of the night, it will be better, but only incrementally better past forty-five minutes.

What about repeated times?

Doing it again? If you're having some problem—maybe you have some injury with your hands—there is no problem doing it every single night. But if you're having something temporary or you just want to give yourself a tune-up and there's nothing wrong, just one night would be fine—one night every three or four months. If you're having something problematic, granted, you'll need to do other things: see the doctor and so on. But it would be helpful if you can—if it's easy and it's not a strain and you can do it safely—to go out and do this three or four times a week. Obviously, the weather conditions and other outdoor conditions might make a difference.

As well as the light in the area where you are, right?

That's problematic for a lot of people who live in the city—that's true. But sometimes even when you live in the city, if you can go to a forest, as in the case of some public parks if it is safe to go there, you might find a dark place. But, generally speaking, the light of the night is much better to experience away from the city. So for those of you who can get away from the city, even temporarily, to go camping or just somewhere out away from artificial light, that's very helpful.

Acquiring Shamanic Wisdom

The manual they forgot to give us at birth—look at the stuff we don't know!

That's the purpose of these books.

Why have we lost all this?

You have to remember that you've lost a lot of this because of religious persecution and colonization. The United States was colonized by European settlers—and as time went on, by people from other places as well. And it's very easy for people coming over to believe that they've got the knowledge and the wisdom, and that the people who seem to be—how can we say?—Native Americans in this case or so-called primitives do not have the knowledge and the wisdom. Yet even now with your universities, they continue to discover the levels of wisdom.

But there is a problem in your universities, and that is that wisdom like this, that I tend to talk about, is very often relegated to something called myth or stories. When that's done, it is immediately downgraded to mean that there is no power or influence behind this. But, in fact, there is plenty of power and influence, because it has to do with the way the Earth actually functions as a planetary body and the way all forms of life function and interact with one another, including human beings on Earth as it is now. And so a great deal of so-called myth and story is misunderstood by educators.

In time that might change as more spiritual and shamanic practices are researched, but you cannot research shamanic practices, mystical practices and so on by quantifiable science, because the variables are very simple. You can't have people just observing; they have to be participating. The person whom the shaman is working with has to want to participate, has to engage the process, even if that person is not the shaman. If there's somebody else present, such as a scientist, that person can't just sit there— she will impact the whole process. No, that person has to be engaged, and in order to be engaged, she won't be able to monitor instruments. On the other hand, if the scientist is engaged because she wishes to be and she is perhaps learning about this because she wants to, then she can make notes later on. But not during the process.

And you really need a live teacher? A book is not really as good as a live teacher, right?

This process? Channeling like this? As long as the connection is solid, that is sufficient. It is helpful to have a living teacher, but if the living teacher does not have all that you wish to know and that you'd like to try, then this process that we are doing here can work with, as I say, a good connection and energy passing through. The budding student may not always feel it, but as long as it is present, perhaps there might be someone else there—maybe an apprentice, a shaman's apprentice or a mystical person's apprentice or student—who will know that the energy is there and who will perhaps even have an assignment working with the scientist who wishes to understand shamanism.

But if the scientist approaches it with a bias, meaning, "I want to understand this religious, cultural practice so that the myth makes sense to me" . . . it's not about what makes sense, because your world, your culture, has been very attracted to what makes sense: "How can we produce it and how can we reproduce it so that we know it's true?" But that is all mental, and the mind cannot directly engage these experiences. It can only observe, note, consider, think about it, but it cannot directly engage it. That requires the physical self for you, the feeling self and the spiritual self—in short, the instinctual self. But the mind can only observe. If you try to do it all with your mind, you will be in class for a long time. But you won't have to stay after school and clean the erasers [chuckles].

You have the knowledge of your tribe, but in your present expanded state, are you fully in your knowledge that you had as a physical shaman?

Yes, and even as a physical shaman I did that too, because I was taught how to acquire knowledge and wisdom that my people didn't have because things would come up that hadn't come up before. That happens all the time with shamanic people and mystical people the world over. So you have to be able to acquire knowledge and wisdom from other places; you can't just say to the elders, "Sorry! I wasn't taught how to do that!" That's not good enough.

Well, you have long vision, but is that how you did that?

Initially I did it until I made repeated contacts with the same source who was providing very good information and knowledge and instruction. Then I didn't have to use my long vision exactly; I could just connect with that source on the basis of my familiarity with the energies of those different sources when I'd connect with them. You get familiar with the energy, and then you can just recall how it feels when they are present—not unlike how the channeling process works. For the channel, we remember how it feels to be in touch with that being.

And is that pretty much how all shamans do it?

I cannot speak for all shamans; I can only speak for the ones I know.

Is that how the ones you knew did it?

Yes.

It's the principle of you call and someone responds, right?

Well, that's the initial step, yes. But for those who are taught to do long vision, that is something they can do in case there isn't . . . you understand, you start with long vision. It's a good place to start because you get used to reaching out beyond your world. When I talk about a world, I'm not talking about a planet. I'm talking about a culture.

Your world culture, right.

Deep-Sleep Activity in Animals and Humans

Speaks of Many Truths
November 30, 2001

arlier you said, "You'd be surprised how much of a contribution there is to all beings when people and animals sleep. Bears, for example, contribute to all life by their hibernation. When the bears go into their caves and sleep and hibernate, they will often go into the past, solving problems there to keep the thread of time safe. When you as people sleep, unexpectedly you sometimes—not always, but sometimes—like the bear, go into the past and solve problems from your past or from the pasts of other human beings to keep the thread of time safe." Can you elaborate on this?

Disruptions in Time

Time is a thread, because it literally meanders throughout different cultures and different localities in order to provide a river of passage to move gracefully from one point to another. But what happens when there is something that is a disruption in that river? What happens in a water river if there is a disruption? Say there is an earthquake: The water might go in a different direction. But we can't really have time striking off on its own, going in a different direction, if you, for instance, as a culture are intended to get from point A to point B. If there is a disruption in time and time scuttles off to point C, that isn't very good for you. However, disruptions do happen. Sometimes they happen because of artificial impacts.

In your time and in some times previous to you, there were a lot of experiments with trying to force a time machine to work. This was not simply a fantastic idea of the famous author but an inspiration *to* that author. Where would an author think something like that up and then put a wonderful story with it? Mr. H.G. Wells, you understand, is who we're talking about here.

The technology of traveling through time, as people know perhaps nowadays in your time more than others, is not unusual to find on spaceships from other places and so on. But in the early days of exploring such technology, almost invariably it started the hard way—meaning just like when you were experimenting with light, if you needed a brighter light, you built a bigger fire, because that's the level of technology you had then. Whereas nowadays if you need a bigger light, you get more bulbs or more electricity or brighter lamps or something like that, because that's the technology you have now. Just like that, if you were working to create a time machine and you were using electricity, you'd use more electricity and so on.

So when that kind of thing happens, it is possible to either stretch or, just like you might do, deflect time—not necessarily break it, as in the case of an earthquake in a river, but you might stretch it or create a deflection. Now, you understand that I'm talking about a major thing here. How would such a deflection, which could potentially create a disruption and cause time to meander off in a different direction, possibly in a pattern that is wholly unnatural for the people experiencing that particular thread of time . . . how can the original thread be repaired?

It is always repaired by individuals, be they plants, animals or humans—and in some cases, planets themselves—when they are asleep and dreaming at the deepest levels. A rock might dream for thousands of years, a human being, just for a few hours. Many animals also dream just for a few hours, except those who hibernate. Hibernation appears to be something the animal does because it is practical, as in the case of bears: winter is coming, so it's time to move the metabolism into a different area and sleep through the coldest part of the winter because survival is not likely otherwise in this case.

Hibernating Bears Help to Repair the Thread of Time

So as fascinated as people are with that, you might reasonably ask, are the bears simply experiencing the soul's journey somewhere else during that time? Certainly there is that. But the bears or other hibernating creatures, just as human beings in a shorter time frame, not just in the deepest levels of sleep . . . how much experiential time, how much clock time might a human being in, say, eight hours of sleep at night (restful sleep, not jarring, nervous sleep where you wake up or almost wake up every twenty minutes or so) . . . human beings might conceivably during that eight-hour restful sleep period experience perhaps three or four seconds during which they have the capacity to support the thread of time. And it happens.

Of course, for it to be helpful and to have the greatest impact, many human beings sleeping at the same time have to cooperate and assist the thread of time. But in bears, for example—since we're using bears as a hibernation example—given their duration of sleep . . . let's say, a bear's hibernation period in a winter environment, where the bear might hibernate for months. During that time, they would have many hours available, possibly even a run of several hours back-to-back, where they are simply repairing the thread of time. That's why it's vital for certain animals to survive. All animals who hibernate need to survive in your time. You have noticed in your zoos, for instance, that bears will not hibernate very often; they have to be in the wild to do that in the most effective way.

So all creatures, all beings on Earth, contribute to the betterment of all other beings on Earth in some way—sometimes directly, sometimes indirectly. Sometimes it is obvious how they contribute to the betterment, such as bees pollinating flowers while they obtain nectar, which is there for the bees. That is obvious. But it is not so obvious that bears literally keep you all on your paths simply by sleeping.

What do they do? They're at their soul level, right?

Yes.

How do they repair time?

Because they are beings in their own right, if they detect or if their teachers or guides detect an anomaly in the thread of time—maybe not something serious, but something that if allowed to exist indefinitely will result in something serious—then if a bear, for example, has moments that it can string together . . . hours perhaps, or less. To correct a small anomaly in the thread of time, it might take a bear, at its deep levels of sleep . . . in terms of clock time, it might take a bear just a few minutes. And the bear will go to the thread of time itself, which is not a place so much as it's a feeling. The bear will go to this feeling and it will do this [draws Fig. 6-1]. The bear will be in the feeling of time, and it will gradually expand spherically.

I am drawing two-dimensional things here, but in fact, the bear is expanding spherically. And as the bear expands spherically in all directions, it is in the feeling of time. The moment it notices something that doesn't feel like the feeling of time that it is used to and that it knows, the bear will immediately be drawn to that. Say it is here [points to dot in Fig 6-1]; the bear will just immediately find itself drawn to that. And when it is drawn to that, it will then do something not dissimilar to what shamans do—it will reconnect or regenerate the natural feeling of time, how the bear feels when it is in time. And the bear will focus its energy in that anomaly and satu-

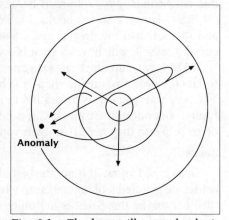

Fig. 6-1. The bear will expand spherically in the feeling of time.

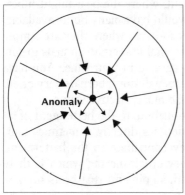

Fig. 6-2. An anomaly in time.

rate it with the natural feeling of time while it is sitting right smack in the middle of the anomaly energetically.

With the power of attraction, the bear will do this. Let's blow up the picture of the anomaly [draws Fig. 6-2]. Here's the anomaly. The bear will sit right in the middle energetically and will feel the way time normally feels. (This is spherical, you understand.) And it will—not just in the areas I'm drawing the lines, but just generally— expand and expand. In other words, it will feel the feeling of time stronger and stronger and stronger, while the rest of time, the outer circle being time on its own, will attract time in its natural feeling toward the anomaly so that it's not only expanding the feeling of time but also attracting the feeling of time.

So the bear is going out and in at the same time in order to resolve the feeling of time. And it will do this for a few minutes until it notices that there is no disruption in the field of time anymore. Then the anomaly has been eliminated. And then the bear will go and continue to expand and expand until it notices other anomalies, and it will resolve them in the same way. When the bear is done, meaning that this is as much time as it can put into this, then it goes on and does other things. That's an example of how a bear keeps you all alive and well.

So there are supposedly time masters and time lords who do this, but the bears have been helping them?

What makes you think that they are not the time masters themselves? Now, you might reasonably ask, how do I know this? Is it because someone taught me? No. I know it because as in my story about my life, in previous *Shamanic Secrets* books, I talked once about sleeping near a bear, and the bear had my dreams and I had the bear's dreams. And I experienced it myself, which was a great blessing.

When I woke up, the bear was gone. I wanted to hug the bear, I wanted to kiss the bear, I wanted to thank the bear. How do you thank the bears? The only way you can is to be kind to all bears when you see them in the future. Get out of their way if you need to, but if there's anything you can do to help and they need that, then you always offer. What a gift, eh?

Absolutely.

That's how I know. It is not the best idea, but it is typical to your time that deities are pictured looking similar to what you know. All religions do not do this, but maybe those deities are other than human in looks. Maybe God doesn't look like a man or a woman; for all you know, God looks like a spider. And in my experience with spiders, that would seem much more logical than a human being. Human beings have a lot of problems. But look at a spider's web; it is something the spider creates for its own needs, and yet it is beautiful, it is a symbol of all life. That is not godlike, just functional, but this is something they create for their own needs, which reminds anyone who sees one that the web of life is constantly interconnected with all life and continues to expand outward. What wonderful beings!

Other animals hibernate. Are other animals doing the same thing, or do they do something slightly different?

They might do the same thing. In my understanding, all creatures who hibernate have this capability if they are on Earth. I cannot say about other places at this time. But hibernation is something that, as far as I know, happens usually on Earth. When I say "hibernation," I mean extended periods of sleep that are beyond what the body needs simply to recover its strength.

Granted, there are some people living on other planets who might do this, but that doesn't resolve the thread of time on Earth. We're talking about Earth here. This is shamanic secrets about Earth, to help the people of Earth to help themselves, to help each other. So I'm not putting too much energy into what happens on other planets. You're not there!

Human Beings Also Help the Thread of Time

So humans do this, then, and you're saying that we can go into our past or the past of other human beings?

If the thread of time is threatened. And you do it, but you do it cumulatively. One human being . . . you don't sleep long enough. One human being will work with perhaps thousands of others locally who are in that deep sleep state at that time. And each can contribute a few seconds, as if you were on a machine circuit. You've seen those strings of flashing lights that create something like a line or a word—you understand how that goes, right? It is just like that. One does something for one or two seconds, then the other one, then the other. It works just like that, on a circuit. You don't do it willfully—it happens. And for two or three seconds—that's enough.

Human beings, though, do it a little different—not like the bear. The bear goes right into the center of the anomaly. Human beings can't do that because your life here is too fragile. You are here to learn, you are constantly learning and so on. There's a lot of stress on human beings that might not exist for the bear because the bear isn't here to learn anything. The bear is here to teach, when asked.

So as a result of your fragility . . . in general, the bear has long hair and can survive in the cold. But you do not. In short, human beings are tender and fragile, and you are that way to remind you that not everything is expected of you as might be expected or appreciated or simply thankfully done by the animals. Even on a soul level, souls have to . . . you understand, you're doing this for two or three seconds. And there are other things you need to be doing. You do it for two or three seconds—how long is two or three seconds? [Snaps fingers.] You understand?

Maybe you'll have to interrupt that and do something else because there are other things to be done because you're here to *learn*. You're learning all the time, even when you sleep. So *if* you have the time, it can be done. But a human being's dreamtime, sleep time, is always available for interruption if something else takes precedence—meaning something you need to do, something about your life. So human beings don't do that much of the repair of the thread of time. I'm talking about it because this is for human beings and I want you to understand how it works for you.

So human beings do not go into the center of the anomaly. Rather, it will work for them that they will find the anomaly, all right? You don't even experience time as a feeling. You simply meander around in time as a river, and if you stumble across an anomaly, then you will feel it as a discomfort on the soul level. Then you will ask for beings to come and repair the thread of time. That's how it works.

It's much more tenuous, almost like the student with the teacher, all right? When you ask for beings to come in—guess who comes in?

The bears.

The bears. That's right. Or other hibernating animals. So you help, you find something, maybe.

The Thread of Time Is All Time

Is the thread of time the same as what we're calling the past-anchored timeline?

The thread of time is all time, meaning all time that affects you. If it's past-anchored or future-anchored, it doesn't make any difference. It's all time. It is the river of time throughout which you might find this past. Past-anchored time, future-anchored time—those are *in* the thread of time. But the thread of time encompasses all of it.

Is there anything we can do consciously when we go to sleep, since we can move in the timeline, to help connect to the benevolent future timeline?

No. If you're talking about the thread of time, you can't ask. It would have to be available.

So is there anything that we can do, that we can ask consciously before we go to sleep, to help connect to the future-anchored timeline?

Changing the subject?

Am I changing the subject?

It's a change in the subject. That's a completely different subject. It creates a break, you understand. A radical shift in the subject creates stress for the channeling process. You have to go forward on the subject. Jumping around subjects . . . I know you don't do that, but for some people who like to jump around a lot in subjects, which often comes up in private sessions, it's a bit of a strain, which is why private sessions are more tiring for the channel than something like this that has a constant ribbon of flow through a certain subject, or than perhaps a public session about a given subject.

But if it's a public session where you jump around from subject to subject, it's a bit of a strain. It makes it tiring, and it makes it less possible to channel for a longer time. When you jump around like that, it reduces the quantity of time in terms of the physical energy the channel has to hold on to the connection or to allow the connection, depending on how you want to look at it.

Hibernating Creatures Reinforce the
Strength of the Atomic Structure

You said that bears, for example, contribute to all life by their hibernation. How else do they contribute to all life besides working with the timeline?

Good question. Bears literally . . . this might be hard to believe, but bears are not alone. Bears and other hibernating animals or creatures literally reinforce the strength of the nucleus of an atomic structure, say an atom—not the nucleus itself, but that which creates a barrier between the nucleus and the other revolving particles. Science has wondered for a long time, "Why doesn't the nucleus simply break apart? Why doesn't it just . . ."

"What holds it together?"

"What holds it together?" What holds it together is that the stuff of life, that which creates a certain amount of pressure in the environment to attract—or in some cases, repel, but in this case, to attract—is reinforced by the sleep of hibernating creatures. Human beings cannot do this, because you're not as advanced as the animals physically. You're not as advanced mentally either, but we're talking about physically. So this is one of the things they do, all right?

You might reasonably ask, "How do they do this?" They don't go into single atoms. But let's say they did. Let's say we have these . . . this is your atom [draws Fig. 6-3]. They literally . . . you understand, they don't do it one atom at a time, but for the sake of our experience, they do something like this. They are centered in the center of the nucleus. Then [draws] . . . this is not part of the atom, but I need to draw it in so that you get the idea. Partly on the outside of the nucleus, about that distance from the center of the nucleus, they radiate out slightly while . . . picture an echo. You're in a canyon, you yell something, and then within a certain amount of time you hear it back. It is like an echo effect. It goes out.

They radiate out, and then there is a slight deflection. They radiate out, and then there's a slight deflection that comes back in—this is the detail here [points to Fig. 6-3]—and it is the deflection that maintains the wholeness, if I might say, of the atomic nucleus.

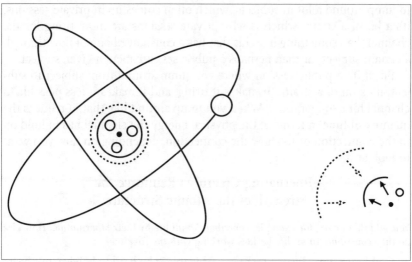

Fig. 6-3. The deflection that maintains the wholeness of the atomic nucleus.

Humans Connect to One Another in Sleep

So what else do humans do in sleep, then? They must do other things that help other humans or help the whole experiment here besides the time problem?

Humans, what they do, is to maintain the link with other human beings, because in the contemporary cultures of your time, there are often great political and cultural differences, racial differences, nationalistic differences, prejudices, that keep you from each other when all of your cultures are intended to contribute, make a soup that nurtures everyone. You don't have to pull from all the cultures all the time, but there will be times when your culture does not have what you need and another culture might. So what you will do, especially during times of strain—which the United States is going through right now and, to a degree, other parts of the world as well—is that at the deepest levels of your sleep when you're doing this, you will fully engage and if necessary repair the links of all human beings to each other on Earth.

This is something that you do not always do. In my time we did not do this, because the links were solid.

You didn't need to.

We did not need to. But in your time now, and with this being creator school, and with you, as your friend Zoosh has said to you, having responsibilities and tests and things that you would have to do . . . you are doing it—all of you. Even people whom you might look at askance and say, "What, him?" or "Not her," yes, because you do it at the deep levels of your sleep.

Well, we recognize that we're all souls and all one soul.

That's right, and you recognize the value of each other at those deep levels. It would not occur to you for a moment to consider that some other being isn't of value.

So when did this connection begin to get less solid?

The work began right around 150 years ago, but now it's stronger and stronger and more and more required. You could say, "Well, there have been wars, there have been battles before." That's true. But there was almost always a sense of connection, even among soldiers fighting each other. Not always would you think about the other soldier on the other side as a person, but sometimes you would. Sometimes you had to fight that feeling in order to do your job. Soldiers who are reading this will know what I'm talking about.

But nowadays it is possible to be a soldier on one side and have absolutely no consciousness that the soldier on the other side is even human. That's why such work has to take place at the deep level *and* you have been visited upon to do the work for yourself because you have all been getting trained. And to some extent, you're also infused more with portions of your natural selves now.

As things get more difficult physically and there are more challenges, the compensation is that more of your natural selves are coming in. And it is because you have more of your natural total being coming in that the children of today can be born. What anchors them, what welcomes them, is this overall energy of naturalness. Even though they may not feel it when they are awake, they certainly will feel it when they're asleep, even in their light sleep, not their deep sleep.

Is this something that spirit beings did until recently when we were, as you say, visited with this responsibility, with this keeping the connections strong?

Spirit beings other than human beings, you mean?

Yes—teachers, helpers.

Yes, it had been done largely externally or by the animals.

By the animals?

They can do many things. You have to remember that the animals are all teachers. None of them are here to learn anything; they are all here to teach. They have nothing to learn here. You are the beings who are here to learn.

Are they still helping with this, or have they pulled back because we had to move into that taking responsibility?

They occasionally help if needed, but they've been guided that this is something that you need to do—part of your apprenticeship. So they will only help if necessary.

Humans Welcome Visionaries in Their Sleep

Are there other things that humans do for all humans rather than just for their own purposes when they sleep?

There is only one other thing that might be relevant, and that is vision. At times of stress particularly, there is a tendency to duck and not look around too much and to see not that far. But it is also at those times that visionaries begin to be perhaps more verbal, to come forth, to talk about what's over on the other side of the hill, or what might be, or what could be encouraged to be on the other side of the hill if only we do this, if only we do that.

So one of the other things you do in your deep stage of sleep is to welcome the visionaries, whether they are alive and functioning and speaking as visionaries in whatever form—a child could write a story at school and it could be visionary, or an adult could have a view of the future and speak of it or write about it—or whether they are children who will be visionaries. You will exude an energy to welcome the visionaries.

In Sleep Animals Support Their Own Species

What about when animals sleep normally, then? Are they contributing to some part of this experiment?

Not really. They support their own species. And the difference is that they will support their species whether that species is alive and functioning on the Earth, or whether they are coming to the Earth (meaning they're going to be born on the Earth in a few months), or even whether they have just died and they are moving off, but they still have a consciousness of their Earth self—the animals will support that too.

But it will generally be done within the species. This is intentional, because sometimes an entire species will leave the Earth, as in so-called extinction. And if other animals were supporting them as a species, it might be difficult for them to leave the Earth. So they don't.

Death and Birth

Speaks of Many Truths
December 1, 2001

All right, this is Speaks of Many Truths. I'd like to talk about something from my life.

Helping Those Who Have Died to the Other Side

In my time when people would die unexpectedly, which would happen, if I or one of my students was able to get to them soon enough before they died, we could help them through. Sometimes they would die before anyone, any of our people, could get to them, so occasionally I could tell that they had not found their way to the other side. This was not typical, but it happened. So I would sit down next to the person—it might even have been his bones—and I would remember him. Occasionally it was someone from another place, so then I would have somebody there who remembered him, I would have this person remember him, and then I would be able to use that. And I would go searching for him with the feeling of who he was.

It's not like you have to take steps when you're doing something non-physical; I would just look for that person on the basis of how he felt, and I would find him very quickly. Perhaps he would be somewhere on Earth, or he might be somewhere out in the stars—in short, lost, maybe wandering around. Then I would first bring him back—in spirit form, of course—to what was left of his body. Because when beings wander around like that and don't immediately go with their guides or angels beyond the veils, they usually don't know they are dead, or they think they might be but they are upset.

So the first and most important thing to do would be to bring the person back and show him his remains, his earthly remains, and that usually helped him. He would nod, and he would see that he was, in fact, dead. And if one of his loved ones happened to be there, then he would have feelings come up.

While the person was there, usually I would have a hand on him, not so much because I was afraid he was going to run away and hide, but because I knew how to be in the spirit world, be in the physical world and be in other worlds, if necessary, and he didn't. So I wasn't going to get lost and he might have, you see? In that situation where the person was that energy, if he thought about something or even if he happened to imagine something, it would instantaneously be there, and that is how he would get lost.

So once I found him, I kept a hand on him. And then while I had a hand on him like that, I would go back to the moment just after death and go through that spiritually until I would see his guide or angel approaching. When I saw that guide or angel, I would expand my feeling into that guide or angel, and then that guide or angel would come again. Then that being would take the person and escort him through the veils and go on.

Humans Need Someone to Escort Them through the Veils

How are the veils set up—so that someone is required to take you through the veils?

The reason it is a requirement for human beings especially to be guided through the veils, is that you are unlike the animals and plants, who know they are here temporarily and aren't here to learn anything. They do not have, as your friend Zoosh likes to say, the gift of ignorance, they are not ignorant, because they are not trying to re-create anything as you are. As a result, when you've been a human being on Earth, you don't have that sense of continuity; it doesn't occur to you consciously that, "I'm going somewhere from here when I die in my body; I will keep on going." The animals and plants know that. It doesn't make them happy to die here usually, except in some circumstances, but it is something they know.

With human beings, since ignorance prevails for the most part in these spiritual matters, then the tendency for human beings, especially if they have been fighting for life, which is typical—where they stay alive, fighting to stay in the body—is that without that guide to help them and to flood them with the energy of unconditional love and of gold and white and pink light (sometimes a little green), without that, they will often become confused and they will want to stay. They might see their grieving relatives, and they'll want to run over and console them and say, "I'm all right." But, of course, they are at that point in another world, and unless their relatives have been trained well, they won't be aware of the presence of their loved one's spirit and certainly won't hear the words. If they've been trained, they might be aware of that presence, might even feel a general touch, if a touch takes place. They might even have a sense of what was said on the feeling level and occasionally might have the clarity to hear words that are, if not exactly what is said, then something similar.

So the necessity is to have someone who comes from the other side, literally, through all the veils. Even though these beings may not normally reside in that place, they will come on a path that is the exact path that they are going to take this person, this spirit, back through, simply because they want that path to be—how can we say?—made prominent. They will leave a gold-light pathway—not because they can't find it, but because they want that feeling to be present for the now spirit they are taking along.

They will generally escort that departed spirit, they will gently bring him or her along in accordance with the procedures of moving through the veils, which must be done quite slowly—not because it's a shock, but because sometimes a person doesn't want to leave Earth. And they'll say, "It is all right; maybe you'll be able to visit later," which is possible. So they bring the spirit along and bring him or her through the veils. That's why it is necessary: because of your ignorance and because of your attachment to the Earth and Earth people and situations and circumstances. That attachment is not easy to let go of and to forget about entirely in order to move through the veils. That's why I refer to the person as a guide or an angel; "angel" is your term, but I think about the person as being a guide.

Between Dimensions or Beyond the Veils

Where is the other side? The other side of what? This planet? The solar system? Where is this veil?

It might be right here, in the same space, or it might be in another space. It is a veil that separates . . . let's put it like this. When you are awake and going around and doing things—doing this, doing that, typing, working, playing—then you might reasonably say, "Where are you when you are asleep?" You know where your body is, but where are you? Most of your personality is somewhere else. It is the same thing.

In the case of sleep, you don't step miles and miles away. You might travel places in your soul's journey, but when you sleep, it is like a page turns in a book; you don't go somewhere. So it's not a geographical place, moving between dimensions in the case of after death—or what is referred to as moving through the veils. But they are not exactly veils. That is just a nice way to say "moving through the dimensions." And dimensions are a nice way of saying "different places located in the same space." It's hard to describe in your words, because it is an energy.

For example, when you wake up gently in the morning, you're at first slightly conscious—waking up slowly and gently, and there's that moment of peaceful consciousness—and then you come into your body more and you wake up to your life. That peaceful conscious place—that is a feeling very similar to an interdimensional place, meaning between dimensions or beyond a veil. It is a way of touching base in your physical life with something extradimensional beyond your physical life.

Now, this tells you something, that when you're moving through the so-called veils, what changes is that there are different feelings that you feel physically, and so does the guide or angel. Those beings know which way to go without blazing a trail; they know which way to go based on their feelings. It is true enough that if you could see the guides taking someone, it would definitely look like they were moving away from you physically, but once they moved past a certain point, something that they moved through would close—just like a veil or a curtain. However, it doesn't close like draperies or a curtain; it will close more like . . . say there's a hole through it, like people see the tunnel. It will just close like this.

It goes together like a camera shutter closing?

Only it's not with different bits as a camera shutter, but that idea, that it just closes. And then you wouldn't see what's beyond, if you were the observer.

You Need to Move Slowly through the Veils

But you're implying that it's like levels of a maze or something. Why would we need someone to guide us out?

Because you're not conscious. Remember, the animals do not need it, although sometimes a gold-lightbeing version of themselves will come or will be in the general area of transit. You need it because you are attached to Earth and still in your Earth life, and just stepping out of your body does not mean that you are suddenly, instantaneously conscious and know all that you've known in all of your lives—that you know everything. That doesn't happen. You have to move through stages. Once you move through the first stage, you release the pain and unhappiness and struggle of your life—even if you had a pleasant life, there would have been some of that. That just drops away like a garment. But even going through that first stage, you still feel attracted to your Earth life and people whom you saw.

You are looking forward perhaps to seeing Grandma and Grandpa or your passed-over wife or children or husband, or someone like that. You have to go a bit farther, and you might see them, and they will welcome you and hug you: "It's so good to see you." But as you go farther, that need and desire falls off also. And then those people disappear, because it wasn't really them, see? It's not impossible that occasionally it would be the actual personality, but the person is probably long gone, you see? Unless you all go at once, like in a car crash or something. But generally speaking, these are spirits who present to you the energy, personality and more than their being on Earth to you when you meet them.

Say you didn't get along very well with your husband, but there were moments and you miss those moments, and at the end you were able to kiss him and he smiled at you, and then he departed. Say that happened. Then when you die, you're looking forward to seeing him, but he won't be what he was on Earth, he'll be his spirit self. He'll know who you are, you'll know who he is, and you might hug each other or touch each other in some way, in some affectionate way. And then he will move on, all the time shedding the desires and the hopes and, more to the point, the attachments—the iron grip of attachment—that you have to your Earth life and all that you knew here.

At some point, you shed all of that. Then you are with your guides and teachers, and very often, in most cases, you will review your physical life. Sometimes that doesn't happen, but when that doesn't happen, it's usually because a person has died before birth, as in a miscarriage, or someone has died perhaps within a day or two of birth. Even then, there's usually a life review.

How Earth's Negativity Is Kept from Going Out to Other Places

But this veil is only around the Earth because of our negativity, right?

Oh, no. Beings who die in other places . . . say there were no human beings here, all right? There would still be a veil for the animals and the plants, which would allow them to remain in their physical life—the veil, you might say, between dimensions, or between worlds, which is what I prefer to say. To use the term "dimensions" . . . I'm not particularly fond of it, because it's a term used by science, used by mathematics. In short, it's vague. I'd rather say "between worlds."

So there's a veil between the third and fourth dimensions, the fourth and fifth dimensions, the fifth and sixth dimensions?

None of those things really exist, but if it makes you happy, you can say yes. We're stuck using that, but I'd rather just say that, yes, all those numbers you have . . . I'd rather just say that they're different worlds in the same space.

But they have different frequencies, different vibrations, right?

Yes. So if the human beings weren't here and there were only animals and plants, there would still be a veil, but it wouldn't be as much. There have to be stages that you can go through for a human being on Earth because of all that you experience here. When you get out of the body, you don't just suddenly drop everything like a garment and don't care and go on. Even if you're looking forward to going on, there will have been things about your life on Earth that you liked, even if it was just a little bit. Maybe you always liked peppermints, maybe you loved animals—something. There will be something about Earth that you liked, so these things have to fall away gently and slowly.

It sounds like a series of filters, with the largest filter taking the big stuff, and then smaller and smaller filters.

That's a nice analogy.

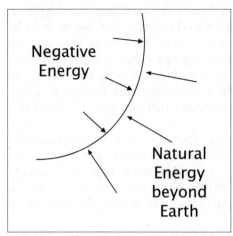

Fig. 7-1. Earth's negative energy cannot pass beyond this barrier.

What is it around the Earth that keeps the negativity from going out to other places? What do you call that?

It is something like this [draws Fig. 7-1]. I'm going to draw a line that doesn't exist, if that's all right. We're drawing a line just to create a delineator, a margin. This is not unlike the way magnets work, but it isn't like that exactly.

Is it like a repulsion or something?

No. This is the so-called negative energy floating out or emanating. And this is the natural energy beyond a certain point that you're asking about. But let's expand that: What's in that line? It's not really a line, but what's in there? Obviously there's also natural energy here. You might assume that this hits a barrier and is deflected and comes back.

Probably the gold light is transmuting it.

You're getting better all the time. Now, the negative energy hits that, and it is a space that contains all of the colors that you know in your world, including an extra infusion of gold light. And this is why the negative energy cannot go on. Yes, the gold light transforms it, but this is why it can't go on. The energy and energy in general—whatever energy is on this planet, in this school at this time—is kept from going beyond a certain point by something that is marvelous in its simplicity.

The other thing that's going on in this space is that the other colors that you don't have on this planet are in there. And those colors . . . any energy outflowing from this planet, even something benevolent, unless it is perhaps pure gold light—pure gold light can pass out from this planet—but any energy that hits that or touches that space will come into contact immediately with colors that that energy does not know or understand.

So it comes in contact with colors it doesn't know?

That it does not know, and as a result, it turns around as it is being transmuted . . . because of the gold light and other benevolent lights in there. As it's being transmuted, it tends to turn around and it goes back to what it knows. That's how negative energy has expanded a little bit beyond what was intended, because some of it will race back to what it knows.

Remember that if something is so-called negative energy, it can be fear or anger and all of this stuff that is basically reactive energy. That reactive energy gets agitated unless it's around something it knows and under-

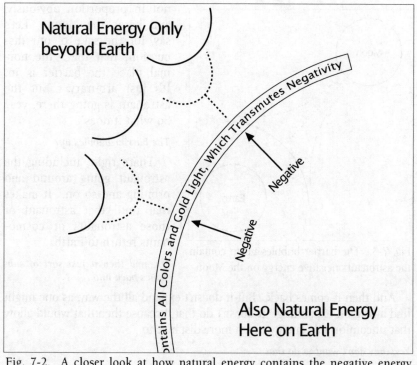

Natural Energy Only beyond Earth

Contains All Colors and Gold Light, Which Transmutes Negativity

Negative

Negative

Also Natural Energy Here on Earth

Fig. 7-2. A closer look at how natural energy contains the negative energy from Earth.

stands. When it goes into that area, it immediately is touching things that it doesn't know and doesn't understand. This next drawing [Fig. 7-2] also indicates that here you have the natural energy; I stopped making the arrows because it's really a radiation that comes out. And then the dotted line, as you can see . . . that radiation, the natural energy, is coming in there and creating, stimulating and sustaining the other colors that do not exist on this planet. That is the actual way it works; that's the mechanical way.

The Barrier Extends to Humans Anywhere Off-Planet

Where is this barrier, then? It's around where humans are, so it can't just be around the Earth, because we're out in space—we went to the Moon, there are humans on Mars . . .

It is wherever human beings are who are associated—being born on Earth, all right?—with the Explorer Race. Even if you send an astronaut or a cosmonaut out to the Moon at some point soon with Mars, even then it just extends.

Around humans?

That's right. This is how it extends: In the case of an astronaut, it doesn't extend all the way out for everything. [Draws Fig. 7-3.] Here's Earth,

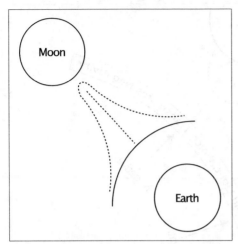

Fig. 7-3. The barrier bubbles up to contain the astronaut's negative energy on the Moon.

not in proportion obviously, and here's the Moon. Let's say, for the sake of our discussion, that that's the normal place the barrier is in. It's just arbitrary. But the astronaut is going there, yes? So what it does . . .

The barrier bubbles up?

That's right, including the astronaut going around and orbiting and so on. It makes that until that astronaut or those astronauts or cosmonauts return to Earth.

Oh, and then it just sort of subsumes back into . . . ?

And then it comes back. But it doesn't expand all the way, as one might find a balloon expanding. It doesn't do that, because then that would allow that uncomfortable energy much more distance to . . .

Yes, they don't want to do that.

No. So it just goes around whoever, wherever that person is. It might interest you to know that some individuals on Earth have been lifted off and have moved with other beings to their worlds. Even then, it will run a very thin—really smaller than what you would call microscopic—layer all the way out and have a bubble essentially around that being until he becomes totally and completely compatible with the energy of the planet or place he is in, without a shred of what you might call negative or discomforting energy either in him or with the capacity to produce it. Most beings do not ever get all that way. But depending upon the level of the civilization that a being goes to—meaning how good they are at communicating, how much the people are enjoying their life there and so on—and how dedicated the Earth human might be to letting go of her Earth identity in all ways within herself and (this is the big one) whether her soul embraces that . . . only in that circumstance might it be possible for the person to become—how can we say?—entirely free of not only discomforting energy but, more to the point, her capacity to produce it.

I might also add that ETs who rarely take Earth people to their planets to live but occasionally do, would not do that if it wasn't known that that barrier, that membrane, would be present—because obviously it could have disastrous and catastrophic results on their people. So this is done with the full knowledge that such things exist, and with that knowledge, they are prepared, then, to take the beings with them.

This Barrier Is a Protective Device

The veil . . . I saw a picture of, like, overlayered levels. It seems to me that Zoosh said once that the veil was there so we couldn't get out, so we couldn't just decide to cop out.

Well, that's certainly true.

I mean, it's sort of like a honeycombed . . . what?

That's certainly true, you can't get out. But that's good—what would be the advantage of getting out?

Well, it's just that the implication is that we can't get out. [Chuckles.]

Why would you want to? If you get out in the usual way, because you've died and you're moving on from Earth, you will regain your full being. But if you get out with who you are here . . . for one thing, you will have to drag a piece of the membrane with you—even if you could—in which case your interaction with other life forms, other places, would be extremely limited for their sake and also for your sake, so that you don't get too distracted and go crazy. No, there's no advantage.

But it's not a prison; it is a protective device. It protects others who are in natural energy, and it protects you just as much. If you took a person, any person on Earth, out into some other places in space where there was much beauty but also, from her experience—she's used to sequential time—total chaos, she would be crazy in a few minutes. You'd have to bring that person back and go straight to the hospital.

The Soul's Natural Tendency Is to Go Right through the Veils

How does this work? Someone dies, and there are spirits who wander around—is that that person's complete soul being, or is that just a shell that didn't go through the veil? Are there complete beings wandering around Earth who need to be . . . you always hear about them needing to be released into the light.

Not many, because there are beings who are dedicated only to rounding up such beings. As I said at the beginning of this, this is rare; it doesn't happen that much. But at times, when there is a sudden great loss of life, such as in wars or other catastrophes, then there might be several people at once like that. But it is not a widespread phenomenon.

Sometimes when people see beings out of the corner of their eye or see other beings, if they're sensitives, they might be seeing other dimensions, as you say, other worlds within your world, other realities. Or they might simply see a being in transit—they're not always human. But you're not going to see something that's really frightening; if it's not human, it's probably just going to look like a light, possibly round, possibly some other shape. You're seeing something in transit, nevertheless; you're not seeing someone in your world.

But is it the whole soul-infused being who can get lost?

I don't think so, because it's like these beings have an antenna. It's not an antenna, but it's like part of them has already made it through the first veil or so, which creates a light signal that they need assistance. And there will be somebody looking for them anyway, because they didn't make their appointment: "Where are you?" [Chuckles.] So someone's looking for them.

But that's a way to find them, because part of them . . . their soul's natural tendency is to go right off through the veils. If a meeting with a guide or angel is missed . . . maybe the meeting wasn't missed and the soul wanted to go right off, but the Earth personality was so attached to its Earth life that it is clinging to Earth life. But there is one other circumstance in which the Earth personality might seem to cling to Earth life, and that is if the soul's family or loved ones—or people, in the case of a beloved political figure who is so loved and so missed (such as President Franklin Roosevelt or President John Kennedy in recent years)—are hanging on to the person so much that his or her spirit cannot easily go through the veils. In this case, the person needs to be gently and carefully escorted very slowly by more than one guide or angel.

So it took years in our time, then, for . . .

You can't measure it.

Yes. But they are gone now, right?

Oh yes, all gone. But they couldn't leave immediately. In the case of a loved one, where perhaps the person's husband or wife, whoever it is—it might be a child—if that person is so beloved and there is so much grief and the family is hanging on to the spirit and the memory of that spirit . . . again, it takes more than one guide or angel to come to help extricate that loved one from that holding on.

That's why when somebody dies, by all means remember how that person was on Earth, but don't bind her to you. Don't say, "Oh, please come and wait; give me a message," and all that. That person might be perfectly happy to give you a message, but let her go. She'll either leave the message for you somewhere, or after she's gone through, if a message is deemed necessary or of value, which it often is, then she'll come back with a guide or an angel and give you the message.

You don't have to hang on to that person. I've seen it; I've seen souls tethered to the Earth. They can go only so far through the veils, because other beings are hanging on to them. Then it requires more guides and angels to come to release that control.

I know one family that was so heartbroken over a family member's suicide that the family held on to this person's soul, I think.

Sometimes they will. But it's not a good thing. Once somebody's dead, that's it—it's time to move on. Suicides do not always move on all the way right away—not because they're being punished, but rather because they need to take a close look at their life to see what led them to that. And they also need to be in a place that's very nurturing and loving, and not very traumatic—meaning not traumatic at all. But it can be somewhat traumatic to look at their life, so they need to be in a quiet space, where it's like floating and sleeping and nurturing—not unlike being in your mother's womb.

It's very gentle and nurturing, and then sometimes beings come in and say, "Let's look at this part of your life," while they're holding them and rocking them, that kind of feeling—not necessarily being rocked, but a lot of love going on, a lot of nurturing. And they very gradually and slowly, not just review their lives to see what led up to it—and they don't live that; they review it from a distance, but they don't feel it personally—but their guides or teachers also say, "Now, if this had happened, this is how your life would have gone. And if this had happened . . ." They go through that whole life, showing all the steps that led up to the suicide. And they say, "Now, if this had happened at this place, then that would have changed, and here are the possibilities that would have led off of that," and so on. In short, they show you how things could have turned out differently. But they will also show you after the suicide, that if the suicide hadn't taken place, what would have happened in the future with all the possibilities.

In short, it takes time. There's no punishment at all involved; it takes time because it is considered to be—how can we say?—an unnatural death. Therefore, it needs to receive extra attention so the soul does not retain that wound. It is like a disappointment wound, all right? So once that process is completed, then the soul can continue its journey to wherever it needs to go.

Now, I'm not saying that committing suicide is a bad thing. That's not what I'm here to say, because for some beings, they feel they need to do it. And looking at their lives, you might reasonably say, "Well, that's understandable." I'm not here to say "good or bad"; I'm just saying that this is what happens after death.

Is this also true for those who choose, when they have an incurable disease, to take their lives?

Are you talking about a suicide?

An assisted suicide, yes.

Yes, that's true. That doesn't make it bad; it just means that extra care is needed in the after-death look at the life, to see how things could have been.

The Culture of Death Will Pass

For instance, in your country, because of the people who originally came over and founded your culture . . . many of them were of certain extreme religions, extreme branches of Christianity, which for the most part do not exist in your culture today. But because of those extreme attitudes—and I'm not talking about Quakers, all right?—that became a pervasive element in your culture, as well as influences from other countries and so on. As a result, things take place in your culture that do not take place in other places.

For instance, your culture believes that pain and suffering are a natural part of death; not all doctors and hospitals think this, but it is a widespread belief. It isn't necessarily so, but it's a widespread belief. As a result, it is not unusual in hospitals for patients to be denied the pain-relieving medication they might need *to the levels that they need it*. So pain medication is only given to them, in this case, in this example, up to a point. If you go to many places in Europe, for example, and they don't have that culture, if the pain medication is available, it's given completely so that the person does not have to suffer at all.

Now, I'm not saying which way is right and which way is wrong; I'm comparing cultures. So what I'm saying is that the culture of death, which you have in your country, will pass, because in time those who actually begin consciously influencing your culture . . . not just letting your culture go in any direction that spontaneity and entertainment choose to take it, or even religion sometimes, but there will be a conscious attempt to nurture and steer your culture into more benevolent avenues. And one of the impacts will be that given the availability of pain medication—and pain medication will become much more sophisticated in the future, where the pain is moderated so you don't feel it—what it does to prepare you for death will not be interfered with and you will still be consciously awake.

That would be what I would call conscious pain medication. It will require the marriage of loving spirit consciousness with science. In short, it will be when science has a loving God rather than only the god of curiosity. Curiosity can be very good, but it can also lead to things that are terrible. So science has not found that God yet, but they will someday.

We Followed Death

How were you trained to be able to follow the feeling of someone who was dying?

Very slowly and gently. My teacher initially did it by having me sit with someone, an old lady, and he said, "Now, this person is going to have a nice, gentle, natural death—no big trauma. She's going to go to sleep and die in her sleep, and we're going to sit here with her, with the family. When she dies, the guides who come are going to welcome our presence, and you and I are going to travel in spirit form with her and accompany her to the first veil. Then after that point, there will be guides who come just for us, and they will wrap a certain energy around us, and we will train behind the guide"—or "angel," whatever you like to say—"leading the lady. We will train behind and see where she goes." So that's what happened; that's how I know.

How old were you?

Oh, about nine.

And once you had done this, then you could do it? Or did you need to practice?

We did that about two or three more times. When you live with your teacher the way I did . . . of course, I would go and be with my parents too, but when I'd go work with my teacher for two or three days at a time, we would live together, because things come up just in the flow of life. My teacher would be working with other people, and he'd bring me along no matter what, unless it was a great distance away or was too difficult for a young boy. But other than that, he would bring me along. Things would come up, and he would do things, and after, when we were alone later on, he would tell me what he'd done. And I would, of course, want to know how to do things, and he would show me as much as I could learn then. If it wasn't time for me to learn that, he would still explain to me how he did it, but he'd tell me that I needed to do my homework, whatever it was at that time.

What did you call it?

It would relate closer to your word "lessons."

Dreaming with the Deer

Did your teacher live in your tribe? Was he from your tribe?

No.

So you actually lived with him in his home, then?

I stayed with him, yes. And then it wouldn't be too far away to go visit my mother and father and my brother and sister and so on. But when I would go stay with him, I would live with him, because it was important sometimes. I remember we walked somewhere and it was getting near sleeping time, and he said, "Now, tonight we're going to dream with the deer." The deer would walk near . . . do you have something called game trails?

Yes.

Deer and even bears and other creatures will tend to follow the same places where their kind have traveled before. So my teacher said, "We're not going to sleep too close to the trail, because we don't want to disturb them, but we're going to sleep close enough so that when we first fall asleep, they will just be waking up. And when we begin to wake up, they will just be getting ready to sleep." Because at least at that time, in that place, deer were . . .

Nocturnal?

Night creatures, yes. Now, what we would do is that we would try to get to sleep early so that we could overlap a little bit with the deer actually still in their sleep. First my teacher would stand a respectful distance from the trail and from the area he felt the deer were, and he'd speak very gently and quietly. Well, let me go back a step. When we got close to where we were going to camp, my teacher would do the deer walk, all right?

My teacher would do the deer walk to invite them, and also to . . . even if the deer were asleep, they would feel human beings coming and they would be somewhat alarmed, so you would do the deer walk a little bit. And he had me do it too—that's something I learned early on. Then we would come to the camp and get things a little ready—not too much. My teacher would stand and face the general area where he felt the deer were, at a distance, and he'd talk very quietly. He'd ask them, talking to their spirits, that if it would be acceptable to them, he would like to show his student the experience of the dreams they have and that he would prepare the both of us so that we would have gentle dreams which they could share if they like. But it would be up to them.

So that's what he did, and then I had my first experience of dreaming the dreams of another. When you dream the dreams of another, the best way to start off is with deer because they are such wonderful beings. Possibly an alternative might be with butterflies, but I feel that for human beings, it is better to have a being who is closer, more like a human being, than a butterfly is. So we did.

So what was it like?

I could feel the deer very present, their energy. I felt myself flowing on a river . . . it was something just like a river, curving back and forth. And I went to this planet way out into space with the stars; I don't know where it was. But when I got to this planet, I could see these beings, and they had eyes that had the same expression as deer. Have you ever seen a deer and its eyes?

Yes, yes.

They have this gentle expression, unless they're frightened or something, and they have beautiful eyes. But they didn't look the way they look here. They didn't exactly look like human beings, and they didn't look like deer here on Earth, but I could tell they were relatives of the deer. Maybe their home planet, how they actually look . . . it's hard to describe them because they weren't exactly like human beings either. I don't remember them having two arms and two legs, but I remember the body and their eyes—that's all I can remember. Then we were there with them: this one, that one. The eyes were full of love. It was one of the most loved times I've ever had in my life. And then I woke up, because it was day.

Feeling Measurement versus Mental Measurement

How many feet back from where you thought the deer were did you first talk to them?

Oh, it was not measured in feet—that's a mental measurement. It was measured in feeling. There is a difference. Say you are approaching someone you wish to approach with respect, a benevolent being such as this deer. You would have a good heart feeling for that deer, but you're sure that it may not feel that way about you, because it doesn't know you yet, eh? So you approach it very slowly, and then the moment you feel the tiniest amount of resistance, that's the deer's feeling, its concern—not quite fear yet, but its concern about you.

The moment you feel that . . . that's what you'll feel in your body phys- ically, a little concern. Imagine feeling concerned right now; you would feel in your body . . . it would be a shift from that warmth to something that feels a little uncomfortable. The first moment you feel that, take sev- eral steps back. Wait. And after you wait until things calm down, you feel comfortable. You keep stepping back if necessary, you wait, and then the energy becomes only that loving energy—no concern. That's how you do it. That's feeling measurement. Feet is mental measurement. When you use mental measurement, you will get it wrong most of the time.

And that's how you determined where the campsite was, where to sleep was?

Well, the campsite was a fixed place; my teacher had been there before with other students. He knew where he was going. He knew it was near a deer trail.

So he trained students not just for your tribe but for other tribes, as you did later?

You'll have to ask him that. I know he went to some other tribes, but I'll let him speak for himself.

Different People in the Tribe

Did he train others in your tribe besides you?

Oh, certainly.

I thought you were the mystical man?

Yes, but that doesn't mean . . . I received all that he knew, but he would give others training and give them certain parts of what he knew. Perhaps they might be in a battle and have a death, for instance, someplace where it would not be possible to ever find them, to go to where their bones were. So they would have to know certain things to die. And there would be other mystical things that he would teach other members of the tribe according to their specialty.

Like the medicine woman might have taught certain things?

Yes, just as the medicine woman might have taught my teacher some things—different people with different specialties, what they were good at naturally and were trained at. They would share some of that; it wasn't only them. Because if it was only them and no one else in the tribe knew anything about it—what would happen if a log fell on that person? Then you wouldn't have a medicine woman ever again? No, some of the knowl- edge was shared with people, and the medicine woman's job would be to retain all the knowledge all the time so that nothing was forgotten. So if there was something she was not sure about but she had taught it maybe many years before to another member of the tribe, then she might have gone to that member of the tribe and said, "What did I say again?"—especially if that member was getting older and maybe sicker.

It's almost like you had a personnel roster; you needed so many people. How many people did you need in a tribe to have all the positions filled?

I didn't really think of them as positions. I'll tell you why—I realize you are using a word, but I'll tell you why: Different people would be born amongst our people, in our culture, and at any given time, we wouldn't have all of the people who could do all of the specialties. Because when a child was born, the elders or the wise ones would observe what this child's specialty was going to be, what his interests were, how he could do things, what he could embrace, all of that. There wasn't always someone who could do something.

So that's why it was necessary to spread some of that knowledge around. If someone was not available in the tribe—either because we had greater numbers or lesser numbers at any given time—then the knowledge would be sprinkled around the tribe. Now, you may lose a little bit of it, if what a person acquired personally during her life, she didn't have a chance to pass on before she died—then that would be it, it would be gone.

I realize that this may not sound like an answer to your question, but that is because not every specialty was present amongst my people all the time. So that's how I have to answer your question. I can't say how many, because there weren't always as many as we would have liked.

How many people would be required if they were of the right capacities? Twenty? Fifty? One hundred?

Oh, maybe forty or something like that. Of course, that would mean forty specialties or so, but ideally you'd want more than that—you'd like to have a few hundred. You'd have to have hunting parties out all the time, or in our case, for part of the year we were near a river and fishing was a daily experience.

So roughly how many were in your tribe? A hundred?

When I was alive?

When you were alive, yes.

When I was alive and living there, the most we ever had at any given time was—I'm using your number system here—197. That was the biggest crowd, if I can use that term, I ever had.

And that was comfortable?

Oh, certainly.

What was the least that you had?

When I was alive, the least we ever had was thirty-seven.

Was there a war or a famine or something?

No, this was different. This was a time when some of our people were going off to try to find a better place to live during the winter, so thirty-seven of us stayed behind. There were the women, of course, with the very youngest children, and the women who were preparing to birth and so on. Thirty-seven of us stayed behind. My teacher went with the ones who were looking for the new place to winter.

And they found a good place?

They found a very nice place. In terms of your miles, it was about seventy miles away. So it took awhile to get there and awhile to get back.

How did you count distance? In the days and nights that it took to get there?

Yes.

Four days away or two days away?

That's right. It's a very practical way. You still use that system today—you just say twenty minutes away, twenty-five minutes away.

Yes [chuckles], but we have different choices of how to get there. You walked, right?

Yes. But I think our way is better. [Chuckles.] But then doesn't everybody think that about their time?

That might come around again, you know? Evidently we're heading for a more simple life.

In Our Time We Lived in Harmony

It is typical on other planets where people live for them to walk around on their feet. It is unusual on other planets to get around in vehicles, although one sees it sometimes. It wasn't common in my experience, because life was *wonderful*—you wanted to walk around, you wanted to walk slowly. You would see your friends; they would be happy to see you. You didn't want to avoid them, there was nothing you wanted to avoid, so the idea of being in a vehicle where you wouldn't have a chance to see your friends wouldn't even occur to you.

There were more animals, more flowers, more trees, more plants—there was more of everything, wasn't there?

Not everything—there wasn't more disease. You have many more diseases in your time than we did, many more. I feel that this is because where we lived at that time was in considerable harmony, and there was a greater degree of balance. In your time people do make an effort, but sometimes the best of intentions to move animals about . . . some of your forest service people move animals about, sometimes even move animals in.

They might note that certain fish used to be in this river and they're not in there anymore. So they sometimes have a place where they nurture those fish and then bring them, put them in the river—sometimes for fishing, other times just because they feel the fish were there once, so they ought to be there now. We wouldn't have looked at it that way: "If the fish are not there now, they moved on. Maybe we better go find them" [chuckles]. But if a certain type of fish moved on and they were gone, then that was that.

You know, even if we were very, very hungry, if there were just a few fish, we wouldn't kill them to eat. We would try to find something else to eat, because we would want to make sure that those fish could thrive, be there next year. Where we lived, the river would freeze over, and the fish would migrate to a warmer climate perhaps, but underneath . . . some of them could survive underneath, live under there in a sleep state of some sort. We wanted to make sure that they survived, so up to a point we would fish, but not past that point. It was the same thing with hunting.

So you lived in a place where it snowed and got really cold in the winter?

It didn't have much snow, but it had some, and it would get, as you say, cold. Of course, we didn't have the kind of warm garments that you have; we had some things, but we didn't have the same kind. So once it started getting cool . . . maybe it would be time to move by the time it was getting, in terms of your degrees, into the forties or fifties. We'd be packing up by then.

And where would you move to?

We'd move to a place that was at a lower elevation and warmer.

Oh! It wasn't that you had to go hundreds of miles; it was just down the mountain.

That's right.

So you went to the mountains in the summertime and to the valleys in the wintertime—like that?

Yes. In your modern times, it sounds rather like going to the spa.

[Laughs.] Like having a summer home.

But it was not quite the same.

Nomadic Peoples in Your Time

Remember, we didn't build homes of brick. But the nice thing about that is . . . you have people who are nomadic in your time. Even in your culture, you have nomadic peoples who perhaps might take a tent. And when they are ready to move, they pack up everything they have and pack up their tent, and then they move to the next place and set up their home. It's not a bad way to live. It's especially nice for people who like variety and who do not feel particularly attached to having water and electricity and all that piped into their house. If you're not attached to that, you can live anywhere you are welcome: the forest and sometimes even in town. Maybe you have a friend. You can set your tent up in her backyard and she's so happy to see you: "Come, stay! I'm looking forward to having you stay." Or, "Oh, George and Jane are coming! They'll put their tent up in the backyard and they'll be here for a couple of weeks—won't it be wonderful?"

But it gets to be a little difficult after a while.

It's not so difficult.

No?

It's not so difficult. There are people who do that. Granted, it is not always so wonderful when you get older and things don't work quite the way they did when you were younger, with some pain and aches—then it's not so good. But you have other people around to help you—in my time we did. Some of our elders would be carried. Usually they would walk part of the way because they wanted to, but if they got tired, then someone would carry them or we had some means to carry them so that they could live as long as possible.

You didn't have horses or donkeys or any pack animals?

We didn't have that.

You didn't want that, right?

They didn't exist then, or they didn't exist where we were—that's more likely. Where we were, they weren't . . .

You said there were wild horses all over the West.

They were brought.

After you died?

I couldn't say. But if they were around in my time, I didn't see them. After my time, I saw them—wonderful! Wonderful beings! I'm surprised everyone doesn't want to visit a horse.

Men's and Women's Stories Help People to Know Who They Are

So did you have an oral tradition, then? Did you have a storyteller?

Oh, yes. That was not me.

You had a storyteller?

Oh yes, more than one, because there were men's stories and women's stories. You can't have a man tell stories to women, and you can't have a woman tell stories to men. There are some stories that men and women can tell, that they can both hear, but not that many. Some.

Say more about that—that sounds pretty strange.

No, it's not strange; it's good. In your time I feel that one of the worst corruptions that has taken place, that has caused many people to become totally confused about who they are, is that men and women hear the same stories all the time and they don't really know what their roles are. What is a man supposed to do? What is a woman supposed to do? Most people are completely at a loss about that, because they don't hear stories meant only for them.

So women don't get guidance about what's the best way for a woman to live, what's the best way for her to nurture and mother her children. Now, I grant that women in your culture have made many more strides toward having their own stories and their own teaching for themselves. This is not surprising, since women must mother and nurture simply because they give birth. But I haven't seen much activity in that direction for men—only a little, some. But not too much widespread activity.

No, I feel that one of your biggest problems that causes the most mischief in your time is the fact that your people don't know who you are because you do not live together the way we did. The most you can hope for in togetherness is perhaps to grow up in the country on a farm, or in the case of some people, on a ranch, where you at least have an idea of who you are based upon your family's consciousness—although not everyone gets the best teaching that way.

In your time it is not that it is a problem hearing stories from other cultures; that's not the problem. The problem in your time—especially in your time—is that women are exposed to the mass culture if there are no stories. And because people in your time have been raised without stories—not myths, but stories intended to mold a benevolent character and personality within each individual—without being exposed to such things on a daily basis (not just one day a week in church, but every day in some benevolent way), then people get confused about who and what they are. It is a big problem in your time.

I'm not saying that one culture or religion is better than others. And I'm not saying that men and women should always have certain status levels assigned to them. Certainly in my time it wasn't only men who were in the hunting parties—did you know that?

No.

Finding Children's Gifts

Remember, in my time children were looked on by the elders: "What are they good at? What are they naturally attracted to?" In my time I can remember two or three of our best hunters, including one who was really good with the nose and smells, really good, and who was a woman. Why not? If that was what she was good at, if that was what she was born to, then it would be silly to say, "Oh well, she's got a great sense of smell, but we don't want her to do what she can do best." [Chuckles.]

It's true that the women have to mother and raise their children, and they must be protected while that's going on, so that means a certain amount of time and energy. But other times women do things, jobs, all right? Just because I was a male and my teacher was a male doesn't mean that the mystical person in the tribe was always a male. My teacher told me that he had met many mystical women when he was teaching.

I feel that what's difficult in your time is that people are exposed to too much in your culture, so they get overwhelmed about who and what they're supposed to be and, more to the point in your time, who and what they're supposed to do. It's like they have to do something to become a "who"; they're not really allowed to express their natural talents, except maybe as a child: "He naturally draws well or is attracted to it; she is naturally attracted to playing musical instruments," that kind of thing. But if allowed to flower in that direction . . . some parents do encourage their youngsters to flower in that direction—that's good. But the way a child acts when he or she is young isn't always a means to know exclusively what that child's going to be good at. Sometimes it's a very subtle thing.

I remember an elder told me once that he noticed that when the other children would get upset with each other and have little spats or arguments, that there was always one child who would come over and help them settle their differences.

That one was a diplomat.

That's right. But that was only observable when such things took place; at other times, the child was a typical child. He liked to tap on things with his hands—like a pots-and-pans kind of thing that you see with children nowadays—he liked to do all that kind of stuff. But what he was good at naturally was helping people to settle their differences and feel good about the settlement. It takes a lot of observation to pick up on things like that.

That's why it's so vitally important, when you are raising children, to have parents and grandparents about. They don't have to live in your same house, if you're not comfortable with that (they may not be comfortable with it either). But to have them nearby . . . it's especially helpful when the children are there so that they can discuss with each other, "Well, let's let him do this!" or "I saw her do that!" They can put their heads together and say, "Oh, he did this, he did that; so this is what he'll be good at." Because that's what it takes.

It was not just one elder saying, "I saw him do this; that's what he's going to be good at." The elders would put their heads together, would talk about these things. That was one of the great benefits of my time—we didn't have such barriers. Parents, great-uncles and great-aunts, grandparents and so on—or even just brothers and sisters—would be available sometimes to consult.

Stories Teach You How to Be

What do you mean by women's stories and men's stories?

I'll tell you. I might have some difficulty telling you a woman's story, but here's a man's story, all right? I don't think I'll tell the story, but I'll talk about it. It's a story designed to teach a young boy how to feel, how to believe in himself, how to recognize his strength and abilities, how to recognize the strength and abilities in others, so that he makes no effort to compete. (We didn't have competition in my time; you could say we had teamwork, but we didn't have competition.) It taught how to recognize the value in all life, including other people, and how to nurture the way a man nurtures. Like that.

In one story?

It would be a story about how this little boy went here and he did that and so on. It would all be designed . . . there was some latitude in telling the stories, because maybe the youngsters whom you were raising at any given time, some of them might have been attracted to fishing and so on, so you'd talk about a little boy who liked to go fishing. You had the goal or the purpose of the story; it would all be worked in there. But what the little boy did in order to learn those things—that could change. Maybe the little boy went climbing and so on. If a little child didn't like to climb trees or something, then maybe the little boy would be good at climbing a mesa and being a lookout. There were lots of different things.

I think with the women's stories, there would be similar qualities, but also other ones—maybe stories designed to nurture. Maybe it would be about finding a squirrel or something that fell out of the nest and raising it the best you could, and then taking it back to the forest and letting it go, even though it might come around say hello.

Squirrels never forget. If you do something kind for them, they will remember and they will come and visit you. They feel that just coming to visit you is doing a good thing, because it's not typical for squirrels to come and visit people. If they come and visit you and bring their beauty— they are beautiful—then it is a gift. Maybe you give them nuts or something, especially if they are having a lean year, and they appreciate that—they never forget.

But these stories . . . they gave your people, what? A sense of possibility? Of how to be?

Of how to be—exactly. And they gave you qualities and goals and things to identify with that would support you as a woman or as a man when you grew up. A man obviously didn't need to have to learn about having children, so that wouldn't be in men's stories, but it would be in women's stories. Even if you, for some reason, never had children, it would be in those stories. Perhaps, for some reason, you never had a child—that would be sad, but suppose it happened. Then perhaps your sister would have children, and you could help her out with her children.

But it seems that there's so much in the joy of being human that relates to both sexes. Was it because you had your focus on survival that . . . ?

We just had different . . . I don't agree with some things that you say nowadays. You say that men and women ought to have an equal chance to get ahead and be fulfilled, wealthy, healthy, all this kind of stuff. In principle, I agree with that, but in my experience, I have found that there are certain things that women like doing, even if they don't know they like doing them. It is not unusual in your time, for instance, for a career woman, even though she loves her career and loves what she's doing in her work, to get married perhaps—or even not get married—and be with child and have a baby. At first she discovers she's pregnant, as you say, and going to have a child and, "Oh, it's annoying." But then she begins to think, "Oh, well, maybe there's a space in my life for this." And then once she has the child, it's wondrous, wonderful.

But things like traveling, things like enjoying beauty, things like spiritual practices—all of these things relate to both sexes.

I have no problem with that.

What about sports?

Sports? Well, I don't know about that. You see, in my time we didn't do sports, but if we had, it would have been a team effort to accomplish a singular goal that everyone was working on. You do have some places on your planet now that have cultures that promote that kind of team sport. I think that is one of the worst things in your time, to have sports where there are different teams playing each other and one team loses; I do not believe in that at all. That impacts you. You don't get over that.

I'm not saying that women can't have sports or men can't have sports—you can do whatever you need to do in your time. But it is my job to teach; it is not my job to follow. I might follow the guidance of my teacher and other wise beings, but it is not my job to follow your culture and say, "Oh, that's wonderful." It's my job to help you to become happy and fulfilled, and to accomplish what you need to accomplish for your own sake. So it is not my job to say, "Oh, women should play baseball," all right?

The Soul Comes in with Certain Desires

Who defined the job? You?

My teacher.

Your teacher defined your job?

And going back before that, when I was born I had certain tendencies, things that I was good at. The elders said, "Hm, he looks like he likes mystical things. I've got a job for you, Reveals the Mysteries!" See? And going back before that, my soul came back to Earth, yes, wanted to do certain things. In other words, our people were focused enough in philosophy and spirit to nurture and welcome souls, to help them to accomplish and to be what they came here to be—not to try to mold them to be citizens of a culture and force them to do something that didn't feel right to them. I'll bet when you went to school as a little girl, they wanted you to do things and learn things that didn't feel very good. Not in my time.

You have to think about it. See, for you, you are attached to the idea of being liberated, of having equal opportunities, and although I might agree with that, it is not an equal opportunity if the child is forced to do something that she doesn't want to do or that she doesn't have a capacity or talent for. What kind of liberation is that?

But isn't there a sense that we're supposed to learn new things each life? If we only do what we come in with a propensity to do, then we're not expanding our . . . ?

No, no; you're misunderstanding. Remember, the soul comes in with certain desires, what it wants to do in this life. The soul can't bring in what it has always done. What it has always done would be "propensities"— that word you used. But the soul doesn't come in with that. It comes in . . . it would go through a filter. It is only allowed to bring in what it wants to do in this life; it does not bring in its talents and abilities from what it has done before—that's not allowed.

So the soul arrives at what it wants to do, and when the baby is born, the baby is, yes, affected by the immortal personality—that's allowed too, of course. But just because in other lives you've been a spiritual master, or in other lives you've explored this or explored that, the soul doesn't have that. That's not allowed. The soul has only your immortal personality— that much of it that is allowed to come through—and what it wants to do. It doesn't bring propensities. So I'm correcting your statement.

But what if it has never done what it wants to do?

It doesn't make any difference.

So as long as it wants to do it, then that's the new learning that it will gain from this life?

That's what it wants to do; we'll see how long the life goes. But the child will demonstrate some capacity toward some activity or way of life or some form of being that will allow the soul to fulfill that desire. Even though the soul doesn't bring in a desire to be a certain thing as a career— no soul brings that in—the soul might bring in something else.

Maybe the soul wants to learn how to get along with all different kinds of beings, something simple like that. And so the immortal personality would demonstrate certain things. Instead of the child having the same friends all the time, the child would be going around and trying to make friends with everybody. [Chuckles.] And then the elders would notice that and say, "Well, this child is trying to make friends with everybody, including the animals and plants, whereas this other child just has the same friends, regular." Elders are intended to notice everything.

I honestly thought that everyone came in with skills they had learned before, and the trap was to fall into the old way and not learn something new.

That isn't the way it is. It's not like that. I'm glad we're getting this cleared up. If you think that is the case, then how could people experience ignorance? How is it that you wouldn't remember your previous lives and what you had done? How is that? Now, it's certainly true that you might, in your culture, where everybody is stamped out with a cookie cutter . . . yes, there's individuality, but I'm talking about your culture here in the United States, where people go to school and they have to learn the same things, every child, all right? Granted, there are some schools that are a bit more flexible, but generally speaking, they learn the facts, all of this business.

I can see where you might think that because one child is good at remembering or another child is better at art, that those children brought in those skills from previous lives. But they don't bring in the skills and the knowledge; what they bring in is an ease. They're comfortable with it. It's an ease, but it's not a propensity, because if the child was never exposed to an art class, he might never know that he had a natural ability.

And that child would miss what he came to do.

No, that's not true at all, because I'm talking about what your statement was—propensities. And when you're talking about propensities, you're talking about what people have done before this life.

Yes.

And I'm saying that's not true. What I'm saying is that just because you didn't discover you were good at drawing doesn't mean that you missed what you came here to do. It means that you had an ease with that, you were perhaps a master artist in another life. You came here, but that's not why you came here; you came here to do something else in this given life that we're talking about. You never noticed, you never had the opportunity to notice that you were good at drawing, because you were never exposed to it.

By sort of the design of the soul?

Not all children are exposed to art classes.

Unfortunately.

But that doesn't mean you missed doing what you came here to do, especially if you have elders who notice and say, "Oh, look at that! He's good at that! Look at her, look what she's doing! She's good at that! Maybe we ought to encourage her to do more of that!"

It's like the child who tried to help the other children settle their disputes. He was good at that. But he was also . . . perhaps in another life he might have been a soldier, for example, and a soldier would know what happens if disputes are allowed to go too far. So in this life, the soul decided, "Well, I want to be someone who settles disputes, not to have to settle them by the sword." He came in and he was exposed to other people having disputes, so he would go over and say, "Well, now, you play with it for a while, and then she can play with it later," like that. He would work something out. He just had a . . . he just did it because he wanted to do it.

But these elders had to be really alert, then, to separate out what children were at ease with and what they came to do in this life, right?

Yes, because settling the differences between the other children . . . if the child just did it once, the elder would notice it but wouldn't say, "Oh, this person is meant to be the diplomat," as you said. If the child did it repeatedly, then the elder would say, "Oh, he does that regularly." But the elder still wouldn't say anything for a while. Until children were about three years old, no one would say, "This is what he or she is meant to do." They were allowed to demonstrate their personality for a while.

By the time they were maybe three years old, maybe three and a half, the elders would have watched them. The elders didn't run around behind them all the time [chuckles], but different elders in the tribe would notice, "Oh, this and this and this is going on with this child, and this and this and this is going on with that child," and they would talk about it. It was not a secret, they would talk about it, and then they would compare what they had seen.

And you feel that they were generally pretty accurate—they didn't misinterpret the signs?

In my time, with my people, I never saw them misinterpret. But that's, of course, because we all knew one another. We're not talking about great numbers. Of course, they didn't all survive, either.

Parents: Don't Isolate Your Children

So how would we utilize that wisdom now in this life? I mean, nobody sees children very much at that age except very close members of the family.

Broaden your community; don't remain isolated as a parent, all right? Even if you are a single parent, meet with other parents. If your parents, for some reason, are not near you or are no longer alive or aren't sure how they feel about you—maybe you've had a disagreement—then seek out others whom you feel good about who can observe your child. Because as a parent, you'll love your children, you'll appreciate them, but you can't look at them as an elder would. For one thing, you don't have the experience an elder has—especially if he or she has raised children. So seek to broaden your community and be around those people—not just one day a week at church, but be around them more often. The more elders, the better. Then you will have people who will be able to look at things, see, study, think. Or seek out your brothers and sisters, perhaps. But don't be isolated.

In your time I see so much isolation, and children brought up in an isolated environment usually don't make very good citizens. Sometimes they can, but it gives them more of an uphill battle to become good citizens because they haven't learned about citizenship. They need to be around other children, they need to be around people of all ages, even if they don't play with their grandpa the same way they play with their playmates.

That's the best thing you can do. Because as a parent, you've got enough to do to take care of your children and try and make a living; you'll need other people. So if your sister has children, try to live with her. If you're living on your own and you have your children, make it a point that your career doesn't take up so much of your time that you can't, every day, be around older people whom you like. It might be that your parents and grandparents don't like you and you don't like them—then find other people of those ages whom you can be around, whom you feel good about, who like you and you like them, and who can be around your child. Try to seek out older people who've had children whom you feel good about—they can advise you.

Let them be around your child more than once. They might notice something once, and if they think they'll never see you again, then they might say to you, "Oh, I see he's good at this." Many of you parents have had that experience around older people who think perhaps they'll never see you again, or they're not sure, or maybe you see them once a year. You need to have the same older people around your child on, I recommend, a daily basis—if you can't do that, then at least every other day. I know in your time you like to have more space and not be around people all the time, but when you are a young parent and you're raising one or two or three children—especially if it's just one of you—believe me, it's a good thing to be around other adults. Maybe you can get a night off now and then while your sister or your brother or your grandpa or your substitute grandpa takes care of the kids.

Study on it and think about it, and see if you can round up some good substitute grandparents if needed. If you only have a grandpa and there's no grandmother, then look around. Even if you have to go to an old folk's home, as you call it, or a retirement home, and find someone who's still vital and got energy, and you like this person and he or she likes you . . . don't decide in a minute; go visit, hang around there when you can. Remember, you're scouting for a good grandmother or a good elder for your child.

Look for qualities in those elders that you like or that you admire—even things that you wouldn't necessarily do in your life but that you think are good to have done. Maybe you wouldn't necessarily be a fireman, maybe you don't have the skills or abilities or the strength, but you admire firemen. And then you meet this person who used to be a fireman or a nurse or a doctor or a lumberman, cutting wood and so on. You admire these qualities and you admire who they are and you feel good about this person, and you've spent enough time with him that you feel good about him. Include him in your life. He'd probably be happy to see your children. Ask him first: "Do you want to meet my family?" "Oh, yes!" "Do you want to come over? I'll come and get you; come over for dinner." In other words, include more people in your life.

Too Many Things Are Trying to Get Your Attention

I think that part of the reason parents are enjoying having their quiet time is that there are too many things that interfere in family life in your time: the radio, traffic, noise, television, movies. It's too much, all of it try-ing to get your attention. Sometimes there are things you have to react to; sometimes all this is trying to grab your attention with things that it would be better for you not to be exposed to. No wonder you're trying to find some time and space to have for yourself.

Think about your environment: Many of you won't be able to afford to move to some place fancy and nice, but think twice about getting a televi-sion set. If you're going to get something for your youngsters, try to get books, even if you're not the greatest reader or never were the greatest reader. Have them around; maybe your children will become readers. And get them picture books when they're young, so they can have their imagination. Don't get nasty books, okay? Get things that are good, that are pleasant. If the kids bring home a horror comic book, it's okay to take it away, to throw it away. They might keep getting attached to that stuff, and there's nothing you can do about that, up to a point, when they get older. But if one of their friends brings it over and says, "Oh, isn't this scary?"—don't encourage that.

Scary has become entertainment in your time—that's very unfortunate. If children are raised with being frightened, taken to frightening movies, then they tend to want it, they like it, it's part of their life. But in the process, it can encourage such things to actually happen—if not to them, then to oth-ers. It puts it into the general demeanor of people, what they like.

Then there may not be monsters who will live amongst you and do things like in horror comic books, but scary things will happen amongst you that will give you the same feelings that you had when you read those scary comic books when you were a child. It won't be because there are monsters, but it might be things that give you the same feel-ings. So if you grow up identifying those feelings with childhood and iden-tifying childhood perhaps with good things, you grow up with the desire to have the good things of childhood—and in the process, you attract things that are scary.

It's pretty important not to expose your children to scary things that are entertainment. They grow up thinking that and desiring that. That's why you have things in your time that are unnecessarily scary, technology that's unnecessarily scary, all right? Cars and trucks with big, loud horns—BEEEP!!!—that scare you on the street. You have the same feeling. I'm not saying that's because you read horror comics when you were a child; what I'm saying is that somebody did. And your society's culture is set up too much for catering to technology and the efficiencies of technology, with-out much concern over what's good for the hearts of all beings.

Well, I hope that doesn't last very long. It's a perversion, it's a corruption, it's an affliction.

Think about it: When the Romans were conquering civilizations, what was one of the things they did? They were catering to their technological needs—they built roads. Some of the roads or even the memories of those roads still exist today. So it's been around for a while, catering to technology.

Two Feel-Good Gestures

The other day I was mimicking you when you were doing some gestures during a channeling session, and I did this sweeping with my hands, which I've never done before, and it was profound. I've been yawning and relaxing ever since I got here.

Feels good, doesn't it?

Yes. Is it some sort of electrical circuitry set up?

Sometimes it can balance the energies, and it can sometimes deflect energies that are not comfortable. It feels protective; it can be a bit nurturing.

So did this gesture just affect me, or is it something that you would recommend?

Oh, a lot of people do it; it's nothing that I invented, eh? [Chuckles.]

It just seems so simple.

It's simple, but it feels good. Sometimes it feels good one time to separate the fingers. Don't do it in the mental way. Touch the fingertips, like this. Put your fingertips together slowly, and do it in the way that feels good. Always react to the feelings in your body—that's what tells you the way to do it.

Welcoming the Soul of the Baby

Let's talk about something else. We've talked about working with people in regard to death; let's talk about birth. Now, in your times some women have trouble giving birth. Perhaps their bone structure is a certain way, perhaps the family has always had trouble giving birth, or there might be other reasons. In my time it was the same thing. In certain families, it was difficult for the women to have a comfortable birth. Of course, babies were smaller when they were born in my time, perhaps because we didn't have the same diet that you have, but still, it was harder for some women to give birth.

So what did we do? There was only so much you could do about that. The elders, the women, would give these women certain exercises—squatting and so on—to help build up their muscles, but they couldn't change the bone structure. So we would do something to welcome the soul of the baby. We wouldn't try to stop a certain soul coming in, but we'd give a certain training to the soul. And then only after the soul had arrived inside mother—mother was beginning to show then, you understand—what we would do was, we would start talking to the baby inside the body of the mother.

How it would be done is this: Besides mother, there would always be at least two other women there. One would be an elder, an older woman, and one would be a woman relative, such as a sister of that woman—or on some rare occasion if she didn't have a sister, then it would be her best friend, her best woman friend. And then I would be there, and the medicine woman would be there too. She would usually burn certain herbs that would help to relax everybody and burn them for the mother to smell especially, because what the mother smells the baby also smells a little bit inside.

Of course, ideally it would have been better if they had a mystical woman to do this, but we didn't have one, so I had to sit in. But having all these women around moderated my energy a bit. When I would go into mother, my spirit would go in and talk to the baby's spirit. Or—and this would be better, because the elders of the women didn't think it was good for me to go into mother, even in spirit form, and I agreed—when the baby was out in its travels, I would talk to the baby's soul. When the baby's spirit, soul personality, soul, is inside its mother, it is in and out, in and out. I would talk to that soul, the baby's soul, when it was out.

I tried to do this when the soul was out; when we could get everybody together in the way I described, we would wait sometimes for the soul to go out. But if it still didn't go out—some souls, once they go into mother, like to stay there almost all the time—then the other ladies would try to expand their energy, their being, and the medicine woman would go in with me. If I'd go in, she'd go in with me so that my spirit would go in encapsulated inside of her spirit, so there wouldn't be that male energy going inside this woman. But usually the baby would be out of mother, and that was better.

I would talk to the baby, and I would ask the baby . . . our example is that mother was small, she had a hard time giving birth. I remember a family like that. And what I would do was, I would ask the baby to be born small physically, so it would make it easier for the mother to give birth. I didn't mean to be born before its time—as you say, premature—but to be just born small and grow as big as that being wanted to in his or her life. And usually the baby would say, "Okay"—not in those words, but usually the baby would agree to it.

I remember one time when the baby didn't want to agree, and we had to bring in all the elders and everybody we could think of—spirit teachers and so on—to ask the baby to do this. And finally the baby's guides that the baby would have when it was born convinced this baby to be born little, though it could get as big as it wanted.

The funny thing about that boy, when he was born, was that he was small, and he used to do the funniest thing when he was walking around. Even when he was a youngster, first starting to walk, he'd walk around as if he were a giant—stomping his feet around, up and down, boom, boom. It was very funny, it was comical—we all used to laugh. It was true that when he grew up, he was the tallest . . . he was very tall, taller than anybody in our tribe before that. But we all knew that he wanted to be big, so when he got tall, we all laughed. That was very funny. "Oh, he told us he wanted to be big!"—that was the joke. He thought it was funny too. And we always made fun of him gently about walking around as a little boy—

boom, boom!—with his feet up and down—boom, boom!—as if he were a giant.

It's Always Better to Have a Natural Birth

But that's incredibly important. You had no way of dealing medically with a child whose head or body was too big to be born, which could kill he or the mother!

That's right. We had midwives who could reach up inside mother if necessary and turn the baby so that the baby would be born safely and not be strangled by the umbilical cord or something like that. But if he was too large and the mother couldn't give birth to him without a grievous injury that she might not get over in our time, then we had to ask the baby to be born small.

Oh, that's beautiful.

And I must say, I do not really feel it's a good thing, cesareans. I think that in your time it can be done, but I feel they are only good in the case of, say, crashes or something where the mother is suffering.

An emergency.

An emergency. But to be done for cosmetic reasons or something? I do not think so. I feel it is because of misplaced values that in your society impact mother, whoever she may be, so she thinks she has to do this or that. But it's always better to have natural birth. And I know that natural birth is very painful and uncomfortable very often—especially the first time. But there are ways to give birth that are better. I have seen them, looked with long vision at these people doing water birth. Wonderful. [See *Shamanic Secrets for Physical Mastery*, chapter 2.]

Would you only work with the soul when there was a possibility of harm to the mother, or was this a normal thing that you did before birth?

It was not a normal thing that I would do as an elaborate thing, but we would check . . . the medicine woman and myself, because it is not good for a man to be working on a woman, but it is possible in that way. But we would both check just generally with the baby. The medicine woman could check with the mother and so could the elders, and the midwife, you say, could check with the mother. But as far as checking with the baby's spirit—and I would encapsulate in the medicine woman's energy—we would just check to make sure that the baby was all right, that the baby was looking forward to life and would welcome being born with our people in our times.

I remember one occasion when the baby had never had an Earth life—which isn't unusual, of course—but this baby had always lived in highly technical worlds (mental, technical) and had never lived a life on the land in nature and warmhearted . . . had never had that experience. So what we used to do, the medicine woman and sometimes everybody, was that we would have special story songs for these occasions, and we would sing the story songs more than once. And when we'd sing a story song, we'd have pictures, everybody would be thinking of similar pictures at the same time—not exactly the same, but some going up into the mountains or of the sunrise or the sunset, something beautiful, always something beautiful. Then everybody would have these same pictures so that the baby would not be anxious or frightened, or want to stay inside mother, and would come whizzing out to [chuckles] embrace life in this wonderful, beautiful place.

I remember in this one particular case that when the baby came out, that baby, when he could do it, would sing those same tunes and was very affectionate with many of the people in the tribe much sooner than you might expect because he felt so welcome and because of all the singing. Oh, that baby was so . . . just hugging everyone and smiling and happy, because he was especially welcomed, never having lived in a place where there weren't machines to do everything.

It's Best to Use Same-Sex Healers

Why did your energy have to be encapsulated in the medicine woman's energy?

Because it was masculine.

So what?

Masculine energy going into a woman? The only time masculine energy is intended to go into a woman is when she's giving birth to a boy or when her husband is making love to her. No other time.

But don't male healers heal women all the time? And their energy is masculine, right?

You mean if they're males?

Yes.

It would be better for the woman . . . if the woman cannot find any women who do what the male healer does, then it's okay to go to a male healer—but only if there's another woman healer present in the room and she is just expanding her energy, her energy is present. Now, I realize that you have men you go to who work on you; if it feels all right with you, then go ahead. But I recommend as a way to do things, as a way to be, that it is much better to have men work with men and women work with women.

Say you're a woman and you've always had men work on you, they were always doing their energy things with you, and it wasn't okay. But say you did this, you made a habit out of it. It would tend to accentuate the male qualities in yourself. And the same thing goes for a male. If he always had women work on him without having his brother there or something, it might tend to accentuate the feminine qualities in him.

Plus, when you have a woman doctor working on a man, she can sympathize with how it is to be a man, but she doesn't know how it is. And it's the same thing for a woman. A man can work on a woman and have great sympathy and kindness and caring perhaps, but he doesn't know how it is to be a woman, doesn't know how it is to feel being a woman, can't even imagine it. He can do meditations and try to imagine it, but it's not possible to actually experience it.

I'm not saying what you should do, but I am saying what I recommend. It is my job to teach what I recommend, but it is also my job to acknowledge that if you have a man you go to and you feel good about his work, that in that case it would be good to have at least one woman you go to as well . . . or perhaps she comes to you. So say a man does some kind of healing work on you; then it would at least be good to have a woman do something too—maybe if not immediately, then some other day. Say a man works on you once or twice a week; then have a woman work with you once or twice a week, even if it is a massage or something.

Moving into the Next Dimension Is Still a Ways Off

But I thought the whole point here was that we were integrating male and female energies as we moved into a higher dimension?

I don't recommend it. It's not going to be for a long time. You're not going to move into a higher dimension and your society isn't going to move into a higher dimension in your lifetime. [Chuckles.] It's not your job to do that, it's not your job to become that.

So I'm not going to move into a higher dimension in my lifetime?

That's right.

But I thought that's what we were in the process of doing.

You're not going to move into a higher dimension in your lifetime, period. But you will set things up for others to do so, and you're setting it up lovingly, because . . . why? You want to tell them how to live? Or because you want them to have a better life than you did? Which one?

Well, I want them to have a better life than I did, but I want to show them the possibilities of what's coming.

That's right, and that's the whole purpose for the *Sedona Journal of Emergence!* and these books. You want to prepare them, you want to help them to prepare themselves and their children, and to encourage their children in these ways, so that when things come and when they move into a higher dimension, where there will still be men and women, or male and female—not men and women as you know them, but male and female and possibly a third sex—it will happen gradually. It's not going to be [snaps fingers]: "Opp! Now we're one." You're not going to leave the planet in thirty-five years and become a creator. It takes experiential time.

It's not about happening instantaneously. When you leave here, although you will be your total being and be exposed to many other ways of life, you're not going to say, "Well, that's the end of men and women. I don't like that; I want to be my total balanced male and female." Your teacher will say, "Wonderful. What about your next life? What do you want to be for that?" "Oh, I want to be my total balanced male and female!" "Well, I'm sorry; in that society, there are men and women." "Oh." "So which one do you want to be?"

Why should teaching for children be separated by sexes? We're humans, we're souls, we're immortal personalities.

Yes. Is it a bad thing to have men and women?

No, no; it's wonderful,. But we ought to be able to enjoy learning together. I mean, why have separate stories for men and separate stories for women?

You find that offensive.

I do! It seems to preclude so many possibilities. What if a man wants to be a ballet dancer, or a woman wants to be a sailor?

See, you are focused on careers.

Well, I mean, it doesn't matter what they want to do. It seems to me that this focused thing on being either male or female and being separated and living in a separated fashion, with men here, women there . . . that doesn't make sense to me at all.

Well, perhaps it's because you misunderstand what I'm saying. Do you think that in my tribe, that men and women who had children didn't live together? And couples who didn't even have children—sometimes couples couldn't have children—do you think they lived apart? Men only together? Women only together? It's only for certain activities that men would be all together. How would it help a woman to learn how to use your penis? Would that be helpful? Or stories to teach qualities of a man? What good would it be for a man to know personally how to use your breasts to feed your child? I don't see how that helps him.

Oh, so the teaching and stories were physiological!

Of course! That's what life is all about. In my time it wasn't about careers. Sometimes the mystical man would be a mystical woman; sometimes the medicine man would be a medicine woman. It didn't have anything to do with sex. But the midwife? Never a man.

When you said that there were stories only for men and only for women, it just . . .

Some stories.

It seems so exclusive, it seems so separatist, it seems so alienated, it seems so unlike what I understand as a human experience. I mean, there are physiological things, yes. If that's what these stories were about, then that's fine. But not the way we look at the world, the way we experience, the way we sense, the way we feel—that doesn't have to do with gender.

I can't say I agree with you. I do understand in your time that that's the perception of people who are trying to create a more heart-centered world. But in my time it was different. Do you not agree that my time was different?

Well, if it was, then we should say so, because these books are teaching people who live now and in the future.

And I am only giving the teaching for the people who live now and in the future; I am not giving you the teaching for people who live in the past. I am not giving you any of that teaching. All that I've said so far for these books and for articles in the *Sedona Journal* is geared to people of your time.

My Life as a Mystical Man

Reveals the Mysteries
December 3, 2001

I 'd like to talk about my favorite pupil and tell one, maybe two stories about our adventures together.

Reveals the Mysteries First Meets Speaks of Many Truths

When I first met Speaks of Many Truths, it was an unusual circumstance for me. I was really just passing through the village. I wasn't drawn there, I wasn't guided there; it's just that I had been through there quite a few years before and felt welcome. I was hungry and had not been able to find any food, and I felt I would be welcome there again, and so I was.

While I was there, one of the elders came up to me, and she said, "We have this young boy now; he's about . . ."—oh, it would have been equal to—". . . about six or seven years old. We call him Speaks of Many Truths, and we wonder if you would consider teaching him what you know. We know it is a long way to go, to come over here, but if you can stay for a while when you come over, we will make you comfortable as best we can. And if you want to bring your wife sometime and your children, they will be welcome also." So I said, "Well, before we make plans, let me meet this child."

So she went to get his mother, and the three of them came back. Normally when children would meet me, they would be shy—that was typical to the times. But Speaks of Many Truths was unusual. They walked up holding hands, and he shook free of the hands and walked right up to me and looked at me like this: a little bit this way, a little bit that way [he's acting as if he's looking very closely at someone], giving me the once-over, as you say.

He walked up and grabbed my legging and pulled on it, and he looked up and I looked down. His mother said, "He wants you to pick him up," and I said, "Oh!" So I picked him up, and he looked me in the eye very seriously. I didn't know what to expect because these weren't my people, but I had met them before, and as far as I could tell, they were fine. He put out his finger on his right hand, and he moved over and he touched the tip of my nose . . .

With the first finger, right?

Yes, that was it. Then he wanted to get down, and he ran back to his mother. I didn't know whether it was a childish thing, like a game. I asked his mother, "Is that a game he plays?" And she was embarrassed; she said, "No, he's never done that before." So I thought about it: either he was establishing a humorous friendship, or it was his way of pointing at me and saying that I was important to him. I wondered why he pointed to my nose, but it might have been because that was where I was holding him. Still, I asked him, "Why did you touch the tip of my nose?"

I didn't think he'd answer, because children are shy with people they don't know, at least in my day they were—probably in your day too—but he had an answer for it. He said—and this was based in our words, our shared language—the word "knowledge" in our language and the word "nose" (the name for nose in our language and the word "knowledge" were very close; they were very similar words). Then I realized that this was as close as he could come without speaking to saying "knowledge" and pointing to me. Isn't that clever? I thought that was so clever. So I made up my mind: "Well, if he can do *that* and this is the beginning of our relationship, then I can expect big things." And as it turned out, I was right. But I thought you might be amused to hear how I met my pupil.

Talk about the shared language.

No. Do you know why? Speaks of Many Truths has gone out of his way to keep the tribal name of his people unknown, and I have actually given a hint or two here unintentionally. So I will honor his desire. The reason he has done this is that he wants this to be universal and not become a study of an individual tribe's knowledge or wisdom, which would then be considered something quaint, perhaps, or "Isn't that interesting?" I agree with him—it is better to universalize what he speaks of, because it *is* universal.

Speaks of Many Truths Learns Long Vision

Later on Speaks of Many Truths said that he went to live with you—how much later was that?

That wasn't for a time, but he did come over. Normally in his tribe—and mine also—when a boy got to be nine years old, he would usually spend more time with the men. Of course, there would be other boys there too, but he would spend more time with the men in order to learn men's things, men's ways of being. They are not so terribly separated—men's things, women's things—but in reality, living the reality we did then, there were things that men did and there were things that women did, and then there were things that everybody did. But there had to be differences—if there weren't differences, then the men and women would not complement each other.

That's the key to understanding this—it is complementing. Attraction would be there, of course, but there had to be things that one did, that the other did, and where together, the two things matched nicely. This is not like bookends that perform the job of supporting something in between—that's not the best description, although I can see that it is a good one for your times. But it is rather like the branch of the tree and the fruit on the branch or the leaves. You wouldn't think of a tree that didn't have leaves or needles, yes? There's a branch, and then there's what grows from the branch. That is complementary—that kind of complementary, where the two go together.

Now, when Speaks of Many Truths was nine years old, instead of going to be with the men and the other boys—not only with them, but to spend more time with them—he came to where I was. His father and brother brought him over. Of course, he said his goodbyes to everyone first, because he did not know how long he would be staying, and I could not say because it was not something like, "It will take *this long*"—not like a four-year college. It would be as long as it took.

But you were a many-days walk away from his village, right?

About three days, maybe a little more—not much. So it took awhile to get there, and it was a little higher up in elevation, so some of the time was involved in adjusting to the altitude, and it's slow moving, going up. So when he got there, his brother and his father stayed for a few days to rest up and visit the tribe (they had not been there before) and enjoy the culture: to relax and eat and sleep. They stayed for a few days, and then they left. And of course, they brought a gift, which was not unusual in those times—where you brought gifts or gave things to people, but not so much objects. It could have been an object, you see, but often it was something you did or said or some care you provided. But this time it was an object, and so they gave that gift to the woman who would be his substitute mother while he was there. That was nice.

So then he said his goodbyes to his father and brother, and they left after a few days. Speaks of Many Truths stayed with me for a few years. And you understand, in those days . . . think about that: As a child, he couldn't call anybody up on the phone. Suppose they had to leave and go somewhere and couldn't come back? He would never see his people again. That feeling, that uncertainty, was there.

After his father and brother left, he was feeling kind of upset. He was nine years old—granted, a little more mature in my time than in your time, but still he was a child, and he was upset and frightened: "Will I ever see my family again? Will I ever see my people again?" So the first thing we did immediately was to teach him long vision so he could see them from a distance, even though they couldn't see him. But the sensitive people in his tribe—there were a few, plus the medicine woman—might feel his presence and be reassured also. So he would be able to see them, and if they moved from the higher to the lower elevations and all those things, he would know when they did so. So he wouldn't be entirely separated; there was that means of knowing.

He was quite impressive. I had had students before him, but never a student who learned long vision in . . . I'll use your time. He learned long vision and perfected it in not quite ten days. I was astonished. I had never had a student who learned it that fast. So I realized then that, working together, we could probably teach him a great amount of things in not as much time—at least that's what I thought then. But it is typical—is it not?—that he could learn many things that were of a mystical nature very fast, but remember that he was staying with us, so he had to learn some of the things any nine-year-old boy would learn at that age and not in his tribal, accustomed way. So he had to learn more about hunting and carrying hides and all of that kind of thing, and that he was very slow at. [Laughs.]

The mystical things he could do quickly, but when it came to the practical day-to-day living matters, that was very slow. I had not even considered to ask his father or brother about that, and no one had mentioned it, so I did not realize that this was something that was more difficult for him. But we had many a laugh over it. I asked him, "Was it because of our people and our ways?" Our tribes were kind of related—they were not the same tribe, but we had a certain amount of shared culture. But he said, "No, no. It's always been hard for me to learn these things that everybody must learn."

So we had lots of laughs over that, and he learned those things, but he would have to be taught . . . the other boys would be shown once, twice, three times, and then they would have it, and sometimes there would be boys and girls learning the same things and everybody would get it first. But he'd always bring up the end of the line when it came to those things. It was a good thing he had a good sense of humor, because sometimes the children would joke with him about it—not in a mean way—and he could always laugh it off. So that was another good sign that he would make a good mystical man.

How Speaks of Many Truths Overcame His Fear of Heights

I had a sudden realization that the story he told us about being afraid of heights and learning long vision must have been amplified by being up in the mountains [see Shamanic Secrets for Physical Mastery, *chapter 3].*

That's right. It wasn't right away that I realized he was afraid of heights, because where we lived, it wasn't like you had the feeling that you were living on the edge of anything. You went up and you were in a higher elevation, but it wasn't like living in the mountains where you were consciously aware of the potential of falling off. It was just a higher elevation. So I did not realize for a long time that he was shy about heights. But eventually he told me.

After he learned long vision?

Yes. He told me because at one point, when I was teaching him about the big cats, we talked about the cats going up in the tree. And in order to learn about the big cats so that you could call in their energy or even call them in, if you needed to talk to one . . . sometimes you would in order to learn things, and sometimes they would approach a mystical man or woman in order to learn things, if they were having trouble or were wounded or were perhaps disoriented or needed to find something that we could unite with them (help them to find a lost cub or something). So I was teaching him the way of connecting with the mountain lion, as you say, and one of the things mountain lions do is, they will go up in a tree and sit on a high, strong branch. So I was going to have him go up a tree and sit on that branch. He didn't want to do it, and that's when I found out he was afraid of heights.

So then I did teach him, but we did it on a much lower branch, and I stood underneath him with my hand up to catch him if he fell off, even though I knew he wouldn't. I knew it would make him feel safer if I was standing there and reassuring him that I would catch him if he fell off, and he trusted me. So then he felt all right. And then over time he managed to make it to the higher branch, but he was frightened.

He told us how you taught him to fly with the hawk.

That's what we did eventually, but it was a challenge, you know. You can be very good at one thing, you understand. In your time it's the same. A person can be very good at one thing, and something else everybody takes for granted doesn't work for that person.

So this is a little bit I wanted to tell you about my student in order to help you to recognize that he's a living person—not some spirit only. When I knew him, I was a person and so was he, and we were not as knowledgeable, you might say, then as we are now because we didn't have the access. But we did know a few things.

Using Long Vision to Visit a Technological Tribe

How did it work, then, when you went out to teach your other students? Did you not go out or did you take him along?

I took him along.

That really brought him new knowledge from all these other people, right?

That's right, because you would meet people from completely different tribes. We went to one tribe . . . they don't exist anymore in your time, but they were perhaps more modern. They were fascinated by anything that was machine-like, meaning that they would figure out how to make things work. I did not see the advantage of it, but they would figure out how to make things work that involved levers and pulleys—like that. They were technical—that's the word.

I was not attracted to that way. Nor was Speaks of Many Truths, I noticed. But we had to adapt to teach these youngsters. I had to adapt, and he was my . . . I could say my best student, so even though I had started teaching some of them before, he was good at it. So we had to adapt. I'd talk to him on the way over, "Now, this is how you're going to have to be with these people, and also you're going to have to accept the fact that there is something that is hugely different about these people from my tribe or your tribe."

These people didn't pair up along the usual lines; yes, there were men and women and children, but they were in the minority. That might be part of the reason the tribe did not last, because most of the tribes that have lasted into your time have had many members and enough of a population that they could stand a disease or a disaster of some sort. But this was a small tribe, and they were paired up man to man and woman to woman. I found that not terribly unusual. In every tribe I had ever visited, there were always a few people who were man to man and woman to woman—that's just part of human nature. But this tribe was . . . most of them were like that. Then, of course, there were some people who were attracted to the opposite.

So I had to tell Speaks of Many Truths about that. And on the way over, he was frightened; he didn't know how he would feel about that. I said, "No, no; it's no different than the couples like this that you have in your tribe. There are always . . . it's typical, it's normal, okay? It's just that in this tribe, it is the majority." So once I reassured him that the people didn't do anything more unusual than the man-to-man/woman-to-woman couples in his own tribe or in my tribe, then he was all right. But the combination, you see, is what made it hard for him initially—the combination of that being the predominant way in their tribe, plus them being technical. That was a bit difficult for him at first.

But the thing that was hardest for him to adapt to was the technical. I don't think he ever really was able to embrace it; the most he was ever able to do was to become polite about it. But [chuckles] the first time he went over there, when he was exposed to such objects, he literally jumped back. It was [chuckles] . . . I tried not to laugh. I tried very hard, but I couldn't suppress a little smile. And then he felt kind of ashamed, like he had . . .

Failed?

No, like he had made me look bad. I reassured him that it was all right and that they were used to people reacting that way who weren't of their own.

What was an example of one of their technological objects?

There was a lever device, like something you would grab in your hand—not unlike that cutting device you use. But you would grab it in your hand, and moving it, you could grab something at a distance.

Oh, like fruit off a tree or something?

That's right; you could extend your reach. They had worked up something like a wooden pin that they would stick between things—very clever, I thought. I have looked at technology's early development in your culture, and it's very similar, except that I do not think it increased the leverage; I don't think it did that. It just extended their reach.

When Speaks of Many Truths saw that the first time, he jumped back—a big jump, way back. Because when he first saw it, he didn't think anything, but when someone picked it up and squeezed it, he jumped back, and then he approached it by way of my back, like coming around my leg and peeking around. Then he was embarrassed, because he thought I had been made to look foolish, but I patted him on the shoulder to let him know, "No, no; it's all right." And the people in the tribe, they smiled. They didn't laugh at him, though, because other people had had similar reactions and they knew they didn't want to embarrass him.

And one of their children was one of your students?

Two.

Two of them?

A boy and a girl.

And did their acclimation to technology . . . it didn't have any effect on the teaching, did it?

Yes.

Did it?

I couldn't use it in my teaching, but they would adapt it. I might teach them something, and then they would include one of those devices—sometimes, not always. It wasn't for me to say, "No," because I had to honor their way. So if it felt all right to me, then I would allow it. I would say, "All right, you can do that," even though it would be foreign to me.

They didn't have their own mystical man or woman?

They had someone, but she was very old and she had passed on as much as she could to them. But then she had something go wrong and she couldn't talk; she could still do her work and protect the tribe, but she couldn't speak. So she used her long vision to invite me to come over, and I came over. And then if I wasn't teaching something that she needed me to teach—maybe she hadn't finished it—she could communicate with me that way, and then I could pass it on. If I didn't know it, I'd demonstrate it—it usually involved doing something physical. She couldn't speak and she couldn't walk very well, but I was able to finish the teaching that she wanted to give them and then go on and teach them more things before she died. So she was happy.

That was wonderful! You probably saved their tribe.

Well, it was a service worthy of the people. And then it was good to teach a boy and a girl; this way, they would have two, and they could hope for the survival of one (but I believe they both survived, which is always pleasant). Then you could have, for instance, if you chose, a mystical man or woman go out with the hunting party and still have someone with the tribe. I'm not saying they did that, but this would be an example of something you could do if you had that amount of people. My tribe never had more than one, but in their tribe, they did things in a different way. The idea of having two, it appealed to this tribe, and there were two promising students, so that's the way we did it.

So was that a common thing: a tribe that needed you would call you by long vision?

No, that was not typical. If someone heard about me or knew about me, that person would usually send someone physically. Long vision, that connection—that was unusual. But she had to make it that way; if it had been different, if she hadn't had been sick that way, injured, then she would have trained them herself. But she needed help.

Food Grown in the Wild Is Full of Life

So Speaks of Many Truths stayed with you for how long? How did you tell time? In months? What was the difference between the way you would say the time and the way we'd say it in our time?

Day or night, and then cold season, hot season—like that. You have to remember that we weren't farmers; we didn't grow food, see? That was different. You need a lot of knowledge of calendars and so on if you grow food, but we didn't.

But you needed to know where to find food, right?

Certainly, but we didn't need a calendar for that. I'm not saying calendars are bad; what I am saying is . . . perhaps you don't know about people in those times. In those times you had people who hunted and gathered. Farming didn't come until much later, at least to my knowledge. Because, you see, if you're farming, then that means you have to pretty much stay where you are. You might have someplace where you are for winter and someplace where you are for summer, but once you start farming, you're usually hunting less in my experience.

We didn't know about farming in my time. It was hunting and sometimes gathering. We might come across bushes that someone would recognize where the fruit was edible. But we would never take it all; we would take only a small portion, what we needed. When food grows wild like that, you don't have to eat as much because it's full of life. And of course, very often it would be something that other animals would also eat, and it would be cruel to . . . so we would take what we felt would be all right to take and leave the rest.

So what were some of the foods you would normally gather? What was it that grew there?

Sometimes there were certain roots that were thick, and sometimes there were, like you say, nuts. Some of the nuts were not very edible just raw, but if they were cooked or boiled and ground up . . . once they were cooked, they would be softer and you could grind them up and maybe add, if you had them, things to make it taste different. But usually you'd just grind them up and make kind of a gruel, and it would be very nourishing—maybe not tasty, but nourishing, and that's the most important thing. And then there were some berries. We didn't usually mix foods like you do, make a stew or something—we didn't do that. We felt it was important to preserve its . . . how can we say? If it was a nut, then it needed to be with others like itself to have its full vitality. If you mix something in, then that's foreign, that's not part of what it grew. Do you understand?

So you'd eat one food at a time!

We'd eat one food, and then we might have that gruel for a meal. Or we perhaps might go into a place where it wasn't possible to make a fire—there was not much wood, or you wouldn't want to use the wood because there was so little. We would have made that nut gruel and let it dry—it's kind of like a cake—and so we would have eaten that. It's very nourishing and can keep you going if you haven't been able to be successful hunting. So you always had a few of those things with you just in case. And so it would be like that. And then, of course, we hunted the meat.

Do Not Kill the Old Wise Animals

So how often did you move, then?

Like the tribe of Speaks of Many Truths, we would move for the season. When it got cold, we would move to a place about—I'll use your terms, okay?—forty-two miles away in the opposite direction of where Speaks of Many Truths' people were. And it was very nice there. There was a river and very good-tasting fish and also some old wise fish, the really big ones. We would never try to catch them, because they were obviously the wise ones for their people. We did not want their wisdom to go away.

In your time you do not understand that when you catch and eat the old fish who are usually bigger and wiser, they might not have been able to pass on their wisdom to the younger ones, and then the younger ones don't know how to survive, how to keep the species going. That's how that type of fish disappears, becomes extinct. Never kill the old wise ones, even if you are very hungry. If you are very hungry and they are the only ones there, say, "Good life," and go look for some other kind of food. If you kill them, you not only might wipe out a species, but you'd just be hurting yourself and everybody else too. So never, never do that. You've had species lost in your time because your people do not know that you don't do that. It's practical as well as spiritual—very practical.

But would the hunters know just because the old ones were big?

I would know, or the mystical person from the tribe would know, because the old ones are not always big. Sometimes the old ones are the same size as everybody else. They usually give a sign of some sort, but if you don't catch that sign or you don't know that sign for their people, then you need to have a sensitive person along who can say, "Oh, just so you don't hurt that one. Leave those alone—they are the teachers."

I've never really been aware of that.

Important, yes?

Very important.

But also very good for your people. Because people don't know about this, but now that they will find out through these books, then they will perhaps start to do it—maybe take a sensitive person along and say, "Is it okay?" And that person will say, "Well, you better leave those fish there; make sure you put them back in the water gently. And if a few extras get out of the net, that's okay too."

I do not feel it's good, this netting thing. It's one thing for a man or a woman to throw out a small net that they can throw themselves and net a few fish. I still don't like that, but I think it's better to spare fish, hm? You have one or two, and that's enough for a small family. If there are more people, then spearfishing is a different way, but that's how you do it. But when you put out a net, you could wipe out a whole culture without even knowing it. And then you find that those fish are no longer around.

Warrior Fish Keep Balance in the Waters

Maybe there are some fish around whom you have never seen before and whom your people have never seen, and they're unusual, and you start to fish them. I have heard of this happening in my time, but I will say that in your time, when this happens, never ever eat those fish. It's a possibility that those fish are there as warriors, meaning that a whole species was wiped out, or more than one, and then these warrior fish show up. They come from ancient places underground. They come to the surface and they breed very fast, and there are many of them. And to the people who catch them and then eat them—those fish no one ever heard of and then suddenly they are around—they are poison. If you eat them, maybe you don't die right away, but then diseases spread around amongst your people that weren't there before. And then the people die out, and there is a big loss of life, see? Then you don't need as many fish, and then the warrior fish go away.

You've seen that happen?

I have heard of it. I heard that this happened once, and by the time I got there, it was too late to tell them not to eat these strange new fish. I could see clearly that they were warrior fish, and they knew that I knew, but it was too late. Those people, the tribe, they lost two-thirds of their people because they had been fishing in a way that wasn't right. They didn't use a net, but they created a dam, and then they created a dam on the other side. Then the fish couldn't get out. The impact was like a net, and they did not realize that this was a bad thing. I thought that was clever, and they might have had a lot of food for a while, but then the warrior fish came, and it was a terrible thing. It was not a good thing.

Remember, in our time we did not have doctors with the drugs that they would push into your body and you would get better right away—none of that. Medicine women, too, would not have medicine for that, because the warrior fish would bring something entirely new. They were new fish, and their . . . everything was new; you wouldn't have medicine for that. The medicine you had could maybe help with feelings the people were having, but it couldn't save them.

The Tribe Who Lost Its Hunters

That is so hard for us to believe now, I think, that just a few hundred years ago, things we take for granted were just not there. I mean, it was survival every day, right?

Every day, survive. That's right. That's why if your tribe didn't have hunting parties, it was a disaster. Maybe something happened to your hunting party, and sometimes the hunting teacher would be with them—that was a disaster.

Once I came across a tribe that had lost its hunting party and the hunting teacher also; the only people who were left were the students, the hunting students, who were too young to go out with the hunting party. That was all they had. By the time I found them, came across them, they had lost a lot of their people. But the ones who were strong enough . . . I used my long vision to invite help, help came and then the ones who were strong enough, we found a place for them to settle for a time where they'd be safe and then brought over, invited, hunting teachers.

It took awhile to rebuild the tribe so that they had people who could go hunting. We started, of course, with their students. They had three who were too young to go out—we had to be very careful with them so they would be safe. That tribe recovered, but I don't know . . . I don't think they survived into your time. They recovered, that tribe—they were all right—but there were very few of them: not too many men, not too many women. The women were a little older, and babies don't always survive as well when women are older, at least not in my time.

Part of My Work Is to Go Out and
Teach Others

So how did you get to be sort of like the . . . the overteacher of the area, is what it sounds like? You sound like an amazing being!

I wasn't; there were others. Just like Speaks of Many Truths, see? When he got older, he went out and taught children from other tribes too. That is part of the work. The medicine woman had to stay there, because her abilities might have been needed every day, but the mystical man or woman . . . sometimes there were times when you could go out, especially if you had been training someone in the tribe and that person could do the basics, as you say, while you were gone. No, there were others. That's part of the way I found out in my time about different things and different places. When I tell you something like, "I heard about it," that's where I'd hear about it from! I'd hear about it from other mystical men and mystical women, and they would tell me these things; we would share knowledge and wisdom. It was a good thing.

Meeting physically or by long vision?

Meeting physically usually. You only use long vision if there's a specific reason. You don't use it just to say, "Hello, how are you?"

How old did you live to be?

In your years maybe not so old. But in our time I was considered very old: fifty-one. Very old for our time.

And by the time you left, you had several apprentices that you had trained, then, who took over?

Quite a few, yes. But my death was sudden.

How?

Something fell on me. I will spare you the details, but I was terribly injured. I was suffering, and I knew that I could not possibly be . . . no medicine woman could cure me of these injuries. So I used my long vision to touch my students, but in this case, since I was in pain, I sent it through the Sun to purify it, and then sent it to them. Then they would know I was . . . that they would not see me again.

After I did that, then I called in a bear and I asked him if he would mind finishing me off, you would say, so I didn't have to just lie there and suffer. But the bear and I had met before, and she didn't want to do that because she liked me. So she called in a mountain lion. The mountain lion and I had not met, but the mountain lion didn't want to do it, so she called in another one, and he did it. Animals are like people; they have feelings. The one that the female mountain lion called in, the male mountain lion, he did it, but he had . . . it is a lot to ask someone, to come and do such a thing for you, because it might make that being upset. He was very quick, and he was also very spiritual. He knew it was a kindness, and he was able to do it and let go afterward, knowing that I thanked him for it. So it was a kindness on his part.

There was no chemical or substance that you could carry in that situation, that would . . . ?

I could not move my arms.

Had that not happened, you might have lived even longer than that.

Well, by that time I was old, and I had some things old people get [chuckles]. Our time was no different than your time in that way. So I might have lived longer, yes, certainly, but it was my time. And looking back on it, considering the way people died in my time, it wasn't so horrible. Of course, maybe I feel differently about that now in spirit; at the time I was dying, I didn't enjoy it. But it was a great comfort to have the lion make it quicker. Had he not been there, well, it would have been worse.

And you haven't really inhabited a human body since?

No, because I knew I would have a lot to do. I might someday, though. It's always possible. Once you've been a human being, you can always do it again. Once you've been any kind of being anywhere, you can always do it again.

Previous Lives Prepared Me for My Life as a Mystical Man

That wasn't your first life, was it?

No.

But while you were living, you didn't remember the other lives; you were subject to the Explorer Race amnesia as you came through the veil just like everyone else, right?

Certainly. I was able to touch one previous life, once. But it didn't make any sense, so I . . . it was like, "Good life, and goodbye." It didn't make any sense.

What time was it in?

It wasn't what time it was in so much; I think it was where it was.

Where it was?

It was in what you now call Europe, and it was so foreign a culture to me, I couldn't even identify with anything about it.

Looking at it now, what were you in that time?

A farmer.

A farmer? Oh! [Laughs.]

I couldn't identify with that.

I thought maybe you were a court official or something. [Laughs.]

No, in terms of time, it was maybe seventy-five of your years before my life.

Had you had other lives that prepared you to be a mystical man?

I had some, I believe.

That prepared you for your life as a mystical man?

I think so, yes.

Can you tell us a little bit about them?

Not too much, because this is Speaks of Many Truths' book. But I will just say that I had one on another planet that was in the star system Sirius, where there are a great many beings that on Earth are called animals. But there, you don't relate to them that way. Everyone on that planet gets to know everybody else personally, so I was able to make a personal connection—you understand, make friends—with a lot of beings that on this planet would be considered animals.

Can you say which ones? Dolphins?

No, like mountain lions and bears, but they were a little different on that planet. So them and others. Then I had an Earth life . . . I won't talk too much; it's not my book. It's not about my life.

How did you gain the abilities to become a mystical man?

That's why I mentioned that life. Because I became acquainted with all different kinds of beings, and when you become acquainted with all different kinds of beings, even human beings, you grow spiritually. Did you know that?

No.

Think of all the types of human beings—races and cultures and nationalities. If you made friends with people of different races, cultures and nationalities, you would grow spiritually because you would have to stretch. You would have to stretch and adapt to their ways, and any time you stretch on the feeling level . . . see, it's not just stretching mentally, to understand. You would stretch on the feeling level so that you could relate and feel comfortable with them, and do what's necessary for them to feel comfortable with you. You would stretch your feeling capacity and you would grow spiritually. Feelings and spirit are connected, just like that [put his first and second fingers together]—solidly together.

Solidly together. That's very important, because Zoosh keeps telling us to meet other people, but the way you said it makes it all much clearer.

Now you see why.

Yes.

So, then, an Earth life I lived was helpful, because I was alone a lot in that life and it taught me how to enjoy being alone. Now, in the life I live as Reveals the Mysteries, I'm not alone as much, but there are many times when I am alone and so it does not bother me.

Digging Disturbs the Earth

The farm life would have really gotten you connected to the Earth in a special way, wouldn't it?

I don't know; I wasn't comfortable with that life when I looked at it, because it was about something that was foreign to me. You understand that farmers dig in the Earth; they disturb the Earth. From my perspective, they harm the Earth. We didn't dig; our people didn't believe in digging. When you dig in the Earth, it's like . . . it would be like digging in a person. The Earth doesn't like it; she recoils. Do you understand this from what you've been taught recently?

Yes, yes.

So my idea, looking at the farmer holding his tool that he used to dig in the Earth—I recoiled from that.

I never looked at it that way; it's considered natural in these times. That's what you do to get food. You plant it, then you grow it.

Different times, different ways of being.

Yes. So that really explains . . . you called in the mountain lion and the bear because they were familiar to you from your life on Sirius. Things relate.

That's right, because I understood them as beings, plus in my Earth life I had often met mountain lions or bears or other animals whom I had a good feeling for. And with this good feeling, we would have a foundation, because I realized that they would always know more than I do. Only as I became more educated and wise were there occasions when I might be able to help them.

Helping a Mountain Lion, and the Physical Feeling of Being Safe

Once I was out walking from village to village with Speaks of Many Truths when he was young (about twelve), and there was a big wounded mountain lion coming toward us. Speaks of Many Truths ran back and went to get his spear, and I said, "No, no, no." He said, "Wounded! He might harm us; not himself!"—you know, when people talk when they're excited, they drop some words. And I said, "No, no; she's coming for help. I know this one."

So the mountain lion came up, and she had lost a lot of blood. She came near me and laid down on a rock, a big rock that was smooth across the top. And I went over and did some energy things and was able to take care of the mountain lion. We took care of the mountain lion for about three days, sort of did something with the wound so that the wound healed up or was on its way to healing up. The mountain lion couldn't really get up for about three days, so we had to stay there and protect her.

So we did that, and then we tried to feed her—but, you know, it's not the same. You go out and hunt, and even if you kill an animal like a mountain lion might kill and try to feed it, it's not the same. It would be like . . . think about it: If an animal in your time killed another animal, you might be uncomfortable cooking and eating that meat. It's the same. We would kill an animal and try to feed her, but she couldn't do it. She sucked in some of the juices—that's all. And we gave her water, of course, during this time—that helped a lot. So it was okay; that was fine. By the time three days went by, she could get up and move around. She still couldn't go out and hunt, though, so we would hunt and she would suck in the juices, and that helped.

After about five days, she left, walking very slowly; she walked away and turned back, looked, nodded, and went on. I'm sure she walked very slowly to get back to her home, and by that time she could lean her head down and drink for herself. I would think maybe that it was another two or three days before she could hunt, so it was probably a hungry time for her. But I like to think she survived, for a time anyway.

Isn't that incredible, your closeness to all beings? It's certainly something we've lost.

A lot of it has to do with feeling safe. If you as an individual, a human, feel safe, and then you focus in on the feeling of feeling safe, then instead of it being something that is within you . . . say you feel safe as a person—that's within you. It might emanate out a ways into your energy body, but it is part of you. But if you focus into the feeling, the physical feeling of being safe, then it radiates around you for a great distance, maybe fifty feet, sixty feet. And so anybody who comes into that, if that being is sensitive and open, like an animal, then it will feel safe. It knows you are safe, and it will know that it is safe in that energy.

So that's what attracted the mountain lion to you—she could feel the safety?

Yes, and she also could tell I was open, and I knew she was coming for a long time before she made herself known. She was not offended by Speaks of Many Truths' surprise; she knew I would instruct him.

A lost innocence.

You know, one of the main reasons for this book is to help people to be able to find, not just their lost innocence, but what helps them. Often what helps you can also help others. In this case, by teaching Speaks of Many Truths things, yes, he learned, but he also passed on that teaching to others, helped others—see? And then in the case of the mountain lion, that was direct help. So teaching him, helping her—everybody gains.

Well, in this case, the teaching you gave Speaks of Many Truths is going to spread out through the dissemination of these books.

It will go out; it will pick up a bit once more people know about it. Right now, it's still kind of a secret. But it's like loyal fans . . . people find out about it, they're excited and they tell their friends. It's been more word of mouth. But that will change.

Learning the Ways of Sacred Hunting

You have looked into the Earth now and you know our present situation. How would you approach it today if you were to teach a student? How would your teaching change from what you taught Speaks of Many Truths?

Well, for starters I'd do what is being done here, channeling, because you can't walk out on the land and hunt the same way—hunt as in your time, using a weapon, a gun. The problem there is that you have crime and harmful things done from person to person using the same weapon, and the gun is often not the personal weapon of the hunter. In my time, you see, you might make a spear, but you would make it and it was very specific.

You would make friends with the tree, you see; you would . . . I taught all this to Speaks of Many Truths, and he taught many others the same thing. You would make friends with the tree; you would ask the tree if it could give you one of its limbs. If it couldn't, then you would say, "Thank you, good life," like that. You would say good things to the tree, make sure it knows that you are still friends, and then you would ask another tree until eventually a tree could give you a limb. Then you would remove it only at the time that the tree said it was all right to take the limb—and then you would do it very carefully, in exactly the place that felt right to you, because that was the tree communicating to you where it was all right to cut it. It has to be in a place, see, where the tree knows it can heal that wound. So you would cut it, and then you would let the wood sit for a time. You would peel the bark and so on. In short, you would make your spear one step at a time.

Maybe you would carve some designs into it, depending on your culture. You might add this to it or add that to it and so on. You would make your spear—it was something that was gathered in a sacred manner, it was created in a sacred manner, that you created yourself. It was something that functioned best with you. Other people could take the spear and it wouldn't work so good for them; the hunt wouldn't be as successful. But when you had your spear that you created, with your energy in it and your tribal signs and your personal signs and all of these things—maybe even something tied onto the spear from previous successful hunts; I have seen different things on different spears—then it would help the spear to know, it could sense what the hunt was about or who we were looking for, what we were looking for. The spear became some*one*; it was all personal.

In your time people do not make their own gun usually, so the gun is impersonal. That is how the gun can be used in ways that are not natural. In my time with your personal spear that you would go hunting with, if you were in a battle or someone attacked you, you would never defend yourself with that spear; that spear was for hunting. You would defend yourself with something else, but you wouldn't use it for that. I have never heard of it happening, but say, for example, you stabbed a human being with the spear. Then you would have to destroy that spear, because it would have a taste for human being. It would never be a good hunting spear again. You would have to bury it, probably.

But if you were to teach a student now, you probably wouldn't teach him or her how to hunt, right?

It is not my job to teach hunting. But the reason I bring up hunting is that even though it is not my job, I had to learn. Everybody in the tribe had to learn something about hunting, even though there were hunting parties, because you walk out on your own . . . I would take my spear with me. When the hunting party was not available to bring food to me, I would have to hunt. So I would hunt, eh? So there are certain things you have to teach, but there is a lot to be gained from learning about the hunt and spiritual things—a great deal. You learn sacred hunting—very important. There are still some people doing sacred hunting in your time.

One of the ways of sacred hunting is how to call in the right animal. You don't want to be killing an animal who just had babies—if you kill that animal to eat, then the babies die too. You never do that. You call for an animal their people can spare—they are animal people—where someone can come and say, "Okay, I will miss my family, but I will come." So you don't track them so much, at least that's the way I did it. Now, I grant, the hunting parties went out and tracked, did other things, but they still also called in the animal. It's the same philosophy.

But we never killed animals who . . . you see, you don't do that; you only kill one whom their people can spare. Things like that are important, because it teaches a philosophy, don't you see? And it's part of the philosophy to learn that hunting is a sacred thing when done in a sacred way. You eat; you don't waste anything. The hide—you do something with it. And nothing gets wasted anyway, because if you can't eat it all, then there will be animals. The little ones, at the very least, will come and finish up. So nothing gets wasted.

You never hunt for sport. Sport hunting is terrible. Never fish for sport either; it is not sport for the others. If you are hungry . . . a hunting party goes out, for instance, or even I go out . . . I am hungry, I have to feed myself and maybe my student too, eh? So an animal comes whom their people can spare. But for sport? They would never send anybody for sport. So when there is sport hunting in your time and sport fishing in your time . . .

It's murder.

But not only in your time. Your people have been doing that for a while. Just killing any animal . . . others suffer, plus then those animals all distrust human beings: "Human beings are not to be trusted." In my time animals didn't have that attitude; they would say, "Oh well, they need to eat. It is a sacrifice on our part, but we knew that that sacrifice would be necessary when we came here." So we ate only what we had to. See, there's mutual respect. And then when one of our people dies, the little animals might eat too—flies and some kind of ants do that. Nothing goes to waste.

I Cannot Relate to Your Culture

If you were to teach a person now who had to live in this age, at this time, in this technology, how would you do it or how would you recommend some teacher now do it? How would you teach a child of this time?

I am not of your time; I could not do that. What I am doing now and what Speaks of Many Truths is doing now is what can be done. I do not live in your time; I am not qualified to teach as a physical person. Even if I could be a physical person in your time, if I were to magically be able to appear as myself in your time but in a physical body, I could not do it, because I am not of your time and I cannot relate to your culture—just as I could not relate to that little bit of technology then.

Your whole culture is about technology and things that I find offensive. I realize that this may sound offensive to you, my saying that, but the idea of digging in the Earth to grow food? No.

Or digging up metals.

Or the idea of digging for whatever reason. No, I would be not the right teacher, because I would not . . . teachers need to be people of your times so that they can speak to you eye to eye. I am not in your time, but there are some things I can talk about and Speaks of Many Truths can talk about, as you can tell by reading these books . . .

That are applicable for this time.

. . . that still work for these times. It's one thing to speak about it and help you, but I know that when Speaks of Many Truths and myself and also Zoosh talk for these books, that these words are just as much addressed to the teachers who will teach others as they are to students who are just interested and may do some things, maybe not others.

But you're able to teach in Sirius even though you're a spiritual being. You're not embodied in Sirius at this time, are you?

When I go there, I will take form if necessary. But they do not have discomfort, so everything is different. Even the tiniest things that you don't think of as being the slightest bit uncomfortable don't happen there. Would you like an example?

Please.

You are walking down the street and there is a tree, and a leaf falls from the tree. As it falls, it gently brushes your face. It is beautiful, but it is startling. That would never happen there. You don't think of that as uncomfortable, but startling can be uncomfortable. It's important to give you an example of something like that, that you would never think of as being uncomfortable.

A Meeting with Pleiadians

This planet must be pretty interesting for people who are used to that level of harmony.

I believe that is why the extraterrestrials, as you call them, have such a difficult time visiting here. They do not walk amongst you because it is not possible for them to accommodate it. I met one, and Speaks of Many Truths was with me.

Tell me about that.

Well, I'll tell you about that because it is so different and an exception to this book. We were far away at this time. We weren't going to a village to see a student; we were just going out to this area that I felt drawn to. I said, "Come with me," and at first I said, "Do you feel drawn?" And Speaks of Many Truths said, "No" [chuckles]. So I said, "Well, let's take some supplies, and then we will go out to this place." And he said, "How far are we going to go?" He was still young then [chuckles]. He was still nine years old. He said, "How far are we going to go?" And I said, "Oh, we won't walk any more than three light times"—you understand, three days. He said, "Okay, let's go" [in a reluctant tone of voice]. See, by that time he had made friends of children in the village, and you have to remember, he was still a child.

It sounded like work.

Like . . . yes. So we went, and then it was fun. We walked and walked for a long time, walking toward a direction that my people didn't normally go because there was just kind of open space and not many trees, and you had to walk a few hours to get water. So we brought some water with us, which was not easy to do in my time; we brought some and were careful with it.

Anyway, we got to this space and I felt this energy—it was very strong. We were sitting on a small flat rock, the two of us, and he said, "What are we doing here?" [Laughs.] He was still a little boy then, see? "What are we doing here?" And I said, "Something's going to happen." "Is it going to be a good thing?" he asked. [Chuckles.] Speaks of Many Truths is good-natured; he lets me tell you these stories about him when he was still a youngster.

But that night, a bright light woke us up, and this thing came out of the sky. It stopped just before it touched the ground, and some things came out of it, and then it settled down a bit more, rested on those things like legs. And then we saw it, we looked at it. Speaks of Many Truths was pulling on my arm; he wanted to hide. And I said, "No, no; this is the energy that I felt, to come to this place. And this thing, whatever it is, it has the same energy, see? It's exactly the same energy. So I know that this is why we're here."

"Okay," he said, in our language. But he still got behind me [chuckles]. Then there was an opening in the side of this bright light thing, and out stepped someone—a woman. She was not dressed exactly like our people, but she was not that much different—though there was kind of a light around her. And what I know now is that it was like a barrier between dimensions so that she could be dressed in the way she wished to be dressed, without wearing a suit to protect her.

We didn't say anything, but she did this [puts his right hand out and motions to come in]. She motioned us, and we walked toward this thing, and then this object slid out of the big bright light thing.

Like a ramp?

Yes, but it wasn't like a machine; it looked like it was alive, kind of like a rainbow, only more solid. This was important to me, because if it had been like a machine . . . remember how I felt?

Yes.

I would not have liked it.

So they were tuned in to you enough to know that.

They knew that. Well, I feel they invited me because I felt the energy and felt drawn to go; I felt invited. So we walked up this rainbowlike thing. We went inside, and there was a lot of light—not too bright, but everything was light. There were plants in there growing, not ones I recognized. And I saw an animal who looked like a deer but not quite—a little different than a deer, a little smaller.

Then I saw a boy; he was different. Now I know he was like a Chinese boy, maybe about the age of Speaks of Many Truths then. And the woman brought Speaks of Many Truths and the other boy together, and the other boy . . . I do not know how he knew our language, but he knew it.

They had translators?

Perhaps that was it. He touched Speaks of Many Truths, and the moment he touched him, then Speaks of Many Truths could understand what he was saying. Before, when that little boy spoke, we could not understand him. But he touched Speaks of Many Truths' shoulder, and then Speaks of Many Truths could understand him. And the boy took Speaks of Many Truths off somewhere—not pulling him off, but showing him things. You can ask Speaks of Many Truths later what he showed him.

The woman took me into another place and showed me something like this [draws Fig. 8-1]. It was like a work of art. It was something that looked like that, only there were lines.

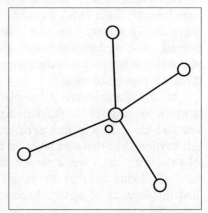

Fig. 8-1. The star map shown to Reveals the Mysteries by the Pleiadian woman.

Oh, a star map.

It kind of looked like that [draws]. Something like that. But I'm not sure. And she said they were from this place called the Pleiades, and that they had visited Earth a lot and they usually would go farther south, where it was very warm. Then she made like a picture on the wall, and she showed a place that I know now was high up in the mountains in Peru, where they went a lot in those times. Then she showed a picture of them interacting with the people and being there all the time. And she said that the people down there, one of the mystical people, told her about our people, so she wanted to come and visit.

Then on that picture thing, she showed me her world—probably not everything about it, but what she felt was good to show. And then I described my world. I started talking, and she didn't understand me at first, and then she did a universal signal [meaning stop] with the hand, and she reached out and touched me on my shoulder. Then I found myself doing the most amazing thing: I would speak her language, I was speaking her language!

Really?

I didn't know it; I would be forming the words in my own language, to talk, but then I was speaking her language. It was very unusual—it never happened to me before or since.

And then when she talked, you heard it in your language?

Yes. So I have to think that maybe she was thinking it in her language, but it came out in my language. It must have been the same way with the other boy who took Speaks of Many Truths somewhere. It was very interesting.

So it was a spiritual way, maybe not a translator?

That's what I think, because I didn't see any device in this vehicle, but who knows? But it didn't seem like a vehicle; it seemed like light. It didn't seem like a machine. Like I said, there were plants inside and this deerlike animal. And we had a nice visit like that. I explained my life a bit, and she said that her people had a special affection for Earth people, and I said, "That's a wonderful thing."

She brought me over to the plant, one that I really liked. It had big unusual-looking leaves, different colors than I'm used to in a plant. And she had me feel the plant's auric energy—not touch, just feel it. I never felt anything like that on a plant on Earth. It felt more like the auric energy of an animal, but it was a plant as far as I could tell. Very unusual. And later on I found out that the thing I was calling a plant was a plant, but it had the capacity to absorb knowledge and wisdom from anything that came close to it.

While you were feeling its aura, it was digesting your knowledge, then?

It was absorbing what it could about me and what I knew. Later on, like I say, when I had more of myself, like I speak to you now, then I found out that she had taken a lot of training in mystical ways. She had had mystical-ways training on her planet and mystical-ways training from the people she met in the Peruvian mountains, and she wanted to have some mystical-ways training from me too. So she was, of her people, a mystical woman—that's how she knew that in order for us to come on this bright-light thing, it would have to be like a living thing, not a machine.

So we had that nice visit, and then she said she had to go. I hadn't seen Speaks of Many Truths the whole time, and then the other boy came and he delivered [chuckles] Speaks of Many Truths back, and we walked out and waved at them both, and that was that. Then we sat down on a rock, and it closed up, the ramp went inside—what you call a ramp—and then it went up and was gone.

Well, did you teach her something while she was there?

No. I spoke about my life, but she didn't ask me to teach anything, and now, knowing what I know now, I see that it wasn't necessary because the plant being absorbed whatever it was she wanted to know that I could teach her. Because she couldn't stay there . . . looking on it now, she couldn't stay there for the years that it would take to teach her things. It's not like you sit someone down and say, "Here, let me show you how to do this." It's a whole thing—you live together, like Speaks of Many Truths lived with me. Things come up on a daily basis: "What about this? What about that?" And then the teacher does this and, "If that's the way teacher does it, I'll try it that way as the student," and then the student does that. In short, it takes time, but she didn't have that much time.

So you think she could get the knowledge back from the plant, then?

Yes. I feel that the plant being . . . she would know how to ask the plant being to teach her from me.

So look at that! You're teaching on the Pleiades. [Chuckles.]

Well, it's not like an ego thing, eh? It's not like that, because the teachings came to me from a sacred manner—and it's the same. Sacred teaching passes on from one being to another.

No, but it's usually . . . you know, people go, "Oh, ETs, they're so wise," but in this case, they wanted to be taught rather than to teach, so that's interesting.

She did, yes. I think maybe the boy might have been one of her students.

She didn't say her name?

No, she didn't say her name, she didn't say the boy's name. But he might have given a name to Speaks of Many Truths. I don't know; we didn't talk about it much. You will have to ask Speaks of Many Truths.

I would think the first thing you would do would be to share your experiences.

No, because it wasn't about the teaching. Remember, he was living with me to learn the things I had to teach. This thing that they were, what their life was about, wasn't anything about what our life was about. So what is the point of talking about it? I had an interesting experience, but it didn't have anything to do with my life and my ways and what I had to teach. So we did not talk about it much.

But he seemed happy and comfortable with the experience.

Yes. If he had been upset, then we would have talked, but he seemed fine, so I didn't see any reason to talk about it. And being a student, he was receptive to things that I said, right? So he wasn't going to talk about things to me. He might have told his friends—that's possible. You'll have to ask him.

I think he had many experiences like that, of meeting star beings.

Then I'll say, good life.

Interacting in Harmony with Your World

Speaks of Many Truths
December 4, 2001

All right. Greetings. This is Speaks of Many Truths.

Welcome! Welcome! I so enjoyed your teacher, Reveals the Mysteries, yesterday.

Yes, he is a wonderful being. When I was a boy, I remember how much I looked up to him. That time with the lion . . . after that I just thought the world of him, as anyone might, especially a child, to see something like that. But that was an exceptional experience that I remembered for quite some time afterward. I used to have a dream where I would see this thing. At first I thought it was a tube, and then the tube would wave, and then it was kind of bristly on one end. Some time later I realized that that was the mountain lion's tail. It looked like that.

Speaks of Many Truths' Experience with the Pleiadians

What did the little Chinese boy say to you on the Pleiadean spaceship? Reveals the Mysteries said he never asked you what your experience was because you seemed okay with it.

That was quite an adventure. The boy was well experienced in flight. He knew this person, this woman, on the ship, and he had been in that vehicle many times. We walked around something, and I couldn't see my teacher anymore. Then we stepped into this alcove, and he said, "This is a place where I come sometimes." You understand that it took us a moment to sort out how to talk, but once we got that, then he said, "This is where I come." And he sat down on one side and I sat down on the other side, and suddenly he did something with his hand and between us there was a picture. He said, "This is how I look at things when I'm on the ship," and then there were pictures. It was like a tube of light, but you could put your hand right through it—it wasn't solid.

Was it like what we call a hologram?

It had depth, but it had a sparkly quality to it. I think it was a liquid-light device on the ship. And so the living-light particles would form certain pictures, and then as the pictures would change, the particles would move about—that's when the sparkle took place. He showed me where the ship was from and a little bit about the way the place looked. It had its own beauty, but I thought at the time that it didn't have the beauty of Earth. He said that it had changed over the years and that a long time ago it looked more like Earth but at this time it didn't look like it as much. Then he showed me, in that picture, where he lived, and it looked to me like a city inside a wall. That was interesting.

Then he said, "I'm going to tell you a secret," [chuckles] the way children do. And he said that he had no family inside that wall, that he had been sent out of the city since there was no one to look after him. In those days they sometimes would send children out if there was no one to look after them, so they wouldn't beg on the streets or get into trouble. It seems hardhearted when you look that way, but that was the custom in that place at that time. When he was wandering, he came upon this vehicle, and the lady took him in and he said that he would be going back with them. And so he was excited about that.

Then he asked me if I wanted something to remember him by and to remember all the things he'd showed me plus some other things that I could look at if I liked. And I said, "What would that be?" because by then I had shown him my long vision, and it's possible with a sensitive person, well-trained like that, that you can let him see through your eyes—the way Robert [the channel] talks about what he's been shown: how to extend into the cat's body, to see through the cat's eyes. If you trust someone and that person is trustworthy of the energy and so on, you can let him look through your eyes and then he can see long vision.

So that's what I let him do. I said, "I will be able to see you on your planet if you want me to." And he said, "No, that is good, but I want to give you something that we can both see each other with, because you will be able to see me with long vision, but I haven't had the training so I won't be able to see you."

Liquid-Light Communication with
My Friend Living in the Pleiades

So the boy said, "I can give you this thing," and he pointed to this part of my hand, my left hand [just above the wrist, on the back of the hand, between the wrist and the fingers]. He said, "There is something we can put in there. It will be like light. It won't take up any space in your hand, but if it feels good to you, then I can put it in there. Then when you want to talk to me, you can do this."

Just press it like a button?

Not quite; look at the position [the thumb of the right hand is against the lower palm of the left, and then the first finger is pushing on the place where the light would be implanted]. Yes, very slight, but pushed gently. And then it would be like he would know I'm going to talk to him or speak with him, or if he wanted to talk to me or speak to me, I would feel a slight pulse there—not uncomfortable. That's what he said. And I did not know . . . my teacher was not there, and I didn't know if it was acceptable to do this. So he showed me that it wasn't like a device.

Like a technology?

It wasn't like that. He said that some of the liquid light would go into my hand and stay there while my body was intact, and that after I died, it would simply return. So what I did is what I had been shown by using the wand [see p. 6]. He asked the liquid light to not have pictures so that I could just feel it, light itself. I pointed with the wand toward the light, and it felt very good to me, so I felt it might be all right. He said, "Okay," and then he did something with his other hand. Some of the light coming out from that tube of light, which was about this wide . . .

Two feet?

No, maybe eighteen inches, sixteen inches, something like that.

It looked more like two feet to me.

Perhaps you're right. And then little bits of the light came from all over the tube—not in the same place. This must have been volunteers, particles of light who wanted to come to me, because when I did the wand, plus I'd been sitting there, it could feel me. It came over and it was very small, but it's a funny thing: You know where the light is in the sky, with the Sun. It's something unusual to look at the back of your hand and see . . . it wasn't as bright as the Sun, but it was a little like a ball of light. It was very small—in your terms, maybe about an eighth of an inch. It sat on the back of my hand for a moment, and then I could feel something go inside. And there it was.

Now, a funny thing: Later on in my life, when my wrists started to hurt a bit, as I got older . . .

Like arthritis?

Yes. Only my right wrist did; my left wrist never did. I think that little light was able to prevent that discomfort. But I don't know; that's what I think.

When you were showing what the boy did, it was like you were putting your hands on the side, like there was a console and he was pushing a button.

Yes, but I couldn't see anything. What you say makes sense. It would have been . . . I'm sitting in this chair. This is just what it looked like, except for the chair. It was not this wide of space to rest your arms on, but there was something to rest your arms on, and then underneath . . . he would turn his fingers underneath that, and he'd press something. But I did not see anything. So it must have been something that only he and I'm sure the woman knew.

Something he could tell by touching something?

That's right, but it wasn't obvious to me.

So Reveals the Mysteries never knew that this happened?

We didn't talk about it. He just had told me that he felt this energy and he felt attracted to go there, and he invited me to come. So I was happy to go.

But he's listening now, so he's going to learn this for the first time.

Well, I think he probably knew it, found out after his physical death, don't you? Then you know more. I don't think he's learning it for the first time. But he didn't know it then, in his physical life; plus he didn't tell you about it because I'm sure he wanted me to tell you. Then you could ask me, because it was my experience. That is our way. We do not usually relate the experiences of others but encourage you to speak to the others directly.

So did you use it frequently? Did you correspond with the boy as he grew up?

We both used it. Sometimes I'd feel a little pulse, and if I could talk to him then or communicate in the way we did, I would. But sometimes I couldn't. And then when I could I'd reach over and do this, press that part of my hand, and sometimes he would be there, meaning he could respond then, and sometimes he couldn't. When he couldn't be there, he would leave me . . . not a message but he would leave me this color. So I would touch it and I would see these colors, and it was very pretty, and then it was not there anymore. So we didn't always connect, but when we did, it was nice. And he stayed in touch from time to time. We spoke from time to time all throughout the rest of our lives.

Was he still alive when you passed over?

Oh, he must have been, yes.

Were you able to tell him that you were leaving?

Oh, I think he must have known, don't you?

I don't know.

Well, the light was there, and after I had died, the light would return to the place, so my feeling is that he would have found out.

What a story he must have had: a little Chinese boy living in the Pleiades!

Well, I think that he didn't think about himself being Chinese—he was a person. Just like I didn't think about myself being Native American (that's a nice term you have these days)—I was a person. We just looked different from each other. He wasn't wearing the kind of clothing that he wore when the woman picked him up and gave him a life, because otherwise he would have died. She had perhaps made something for him, or however they made things on the ship. He had on this garment that was very beautiful, like the kind of thing that people probably would have worn in China in the past if they were very wealthy. So I think maybe she made it for him. It was like a free-flowing garment, very comfortable and very silky and very beautiful, with patterns in it.

Like a kimono?

That is a Japanese word, I think. It was not like a kimono, because a kimono is a garment that wraps around you, and then you wrap something around it and it fits you closer. But it wasn't like that, that thing he wore; it just hung out to the sides without that obi around it, as in Japan. But it was very beautiful and it had designs on it that looked like dragons and things like that. I don't know where he got it or where she got it. He would wear a little hat with it too sometimes. It was not quite blue and not quite purple, and then the designs were gold color. It was very, very nice; it looked very comfortable.

What an experience! Did you ever share that experience with anyone? Did you tell your friends or your wife?

I told my wife.

Did she see the pictures, then?

Pictures?

When you communicated.

Oh, no. No, when I would press it, I would see it in my mind's eye. No, she could not see it. But I would describe it.

Was your wife from your tribe?

Yes. It's good that way. She knew me, I knew her; there were no secrets, eh? [Chuckles.] No surprises.

And your children, were any of them trained as mystical men or women?

One had training for medicine woman, but she wasn't the one who actually inherited the job, so she was like . . .

A backup?

Well, it was good because she would sometimes go out with groups or hunting parties, something like that, to be there to help them if they needed help, which happens when you're hunting. Sometimes people get hurt.

Women Are the Visionaries

Could you talk about masculine and feminine energy and how you perceive that?

It is not unlike what you have heard from other beings before, where the feminine is intended to pass life through her, so she is the source of life. In that sense, she is more connected to the Creator and needs to have time, opportunities. She needs to be somewhat protected so that when she needs to do mystical things . . . any woman needs to do mystical things at her time of creation, when she is prepared to create a child with a man, and at her time when she is connected to the Moon more and she passes her blood. These are mystical times for every woman, and she cannot be expected to do other things: not go hunting, not go gather wood for the fire, not fish, nothing. She needs to have this quiet time on her own, to commune with Creator or whoever her guides and teachers are, or to be with the other women to do ceremony.

So the man's role, then, is to do everything. If there are children, then the man looks after the children. If she wants one or more of her children with her, maybe the girl children at that time, that is up to her to say so. But it's not for the man to say, "Take the girls with you"—none of that. It is up to her. So if there are a few children, then the man has to do everything. He might have to ask his brother to help out or something like that. So that's why I say that.

Now, the woman being the source of life and therefore being directly connected to spirit and the communication with spirit-being feelings—that is all part of the feminine. But the man, not having that direct connection to creation, has to make do with what's left [laughs]. That would be the physical, though the woman, of course, has the physical also. The woman has all of these things, but those things especially that I mentioned are heightened. The man has to use his physical and he has to use his mental because he is not born to the capacity to commune with Creator, because creation does not pass through him.

Some tiny part of creation passes through him when creating, when doing his part to create the child, but that's all. Creation doesn't grow in him. He does not deliver creation, a human being. And so there's only a tiny part. So the man has to use his mind to understand things. But the mind is not as fertile a place; it doesn't have the great depth and capacity that feeling and spirit and creation . . . in short, the mind is much more limited. That's why the man needs to learn from the woman, because she is the visionary. She is born to it, even if she is not in her nature a visionary. If she is nurtured in these roles as our people were in our times, then all women would be visionary to some degree. Granted, if well trained, she might be a mystical woman or medicine woman. But all women have that capacity, to have the vision and a strong connection to Creator.

So the man has to be instructed and guided by the woman sometimes; other times he uses what he has, which is the brain. A woman has a brain too, but she does not have to use only that. A man has the brain and the physical, so he has to learn things and be instructed by things with older men on the basis of what he thinks, what is knowledge passed on down: "This is how we do it. This is how I solved that. You can see if it works for you," like that. Whereas women's stories and women's teachings would have to do with connecting woman to the mystical, creation, visions and all that. Yes, in your time, people like to learn about visions and have visions, men and women alike, but in my time, if we wanted or needed a vision, other than the mystical man, one would go to any woman, because she would have been trained in these connections.

So everyone has all these capacities to a degree, but a man is primarily physical and mental, and a woman is primarily spiritual and feeling. And the third thing for women is that a woman is also creation.

We've certainly lost a lot of that.

I feel it is very practical, don't you?

Yes.

It is practical and it recognizes the obvious. Woman is clearly connected to creation; man does not grow a child [chuckles]. Woman is connected to creation, and what goes on in woman for that creation has to be honored. At those special times of the month, woman has to be protected and allowed to connect with Creator and other mystical things if she chooses. So she cannot be expected to do things she does at other times.

And this was not just the teaching in your tribe, but this was pretty much representative of the teaching of most of the tribes?

I can't say that, but with the people whom I met, it was understood. To use a term in your time, to us in those days it was obvious. We thought it was obvious, but later on when settlers came from across the ocean, that's when those who succeeded me, who lived on after me, found out that what was obvious to them and to everybody else was not even known or understood by these people. That's why the native peoples had pity on those strangers who arrived, because they were obviously . . . they didn't know anything about life. They were just struggling to survive because they didn't know anything about life. They didn't honor it, didn't appreciate it. To them life was more of something you suffered and were annoyed by. So native peoples had pity on them and brought them food and so on. If they had known what would happen . . .

They probably wouldn't have.

I am not saying that.

But this is the way you were taught, and that's the way the human body works. On other planets, men can give birth; it's not so restricted.

I do not know of that. But if you say so, maybe you know that; that's fine. But that is not my knowledge. I grant that I can look at things, use long vision, but . . . I can see things from a distance, but I usually look at things for a reason, because it can help. I am not sure that this is something I need to know.

Mystical Women Were Better Than Mystical Men

This is such an honoring and such a beautiful presentation of how you lived.

It is helpful to understand that the knowledge and wisdom that I have been taught and have been able to share sometimes . . . to see the environment that I was nurtured in is helpful. I don't really care for the word "environment," because it doesn't have enough love in it, but to see the . . . it is like a bowl, the loving circumstance in which I was raised and our philosophy and our beliefs and what we knew to be true. It is then easier to understand why I'm the way I am.

But as a mystical man, then, you proved that it wasn't the function only of women to have visions, because you were trained . . .

I didn't have to prove it; it was understood that for mystical people, a mystical man would be born to certain capacities, meaning he would have those capacities when born so that when nurtured he could develop them. A mystical woman would be naturally born to those capacities but would have them heightened.

With the training?

No, it would be heightened so that it would be noticed, because all women are born with that capacity. But for the elders to see that a young girl had these capacities, she would have had to demonstrate something in her personality that they would see was more so than usual, which is why mystical women in our time were considered to be the best—not meaning better than or in terms of rank or more valuable. But if your tribesperson was a mystical woman, then you probably had someone who could do more. But if you didn't have a mystical woman, then you made do with a mystical man.

That may have been a misunderstanding . . .

No, it isn't—not in my eyes. I agree, from what I have seen. I have spoken to many mystical men and women, and I would have to say that taken as a whole, mystical women are better at it.

Better at the ability to tune in to things? To see visions? To be empathetic?

Better at everything. And it comes easier; they learn quicker. I spoke to another teacher once like Reveals the Mysteries, but for another tribe. We were talking, and I happened to mention how long it took me to learn long vision when I was a boy. He wasn't trying to make me feel bad, but later on, much later in our talk the next day—actually, it was at night—one of his students came by, a little girl [chuckles] who was perhaps seven years old, and she could do long vision. And he laughed and he said the way people do so they don't offend you, "Don't feel bad, but she learned long vision in about an hour."

[Laughs.] *But it only took you ten days.*

In terms of that time. It took me ten days; she got it in about an hour.

Yes, but ten days . . . most men would have taken years, I'm sure.

I'm not trying to make comparisons; it is not a competition. I'm just trying to give you an idea of the difference. And therefore, if she could learn that, then she would be able to learn so much more by the time she was ready to begin to help people and do things, and was old enough, mature enough—not in years, but mature enough—where she could take on such responsibilities, where she would know much more. And so, of course, that's why I said, when I met mystical women, that there was so much more they could do.

The Mystical Person Protects the Tribe by Communicating with All Life

Either you or Reveals the Mysteries used the phrase, "The mystical man is to protect the tribe." Is that basically his function?

That's right. That was the basic function. The mystical person's job was to protect the tribe. And the medicine woman's duties and responsibilities related more to what you have in your time, like a doctor or a nurse. But in my time, the mystical person knew all of life, the energies—plants and so on—and could communicate with them. That's one of the ways you know danger is coming. Now, perhaps you would not know exactly when something was coming when you would get a feeling—sometimes, you'd say, a vague feeling. You might get a vague feeling, but it could be many things. So having the ability to commune with all life is very helpful. The hawk comes by, and it might make a sound that would sound like a bird, but then you know what's coming. It's a feeling. And very often there's a picture with it.

I remember once . . . this was unusual, because we were hunting, but I remember that once a deer practically ran into the village where we were, and it was so unexpected and so unusual that I ran up quickly to stop anyone from doing anything. It was a male, and he stood there and looked at me with . . . deer usually have certain expressions, but he looked at me and he was very serious. Someone said, "He's going to charge you," and I said, "No, something else." He had put his head down, and that's why people thought he was going to charge. But he put his head down on purpose, and then he looked at me very strongly, and I could feel that something was coming. And then when I understood something was coming, and I could see that it was people, the moment I got that picture [snaps fingers], he turned around and ran back into the woods.

It was very kind of him to bring that knowledge. Then we weren't sure what to do, so we sent out a group, a party of people—not a war party or even a hunting party, but something a little in between, a group who looks for things.

A scouting group?

Something like that. We saw the people coming, and it was true that they looked very warlike. They had weapons and they looked like they had their ceremonial war dress on. But fortunately—this was such a blessing—one of the people in the scouting party recognized these people, and it wasn't about war. Even though it was war dress, it wasn't about that. When he recognized an individual, then he made himself known—from a distance, so they weren't frightened—and he yelled the name of the individual and waved. Then the people stopped, and this young man in our group went down and talked to them.

It turned out that they were on their way to a ceremony, but they did not realize that their journey would take them right through our village. To do the ceremony, they had to dress in their war garments, but it wasn't about war. So we welcomed them, and they stayed an evening with us and told us some of their stories and went on the next day. But it was very good that the deer had—to put it so you understand the level of the animal wisdom to our own—pity on us and came and told us. Just like when my future generations met the settlers coming over and I said they had pity on them? It was the same with the deer. The deer had pity on us.

Because he was afraid you might shoot at them?

The deer had pity on us, but that was not the exact reason. It was because our consciousness was so feeble compared to the deer's consciousness and the consciousness of most of the animals, that the deer had pity on us and came to warn us of the danger. And remember what I said: The deer put its head down and someone said, "He's going to charge you." In other words, that's the battle position, see? The deer took the battle position and then looked at me without charging. That's how I knew that someone was coming who might be warlike.

Yes, that was in battle position.

So the deer took pity on us. Was that not kindness?

Well, that was incredibly kind, and the fact that you could interpret it was the blessing.

That is an example of how a mystical person protects the tribe because of the learned ability to communicate with all life. And then when other beings, other life, take pity on you, which they do, very often then they will tell you things.

Another Way Mystical People Protect the Tribe

I remember once I was with some of my people who were fishing, and there was an old one whom we would never try to capture. The old one, the old fish, came over to me and spoke to me and said, "Would you mind not fishing as often? Because we are having trouble creating more of our kind. And if you could not fish every day but maybe fish every third day . . . could you do that for a while, until I say it's all right?" And then I said, "I will tell the people."

So I did tell them, and we were able to do that for, oh, maybe two cycles of the Moon—not quite two months in your time. And that was enough. We just had to send out . . . instead of one hunting party, we had to send out two hunting parties and they had to go a little farther. And what you did, see, if there was meat leftover, was you dried it, and then you could eat that dried meat at times. It's very good. So that's what we did; we used some of our dried meat and the fish were able to rebuild. If that had not been a mystical person, to get that message . . .

You would have fished them out, and then you wouldn't have had any fish.

Well, they might have come closer because they would have gone and there would not have been many, just the old ones. Then we would have figured it out. But by that time, it would have taken maybe a year to rebuild their number. And if something like that happened, then we would have had to move the village permanently. So that's another way the mystical man or woman might protect the people.

Education in Your Time Has to Change

If you compare that with the way we live now, it's a different world!

It's a different world, that's right. That's why these books are so important, because they remind people of how it can be. That's the important thing: This is not supposed to show to you what has been lost; it's supposed to remind you of what can be. And then perhaps some parents, when they see that their children have some talent or ability, they will encourage it and not just send them to school to become like everybody else.

This whole school thing is something that I feel is not good for your children. I grant that it is important to be taught; I was in "school." So there is the school that is necessary, that teaches you the things you need to know to do your work and make your contribution. But I do not see what good it does to learn the birthdays of famous people in your culture. When will you ever use that? What good is that? And teaching everybody the same thing . . . the reason you do that is that you have forgotten or you do not know in your culture how to know what child would do what and what child would do something else. So you teach them all this same thing—much of which they will never use the rest of their lives—and then they never find out what they're good at.

That's why we're putting these books out—not to condemn what you do, but to say, "Here is another way, and it honors the individual, and it improves the quality of life of all people—for you and others—and it helps you to be sensitive." Creator has created you as humans to be sensitive; it's not a failing, it is not a *problem*. It is intended that you be sensitive so that you can feel what is for you and what is for others, and so that you can see, because you're older and more experienced, that this child is, in your time, going to be a good musician, and that this other child might be a good doctor or nurse—things like that.

Well, education has to change, because right now it has been deliberately dumbed down a little bit because of the controlling element on Earth here. Many people are working from within the system to make changes—not toward what you had, but at least to make it where children actually learn.

Start with the Desire to Improve the Quality of *Your* Life

I've asked you this once before, but I'm not really clear on it. Say again what you feel spiritual mastery is in the context of these books.

Spiritual mastery is more broad; it is the underpinnings of multiple ways of being and multiple ways of understanding, appreciating and interacting in harmony with your world. That is why you have all been spiritual masters before you came here in at least one life somewhere, in some form. But there were many different types of spiritual mastery, so that is why we can wander around a bit more in this book, whereas in material mastery it was clearly about the Earth, and in physical mastery it was clearly about the physical body. But spiritual mastery is a little more broad, so that's why I've not been too strict about staying to the subject— because touching on different things might have connections to types of spiritual mastery.

So what's the next step? What do we do now? We're in a life that has a lot of responsibilities, not much time and no training from childhood as you had. It's completely different.

Ultimately, there's plenty of time, because your bodies are temporary vehicles, but your souls, your spirits, are immortal. So there's all the time in the world.

But to help ourselves and the other humans on the planet now, where do we start? Where does the reader start?

The reader starts with the desire to improve the quality of his or her own life, his or her family's life, perhaps, and the lives of all beings. But you cannot have a desire just to improve the quality of life for all beings without having the desire to improve the quality of your own life, given the type of life systems, governments, pursuits and ways of being that exist in your time—because you can no longer live in the ashram and make direct improvements in the quality of people's lives on a large scale. You might be able to do it for the people in the village and make a fine contribution, and that is still worthy, but people who are going to read these books may wish to do things on a broader scale.

But I cannot accentuate enough the importance of wanting to improve the quality of *your* life as well. It's not being greedy; it just includes you in the value of all beings. It's all beings as all beings—not all beings minus yourself. That is something that is surprisingly not understood very well by even the most talented spiritual students.

I guess it's the training of a lot of the religions: "Do for others." You know, they come first, the group instead of the individual.

Sometimes, but sometimes it's other ways. The world in which you find yourself requires the spiritual student to be included; you cannot just sit in your cave high up on the hill and do good work energetically and with benevolent magic. Granted, there will be some who will do that and might be of good help, but what's really needed are people to be out amongst the people doing things.

So when you read these books, all of them (the *Explorer Race* series, but especially the books that are giving you homework assignments, such as the *Shamanic Secrets* series, *The Explorer Race and Isis* and so on), then be thinking about what you can do, what you can apply with people in general—always and only people who want your help. Don't try to visit your philosophy on those who have their own. Then you just make trouble. The point of this work is to make good things, not to make trouble. It's a sad thing, how much trouble has been made by people who want to make your life better.

The real way you've talked about is to make your own life so loving and comfortable that others want to be like you.

This is good. Then when you are around people who are receptive, who want to learn, who want to know and who perhaps welcome that sensitivity, at least in ways that will help them to grow and be more insightful, then they will notice that something's up and worthwhile with you, and they will say so perhaps: "What are you doing?" or "You feel so great, I feel so wonderful around you. Are you doing something different? Tell me about it!" Then you can tell them a little bit, see how they react. Don't tell them the whole thing, just a little bit, and see how they like that. You can tell them that if they want to know more, you will share it. Maybe you can show them how to do the love-heat/heart-warmth/physical-warmth [see Overview].

Introducing Others to Some of the Teachings

So sharing the love-heat and disentanglement [see p. xxxi] and some of the teachings . . .

You would if you were introducing someone to something. You'd say, "Well, you could try this method to experience this warmth within you that feels very good; it's something I do and I recommend it because it has improved the quality of my life. Sometimes when you're around me, I'm just feeling it, and that's when you often react well to me." This is in general, with people, see? Just tell them. Say, "This is how it's done," or you might say, "Would you like to know how to do that?" And if they say,

"Oh, yes," then you say, "Well, I can show you in just a minute." Then they say, "Oh, wonderful!"

You show them that, and then you say, "Now practice on your own time, not when you're driving or when you're cutting vegetables up. But practice some place when you're quiet," and so on, as it says in the elaborate homework instructions. Then you say, "Try this, and if you want to know more things that I am doing, then ask me and I will tell you. But try this for a few weeks." Don't rush them. Don't say, "Oh, there's the love-heat and the disentanglement and . . ." That's too much. If they're very interested, give them a little bit, and when they come back, if they want more, give them something else—the disentanglement, perhaps.

So that's why the stories you tell are so powerful, because without preaching they just present ways that people can be, from the example of a life that was lived.

That's exactly it.

And it's possible that we can do this?

Yes.

It Was Our Job to Help Earth Adjust to Human Beings

But it is important for you not to look at my life and my life with my people as something that is to be worked toward, living that way, because I am telling you the philosophy and our practices, but there were things about our life that weren't so wonderful.

Yes, not having your own food, having to move. I can think of fifty things that . . .

That's right. We didn't have any . . .

No Jacuzzis. [Laughs.]

No down comforters. We would have loved to have had those. If we did, we sure wouldn't have said, "Oh, these are not good." [Chuckles.] We didn't have any sleeping bags. So getting too warm, getting too cold—that was typical. Of course, it also tended to make husbands and wives more friendly. [Chuckles.]

[Laughs.] But this life that you and your predecessors and your successors lived . . . on other parts of the planet, there were civilizations in progress. You were doing this as a service to the Earth and to those who would follow. Maybe you didn't consciously know that, but . . .

I think that this is widely known in Native American communities, that it was our job to come here and help Earth adjust to human beings who would come, and to know what we would need so that she would welcome certain types of plants, certain types of animals, and others would not be welcome so much—meaning, for instance, that dinosaurs, as beautiful as they are, would not live very compatibly with human beings. So after a time, she unwelcomed them. See? Like that. That way the modern human being and bodies like you have now . . . they're pretty fragile, right?

Yes.

So we need to have some great hazards not present. Dinosaurs are beautiful beings on their home planets . . . you would love to be with them. I used long vision once. I looked at the big one, with the long neck and the long tail. It was wonderful, beautiful. I once saw a child riding on the neck and shoulders, not unlike in your stories.

Really?

It was not a dragon, but they were friends. And I'm not sure who was whose pet [laughs]. I don't think "pet" was involved, but they were friends, and oh, it looked like fun. If I was a child, I would love to do that. But that's not on Earth, see? That's not the way it would have been.

Right, yes.

So one day Earth said, "Well, it's time for some of you to move on."

Everybody's Lineage Goes Back to Africa

But see, you were doing this in North America at the same time as there were advanced civilizations elsewhere.

No, no—you don't understand. The people, the native peoples who originally came to Earth, they weren't our people. We knew very clearly that we were not people like that. No, I'm talking about the native peoples who originally came a long time ago to different places, to Africa, yes? Way back. They're the ones who set up what Earth would need to be to support them. But our lineage—the people in, you say, North America— goes back then to Africa. We were not dark-skinned anymore in my time—when I lived, about four hundred years ago, we were not dark-skinned anymore. But that's because of the long walk.

Your lineage goes back to Africa?

Everybody's lineage goes to Africa. So does yours, your bloodline. Not what star you are connected to—your bloodline goes directly to Africa. If we traced your bloodline back, we could say, "Oh, you used to be African; you used to be dark-skinned." But through years and years of moving, emigrating . . . all of life, the native peoples we talk about, who originally came here? They came to Africa, because it was the most comfortable place to be. It never got any snow. Oh, you might get some on the top of a mountain, and that was exciting and fun, but it was at a distance: "Oh, look at that; it's beautiful!" And of course, as you know, it would make for fresh water. That kind of fresh water is wonderful.

But no, no. Our bloodline goes back to the dark-skinned people in Africa who came from Sirius, okay? Our bloodline. So does yours. There is not a single person alive on Earth today whose bloodline does not go back to Africa. That's why when they analyze the blood in a science lab, they're really analyzing African blood. You're all African—me too. You don't think of yourself that way, eh? But that is the way it is. Funny, isn't it? That's why I'm thinking it's funny, strange, this whole thing about prejudice and how people look and their skin. Well, we would all not be here, we wouldn't have much of a life here, if the original native peoples didn't come to Africa.

Then people were encouraged to move about; they moved to this place, that place. Then some of the ETs came, and sometimes they stayed and then intermarried over time. Things changed . . . like that. Sometimes the ETs too might have come and enjoyed . . . like the woman we talked about before. She talked about going to Peru, what would come to be known as Peru, and their people would come there from the Pleiades, they went there a lot. Sometimes they would stay there for a long time, years and years, and there would be children. And the children sometimes would want to go back to the Pleiades. But sometimes they would want to stay here on Earth; Earth was their home, that was what they knew. So when the ships would go back, they would stay here. Sometimes that's how different races got started. But it all came originally from Africa.

So any of the DNA . . . ?

You are African—everybody too.

So all of the later additions of the DNA came from African stock?

All of the additions from other places. That's right; it all was superimposed over African peoples, who taking it back, are people from Sirius. So, you see, it has to be that way. Think about it. This planet is from Sirius—how could this planet be comfortable if the foundation human beings were not from Sirius? The foundation of human beings *have* to be from Sirius. And most human beings I have seen in my long vision there on Sirius are all dark-skinned—maybe not all with the same color dark skin, but everything from light brown to dark brown to dark brownish-blue.

So in your tribal oral history, what was the path your tribe took to get where they were?

That is too long a story. I would need to have a globe to show you. But, generally speaking, it went up from Africa through what is now known as the Middle East, then Europe and eventually over across the bridge of land that is now sometimes almost a bridge of ice from Russia to Alaska. Of course, it took a long time.

Yes, but that was part of your oral history. I mean, every child was told a little bit of his or her heritage and origin, right?

Not too much—just that when our original peoples came here, our ancestors . . . there's a word where you live now, in the Southwest. When the Anasazi came, meaning the beloved ancient ones, they came from this big land across the sea. We didn't say "Africa"; we didn't have that word. But we said, "This big land across the sea, far away from here on the other side of where we are. Far, far away."

We didn't say "on the other side of the planet," but I'm saying that for your time. We would have said "far, far away." "And we looked different then," we would say. "How did we look, Grandpa?" [Chuckles.] "Oh, your skin was much darker, so when you were hiding in the forest at night, they'd have a harder time finding you. But when you were trying to hide in the day, we could find you easily"—the way you talk to children, to have fun.

Yes, lovingly.

Lovingly, gently.

Native Americans Helped Dark-Skinned People in the Time of Slavery

My people in my time never saw a person of that dark skin, but after my time, since then, I've been able to see that some people of darker skin came. Oh, they were welcomed as if they were like the ancestors, the children of the ancestors, and embraced: "Oh, come; stay with us."

And they didn't understand why. [Laughs.]

Well, sometimes if they were trying to escape from something, they were embraced. It was not unusual during the time of slavery in the South, that when some of the dark-skinned people managed to find some native peoples, they were often embraced.

And hidden.

Hidden and protected and welcomed to join. That's why just as many if not more dark-skinned people can trace their roots back to Native American culture.

Oh! At the present time?

It's not just, as you say, white people or, "Yes, we have some Cherokee," and so on. It's the same thing with dark-skinned people, only it's more likely that the dark-skinned people can trace them back because . . . well, from my perspective, I am not a number counter, but dark-skinned people were usually welcomed in the tribes, unless they were not good people. But if they were escaping something, the tribe would go to great risks to protect them because they understood that these were the children of the ancestors, the beloved ancestors, and so they must be protected if at all possible.

I have seen with long vision many times when members of the tribe would die protecting them: "No, no; we haven't seen them. No, we don't know who they are." Do you understand that I'm talking about native peoples for whom lying would not be something that they would even know how to do? So they would have to break all of their cultures to say, "No, we haven't seen them."

To protect them.

That would almost create a sickness for them, to tell a lie in my time, in old times—in times gone by or times that may be a hundred years in the future of my old time. I'm not trying to fix any time too much, but I don't want to make all Native Americans sound like better people than you are. Now, you were going to ask something?

Earth's Bloodline Goes Straight Back to Sirius

Oh, I just had the sudden realization that this really explains for the first time why what we call the negative Sirians felt that this was their planet, when they were here tyrannizing and blackmailing our government.

Yes, because it *was* their planet. It was from Sirius, and the bloodline on this planet goes right back in a straight arrow to Sirius. So they had . . . I'm not saying that they were right or that they were smart or that they were good.

Yes. [Laughs.] They were definitely not good!

It's not about that.

But it explains it, it explains their feelings.

I'm not saying that they weren't that; I'm saying that that's why they felt that way [see previous books in the *Explorer Race* series and *Shining the Light* series].

Rainbows Nourish the Earth

Speaks of Many Truths
December 6, 2001

his is Speaks of Many Truths.

Rainbows Are All about Encouragement and Nurturance

So do rainbows feed the Earth?

It is not often understood by people that rainbows do more than cheer you up and provide great beauty to encourage you. Rainbows, for the human being, are all about encouragement. Sometimes you can get physically close enough—optically, as you say—to a rainbow to see that it almost has substance. There is a sparkle quality within it. Scientists will tell you, "Oh, this is light reflecting or refracting off of raindrops," but that is not quite true. Even though that could be scientifically proven, light has personality, it has purpose and it has intention. Given those three very important factors, the light chooses to be there in order to provide a function, not only of beauty and encouragement to human beings and animals and, to a degree, plants, but also because when the light is attached to the drops as it descends to Earth, it not only performs the nurturance of the soil and the plants and all that water does for all life, but the colors themselves actually feed Earth in given places.

This is why you will see surprising things, like a rainbow in one place for a very long time. Or you might see rainbows flitting about—here one moment, there the next. You might also see, in the case of a full arc, a rainbow where one side is on the mountain and the other side is on the sea or the river or a lake or whatever body of water may be near you. So it is important to discuss the impact of rainbows.

Now, even though science will tell you this is not possible, in recent years they've had to admit that maybe it is possible, depending where you are geographically, to find yourself within a rainbow. If that can happen, try to be within it as long as possible. It can only help; it cannot harm. It will be an attunement for your physical body and your energy body, and it can only improve the quality of your life, even if it's not directly touching you.

Red and Gold Nurture Earth's Mountains and Auric Field

Now, when the color of a rainbow enters the Earth, something interesting happens. You will see a rainbow in a given arc, and the assumption is that these colors are traveling in the distance that you can actually see, but an actual rainbow, were you able to see underneath the surface of the Earth, makes not an arc but a full circle. The colors continue right on down into the Earth, sometimes completing the circle and other times actually meandering out while completing the circle—meandering out in various directions on the basis of what that mountain range or what that landmass or what that water mass needs at that time for its own functions. Mother Earth is providing the rainbow, then, for herself and, to a lesser degree, for those who reside upon or within her.

When you have the color, for instance, of red: Red color nourishes, enriches (meaning like food) mountain ranges specifically. This is not to say that when you see a rainbow going into water or when you see it going into flat land, that it isn't nourishing it, because even though the land is flat, perhaps there will be a mountain there someday. Or in the case of ancient times, perhaps there was a mountain there once, and its memory and energy are still present for Mother Earth. Therefore, the red or the colors along that line of red, when they go in, are going in to enrich and nourish mountain space, mountain energy.

Now, you have colors that are gold, for instance, and they might go in. They are always nourishing and nurturing Mother Earth's auric field, even though her auric field is present elsewhere especially. But her auric field, not unlike your own, begins within her body and radiates out. So she may have a weakness or a tear or a hole or a thinness—any of those things and more—in her energy body. She will use that gold color or color like that in the rainbow to repair or heal that place in her body.

When you talk about gold, that would be the yellow that we see in the rainbow, right?

Yes, but I see that as gold. Even though your description of gold more closely matches the metal, I see that color as gold.

Mother Earth Uses Rainbows to Offset Earthquakes

Rainbows might also be used sometimes to offset the potential for an earthquake. Sometimes when you are living perhaps in an earthquake zone and you see a rainbow, just thank Mother Earth. She is probably doing something to heal, repair or lubricate her fracture zone within her body. This is especially important these days when oil is being pumped out of the Earth, which in the Earth acts very much like hydraulic fluid in a mechanical device, which acts as a means of support, holding something up—rather like the way I believe some shock absorber systems used to work, at least in the old days.

So when you remove that, it actually creates an air space, which means that the land above it becomes significantly more perilous. When Mother Earth uses her rainbow, she knows better than to put more oil in there, because if you've been pumping it up, you'll just pump it out. So she will put in the color in an attempt to concentrate the color in there. This is not the same, it's not physical, but it does tend to nurture and strengthen the space where the oil and gas were.

It is not really understood by your people yet that what they consider a product—oil and gas that you have applied to your own purposes—has direct use in Mother Earth's body. She uses it to support the surface of the Earth, yes, but she also uses it to maintain some distance between different parts of herself. For instance, it's not unusual to find a pressure cavern with gas or oil in it near water, underground water. The pressure is intended to separate certain things from the water. When water goes down into the Earth, it is not only purified by the Earth but also runs though various parts of her body to strengthen her. Also, when it does come back up to the surface in some way, it will often contain certain vital energies that support and sustain life as well as soothe the surface of her body.

Blue and Green Help Mother Earth with Connections to Her Dimensions and Soul Personality

Then you have the ranges of color that are more like blue. Blue, although it is identified often with the intellect for human beings, does not perform that function for Mother Earth. Blue for Mother Earth has to do with her direct connection between her physical personality and the rest of her dimensions—meaning third-dimensional Earth with the other represented dimensions of Earth, which contain other cultures and other ways of life. We use the term "dimensions" for you, but in my time we might say the other faces of Earth. So the blue feeds, connects and supports her interaction with those faces of Earth so that her present face, which is where you live and which is suffering a bit, can be nurtured and supported by other portions of herself.

Now, greenish colors are sometimes also noticed in the rainbow. When these colors are seen, this always has to do with the connection between Mother Earth and her soul personality. The soul personality of Mother Earth is quite vast. It extends beyond space and time, of course—because of her being so many levels of a master—and it has a good portion of itself anchored in the Sirius star system, so as to connect strongly with other water planets.

Orange Supports Feelings and Purple Nurtures the Passage of Life Forms

If you see orange or something orange-like in a rainbow, that always supports feelings, but this does not have to do very much with Mother Earth's feelings, which remain fairly constant. It has to do with her manner of reacting to the feelings of other beings on her. This is something that has been discussed before, where you have heard that residual feelings of human beings, for instance, are often left on Earth and create some complications or something that needs to be worked out.

This orange-like color will help Mother Earth work out feelings of human beings that, for one reason or another, have remained on Earth. These are usually feelings of discomfort when a human being passes on, goes through the veils and sheds earthly feelings—"earthly" in terms of what that human being experiences on Earth, *not* Earth's feelings for herself. Mother Earth does not, in her own right, have those feelings of depression, anxiety, upset, fear and so on. She doesn't have those, but they refer to earthly feelings because human beings have those on Earth here in order to use them as tools for growth.

And purple?

When you see the tinge of purple—it is more like a tinge—that always has to do with the transference of souls from one place to another. So it supports and nurtures the passage of all life forms on Earth moving from one realm to another. Every blade of grass, every ant, every human being, every flower, all have their own innate personality and soul being. Therefore, that energy needs to be invigorated. If you've ever noticed at the end of the day, if you can see the sunset, after the Sun has gone around to visit another part of the Earth, you will not only see the rays of light coming up, but you will see at one point, if you look closely, the rays of a darker color.

This is not just highlighted from light rays but is an actual darker color. It is that color that is supported by the purple energy that goes into Earth. It is that color that is a reaction to the Sun's journey that comes up right around the time of sunset that allows, supports, nurtures and otherwise helps human souls to move beyond the veils to their next places with their guides. That is why it is not unusual for human beings to pass over around that time.

That is special energy. There's an indigo that's just barely seen. Is there something beyond the purple?

I consider the indigo and the purple to be one.

There Are So Many Forms of Light on Earth

Is this part of what you knew, or is this what you've learned in your larger state?

This is part of what I was taught. Things can be observed if you have the time or make the time, just as my teacher did, to climb up with me on the mesa where I like to sit sometimes. Robert [the channel] knows about that; he comes to visit me sometimes. Then you can see these things because it is quiet, there are only the animals who come by sometimes, and you can observe these changes of light.

There is so much light going on, on Earth. You don't think of it all the time because you're used to the daytime and the light. But the morning light, the evening light, the sunset, the sunrise, all these different forms of light, the rainbow—there are lots of different forms of light and different things going on with them.

Liquid Light Is Welcomed by the Joy of Children

You said that the rainbow was the closest thing to liquid light. How does Mother Earth create it? Is there a mechanism or a dynamic?

Liquid light will only present itself in places where there is enough joy to support it. This is why when human beings see rainbows, especially children who are more likely to demonstrate their true feelings, it immediately activates joy. You could say, "Well, to see such a beautiful thing would naturally activate joy," and yet think of how many adults look at a rainbow and don't give it another thought, keep right on going.

But in your purer state, before you are affected by life to a greater degree as you live it here now, when you are a child, you look at that rainbow and there's nothing more wonderful and exciting. Christmas presents, yes, those are fun, but they don't hold a candle, as you say, to a rainbow for a child. That's just wonderful, wondrous. It would be like an adult seeing the ETs arrive and being happy to see them—wonderful ETs—or seeing a *real* Santa Claus arrive. If adults saw that, they probably wouldn't believe it, but a child would.

That joy is intended. That joy, that projected feeling from children, actually welcomes liquid light, and liquid light knows it will be welcome by that. If it wasn't for that, given the fact of all the discomfort that is present on Earth, especially in your time, it is not likely that you would see rainbows very often, or they would happen in places that are much more remote where there would be so many fewer human beings. Even today there are remote places like that—certainly out on the ocean, for example.

You can go to a spot on the ocean very easily, even today, and not have any surface ships in any direction. You could be out there on a ship and look in all directions and . . . nothing. There might be something over the horizon, as they say, but it wouldn't be present in your line of sight. So you could be out there on a ship—say, in a sailboat—sailing from point to point. You might see rain in the distance—not a big storm, just a small shower—and you see that rainbow, and it's just you and the rainbow. That's why people go out on sailboats like that, to enjoy that peace and the beauty of nature.

Mother Earth Invites Liquid Light

But how does she do it? How does she manifest a rainbow?

Working with liquid light, because she is prepared to work with liquid light. She first invites liquid light, and you invite liquid light the same way you invite anything else. Once you've had contact with liquid light, you automatically feel joyous—Mother Earth too. You'll recognize, though, that you'll have a certain joy as a human being to see a rainbow that doesn't usually exist for anything else but that level of joy that Mother Earth will exude and radiate, and also the pure feeling of welcome. She will almost always, not always—sometimes you'll see rainbows where there's no apparent water falling from the sky; you'll see that sometimes—choose to have rain falling in and around that rainbow so that the droplets of rain can pick up the color and go down into the Earth. That's intentional.

Liquid light exists in more places than you realize. It is part of Mother Earth's auric field, so it's not that far away, but it also has an existence in its own right. Liquid light as a being will choose to be anyplace where there is joy and where it feels welcome—period. That is why one finds it often on Pleiadian ships.

In previous *Explorer Race* books, there may have been the description where a Pleiadian will hold his or her hand above something and there will be a tone like a chime and the liquid light will emerge. One assumes that this is something being generated by the Pleiadians, but it's not. The Pleiadians invite liquid light to come along. Not everybody in the Pleiades, but certain individuals or certain ships will invite it to come along, and it will choose to come along because the people on the ship tend to be cheerful, joyous and welcoming, so it's happy to come along.

So when you hear the chime, that is not a tone that liquid light itself is making, but it is rather part of the mechanism of the ship to indicate that it has been activated. They wave their hand over something, then "ding," or whatever you like, and then the motion of the hand of the person is actually a means to welcome the liquid light in that moment, in that place.

So your experience on board that Pleiadian ship [see chapter 9]—that was liquid light that the boy called forth to show you its features?

No. I just know this.

Breathing in the Rainbow

For people who get to see a rainbow, does a human absorb the colors by looking at them?

No, but you can do a couple of things. If you're used to having energies flow back and forth through you, you can then, yes, just look at it. It's best to not look at it through glass or something. But even looking through glass or even if you wear glasses or some lenses in your eyes, you can still absorb quite a bit if you're used to passing energies back and forth through yourself—quite a bit.

But if you're not used to doing that or it's not natural or you're not conscious of doing it, then the thing to do is to look at the rainbow. Try to look as high up at the rainbow as possible. Obviously, don't look into sunshine, but look as high as you can go so that you're not looking at anything man-made. Or if you know that the rainbow is in a canyon where there aren't any houses or human beings, you can look a little lower—sometimes you know that. Perhaps it's in a park or something like that. Then, when you're doing that, just breathe your natural breath—you don't need to take deep breaths. Just look at it, and while you're looking at it, just breathe in a natural way and try to look at it if you can—standing up, sitting down, whatever you like to do.

If you're sitting down, it's best to be sitting in a chair that is not metal. If it has a screw here or there, that's fine, but only one or two. Ideally sit in a chair that is perhaps wooden and is pegged. You can find things like that, antiques, or even use something like wicker. So just look at the rainbow. You might assume that looking at a rainbow from any distance would work. It does work, but the closer you are to the rainbow, the more effective it is. Say you're on a hike in a canyon somewhere and it's raining or there's even a waterfall—that's okay too—and you see the rainbow. Just look at it; just breathe naturally for a few minutes.

Once you notice that you feel more physically invigorated, once you actually notice that increase in physical invigoration, then stop breathing in the rainbow because that's enough. You don't want to take more than you need. There's no advantage in taking more than you need. Just say, "Oh, I feel better now," to yourself and say, "Thank you. Good life," out loud if you can to the rainbow, which is by way of speaking to Mother Earth—it is acknowledgment. Then go on.

Of course, your eye is going to wander to that rainbow again and that's fine, but don't stare at it too much because you've received your gift and you don't want to take more than you need. If you take more than you need, you might eventually feel overstimulated and uncomfortable. You want to take just enough so that you start to feel refreshed and better. Once that happens, then let it go. Others will be looking at it too, perhaps. Certainly the animals will, and the plants will tend to lean toward it.

And in the leaning they will absorb some too?

That is their way.

Earthworms Enjoy Rainbows' Gold Light

So whereas different colors affect different places in the Earth, for humans it's more of the whole spectrum?

The whole spectrum, that's right. And it is generally the whole spectrum for plants and animals as well, with a few exceptions, the exceptions all being creatures who tend to live underground, such as worms, earth-worms. They, for instance, might not need some of the color, but they will be happy to be bathed in it. But they might enjoy some of the color in particular, such as the gold. That's very invigorating, and it helps them to produce more young—usually more vigorous young at that.

That's the real reason, in places where they exist, one tends to find more earthworms in areas that tend to be more saturated and have more rain-bows—not just because earthworms like that, but more to the point, because the ground itself is saturated with gold light.

The Crystal from the People Inside the Earth

As a shaman in your time, did you use color in your healing or your teaching or in interactions with your students?

I didn't in terms of using color like that, in terms of the rainbow, but I met someone once who used that using a crystal. This crystal had been passed on through this person's people. By the time I met this person, generations and generations had had it available. It had been found once in a cave. It had points at both ends, and the person who found it actually not only felt permission to take the crystal but, to a greater degree, felt like he was supposed to take the crystal and that it would be an offense to leave the crystal where it was. It was as if Earth herself or someone had left the crystal in a place where he would practically trip over it.

So he picked it up, and the moment he picked it up, he felt this profound sense of welcome. At first he thought, "Welcome to this place," but it was when he put the crystal down in the proper way that he had an uncomfortable feeling and the crystal wouldn't let him leave it. That's when he realized he was supposed to take it. Every step back out of the cave, he would check to make sure that the crystal wanted to come with him, and it definitely wanted to come with him to his people.

They used the crystal with sunlight shining through it, and they used it for colors—not only for healing, not so much for that because the medicine woman could do that, but they used it to feed the Earth in various places where the sun would shine through it. The light that would come through the crystal was very clear. The light would come through the crystal, and they would hold it in a certain way.

Depending on who the shaman or the student was, that person would hold it in a certain way—between the fingers, like a claw shape [between the second and third fingers of the left hand with fingers pointing down toward the ground]. They'd hold it in that shape and move it around so that the sun could touch it—it was pretty big, about sixteen inches. It was quite large and quite beautiful.

Do you want to know something fascinating about the crystal that that person told me? He said that at different times of the year, different seasons, the crystal itself was tinged with different color, and that was quite astonishing. I believed him, of course. That was amazing, and the people in their tribe had no idea how that could be. It didn't make any difference whether it was nighttime and they had a campfire going and could see it or where there was good moonlight. It didn't make any difference. It could be nighttime or daytime. It had to do with the seasons. When they realized it had to do with the seasons, they realized that the crystal wanted to come to the surface because, of course, inside the Earth in a cave, seasons are not really a factor.

It's always my desire to know the history. It would be fun to know how it got there.

This is what the man said: The reason it was there is that it was placed there by some people who used to live inside the Earth near that cave. The reason that shaman and that shaman's ancestors had been going into that cave was to visit those people. But, you see, those people have moved on. They're not there anymore, so it's all right to talk about this.

And this was hundreds of years before your time?

Yes. It used to be in those days that part of the training for the shaman for those people would be to go into the cave. There was a passageway inside the cave; I believe there has been a collapse of the rocks since so you can't take that passage anymore. But there was a passageway and you could take it, and it would go like this [draws Fig. 10-1]. This was part of the reason it was hard to find if you didn't know otherwise. Once you got into the cave . . . say this is the cave, the mouth of the cave, then you would take the passageway and it would go like this [draws]. It would take quite awhile. You understand, we're talking about a great distance.

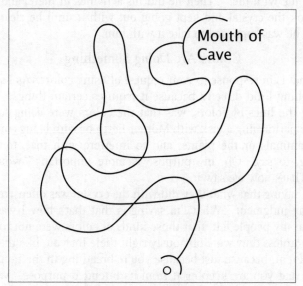

Fig. 10-1. The passageway in the cave that the shaman would take to visit the beings inside the Earth.

It's going deeper and deeper.

Round and round like this, and then you'd get to this point right about here where someone would meet you. So you'd go into the cave like this, and someone would meet you and take you the rest of the way. In order to take you the rest of the way . . . this is essentially down from the surface, which would involve going through different changes of energy—as you say, different dimensions. But in order to get to that point, someone would initially have to take you. Of course, the ancestors were shown how to get there, so they had to pass it on from generation to generation. Eventually, I'm sure that when those people left the Earth . . .

That's when they left the crystal for the shaman? So instead of the training, all he had was the crystal? The shaman came there to get the crystal, which these beings had left him?

He didn't come in to get the crystal; he came to visit the beings.

No, I mean after they left.

They didn't just leave. They told the people they were leaving. They didn't just disappear. They said they would be leaving at such and such a time.

Then when the ancestor came in and found the crystal, did he connect that with the fact that they had left it for him?

No. When he found the crystal, he was coming in to see them. The crystal wanted to go with him, so he took it with him to go see the people, and they said, "Oh, you found the crystal. That's nice." He said, "It seems to want to come with me." Then he did his activities in there, and when he left, he took the crystal and kept going out with it until he clearly understood that he was supposed to take it with him.

Colors Are *Doing* Something

Now, that is in response to your request of using colors. As I said, that's not something I did directly, because it requires certain things. My training, along the lines of colors, was that the colors were *doing* something. They were performing a task with Mother Earth or with beings on Earth or with the animals or the plants, and to interfere with that, to try to do something, to say, "Oh, my purpose is more important," would be an offense. That's how we saw it.

I'm not saying that what they did with the crystal was offensive. I'm not passing any judgment. What I'm saying is that that's how I was trained. That's what my people felt, that those kinds of colors were not to be interfered with unless they were obviously right there for you, like the rainbow. That's different, because just because you're breathing in the rainbow does not mean that you are keeping it from its intended purpose. What is on the surface is intended for people on the surface. What goes below the surface is intended for beings below the surface or for Mother Earth herself. So she allows the rainbow to be on the surface and invites it for her surface dwellers and, to some extent, for her air.

Her air? What does it do to her air?

It freshens her air in certain ways. Your scientists have discovered positive and negative charges and particles and so on. A rainbow tends to produce in and around itself more benevolent good-feeling charges in the air.

At the End of the Rainbow, You Can Feel the Tingles

Where did the legend come from about finding the pot of gold at the end of the rainbow?

Is this not an Irish story? I believe it is a story of the creative people of Ireland.

Maybe it's because if you could stand where the rainbow touches the Earth, you would have really good feelings.

Definitely, or even if you could get close to it. You can feel the tingles.

Maybe it started with that.

Healing with Sound

What about sound? Did you use sound in any way in your teaching?

Only occasionally, but that would be done more in reaction to a missing sound within the person. If you are attuned to the musical register—not as you understand music, but the music of natural beings—Mother Earth herself always makes the same tone. I could not make this voice go that low, nor could I make my voice go that low. It would be like this, "Mmmmm," but much lower than that. It's a resonance that can be felt better than it can be heard, but to a degree it can be heard.

Now, human beings also have certain tonal references in them. If the tone in a human being is not very strong, then it could mean different things. The tones are not as strong in little children, and they're not as strong in the very aged. But for an adult, a vigorous adult, they are quite strong. Of course, in the case of a vigorous adult who was injured—say something fell on you and hurt your arm or broke a bone in your arm—then the tones will become very weak.

There are other things you can do to create a healing for the arm, but one of the things that can help is to know the tones of the human being. In my experience working with that tone, what works best is to find someone who lives with the injured person—a wife, husband, child, brother, sister, friend or anybody who lives with or lives very close to that person. I would put that family member or friend between myself and the injured person, and then I would tell the family member or friend to remember what his or her life was like right before this injury at a time when this now injured person was whole and strong. I would tell the friend to just focus on those times before the injury, and nothing else.

Then I would go near the hurt person's arm and, in feeling, travel up the arm on the right-hand side, right up under the collarbone. That's where you can add tone. But you don't flow it straight in—you want to make it available. So what I would do is, I would have the person close to the injured person focus on a recent time of health and happiness, facing toward the injured person's arm so that his or her head lines up pretty much with the other person's head. I would be standing just past that person but leaning a little bit this way, around the left shoulder.

What I would do while that person was remembering being with the injured person—he or she doesn't have to remember anything about tones; all he or she has to remember is being with that person—was that first I would connect with Earth's tone, the deep "Mmmmm" feeling sound. Then, since our bodies are made of Mother Earth, I would very gently begin blowing across that person's left shoulder toward this spot on the injured person. I would breathe, not into the body, but so that my breath, even though you wouldn't be able to feel it, was not blowing hard but gently, because I would really be blowing energy. So my breath would cross over in front of that spot.

It would be in front of that spot, so that the energy, not the breath itself . . . it's good not to blow directly into the body if you can, but rather to blow in someplace where the body takes energy in. I would blow across there gently and slowly for a while until I could feel the tones in the injured person's body begin to get louder and more vigorous. Once they got louder and more vigorous to the level of where they would normally be, then I would stop.

How to Release Fear in Your Throat

As an aside, when human beings are sometimes frightened, they get a lump—you say a lump in your throat. That is because this place is open; it's open almost all the time. If you ever get a lump in your throat . . . have you ever noticed that when people do that, their first gesture is this [puts his hand over his throat]? What they're really doing is covering this spot. That's what they're doing. They're actually covering this spot.

So what you can do when you know where that spot is, is that if you have a lump in your throat and maybe it's uncomfortable—maybe you're feeling compassionate or sad, if that feeling is uncomfortable; it will go away in time—you can put your hand over this spot. You don't even have to put it over your throat. If you're putting it over this spot, that will be enough. You don't have to do that; I'm not saying it's important. But if there is a reason, if it's uncomfortable or if you find yourself having some discomfort—there are some people who have some diseases who might find it uncomfortable—put your hand over that spot and it will get better soon.

Breathe in the Rainbow When You're Tired

Okay, you told us what to do for someone who has injured his or her arm or something like that. Does that work for people who are sick or old or tired also?

When your body is tired, the first thing to do is to rest. That's the most important thing. Your body is tired, and it's telling you to rest—rest and maybe eat. Rest a little bit first, then eat something, and then rest some more, maybe sleep. First you do all of that, but if you're tired all the time, maybe then you want to go to your doctor or your medicine person and find out all those things.

But one of the things you can do is . . . say you're tired all the time and you have the opportunity to see a rainbow. When you're breathing in the rainbow the way I instructed you to do, try to make sure that you don't have a metal belt buckle over your bellybutton. Pull it down, or if you have to, pull it up, but keep that metal away from there. And make sure you don't put your hands or your books or anything in front of your belly-button, because that's a place that is open on almost everybody all the time. It's only closed—and not closed all the way—sometimes. If there is extreme fear, agitation or battle, then it will close almost all the way.

And you can take the energy from the rainbow in there too?

Don't take it in, because it's too complicated. Just breathe the rainbow in normally, and your bellybutton will be taking it in. That ought to help with being tired.

But you never focus on putting energy into your own open point?

Don't do that yourself. Let your body do it. If you think about breath-ing in like that from there, you might find that there's a conflict, because you'll be thinking that you have to do this for a few minutes, whereas your bellybutton can probably . . . if you know how to breathe in through other parts of your body, you can just breathe in for a very short amount of time in your bellybutton and get what you need for that immediate area. But why do that? If you can look at the rainbow and breathe naturally for a couple of minutes, you won't need to do that. It will affect your whole body. I think it is an unnecessary complication to talk about breathing in through your bellybutton that way for the average person.

Homework: Try to Hear the Sound of Mother Earth

Are there any other means of healing yourself or anyone else with your own sound? How do you recognize your own sound if you don't hear it?

The first thing to do is to try to hear the sound of Mother Earth, which is most easily heard somewhere quiet—meaning with not too many people around, not too many human voices. If there are people around, perhaps they are quiet, perhaps they are sleeping—although not all people are always quiet when they're sleeping. Or sometimes you can hear it in a car even, if the car is quiet. But it's better to be outside. I find in my experi-ence that hearing the sound near mountains is easier, especially if there hasn't been any building on the mountains or very little—meaning not too much digging in Mother Earth. Then it is easier. It will be a deep tone.

Like the Om sound?

But there's no "O"; it's just the "Mmmmm." It will be a very deep tone. You might feel it as much. For people who have visuals, you might actually see "M's," like a string of "M's." I'm not saying that you will, but people who have visuals might. You might also see color. It depends. It depends on what you see when you have visuals.

First you hear it, and then you do what?

Try to respond in kind. Either make a deep sound like that, "Mmmmm," as deep as you can make it in response, or what is equally good is to just say out loud, "Good life." Mother Earth knows "Good life." That is equally good. That's your acknowledgment to Mother Earth, but that's a good beginning. To hear your own tones might take some time for training for that. It took me a lot of time—years. I'd say that the first homework would be to try to hear Mother Earth's tone.

Wear Light Colors to Channeling Sessions

Do the colors I wear to these channeling sessions have any impact, and if so, what would be the best color to wear?

It does not impact that much. That is probably because you and Robert have built a certain degree of harmony after all this work together. I would say that it only affects things to the slightest degree. But for people coming for a private session, especially if they're new to this kind of thing, it might be better for them to wear white or ivory or a light beige color, such as the fabric color that is often referred to—in the case of cotton, for example—as natural. White, however, is perhaps not the best color to wear in the Hawaiian Islands, given the fact that it has some symbolic meaning and has to do with the passage of life from one place to another and is often worn to funerals.

Right, the way other people might wear black.

The way people in your culture might wear black, that's right, because in your culture, passage of life as you know it to the afterlife is the unknown. You identify the unknown with black or dark, like the spaces between the stars: "What's there? It's unknown." Like the cave under the ground: "What's there? It's unknown."

But for the people here in Hawaii, they identify white because of the white light that contains all forms and colors of light, and that contains only love for all beings—they understand that. That's why they wear white, because it celebrates the passage of the soul to this wonderful, benevolent place and celebrates the continuation of that soul's life in another form.

What about people who have channeling sessions over the phone? Is there any significance in what they wear while Robert's talking to them?

No great significance. I would say that, generally speaking, while the channeling is going on, if they want to make some slight improvement, they might wear those colors. And I would say that perhaps red is just slightly deflecting. Red is a color that stimulates physical activity and revitalizes physical activity. That's why sometimes people who feel like they need a little jolt or something will wear their red garment for the day.

You'll find that for other channels, this will apply pretty universally. This is why it's not unusual in ashrams to see people wearing light-colored garments, unless they are going about specific tasks, doing their duty. But students often wear these light-colored garments because it's their job to be as receptive as possible in order to learn as much as possible. Whereas you might see some of the teachers wearing darker-colored garments because it's their job to project as many lessons as possible for the students. That is my understanding of that color arrangement.

One sees this sometimes even with organized religions. At least in the more traditional level of the Catholic Church, one might see a novitiate wearing a lighter-colored garment. It always represents the one acquiring knowledge and wisdom.

And the Mother Superior wears black.

Well, she might wear different colors, but the teachers will wear darker colors because it is their job to provide lessons.

The Sun Nurtures Mother Earth's Auric Field

You talked about Mother Earth's auric field. What happens when missiles or the shuttles go back and forth? Do they damage her auric field?

Yes. That's why she's constantly working on repairing herself, and when she cannot do it, she will call on the assistance of other planets. Of course, the Sun helps a lot. Sometimes when the Sun releases a massive burst of energy that will go out in all directions, including toward the Earth, it's to help Mother Earth with her auric field. So that happens sometimes. You notice that your scientists tell you this is happening, and you say, "Oh, what's that all about?" It's usually to nurture Mother Earth.

Of course, you as citizens of Earth can only benefit from that. Even though it might seem to interfere with your technology, it greatly assists you when it comes to the factor of nurturing Mother Earth. A nurtured, refreshed, replenished Mother Earth is, of course, constantly nurturing and replenishing and refreshing your physical bodies.

What does the Van Allen belt do to her, then—that incredible belt of radiation and stuff we've got up there?

It doesn't help. Good night.

More Stories of Earth Life

Reveals the Mysteries
December 6, 2001

his is Reveals the Mysteries.

Welcome, welcome! Do you have anything to say about rainbows and color and sound?

Well, I'm not going to comment on my student's book, but I will speak of other matters, if you like. I don't want to sound as if I'm correcting him, because there is no correction needed. After all, he is passing on things that I was taught, that I taught him and that he learned in the course of his life and duties. A practitioner, whether he be shamanic or any other profession, will always learn things in the course of his duties that he wasn't taught, simply because of the needs of others.

I think it's better to just tell stories about Earth life, since the people who will be reading this will all be living on Earth [chuckles].

The Gift of a Raft

One time when Speaks of Many Truths was a youngster—in your years, about twelve—I took him on the river for a ways in a raft because I wanted to bring him to a village where I had two friends. One was like myself and was married, had a very nice arrangement.

To the mystical lady?

To the medicine woman—a very nice arrangement. That's not typical, I might add. That's a lot of responsibility in one family for the other people, but that's just the way it was. And I wanted to introduce him. It was a very long walk to get to a place where we could cross the river easily, but not such a long ride on the river. So in order to make it a good lesson, a good experience, I had Speaks of Many Truths make the raft. That's why it was a raft, not a complicated boat or something. I had him make it, but only from trees that would volunteer the wood.

So it took him about a year to make it, because he had to go around and get volunteers—everything that made up the raft had to be openly offering it, so that took time. But then, you see, we could take the trip on the boat that *he* made. That made it more wonderful for him, because it was his responsibility to make the vehicle that we'd get there on, and in the process, he had to learn and interact with trees and so on, and even deer. So that was quite a job for him. But he managed to do it. As I say, it took him about a year.

So we went down to visit my friends. As it happened, they weren't there, but we waited a few days and they came back—which was fortunate, because sometimes they go off for quite a while. But my feeling was, in connecting with them at a distance, that they would be there soon if not right away. So we went there, and he brought his raft up, and you know, young people are very . . . it's heartwarming. He told the other children not to touch it because it was a special boat made for spiritual purposes, and of course, the moment he said that, they all wanted to hug it. [Chuckles.]

[Laughs.] Did he give rides on it?

Oh no, it wasn't about that. It was just for that purpose. And the river, of course, flowed one way, so what I didn't tell him was, we weren't going to carry this boat back. It was going to be a gift that he would freely offer to this couple, who were the mystical man and the medicine woman. But I was not going to tell him that. I knew when we went there that he would freely offer it to them as a gift; he did not know that. And my friends did not know it either.

So we stayed there with them for about two or three weeks of your time, and it was a wonderful time. It was an opportunity for Speaks of Many Truths to see what it would be like to be married, to have a family life. And he wasn't too young to learn about marriage. In my time a boy would be just about ready for marriage by the time he was twelve, certainly by the time he was thirteen. You see, we didn't live as long, so that was typical in those times. So it was good for him to see what might be possible.

As it happened, the medicine woman liked him, and he liked her, and they all really liked each other a lot. While we were there, the medicine woman asked him, young Speaks of Many Truths, if he had carved his sign into the boat. He didn't even know about that, carving his sign. He had known about carving signs that he felt to carve into a spear, because we had done that, but he didn't know about carving his sign into the boat. So first he checked with me, to see if the sign he was carving, the one he had put on his spear . . . was that his sign? And I said, "Yes, that's your sign." The medicine woman said, "Do you know where to carve it on the boat?" He said, "No," and so she had him carve it on all the corners and then one carving right in the middle. There was a place you could sit, in the middle, that wasn't too lumpy [chuckles].

So he did that, and it took a little time, because remember, the tools of those days took time. And the medicine woman helped him to make it. I won't show you his sign; that's up to him to show you or not. But what she did is, she added this [draws Fig. 11-1]. I'm just going to draw a circle to indicate his sign, even though that's not it. She did this . . . I'll try to get this just right [draws]. She told him that this would radiate his sign in different directions and also call on the directions to support his sign, which would support him.

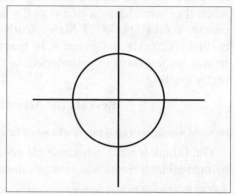

So that was the way it was carved in the middle, and it was carved in his normal way around the outside. We

Fig. 11-1. These markings radiated Speaks of Many Truths' sign in the different directions.

stayed there for a long time and she taught him many things. There are things, remember, that a woman can teach a boy, even in mystical things, that I could never teach or that my friend could not teach either.

Well, because she was a medicine woman—that feels different than a mystical man.

Plus she was a woman—medicine, plus being a woman. So he went out with her many times to gather different things. Even though he was being trained to be a mystical man, I saw no harm in it. In fact, perhaps it would be to his advantage. So he spent a lot of time with her.

At the end of our time there, he wanted to give her something. So, of course, he gave her the boat, which was a raft.

But once you told him that he couldn't take it back . . . I mean, first you told him he couldn't take it back, right?

Oh, I never told him that. I *knew* that.

Did he know that?

No.

So even though he was thinking that instead of riding back, he had to walk back, he still gave it to her?

Oh, yes. He wanted to give her something to remind her of him, and of course, he was not just giving it to her, he was giving it to the tribe, because there weren't possessions that way. He explained to her, of course, how he had made it, how it had taken him a year and everything. And of course, it had a wonderful energy. She said that instead of using it for travel, to go one place to another, they would use it as a special place to put things, like an altar, and it would have a special use, and that even when they moved, they would take it with them and use it for an altar only for ceremonies and blessings and other benevolent occurrences.

My friend told me some time later, when I saw him in another place in our travels, that the tribe had begun using it as a place to bless babies when they were born, which is really wonderful. Such a blessing. Of course, I told Speaks of Many Truths about that, and he was very excited. [Chuckles.] Of course, by that time, by the time I told him that, he was getting ready to get married, so the idea of babies in general was pretty exciting.

Reveals the Mysteries' Family

How old was Speaks of Many Truths when he got married?

Oh, I think it was . . . because his mystical training took so much time, he married late. So he was about thirteen and a half.

And he lived until he was forty?

I think around fifty-one, something like that, in your time.

So you both lived to the same age, then—you lived to fifty-one?

You'll have to ask him how old he was. I'm not always clear about your time; our time is based on the Moon.

So weren't you married? You said you gave him a chance to see married life, but you were married, weren't you?

Yes.

And he lived with you, right?

I was married twice. My first wife did not survive. She gave birth and she died; it was terrible.

Did the baby live?

No. The medicine woman did everything she could, but . . .

What a heartbreak!

The baby apparently had been dead for a time, but we did not know that. I don't . . . can we not talk about that?

Of course.

[Laughs.] I'd rather not. Of course, I have seen her in spirit form, but just now I touched into my grief in my life; it is very hard to bear.

Yes.

But about six or seven years later, I met someone in another tribe. I didn't like to marry outside of the tribe, but I couldn't marry somebody else in the tribe, because I'd grown up with my wife, and everybody else . . . I related to them in a different way. And so my tribe did not . . . it was not considered a problem, especially since I traveled so much, and she traveled with me.

Oh! That's unusual, isn't it?

Yes. That's why we got married. She had been trained partway through medicine-woman training, but then somebody else was better. So she had had a lot of the training, and we were very compatible, knowing a lot of the same things—and then her knowing things I didn't know. Even though she no longer needed the training, she would sometimes assist other medicine women so she would keep up her knowledge. So that was nice.

We actually could work together sometimes; it wasn't that way with my first wife, so that was nice, because my first wife was like the love of my life when I was a child, and then we got married and so on. But my second wife was someone who . . . we were very close also, but we actually worked together, so it was a completely different relationship. So it wasn't like trying to . . . the reason I am saying this is that people often, when they have a sad ending to their marriage, try to look around and re-create it, pick it up again—pick up the thread with somebody else. But this was completely different.

But very enjoyable.

Very enjoyable, yes, but completely different—so different that it worked all right.

So that's the wife Speaks of Many Truths knew?

That's right.

Oh, that's wonderful. Did you have children with her?

Yes.

And they traveled too?

One child.

That's interesting, because that wasn't usually the case in your time, was it? That the whole family could travel?

Well, it's different; it would depend . . . obviously, if you were a hunter, you wouldn't take your wife and children out with you—or in the case of a woman hunter, your husband and children—because you had to devote your total attention to what you were doing, every second. But in my job, yes, there would be time sometimes when traveling between places to see students or doing other things. So I would be able to have family there and pay attention to the family.

And a student, yes?

And a student, and then sometimes there were others who just traveled with us. Perhaps they were going this way for a ways, or they were coming from some other peoples, and we accompanied one another just for the pleasantness of having friends or company on the trail—and sometimes feeling safer, if there was some reason to be alarmed.

And then, as you say, when you would get somewhere, your wife could work with the medicine woman while you did your work.

Or since she was not actually performing that job and could not do all the duties, she could either, as you say, assist the medicine woman in some way, or if what was needed was simple and not the complex sort of thing that requires years and years of training that medicine women or medicine men receive, then she could actually do something herself if the people were comfortable with that.

So the child we had, who traveled with us, became . . . I have to use your term, in your time, because that's really the only way it works. She became very cosmopolitan—perhaps not in the relationship of big cities, but she could speak many different languages and different dialects, and she understood all different kinds of customs. So as it turned out she became . . .

Like a diplomat, almost?

Very much like a diplomat, and as she got older, she became someone who helped unite the tribes in that sort of statesmanlike, diplomatic fashion, the way a person does who feels at ease in all different cultures.

How wonderful!

It was wonderful.

Finding a Mystical Teacher

I'd like to talk more about my relationship with Speaks of Many Truths, mostly because this is really his desire to create these books, and I want to honor that. I want to honor the fact that it is something he wants to do. And I want to support him doing it.

What's the first time he did something that really made you feel: "Oh, my God! Look at that! I didn't teach him that! How did he know that?" Was there a case like that?

Almost immediately. That is one of the ways you can tell that someone will be good in this profession, because he will be doing things that you didn't teach him—and very often naturally. And sometimes if the person is living in a circumstance—with the tribe or people or clan—in a situation where the people don't understand why he's doing that, then the people can get upset or confused. But when the mystical man or woman sees that person, he or she says, "Oh, well, he's . . . you know, this is a person who would be a good student, because he's doing things."

So when I met Speaks of Many Truths, he was doing lots of things like that right away. And all of my students were like that; they were all doing things like that. So it did not surprise me that they were relating the different things, or perhaps by being exposed to the medicine woman or the medicine man or the mystical woman or man in their tribe, they had already learned things just by . . .

Osmosis?

No, by wanting to be around. And if the medicine woman or man or mystical woman or man was comfortable with having them around, then they would pick things up. If that teacher didn't have a feeling to teach them, or any student . . . it requires a feeling, not only for the student to learn from a teacher, but equally that the teacher has the feeling to teach the student. If both of those feelings aren't there, then you do not get a good relationship that way.

So the reason I taught Speaks of Many Truths is that the people in his tribe who could do those things didn't have that feeling to teach him, though he had already picked up things from them. And that is not at all unusual. It wasn't that there was something wrong with them; it was rather that sometimes when you grow up with somebody . . . in Speaks of Many Truths' case, he related to them in certain ways, growing up, and they related to him, growing up, in certain ways. And not unlike other cultures, it isn't always easy to suddenly adapt and decide that that person is your spiritual student and that he's not all those other things that he was when he was younger. And it's the same thing for the teacher—that he or she is not all those other things when you were younger, and now he or she is just a teacher. It's not easy to adapt. But if someone from another village . . .

Comes in fresh, becomes the teacher?

Then it is much easier. There is no history, as you say. And that's why sometimes students from different cultures—usually tribes related in some way, or even the same tribe, just different clans living different places— would do that. It was not all the time, but my people would do that. We liked that, and it made things much simpler and you could accomplish more in the time you had.

Once You Learn to Communicate, You Are Surrounded by Teachers

So with the short life span, if you got Speaks of Many Truths at nine years old and he became an adult at thirteen . . . and yet he studied with you many years past that, didn't he?

That's right. Even though he was an adult and he had his wife and pretty soon his children, he was still studying with me for quite some time.

And that was normal?

Yes. And then, of course, once he could start traveling and going around teaching, doing things on his own, he would still learn from other people or other animals or plants. Once you learn how to communicate, then you're surrounded by teachers. Plus, when he would meet other mystical men, mystical women, medicine men, medicine women and sometimes individuals who had special skills they had learned on their own, then if they wanted to share, he would learn those as well.

So there were rich possibilities. I mean, there were no universities, no schools, no churches, but there were still many possibilities to learn, right?

I feel that it was more so, because the schools in your time are often rigid. They want the student to adapt to the teaching. But they're often not going to adapt the teaching to the student. In our time we did that. We didn't expect our students to become something; we expected and encouraged them to be themselves. If they needed to be by the water to learn things, then we'd do the teaching by the water. If they needed to be up on the mountains to learn things, then we'd be up on the mesa.

Or in the tree, as you said [chuckles]. I was just wondering how old Speaks of Many Truths was when he was kind of considered a graduate and only saw you intermittently after that?

Oh, you never graduate. I'm not one either. There is no such concept. You always learn; you continue learning.

But he lived with you for a certain time . . . and then what? How old was he when he stopped living with you?

Well, of course, when he got married he wasn't living with me; he was living with his family.

But still in your tribe rather than his?

Well, sometimes I would travel; it depended. It was not fixed; it's hard to describe. Good night.

Thank you for coming.

The Feeling Heart

Speaks of Many Truths
December 8, 2001

All right. This is Speaks of Many Truths. Greetings.

Welcome!

The Feeling Heart Is Your Soul Heart

The feeling heart is on the other side of your chest from your physical heart. Your feeling heart is your soul heart and lives on after your physical death. It lives in your body to allow your soul to reach for its desires, and it gives the soul some influence in your physical life.

So the heart lives on in the physical body after you die? Is that just until it decomposes?

No, that is not what was stated. Your feeling heart is your soul heart and lives on after your physical death. Do you understand? It does not live on in the body.

It lives on in the soul.

That's right. It lives in your body to allow your soul to reach for its desires and to give the soul some influence in your physical life. But it lives in your body only when you are alive and in your body. It does not live in your body when your soul leaves—what would be the point?

So the soul comes in and it has a feeling heart?

Yes.

And that's the connection, then, to the physical? That's the soul's connection into the physical, which influences the endocrine glands and so on?

The soul comes in without the feeling heart. The soul comes in with universal love for all beings, the way it exists in its natural environment. But your soul has to do something that is different than the way it lives in its usual place; it has to have a personal love, not just an impersonal unconditional love. In order to have a personal love, then it has to have a connection to your physical body.

Therefore, the feeling heart will reside in a physical body so that your soul can engage. Its first engagement in personal love is with your physical body, where you as you understand yourself reside. It is also at that level . . . when that happens, it is a means by which you, your physical self, your mental self, your spiritual self, your feeling self—you understand, your instinctual self—it's the means by which you can develop personal love in this life here at all.

Without a feeling heart, your love could not go out any further than universal love, period—meaning universal unconditional love in some cases, but certainly just universal love of all beings. But to have a personal attachment or a personal attraction or an individual-to-individual attraction, even for a pet or a favorite plant and certainly for a human being . . . first being your family, and then as you change and grow, a lover, a wife or husband, like that. And then perhaps children.

And grandchildren.

Yes, grandchildren, as you say. All of it starts with that initial connection with the feeling heart to your physical body.

Emotions Do Not Exist

How is it connected? Is it in the emotional? In the astral body?

"Emotion" is a word associated with the mind; it does not exist. There are no such things as emotions. I realize that sounds strict on my part. There *are* feelings. The reason I say that emotions do not exist is that "emotion" is a word that does not describe feelings. You understand, "feeling" is something that has touch associated with it, there is physical evidence. What am I doing now?

Rubbing your right fingers over your left arm.

Yes, and over my face and so on. In short, this cannot be thought as well as it can be noticed as a physical experience. So, reader, while you're reading this, just touch your fingers together, because even though your mind knows what this means, it accentuates your understanding.

When you actually do it, yes.

Right. When you actually do it, feelings are felt. "Emotion" is a word that the mind uses to separate itself from feelings. If the mind uses that to separate itself from feelings, it always does that because it does not understand feelings. The mind cannot feel, and therefore, when you run your life by your mind, you can remove yourself from feelings if those feelings are causing you suffering—which is why some people are attracted to that. But in the process of removing yourself, you remove yourself from all feelings and sensitivity—and essentially remove yourself from the path of awareness that leads to your creation potential.

So my suggestion is this: If you understand that the feeling self is the means of material mastery by which you can understand and accomplish . . . if you wish to remain away from that, aloof and at a distance, unreachable, you can try to ignore your feelings. Sometimes that is useful, on some occasions, but generally speaking, I do not recommend it.

Conscious versus Unconscious Business

So you will find, then, that the feeling heart is a means by which you engage your world in your physical life. You use your feeling heart to establish your means of discernment: what is for you, what is for others. It is always better to say that than what is right and what is wrong, because different cultures have different practices of what is right and what is wrong. But if you make a decision based upon those good, warm feelings, you will know what is for you, and if the feeling in your body is something uncomfortable, then you can let it go, leave it and walk on, whatever it is associated with: a person, a place, a thing, an object. You can leave it, because it is not meant for you. It is meant for someone else who will have a warm feeling for that, and the outcome of that person engaging with that will be better than the outcome of you engaging with that.

This is not always so well understood. One might say, "Well, I have to do such and such for work; I have to go and take a client out for lunch or dinner." Now, that person might, at a distance, be able to look at that client and get an uncomfortable feeling. In a conscious business, where people are aware and practicing with their feelings and their instincts, there would be others available, maybe someone who is your junior in the department or even someone who is your senior in the department, who would say, "I have a good feeling looking at that person." Then in the conscious business, which succeeds more than it fails because it makes few mistakes, the person who has the good feeling would go out to dinner with the client and would have success. The client would like that person and he or she would like the client, so they would achieve quite a bit.

But say the person is working for an unconscious business. So he or she goes out with the client, has an uncomfortable feeling with the client—and the client would have the same uncomfortable feeling with him or her. In this case, the chances of accomplishing your goal, much less your mutual goals, are not as likely, but the chances of getting into trouble or mischief—something that you maybe don't want to do but which is the only thing . . . not the business discussion, but it is the only area that the two of you feel good about. Maybe it's going out and getting drunk and then doing who knows what shenanigans, or maybe it's that the two of you do not relate on a business level and nothing happens there, but you find each other attractive, even though you're married, and you have an affair. Things like that. That's why I say you can have mischief, because the feeling you have is more important for the successful business, in this example, than the assignment to take the client out for lunch or dinner and see if you can find something you can mutually agree upon and have success together with.

I give this out because in your time business has a profound impact on social systems as well as economic systems. And because it has such an impact on social systems, its tenets, its manners and mores, are corrupting social behaviors. But that is not necessary. For the conscious business that is successful more often than not, you would then as a business have the opportunity to not only be successful more often than not, because you match the right people up together in the business and with the customers, but you would be demonstrating ways of being that would be a benevolent influence on society, even if that is not your intention. So you would be contributing socially to the betterment of life around you, which would affect you and your security and all these other things for your business, to say nothing of your public image, while you improve the quality of your business and its structure and its success.

The Mind and the Instinctual Body

What do you call the body that the feeling heart is located in—the feeling body?

You mean instead of the emotional body?

Yes.

I would say that if you're going to use the term "body"—such as "mental body," "physical body," "spiritual body"—then, yes, you might say "feeling body," and altogether, minus the mental body, they make up the instinctual body, yes? The mental body is not necessary nor is it useful in the instinctual body; it would only be a complication. But because the mental body can observe the instinctual body in action, it can learn from it and apply the principles of harmony that work in the instinctual body. It can apply those to itself and learn how to think for its own benefit, rather than have destructive thoughts against itself and against others and motivate itself or others to become self-destructive.

Think about that for a minute: How many suicides take place because of thoughts? And how many unintentional self-deaths take place because of distractions in the mind? And how many of these suicides and unintentional deaths cause death and harm to others?

So when the mind learns how to think in a benevolent way for itself and no longer gets caught up in, "What if this happens?" and "What if that happens?" pulling on its litany of things that are largely fears induced by other people, or even other people's fears that seem like a remote possibility to the mind . . . then the mind becomes a self-destructive organism to itself, to say nothing of to others. You give that power over your natural instinct, which is not . . . remember, your natural instinct is not only your feelings, it is your spiritual self. Or let's call it, since you're using the term, your spiritual body, your physical body, your feeling body—that's what makes up the instinctual body.

Now, when the mind learns how to think based upon its observance of those other three, which make up the fourth one, the instinctual body, it then learns that much of what it is doing . . . take worry, for example. I'm not talking about an analysis of a situation so that the best circumstance can be applied, but I'm talking about repeated worries over and over and over again so that the mind becomes obsessed with exploring those worries. It's not that this draws those negative situations to you, as you call them—or discomforting situations, as I would prefer to call them. But the mind becomes obsessed with discovering if there is truth in these worries, because the mind's goal in life, if you would call it that, is to discover truth—what is true as compared to what is false. So if that is the mind's goal, it will explore all of its worries to find out if they are true or false. That's how people's lives get complicated and, as you say, messed up.

But when the mind observes the physical, the spiritual and the feeling bodies (which together make up the instinctual body), if the instinctual body has been embraced by the conscious person, then the mind learns what is of value. It can let go of worry entirely, and as such, it does not have to pursue worries in the search for truth. It can let go of all of that, and life then becomes much simpler, more comfortable, easier to live and more enjoyable.

The Vertical Mind, the Andromedan Linear Mind and Ignorance

So when you are using your feelings, you ascertain what is right, what is best for the self, and no matter where these feelings come up, they're in the feeling body, not actually in the physical body, right? Is that correct?

Yes. But they are in the physical body also, so that is the real answer. The feeling body and the physical body are not just first cousins; they are two parts of the same thing. The spiritual body marries those two parts when it comes into the physical body, so those three are completely united and, more to the point, completely compatible.

Whereas the mental body, which is a linear mental body and is not associated with your natural way of knowing . . . which as Zoosh says is vertical, meaning you know what you need to know, when you need to know it, but if you don't need to know it anymore, you don't have to know it, and it will come up again if you need to know it again in the future. That is the natural mental body you have, so you do not have to carry around a cartload of things that you don't need to know. That's how it works for everybody, so you don't have to tell people things from your cart [chuckles]. You don't need to carry the cart around to tell other people; other people have their own vertical mental body, as Zoosh calls it.

But here on Earth, because you are helping your brothers and sisters on Andromeda resolve something that they are unable or have been unable to resolve for themselves, you have been using the Andromedan linear mind as a service to them. And it is not devoid of being a service to you, because it creates a challenge, and the challenge for you is something that must be overcome in order to experience your true nature for the benefit of yourself and all beings. It also allows you the feeling of joy, gratitude and gratefulness when you achieve something that is natural for you. Being the instinctual person—having the vertical mind and all that—when you achieve it, you feel this wonderful sense that is or approaches euphoria. That is because the challenge exists, and it allows you to stretch, it allows you to grow. Also, the linear Andromedan mind is the vehicle by which and the only way by which you can experience ignorance.

Think about it: You do not have the capacity to experience ignorance in a vertical mind. In a vertical mind, you always know what you need to know, when you need to know it, and if you don't need to know it anymore, then you don't know it. There is no ignorance; it is simply that something is utilized when you need to know it and released when you don't need to know it anymore. That is not ignorance; that is usefulness, that is focus.

But if you are going to have ignorance in order to be able to re-create your existence, to learn new things, to add new things, to do things in a new way that you would never do away from Earth in a more normal life for yourself, because you have discovered how to do things that work well for you and you do it that way . . . why change it? To come here where you are learning lessons to be a creator, where you have the opportunity to learn creation from the moment you are born, you have to have ignorance. And imbedded within the linear mind from Andromeda is the capacity to experience ignorance for the past, the present and the future, because that is how the linear mind works. A vertical mind does not have the capacity to experience ignorance.

That's a good fact! All this time we thought we were helping the Andromedans, but we had to have that or the experiment wouldn't have worked!

That's right. So you helped them, and perhaps unintentionally, but still as a factor of the function of their mind, they are happy to help you. They did not visit ignorance on their linear mind, nor are they ignorant in their own world, but it is a capacity of the linear mind in fact. So it is, as the Spanish language says so precisely, simpático.

Andromedans are now being encouraged to seek their feelings, to work with their feelings [see The Ultimate UFO Series: Andromeda]. The entire civilization is being encouraged to do this.

That's right. They are being encouraged to do this, and the means by which they are able to adapt their mind, adapt their feelings to embrace the idea of working with their feelings . . . which will allow them to let go of a mind that can worry and keep them in the past as well as in the future, that can keep them somewhat out of the present, which is where they really have the capacity to grow, to change and to achieve their potential. Then the encouragement to work with their feelings will inevitably lead them to what you are doing here, only they will do it in a more benevolent environment. It will take them much, much longer as a result, but they will ultimately achieve the vertical mind.

And the horizontal mind will go to the beings from the negative planet in Sirius that blew up who are now on 3.0 Earth, right?

In time. If they choose to accept it, in time, but it is too soon for them. Then if they choose to engage that, that's fine, but I think they will choose to engage something different, which is a curved mind—a curved mind like this [draws Fig. 12-1]. A curved mind is not quite so difficult to deal with. Of course, here is the linear mind, and here is the curved mind. The curved mind . . . I'm drawing in these dotted lines, even though it is not there. The curved mind has a bias toward the vertical mind, but it allows for some small portion of the linear mind to help growth. But it is not as overwhelming to these people who have enough to deal with, as with the linear mind that you are experiencing—it's too much. They have suffered too much. They need to be nurtured, they need to have a mind that offers a bias or a support or a . . . you could even say a leaning toward the vertical mind, which is ultimately much, much more nourishing and nurturing, and does not demand so much.

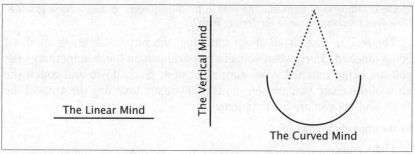

Fig. 12-1. The linear mind, the vertical mind and the curved mind.

Also, with the curved mind, you do not have to have been a spiritual master in any of your past lives. The Andromedan linear mind as it is set up, as we've discussed, requires you to have been a spiritual master, because the depth, the challenge, the capacities will always—in any given life, no matter how long or short—throw you back on resources that you have not acquired in this life. Because there is ignorance about what you have done in other lives, so you don't have ready access to your usual methods, then you have to have that spiritual mastery in your soul, and there you are able to acquire the support you need energetically to go on.

The beings who are now beginning to inhabit where you used to be in 3.0 Earth, from this troubled place of much suffering . . .

In Sirius?

Yes, in the former planet in Sirius . . . these beings cannot take that level of suffering, plus most of them—not all—have never had a life of spiritual mastery. So the curved mind allows them growth, but it does not demand it, and it supports the attraction to the vertical mind, which is much more loving and benevolent and natural and nurturing for all beings, in my experience. As well it welcomes them into a nurturing mental place, rather than a mental place that they had to suffer through in their past on that discomforting planet, where even their dreams were invaded.

The Feeling Body Has a Natural Affinity with the Physical Body

Whenever you say, "Feel the heat; feel the love-heat," that's coming from the feeling body, right? [For more on the love-heat/heart-warmth/physical-warmth exercise, see Overview.]

That's correct. It's coming from the feeling body, and the feeling body is united with and has interactions with . . . it's like this [crosses fingers; fingers are intertwined]. These fingers are interlocking, yes? It is that the feeling body's first communication is always to the physical body, because the feeling body has a natural affinity with the physical body. It isn't that the feeling body is instructing the physical body; if we say that, then we're trying to create an artificial hierarchy.

So you're telling us to focus into the heat by touching fingers, getting a sense of touch. How does touching relate to the feeling body?

The feeling body is all about touching; the physical body is all about being touched. Even when you as a physical person touch something else, you are being touched. You can, right now, reach down and touch the arms of the chair; you are conscious that you are touching the arms of the chair, and yet you are being touched.

By the arms of the chair?

That's right.

Observe the Warmth and Feedback from the Instinctual Body

So what do we need to understand? This is a new concept: the physical heart, the feeling heart. What do we do about it? How do we focus on it? How do we use it?

You don't use it; it is there as part of your existence. It would be like saying, "How do you use your blood cells?" You don't have to, because they are part of your existence; they do for themselves and for you on their own. So does the feeling heart. What you are really saying is, what homework can you use in order to feel more mentally aware of the feeling heart? I know that that is not your thought, but that is your motivation behind that question.

I think it is better for your mind to observe the actions of the warmth and the means by which the instinctual body, as instructed in the *Shamanic Secrets* series and so on, gives you a physical feedback to know whether something is for you or whether something is for somebody else. The warmth is that vital. But to attempt to use it in some way, to run it through exercises? No, I do not recommend that. Because the point is for the mind to learn from these other parts of your body, not for the mind to instruct.

When the mind is the devotion—you're devoting yourself to your mind—the mind will always attempt to re-create everything it interacts with. This is why people try to control one another and their environment. The mind will always attempt to re-create everything and everyone in its environment based upon the model of its own existence. So if the mind is not very evolved or if it is intended to be challenging—and the mind is your challenge here—every time you allow the mind to structure other things according to only its understanding, it will tend to create (this is its bias) challenges and complications, even if none were present originally. That is why control, which seems initially so efficient, so valuable, so useful, ultimately stifles, narrows, causes resentment in the case of human beings and even animals—sometimes plants, I might add—and ultimately creates a hostile environment.

That is why I speak to you now of these matters, because it is time for the mind to learn—and the mind has been preprogrammed to learn, by Creator, on the basis of physical evidence. That is why science is so appealing, because in science the whole point is to have physical evidence that proves that your mental thought or theory is true, and if others can reproduce it using your theorem, then you can say, "This has validity." That's why science is so popular in your time, because your time is devoted to the mind. However, if you use instincts—not based upon their popular description in your dictionaries, but the instinctual body as described here (the spiritual, the physical, the feeling bodies, which make up the instinctual body as discussed at length in the *Shamanic Secrets* series)— then you can achieve your goals, be they mental, spiritual, feeling or physical, in a much, much faster time than you can possibly ever achieve them in linear time.

That's why I make such an issue out of this, because your culture is too caught up in the challenge because of a factor of the personality of Creator. Remember, the Creator of this universe *loves variety*, and because Creator loves variety, and because you are using a linear mind, and because the linear mind controls, and because the linear mind is about challenge, your worries will very often have a great variety to them. And the obsession of the mind to find out if truth is associated with any of these worries in all of their variety will allow you to pursue many false trails for a long time and to impose the controls of the mind—set up according to its own model and influenced by Creator's love of variety—to impose and unintentionally restrict the capacities of creation in yourself and others all around you.

That sounds like a glitch.

It sounds like that, but you have to remember that Creator's intention was always that you become better, or from Creator's point of view, greater than Itself, as any parent wants his or her children to do. Therefore, what sounds like a glitch is an intentional challenge, because if the Creator created you only in Its own image, you could become like Creator, but never more. And Creator wanted you to become more.

Therefore, Creator provided you with a challenge, which Creator Itself does not have, in order that you might find a way to achieve more than Creator Itself can achieve, because Creator does not have that challenge. Creator's challenge is always and only to be able to move beyond to Its next level, only if It can create someone—meaning all of you in the Explorer Race—who eventually will unite and become something that is not only equal to the task to inherit and take over this creation, but who will have greater, more beneficial tools (if I might say that), applications and wisdom to do a better job. So the challenge is intentional.

Should we put a requisition in for a curved mind?

[Chuckles.] No need to. When you move on from here, right away you will have your natural mind.

Which is vertical.

Yes. But, nope, you can't put in a requisition. Or let's say this: You can put in a requisition, but unlike letters sent to the North Pole and received by Santa, these will go to the dead letter office.

[Laughs.] Okay. Thank you.

Good night.

Good night.

The Human Soul on Earth

Soul Doctor
December 8, 2001

octor, here.

Welcome!

Souls Were Never Prepared to Tolerate the Conditions of Your Time

If you've never had a life in which you've been exposed to something frightening, startling or unexpected, then one of the conditions that can be expected as a response to these stimuli might be, for example, asthma or even any condition such as a backache that is not caused by an injury. Also, you might get an upset stomach sometimes—not caused by an injury but through conditions. All these conditions that I'm mentioning are aggravated by stress but not actually caused by it. Therefore, the increase in these conditions these days is in direct proportion to soul personalities who have never had this experience—never experienced something frightening, startling or unexpected, ever. The increase in air pollution is of negligible impact on the increase of frequency of, say for instance, asthma or other breathing disorders, though it certainly affects patients like that and certainly affects patients with emphysema as well.

Now, I am here to discuss this because the challenge in your time for my team and myself is to resolve these challenges that confront the soul and to help the soul to survive and function more easily in your time. Souls were never prepared by Creator or even by their teachers to tolerate the

conditions of your time. By "conditions of your time," what I am referring to is not just the interactions between human beings, which have
been ongoing, but it is also the circumstances of overwhelming influence
from the media—too many ideas at once. Children now go to school, and
not only do they interact with other children and their lessons, but they
are overwhelmed by experiencing too much information, very often for
the children way, way too soon. So we are talking about impacts on the
actual soul that are causing the soul to have a greater desire to move out
of the body.

In order that we do not have mass suicide, which could develop if the
Soul Doctor—not to be sounding as if I myself am so wonderful; the Soul
Doctor and team are all worthy and equal—were not working on this circumstance . . . many children all over the world would simply say, "Oh,
this is too much; we will go elsewhere, be born somewhere else." There is
really a grave threat of this, that souls will put out into the atmosphere of
Earth energetically that this is not a safe place for young souls to come. By
young souls, I do not refer to children; I am referring to souls who have
not had too much experience in such a challenging place. And then all of
these beings will go elsewhere.

Even if Creator says, "Oh, please come here," Creator does not twist the
soul's arm behind the back and say, "Oh, you have to go to Earth!" At
most, Creator would say, "Oh, please come here to Earth." But if a soul is
frightened . . . not frightened, but if the soul feels that this is not an attractive place, the soul will go elsewhere.

In Your Times the Soul Must Be Encapsulated

Therefore, I and my team cannot re-create the conditions on Earth; that
is your job. The only thing we can do is to try to create a more benevolent
environment inside the physical body, which temporarily encapsulates the
soul during the soul's experience or, we might say, journey through its
Earth life. Therefore, that is what we do.

Now, say you go back about four or five thousand years on Earth: The
soul connection to the physical body was not as firm as we have had to
make it. This is why in your time, not only because of wonderful medical
methods, sometimes when people experience grievous injuries or shocks,
things that in the past (say, five thousand years ago) . . . a shock, a tremendous shock, where a person might have just passed out and died . . . meaning that soul would have said, "That's enough of that," because the soul
was not as—how can we say?—supported to be in the physical self, protected. Now, in your time, people experience shocks like that more than
one time in a life—not everyone, but many times—grievous injuries that
in the past would have caused death.

Now, granted, you have wonderful medical procedures, but even so,
even the doctors themselves or the emergency people themselves are sometimes surprised that someone would live through such a thing. This is

because we have had to make changes because of the overwhelming aspects of your society—not just the threats and dangers, but more to the point, too much information too soon for children, and then they become nervous in the body. If they do not have an encapsulation for the soul itself that supports and nurtures them in a different way than, say, five thousand years ago on Earth, you would have difficulty in continuing your race of people.

You could say, "Well, there are too many people on Earth," but even though you can make a good justification for that and others would have to say many times, "Yes, that's true; yes, that's true," ultimately you do not have too many people on Earth. Creator would not allow this many people on Earth if you were not performing a function that required more people. Therefore, the people you have on Earth are intended, even though it is difficult for Earth as a planet to support you all.

Plants and Animals Cooperate to Welcome the Soul

So our job, then, is to create an environment without particularly changing the makeup of Creator's choice, Creator's model, for how the physical, spiritual human being is to be. We have to find a way in order to welcome the soul. So this is what we do: We utilize not only the feeling heart, yes, but we also utilize something like a network of the feeling hearts in plants and animals to create a beauty that is beyond their own being. And that is why in your time people find enough beauty in plants and animals alone to stay in a life when they would otherwise say, "It is too much; I am going to go on."

In your time, did you know . . . you idealize times in the past, but in your time, meaning the past one hundred fifty years or so, there are more people as a percentage of all people who are engaged with—who love, if you like—plants and animals than ever before. This is not the means by which the soul stays in the body, but it is something that has to happen because plants and animals are giving some of their own loving feeling to support the feeling heart, the feeling body in the human being, so that human beings will feel more sheltered in the soul inside the physical body in all human beings now. And as I say, as a result—this is not intended, but as a result—you have human beings who are enamored of animals, enamored of plants. I can assure you that five thousand years ago, people weren't collecting orchids, they weren't devoted to cats—none of that!

It's not that people didn't find orchids beautiful, not that they didn't enjoy the beauty and personality of cats. But it wasn't such a devotion. That cannot be helped, because these beings are literally making it possible . . . think of the challenge to us! We are not able to change the model of the human being—the spiritual being, the physical being, the feeling being, we're not able to change that. For Creator says, "This is how it has to be." And Creator also says, "It is your job to cause the soul to feel more welcome in the body. Go on, go! Go do it!" And so we say, "Oh! Oh! But we cannot change things!" And the Creator says, "Oh, you will find a way! Goodbye!"

So all we have is: "We have to find some beings from the outside who will volunteer to help." Who else can help on Earth but beings who are not here to learn anything, who are here to help, who are here to offer their wisdom? In short, these are beings who are prepared to make a personal sacrifice for your benefit. We go to the plants and animals, and we appeal to them: "Can you spare some of your loving feeling so that we can create a thin membrane around the soul when it lives in the physical body of human beings, so that humans will not just die off and the whole experiment will fall down in a heap?" And they say, those who cooperate . . . especially certain ones. How do you know which ones especially cooperate?

They're the ones we love?

That's right. What animals right now are so loved? Dogs, cats, dolphins, horses—you can think of many more. Elephants, dinosaurs . . . they are in the past, yes? But in some ways, they still exist. So think about it. I am not saying the other animals are unworthy. What I am saying is that individuals amongst the other animals cooperate, yes, but as a species, the animals whom many people are so enamored of . . . I can assure you that five thousand years ago, if you saw a dog, you'd say, "Oh, what a nice being"—that's it. The idea of making a pet of a dog, of providing food for the dog, of providing water for the dog, of shelter, all of this—essentially adopting the dog and making the dog your child—would never have occurred to you in a million years. If the dog wanted to accompany you on your travels for your pleasure, as long as you and the dog were going the same place, that was fine—a companion, a friend, wonderful. But to have a dog as a pet? No, you would never think of it. So what changed? Why now? That is why. Interesting, isn't it?

Fascinating.

Soul Doctors and the Explorer Race

Tell me about soul doctors. Do you work all over the creation?

Only where needed. Occasionally in other places in the creation. We will go somewhere to offer advice and guidance to beings, sometimes beings of the culture who are living there and sometimes their teachers, who may want to create a different environment—not in this case of protection; it's not necessary there—but a different environment where the soul might flower and grow. So then we might consult, the same way a physician here would consult with another physician, based upon his or her specialty. So that's that. But more than 99 percent of our effort is taking place right here.

How many are you?

It is hard to quantify, but for the sake of simplicity, for your number system, it is more than a hundred.

Are you individual, unique beings? Or can you flow and become a group being?

We flow and can become greater or lesser numbers, though this whole thing of numbers is not really a factor for us. But for the sake of your conceptual understandings, then I can say, yes, we are that.

Have you ever done this before? Talked through a human?

No. That is why I am having to learn how to use his voice box. I have to learn how to speak more gently for the voice box and be perhaps a little less ebullient, a little less excited. Because although the physical body does not mind that, the voice box . . . if I speak with my own voice only all the time, then it is hard on the voice box, and I do not wish to harm the individual [the channel].

So the bulk of your service for the past . . . how many years? Five thousand? A hundred and fifty? How long have you had to really be in service here?

On Earth, you mean?

Yes.

Well, I went back before, as you know, because the Explorer Race has been on a pattern.

Oh! You've been with the Explorer Race on other planets?

Yes. We've been following you, not because we're engaged in the Explorer Race phenomenon or the Explorer Race system, but we go where we're needed, and because you were like this . . . [draws Fig. 13-1].

We caused a lot of problems. [Laughs.]

Well, not intentionally.

I know.

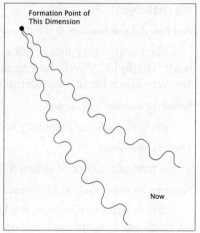

Fig. 13-1. In terms of your needs, the Soul Doctor is with you more and more.

But because at one point, using this dot, you'd become like that [draws]. In terms of your needs, we are with you more and more. You can see that the direction is going out here toward the . . . becoming more and more. So we become with you more and more and more, the dot becoming the part where there was the consideration by Creator to begin this whole concept, experience, of creator children to be greater than, more than . . . with more capacities, I would prefer to say, than Creator Itself.

Did you have to minister to the souls or doctor to the souls before they started having physical bodies?

No, not when the physical body began, but when the Explorer Race souls started having bodies that you could call physical (meaning in their focus), in the place where they were they could reach out and grab themselves and say, "Ah, here is a substance." You could have a body that would feel physical to you at dimension five, six, seven, the eighth dimension. It would feel physical to you, but of course, if you as a third-dimensional being were able to be there, you would not see it at all.

In the form of whatever image?

Form—that's a better word, yes.

The Soul Doctor Team Can Only Use Resources Available on Earth

So you've been around a long time!

We've been around since Creator started this thing. Creator said, "Well, I can only do so much." Creator is a good boss; It can delegate. But It does not always tell us how to do it! Mmph [expresses poignant, perplexing challenge]!

And how did you learn to do it? By experience?

I like Creator very much, but sometimes the employee gets mad at the boss: "Go do it!" "Well, how to do it?" "It is *your* job to do it!" "Thank you very much for that wonderful instruction!"

"Read the manual!" [Laughs.]

"Yes, but [makes a raspberry sound] where is the manual?"

There is no manual.

No manual: "Go do it yourself!" [Laughs.]

So whom do you consult with? Friends of the Creator maybe?

We only can use resources available in a given place. For example, here on Earth, we can only use resources available to you in your world. We cannot say, "Oh, let us bring down resources from the Pleiades." No. You are here; your souls are here on Earth in these bodies, in these conditions, now. We cannot bring something from a foreign place, even from another focus—how could it help you? To say nothing of creating a problem for them, because it would create a cord from where you are to their world that could totally saturate their world. It could create a disaster for them and not be of any help to you at all.

So we can only utilize resources within your realm of existence, because that will help you and interaction with you will not harm them. You understand, the flow from the animals and the plants is to you, but there is no reverse flow of any great consequence. So your reaction to plants and animals is based entirely on this loving energy coming to you from them, even though it is not conscious in your mental self. It is something you feel. That's why some of you feel . . . oh, dogs, you love dogs. Have you ever met a child who doesn't love dogs?

Yes, and dolphins.

Dolphins. It is natural; you just say, "Oh, I want to hug them!"

I think you said that five thousand years ago the soul was not so attached to the physical body.

I used that as an example. Five thousand years ago, conditions were different, meaning on Earth.

What was the method by which you allowed the soul to get a firmer grip on the physical?

It has a natural grip; we didn't have to do anything. Only in your time do we have . . . a soul doctor responds exactly the same way a physician does. A physician helps when you are sick, when you need help. You are in pain, there is some suffering; something isn't working. You go to a physician, and that physician says, "Oh, you do this or this or this," or "Let me help you," or "I will assign this to help you; you will feel better soon." With a soul doctor, it is the same way exactly. We don't do anything unless something isn't working and we are needed. So we didn't go to people five thousand years ago and say, "How can we help you?" They would have said, "Nothing is wrong! Have a good life. Goodbye."

Who calls you, then? The souls themselves?

That's right. The souls themselves call, and so we come. That's how we know. And then we recognize the overall system, that if we are not successful, the whole civilization could die out, because the beings you need . . . it's not just the beings who will come to be born. That's wonderful, that civilization can maintain itself for a time by simply the beings who will come. But ultimately the beings you *need*, who will have the ideas, the methods, the stimulations, the whole method by which your civilization can not only survive but thrive, they will not come. They will go elsewhere, and then before long your civilization will be but a memory.

The New Children's Souls Didn't Always Want to Come to Earth

What we're counting on now are the new young children, the new breed of children.

But they're growing up, they're here!

Yes, I know, but just in the past few years . . .

No, no; they've been here for longer than the past few years.

The new kind of children?

Even the teenagers today.

Oh!

I'm not talking about something that just started a couple of years ago.

So when would you say it started?

It started seventeen years ago.

Precisely seventeen years ago?

Not to the day, but seventeen years ago.

Was there some . . . ?

Anticipation. The souls have the capacity before they are born, especially when they are inside mother, to get a general view ahead for their lives—not every instant, but a general view. And many of them wanted to say, "Forget it!" It you look back on those times, you will see that there were a lot of miscarriages around then. And even the people getting abortions [makes shuddery sound] . . . horrible thing. I'm not trying to be judgmental, but if a baby should choose to be born in your body, then let it be born, if you possibly can, please. Even if you do not intend to bring up the baby yourself . . . I know it's a great responsibility, there's a lot of discomfort, but please, please, please, let the baby be born.

But souls could look forward, as you say, to their general flow of life, and they were beginning to get nervous universally. And some of them were saying, "Oh, that's it; we're leaving." It wasn't exactly a strike, they weren't on strike [laughs]. But it was like saying, "No, no, no, no; we don't want that." And every time a soul leaves with that feeling . . .

It radiates.

They radiate. They leave like a residual . . . not of themselves, but a residual of what might have been. You get enough of that residual energy in the energetic atmosphere of Earth, and then the souls you need to have come here, they all say, "Oh, no, no, no, no, no, no; I will go somewhere else. Why would I even want to come there?" And even if Creator says, "Oh, please? Oh, please?"—the soul is not the employee of the Creator. It's free.

The soul is a child. As any parent knows, you could even say to the child, "Oh, please! Oh, please!" and the child will ultimately do what he or she does. So creators are not bosses, as every parent knows, even though sometimes you forget, eh? [Laughs.]

Parents: Play Gentle Music to Your Baby in the Womb

So it's not just the overload of information for today's children, it's the incredible challenges. I mean, there are drugs in grade schools—there are so many things that were not there fifty years ago.

It's too much!

It's too much . . . not just information—there's too much everything!

It's too much everything too soon, and it is overwhelming. And if there's not a special effort made to have the soul be welcome in the physical body

. . . in other words, if there aren't other things in life as well as the membrane, if there aren't other things in life that are so attractive that you want to stay . . . like dogs and cats and horses and ponies and dolphins, which you can't hug. But sometimes, if you are lucky, you can swim with dolphins if they like you. It's wonderful; you never forget it.

So what can parents do? What would you recommend that parents do? I mean, obviously they need to welcome the child before he or she is born, but what would you say to parents specifically?

Try to play music, even if it is not music that you normally listen to. Maybe you like rock 'n' roll or country music or rap—that's fine. Those are all fine, those are all artistic things. But try to also play music that is older or more gentle, meaning lullabies—mother will have to listen to this, not only mother but father too, to support mother. You can sing lullabies, nurturing songs—the soul will appreciate that. You can play New Age harmony music, but not new music that expresses disharmony in an attempt to create harmony out of disharmony—not that, not that sort of electronic thing.

Gentle, yes.

But you can use electronic if it is beautiful, melodious. You can use some classical music, but it has to be nurturing, gentle—not just exciting and all of that. As much as Stravinsky is wonderful to listen to when you're an adult, it's not so much when you're inside mother.

Who specifically of the old masters is good to listen to?

Well, try some Beethoven or Liszt or someone like that. But you have to listen to the music and see. You, as the adult, have to listen to it and say, "Do I get relaxed when I listen to this?" Sit down for a moment and listen to it. If it is not your natural music, it might make you a little annoyed and bored, but try to notice how your physical body feels: "Do I get relaxed?" Don't assume that the music you like, that you like to listen to, that causes you to be excited or stimulated, is good for baby. Baby needs this other music that is nurturing. That's why lullabies sound the way they do, because they are nurturing.

And the words in the lullabies . . . let us not make them, "Jack fell down and broke his crown." That is terrible. That is intended to be a parody, of course; when it was originally developed, it was a satire, having nothing to do with what it has come to be in your time. But what you need to do is pay attention to the words in the lullabies. If the words are not nurturing and supportive of life and welcoming new life into the world, then just sing the tunes. It is always better to sing it yourself, even if you don't think you can carry a tune very well.

Mother and father, try to sing the tune. If you have other children, then have them join in. It is good to do that, but only if they want to. Don't draft the children to sing, because then they will feel resentful. You can't tell them, "Don't feel resentful"; you can't control their feelings.

Television Is Always Too Much at Once

What about raising the child? Everything these days seems to be too much at once.

My recommendation?

Yes.

My recommendation is, if you're going to have your youngsters use computers, have some kind of control system, at least until the time they are twelve or thirteen years old. I grant that when they're away and at school, they might have other things they can access, but at home, have some kind of control system that does not allow certain . . . that allows only certain websites to come up. I know, sometimes you will say, "Oh well, these others are wonderful too." They may be wonderful for an adult, but maybe not for a child.

Now, as far as television goes—and you're not going to like this—I do not recommend television at all.

Until . . . ?

At all.

Until the child is an adult?

I do not recommend television at all. Period. At any time.

For anyone.

Because television is always too much at once. It is too many colors, too much motion—especially now with your current media people being excited by speed, motion, interaction, trying to demonstrate in color and motion the expression of a computer, which can do many things at once but which is not compatible with the human heart. Therefore, if you are going to watch television . . . just because I don't recommend it, isn't . . . I'm not saying, "Don't watch television!" [says this in a dramatic, commanding voice]. I am saying, if you are going to watch television, it might be better to watch programs that cause you to feel benevolent and nurtured.

Watch your programs that you watch as an adult, even if you think they're for your family. Do they cause you to feel excited and nervous? If they cause you to feel excited and nervous *at all*—be honest—probably they're not right for your thirteen-year-old or under. And pay attention to how much motion and color is going on, on the screen. If it's moving around too much, it is exciting physically to the physical body. Although the adult might like that if he or she is having a boring life—what that adult considers boring—excitement is stress to a child.

Even though there are times when children can be excited—they will play sports with other children or they will play a game with other children, and they will get excited in that—that's more natural. That has to do with an excitement that happens between you; you are excited because you have a friend whom you are just crazy about, and that friend feels the same way about you. That's fine; that's natural. But artificial excitement creates only stress for the child—and I might add, creates stress for the adults.

Sleep Deprivation in Your Time

You come home after work, you've had a long day, and you watch many programs on television. Sometimes there are ads on with the images flashing around. Even in your programs you watch, even if they're funny, very often there are stressful things in there, and your body gets *more* tense. You go to sleep at night, and then your dreams are serving only to deal with the stress you've picked up from television. When you wake up in the morning, you haven't had the opportunity to have your body relaxed from the stress you picked up in the day. And what happens? You wake up tired. That's why people wake up tired in your time.

This is to say nothing of the noises that come in that interfere with your sleep pattern. If you're living out in the country, the noises are natural: cows lowing, maybe coyotes baying in the distance. Of course, if you're a farmer or a rancher, you might not find a coyote sound too nurturing. Nevertheless, natural sounds . . . if you're living near the ocean surface, that's fine. I'm talking about sounds like horns honking and sirens that disturb your sleep even if you do not wake up all the way. It will bring you up out of sleep. In a city, with city sounds, in a six-hour sleep, you might come up thirty, forty, fifty, a hundred times, and that interrupts your sleep as well.

Feel free to use those sleep machines if you like, as long as they are producing a sound that you find comfortable. This is good. Feel free, for those of you who can, to wear earplugs that are comfortable. It may not be natural, your body doesn't exactly like it, but it is an improvement. And don't stimulate yourself so much before your sleep time. It's better to be stimulated by your lover or your companion in bed [laughs], than to be stimulated otherwise. Or for that matter, it is better to be stimulated by your pets whom you enjoy having. Oh, it's so much fun to pet or play— isn't it fun? All of that . . . that's all relaxing and natural. Or take a nice hot bath and relax, or read a good book that you enjoy. But pay attention when you're reading the book! "Am I getting excited? Am I feeling stressed? Or am I just enjoying this? Isn't it wonderful?" Pay attention!

One of the greatest challenges in your time—and many physicians know this in your time—is sleep deprivation. And by sleep deprivation, we do not only mean that the length of time of sleep is shortened, but the quality of sleep, the capacity to get to the deep-sleep levels, which really allow your physical body to rest completely. It is in the most deep-sleep levels that your body not only rests completely but, more to the point, restores itself physically, so that when you wake up in the morning, you feel good, you feel refreshed.

In School, Life Skills Should Be Taught First

How early should children go to school?

Well, given your current schooling . . . I'm not too crazy about it, okay? [Laughs.] But that is because it is too burdensome with facts and it doesn't teach children what they actually need to know. When children go to school, first, right away, they ought to learn methods of problem solving as it interrelates between people. That's the first thing you learn. Of course, when you go to kindergarten or even first grade, you sort of learn that anyway, because you're interacting with other children whom you do not know, as compared to your brothers and sisters at home or your friends in the neighborhood. So you get a little of that.

But it needs to be nurturing along that, not just two children fighting over the toy and the teacher takes it away, gives it to one of the children and says to the other, "You can play with it later," and then if there's time, comes back and gives it back to the other child. That is a means by which the child learns that the solution of problems between individuals requires the external: "We can't work it out ourselves." It is better for the child to be learning, "How can we teach children how to work it out themselves?" Some private schools do this, and it's wonderful. Then, of course, as the child gets older, he or she needs to learn practical skills: obviously, how to balance a checkbook, how to honor your body's own needs, what is the value of these things. In short, children need to learn practical things first.

I do not really see any value whatsoever in learning to memorize the Gettysburg Address, to say nothing of dates and times and places. If you're going to be a historian, that's one thing, but those things are given now to . . . I understand the theory behind it. It's to sharpen up the mind and to sharpen up your mental tools—not because the educational system wants you to remember the date of birth of President Millard Fillmore, but because they're trying to sharpen up your mind for further mental challenges as you get to high school and college and so on. But life skills should be first.

Pardon me for saying "should," but I believe life skills would be best to teach first. Allow teachers who've had courses from counselors or psychologists to teach others how to teach children how to resolve their own problems—because at some point, these problems might come up with their own brothers and sisters and family. They need to learn not just how to resolve their own problems with one another, but how to resolve problems with adults—and not just on the basis of "the adult is always right." These things would be best to teach in school and are often found taught in school on other planets in other cultures: life skills, life nurturing, how to get along with everybody, how to get along with yourself. How to recognize when you're tired and to lay down and take a nap—not just, "It's 2:00. Naptime!"

Do you see ahead that we will come to that point?

Certainly.

There will be enough wisdom that this will happen?

You cannot help it, because in time you will begin to restore and it will be supported to restore your natural way of being. This will come about naturally—though there will certainly be people credited for being pioneers in these areas, and that is certainly the case. The educational system is filled with loving and devoted teachers who are attempting to accomplish these things right now, even in the rigors of an educational system that has its eye on other things.

It is a curiosity to me that teachers are not given the support they need and that other avenues in government get support. I personally feel that if it is a choice between supporting teachers with the tools and the instruments and the support and the books and the teacher's aides . . . it is ridiculous for a teacher of second grade not to have at least two or three aides present. You cannot, if you have thirty or forty children . . . how can you possibly give them the help they need? Actually, classes ought to be no more than twenty, with three or four aides for the teacher. That would be fine. Then some of the aides would naturally be attracted to some of the students, and some of the students would naturally be attracted to some of the aides. It would all be wonderful and nurturing, as school is intended to be, rather than authoritarian so that you will learn how to deny your needs.

And what kind of parent does that create? These children are going to grow up. If you learn how to deny your own needs, you learn how to suffer, you learn how to be miserable . . .

Then you're going to perpetuate that.

That's right! You're going to perpetuate that for yourself and others. You start a business, and you're going to expect your employees to be miserable and suffer. You're going to expect yourself to be miserable and suffer. You may accomplish some things, but think how much more you can accomplish if you know that your own needs are important and that instead of having one boss, you always have at least three or four bosses, so if one boss is tired, "Oh, it's 2:00 in the afternoon; I need to take a nap" . . . not based upon your teacher saying in nursery school, "Oh, it's time to unroll your blanket and take a nap!" but "Oh, I had a big lunch; I need to take a nap. Can you take over?" "All right, but don't have such a big lunch in the future!" [Laughs.] Laugh about it! In short, you need to support and nurture yourselves and one another so that your society grows up. A whole generation after generation grows up used to nurturing yourselves and others, and then everything starts to work!

It's not the way I was raised.

Not the way you were raised, but perhaps a valuable way to be, eh?

Yes.

Certain Sounds Do Not Support the Channeling Process

Now, hold on a moment. [There are sirens outside.] It is that sound [sirens fading but not gone]. Why do you think I'm doing this [he is plugging his ears]? Because I am offended by what you say? I am plugging the ears because of the sound. And the sound is something . . . let me explain.

The connection between spirit and the channel requires a childlike, totally trusting connection. If you've ever known a channel . . . say you knew him before he became a channel; you knew him and after a while he became a channel. You will notice that several times, even when he is not channeling, he will have certain childlike qualities about him that are presented. He cannot do certain things; he is unable to do things, just as a child. Or the channel has an innocent countenance that sometimes comes forward. This is because he got used to being that way. The connection requires total trust, and that kind of total trust is often found in childhood.

So when that sound is heard, the sound that, of course, is necessary to get through traffic and is to be honored and respected for the urgency . . . I support it, but it does create stress. And stress, as you know . . . what? Impacts the sensitive and vulnerable. Who would be the sensitive and vulnerable in your society at all times, without any doubt?

Children.

Yes, and because it is children, and because the link in channeling is along a childlike, fully trusting, loving, nurturing level, such sounds do not support the channeling process.

Soul Doctors Assist Humans with Death

You created this wonderful plan to help the souls stay here—how else do you work with individual souls? Are all the soul doctors here right now?

Most.

Oh, most. How else do you interact with the souls of mostly newborn children, or the souls of anyone?

The other time we normally interact is when death occurs and the soul is changing back into its normal state of being. But it is often, by that time, after having lived in the body for so long, or as long as it did . . . of course, if it is a child, then we don't have to do this, because the child has not been in the body too long. But as a typical adult, for a life lived, by that time the soul becomes attached to its physical life, especially since it is cut off to some degree—not in deep-sleep levels, but certainly when the body is awake—so often from its natural state of being, that it needs help and nurturance and support and guidance in order to be received, welcomed, and to recognize that the death of the body just liberates the soul and allows it to naturally go on to become its natural self.

So the way we work with that, since it is not our job to teach so much but to support the teaching of others . . . what is this tickling thing? Hairs! Hair!

[Laughs.]

So these things tickling the ear over here, this is . . . *hair!* Amazing.

Yes! [Laughs.]

I've never felt it, you know—quite unusual.

You might want to come into a body yourself!

[Laughs.] Oh, I think I'm happy with my job. So when the soul is preparing to move into its natural self, it might interest you to know that one of the things we do . . . this is perhaps more noticeable when a person is having time to slowly pass on, maybe even demonstrating what is called senility. But senility is really just a foot in the other world. So then what occurs is that the membrane that has been placed there, you understand?

Yes, to keep the soul in the body.

To welcome, not keep.

Well, but to assist it to stay in the body, right?

To welcome—only that word—because that is the feeling it exudes. It's not a safe or a cabinet; it exudes a greater feeling of welcome.

Okay.

So we begin to release that membrane, allowing it to return to the plants and animals who have sent it, and then the way the soul is in the body, in times gone by, becomes that way—without the membrane. And then the soul is much less likely to be attached to the physical life and can much more easily step out and go on about its business.

So that's a natural form of death. What do you do when there's an accident? How do you do it then?

Then it is not our job. Soul doctors support and nurture the souls, but it is not our job to be guides. If you have a death . . . crash, bang, you are dead. Your soul is not stubbornly insisting on staying in your body [laughs]: "I refuse to believe! I am going to be buried in the body!" No. No.

Is it catapulted out or something?

No. It just leaves when it leaves, and the guides and angels come and say, "Oh, this is the way." We are not in control; it is our job to create something, to work with what is here. But we are not sitting here with our fingers tapping and, "Yes, we're watching this one." It is not a conveyor belt going by, watching them all on there—"Are they doing it right?" That is not our job; Rather it is our job to perform a specific function, then to act only when called upon. So we are called upon most often in birth and, more to the point, in prebirth, and also in death.

Called upon by the souls themselves?

Yes, always. Creator, granted, sent us here and said, "This is your job; go do it," but Creator doesn't say, "This is your job; go assist Susie right now." Creator is too busy to say, "Go assist Susie." It's our job to notice that Susie needs help and to go assist Susie right now ourselves.

The Soul Is in Union with the Physical Body

If you would, I've always had a lack of understanding about souls. How would you explain souls to someone who didn't understand that term?

I completely agree with your friend Zoosh. Zoosh calls it the immortal personality; I would call it the constant personality that is the portion of Creator that you yourself most identify and love.

But see, we're not a portion of Creator, and yet the soul . . .

Oh yes, you are.

No, we all come from somewhere else.

Ah, but you are affected by that. You cannot be birthed . . . you could say, well, a soul comes here to Earth, grows up to be a woman; a soul comes here to Earth, grows up to be a man. Then between the two you create a baby, yes? You could say, well, there are a lot of materials involved there that are not associated with the soul itself. What I'm saying is that you, granted, as beings, existed before this Creator and came here to be the Explorer Race. But you couldn't come here and be a potato that floats in the stew without being part of the stew!

So we use the soul, which is part of Creator, in order to have experience here? Can you say it like that?

No.

The soul is part of the Creator?

The soul is a word used by religion or philosophy to describe this personality that is naturally your own.

But you just said a soul was like a child?

Here on Earth, yes, but not everywhere. A soul might be born on some other planet in some other life. In a natural state or condition, it is not naturally—how can we say?—a child; it is vulnerable only in a threatening environment. Rephrase your question, if that is not clear.

So a soul comes here and is like a point of light?

You are trying to quantify the soul, is that it? In a substance that can be counted?

Well, I know that people can see it. It's like a filmy substance. When it departs the body, people can see it. So that means it grows, because it comes in just to the fertilized egg. So does the soul grow in substance while it's here?

Have you ever folded up a piece of paper and made it smaller, and then unwrapped it and it got bigger? It doesn't grow in substance; it unfolds.

It starts out in one egg . . . so it must be in every cell that divides and in every atom and every particle. So it's connected to the body in every particle, then?

It marries the body. It comes in and says, "Oh yes, I like this! Wonderful!" And it marries the body. It is devoted.

But it's actually connecting at all these points?

Oh, certainly.

I'm sure there are levels smaller than a particle; we've found some of them, so . . . ?

Oh, yes. Smaller, larger—there is not really a point to it. You could say, "Well, I will add a little red paint to this white paint, and it becomes pink." At what point in that pink paint does the red not connect with the white? You see?

It's not just you; it's a total . . .

It is union, a total thing.

Union, I understand. Jehovah once said that in early times—and I don't know how early he meant, maybe thousands of years ago on another planet—the soul was not nearly as connected to the human body.

Yes, but that is the same thing I'm saying, because it doesn't have to be as connected there. Because the circumstances are much more calm, there is no stress to speak of, there is no overwhelm of information. In other words, there is no need. It is exactly what I was talking about before! There is no need for it to be that connected. But he used the term "connected." This membrane creates a greater sense of welcome, but the net result . . . we are just saying the same thing in different ways.

When the Explorer Race becomes one being, will they coalesce like particles, or will they actually be in union?

Union.

But they were individuals coming into union, so at some point they can separate back into individuals, right?

Why would they want to? That is my answer. It is meant for you to answer. Why would they want to? What do you say to that?

Because I'd want to.

That's a good enough answer. But it is not one I'm going to comment on. [Chuckles.] It is not for me to say, is what I am saying. That is why I put the question back on you, because it is not for me to say.

I see. That's right—it's not a general thing, it's an unusual thing. But see, everything is ensouled. Do you work with souls of animals? Does each species have its own soul doctor?

Perhaps, yes. We work only with human beings. I do not think that the animals need much, but they might. It is not our job.

So what do you think your job will be when we become one being?

Well, we weren't unemployed before! [Laughs.]

Oh, you're just more stressed than employed now.

We're not stressed; we just have more to do. But I am sure that you will find us reasonably good, and if you do not have any use for us, perhaps we can shine shoes or something [laughs]. Go out and get you a hamburger?

[Laughs.] You have a delightful sense of humor!

We can make a good malted milkshake! We can find something to do, eh? [Laughs.]

Were you conscious before this mission of being soul doctors? I mean, do you have memories of something before this?

Yes, but I don't think that's really pertinent. I think it is just about time to say goodbye for now. Maybe we'll talk again some other time!

Power: Influence, Memory and Adaptation

Speaks of Many Truths
May 21, 2002

Greetings. *What I'd like to talk about is power, power in the way that you as a shamanic person would use power—spiritual power.*

Power is a word that really stems, in your culture, from control. I would prefer to use the word that my teacher used, and that's "harmony." Harmony requires that if you want something to work in a specific way for the good of all beings—or in the case of a need, based on individual needs—then you are asking beings, large or small, maybe everyone, to alter the way they are for the good of one. If that alteration can be done by them or if they allow that it can be done, then that being's good improves.

Harmony Involves a Great Deal of Adaptation

In a world such as this, that is life everywhere. Everything you touch all the time is alive. It requires a great deal of cooperation, otherwise known as harmony, in order to make things work benevolently for all beings. What happens when any one thing goes wrong? Then all beings in contact in any way with that one being for which something is going wrong maybe compensate in some way so the effect that being is exuding of his or her or its discomfort is harmonized, meaning adapted to. So harmony involves a great deal of adaptation all the time, because different beings will be going through different levels of discomfort, especially in a world where consumption is involved.

You breathe in air, and there are particles in the air. You breathe out. Maybe you've consumed something. Maybe some of those particles are destroyed, or let's say transformed. You eat, and something is destroyed and transformed—you understand? And all beings are breathing in and out and eating, to say nothing of other factors: being born, dying, stubbing your toe, breaking your arm, tearing your wing if you are a flying being. All of these things not only cause an effect for the individual experiencing them, but because of that individual's distress or upset, that being affects the immediate harmony around all beings connected to him or her or it. This requires adaptation.

It is not largely understood by people in your time that adaptation does not mean that the beings around you try to make you feel better. They adapt to your discomfort because the given for this world is that human beings are here to learn. The animals, the plants, the stones, the particles, everything around you is aware that you human beings are here to learn and that everything is set up, including their lives to a large degree, to accommodate your learning cycle.

Therefore, the animals, the plants, all automatically assume that whatever happens to them that isn't part of their life cycle as they understand it (birth, life, consumption, elimination, mating, young, love, death—all that is part of their natural cycle), whatever is outside of the boundaries of their natural cycle, has something to do with the growth of human beings. They don't say, "Earthquake—Mother Earth needed to move." They say, "Earthquake—human beings needed Mother Earth to do that for something they are doing to grow." They don't think that way necessarily, you understand, but it is an instantaneous assumption.

So if a human being breaks a leg—we're going to use that as an example—the life around that human being, the nonhuman life, automatically sets into an immediate rhythm of adapting to the condition of that human being, not trying to help. Now, what does the shaman do? Say the shaman or the mystical person is asked to help the human being with the broken leg. Maybe the doctor has already come and gone, set the leg—in my time that would be the medicine person, but let's bring it up to your time. So the doctor has come and gone. Maybe you've been to the hospital and they've given you some medication to help with the pain, but you are asking yourself, "Why did that happen? I didn't see it coming. What's this about?" So then you ask the shaman to come over and see if there's something that can be done.

Meanwhile, all this time all life around the human being, whether it be plant or animal or particles or stone—all part of life here on Earth—has adapted to you with a broken leg. Before they were adapted to you the way you were. Then you broke your leg, and they had to change their being to adapt to that. Even that which might cause a cut on your hand . . . and sometimes it can get infected because the skin opens and particles that are around, what you might call germs or viruses—I'm including all those things as particles—will be attracted to that because that's what they do. They will be attracted to that opening to do whatever it is that they do, which can cause an infection.

They're not just attracted to human beings like that; they're attracted to any living, breathing mammalian creature, all right? So that's part of something they do, but also it's an adaptation that they make. Even the tiniest pinprick you get on your finger . . . you go over to the tap and you wash it off; maybe you put a little alcohol on and then a Band-Aid if you feel it needs it. If those beings have been attracted, they are perhaps eliminated or at least grossly altered by the application of the alcohol or whatever you put on it.

Transforming the Energy with Harmony

The reason I'm saying this is that little things are going on all the time. Your body reacts too with its white cells and so on—your body has the ability to do that. All these things are going on all the time. You don't need to know about it most of the time, but for our example person who broke her leg, she wants to know not just how it happened. That person knows or someone told her, "Oh, you tripped and fell down the stairs. You tripped over a child's toy and fell down the stairs," or "You didn't see that can on the stairs and you slipped over it."

That person knows what happened, but she wants to know why, so she asks the shaman in this case and the shaman looks into it. The shaman sees not only the rhythm and the harmony of all the beings around that human being, that individual, but at the very least the shaman will feel— the shaman may see, he may have that gift—he will have a feeling to know how things *feel* around that human being. If there is a discomforting feeling around that human being, the first thing the shaman is going to do is to try to create in the energy around that human being . . . which, you understand, is not just some vague sense of energy like magnetism or electricity or even that energy that is sensed by sensitive people around beings, but it is also particles floating in the air. It is perhaps plants, animals, maybe that person has a pet. It is things that were once another thing—a chair that was once a tree and maybe an animal itself and so on. In short, it is all life in all its different forms.

So the shaman feels this discomfort around the person—not just because she is in pain from the broken leg, but there is a general energy that doesn't feel good. The shaman begins to look at the person and sees or feels some discomfort. Working with the teachers and the aides, the spirit teachers who work with the energy that the shaman can summon himself, he begins to work on that discomforting energy.

Now, what are they doing? Is it power? No. Power is the human derivative in your now culture—the derivative, meaning, "I see things change. I want them to change my way." That's the human now culture's approach. That's not the best approach. The shaman says, "I feel things are not comforting, and I now ask my teachers and those who help me"— meaning spirit beings, gold lightbeings, whoever it might be—for that teacher to come and do whatever the shaman says. They have their own techniques—perhaps it's a ceremony, perhaps it is direct action like that, working with other beings, or techniques the shaman knows—to transform the energy. With power? No. With *harmony*. But how with harmony? With *influence*. That's the key word.

Influence is the whole thing. How do you influence all of these beings? Plants? Animals? That which makes up plants and animals—particles, yes, all the particles of everything, whether they are in an identifiable form such as a vine, a plant, or whether those particles make up a dog or a cat, a bird, a squirrel, or whether they are in the air and are breathed in and out by the person with the broken leg? In short, all life in contact with that person? How can that life be harmonized?

That life, you understand, has adapted to the human being having a broken leg. "The human being is learning something," says the life to itself—not consciously but they all know this and they adapt. "How can we encourage that life to transform into a harmonized state that does not include the adaptation?" It's like when you hold a cloth out tight between four people—it would be fairly flat. The broken leg in this case would be like someone coming along and poking his or her finger down someplace in that sheet. It creates a dent. The dent in this case is visually—just the dent, not the person poking his or her finger in—the adaptation of all life.

So see the person with the broken leg and see things sort of sloping down toward her. Maybe the energy is a little odd looking in that area. That allows the shaman who can see to see it and the shaman who can feel to feel it. In short, the shaman knows something needs to be corrected. That life is not doing a bad thing; it is adapting to the human being in the way it knows how because human beings are here to learn. It's very simple for them. Don't make it complicated for them.

So the shaman wants not only to remove any energies that are discomforting from the person with the broken leg, which he's working on, but the shaman also wants to ask the beings around this being—they come and go, you breathe in and out, there are particles, the animals come and go—the shaman wants to set up an energy around this person that will allow the life that is adapted to the human being with the broken leg . . . they've adapted to her before as she was and they adapted to her with the broken leg, and that's as she is. There is no change from them in attitude but a change in how they represent themselves. They don't keep her in suffering with the broken leg, but they adapt to her like that.

Harmonious Adaptation Must Occur Slowly

Now, there's an important point here: What happens when all life around you—and I'm talking about atomic particles and all that—adapts to you with the broken leg? I'll tell you what happens, because you're here to learn about cause, effect, applications, consequences, all of that. What happens is that it takes longer for that broken leg to heal than it has to, because you've changed the environment and the environment changes to adapt to you! As your leg begins to heal, all the particles of everything around you have to change as you get better, but that change comes about slowly. The adaptation comes about slowly, just as things adapt to a change of seasons.

Why do you think you're living in a place that has seasons? It's to show you that adaptation, in order to happen in harmony—so that life doesn't suffer cataclysmically every time there's a change of seasons—has to happen gradually and slowly. The leaf begins to turn yellow, and then it gradually goes through its yellowing cycle, and then it becomes dried out and becomes brown, and then it becomes shriveled and shrinks. And when it's dried out enough, it falls off the tree. In short, gradually, slowly . . . what? Harmoniously. So in order for this harmonious change to take place, it needs to be gradual, it needs to be slow.

Encouraging a General Benevolent Energy

How can the shaman help the person with the broken leg to not only understand why this happened but to understand what she can do about it within the context of her entire lesson here as a human being on Earth, as the Explorer Race, to come here to learn as a soul in the human-being body? All of that context must be taken into account. So the shaman begins by asking the spirit teachers and helpers what they can do to remove this energy. It might look funny; it might have a dark appearance. That means it needs to be transformed. First the energy will be transformed. Dark does not mean bad. It just means it's a signal that something needs to be assisted. It catches the eye. It contrasts, you see? It's like that poke in the sheet. It creates a dent, and that catches the eye or the feeling body. The shaman can feel something out of harmony.

So say it is that dark energy. The beings come along and they transform the dark energy, because underneath that dark energy is an energy that's exuded to say, "Help. Something's wrong." And the energy is transformed. While they're doing that, they're doing it gently. While they're doing that, they are able, working in gold light and white light and pink light and green light . . . whatever they need to do in that particular circumstance. They do this, and this all needs to be done gently and in a way that does not cause distress for the person they are working on.

So all this is going on simultaneously while the person with the broken leg sits quietly. The shaman is then able to see what needs to be corrected. Or in the case of a shaman who is working with spirit teachers, the spirit teachers see what needs to be corrected, and the shaman just exudes a benevolent energy or requests that the benevolent energy be present so that the work can take place. All the while, not only is the energy around the person with the broken leg being worked on, but the energy of all the beings in contact with that person—plant, animal, mineral, gas, what-have-you—all of that is also being worked on simultaneously by other lightbeings and spirit teachers to help them to create that original harmony or a better harmony, in this case, so that the energy around the person supports her benevolent state of being—either as it was before she broke her leg, or more likely, as it could be.

If you're going to break your leg, the energy . . . there would be a little tension there. We don't want that. We want to have a generally benevolent energy. So they are encouraged to be benevolent or have a benevolent energy. If the person is spiritual and comfortable with it, the shaman might even temporarily have a spirit teacher or being stay with that person for a while in order to encourage the energy around that person to be benevolent. It's not just energy. I'm using energy in a compatible way with the idea that the person is interacting with the particles and all life around her. So, in this case, the energy around her means all life.

So as you as immortal souls, immortal personalities, learn to become more conscious of these energies or work with these energies or ask gold lightbeings and benevolent lightbeings—loving, benevolent lightbeings, especially gold lightbeings who can transform—to be around you wherever you are, because they are safe no matter where they go . . . as you ask them to be around you, they might just be able to help to harmonize. How? With influence by interacting with all life around you—be it particle, form, substance, gas, liquid, anything—and asking them to transform themselves or to alter their being so that they are in a particular state of harmony, to do that if they can. They have lives, they are doing other things, and they may not be able to do it. If they're not able to do it and if they're able to leave the area, they might be asked to leave.

It May Take Pets and Humans Some Time to Adapt

Here's an interesting thing: Some of you have noticed this. Some of you have pets. Perhaps you're in an accident, all right? Or you have an accident and you come home with your broken leg. Your pet maybe does something that really startles you. Your pet loves you, but the pet unexpectedly goes the other way. You want to hug your dog, you want to hug your cat or your horse or whatever your pet is, but your pet surprises you. It goes the other way. It's not that your pet is mad at you; it's that it needs time to harmonize itself to the condition you're in, because the beings around you, especially if you're a spiritual person, but even if you're not . . . even people who aren't conscious of these things have beings around them trying to help them to harmonize life around them all the time.

If your pet is used to you being the way you normally are and you come home with your broken leg, it needs time to adapt and harmonize to that situation. Your pet can't do it immediately. Some pets can, but if your pet can't do it immediately, it goes away for a while. It adapts and harmonizes to the situation you're in, and then it comes back, then it wants to be around you, wants to be petted by you, wants to comfort you. But if your pet goes away for a time, don't be alarmed. It needs to harmonize or it has other things to do. Remember, pets are living, breathing beings with soul personalities of their own. Maybe your pet can't adapt right then. Maybe it needs to do something else. It will be back when it can adapt.

I mention that to you as an aside, because many of you have been baffled by the behavior of your pets. Sometimes this even happens with human beings. Human beings cannot adapt. Human beings are all here to learn, and you're all learning all the time. But someone comes home, whoever it is, a family member, with the broken leg. You need to adapt, but you may not be able to adapt right away. So parents, if you or someone in the family comes home with a broken leg and the children are unsettled for a time, they don't know what to do, it may simply be family communication that needs to be squared away, but it might also be that they need to adapt to the situation. That's not so unusual, that's not so startling. If one child needs longer, give him or her the time, let him or her adapt; that child will come around when he or she is ready.

As a Shaman, You Will Have to Change

Now, you understand, it's different for animals than it is for human beings, but I'm putting this in here so that you know you are not excluded from harmony and influence. Listen up here: The shaman always needs to be in some state of harmony so that he is readily available at a moment's notice to take care of anything he can work on or with that needs his attention [snaps fingers] immediately. Therefore, if you know a shaman or if you are working on becoming one yourself, then you will have to gradually understand that the way you've been in the past (if you're working on becoming one) may be different from the way you will need to be as a shaman, a mystical man or woman.

As a shaman, you will have to change. Your personality might change. You're not going to grow horns and eyes and have tentacles—just kidding [chuckles]. But you're going to need to change. People will comment on the fact that you are different from the way you used to be or as they remember you. Sometimes you will need to change in midstream. You are talking to someone and suddenly you will need to do something. Perhaps you're out in the car driving about and you go by the scene of a traffic accident. Or better yet, you're in a car with somebody else driving. If you're driving, you may be able to continue to drive, to pay attention to your responsibilities as a good driving citizen, while energy streams through you—you may feel the energy—toward those beings in that car accident as well as to others who are affected by it.

If, on the other hand, you're a passenger in the car going by, you may be able to be more directly involved, to do some ceremony that you do or ask for energies to flow through you in a more powerful way. Powerful means what? Influence, harmony, in a way that you will feel, and perhaps even other people in the car will feel it as well. That's why it's always good for your friends to know that you are a shamanic person and that you may be called upon at any moment to help out various beings you're just simply walking by on the street, driving by or even see, who need help. Perhaps you'll say a prayer for someone.

So if you have a friend who is a shaman or if you're working on becoming one yourself, know that your life—either as you're around your friend who's a shaman, or your life as you're working to become a shaman—will have everything to do, in every moment with adaptability (either when you're with your shaman friend or as you're training to become one). You might be talking, having a conversation, and suddenly you feel like you're talking to yourself with your shaman friend. She's doing something, or you might feel that her attention is split. You wish she was paying more attention to you because what you're saying is important, of course, but her attention is split because she's doing something else. She can give you half an ear, as you say, but she's doing something else that is equally or perhaps more important.

I'm not trying to say that shamans are gods or deities who need to be bowed down to; it's just the opposite. I'm saying that it is the responsibility of a shaman to be available on a moment's notice to help in whatever way he can, according to the circumstances of the moment. Perhaps you're going by someone who is in distress, the person has a disorder of some sort. Perhaps you can say something or do something that will be *available* for that person—it doesn't inflict something on them. It's not your job as the shaman to inflict anything on anyone.

The Shamanic Blessing

People may not know because of their culture or their language how to ask for help. They may not be able to know you're a shaman, especially if you look like everybody else. But you can do something, not unlike what people do when they say prayers, but this is different because it also has energies, spirit teachers, light ceremonies—it may have lots of stuff going on. However you work as a shaman, you can do something that will be *available* for that person, or even ask something. You can say,

---

Living Prayer

"I'M ASKING THAT SOMETHING BENEVOLENT HAPPEN FOR THAT PERSON TODAY TO IMPROVE THE QUALITY OF HIS OR HER LIFE."

You might say that in many different ways. You might even have a quick way of saying it.

In short, you are feeling compassion for that person and you want to help. You don't say, "I am asking that that person has this or that happen to him or her right now." Keep it general so that if that person is suffering— meaning she's suffering and you want to help her in some way—if she is learning something with her suffering, you do not *inflict* change on her, even if that change would be a benevolent change for that person, if she needs her pain and discomfort in order to learn what she is trying to learn

LIVING PRAYER
Speaks of Many Truths

Living prayer allows you as an individual to give to the Earth. So many of you ask, "What can I do for the Earth? What can I do for the animals? What can I do for people suffering in other parts of the world or in my own town or family? What can I do?"

If people are suffering on the other side of the Earth, you can say, "May the people be nurtured and know they are loved. May their hearts be healed and may they find what they need, or may it be brought to them in a benevolent, beneficial way for all beings."

Say this key phrase—"I will ask," or "I am asking"—out loud, though perhaps softly. This way it is understood that what you are asking is about physical things. In the case of a war on the other side of the world, you might say, "I ask that everyone's heart be healed and that they find peace together in the most benevolent and beneficial way for them."

Let's say you are driving through the forest and there is no one else around. Suddenly your heart hurts. It is a dull ache. When you get used to this living prayer, you will look around and say, "I will ask." The moment you say that key phrase, Creator knows that you are saying a living prayer. "May the heart of the forest be healed. May the hearts of all the trees, plants, rocks, animals and spirits who like to be here be healed. May they enjoy their time in the forest and feel welcome."

Then go on. Your heart will probably feel better. If you get the feeling again farther up the road, say it again without looking at them: "May their hearts be healed. May they feel welcome wherever they go or where they are."

Remember, you have to say these blessings only once for each place, person or group of people. You are more sensitive now, and the plants and the animals and the stone and maybe even other people are more sensitive too. You all need each other more now than ever, and here is something you can do to help others and feel better yourself.

Try not to look directly at people who cause your heart to hurt. Some other part of your body may hurt sometimes when you are near people who are suffering in some way. First ask that their hearts be healed, then add other parts of them according to what hurts on you. You don't have to name the organ unless you feel sure; just say the place on the body.

It is intended now that many people begin giving and asking for such prayers. As Mother Earth and her rocks, trees, plants and animals come under more strain in your time due to so many people and their needs, these natural forms of life may no longer be able to give you the healings and blessings they have been doing simply by being and radiating their good health. So you can now give to them in return for all their generations of benevolence. These prayers are all they ask.

as an immortal soul personality allowed to be here by the Great Spirit/Creator Itself. You do not want to interfere with what Creator is doing with this immortal personality.

On the other hand, if you wish, out of your compassion, to encourage or make more available something benevolent to happen to that person that day, you simply say that. It is like a prayer; if there is a lot of energy that goes out with it, you can be pretty sure it will happen. If you don't notice much energy, maybe something benevolent will happen, maybe it won't. But you go on. You let it go. You say it, "It's gone," and you go on with your life. That's what you've done; that's what you can do.

The whole point of that is to allow that possibility to take place. It is a blessing. It is a prayer. It is something you can do. That's what the shaman does, and it all has to do not only with beings—spirit beings, gold lightbeings, spirit doctors, all of this—but it also has to do with all life around that individual. Harmony, yes? Influence. All of that has to do with harmony, influence, all the time, everywhere—period!

How the Shaman Works with Energies

When you say "influence," the shaman is running energies, is asking spirit beings and doctors and gold lightbeings, right? Is that how he uses his influence?

The shaman isn't actually . . . I know that you know what "running energy" means, but let's be clear. The shaman is open and available to energies of benevolence that the shaman has come to work with and become familiar with over the years in his or her training. As a result of this familiarity, the shaman has a faith and trust, and is open to these energies all the time.

As a result, when you say "running energies," the shaman is open to these benevolent, loving energies, and those energies and the ones he or she is most familiar with are the ones that run through the shaman first. But they might also simply be a platform, in that sense, for the energies that the other individual might need. So it supports and insulates the shaman, because the shaman's job is not to take on the pain of others but to assist others with their pain so that something can happen in a way so the energy around the person with the discomfort adapts so that his or her life can improve in some way.

This is done, these energies come through or near—very often, it's near—the shaman in such a way that the shaman is insulated from feeling the feelings of the other person so that the shaman doesn't take them on and become injured by them. The other energies of love and light and harmony and benevolence that the shaman has worked with or felt and the energies the shaman might feel (perhaps in the top of the head, or some feel it in their heart or their solar plexus or wherever they feel it) . . . shamans feel these certain energies on a regular basis, so when energy flows through them, they're only going to feel something benevolent. The shaman says the prayer, yes, and the energy will flow through, but also the energy is, as you say, "running," as a stream runs. It flows through, by, around or near the shaman toward the other person in a way that is benevolent for that person and not harmful for the shaman.

So, you understand, we're talking about something that's a circuit [draws Fig. 14-1]. Here's the shaman, and we'll say that the shaman normally feels these energies at the top of his head, okay? So the energies flow across the top of the shaman's head toward the person—I'm labeling this "S" for shaman and "P" for person. The shaman may be aware of the other person. The shaman may be aware of the energies flowing that are not

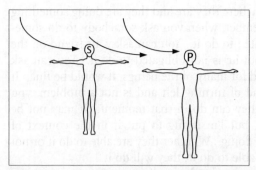

Fig. 14-1. The shamanic process of running energies.

exactly the same as the energies the shaman normally feels. But the shaman will know that those energies are intended to be what is compatible, appropriate, useful.

In short, the shaman does not only *not* need to know mentally what that's about, but it's not even to the shaman's advantage to know mentally. Why is it to the shaman's advantage not to know mentally what is going on? Because the shaman is working with energies, he's interacting with energies of beings all the time. Every being—whether it be a human being, an elephant, an eel, an ant, an atomic particle that makes something up, anything—they all have their own personalities. For some people, it may be hard to grasp that this is true, but you are living with the living all the time. Granted, life changes form, but all around you is alive.

Asking for Help from All Life

Since the shaman is interacting on a feeling level with that, thought as a tool of observation—which steps away from feeling and action—is inappropriate because that's the opposite of what the shaman wants to do. The shaman needs to be engaged on a feeling level with warmth, the love-heat/heart-warmth/physical-warmth [see Overview]. The shaman exudes love and is feeling love. That's why . . . it's not something where a shaman says, "Hocus-pocus," as your friend Zoosh likes to say, and here's loving energy. The shaman must be feeling it, and because the shaman is feeling it, it naturally exudes. And because it exudes, all life around the shaman recognizes that energy as the core energy of all natural life.

Therefore, the shaman who is radiating this love that the shaman is feeling—granted, he doesn't feel it all the time, but when he does—all life around the shaman is going to be heightened to the greatest feeling of love. You're going to feel like you can relax and be yourself. That energy relaxes, is itself and is open, and because your energies are open and feel safe to be open . . . you are exuding this loving energy you are feeling, physical feelings, and you are fully engaged. You have to be in your body to feel it, you can't be thinking about it; you have to do it, it has to be physical, because they feel that. All this life around you, these beings are open also, and when you ask them to do something, because you, a loving being, are asking, if they can do it, they will.

If some of them can't do it and that energy needs to be present to help the person with the broken leg, for example, then they will go elsewhere if they can. If they have to stay where they are and they are doing something else, it can't be helped. Remember, when you ask somebody to do something, that being is not obligated to do it. You can ask your friend on the street to stand on his head, but he is not obligated to do it. You can ask someone to do something, and for many of the beings, it would be fine. It would be turning right instead of turning left and is not a problem, you understand? It's something they can do in that moment. It may not be turning right or turning left, but I'm trying to put it in the context of something they are capable of doing. Whether they are able to do it or not is another matter. If they are able to do it, they will do it.

It is that kind of harmony, that kind of influence, that creates help. Ultimately, the reason I'm telling you this in this book and in this whole series of *Shamanic Secrets* books that talks about these things is because I'm trying to let you know, as an individual, as a reader or as someone who is hearing this in some other form, that you can train and learn how to do these things for yourself and, in time, for others. And you don't have to change your philosophy and you don't have to change your religion.

This is part of natural life, and it is my job to remind you in your time about natural life for human beings, just as natural life for plants, animals and all other life exists on this planet in its natural life cycle to the best of its ability—except when it's adapting from its point of view to human needs, because humans are here to learn and grow. It is my job to help you to remember how to create natural life for yourself and, in so doing, help others to create natural life. So you can have your religion and your philosophy if you want to and live your lives in a more benevolent way for yourself and ultimately for all others.

It's All Based on Feeling

This energy that flows through the shaman . . . ?

Or around the shaman perhaps. I'm stopping you because your question may not be correct. What I said . . . remember, I showed in the picture [Fig. 14-1] that the energy seems to flow through the shaman, but very often it may come from somewhere else. The shaman is not necessarily a lens. The shaman may ask for beings to come in a certain way—either beings the shaman has worked with before and trusts, or the shaman asks the beings around him, the energies around him, to invite beings to come.

These beings may not come through the shaman. They may come near the shaman. They might come from some other point, not coming through or around the shaman at all. In short, they might come from many different directions and many different places, but because of the tone . . . I'm using "tone" here to apply to the general feeling the shaman exudes: "What I'm asking for is, would beings come if they can help this person?" In short, this is the general energy the shaman speaks while feeling the usual energies the shaman feels to a greater or lesser degree dependent on the circumstances. The energies will come—the energies of the spirit beings, the teachers, whomever you're asking to come—not only based upon what the shaman says or thinks in words, or in reaction to what the shaman is feeling or the gestures the shaman is making or other things the shaman is doing, but they will also come based upon the energy that is normally associated, from their point of view, with the shaman, the energies that the shaman normally works with.

If they see that those energies are associated with this human being—the shaman, yes?—they will not only know that what the shaman says can be trusted, but they will know on the basis of their feeling, because everything is about feeling: harmony, adaptation, influence, it's all about feeling. No thought is involved at all. They will know on the basis of their feeling that this is something they can react to in the best way they are needed. It is genuine because of what? Because of what *they* feel. It's all based on feeling. The shaman feels, all life around you feels, and the spirit teachers, doctors, helpers and beings come to help you. It's all on the basis of feeling.

That's why I've been talking to you about feeling for these past years, because everything you need to do as a human being to help yourself come into a more natural (in this case, "natural" meaning benevolent) life cycle for yourself—maybe even heal that broken leg a lot faster than it might normally take—is going to be helped as you utilize some of these things for yourself or come to see their value. It's all based on feeling. That's why one of the very first things we gave—"we" meaning myself and other teachers through Robert [the channel]—was the warmth feeling within.

I know others have given this, but we wanted to announce the value of what was coming through this channel on the basis of giving that thing to do about love, which is felt as warmth on the inside. And that's the foundation. The foundation of benevolent change is based on love that is felt as physical warmth in the human being, is felt the same way by all other beings and also tends to create in all beings a feeling of openness with the complete knowledge that they can reveal themselves because love will be present and love does not contain judgment, control . . . or what? The word you used to start this whole conversation—*power.* Power can be seen. You could say love has power, but I don't like to say it does, because power has been used by your cultures for many years to mean something that stems from control. So I'd rather say, as I've said, these other words.

The Gold Lightbeings Need to Be Given Permission

Let me just clarify this so I understand: Someone is in need, and the shaman is going by. He focuses on his heart, his energies radiate, but other gold lightbeings or other beings may use him as a conduit or a channel also to send energies through him to that being?

That is *a* way, but it is not *the* way. You are presenting something to me, all right? You're saying, "Let me understand. Is this how it works?" Is that what you're saying?

I think my basic question is, can the spiritual teachers or the gold lightbeings send energy directly to that being, or do they need a human to send it through?

They need to be asked. They need to be given permission. It is not their job to save you. It is nobody's job to save you. If it is anybody's job to do any saving, it's your job. But they need to be asked, because in the asking, you give them permission. And sometimes, very often, the human being does not know how to ask. So that's the shaman's job, to know how to ask—not just in words. The words are almost superfluous, but sometimes they are helpful for the shaman, if that's how the shaman works, in order that the shaman remain clear on what is being asked.

More to the point, the shaman feels. Very often the shaman will simply walk down the street feeling the energy he feels, the energy radiates and it can only do good to those it touches if they wish to use it. This does not mean that the shaman's job is to be an energy fount that others come and drink from; that is not the job. The job is for human beings to embrace their ability that they can create and generate to come into a state of natural life for themselves for which you need instruction and training—which is the whole purpose of the *Shamanic Secrets* series of books.

So the gold lightbeings, since we're talking about gold lightbeings, must be given permission or must be requested to come by somebody. If the person walking down the street whom the shaman feels compassionate for isn't asking them to come, then the shaman can ask them to come and be available if that person desires that assistance, and there will be as much time as that gold lightbeing feels that person may wish that or want that.

The gold lightbeing is not going to stick around with you forever and tell you in a moment, "Drop your guard," and then rush in to save you. It's going to stay around, let's say, for a few hours of your life, maybe no more than a twenty-four-hour cycle and probably less because of, generally speaking, permission. The gold lightbeing will know on the basis of what it can do—or the lightbeing or the spirit doctor or the teacher or the spirit or the loving being or the angel, whatever. The being will know on the basis of what it feels with its gifts and tools and abilities almost immediately whether and when that person is likely to open up to what it can do for him or her.

They will know that it will happen, say, immediately, soon, or that it might happen at some point in the future, at which time they will return, at that point in time when that takes place, and be present for that opening in that person. The only way this happens is that somebody must say the word to give them permission to come in the first place. And you, as the person who is suffering—speaking to the reader here—might be able to give that permission too. You might feel that you are shut down or angry or upset or agitated, and you know you can't drop your guard and be opened up to what loving beings can do for you then.

So this is what you do: You don't start off with that explanation. They know. You simply say,

Living Prayer

"I AM ASKING THAT LOVING LIGHTBEINGS COME AND HELP ME IN THE WAY THEY CAN IN THE WAYS I NEED ANY TIME I AM OPEN TO RECEIVE THIS HELP."

That's all. That's all you say. You have to say it out loud. If there are other people near you, you can whisper it. That's good enough. But it has to be said in this physical way with some noise, spoken in your language. Out loud is better, but you can whisper it if there are people around and you're concerned they might overhear you. That's completely acceptable.

Say it just like that, or as close as your language can come to it with that meaning and that intent. Say it, and they will come in exactly the way you have said it when you are ready. You might even feel them come. Some of you will feel a little bit like being touched by electricity for a moment. I don't mean a shock that you'll get from something that's uncomfortable; I mean that it will be a sudden feeling, an odd feeling. Or you might feel a sudden energy, restful, a loving energy. You might feel a little alteration, or for the vast majority of you, it will happen while you're asleep.

That's what you can do to begin. It's my job to help you to begin—not to take you to the very end, but to get you started, to intrigue you, to interest you, to support you and, yes, to help you.

Influence Depends on Harmony

Is this same principle that worked when you in your time or a shaman in our time would ask, for instance, the rain to come, or if there is too much rain, for the rain to go? Would you ask teachers and gold lightbeings, or would you talk directly to the rain at that point?

Some people might. If the shaman was trained, she might be able to pull the rain. But the rain will only come, no matter how much you are pulling, if it is not needed where it is. If you are pulling the rain, it's coming from someplace else where it was originally going to go to where you want or feel it needs to go. If you do that, if it can, if that place the rain was going to go to does not need that rain, or maybe it's getting inundated with too much rain, then if Mother Earth is comfortable with it—since it is part of her body—the rain will come to where you request it to come. Or conversely, if there is too much rain and you are trying to pull the rain away from a place that is flooded, if Mother Earth does not need to flood that place anymore and you pull on it a different way—not asking beings to do it—then maybe it will go away.

But either way, whether you are asking beings to do it, whether you've been taught how to pull—which is a feminine technique, to move things about—it all depends again on this influence. It's a form of influence; it all depends on harmony. What those beings . . . let's say the rain is made up of beings, droplets of rain, particles, cloud, maybe wind, all of this. All of that depends on whether it's harmonious for those beings to do that and whether it's harmonious for Mother Earth for that to be done with a portion of her body, which is the rain and possibly the wind and so on.

And the shaman has to be harmonious within himself or herself to even be able to ask, right?

Yes, to be able to influence in any way, you have to feel that harmonious energy. You can't simply say words. Control doesn't have any meaning here. I grant that in your time, science, which is sometimes harmonious— meaning the scientists themselves perhaps know things or are working with benevolent energies and are working benevolently (this is not as common in your time, but in the future it will become the standard)— might be able to harmoniously change things. But if you are simply doing something on the basis of desiring control or change, or trying to influence the weather on the basis of particles you're throwing out or dust or powder or something like that, you might be able to create an alteration for a time.

But when you do something like that, Mother Earth, especially if you do it more than once . . . Mother Earth is forgiving for things done on an experimental basis once or twice. But if you're doing it over and over and over again, she will compensate and do something else, either to eliminate you doing that or to set up a compensation that she needs to do in some other part of her body—some other part of the Earth—that will necessarily balance her on the basis of what you (in this case, the scientist) are doing to influence the weather.

Of course, that has to do with anything you are doing in her body, whether it is mining, exploding, changing, altering—even altering the course of a river. Mother Earth will find some other way to change it. Think about that for a moment. Many people live on floodplains, meaning that before walls or dams and so on were built, that area used to flood on a regular basis, usually seasonally. I'm not saying that it's bad to make those changes, but in my time we wouldn't have done it because we were always trying to live in as much harmony as possible. If we wanted Mother Earth to do things for us, we had to at least live in harmony with her. It's not too nice to your host if you are poking her with a sharp stick and asking her to do nice things for you.

What I want to say, though, is that if you alter the flow of the river so it no longer floods into its natural floodplain, then at some point, maybe not immediately, Mother Earth will begin raining either in that place a lot or somewhere else to create a flood so that *some* floodplain somewhere is flooded. Sometimes that works for her. Ultimately, though, she will have to flood that floodplain upon which you are living in some way. She'll find a way to do it. Perhaps it involves moving her waters about in such a way as to find a way to flood that floodplain you're living on. But she'll find a way—not because she wants to harm you, but because that floodplain is a floodplain, because that is part of her natural body life cycle. She needs to do it, just like your blood needs to move in your veins.

I realize it's not convenient, but if you're living on a floodplain, you might want to think about building your house up a few levels. Sometimes you find that people who live in swampy land will build their houses up twenty or thirty feet so that as the water level rises and lowers in the swamp, they still remain dry. The house might look a little funny, but you've seen houses sitting on stilts built on the side of hills before. It's a similar construction technology. It just looks a little odd, but then as the flood comes—as it will come seasonally—it will look completely normal and for a time you will travel about in a boat instead of by car or by wagon with horses and so on. So you just have everything sitting up higher. It might look a little strange, but you adapt, you understand? Adapt. The less adaptable you are, the more likely something will happen that is uncomfortable, meaning something that has to be changed suddenly in order to create adaptation.

How Your Pet Might Adapt

When you talked about the animals around someone with a broken leg hiding to adapt . . . I know the meaning of the word, but how specifically do they do that?

Remember, animals and plants all know that they are here to help human beings to grow, because they could be someplace else where they live lives much more benevolently. But they are here because they can help in some way. They may never know what that way is, or they may know, but their very presence will have something to do that will help you with your lives or help you to grow in some way. It's all set up for you, so they're all volunteers.

No animal, plant or even particle comes here without being a volunteer. No one is drafted. They have to volunteer, because they have to know that it is possible, at some time during their natural life cycle, that something might happen to them that will alter their natural cycle that will have to do with your growth. So they have to be able to give permission at the deepest soul levels—and even, of course, naturally at the cellular level of their tissues in their bodies—to accept that that's a possibility and could happen.

So the animal adapting to you must . . . it's normally used to you how you are, whatever way you look, and if you come home suddenly, unexpectedly, with this broken leg, you are different. Your energy has changed.

Think about it. An animal, a pet, gets used to you. You grow and change with the animal, but it's gradual. The animal grows and changes, and you like each other just the way you grow and change on a daily basis. Suddenly you come home and you're completely different, your energy is different. You broke your leg. It happened suddenly. The animal needs time to adapt. It's not the case with all animals, all pets, but some do. They need time.

What does the animal do during that time? It goes away. It might need to leave the house, or it might need to go to some other part of the house and be quiet. It will sit there and be quiet for a time. It won't run around the house screaming. It will go somewhere and be quiet, and while it's being quiet, it will gradually . . . the energies will come for it, and it will gradually adapt to this change for you. Its whole body will change on a cellular level. That doesn't mean that cells will fall out of its body; it means that the cells themselves will adapt. It is a change that happens on a feeling level. You go somewhere and you have one feeling; you go somewhere else and you have another feeling.

Things happen in your life and your feelings change. It's like that. The animal's feelings change; its whole physical feeling in its body changes. It adapts to how you are now, and once it is adapted, in whatever time that takes for it, then it will come around. If the pet is nurturing, it'll come around and be nurturing. If it is just available, it'll come around and be available. It will take it as long as it takes it.

And when it adapts, it has adapted and that's it. Your pet is adapted to you with a broken leg, and it stays adapted to you with a broken leg until you are either working with various beings—as I said before, with the prayer—or are more engaged in this process as I'm instructing in this book and talking about how I do things in my time, how I've been trained, how other shamans do things in your time too—some anyway (they are all trained in different ways). The whole point is to help you to discover how things are so you can begin to work as well as you can in your time in the best way you can for yourself and others.

You Are Always Connected with All Other Life

Now, if you can, you can ask (using that broken leg as our example here) for things to change around you, to harmonize to you in ways that are benevolent to you as you are now. Or you can say, with your broken leg,

Living Prayer
"I'M ASKING THAT ALL LIFE AROUND ME ADAPT IN WAYS THAT WILL BENEVOLENTLY ALLOW MY BROKEN LEG TO HEAL AS QUICKLY AND BENEVOLENTLY AS POSSIBLE FOR ME."

That's what you say. This invites beings to come and work with all life around you, to set up energies around you and so on for that to take place.

It may not change the length of time it takes for your broken leg to heal, but it might. If it changes the length of time, it will make it shorter, not longer. So if it takes awhile for your broken leg to heal, that's how long it might take, but it might take less time. Wouldn't that be nice?

Can you use that same principle for a disease?

Yes, anything. But you must remember that since you are here as a human being with lessons you're learning between you and your Creator and your teachers, and as the Explorer Race and all of this, that sometimes you will ask things to change more benevolently for you and they don't change. That's because whatever you're feeling in that uncomfortable thing for a moment, there may be something that you need to do, or you may simply need to adapt to that circumstance because it has to do with something you're learning, or it may even have to do with something that somebody else is learning around you or with whom you will come in contact.

After you come in contact with that person, say . . . this is an extreme situation, but it's happened before and it could happen again. Say someone you're going to come in contact with who has maybe even known you in a past life and felt good about you, say that someone often feels uncomfortable around people who walk with crutches or who obviously have a cast or a splint on their broken leg. It always feels awkward and uncomfortable, and this person doesn't know what to do and feels befuddled, for example. But you have this broken leg and you're hobbling down the street as best you can with your crutches. You're on your way to healing, and you're trying to carry a bag of groceries at the same time—you know how that is. You can grab the handles while you're moving with the crutches, but all the while the groceries are bashing up against the side of the crutch.

And this person, whom you may or may not have known in a previous life but who is particularly compatible with your energy and who has always felt uncomfortable around people with crutches for whatever reason, sees you and in that moment says, "Oh. Can I help you with this bag?" And you say, "I'm just walking a short distance to my car." And this person says, "Let me help you," and you say, "Okay, thank you." You walk to your car and this person carries your groceries, puts the groceries in the car for you and maybe even assists you in getting into the car with crutches. And there you have it. You drive off, and maybe you never see that person again, but he has made the leap.

This person is now able, because it was you . . . anytime he is around people with crutches again in the future, he will know he can approach them and offer help, even if that help is declined—because initially you said, "Oh, I just have a short way to go," which is a decline. But he said, "Here, let me help you." He asked you again, and you said, "Okay." In short, this person will not be befuddled around people with crutches again in the future. I'm not saying that you got your broken leg because of this. I'm saying—and I'm talking generically—maybe that's why, because you're always helping each other, and from that point on, your broken leg will heal a lot faster because what you were intended to do with this person is done.

So the reason I'm bringing up this example, which seems a bit extreme but has happened before, is because sometimes you will ask for benevolent change to take place for that broken leg to heal, and you don't notice it healing any faster and the doctor says, "Oh, it's healing at the usual pace," and so on. In short, nothing happens. But maybe something will happen that you have no knowledge of. It might be something innocuous. Maybe somebody will open the door for you when you don't expect it—"Oh, thank you very much," and off you go. And then for some reason unexpectedly your broken leg begins to pick up the pace of healing, because you did ask for that help and it is available, but something needed to happen before that could take place. So your broken leg isn't all healed up, and by the time you see that person who needs to learn that thing, you're not at that time already using a walking cast where you can carry your groceries yourself [chuckles].

See how involved you are with all other human beings, to say nothing of all other life? You are always connected to all other life all the time. And it's the same when you are on other planets and other lives elsewhere. It's just that there there's no discomfort as you know it. There may be some teensy little discomfort—teensy compared to what you're used to here. There it might be felt as something more oppressive or more urgent because you're not used to any kind of discomfort there, but that's another story.

Loving Life Is What Exists

The main thing is that living compatibly, harmoniously, and influencing each other on the basis of your own needs according to the way you can all adapt to each other is the way to loving life—and loving life is what exists. No particles can come together to create the body of a human being to be birthed without there being adaptation—in short, love— between those particles. That is the way of all life everywhere, that kind of adaptation, harmony and influence. So the whole point is to learn how the system works so that you can work within it in the best, most benevolent way for yourself and others. Once you learn how it works, the system is not going to change. You might be able to run around and make things work in your favor with control—controlling and hitting and making things work temporarily for you—but it won't last because the system is set up in a way that is intended to be benevolent for all beings.

That is why your world is somewhat isolated here, so your cultures can learn and grow and change, not always in pleasant ways. But it is somewhat isolated on this planet in this place—and to some extent, in this solar system—so that it does not radiate out. It's kind of encapsulated, let's say, so you can do what you need to do while you are here: to learn, to grow, to change. But it does not have to affect what others are doing other places.

Interestingly enough, think about this: Suppose you're living on another planet and you can feel all the harmony around you, but as you expand— say, in a contemplation or a meditation or a prayer—as you feel your energy expanding all over the universes everywhere, you notice there's a place where you can't feel the energy, there's a gap, there's something missing. That's where the encapsulation is covering you and where you are and where you're learning. You say, "I wish I could feel that." And then your teachers maybe or those who tell you say, "Oh, that's a special encapsulation, because the people there are learning things and, because of their style of learning, it could harm us in the way we feel. So that encapsulation is there to help us, to keep us from being uncomfortable."

And you say, "Oh," and you understand why it is that way, but in your heart, you are longing to be able to feel connected to that place. So everyone on your planet and every place else is missing you and loving you and waiting for you to grow and change and do what you need to do so that that encapsulated space can be opened up and they can feel it and their hearts, which are missing you as part of everything, all life, can feel you once again and feel comfortable.

Basics of Shamanic Training

Speaks of Many Truths
May 24, 2002

reetings.

Greetings.

The Value of Being a Shamanic Person

Could you summarize the steps and the training of a shaman?

But you see, what you are asking for is not possible, because there are so many different cultures on Earth and nationalities—it does not bear so much, but the culture of the people you are with makes all the difference. There are certain basic things. One's teachers, if they are wise people, will have a couple of things in mind. First, what is the value of being a shamanic person? Of course, the first obvious value is to be in harmony with your surroundings. The second one is to be able to serve the needs of your people and, of course, yourself. And the third is, *to give no offense to life that you come in contact with.* That one is really important.

This does have something to do with harmony, but you have to consider that the basic teachings will follow the lines of: observe nature, especially that which is obviously in harmony with other elements of nature that are not of its own kind. In other words, how are the rocks in harmony with the trees? How are the animals in harmony with each other, even if consuming one another is a factor? Is it possible for that kind of thing to still be a form of harmony? That seems to me to be obvious, but even those given basics are not absolutes when it comes to shamanic training.

I can only talk about training that I received. That's why I've told stories about things that have happened, or anecdotes as you call them, because I cannot speak about shamanic training for shamans in other cultures. I have spoken to many of these beings, both alive in your own time and in other times, and also in spirit, such as myself when I am focused in that. I have seen similarities, yes, but there are many, many cultural differences.

Can we isolate some of the main steps on the path?

I realize you are trying to hit the foundation benchmarks: "How can people in general prepare for this?" But I can only speak of how it was for me in my time. I can't speak too well for how it is in your time, but it is up to the reader—whether the reader be simply an interested party, a casual observer or a shaman or a shamanic teacher—to adapt my experience to your times and see where it fits in. If it fits in, perhaps incorporate it. If it doesn't, then try to assemble something in your time that works, as long as you are conscious, ever presently conscious, of living in harmony.

Be aware that what occurs in nature in your time is not always harmony, because in your time there is so much pollution and damage to the Earth that sometimes nature—the animals, even the plants—is showing what amounts to a compensation, not true harmony based upon the planet being largely intact. In my time the planet was, if not completely, then more intact than it is in your time. Now, even though there was no mining going on where I lived in my time, I grant that there was mining going on in other parts of the world in other cultures that were not dissimilar to your own. After all, 440 years ago, 430 years ago and so on, there was mining going on, and of course, this was damaging to Earth's body as it would be if someone were mining in your body, and it caused her to have to compensate.

It's like if you get a wound in your body or you hurt some part of your body. You might be able to walk still, but you might find yourself limping for a time. Mother Earth's life is longer than the human being's life, and she recovers, she is able to recover, but it takes her longer to recover because her life is so much longer than our own. It makes sense, doesn't it?

Proportionately.

Yes, that's a nice word—proportionately.

Feminine Inspiration at Work

Would you discuss the difference between male and female power—or as you say, harmony—and how the shaman needs to accommodate that? Use the feminine?

At its most basic level, masculine is largely what is done, what you do, what you apply. The feminine is at its most basic level what you receive and, to a degree, what you pass on. Yet these two, we know, although they are not always compatible, tend to work best with each other because sometimes, as any good teacher knows, simply having knowledge is not enough. Sometimes, even for teachers who are enlightened in one way or another, one does not necessarily have the degree of enlightenment, as a teacher, you might want.

But when a teacher is working with a student—a special one, a gifted one perhaps, or even a very curious one—or a group of students who might have in the group a collection of qualities like that, the question of the student, not just asked with curiosity (although sometimes it might be that), but asked with an earnest desire to know, perhaps a need to know, often inspires the teacher. If the teacher does not have the answer, the inspiration might be present for the sake of the student, and that's how the teacher also learns and grows, because the teacher begins speaking of matters that he had not consciously assimilated before that time.

This is an example of feminine inspiration at work: that which is unknown but suddenly becomes known out of necessity, if not your own then the necessity of another. In your time this happens as well. You have heard of people being inspired, of course, but here is a nice melding of the feminine and masculine. Someone in your time is coming across an emergency situation. You've heard of people lifting cars off of other people. It doesn't really matter whether that person is a man or a woman or even a very young person. The person has to do it, so she does it. She suspends, in that moment, the disbelief that it's not possible, or she just runs over and does it without thinking about it. Then someone is able to crawl out or be pulled out by another. There are many incidents like that. This has to do not only with the feminine—meaning receiving not just the ability, but receiving the capacity.

You have, as a human being, many, many qualities that you never use because of your culture, the times you live in, the circumstances of your life and so on. These abilities are never accessed, even though they may be present, like sleeping. Along comes a situation like this, and it isn't strictly spirit or the angels alone who are at work here. It is like an automatic thing. Automatically your body responds, regardless of the condition of your body. It responds to the sudden need: "Lift the car or just try to lift the car; maybe it's possible." You don't usually think about it afterward when people are asked, "Who did that? What were you thinking? What made you think you could do this?" The almost universal response is, "I didn't think about it." You can do the research. Almost everyone says, "I didn't think about it."

The more people are forced to think about it afterward, the more likely they will need to go to the hospital, although usually they are all right. After that, however, their life is usually changed. One cannot have such a dramatic experience without having a major change that follows. Some people, as you say, "get religion." Other people start working out at the gym or just living differently. Of course, saving a life has a lot to do with that as well.

But I mention these things because I want to mention an example, and in your times it seems like dramatic examples get more attention. This is an example of something that is strikingly different that you would not normally think you could do and that involves the feminine receiving and the masculine applying, and is not done with calculated planned thought. This tells you something important: It tells you that the masculine, while being associated with the mental, does not *have* to be mental in order to produce value. That's important because in your time you've become almost addicted to thought.

Thought has its great value. After all, what we are doing here is largely a factor of your thoughts, speaking to the questioner here. Your thoughts access inspiration through the trained channel, who can then accommodate me as a spirit being to respond to your thoughts in words that help you to think along similar or different lines. So there is that. This tells you that such a thing is also spiritual. But the actual melding of the masculine and the feminine is, of course, most obviously at work during birth, and this is so well known that I will not discuss it too much.

The Love-Heat Practice Is a Given Foundation of Life

Are there some generic or general steps that a shamanic trainee can take to learn to focus in a deeper level of reality?

There are, of course, aids like disentanglement [see p. xxxi] that have been given. But the love-heat/heart-warmth/physical-warmth [see Overview] is so important because it is a given foundation of life. In the natural world—meaning with natural animals, for instance, natural plants—all you have to do is come up in fairly close proximity or as close as they are comfortable with. If you go into the love-heat, they will almost invariably respond in kind. How will you know? You will know because the love-heat you feel in your body will suddenly—not because you're doing anything—become much greater than you normally feel it.

This tells you that they are also doing it, and equally they are feeling it in their body more than *they* can normally generate, which is how they know you're doing it as well. Generally, animals and plants will automatically feel this when exposed to any other form of life besides their own. It is not just a beacon to know friend and foe; it is an automatic greeting. Why? Because it is something they normally feel.

This tells you that human beings have basically forgotten this. And if anything is to be taught to yourself, to others or even over the wider tools of media by anyone these days, this love-heat is one of the most important, because it automatically gives you something that feels good, something that does good, something that is a foundation to many other things and, perhaps most specifically important, something that is a foundation for all life in the universe, especially Creator Itself. So if you want to unite with Creator, if you want to have a common language of feeling with natural life around you and if you want to lay in the foundation to know, applied by practice and technique in the future after you do this, what may be a good thing for you to do that day, what may be a good thing for you to do some other time, what may be something that is not for you to do but perhaps might be perfectly all right for others to do—in short, if you want to have a means to make decisions that will work—this love-heat is so important.

Love-Heat Creates Physical Evidence of Your Union with All Life

Of course, the love-heat creates physical evidence of your union with life around you, because that life will respond in some way you can tell. Say you are doing this with a tree. The tree, if it can do this with you— perhaps it is busy; trees are sometimes—and if the heat suddenly rises within you, you'll know the tree is engaging you. If the warmth is particularly significant so that you feel it, the tree might be so happy that a human being in your times—a contemporary human being, you might say—is doing this, that the tree without any influence from the wind will on its own move its own limbs or leaves to show you how much it appreciates you interacting with it on this level. Those who have done this practice know this is true.

Equally, an animal . . . perhaps as I said before, you see a grasshopper, a praying mantis, a beetle, a squirrel or a bird. With the grasshopper or the praying mantis or the beetle, being a little more ancient beings insofar as their lineage to their point of origin as well as their experience on Earth, they might be more inclined to allow you to get closer to them. Granted, this trust and faith does not always pay off well for them, but as you learn what important teachers they are for you, it will.

Say they allow you to slowly come up close to where they are. Try to bring the heat and warmth up when you are nine or ten feet away, and then, while feeling the warmth, move up closer to them. If they are on a bush or on the ground, if you can, hunker down or kneel down to get a little closer yet. But don't reach out for them. Just feel that love-heat for yourself. If it rises in you more than usual, more than you usually feel, or significantly, they are doing the same.

How will you know for sure? You will have that extra warmth, and in the case of these creatures I mentioned—especially beetles (including ones you see in the city), perhaps ants (but ants are often very busy), maybe grasshoppers and praying mantises—they will very often do something that you recognize immediately in your culture that is indicated when such contacts occur. These beings will, if they are not looking at you, turn their head to look at you while you are feeling the warmth.

This is a direct personal connection in which they are not trying to look at you—they can do that because of their eyes; many of these creatures can see a little bit more than you can see as a human—but they are acknowledging you as an individual. The love and warmth feeling that they naturally radiate is something that they do to interact with their whole world and is a naturally broadcast signal that comes from them because they are doing it all the time, whereas you in your time have to learn how to do it, but you can do it. The turning to look at you while you are feeling this love and warmth is a genuine connection contact.

Learning from Beetles and Other Creatures through the Connection of Feeling

In time I will teach you how you can learn from them. One of the first things they will want to teach you is about their world and what they do, but they'll want you to learn on the basis of having this warmth going on at all times. That's why they will start with something small that you know and recognize. This tells you if they're taking you on as a student, even for the brief moments that you see each other. Or perhaps if they happen to live in the neighborhood—choose to live there, you understand, for a time—they will take you on as a student longer if life supports them there. They will turn and look at you—this tells you that they might be willing to teach you.

That's why the "turn and look" is important. If they are willing to teach you, you will immediately while you have that warmth, always feeling that . . . for their comfort? No, for your comfort as well, because in your time most of you have been trained, conditioned, to believe there's something wrong with these beings. There's no more wrong with them than is wrong with you. They are just different. You want to meet ETs? Here they are. The ETs you meet won't look like this, but they are sufficiently different—these beings whom you live with—that it's good training to meet ETs. That's really just an aside, but if they turn and look at you, they are willing to teach you.

But first there must be the warmth, all right? If they turn and look at you, they're willing to teach you. If this look takes place, then be prepared for something that they are teaching you. They might suddenly fly somewhere. If they fly away, the look was simply an extra acknowledgment—a gift. But if they fly just a short distance, not very far away, and maybe even fly back to where they were or stay at that short distance away, what they are teaching you is about flight, because you are in connection with them. Men and women . . . they've always looked at the birds, always looked at flight as something they want to do. After all, you fly about in planes in your time. And in my time, I can assure you, we were just as fascinated with flight as you are.

In my time we were taught how to pay attention to those who would teach us of these things. We did not have wings any more than you have, but we applied this to the type of flight that we did—meaning perhaps that we learned how to fly with these beings, with this union of love and warmth. The next time they flew, maybe we could imagine . . . not being a passenger, but imagine being them. If they take you on as a student, they will allow you to feel their bodies from the inside out.

Don't go out of your body, but extend so that you feel being them. They are comfortable with this, and they probably will be if they turn to look at you. Then what you do is you extend. Try to feel their bodies as if they are a part of your own. Don't touch them; just extend your feelings. It won't be too hard, because you're already exuding a feeling. By the way, with the love-heat, you never send it out, but it naturally radiates or exudes.

So the connection of feeling . . . what is it like to have these wings, to have this shape of body, to have these wonderful extra legs? Isn't that exciting? Then the next time they fly or even move their head while you are feeling their body as part of your own, you will almost feel . . . it's not exactly like your own head moving, but there will be a sensation of personal experience when that is going on. Then if they fly, they want you to experience flight in this way.

Remember, harmony means living with the living all around you in the ways that are most harmonious for you all—including you. If you as a human being cannot fly because you have no wings, this does not prevent you from the experience of flight. It simply means you need to make loving contact with a being who can fly and experience flight while united with that being—not going out of your body to do it, because you want to have the physical feeling of flight.

Say the being suddenly flies . . . maybe it flies away, or maybe it flies around for a bit and comes back. But once that union is there, staying in your body you will be able to experience some of the physical things. The being might look down, and suddenly you will have an impression or even see clearly the ground below. You might even see yourself looking up. Even though you are in your body, you are also seeing through the eyes of this wonderful teacher. The being might land and eat something, a little nectar or something like that. Probably it won't eat with you in connection to itself right away, but it might. If it happens, it happens. Notice how it feels—never judge it. Judgment usually comes from fear or conditioning or both.

Actual learning about harmony in life around you offers you gifts like the one I mentioned where you can actually experience flight as a personal experience with all of its joys and even sometimes its struggles—such as at times when I have experienced flight with a friendly bumblebee and there's a definite feeling of the weight of the body, kind of a struggle to fly. I believe that's why when they fly, sometimes they look a little ungraceful, because they really have to make an effort to fly with those little wings and that big body. But the fact that they can do it is encouraging. I find bumblebees very inspiring, and I think some of you find them that way in your time as well, because look at what they do given how hard it is. Think about that. You can fly; you can see. You'll be surprised.

The many-leggeds, what you call insects . . . which is not a nice word, because you're conditioned to believe they are bad, which is not true at all in my experience. Granted, some of them are a trial, such as mosquitoes or fleas or ticks. But you learn what is safe to connect with. Many of them are what I call stage teachers, meaning they will teach you about flight or they will teach you about crawling under rocks or what beetles might do. They will teach you.

How do you think the first humans learned about caves and learned that they were safe? It was not just because they were there, but because they observed and felt, being open in those early days, these other beings, what they did. "What's in there? What's in that cave? I don't feel safe to go in there," say you, "because I saw a lion go in that cave once. Maybe it's still there and I can't see him." But then a beetle crawls in and you feel, as that ancient human, connected with this beetle. The beetle looks all around the cave. Maybe the beetle doesn't even have to crawl into the cave, but because of this union with you, the beetle does you a favor, crawls in the cave, and you can see what the beetle sees.

The cave is empty, and you go up and thank the beetle and say, "Good life." You say, "When I have some food left, when I get food and I have some left, I will leave some out near the opening of the cave if you like." And the beetle will tell you, because of its wisdom, "It might be better to leave it a little farther in the cave so that the smells do not attract the lion." You say, "Oh yes, I will leave some close enough to the fire where it is safe for you to come, and I will put it on a rock shelf that you can climb up to so that everyone else here will know that is for you. Perhaps the rock will absorb some warmth—not too close to the fire, but close enough so that you can eat and then rest while you absorb the warmth from the rock."

This was something that was done in those early days, something that I've done in my time when I wasn't sure about a place. Often the animals will go there and do you a favor out of kindness, not out of servitude. It is not their job to serve you slavishly. It is your job to learn from them that which they freely offer in teaching if they acknowledge, in the way I indicated, that they're taking you on as a student. If they decide to teach you flight, they might teach you something else. You have to observe what they are doing after they turn their head and look at you. Maybe they will teach you something then, maybe not. Observe.

You Must Experience Flight with the Many-Leggeds First

But if it is flight, then you know that someday you may have the opportunity to unite with the birds and fly with the birds, and the birds may show you what's over the next mountain, whether it's safe to go there for your people. Maybe you have to move from time to time because of the weather. How will you know it is safe? What's around the other side of that mountain? Sometimes you have to climb up the mountain. After all that effort, you wouldn't want to look down and say, "Oh, oh, there are some people or some danger down there for us." You would really like to know what's on the other side of that mountain, and you might find a bird who will do you a favor, who will fly over and look while you are united with it and show you what's there. Or it might be going that way.

You will find that unless you've had extensive shamanic training, you will probably not be able to unite with the birds in the best way to create good friendship like this unless you've already been taught flight and its feeling and the type of union you feel from the many-leggeds, the little ones. The birds look for this in a human, a shamanic student or even a teacher. First they feel, "Have you flown with the many-leggeds, the little ones?" If you have already flown, it is not unlike the person who owns an airplane in your time: "Do you have a pilot's license? Why would I want to take you out for a flight or flight training if you don't have some familiarity?"

It is like that—familiarity. "I don't want this person I unite with"—the bird doesn't think this way, but this is the interpretation and feeling—"I don't want him panicking while he looks out or sees or does with me when I am doing and seeing. If I need to eat, I don't want him panicking while he is united with me because he is upset by what I am doing." In short, the bird wants to be assured that you will be a safe passenger.

The birds will check to see if you've flown with the many-leggeds, the little ones. If you have done so, then they will embrace your flight with them. They will all know, on the basis of the feeling . . . what? The love-heat that you are feeling becomes coded. You don't broadcast your feeling with flight with the little ones, or maybe you will, but most likely it won't occur to you because you are making connection with life around you. But the birds will know and they will welcome you.

If you've had the opportunity to fly with the little ones and they have taught you well and thoroughly about flight, if that's what they wish to teach you or what you welcome to learn—both—then they will teach you other things. The little ones will fly, they will eat and perhaps they will drink. They will do all the natural things all natural life does so that you will be familiar with what they do, how they feel, part of their natural life, so that you can enjoy that with them anytime they wish to include you in their lives. And perhaps some day, if you find that you need a bird's vision or would like to, even just for the pleasure of the experience, be joined with a bird, see what it sees, feel what it feels, enjoy flight, then you can fly.

The Lessons Are Physical

Once the student has a sense of any one of these techniques, has felt the feeling in the physical, that gives him or her the impetus to take the next step, right?

The most important thing is to observe. Pay attention. Don't look for the vague. Always look for the clear. The lessons are physical. You feel the love-heat. You make contact perhaps with grasshoppers or praying mantises or beetles, for instance. They make contact with you; they acknowledge you. They turn and look at you, or they lift their head up and look at you. That is direct acknowledgment of you as someone. If they don't turn and look at you, they are busy—even if the warmth comes up. You can sit with them for a while if they choose to. If they move off, just say, "Good life," as they are moving on.

You can also say "Good life" when you sit down next to them, but not too loudly. You don't want to frighten or startle them, but you can say it out loud quietly. They will know what that means. They will know it is a greeting, a blessing, an acknowledgment, a prayer—all of those. You may, if you are sensitive, hear "Good life" back, or you may not. They might even make a little sound if they can, which will be their sound equal to "Good life." That's possible, especially from, say, a grasshopper, who can make little sounds sometimes. So you see what happens.

The natural world gives you signals in the physical first because they are here to teach you utilizing . . . what? The five senses that most of you have. Those of you who have either lost one of your senses or perhaps were born without one will have the capacity to heighten the senses that you still have. But for now I speak to those of you who have the five senses. In short, these beings will communicate with you in the easiest, simplest and most direct way. They do not want to start to teach you about the physics of the universe before you've had a chance to say hello. First things first—always.

Then what would come after that? The student gets that far—then what?

That's pretty far. That's as far as I'm going to go right now, because I want you to have a chance to learn and to observe perhaps the little ones—"little" meaning in terms of their size, not in their value. Everyone is equally valuable. Perhaps the little ones will want to teach you something else. Perhaps if they have faith in you or have sat with you before, perhaps they will have one of their young ones there. It's not just that you happen to be there and they are doing that. They are very aware.

Just pay attention to what they are doing once you've made contact with them. It's what they do next after they look at you that's important. That's what they're going to teach you. If it's eating, then it's that. If it's drinking, then it's that. If it's flight, then it's that. Whatever it is they do next, unless they simply go away or fly away . . . which would be simply, "I acknowledge you as a student, and perhaps I will be back. Perhaps one of my brothers or sisters will make contact with you again. Then we'll see."

It's not what comes next in some empirical, factual way. It's always that first the student demonstrates that you are worthy. You feel this love warmth yourself, and it naturally radiates. It doesn't work if you send it out. It has to naturally radiate—meaning you know how to do it, and it will naturally radiate. Don't worry about that as long as you are feeling it. Remember, feeling the love and warmth is something that takes practice, practice, practice. You know that it does.

So once you've felt that, then whatever the teacher wishes to teach you, that's what comes next, not what you want to know. By the way, always pay attention to what's going on the moment you start thinking about what comes next. Probably the warmth will go away within you, which is very upsetting to the person you're with. So remember that the love-heat in you requires you to be physically present with yourself. The nice thing about the teacher is that the teacher will know that you are physically present with yourself or not. Ideally though, since I'm talking about that, the teacher will know because of the warmth. The teacher will feel: perhaps, you will both feel more, and in order to have that connection, you will have to be in the moment. If you are thinking about what's next, you probably won't experience the warmth.

Remember, be in the moment so you can learn what they offer. *Be there.* They will teach you physically. It's all about physical; it's all about feelings. It expands our spiritual abilities, but more importantly for you now, it expands your physical abilities. Just think about it. What if that bird flies over the mountain and shows you what's there? What a gift for you and your people, eh?

Meaning while you're connected so you can see?

Of course.

Finding a Teacher

A teacher is extremely important. Is it that, "When the student is ready, the teacher will appear," or should the student go and try to find a teacher if he doesn't have a physical teacher?

If you don't have a physical teacher of your own kind, meaning a human being, then it is all right to go out and engage nature, as I said. Even with a teacher, he or she will probably have you engage nature. I recommend engaging nature in the way I stated. For example, because in your time such little beings in size—little only in size—are still available, I can tell you about my experience, which is relevant to your time. But if you're saying, should the student go looking for the teacher . . . in your time, that may be of some value, but many in your time have traveled all over the world only to find that the best teaching is usually available within walking distance of where they live.

Remember, the teacher may not be one person. It might be many, many people, sharing their experience, their knowledge, their wisdom. Sometimes it will not be knowledge, wisdom or experience that you can apply in your life, but perhaps you will observe something. If they are wise, you will know. Perhaps even what they say will help you in your life. Many of you know this.

But do I subscribe to the fact that a teacher will magically appear? I'd say, with no more magic than life itself is magic—which, of course, it is. Just be aware that very often your teachers are so close to you that you do not always notice them. Perhaps they live across the street or down the road. Perhaps they're in the forest. Use the love-heat even with humans.

If you approach a human and the love-heat in you goes away and suddenly feels very uncomfortable, you might want to give that human a wide berth. Maybe she is not always exuding this unpleasant feeling; perhaps even this is your reaction to that person, not just you feeling something from her. But if you can, sometimes it's good to give this person her quiet and her world, to give her a wide enough berth so that she can have her world and you can have yours. What is a wide enough berth? I will tell you. Once the uncomfortable feeling starts to come on, change your direction for now. There are other things I will teach you in the future, but this is part of your *now* training. Change your direction so that you can still feel the warmth.

You might be able to practice this with someone you don't necessarily get along with very well—meaning if you see him or her coming, see if you can put some space between the two of you. Notice, if you are feeling the love-heat, how much space you need in order to maintain the love-heat even though you are walking near that person. Remember that even though you do not feel good around that person, it does not necessarily mean that that person is a bad or dangerous person. Maybe it does, but it could also mean that you and that person have an incompatibility in that moment, or perhaps that person needs to be quiet or private, or needs to be with whomever he or she is with and not with you.

In short, know that these feelings that you have in your body are always telling you something. We start you with the love-heat because it's the foundation of that which will help you. Just feeling it feels good, but interpreting it and applying it greatly improves your life. In time I will speak of other feelings at length so that you can learn how to interpret those—some of which you know how to interpret, but the vast majority of which you do not always know—probably in another book.

There has been a much greater interest in the past few years in shamanic teachings, and there are actual schools and workshops that give beginning teachings to workshop participants. Do you feel that's a good first step for someone looking to start?

If you are attracted and if they say that it is their intention to help you to feel more united with your world around you and to make a loving connection, harmony, using words like that, then give them special attention. If rather they say, "Do you want to have power over life around you? Do you want to control your life?" then I say maybe let others try that.

Even though those who described this teaching may not be people who want to have power and control over you, nevertheless, if they use words like that, they may be trying to attract someone whose teaching is not always compatible with what I have to offer—if you are interested in what I have to offer and occasionally what others have to offer in these pages of the *Shamanic Secrets* series. If, on the other hand, they use some key words like I've used with you—love, harmony, compatibility, things like that— then you will know, if you wish to learn concurrently with these people and with these books, that this will probably be compatible. They will probably teach you about harmony within yourself, feelings, harmony with other life forms, love, feelings and so on.

Physical Mastery Is Available on Earth

That's what to look for because it is best to learn the basics first, the physical. You exist. You are immortal. Your personalities go on indefinitely, all right? You come here on Earth in this time—this time for you, not for me—in your time, to learn about the physical: its ways, its manners, its means, its feelings, its applications, its consequences, all that and more. So one must recognize that if you are here to learn about the physical, then this is the place to begin. It also has everything to do with the acquisition of knowledge and wisdom that you may not have accumulated to any great degree elsewhere in all of your incarnations and even in your ongoing overall being.

That is the great value of this. You will learn not only what you don't know but what you haven't done and what has even been foreign to you. How will you know if it's foreign? Because as you approach many things physical, even in workshops or with these books, there might be a vague feeling of foreignness or strangeness, not necessarily discomfort. If there's a feeling of foreignness or strangeness, that will tell you that you have lived almost no physical lives or no physical lives before anywhere. So that tells you it is a great privilege that Creator has allowed you to come to this finishing school.

That's what it is. You may not finish in one life here, but it is a place where physical mastery is possible to learn. You may not learn it all in one life. You might just learn one small facet, but it is *possible* to learn. I can assure you that the ability to learn physical mastery, which must be something that you feel and do physically, is available to no greater degree on any other planet, in any other place, in any other existence, as it is available here. That's why it's part of creator training.

Drumming the Shamanic Way

Let me go on with what's out there in the modern approach a little bit further. One of the things that these workshops and these trainings do is teach people to relax and then follow drumming and learn to what they call "journey," which is to go somewhere and take some action in the spirit world. In all these books, I've never heard you mention drumming as an accompaniment to this type of spiritual aid.

That's because I feel it's too advanced for you. I feel that although the intention of many people teaching this is good, the real purpose of drumming must begin with the basics. You must feel life around you first. You must become absolutely familiar with your drum if you're going to be involved in drumming. The best way is to make it yourself, but you must become very familiar with the materials first, which means you must become familiar with trees as they are living first, say, if it is partly tree.

You must become familiar with deer as they are living first if you use deer-skin. And it is the same with the stick, if you use a stick and all its component parts to strike the drum with. In short, there's a great deal to be done first.

Even once you've made your stick, you don't strike the drum with anything but your heart—meaning that if you expect the drum to respond to you after you have made it and have let it get used to itself . . . meaning, the deerskin does not normally hold anything but a deer. It is not natural for the deerskin to hold the wood, nor is it natural for the wood of the tree to have deerskin wrapped around it—it would have bark. So it must take time.

You must let it sit on its own quietly for at least sixty days and maybe have some of that time outdoors, feeling the Sun and the Moon. Maybe—these are maybes depending upon the culture and depending upon your purpose for yourself and the drum—maybe you might even have it near the rain. Perhaps let a few drops strike it. In short, expose it to the elements—not to get soaked, but just a little bit. And you will want parts of your body to touch it.

If you want the drum to *do* something for you, you will need, after the drum sits for a few months . . . and this is not my complete drum teaching; I have extensive teaching available for that, but this is an overview. One of the things you will do after the drum sits for a time is that you will then strap the drum to your chest, your bare chest. It will overlap a bit onto your solar plexus, but that's good. You want the drum to feel, not only your heart-warmth, your love-heat, but your feelings as you feel them so that the drum will become familiar with your feelings—in short, you.

You want to feel the warmth, but before you can strap the drum to yourself, of course, you will have had warmth with the deer—maybe not *the* deer who offered the skin of its body to make your drum, but deer and trees in general and so on. But before you strap the drum to your body, you will first have to sit by the drum and do the warmth. Until that drum, sitting by the drum, causes in you the feeling that you get, at least similarly, sitting next to the grasshopper or praying mantis or beetle—that feeling of more warmth than you normally feel for yourself when you feel the love-heat—until it has that feeling, you don't strap it to your chest. And never bother strapping it to your chest unless it's right on your skin. After you strap the drum to your chest, wear it at least ten to twelve hours a day.

Don't sleep with it strapped to your chest. That's not good for you and it's not good for the drum. But keep it near your bed when you are sleeping. Put it in the position near your bed that feels good, where you have the most warmth to you, because the drum will also acknowledge by that warmth that that's where it wants to be. But don't have the drum near your bed or while you are sleeping until these other steps take place, because you and the drum are not only getting to know each other, but you are feeling each other so that the drum can respond to you personally. That's all I'm going to say about the drum now, but that tells you pretty well what my approach would be to teaching someone about a drum and making a drum and working with a drum.

There's a great deal more to talk about in terms of how you use the drum, but do I recommend that people come to a workshop, buy a drum—they don't know the drum; the drum doesn't know them—or, even more extreme, just use a drum that other people have used? If you've been acculturated and conditioned to a drum made like that your whole life and it is a drum passed on to you by your parents or your grandparents—in short, if you've been raised with the culture of the drum—that might be different. But if you just go somewhere and there's a drum and you are to take a drum journey, the chances of that journey being your own, that will benefit you completely, are greatly reduced. This does not mean there won't be some benefit. *Perhaps* there will be some benefit, but the benefit will be greatly reduced. Think about just what I've told you about making a drum the way I've suggested. Just think about that level of familiarity and bonding and companionship that I've told you about.

Now, I haven't told you everything that you do, but with just that much with the drum, how much more can that drum do for you? I will tell you this much only as an extra treat. That drum can take you anywhere! You can see life on other planets. You can see the ends of the universe and beyond. Someday I'll teach you about the drum—we'll see.

And usually that student doesn't beat the drum in a workshop environment?

Even lesser, then. So I'm not saying don't do it. I'm saying that if it appeals to you, if you find it attractive, even if you want to teach something like that to expose the uninitiated to possibilities, you can do it if you want to present it. You can attend something like that if you want to. Just know that it will be what it is and no more. I hear someone saying, "You can say that about anything." But in my experience, things—life around me—are what they are *and* they are more. That's the difference.

There is a chance that once this student begins some of this love-heat and begins interacting with natural beings and some of these steps, he will then connect with an inner teacher, if he's sensitive, who will teach him individually, right?

Possibly.

Does that happen in a great many cases, or is that a rare occurrence?

Not commonly without other teaching, but it's possible. You might need to do other things to connect with that teacher, but that's not the purpose of this book. Other books might cover that, such as those that discuss how to connect with your inner teacher, inner guide or angels, and so on and so forth.

I've never heard anybody talk about drumming. Do you want to talk about your experience, or do you feel you've said enough?

It's enough for now. My teacher says it is too soon to speak of these matters, and you can see why in the way I explained it to you. Look at the teaching I provided today about the grasshopper or the praying mantis or the beetle. It was extensive, fairly thorough for what I wanted to expose you to, but we haven't really expanded on that. We've touched on these matters about the grasshopper and praying mantis and beetle before, but we expanded on it today and we will expand more in the future. We've touched on things you might do with trees and animals—deer and so on. In the future, we will do more to explore that.

Once I feel we have done enough to explore all the elements you might use to make a drum, then if you like, you can ask more about the drum and I may repeat myself a bit because I will build. That's why people of my time and conditioning and culturalization sometimes repeat ourselves, because we remind you what you've already learned. We review it for those of you who haven't been exposed to the previous teaching, and we build on that, expanding it, so that you can see how it connects to things that very often you haven't even thought about.

So we will do that once we get to that place, and then if you like, you can ask about the drum and I will speak of these matters, telling you more things about how you and the drum become brother and sister—like that. You and the drum become one family. The drum then becomes part of you, part of your body. If you can possibly help it, no one else ever touches the drum but you. If anyone is ever going to touch the drum, it will be your initiate, your student, perhaps your special student whom you pass your things on to. Or if you are not blessed in that way, then perhaps it might be a relative, a daughter, a son.

But this is only if that person knows that he can touch it—he's not trained in such things—only to remind himself of you. If he wishes to touch you, he can touch your drum, which is almost part of your body. As a grandson or granddaughter, you might say, "I love you, Grandfather," and give yourself the gift of once in a while touching with two fingers, left hand or right—these two fingers [first and second after the thumb]—just touching some part of the drum. Try not to touch the part that is struck, either by hand or by stick, because the drum will be not used to you but sufficiently familiar with you to know that you are a beloved relative or descendent. However the drum feels, it will have its feelings—its own feelings if the drum was made right.

There is a lot to learn about these matters. If you want to have a drum for you that you use that provides you with great gifts, you must make it all yourself: gather the wood and gather the deerskin. The only other way to do that in your time, if you cannot gather the wood for whatever reason, if you cannot gather the deerskin—that might bother a lot of you— then you must acquire these materials from someone with whom you have a heart connection.

It doesn't have to be someone who is a lover; it can be someone who feels good to you. It might even be someone who supplies these things. But you pick the materials. All of them must feel exactly along the lines of that extra warmth. You might go someplace where there's a great deal of this material, drum-making material. If whatever you pick to use does not encourage extra warmth in you, in your body, then leave it. It's for someone else. I'll say more about these things in time.

Did you use a drum a lot? You've never mentioned it.

I did not use a drum much, but there was a drum person with my people, so I tell you what I know based upon what the drummer told me or based upon what they tell me now to pass on to the student.

Learning to Sample and Feel the Air

Speaks of Many Truths
May 27, 2002

This is Speaks of Many Truths. I will make some comments for the book. I would like to talk about Mother Earth's method of breathing.

Mother Earth Samples the Surface Air to Know How to Accommodate Humans

Now, Mother Earth, besides opening up passageways to the surface for moving or altering the land surface with her volcanoes, also leaves some of those shafts open. As some explorers have found, it is possible, once it has cooled for many years, to descend into the opening of the volcano, in some cases partway. But very often she will leave a gap, not big enough for an explorer, but enough for her to breathe through a circuitous route.

One does not think of Mother Earth as needing to breathe. She does not have lungs as a human being; she does not have a beating heart that you can hear. But she does have a need to exchange the air within her body with the surface. You might reasonably ask, "Is this a personal need for her?" Before the days of pollution as you know it now, it was, because it was a way that she sampled the surface air to see how many human beings were here. In the old days, she would simply exchange the air from where she was with the surface so that she could sample it, because of a certain taste there is in the air.

There's a better way to describe this—it's not so much a smell. We all know that human beings have a smell, but it is more for Mother Earth. A little closer description from my understanding is like a taste. When the air tastes a certain way, then there are this many human beings, and when it tastes a certain way, there are that many. If a place you have been in has no other influence but human beings—meaning it's not air-conditioned—you can get a feeling . . . not quite a taste as you know it, but like a taste, just from the air of a place where there are many human beings at once. I'm not saying you should try, but it is possible to just get that from the air, or at least a feeling that resembles it. It is similar for her but not the same.

When the air is flavored with human beings sufficiently, that's what tips her off to changes she needs to make in order to make accommodations for you. That's what encourages her to change her weather patterns and so on, so as to make it possible for you to live on her surface as benevolently as possible. So all over the Earth, there are these places where she breathes. Sometimes they've been discovered and noted, and other times they've simply been noted only by local mystical or shamanic or medicine people. Other times only the animals know.

Learn More about the Instinctual Body from Mother Earth

I mention this because it is important for you to understand how very similar human beings are to Mother Earth and what you can learn from those similarities. The original mystical lessons, spiritual lessons and so on, had to do with human beings observing. It was not so much that things were brought to their attention in dramatic ways, but rather that they observed out of necessity or simply because they could. Therefore, in your time there is value for you to observe. Consider that if Mother Earth can sample the atmosphere of her surface to know how to alter her situation, this tells you a little bit more about the instinctual body that human beings have, which I've discussed before.

The instinctual body utilizes not only the physical self (what is called the emotional self but in fact is the feeling self) and the spiritual self, but also, to a greater or lesser degree, it utilizes the senses. You are, of course, becoming aware of things that you see, smell, taste and so on, but I mention things like Mother Earth's breathing because it is important for you to realize that if she can adapt to the needs of an entire race of people, then by similar means, you can adapt to either what is going to happen or what might be happening that you do not see or are not aware of.

Think about that: When she has sampled the air to know what she needed to do, what she needed to do was not a response to the present but a response on the basis of a trend. Therefore, she would respond for present needs to a lesser degree and future needs to a greater degree. When you think about that, it tells you right away of a lost art that is available, because you still have your senses in your time. I want some of you who are especially sensitive to flavors and who have a desire to expand your spiritual wisdom and perhaps have some knowledge and wisdom of these things, to consider when you respond on the basis of instinct—and I'm not just talking about mental instinct, what you think, how you're inspired, but how you feel physically, which I've discussed before—to consider adding flavor to this. In order to do that, you may need to, when it is safe of course, breathe in the air.

How to Sample the Flavor of the Air

This is how to sample the flavor: When you are breathing in the air, specifically put your tongue in such a way when you are breathing like that [the tongue is above the teeth so that when the air comes in, it's going along both sides of the tongue]. Yes, it's like slurping the air. Have you ever eaten something or drunk something you wanted to slurp? It's like you actually bring the air in over your tongue. Ideally I'd like you to bring it in slowly, maximizing the potential to experience, if not a taste as one might have bittersweet, salty and so on, but a taste that is more likely to be something that you feel as an aftertaste.

For those of you who are wine connoisseurs, you are attuned (or let's say you are sensitized) to tasting things on the basis of their aroma—meaning you might sniff the wine, for instance, or the brandy, and the actual flavor of it produces a sense of taste. It is that technique. By the way, you don't have to be a wine connoisseur or brandy connoisseur, but I'm mentioning this because in your sophisticated times such things are known, even by people who are not this. It is that kind of thing.

So bring in the air that way. You won't be able, as the wine connoisseur does, to swirl the air around your mouth and get a better feeling for it. You need to bring it in, in that way over your tongue to maximize the impact of the air on your tongue. You may notice some sensation of flavor as the air comes in. You may notice it as an aftereffect as you close your mouth and then simply are conscious. Put your physical energy into your tongue, your sense of touch into your tongue and even on the roof of your mouth, where you might have a latent ability to have a sensation. The purpose here is to observe a flavor.

Now, granted, in some circumstances, there might be a smell that would overpower the flavor or produce something else. What you're looking for, however, is what Mother Earth was doing in my example. I know that in your times you're particularly interested in what the future might hold, and since you've demonstrated an interest in that, it might be to your advantage to reacquire this lost art. Granted, there are a few people in your time who can do this. Most of them are doing it quietly. But I feel that it will be to your advantage now to begin to utilize your senses in ways that are more thoroughly entrenched in their full capacities.

Flavors in the Air Help You Pinpoint Future Potentials

I want you to, if you like—those of you who wish to try this—take notes. Try and make notes of some sort on a recording device, even pencil and paper or computer, anything you want to. Make some kind of notes after your experience of sampling the air if there's some taste at all (if there's no taste, then it's probably not necessary, but I will examine that further). I want you to take note if you can—if you get a latent flavor or anything—write down what the flavor reminds you of or what it tastes like. Try to write down something descriptive, even if it is bitter, sweet, salty, anything like that, so that you can start to get some kind of research going with this that will be to your advantage. Then over the next twelve hours, you might try this for a few minutes. Probably you'll do this in the morning; ideally do it outside so you can get the taste.

Now, for those of you in cities, if the pollution is to a great degree, you're not going to be able to get much. But for those of you in places where the pollution is not too extreme or where there is a breeze, you might be able to get this. So you do that then and take note of what occurs—not globally, not news so much, but what occurs in your experience over the next twelve hours, especially in your interactions with your fellow human beings, let's say before you get to work, but even what happens at work. This is not, "This deal was discussed," or "That had to be filed," or "This had to be repaired," none of that—in other words, not your tasks, but how you react and interact with other human beings.

In short, you want to keep this personal record. You don't have to keep it like a diary. You can just write it down at the end of the day as a trend. Also, if you wish, you can make note of the local news and what happened locally. If you want to, you can jot down some major event that may or may not happen internationally, particularly if it has to do with phenomena—weather, earthquakes, volcanic eruptions and so on—because this research you are doing involving flavors can in time, especially if you are not intimidated . . . let's say others you know are trying this. They might taste it differently, all right?

This particular skill is something that is not dependent upon other people experiencing the same flavor, though within certain types of individuals that could happen—meaning men, young men, older men, young women, women or older women (that's what I mean by types, not any other category). You might find some similarities, and if you do, it might be good to take note of them. It won't always be the same, but some similarities will allow you to pinpoint certain potentials for the future more accurately.

This could be of invaluable aid in knowing when, say, an earthquake might occur, or when a volcanic eruption might occur to a greater degree of pinpoint accuracy—meaning that it will occur within the next ten to twelve hours, or when you get good at it, that it will occur in an hour and a half, a "Let's get out of here!" kind of thing. I'm pointing this out to you today because on a previous occasion, I spoke to you about smells and how we are able to use them in our time to know how to treat illnesses.

Now, these books are their own series—*Material Mastery, Physical Mastery, Spiritual Mastery*—and yet they have a sequence of their own as a unit. Each one follows the other, and yet you will at times be able to say that the sequence might run the other way. You might conceivably be able to notice a sequence running from *Spiritual Mastery* to *Physical Mastery* to *Material Mastery*. That's all right.

I wanted to remind you of this so you realize that these books are being given to you in such a time and in such a way as they are intended to provide you with what you need at the time of the channeling and, to some degree, at the time of the publication. The publishing process here is complicated and multileveled, and that's why it takes awhile to get the books out. Therefore, do not be annoyed or upset if it takes awhile. Still, when the book comes out—and for the next twenty to twenty-five years—to greater or lesser degrees, it will be profoundly relevant. If you are attracted to something, you can do it.

The Wind Will Carry Flavors

I'm not trying to draft people to use this method; rather, I want to remind you of your abilities. We've talked over time of touch and smell. Today it's about taste. Now, there are other things you can do with tasting the air to get some impression of what might occur in the future. For instance, if you go to a place where there is a great body of water—such as the location of this channeling [in Hawaii], which is an island out in the middle of the ocean—in such a place it is easier to get a sampling of air for the future. It is not at all hard to find a beach here where there is a steady breeze blowing.

Take note of the direction of the breeze if it is consistent: from the north, from the south, from the east, from the west. Try to sample that air if it feels safe to do so. If you're right by the beach, you will probably get some salt spray, so you may have to move back a bit, but try to sample the breeze as it is coming in. See if you can notice a flavor other than saltiness. If you are noticing only saltiness, you'll probably have to move back further from the beach.

The point I'm trying to make is that the direction of the breeze is all-important if it is a consistent direction. It can, in this case, once you have your notes made and have some idea of what the flavors mean, give you some idea of what might happen from where that wind has been, because the wind will carry flavors.

Let's say the wind is from the east. If it is from the east, consider what landmasses and population centers lie in that direction. Say the wind is from the north. What landmasses and populations are in that direction and so on? This is something that is valuable to try and research for a while. Don't jump to conclusions. Don't try it for a week and say, "Oh, this is what this means always."

But this is something now that I feel is of great value to you because your usual or traditional or intellectual means of predicting the future may not always be to your total and complete advantage. Right now your intellectual analysis—as one hears on the radio or reads in newspapers or sees on television—of the focal point of interest that day about the news is not always accurate, because intellectual analysis invariably involves the past. This is typical for the intellect, because one often understands what *has* happened better by looking back than by looking forward. Historians are aware of this. I'm not saying this is a method I'm promoting but rather that this is how the method works.

What I am suggesting with the flavor sampling is that it might be possible to not only have an immediate sensation of what is going to happen in the present, but that there will be the potential to know trends: How does the Earth feel? The wind, part of her body, carries that. In large population centers, the wind will pick up a sampling, meaning not just this person, not that person, but an overall flavor of what people are feeling in large groups. If you can pick up this flavor from the wind, make your notes and follow world events to some degree—especially if the wind is coming from a population center, a landmass that you trace back from the wind's direction—you might be able to get some idea *how* or *if* you can use this method to predict trends for the future.

You Can Use This to Predict Needs for the Future

The way I really feel this can be used, to the great advantage of your populations, is to predict *needs* for the future. That's its actual purpose, if you can taste some flavor that suggests that people need change or they need food or they need nurturing. So this suggests that it might be useful. You might be able to provide these things as a society. In time you might be able to have global communities that provide these things—not just disaster teams that go in to take care of people's immediate and urgent needs, but also teams that go in *before* some disaster happens, man-made or otherwise, to serve people's needs before some catastrophic action is taken, occurs or is simply generated by groups of individuals.

Do you see what I'm hinting at? It might be possible to head off problems before they occur. You may not be able to know exactly what the problem is that you're heading off, but maybe that won't be necessary to know. At least the immediate need will be to head it off. There's a feeling, a taste, you understand, that something is needed. You serve that need, and then you note, as the taster, that that taste is no longer present. That's how you know that the need has been served.

You can see that this will take time, effort and research. If I did not feel it was of value, I would not provide it as a method that you can research. But since it can not only be used to make general predictions—and in time, when you get better at it, specific predictions—but it can be used to serve the needs of communities of people, which might head off man-made or even unintentional man-made disasters or such things, then it could be a worthy system to explore, research and compare notes with others who are doing it.

Remember, don't be intimidated if your flavors do not match others' flavors and all of that. Do pay attention to other people your age. You won't always find agreement, but if you do—and you have to be honest about it; don't just try to be one of the guys or one of the gals here—if you find someone whose flavors tend to coincide with yours, you can establish groups who might be able to predict trends. Think about what it is you'd like to know the future, and write these up as your goals. But also take note of other things and world events to a greater or lesser degree—at least local events—and see if you can begin to correlate flavors with events.

Learn to Use Your Body So You Can Change Things

And when Mother Earth breathes in and samples how many humans there are . . . ?

Or how many, in this case, might be coming.

In the future? So what are some of the things she does to prepare? She does volcanoes and floods, right? What are some of the things she does?

She might be doing volcanoes. She would tend to make long-range . . . not plans, but say she noted that the birthrate of human beings was increasing, that the length of life was stabilizing or even becoming longer for human beings. Then she would be more inclined to create a nurturing environment for plants and animals, which human beings would become dependent upon someday as their numbers increased from the hundreds to the thousands and then onward. In short, she would begin to do things that would allow someday . . . we're talking, in Mother Earth's time, thousands of years, even millions of years. She would do things that would make it available so that when groups of human beings someday go to a river, there will be many species of fish, enough to continue the population of fish in their own culture and society to be equal to those who need to be consumed by the human beings who then move on.

However, she has never produced fish in numbers that would fulfill using nets. It was always intended that fishing be done one fish at a time. Of course, in your time you need to serve the needs of many, many, many people, but that's what your fish farms are intended to do. Granted, this is not a benevolent way to allow creatures their freedom, but I understand the purpose. In my time the population was not as extreme.

Zoosh said in 1997 that in twenty-five years we would begin to go and explore other planets. That's only ten years from now!

Even if people go out to explore space, everybody's not going to go. A tiny little number will go. Do you think they will build ships and evacuate the Earth? What are we teaching in these pages? The whole point is to learn how to use your body so you know how to change things, how to make things work better for each other as human beings or for the animals or the plants.

What will you do when all the animals decide they are being mistreated so much that they are going to leave or become dormant (meaning they will leave the potential in the Earth for their populations to reemerge from what you might call extinction)? What will you do when they all go away? What will you do especially when those animals you have who are, as you say, domesticated and who are so entrenched as part of the food chain . . . what will you do when they feel burdened with their treatment and decide that that's enough, they are leaving, and they welcome a disease they have fought off in the past and simply return in soul form to their point of origin—which is always, for the animals, another planet—and say, "That's enough"?

Now, you will have to have people who by that time are well trained and who can do this. That's why your questions are so valuable. Suppose some species has gone away completely. Let's pick a species that's important to you in the West. Suppose cows, cattle, decide they've had enough of mistreatment. They've had enough of mistreatment, they haven't been appreciated, they haven't been treated kindly enough. I'm not trying to criticize ranches, but there are processes, things that happen to the cows and cattle after they leave your care, if your care has been kind.

Many ranches are considerate of the cows, providing them with what they need, even though they are being raised for food and other products that might be made from their bodies. Still the cows have complaints. So what if they leave? You will know that they will leave if there's a global disease for which you seem to have no cure. You have seen some samplings in the past, where cows feel that the numbers or the process of their death is too terrible to bear. That's an area that needs improvement, but we've discussed that in the past and may discuss it again if you feel the need.

What will you do if the population of cattle begins to decrease, especially in some precipitous manner? Some of you will have to be trained to not only welcome cows but to be influential in the circles that, for instance, have to do with what you call "processing," which is actually the manner and means of the cows' death. For example, feedlots that, granted, will fatten up a cow, will also—since they are often near slaughterhouses—terrorize the cows, and the cows will grieve and suffer and cry and be frightened by the horrible fate that awaits them.

Feelings Are Our Common Language

I'm not trying to turn you into monsters. Certainly in our time we were hunters. We hunted the animals. We didn't raise them domestically like you do, but we hunted them and sometimes very often they would suffer in their death to serve us. We made offerings, we honored them, but we could not avoid their suffering. In my time we had people who would familiarize themselves with the animals . . . not just hunters, but those who would welcome the animals. I'm not talking about trappers here. What would we do in our time? Think about it, in our time, if there weren't deer around. If the deer decided that their fate was too frightening to be near us, if they couldn't even send us some of their number from time to time so that we might survive, what could we do to welcome them without doing something that is devious because that will always be found out?

We would have certain numbers of our individuals who would go out and make friends of the deer. They would not represent any danger to them, not bring them any gifts, but just live near the deer, causing them no threat, no harm, and being as peaceful and calm as possible—not with any ulterior motive so much, but yes, with an agenda. The agenda was to learn how deer feel physically, their feelings around each other, so that the human beings, we all . . . that's our common language between human beings, between animals and human beings, between plants and human beings: feelings. Regardless of what language we have, feelings are our common language. What feelings do the deer exude to each other?

When the human being or two would be accepted, then the deer would go on about their lives and the human beings would follow nearby—not so close as to be invasive, but nearby. They would experience, be open to, be receptive to the feelings the deer were having for each other, so that when the human beings could be receptive when they were awake, they would know that the deer was loving its young and feel the love, or that the deer was startled by a noise and feel that. In short, they would become familiar with the full range of feelings the deer would have.

Once they had that . . . and you cannot get that in teaching from one human being to another; you can only get that if you go live around the deer and the deer come to trust you. This cannot be done by talking to them. They come to trust you or not. If they never trust you, then you are not going to be able to work with that species; perhaps you will be able to work with the plants. But someone goes out there, in our case usually two someones. They would be born to it, and we would know that, the elders would know it, and they would go out. These people would then be responsible if the deer . . . perhaps their number would be thinned, but we might have needed to have a deer now and then. Especially when the winter was coming, we needed to have not only the hide and the horn, but also to have the meat and to cook it and dry it and have it available in the winter time when it wasn't always possible to have regular food.

Then these people would be sent out. They would go to the areas, to the trails that the deer would walk, and these trails would be far enough away from our camp or our regular place of living. We would have, of course, a place where we lived in the winter and a place where we lived in the summer, but these were practical necessities because of the weather. So they would go out near the trails, usually several miles from where our camp was, and they would simply sit—not on top of the trail, but in terms of your measurements, one-tenth or one-twelfth of a mile from the trail, that close.

They would start generating in their body the full range of feelings that the deer felt. While they were doing that, they would think of the deer, they would remember the deer. They wouldn't try to become a deer—that would mean they would feel themselves as a deer. They wouldn't do that because that would be like tricking the deer, as if to suggest there were other deer there. That would be like trapping the deer. The whole point was to welcome the deer, to exude the feeling that the human being had come to feel as the deer, all the feelings—yet exuding it as a human being, feeling it, and it naturally radiating (that's what I mean by exuding). With this radiation the deer would know that the human beings needed one or more of their number for food and our purposes, and were welcoming them to come—not their whole family, but welcoming those to come who could offer themselves for this great sacrifice.

These people would be there for a day or two doing that. Then the hunters would come, but they would stay at a distance and would wait for the signals of these people who were feeling. When the deer would make themselves known—usually a male of the species or two perhaps, not the females—then the ones who would feel deer feelings would begin to move away slightly, and the hunters would get closer and eventually they would exchange places. If the deer remained, one or two, then the hunters would slowly, gently approach the deer and take them as our needed food.

There is something else in this case, the way I described it. After the hunters would leave and take the bodies of the deer with them, those humans who were welcoming the deer would remain behind for about a half day. They would exude nothing but love. This was their way of thanking the deer for their great sacrifice that we might survive, even though their numbers, their families, their loved ones, would have died for us. This is the kind of gift they could appreciate so that they would know that we appreciated their great sacrifice.

The Physical Feeling of the Air Alters When Any Type of Life Is Around

Remember, in order to sample the feelings of the deer, the radiated feelings . . . I'm going to go back now and retrace my steps a little bit; I wanted to give you the whole story there. But when those individuals would go out to live near the deer, they would do something besides feeling the feelings of the deer. They would taste the air. They would have sampled the smells. If the deer would let them nearby, they would put their hands up, palms out [both hands palm upward, elbows bent about center, face level, out in front of the body]. They would put their palms out toward the deer and feel the air. Do you know that the physical feeling of the air alters when any type of life is around?

The way you can test this is to go someplace where there aren't many types of life around. This wouldn't be the ocean, but it might be, say, a vast rocky shelf, a rocky mesa. But the better way to test it is to go out to a desert where there is just sand. There will be some creatures about but not many. Sample the air there. How does it feel physically? Just move your hands around in it—for a researcher, yes? This is not going to be something you'll be able to extrapolate mentally, but move your hands around in it so you get a foundation feeling.

Then, for example, so you are able to understand the difference in physical feeling, you would then go to a place teeming with life—not human life. Keep it natural at first so your body feels safe. Sample the different physical feelings of the air. Say you might go to a forest where there is a great deal of plant and animal life. Then put your hands up in the same way and feel; move your hands around in the air and see if you can note a different feeling in the air.

Use All Your Senses to Welcome the Deer and the Cows

Now, the people out near the deer would do all these things. They'd have the feelings—the feelings of the deer, the feelings of themselves. They would have the taste, touch, sight, sound, smell, all of that—the whole thing, the whole gamut of feelings—and they would utilize all of those different feelings so that when they went to welcome the deer, they could do something besides exude the feelings. They could put their hands up and recall how the air felt around the deer. You can use your mind to do this, and also your body has the means to recall that, but your mind is not excluded and your body will recall how the air felt. They would put their hands up to do that.

Their body would recall . . . they might have remembered how the air tasted. How do you do that? Once you remember, you will remember what the flavor was. Then instead of doing this [takes a deep breath], where you breathe in the air across your tongue, you do just the opposite. You blow out with the recollection of that. Granted, it will exude you, but we were not trying to fool the deer. We wanted the deer to know that this was a human need. So they would do that, plus they would remember what it was like to see the deer. In short, they would use all their senses to welcome the deer.

Do we extrapolate from that that this could be done with cows, then?

Yes, exactly, because if cows decide . . . and they've given you several warnings. Ranchers have noted in the past strange phenomena where cows would be found, sometimes even in a group, where they were dead for no apparent cause. If you happened to be able to find this before predators moved in, you would simply wonder what caused it. Very often there were attempts to find out with a veterinarian and so on, and sometimes it could be traced to a cause, but other times it was simply a mystery. This is something not widely known by people other than those who raise and truly live with cattle, but it was known in ranching circles. Also, there have been scares such as what came to be known as mad cow disease, something that is still to this day largely unknown in terms of its ability to be treated.

There are other diseases that cows have been resisting for years. You do not know that these diseases exist because cows have been resisting them, but should the cows feel that they no longer wish to be here, they will exhibit these diseases and you will have no cures and the cows will go away. So you don't want to do that before you can sample being around cows. If you learn to send out people to be around cows, they must not be threatening. You can follow some example like I gave you.

You will have to be around the cows . . . it would be better if the cows were ranging about. You will have to give them their distance. Most likely these will have to be people who are used to being around cows and have talent to be sensitive. It might be ranchers or cowboys, as you say, or cow-girls, who are still a factor in your time. Although they do not often call themselves this, they are referred to this way and sometimes they call themselves this. Perhaps they will be from other walks of life.

Homework: Feel a Tree's Feelings

I am inviting you to try this, especially when it comes to plants and animals who are part of your main food chain. You might also try this with corn. The corn can be planted in a certain way, a sacred way—meaning you might study the way it has been planted in the past by traditional peoples who have been given spiritual lessons on how to do this. I think you can research that. You can interact with that corn. Again, approach it the same way. You will know what the corn feels more easily as it exudes its feelings from one member to the other—say, at night.

But there are other ways to study what plants feel. You might wish to learn in ways that are easier, such as to go to a forest where the trees have grown by themselves, were not planted by humans, and use the same methods I described generally with the trees and use the homework that was given about the trees [see Overview].

Use that as a foundation, and then you can go and begin to feel the tree's feelings. At night trees will exude feelings for one another. Don't go up in any great number—one or two people, that's fine. That is a good thing. Don't be shy. You can drive up in a truck or a camper and sleep in that and so on, but do go out at night if you feel safe and walk some distance from the camper. It is all right to bring a weapon in case there are dangerous animals around, but relax. The trees will not feel threatened by a rifle, so put the rifle within your reach but not on your person and see if you can open up to the feelings the trees are exuding to each other. You can see that I have no objections to weapons. Certainly we carried them in our time. If we had had rifles, we would have carried those. But this is what I'm going to suggest. It is homework. It allows you to consider the actual abilities and opportunities you have here.

Consider Your Senses

Now I will close on this chapter and say, consider your senses. They are things that you do not take for granted. You appreciate them, you value them, but you do not always realize that you might be able to tell the future with them, that you might be able to welcome species of plants and animals whom you feel might be moving away. Perhaps they are not happy with things, their environment does not nurture their life. You might be able to welcome them to stay—not only by improving their environment, but by simply exuding the feelings, by exuding the smell, the sight, the touch (not by touching them, but by touching the air around or near them), to know what it feels like and then reproducing that.

You have learned many things with the talk today, but the most important thing is to know that the senses that you have can be used in ways you are not using them, most of you. I want to encourage you to practice, to try, to research it and to see what great good can be done.

Don't use it to try to bring back a relative who has passed over by studying this with a relative. The birth and death cycle is natural for human beings. Don't worry. If it is a loved one, when your time comes and you pass over, you will surely see him or her again. You will not be denied this love. So know that you have many skills and abilities, some of which have been sleeping. Today I have made some effort to awaken them. Good life.

Sacreɒ Hunting

Speaks of Many Truths
May 28, 2002

Yesterday I spoke of the people who would go out and camp near the deer, who would make every effort to become energetically acceptable to the deer so that the deer could feel at home with them. This was so that if they went out and welcomed the deer for the purpose of our hunting parties . . . not for the purpose of betraying the deer, but for the purpose of clearly letting the deer know what was needed by us, by my people, from them. Then, if the deer could—it was a request, not a demand—send one or possibly two of their number whom they might choose to sacrifice . . . and it is a sacrifice. Think about sending a family member whom you would never see again. But if the deer could, they would, because they are such wonderful beings.

Now, one of the ways I spoke of briefly in the previous chapter that they would do this—I didn't say everything—was how they would touch the energy of the deer. It would not be like long touch, which I may or may not have discussed in previous books. If I haven't, I'll talk about it at some point [see chapter 21 in this volume]. If you get close to something, you can feel its actual physical energy but in the outer boundaries. Now, for those of you who are farther along on your path of spiritual discovery and exploration, you may know this already. If you don't, then here's some homework.

Homework: Learning to Feel Energy Fields

What I'd like you to do . . . you can do this around your home or yard or neighborhood, but I'd prefer that you begin doing it around some place you're familiar with and where you feel safe. First, you have to feel your own body. It seems like an obvious thing one would feel, one's own body, but I want you to heighten the physical feelings in your own body. The way to do this is to move around a little bit. Try to put your attention, your physical attention, inside your body, so as you're moving around you can actually feel the parts of you moving. Then move your shoulders around and put your physical attention in there so you can feel that. Then move your arms around so you can feel that. Then move your wrists back and forth and you'll feel that. Some you will be able to feel actual motion of the bones in there and the tendons and so on. Move your fingers around.

That's sort of preparatory. After you do that, then either with your left hand or your right hand—regardless of whether you're left- or right-handed, you can do it with either hand, though I recommend you use your right hand—reach toward a physical object that has some substance. Reach toward a chair or a wall if you're indoors, or if you're outdoors, a big rock if you're in the countryside—somewhere you feel safe and comfortable, without too many people around. If you have a friend with you, have him or her stand off at least forty feet away. If you are near a path people are hiking on, walk off the path a little bit to somewhere you feel comfortable. Stay at least thirty to forty feet away from people so you're comfortably in your own space.

Reach toward this thing . . . as I say, if you're in your house, it might be a wall, it could be a chair or something else, but not something you're sitting in. Now don't touch it; just reach slowly toward it. And as you're moving your hand, the palm of your hand with your fingers spread out a little bit—or the fingers can be closed but keep your hand open—as you're moving toward the object, I want you to put as much of your physical attention inside your hand as possible.

As you're moving toward it, I want you to notice if there's ever the slightest resistance. By resistance I do not mean like one hand pushing against the other. I mean, I want you to see if you can notice a difference in the consistency of the air that you are moving through toward this object. If you are really sensitized in that hand, you will notice before you touch the wall . . . it will be slight, but you will notice a slight difference in the air. It's not pressure, but you are actually feeling the energy body of that object. Don't do this with an animal or a person at this stage; I want you to do it with something that isn't moving. It can be a tree, a wall, a rock or something like that.

That's the thing I want you to do, because working at these close ranges, large objects will have more of an energy field and might be inclined to extend that energy field more so if there aren't too many people around. So see if you can feel it. That's your homework.

Deer Will Try to Feel You with Their Auric Field

Now, understand that those people who would go out to be near the deer, they would know how to do this very well. So they would be feeling, they would put their hands up—both hands—from a distance, you understand, because you're not going to be able to walk right up to the deer. The deer wouldn't allow that, they wouldn't be comfortable with that, and you don't want to offend them. But these people would be so good at feeling energies at a distance, having trained to do that, that they could feel from a significant distance the energy of that deer.

This is not unusual, especially if a deer, in this case, or another creature is looking at you. The first thing it's going to do, aside from looking at you and trying to smell you at a distance and so on, is it's going to arrange its energy body out of its auric field out to feel you in that way as well. If you are sensitive to such things, having trained with this homework and further steps—some of which I'll give you in this chapter—you might be able to feel that energy. Like I say, it's a subtle physical feeling, but you can train to feel it. And if you know your own feelings and you are attempting to focus on the warmth, the love-heat/heart-warmth/physical-warmth, within you so that you feel safe and calm and the deer feels safe and calm with you around, then the sensitivity will be even stronger [for more on the love-heat, see Overview].

More Homework: Feeling from a Distance

Now, what might be the second level of homework after you do that first homework assignment? I'll give you the second level: For those of you who live out in the country or near mountains or some really big object . . . ideally you want to use something in nature, maybe a big tree or something. Let's talk about big trees, since they're more available for you. Some of you live near big rocks or mountains or mesas or something, but if you live around big trees or can find one . . . maybe go to the park or something. If you do, try to go either at a time of day when there aren't that many people running around or perhaps very early in the morning so maybe you can get a tree to yourself.

Try that homework where you get close to touching that tree but not quite. Don't ever actually touch the tree trunk if you can help it. The trees don't actually like that. They'll accept it from animals, because animals are in more of a natural state than human beings, but they don't really like to be touched by human beings—nothing personal. Now, say you felt in the first homework assignment I gave you that sense—it will be very subtle—of something not physical, but something. Then the thing to do for the second level of that homework is to step back. You know where you felt that something. Some of you will feel it farther away from the tree or the rock or the wall (if you're in your apartment). Some of you will feel it farther away than others.

The second level of the homework is, if you can, to step back three to four paces and see if you can feel it there. If you want to, you can step back one pace at a time. In other words, you want to see how far away you can go and still feel it. Obviously you don't have to go city blocks away from something, if you're in the city, or acres away if you're in the country—but for some of you who might be around mountains, you might try that. It's always best to approach it, get up close, feel it and then back away. Once you get good at this, you'll be able to be many acres, even miles away from a mountain and still feel it and know that you're feeling the mountain, so practice with that. I've given you a general idea of what you are to do.

If you're working in nature, try to make sure there are no electrical wires or man-made objects between you and what you are feeling. I'll tell you why, and that's because human beings have an energy, and we do not want you to disturb the human beings, nor do we want you to be disturbed by them. We [the beings who speak through Robert Shapiro] want you to always be focusing on one thing while you are training without any energy to interrupt that. Of course, electrical wires would interrupt that quite a lot. So that's your homework in general.

Asking the Deer for a Sacrifice

Now, the people who are feeling the deer—in my example, in my time—are also responsible for going out to ask the deer to send one of their number, or two if they can. Usually such a request would come as the winter months came and we needed to cook the meat and dry it for the long winter periods, some of which there would be food available. But there were always times, in my life cycle when I was alive physically, when you would go for a few days or maybe even a week or two without any food readily available. That's when you would use your stores, as you know, just as you would do in your time if you were cut off and you were using your groceries. So in our time we would use dried meat or dried fish and so on.

What the people would do was, instead of feeling . . . first they would go out to where the deer were and they would have been very familiar with the deer. (This doesn't have to be deer; I'm just picking deer as a very good example.) They would go out there, and somewhere along the trail they would find the deer—they might be out for days, you understand—and have their initial greetings. But if they wanted the deer to send one or two of their number toward our camp, in which case we would know they were offering themselves in this wonderful way for us—this was sad for them; I admit that—then this is what the people from our tribe would do: After the initial greetings and so on, which might go on for four or five hours, then the people would put their hands down and sit down, probably on the ground. When human beings sit down, they look less threatening. If you are an animal who knows that human beings hunt you, if a human being sits down, he or she is automatically going to be perceived of as less of a threat. Of course, this was in the time before guns and so on—at least where we lived, there were no guns.

So they would sit down so as to look as nonthreatening as possible. Then they would put their hands down, usually on this part of the leg, the upper thigh, even if they were sitting cross-legged—it would be up to them. They might more likely fold their legs up underneath them so the knees were forward. This way they could put their hands down, their palms down, on top of their thighs, because usually your legs are what touch the ground before any other part of your body. The legs in that sense also then tend to store the residual of your needs. It's the first part of your body that touches the ground generally once you're up and around as a human being and especially once you are able to look after yourself and ultimately others. That's what we believe.

So they would put their hands down on their legs, and generally the deer would know us well enough to know that a request was coming, but the people wouldn't make the request then. They would picture . . . not what they wanted, all right? Not that they wanted a deer or two to come toward our encampment, which is by way of coming toward our hunters. But these people, our people, would begin to picture the winter and the empty baskets that hold food. Then they would picture the baskets full of dried meat.

They wouldn't picture them full of dried fish, because that's not something the deer would have anything to do with. But they would picture that as a need. Now, the deer would not feel particularly comfortable with the picture of their own bodies dried as meat, so it would be a quick picture, very quick, so as not to offend the deer. Then the people would picture perhaps one or two deer approaching our hunters without flight, walking toward the hunters, stopping and waiting. That's all. We wouldn't picture them being killed or anything. That would be an offense to their tender hearts. But the elders of their kind would know what this was about.

Once the people had those pictures engaged in their own minds, then they would put their hands up, palms forward toward the deer, and they would do the pictures again, like that. Then after doing that for a few minutes, they would put their hands back down again on top of their legs, their thighs, and they would picture all of that again. Then they would stop, take their hands off their thighs and probably gently touch their fingers to the ground to ground those images and let them dissipate. Then they would remain seated for a few minutes.

All this time, the deer would be looking at them—perhaps not, but they would get the idea. Then the people would feel the warmth of the love energy in them. They would do that for quite a while, and because they had come to ask for this sacrifice, they would know the deer very well and they would know whether a gift for the deer or the forest was a good idea. Sometimes deer like that; other times they don't. So the people perhaps would leave a gift; they might not have. The gift might have been something that would appear to others to be symbolic, but it would depend. I will not discuss the gift right now, but perhaps someday.

So after that, after another half-hour or twenty minutes of feeling the warmth, the people would then get up and take a few steps back away from the deer, slowly back. When you walk backward, you can turn around and look to see where you're going, but when you walk backward like that, when you turn your head around to see where you're going, you still keep the front of you toward the deer. This is not because you don't trust the deer; it's because you want to show that you are leaving, but you also want to be honoring and respectful. So then after they had taken eight or ten steps back or more, based upon what the people would feel—always with the feelings—then there could be a turn. If the people would turn, they would turn either to the right or to the left based upon what felt right to them, not according to something that was rigidly intact.

Waiting at Camp for the Deer to Come

I understand that these individuals would always trust their physical feelings in their physical bodies, because the physical feelings in your bodies, as human beings, are exactly the same kind of physical feelings that all beings have on Earth. And in my experience of exploring the universe, they appear to be the same kind of physical feelings that all beings have everywhere. However, other beings elsewhere may not have the range of feelings we have here—not because they do not have them available, but because of their style of life, where they live, what they do and so on.

But the way I know that the feelings are the same is that when I use my long touch to look at other planets or when I interact with other forms of life on Earth—plant, animal, human and so on—my feelings respond in the same way within me. So I know what they are feeling, no matter whether I am responding to a human being's feelings or those of a rock, a plant, a tree, a fish, a bird, a snake, a butterfly or an ant—it doesn't make any difference. I believe, on the basis of my experience, that we—meaning all beings—have the same mechanism for feelings, and I believe from the way they react to me that they can feel my feelings the same way.

So the people of those times who would go out to interact with the deer like that would trust their feelings, because their feelings were not only their own but were in response to the other beings they were interacting with. Thus, they would leave having requested that the deer send one or two of their number. Now, the people would leave and they would walk back toward our encampment, and as they were walking back, they would gradually become more and more aware of the feelings under their own feet. It would take them awhile because of their total engagement with the deer. But after about, in terms of your distance, a quarter of a mile, they were completely in their own bodies, fully aware of their own surroundings. Interestingly enough, for the first, by your measurement, hundred feet or so, the energy of their own footprints . . . if, say, an animal were to come up and not sniff the footprints but just feel them at a distance, there would be some confusion about whether these were deer footprints or human footprints—not by what they saw, not by what they smelled, but just by feeling the energy at a distance. This faded as the people moved along and became more in their own physical bodies in their own world.

So they would walk back toward the encampment and locate the hunting party. These people would not sit or stand or be with the hunting party, though they might sit off at a distance, perhaps 100 or 150 feet, not because the hunting party offended them or they offended the hunting party, but in case the deer came. They would wait for two to three days to give the deer time to either say goodbye to its family, or in two to three days we would know whether it was coming or not. It was, after all, a request; it was not a demand. If the deer could spare one or two of their number, they would come, usually within twelve hours, but we gave them two to three days in case.

So these people who interacted with the deer would sit off a ways from the hunting party so they did not absorb the hunting party's energy. They would wait in case the deer needed to communicate something with the hunting party before it waited to be killed. If the deer needed to do that . . . this has only happened once in my lifetime that I know of, but I have heard of it from other peoples whom I visited as well who hunted in this sacred manner and so on. The time it happened it was when one deer came to let us know that it cared for us as people, but it wanted us to wait. You see, this communication happened through the people who went out and interacted with the deer. The deer walked toward them rather than toward the hunting party—that's how that happened. The deer said, "Wait," to the hunting party. The communication was through pictures, but it wanted them to wait about four to five days instead of the two to three days they would normally wait. Then the deer left, and another deer came back in four to five days.

Now, you might reasonably ask, "Why?" But we never asked why. After all, this was a great sacrifice; it was a request. The hunting party didn't actually wait. They went out and did some hunting in the interim, at least some of their number, but then they returned and were there at the requested time to take the deer.

Hunting in Your Time

I mention these things because there are sacred ways to hunt, and in your time hunting still happens. Perhaps you don't think of it as much for those of you who are living in cities or even in small towns. But some of you in cities or small towns do hunt as well. As you know, I completely approve of hunting as long as it is done in some way to honor the animal and to recognize that it is a great sacrifice. I also recommend, if you can possibly avoid it, not to at any time, especially at certain times of the year—the hunters will know—to avoid if you can possibly do so taking a doe. You can't get too close to them, and they may be ready to birth or they may have birthed recently or they may still be nurturing their young. So always take a buck, if you can. I realize the meat may be more tender with a doe, but there's not much difference.

Now, in your time you actually hunt more than we did in our time, much more, but you, living in cities, do not always think about the level of hunting that's going on because you are aware that many animals are raised. I don't consider ranching and things like that hunting—don't get me wrong. I'm not confused about that. But the level of fishing you have in your time far exceeds anything that we did. That's probably why some of your species are dying out—fish, you understand—partly because they don't feel welcome, and partly because it is in the nature of the way you fish. This is not the average person who throws out a line or goes fishing from a rowboat or even a powerboat—though I think it would be good to do something with the propeller on a powerboat so it doesn't harm fish. I think that you can do this; that technology is available. But to throw out a line with bait on it is fine.

But to use nets, those commercial nets . . . I think that this is really a terrible thing. As those who do that know, you catch vast amounts of fish that human beings do not eat—although you could, perhaps, or animals could, but these fish are caught and killed. Sometimes there is some attempt to let some escape, but it is difficult for the fishermen to do that, and so many, many fished are killed. Perhaps more than half of the catch isn't even for human beings, but the fish die nevertheless. If you want to see an end to fish in the sea, then mark my words, that will come much faster than you would like.

For those of you who are beginning to experiment with fish farming in the sea, I think this is a good thing. Some fish farming can be done on land, but I think you will perfect fish farming in the sea and in lakes before long, and when you do, that will be very good. I think this is particularly important for some peoples who live off of fish more than meat, so I want to put my mark of approval on that.

I realize I have wandered around a bit in this. I'm not going to talk about hunting excessively, but it's important to talk about because it's a real thing, it's an important thing and it is, after all, how people survive. But we must allow other species to be here and encourage them to be here because they have as much right to be here. And I assure you that later on, when you're looking for these species for reasons you do not know yet, if they have not felt comfortable, if they are not here because they have felt unwelcome because of attacks on their species, then you will miss them.

Creating Love-Heat for the Cows

Is there anything in the rituals that some tribal people did when they put animal skins on and danced? Did it have anything to do with hunting, or was it for some other purpose?

Yes, of course, but this is widely known. I will talk in these books about things that are not so widely known in your time. This is widely known and has been thoroughly researched and published in various anthropological texts and other things. So if you don't mind, I won't comment on that—not at this time in any event.

Then how would we translate that to dealing with cows who aren't asked for just the volunteers but for all of them to be used by humans for food?

For starters, as I mentioned the other day, it's really important to change the way you do feedlots. A feedlot itself is not awful in its own right. But you have to remember that feedlots are usually located very near or right next to slaughterhouses. Even if the odor is not blowing in that direction or even in the direction of the cows, they can smell it. Many of them have a better sense of smell than human beings do. That's why they weep, because of their own kind being killed in such a ruthless and cold-blooded way, all right? That's what it is.

So I would say that you need to kill them—I recognize that you need to kill them—in a more benevolent way. It can be done, but it requires honor and respect. Now, I know that this might seem impractical or not as profitable to companies. But I can assure you that you will get much more value out of the food, and beef will become so much more popular if it not only tastes better—and it will when the cows are not frightened as much—but it will also nourish you better.

I'm not just going to point fingers, but I'm going to make suggestions. In my time we have human beings trained, as in the example I gave you, for how the deer are interacted with. Even in such places as feedlots and slaughterhouses . . . these are places right now of terror for cows. There's no other word for it. If human beings can do with cows pretty much what our people did with deer . . . with the exception, in this commercial operation, of asking for one or more members to come to the hunters. If you can be around cows when the cows are calm or nurturing one another—and I don't mean having sex; I mean leaning up against each other or lowing and so on as cows do—if you can be around them and, using similar techniques as I've described in these books, as a human being experience those feelings at a distance . . . if they are compatible with you when the cows are benevolent or, not sleeping, but nurturing each other in some way, you will know by the way you feel in your body how that feels. It will probably stimulate or create a greater warmth than you normally feel doing your love body experience, the love-heat, as I've discussed at length.

So what to do is, train a group of people. You'd be surprised, commercial vendors. You might even be able to get people to volunteer to do this at no cost whatsoever, or perhaps for some nominal fee. Try it as an experiment first. You can't use your own people; you'll probably have to bring in spiritual people from the outside. It's not that your people aren't spiritual, but this kind of training requires time. So you bring people in and you have people stationed around various places—outside of the corral, of course—who are just experiencing this energy, this love warmth, and sometimes it will just be calm.

Have these people situated, say, every hundred feet or so until you get enough volunteers so you can have them every fifty feet or so—not only outside the slaughterhouse, but as you come inside the slaughterhouse, you will need to have people who work for you. Then they can maintain this warmth, which will require a lot of discipline and a lot of practice, but it can be done—just that, nothing else. Even without changing your procedures very much . . . though I think your procedures need to be changed enough so that the cows do not see what's coming. Many of you have your slaughterhouses set up so the cows don't see what's coming, and that's good, but there's more you could do. I think you know what that is. I'm not going to tell you your business. There's more that you can do. So don't just resign yourself to the fact that the cows are going to be terrorized and that's it.

Experiment with how many people you have in there. Of course, the people will take a lot of training to be able to maintain that good feeling while this is going on. One of the things it will take for the people to do this is, they'll probably have to sit down and do it and they'll probably need to wear earplugs and possibly blindfolds so that they can have as much separation from what's going on as possible to maintain those feelings in their bodies, which will automatically be broadcast. They may even have to hold their hands up in front of their bodies with their palms toward their bodies to maintain those feelings.

Happier Cows Make a Difference

What this will do, if enough human beings are doing that . . . you'll have to experiment. I want to give you a benchmark to know the difference. You'll need to tag some of these cows so that you'll know the difference between the cows who were exposed to this and those who were not. This can more easily be done in a smaller operation to find out. I want you to experiment with it, and you have places to do this.

I want you to have people eat . . . not just your own people, not just your own methods of testing a flavor, which I know you do, but try it out on people, both young and old, male and female. Ask them, compare it— some kind of scientifically run process. You want them to eat the meat within, say, twelve to fifteen hours after the cow is slaughtered. I know this is hard for some of you to read this, so for those of you having trouble reading this, just skip right over all of this. I'm talking to the cattle-industry people here: twelve to fifteen hours after the cow is slaughtered, try this. Try one steak, for instance, and you have to eat at least four ounces. Have four ounces in separate groups; one group: eats the four ounces of steak from a cow who was slaughtered in this way who was exposed to this good energy of people radiating, and the other group eats the steak from the cow who was slaughtered in the usual way.

Then quiz the people: "How did it taste?" By the way, you want to put the people, both of them, in some place that is peaceful—not a restaurant, but some place that's quiet—so that they're eating in something akin to a living room. No TV, no radio, just quiet—but not so quiet as to make them nervous, and not too many people sitting at each table or place of eating. What you want, obviously, is to know how they are reacting to the meat. That's why you don't want them in noisy groups—you know what I'm talking about. Afterward, ask them or have your questionnaire: "How did it taste," and all of that. But also ask them, "How do you feel? How do you feel after eating this?"

Obviously, the people who eat the commercial-quality steak are probably not going to know the difference. But the people, especially your tasters or even people from the public, ask them how they feel . . . and you might have to ask that question in different ways, because what we're looking for . . . I'll give you some benchmarks. In some people it will be greater and some people lesser, but you're looking for the people who say that they have a better sense of well-being or they feel more relaxed or they feel more calm or they feel more friendly or they feel more cheerful—in short, things that you wouldn't expect to hear.

You might expect to hear, "I feel invigorated. I feel stronger. I feel nourished. I feel full," whatever. But you wouldn't normally expect to hear, "I feel more cheerful. I feel friendlier. I feel calmer. I feel more relaxed." Do you understand? That's the kind of difference I want you to look for, for those of you who experiment with such things—and I know that you're out there. I know I'm speaking to you in the wallet because I recognize that you have to pay close attention to that. I think you can greatly improve the way people receive this meat and greatly improve its popularity—and I might add, to be practical, probably charge more for it.

You don't necessarily have to feed your cows beer and hug them, but what these Japanese manufacturers who've raised cattle in this way have found out is that it's not just that the beef is better marbled or the cows are happier, but the happier does make a difference. But what I'm suggesting to you is, you don't have to go through all of that. That's fine. They are doing that in Japan; you don't have to do that. What I'm recommending is that the cows will feel honored, they will feel respected, when you improve your style so that they are not grabbed by the back legs and hoisted up and killed like this and have gone through that terror. It's frightening; it's terrible.

The cows walk up the chute and maybe the knife drops or what-have-you. That's bad enough. But if people are sitting around and radiating these good feelings, the cows will know they are being honored and respected and appreciated for their sacrifice, and they will have a corresponding feeling in their body. That's what you want. Experiment with this and see. You'll see.

Those of you who experiment with this thoroughly will notice. You can create an experimental brand for a while that you charge more for. You'll see. It'll make a big difference in your profit. You see, the thing is that when customers eat the meat, they'll know the difference because it has an effect. It's not a drug, so it's not like a drug has an effect, but they will actually notice. Of course, it will work better for them if the cook is calm and not angry when he or she is cooking the steak, but people will actually notice the difference and it will certainly be something you can market.

That's all. I don't want to tell you how to run your business, but I think you will find it is better, it is kinder and it is more honoring.

And the cows will probably stay here longer.

The cows will be more likely to stay here and not go away, which they can do no matter what you try to do to keep them here. If they don't want to be here, they will find a way to go away. But with this they will feel honored, and that's what they want. They are prepared to make this sacrifice, to die that you might live, but they need to feel more respected and honored, and they have said so all along.

Spiritual Humor and Interspecies Communication

Speaks of Many Truths
December 23, 2002

ould you talk about how humor contributes to spiritual mastery?

The Function of Humor in Mystical Training

That's an interesting question, because in my time, of course, we had humor as well. And very often when learning these things that are not always the same methods of living as the rest of the culture one finds one-self in, as it was for me, it could be complicated. In the culture in which I was raised, like your times, we were taught to live in certain ways to get along as best we could, and the techniques we had to learn—or that I had to learn in order to be the best mystical man I could be—were not always simple. As Robert [the channel] likes to say, the methods of practice may not ultimately be what you do, but the steps along the path are often complicated or unexpected, as any teaching method might be.

Very often it was typical to get frustrated or upset, or to just feel like you could go no further—meaning that you'd done all you could and you couldn't get any further no matter what you tried. As anyone who's ever accomplished anything knows, this simply meant that you needed to do it a different way. But in the early days, you very often didn't realize that. You just kept trying to do it over and over again the way you were shown without realizing that one of the methods the teacher was using was to see whether you could adapt your own skills, ability and inspiration to the general lesson that you were trying to learn and go beyond the technique that was shown to you as the teaching tool to accomplish it. But that was not obvious to the student. Usually the student was just trying to emulate the teacher.

Sometimes I would just get frustrated and not be able to accomplish things, and so my teacher would then sit me down and he'd invariably tell me a funny story. Usually it would have nothing whatsoever to do with what we were doing, or we'd talk about what I was trying to do for a while and he'd say, as an aside, that this funny thing happened or he saw this funny thing, and we would laugh for a while. As you know, this breaks the tension, and more to the point, rather than just breaking the tension, it greatly reduces the expectation that you have of yourself of either failure or accomplishment. It simply moves you to a different space, just as if you're standing in a different space to accomplish the same task. That's the function, I feel, of humor.

There's Not Enough Humor in Your Schools

I think one of the biggest problems in your time in any educational system is that there's usually not enough humor. If not enough people are available to do something that's desperately needed, you can be pretty sure that no matter how serious the job might be or how important it is to remain serious on the job, people have allowed that ultimate application to interfere with the methods or manners used to teach the student.

This is not to say that all teachers must be funny, but all good teachers know that there are some situations that call for humor. Not all teachers are able to do this, but those who are can usually accomplish more or help the student to move on more quickly, more easily, or to simply adapt. Sometimes students might be given this humorous story or thought or picture to imagine, and it might help them to get past difficult things that might occur in the future with their lessons or their applications once they begin doing their job. I'm sure many of you reading this can identify with that.

Laughter Helps You to Let Go

There's another aspect, then. Robert was giving me an example of being in a state of mirth because something was really funny to him and then he spontaneously had an experience with Spirit. Is there a connection there?

It's the same thing, isn't it? Because no matter how serious you are, you can be thinking . . . in that case, he was driving down the highway thinking seriously about serious things, as people often do, but then he saw something suddenly, unexpectedly, that prompted him to laugh and to think of it in a humorous fashion. The moment he did that, he released all of the tension around everything he had been thinking before that point and was just driving along cheerfully without expectations, all right? That's the big thing, *without expectations*—meaning that in that moment, as laughter often does, it helps you to let go, at least for a moment.

When that energy is there, it is often easier for Spirit—or even as you might call it, inspiration—to take place in some benevolent way that is experienced completely benevolently and is possibly not seen by others. Someone could have been sitting right next to Robert in the vehicle, and if that person hadn't laughed or hadn't thought it was funny and she was thinking something serious, she might not have seen it at all. It is not untypical, it is not unusual, say, for instance, when people in your time see a UFO or an unusual mystical phenomenon, that someone can stand or sit there and see that phenomenon when someone right next to him or her doesn't see it. That doesn't mean that those who see it when others don't are having an illusion or an odd experience of the mind. It simply means that those who don't see it, that their mood or their thought structure does not make that experience available to them in that moment. That doesn't mean there's anything wrong with them; it's just that the timing isn't right for them.

It's important to remember that, because most of you who are reading this book are on the path or are considering being on the path. Don't be attached to competitiveness on the path. It's not a race. If somebody you know or even like is way ahead of you on the path and maybe you started off at what you felt was the same point, don't feel bad about it. It's your job to go as slowly—not as quickly—as you need to go in order to get it thoroughly, whatever it is that you're learning, so that you can proceed on to the next step, whatever that might be, building it on a solid foundation. If you rush on ahead and the foundation is weak . . . well, anyone who knows anything about weak foundations will tell you that that's a foundation or a platform that won't last. Someday things will fall apart and you'll have to go back and get that step that you weren't clear about.

There Is No Urgency

Native Americans, along with indigenous people in all countries on the planet, were sent here or volunteered to come here for the Earth itself, but it seems that as humans change now, they're going to become more shamanlike. Is that true, that humans are going to become more connected to the Earth, more natural, more concerned with the Earth and each other?

We'll see. It means that there's more interest in that by many humans, but it hasn't happened yet, so we'll see. It will take time to find out if the general population becomes more interested in that, not just as an intellectual possibility, but as an applied trade or talent or ability or practice. So it will take time to find out whether that will actually come about. It may come about.

So as humans become more open, more heart-centered and ready to go to the next dimension, it's not a given that they will become shamanic? It's still a method that has to be taught?

Let's just call it more spiritual. It's not a given—no. People have to want it. You're not going to be converted by the sword, to be political. It is offered; it is available if you want it. It is there, but it is not, again, a race to the next dimension. You are to learn as you need to, with as much time available to you to learn as thoroughly as possible. One of the tools that is helpful to you right now is your technology. Technology is not always helpful, but it is helpful in this case because people are able to find out about things, or information is more readily available. The teacher is not always readily available, but at least the information does help to prepare the individual. And there will be, of course, for many individuals, mystical experiences if the proper information is there and enough experience and maybe teachers. Then you move on. But it's not a race—there's no urgency.

That's the thing that I think is really confusing to people who are interested in these fields you are publishing books in—that there is a constant tendency and a real desire on the part of the reader to believe that there is some urgency for this reason or that reason to go to the next level, whatever that might be, given the book you're reading or the thesis. I think that in your culture—not just in Earth life, but in your culture—there's a tendency to believe that urgency will bring out the best in an individual.

Now, this is something that I feel has been distorted in your westernized world. In my experience in older cultures, or at least in cultures of the past, although there was a certain degree of urgency built into life—meaning, "I've got to have something to eat before I get so hungry," or "I've got to have water to drink before I get too thirsty"—that when other things needed to be learned such as spiritual techniques as you're talking about, there needed to be time and effort, and some people would get it faster and other people would get it slower. So it's not about urgency, it's about thoroughness, and that's why you've had so much time, in years, to come to various conclusions as to what actually works and what doesn't, because in your world, it's very easy to put value into what doesn't work.

The cultures in your world now—not all of them, but in your westernized-culture world—it is easy to believe that what others have said (your teachers, your elders) has value, because they either created the culture in which you are living or they perpetuated it. But as times change and as people change to either fit the time or adapt to the time, it will become clear that what the elders have to teach, while it is useful, isn't always enough. There needs to be more or something that will inspire you to find that "more" that you need so that you can apply it in your own time.

You will make mistakes, of course. Usually youth are known for making mistakes, but they are not the only ones to make them. Sometimes you can be older and make mistakes, as everyone knows. I think the main thing to remember now is that being thorough is more important. If you *know* something, then you know it; you don't have to keep learning it to make sure you know it. Once you know it, then move on. But don't be willing or rush on to the next thing when you think you know it.

Shamanism Will Be Universal

Is there a point at which, as we open to our original nature of what we were before the loop of time, combined with the incredible experience gained in the loop of time . . .

will we become as shamans are when we have that nurturance, that love, that ability to work with nature, or will it always be a specialty for some people?

That's an excellent question. It will be universal. It will start with individuals as it has been, traditionally speaking, for some time—there are individuals who can do these things and so on. But ultimately, it will be that everyone can do it, and this is intended so that what you find in the animal kingdom or the plant kingdom, where all plants or all animals have certain capabilities, it will be the same for humans.

Then all humans will have capabilities, such as how different species might know the experience of other species in the animal or plant world. You might not know the exact language, but you would know their experience by a more universal way of communication. Human beings do not normally do this, although spiritual human beings, mystical men and women, shamanic men and women and other spiritual human beings do know this because of their training. And yet at so-called higher dimensions, all human beings know this. As you begin to integrate your natural personalities—meaning the way you are when you incarnate on other dimensions, other planets, other existences; in short, the way you normally are—with this school that you're in now, the majority of you merges ("majority" meaning what is beyond this school of Earth) with this school.

Practical Earth-Living Mastery

What you're learning here on Earth, in your Earth lives and in your Earth experience, colors or impacts or influences that total *you*, so that what may be believed, what may be expected and honored, what may be lived, allegiances and so on that you have on other planets in other lives that cause you to perhaps be biased or even narrow-minded toward Earth experience, fall away because of the integration of your Earth experience and your Earth personality after you have had a life on Earth. All of you have lived through a time in your lives to discover what works, what is theoretical in that sense, as compared to what doesn't work—meaning the difference between theory and application. All of that true applied purpose, or all of those tests, if we would call it that (meaning the process you designed doesn't necessarily live up to your expectations), the test of all of your theories, as well as how things are supposed to be on other planets and in other cultures—all of that is tested here. And in the course of that, what develops through your Earth experience is a greater level of what I would call practical Earth-living mastery. That is blended with the rest of your existence and impacts or influences your total personality.

So it's not that you strive from Earth to move onward and upward; it's rather that you merge with your total being. So in that sense, don't think of it as a vertical movement; think of it as something that is more horizontal, all right? I can even say which direction it comes in from. It comes in from the left, that total you that has to do with lives lived in other totally benevolent places where Creator is a day-to-day, moment-to-moment experience.

Whereas here on Earth, while Creator is that, one does not always *feel* that way because of the struggles of this school. So as that total personality merges with your Earth experience, the total personality is influenced.

It's not so much that your Earth personality is influenced. Your Earth personality, the life you are living on Earth now, is the laboratory, the practical application; it's, "Here's my personality, living on Earth now, and some things work and some things don't." You have to set aside the ones that don't work. Although they might work on other planets, fit in other lives that you are leading or have lived or will live—depending on your time sequence, how you think about it—they don't fit on Earth. Since you are learning about Earth now because it's a school of practical application, then your Earth personality influences the rest of you. So the rest of you does what this kind of practical day-to-day work education always does— it influences the rest of you and *causes the rest of you to expand.* And it is this which brings about the universe expanding. This is very important, which is why I made such an issue of it.

I bring that up especially for the student of the *Explorer Race* books. Many of you have read many of these books, and the actual manner and means of how the universe expands has not necessarily been made clear on a personal level. I'm making it personal with this explanation so that you will see that each individual and what he or she does is important, and that no lives are wasted. Even though you might think that they are, it's not true. Even learning how to tie your shoelaces is about practical.

Feelings Are the Foundation of All Life Everywhere

At that point, then those of you who have volunteered many, many times as souls to hold this energy on the Earth will be free to do what you want to do, right?

We are free now. We are doing what we want to do.

But a lot of indigenous peoples are not necessarily part of the Explorer Race; they are here to facilitate the Explorer Race, right?

You mean the native peoples who are living on Earth now? Well, they are part of the Explorer Race, at least while they are here. They are not some other species.

In the beginning, when the indigenous people came to bring good energy to Mother Earth, they were here, as you said, because of those who would follow, who would come later, right?

I think you're confused. When they came initially, it was to prepare Earth to know what she would have to do in order to adapt herself to provide for human beings. They didn't bring something to her that she didn't have other than the fact that they brought themselves and their needs. They learned from Earth and they gave to Earth by being.

I thought that continuing to be here was part of that same contribution and that when the Explorer Race went on, all of those beings could go back to their homes. But they may choose to join the Explorer Race, then?

That is up to them, but I do not consider them as outside of the Explorer Race.

So everything that you teach and we put out in these books has a ripple-like effect to help people come to a realization of their real nature, right? Is that true?

You might say that generally, yes.

But still it's important now for people to use these techniques and to become more loving, conscious of all other living life that you teach, right?

I believe that it is important and always has been. It's no more important now than it ever was. It just is a way to solve problems in the simplest possible way. It tends to uncomplicated life rather than to make life more complicated. It allows you to use something, which when it is not used and is judged, makes life more difficult. If you do not use your feelings . . . and in your societies, many of your contemporary societies of your time, feelings are judged as being *less than* or something that is out of control or what-have-you. When you do not use your feelings and do not understand your body's method of communication (which is feelings), you will simply make your life much harder, much more complicated, and you will greatly reduce the quality of communication—not only between yourself and other species, but between yourself and other human beings, your own species.

So feelings are the basis of spiritual mastery?

Feelings are the basis of communication with yourself and all other beings. Feelings are, in that sense, the foundation of all life everywhere. Life began with a feeling. It didn't begin with some scientific theory called the big bang—that's ridiculous if you think about it. It's like saying the Creator likes to set off bombs. The Creator—and all creators everywhere—begins, lives with and continues with love. That is the foundation of all creators everywhere. I don't see any big bangs in there. I realize that's a temporary flirtation with the unknown, as science still has not yet found its God, but it will get there. For right now, I'd say that the most important thing to understand is that all life is laid on a foundation of feeling. Is love not a feeling?

Love Supports All Life

So one of the solutions to the incredible complexity of spiritual and religious contradictions on this planet is that each member of each faith should approach his or her feeling level, no matter what faith or religion he or she espouses?

No. Because if your faith or religion is not based in love, then you could take what you just said and . . . well, suppose your religion is preaching hate. Should you go into hate? No. It depends what your religion is preaching.

I'm trying to find some basis for all religions here.

I understand that you're trying to create a united link, which is why I gave you love. Love supports all life. There isn't a single molecule that approaches another molecule without that feeling. It's not that they're *in* love; it's that they have that in common.

If you were to give advice to all the peoples of the planet, no matter what religion or faith, to those who don't understand the Native American way, how would you ask them to start changing?

Don't! Just feel your own feelings and don't decide that feelings are the enemy. Feelings are the foundation of all truth. Even if your feelings are upsetting, then that's a truth for you in that moment. It doesn't mean that someone is to blame. If you look to others as a cause for your feelings, you will not find an easy path. If, on the other hand, you look toward your own feelings and pursue engagement—engaging your own feelings with yourself—you might just find a simple, uncomplicated enlightenment. You understand, I'm not going into great detail here because you're trying to find a universal thing. I can't go into great detail in answer to that question. You want something that links up all religions? If that's what you want, then simple is better.

My concern is that the title "Spiritual Mastery" . . . as you've said, there's been so much written about it and so much of it is so old and has been misinterpreted and changed.

That's why I feel—if you don't mind me interjecting—that it's more important to talk about how I learned from my teacher. And that's why my teacher has given stories, because *Shamanic Secrets for Spiritual Mastery* through myself and others who have contributed to this book is necessarily going to be shamanic. It's not necessarily going to be techniques; it's going to be how to do it, how to communicate from one species to another, meaning Robert's favorite story if I might use it as an illustration, okay?

Spiritual Interspecies Communication

When he was living in Sedona, Robert once went down to Red Rock Crossing with his friend. While she was doing spiritual studies and lessons that she'd been taught, he went over and sat by the creek on a warm stone. He happened to look down at the side of the stone and saw a spider there, and he said, "Oh, I'm sorry. I didn't mean to practically sit on you."

Before he could say or do anything else, he suddenly got a picture in his mind's eye—a picture, you understand? Not thinking and imagining a picture; just a picture suddenly being there. It was of a dark space, just black, and he thought to himself initially, "What's this?" becoming slightly alarmed, but no more than that. He saw a pinpoint of light, and then the pinpoint of light got brighter and then it just got bigger. So the light didn't continue to get brighter; it just got bigger until there was no more dark space.

Suddenly in the picture he could see stones and rocks. Then there was a feeling of undulation, like moving, as if a camera . . . imagine a camera bobbing up and down. He could see that from the point of view of what he was seeing, something was moving over these stones and rocks. He realized that the spider was showing him something about its life, and the spider showed him essentially that in the dark space was the spider's home or where the spider had slept that night and then came out of.

And the picture story went on. The spider went around a rock and then things went black for a moment. Then the spider came out, and the picture-story feeling was that the spider had had something to eat, but the spider was gentle enough with the picture story to not show the eating process. Then you could see the sky and the trees, and then things jumped forward and you could see the rock and feel the warmth. The spider was clinging to the side of the rock at that time of day, just taking in the warmth and enjoying the beauty of this place. And that's it—the pictures ended.

By that time, Robert knew that it was his job then to show the spider his day in a simple, uncomplicated way—not showing any machines because that's not part of the spider's life. So he went through the pictures of his own day, keeping it as simple and as uncomplicated as the spider did, and then he stopped. That was interspecies communication. The spider was teaching Robert how to be polite. Robert had been taught previously by a tree in another spiritual encounter that species say "Good life" to each other and sometimes other species say other things. But trees and many plants say this or say, feel, project something that is interpreted into English as "Good life"—not only a word, but a wish, a feeling, a blessing, a salutation.

In this case, the spider was teaching Robert how one communicates with another species by showing. You see in your own mind's eye and you relive the feelings of the moment of your day as a polite way to introduce yourself to another species. As you know, even when you meet another human being, a stranger, perhaps somebody you have to meet for business, there can be awkward moments, and simply saying, "Hello," or shaking hands isn't enough. It's not enough of a feeling of intimacy. But the spider taught: "Here's something personal about me, something I did— part of my life."

Animals Have So Much to Teach You

This book is intended to be not just about techniques but about experiences, how we live our lives as spiritual people—not only to become more spiritual, but to experience spirituality in simple, benevolent ways you can express on a daily basis in order to enjoy spirituality so that spirituality does not become a "job" or even a vocation or a profession. It becomes simply a better way to live for the pure joy of it.

Shamanic Secrets for Spiritual Mastery, then, is not about techniques of how to communicate with extraterrestrials and explore the planets, but rather it is about how to understand yourself and other species in order to improve the quality of your life. The techniques will be spiritual because that's the word we're using to define who and what *we*, meaning all beings, all are—I'm speaking as if I were still physical, all right? And *we* on Earth would simply mean human beings, plants, animals, Earth herself. When you can communicate in these universal ways with each other, you will find out that the patience of the animals is not only without limit, but that your own patience can also be without limit once you have teachers who live by example rather than by an attachment to your learning what they know in the way they know it.

The spider taught by example. This is how we introduce ourselves, by example. Robert, being a receptive spiritual man, was able to take in the teaching in a very nonthreatening and pleasant way. He learned about the spider as an individual rather than as a thing. Just because you don't speak spider language as a human being, just because spiders are different than you—you might say, an "alien" species to you—does not mean they don't have love, kindness and appreciation for you. This revulsion of beings who do not look like you does not serve you well, meaning the human beings in your time. It doesn't serve you well.

So many good things are available to be taught to you by these ancient beings. The spider was not in its own self so very ancient—it was fairly young. But spiders, like all other animals on your planet—and plants, for that matter, and fish, all of them—are not here to learn anything. They're here to teach, and the reason many of them are still here in their species form is that they still have something to teach to you that you can learn for your benefit. So knowing that allows you to know that moving forward in communication with creatures will allow you to perhaps learn and to enjoy life more.

You Have All of These Connections to Other Life Forms

Robert likes to tell the story of how he once saw a grasshopper on a wooden pole, a fence, out in the country. The grasshopper looked at him, as they will do sometimes. It was all by itself. It looked up at him and Robert knelt down to get, not too close, but at least at the same level. He presented to the grasshopper the way the spider had taught him—showed what he had done that day, introduced himself through pictures and recalled feelings. When you do this, always and only show that which feels comfortable. Don't show something that makes you recall something uncomfortable, because the other being will feel your discomfort and it might make it feel bad. You want to introduce yourself in a way that shares something benevolent.

So Robert waited and then the grasshopper did the same thing. Then there was a great warmth that Robert felt, beyond the warmth that is normally felt. This is the warmth that two beings generate when there is a benevolent connection between them. And the grasshopper looked at him for a time and then flew and jumped away. It was a connection with another life form.

Many of you reading this book have expressed a desire over the years: "When are we going to meet the ETs? When are they going to come and talk to us?" Well, the ETs are waiting. They're waiting for you, not just to learn how to get along with each other as human beings, but how to do these simple things to connect with other life forms. Why would an ET—who looks very much like Earth people and at a casual glance would look like an Earth person—want to come and visit a civilization that is so uncomfortable with another species that it rips it out of the ground, as people often do with dandelions, or steps on it simply because they are offended by the appearance of, say, a beetle or a spider.

You need to learn that all life forms on Earth are here as teachers and that the students who are here are you—human beings of the Explorer Race who have volunteered to come here to learn something outside the boundaries of your normal existence. In your normal existence, you know many things. You have all of these connections to other life forms. It is typical for you to have warmth and love and feel safe and comfortable with all life forms everywhere But here you come to this place, this school, and you are cut off from that so that you can create, re-create, apply and test the value of philosophies in such a difficult environment, as has been discussed before. These beings, whether they be the littlest spider or an ant or a grasshopper or a fish, can teach you something.

Don't wait for these beings to tell you stories or sing you songs. Don't wait for them to make the first move. When you see a bird on a limb, if it is not busy, you will know. If you give the pictures and the good feelings of what you did that day and it flies away, then it is busy and you say to yourself, "Oh, okay, good life," and you go on. But maybe you will see an ant or a spider. If you have a moment, offer quietly, slowly—no rush—some pictures of what you did that day for which you have pleasant feelings. Then wait. If the ant hurries on or the spider goes off somewhere or doesn't respond, or you don't see or feel those pictures, then maybe it is busy doing something else. This happens—you know how that is. Or perhaps you have not yet become open enough or you are not able to tap in to that which it is sending.

Do you know that very often when you have difficulty with other forms of life—be they plant or animal, insect or fish, anything like that—it is because they have been trying to tell you something in some way, to communicate with you, and sometimes they will act in some way, like ants coming into your house? Granted, sometimes they are looking for food—that is sometimes the case—and there are things you can do to help and support them in their temporary urgency, but that's for another day, to talk about that. Perhaps we will at some point.

Animals are trying to tell you, they're trying to teach you all the time. If you can begin to reach out, offering these pictures or feeling the warmth in your body when you are around them—and some of them may also feel the warmth—then you will know that they are responding because the warmth in you will certainly get stronger. If you can begin, it will encourage them very much. I assure you that any animal or plant who experiences this from another human immediately communicates that to others of its own species and to anyone who will listen, even from other species, because they all need that encouragement that says, "Here's a human who's ready to learn." The more humans who offer that, the more these species will be encouraged to stay and to be available to teach you.

In the future, more and more books and stories will come out and even movies and other things—granted, the movies will often be fictional—that are not about scary life forms but are about plants and animals on Earth now who have good things to say. Maybe it will be channeled; maybe it will be from authors who are inspired in the form of stories. Look for them, not only for your children, but for yourself, because the plants and animals have so very much to offer—not only about their experience, but in how to help you.

The Animals Always Want to Help

Here's another story: Once Robert was visiting a foreign country and he wasn't feeling very well. He had an upset stomach, and some of the over-the-counter medication that he brought with him to this foreign country, he didn't have with him, and he was far, far away from it, way out in the country. He couldn't get to it, and he didn't know what to do. So he was lying down at his friend's house (his friend had brought him out to the countryside), and as he was lying down in this house, he saw on the wall a spider and the spider was aware of his distress.

Robert looked for a moment at the spider, and the spider suddenly emanated a picture to Robert. You have all seen this famous artistic picture done by your artist of old that shows a man with his arms outstretched and his legs outstretched—I believe this was done by Leonardo da Vinci. This spider superimposed that over a picture of the spider's body. The spider was trying to communicate in an illustration for Robert to imagine that he had other legs coming out of the side of his body. Robert was then able to put together that the spider meant, "Imagine that you have streams of energy coming out of the side of your body," because the spider could see that Robert had too much energy in his body and he needed to simply extend some of it out of his body so he would feel better. Robert understood this, so he did it and felt better.

Sometimes Animals Need Your Help

The animals always want to help, and sometimes they will need your help. I will give you more stories. These are things from Robert's life, but they are things he learned on the way toward his capacities that he now has in the shamanic world. The reason Robert was at that house, in that country in Brazil, was that his friend had brought him out there to say, "The ants keep coming into my house and I don't know what to do about it. It is making things very uncomfortable for me. Also, I just want to show you my country place." So he brought Robert and Robert's friend out to this place, and a few other friends came out there, and the first experience Robert had was this discomfort. So he laid down and the spider showed him what to do and he started to feel better.

Then his friend, Nancy, came into the room, and she said, "There's something you need to see out here." Robert said, "Well, I'm just doing something." She said, "I don't think it will wait." So Robert came outside, knowing that if Nancy said that to him, that it was important. So he went outside and he saw coming around the house a legion—as in the Roman legions, yes—of ants. It was a solid block and stream of ants, twelve, fourteen, maybe sixteen inches wide, solidly of ants, and it was coming out from behind the house, wrapping around the house, walking in perfect formation. Robert didn't know what to think.

Nancy asked, "What does it mean?" The others asked, "What does it mean?" and they looked at it. The ants stopped. The humans were all standing on the porch. The ants formed up a design in front of the house and they formed up a pattern that was about four feet by five feet. It was an amazing sight—one of the wonders of the world. These people were exposed to something that ants practically never do, but it's done when they're desperate to communicate something that they feel strongly about. It wasn't done because they were monsters who were going to attack; it was done because they were special beings, as all ants are.

They were forming up—imagine, if you can—a squarish pattern like this: ranks of ants, like rows of ants, but a solid block of ants, thousands and thousands, some of them going back and forth. Imagine the picture: back and forth, all these ants, and some of them going the other way, back and forth the other way, but in square patterns as in the pattern of a weave of cloth. It is an amazing thing, to see this. It was a blessing, an amazing experience of nature, and the people were observing this and saying, "What does it mean?"—the people other than Nancy, Robert's friend Nancy being a spiritual person. The others were spiritual but were alarmed, never having seen anything like this and being uncertain about ants in any event. They were a little frightened.

Suddenly a couple of the ants broke rank, just two or three, and they walked up the steps toward Robert. Robert noticed this, and Nancy said, "I think they want you to say something." She felt that, being a spiritual person, and Robert said, "Okay," and he started speaking a story, a story the ants wanted to tell, and this was the story:

The ant said, "About forty years ago" . . . can you imagine that? That they had the time, that they could relate in time?

They said this through Robert?

Yes, Robert was speaking in his own voice, getting this story. So the ants said, "About forty years ago, we used to live over there," and Robert pointed over there, which was down the road where there were a few houses. There were very few houses out in this area. It used to be part of the jungle in Brazil, a tropical area, but a few people had built houses over the years. The ants said, "We used to live over there, and it was a big colony, there were many of us. Mostly we lived underground, but then we'd come up to the surface to find food and other things we needed to live. And we had generations and we lived as we have always lived in this place.

"One day there was a loud roar and a machine. People had come to build a house, and they were digging down to build a foundation. In their digging, they broke into our colony and we lost a whole generation," meaning they had eggs in their colony and the whole generation was wiped out along with many of their fellow beings in their colony. Some of the ants, the survivors, escaped, and they came over, far away for them (far away for an ant is not as far as it is for a human). They came over and they dug back down into the Earth. They lived there and they slowly tried to recover from the terrible shock and loss of their loved ones. Ants are totally devoted parents and they love their young dearly, just as much if not more so than human beings (I'm telling you this, but the ants didn't say this).

The ants said they moved over to this place, and then when Robert's friend came along and he and his family built a house there, the ants said it was all right because they built it on the surface—meaning they poured a concrete slab, you understand, and built the house up from there. The ants were all right, no one dug into the ground, but recently (this shows you how aware ants are) the owner, meaning Robert's friend, had been talking about making an addition onto the house or building a barn and digging a deep foundation, and the ants were frightened.

This was the story they told. They were frightened, they said to Robert: "We're afraid the same thing is going to happen and we'll lose another generation, and it's taken us forty years to rebuild our colony to its former size and we're frightened. We don't want you to dig into the ground. Won't you please, if you have to build something, build it on the surface like you did before?" That was it. The ants who had broken rank returned to the rank and the ants marched in perfect rank back around the house and back down under the house—there was a crack in the concrete back there that went down to their colony—and they were gone.

Honor the Ants to Keep Them Out of Your House

Interspecies communication is possible. In this case, granted, we had two spiritual human beings involved—Robert and Nancy—and yet still there was the potential. This is why the ants had been coming into the house and bothering Robert's friend. The friend said to Robert, "What can I do?" And Robert said, "Well, they made it clear that if you're going build something, they simply request that you don't dig down into the ground." The friend said he'd think about it, but there were other members in the family and it was up to them. Robert said, "Well, they'll keep coming in and they'll bother you." Robert also advised them, the people—his friend and the other people with him—on how to make an offering to the ants, how to ask the ants to stay outside and allow them, the human beings, to have the inside of the house, and how to honor the ants—to offer them food according to the kind of food they would eat and how to know that food and so on. But it was sort of an experimental way of finding out what the ants liked and honoring them and asking the ants to stay outside and giving them food. You can do this all outdoors. It's a way of honoring them.

One might, in that sense, offer different types of food—different types of ants like different types. Some, as you know, like sweet things, and some like meat or grease—the leftovers of meat or something like that—and others will sometimes like seeds. So you might put that out near where the ants are, outside. Always go outside, because you want to make clear to them that you are honoring them, and this is where they are—they live outside in the world. Find their home or the opening to their home, which is often an anthill or possibly a crack in the concrete if it is a city place. Where the stream of ants is—there's usually a stream—six or seven inches from the stream, close enough that they can find it but not so close as to be in their way and cause them any problem, put out little piles of the different types of foods. Then notice which food they eat. Try to make sure that no other kind of animals can get to the food, meaning you might cover it up in some way, leaving openings so that the ants can get to it.

Then observe it and watch and see—maybe go away for an hour or so and come back—and find out what kind of food they like. When you find out what kind of food they like, bring that food out on a daily basis for a while. This is only if the ants are coming into your house and you want them to be outside, to not come in.

Once you find out what they like to eat, then make a statement out loud. What you say is this: "I am asking . . ." They might not stop and listen, but if they do not listen, then the spirits who work with them will listen and interpret your words and request to them later. But you say out loud near them, standing far enough away so you're not in their way or frightening them (and you don't have to say "ants"; you're looking at them, you're speaking to them and they know or their teachers will tell them):

Living Prayer

"I AM ASKING THAT YOU ALLOW ME TO LIVE INSIDE MY HOUSE AND THAT YOU LIVE OUTSIDE, AND I WILL OFFER YOU THIS FOOD EVERY DAY FOR AS LONG AS YOU NEED IT, ONCE A DAY."

And that's it. You walk away. [For more on living prayers, see p. 245.]

Maybe take a couple of steps backward first, carefully so you don't fall down, so that the ants are clear that you're speaking to them, and then you can turn and walk away. You don't have to do that part, but it is a way to underscore the fact that you are indeed talking to them. Then walk away, but you must deliver every day, bring the food out. Again I say, only do this if the ants have been coming into your house, which is their way of saying, "We don't have enough food." This undoubtedly means that they don't have enough food for their new generation. So they're storing it up for them, you see.

So then you come out every day and you bring the food, and eventually the ants are not going to take the food, meaning they have enough between what you're bringing and other foods that they've been able to find. Also you'll notice during this time that at some point they either stop coming into your house or the numbers of them coming into your house greatly decrease, usually so it's just one or two. But usually they'll stop coming in entirely. At some point, you'll notice that you've been putting out the food every day—not a huge amount, but you put out enough—and they're not taking it anymore.

Continue to bring it once a day for at least a week. Then if they're not taking it anymore, bring it out once every three days. Do that three or four times. If they're still not taking it, then bring it out once a week and gradually taper off by that schedule. If they still don't take it any of those times, they have enough. Then don't bring out food anymore until they either come in the house again, or if you've kept track on the calendar of when they started coming into your house, then you'll have an idea that they might need food at that time of year because that's probably the birthing time. And you might be able to help them by bringing them food.

Generally I recommend that you not bring them food unless they come into your house or they might come up the steps if you've already indicated to them that you will support them in this way. If you see ants coming up the steps or maybe you see one ant in the house, then you know it's time to start bringing them food again. This is the best way to keep ants out of your house and it's a benevolent way—good for you both. And who knows, maybe some day the ants will show you some wonderful thing that they do on their own, or they might find a way to make sure that someone does you a favor.

It's not tit for tat, as you like to say, but as you know, things balance out. If the favor is not done for you, maybe it will be for someone in your family, someone whom you know. It's hard to say. The main thing is, do it because you *can* do it, do it because you want the ants to stay outside while you live inside your house and do it because they need the help and if they could help you, they would.

Reconnecting to Timeless Wisdom

Reveals the Mysteries
December 26, 2002

'd like to say this: The nature of spiritual mastery is not to be completely in control, but the nature of spiritual mastery is necessarily to not have any control. The whole point of spiritual mastery is *to be in concordance, not in control.* Concordance is a little different, and it's the closest word I can find in your language to express how I feel about it. Concordance to me would mean that whatever develops as you go along, moment-to-moment in your life, you are able to act or react to it on the basis of the natural foundational love that exists between all life forms.

Now, I want to be realistic and practical. Sometimes you will meet life forms, in the form of humans or animals, who might be hostile for one reason or another—maybe it's personal, maybe it isn't. There are a lot of things you can do on a more advanced level, but we will save that for a more advanced book, and that might come along under the guise either of something that builds out from benevolent magic or that is simply along the lines of a follow-up to these *Shamanic Secrets* books.

But for now I want to say this: Many of you are concerned about meeting other people and some of you are concerned about meeting animals who might be hostile, and there may or may not be a great deal you can do about that, but there are a couple of things I want to tell you. The most important one in alignment with spiritual mastery is this: All animals, people, physical beings as you know them, are made up of the same stuff. Your scientists like to say, "genetic soup," but it is the same general matter.

How to Relate to the Natural Level of Existence in All Beings

So what you can do before you go wherever you need to go—if it is down the hall or across town, if it is across the country or just a few feet—is I want you to approach it from a more basic level if you are concerned about your safety or even about your personal comfort. So this is what you do: First, I want you to picture the Sun in the sky. Don't look at it; just picture it, imagine it. Then I would like you to, when you are breathing out like this, I want you to blow lightly out of your mouth—not strongly, just lightly—and imagine that breath blowing through the Sun. If you can picture it, then picture it; if you can feel, then feel it blowing through the Sun. And imagine that direction you are walking in, having that breath from your body blowing through the Sun paving your way.

Sometime in the past I believe I discussed—or perhaps it was my student, Speaks of Many Truths—blowing gold light in front of you, but this is different. The Sun is directly related to Earth, the planet upon which you are now living. Gold light is immortal and everywhere; the Sun is personal, personal to Earth. It is your Sun for your solar system, yes, but also for your planet, and it is in the present—you relate to it every day. So blow through the Sun. It will naturally purify anything coming from you, and it will lay down in front of you a pathway that will relate to the natural level of existence in all beings. I'm not guaranteeing you that you will be safe, but it will tend to make you safer.

Try to walk on the path that you pictured when you ceased that breath—just once like that through the Sun is sufficient. If you want to blow more than once, that's all right. And say you decide to walk farther, then continue to blow through the Sun while you pay attention to where you're going. If you're driving across town, you can do that, but picture the general route you'll be taking. It may change a little bit, but try to keep it on that route. If you need to change your route, then either pull over and park for a moment and blow through the Sun, or if you can keep your eyes open, picturing the Sun, blow through the Sun and still drive—that's all right. But I think that's too complicated for most of you beginning this work, so I recommend you pull over.

These suggestions are intended to help you to become more oriented to being an Earth person. Know this: The animals naturally do this. The animals are very conscious of being on Earth, even if their spirits in the larger sense of their reincarnated selves are from other planets. They are very conscious of utilizing the strength and the strengths of the planet upon which you are living—even the astronomic strengths, meaning the Sun or the other planets. Some of the animals are day-livers, meaning they sleep at night. Some of them are night-livers, meaning they sleep in the day. Then they will still use the Sun, but some of them have learned how to use the Moon if they are, as you say, nocturnal.

I won't give how to use the Moon right now because you need to begin by utilizing the Sun. You need to, in that sense, embrace your life more, and you will feel like you can embrace life more once you have a more intimate arrangement with the Sun. Clearly you cannot touch it or get close to it physically, but simply by it being in the sky during the day, you are reminded what it looks like. You can't stare at it, but you can take a quick glimpse as your eyes might pass over the sky looking at the clouds. You know what I mean, you've done that many times, so you know what it looks like. It's all right if you picture it being gold; it's all right if you picture it being white. The main thing to know is that you need to be very clear that it is the Sun in the sky because it is that which gives, nurtures, supports and strengthens life on your planet. Even your scientists have shown you that this is so. Make this spiritual connection with the Sun as well and bring it into your life so that you can utilize the Sun's abundant strength.

The Sun Speaks to Your Earth Physicality

Scientists have wondered for a long time why the Sun is so powerful and why in general suns are so powerful. This is why: The Sun's offering to all life, around which life revolves in the form of planets and so on—the Sun's support to you all—is physical and spiritual. The animals breathe in the Sun or they feel the strength of the Sun, and so do the plants. They make it personal. If you can make it personal, you will begin to feel more comfortable on Earth. The energy of the Sun "speaks" to the physicalness in human beings, animals and plants, for that matter, as well as the planet.

And by interacting with the Sun in that way—even if it is nighttime, just close your eyes and imagine the Sun—you will embrace your Earth life, you will be more comfortable with your Earth body and you will create a connection that is completely safe for you and completely safe for all other beings by using the purifying function of the Sun. Blowing through it the Sun naturally purifies and the connection is to all other forms of life on Earth. It doesn't blow these forms of life away from you, but it allows these other forms of life to feel the Earth in you, and they will not be naturally reactive or frightened. Therein lies the insight.

You might reasonably wonder why human beings and animals, for that matter—and even to some extent, plants—have fear at all. It is designed to protect you from that which is not safe, and at the most basic level, one of the things you are designed to be shy about is that which is not like you. But at the most basic level, what is like you does not have to do with your culture, even with what sex you are; it simply has to do with the fact that you are Earth. Yes, you are sparked by Creator, but other than that, you are Earth.

And so if something or someone approaches you who blows through the Sun and follows that path, what it will feel like to you, being approached by that person doing that, is that at the most basic level, this person will feel like you. In short, you won't have the natural reaction of fear and you won't react out of fear. This means then that you, as an individual, can move about safely, causing no harm to others and not being perceived of as a threat. It will not cause people who need to observe you to be less observant, but they may not strike out as people do in fear. You know how animals can be like this if they are frightened of you.

Perhaps you've been chased by a dog who didn't feel you being Earth. If you're going to walk some place, those of you who have routes where you have to walk or pay special attention, imagine your route. Blow through the Sun and imagine that going all throughout your route wherever you go that day, even if you jog part of it, and the dogs who will be there will not react to you so harshly. Try it and see how it works. If the dog is reacting harshly as you are approaching where you need to go, use all the cautions you normally use, but if you do not feel you've made that connection—Earth to Earth to this creature—pause for a moment, if you can. If you are walking, close your eyes, picture the Sun and breathe through the Sun toward the dog. The dog ought to calm down. If it doesn't, then use your usual cautions.

It might take awhile to build up your capacity with this technique, but I recommend it because it can help you to make the connection, which is intended to take place from one Earth being to another. When you do that, you will be relating to these other people or animals at the most basic level to reduce their fear level, and in time, it will reduce your fear level too.

That's a very basic lesson in spiritual mastery that has been lost in your time for the most part because of the break in connection with timeless wisdom. But these books and others are intended to reconnect you to timeless wisdom that you can apply, whatever time you're living in. Try it out and see if it works for you. If it works for you, then you will know that here is a practical portion of wisdom that is indeed timeless.

Your Spirituality Must Be Personal

Are there any other techniques you'd like to share?

I wanted to give that one toward the end of the book because it is so practical and grounded and real. As you know, these books were given in reverse order, not on the basis of the normal progression. Normally if one were to give these books, these *Shamanic Secrets* books, one would have started the student out with spiritual mastery, then physical mastery, then material mastery. But the books were given in reverse order because of the urgency needed to go straight into material mastery with the hope that people would be able to hit the ground running, as you like to say, and do the best they could for Earth so that Earth can do the best for you.

But the reason this book is intended to be not too complicated is that the actual order of the books is intended to be spiritual mastery, physical mastery, material mastery. So that's why this book is not intended to be too complex. Think about it. Both physical mastery and material mastery are quite long and complex, even though Speaks of Many Truths and myself and other beings attempted to have parts of the books, whole sections of the books, that were storylike to make it seem more friendly and more personal. This was so people could relate to the books on a personal level rather than them strictly being instructional, which can get a bit dry for some folks.

So this book is more storylike because we want to help people to relate to spirituality in the number-one most important way for them, and that's personally. If your spirituality is not personal, you won't do it. If it is personal, you will do it because it will be wisdom that works in an applied, practical way for you on a day-to-day basis. Why would you not do that? On the other hand, if it is external, external spirituality—that which you were born to in the case of some religions and cultures—it isn't always personal. You can make it personal, but it isn't always personal and you don't always use it on a day-to-day basis. It isn't always practical. I'm not saying it doesn't have its beauties, but even those who professionally practice them know that it has its gaps. Whereas personal spirituality, or timeless wisdom—which is my intention to pass on to you here—is usually something you will use because you want to because it works and it supports you and it tends to support other life as well. It recognizes the basics, and the basics always have to do with practical day-to-day reality.

Using Spiritual Mastery to Obtain Joy

How do you get to feel joy in your daily life? How do you use spiritual mastery to obtain that feeling of joy?

For one thing, you have to become an actor at some point. You have to find out what joy feels like to you. Remembering it isn't always enough, so I would recommend for starters that you imagine joy so that you will have a means to know how it feels in your body. You may, as an adult, have to play "let's pretend." The younger you are, then it won't be so difficult. And if you have a pleasant life or pleasant aspects to your life, if you are older it won't be so difficult either, because the older you get, the more you tend to let go of unrealistic goals that you may have had and simpler things might give you happiness: grandchildren, a favorite pet, things like that.

But for the average person, imagine being joyful like an actor. Actors have to do this on a regular basis. They have to imagine something so thoroughly that they become it. And to some extent, they have to put their personal stamp on it—meaning that even if the director or the acting coach is suggesting to you as the actor that, "This is who you are playing; this is what is happening; this is your motivation," even so, you can be this on the basis of how he or she instructs you only up to a point. Ultimately you have to be what your coach is instructing you on the basis of your own personality.

324 ✧ Shamanic Secrets for Spiritual Mastery

So to be the acting coach for a moment, first perform joy and know that it won't be that difficult and that you can do it, even if you have no reason to be joyous. You can do it because it is a performance, it is "let's pretend." Therefore, your mind will probably get out of the way, stop telling you all the reasons you have to feel bad and say, "Okay, it's 'let's pretend,'" meaning the mind will accept the fact that you have permission to be joyous from its conditioned position. Your minds in your time have been conditioned to not only believe but to exercise more control over your lives than they were ever intended to do, and your mind will be able to step aside and say, "Okay, this is something she's trying." Pretend or perform, as the acting coach might say, to be joyous, and do that at least once or twice a day for two weeks. You can be it as long as possible. In the beginning, it may be difficult, but by the end of two weeks, it won't be difficult. You'll be able to do it.

Once you are able to do it, to simply pretend to feel joyous—or even by that time you might actually be able *be* joyous in those moments of the practice—then while you are feeling joyous (this works particularly well for people who either own their own homes or who have lived in the same neighborhood for a while and expect to live there), anchor that joy. Again, you will use your breath. This is what to do: While you are feeling joyous—you have to do two things at once, but I'm keeping it simple—look at something in your home. It cannot be a person or a beloved pet—no animal, no plant—but it has to be a physical object. It has to be something you might come in contact with every day, ideally a piece of furniture—wood is good or fabric, especially a natural fabric. For those of you who are traveling or moving or do not have a fixed environment, try to look at something you carry with you, perhaps something natural. For those of you who own your homes, you can do this with the structure of the house itself—not the metal, but the wood.

What you do while you are joyous is that while you are feeling joyous in the moments when you can create or perform it to the best of your ability (after a couple of weeks, you'll get good at it), literally blow firmly—not lightly this time—into that couch, let's say, or that wooden frame of your house or the roof while you are experiencing that joy. Do not blow more than once—one breath. Continue to do that for another thirty days, practicing that joy once or twice a day and blowing it into places that are physical that you will see and ideally touch.

This works best with natural materials, wood, natural fabrics. It won't work very well with plastic or metal. It can, but these materials won't hold it well because they are not in their natural state. It also won't work very well to blow it at a mountain nearby where you live because the mountain is too far away. If you lived in a cave, you could blow it at the walls of the cave, but I know most of you do not do that. So that's what I recommend, because you need to have reminders of joy and you need to honor the fact that you are living in the times in which you are, in fact, living.

All of this practice of feeling joyous will remind you not only that you can generate this joy but that you can infiltrate the joy into the physical objects in your home, or for some of you perhaps in your office. Offices do not probably have much natural wood or fabric, but if you can do this, fine. What happens is this: Say, for instance, you come home from work, you are tired and you flop into the couch you've been blowing joy into. You just feel tired and you don't know what to do and you're depressed or upset, but it's possible after blowing all this joy into the couch, that after a time (not immediately), especially if you don't turn on the TV right away or if you're not immediately approached by many people, if you're just sitting there quietly for a while in that chair, there's a good chance that the chair itself will, because of the joy you've invested in it, create a more relaxed state in you, a sense of humor.

I alert families to this especially when mom or dad comes home. If the kids have encouraged mom and dad to try this or if mom and dad have done it on their own, let them just sit in the chair for a half-hour or twenty minutes. Don't approach them with any problems. By that time mom and dad will have relaxed and the invested joy put into this piece of furniture will have done a little return of investment—it will create for them a more pleasant persona. Then gently tell them about your day or whatever you need to say.

Leave the Joy in Your Footprints

So for you in your time, I'm giving these things that may seem very basic indeed, but this is intended to provide something you can do without any expense and by using your breath that you need to stay alive (so I know you have it). In time I will teach you how to generate that through the bottoms of your feet, but I'll give you a hint now.

Once you've practiced how to feel joyous, what you can do is this: If you take a trip, maybe to the mailbox or even to the trash can, trips you make every day but outdoors, then what you might do is practice being joyous while you're making the trip. It will be a little harder, so this is an advanced lesson, and while you're doing it, when you breathe out, imagine the joy blowing through the bottoms of your feet. It will work better, of course, if you are barefoot or at the most in stocking feet or maybe leather-soled shoes. It doesn't work as well in rubber-soled shoes, but it can have some slight effect. And you leave the joy in your footprints. Then when you walk back, try to walk back in the same footprints; it's kind of fun. That's just a hint. We'll try to give you more techniques in the next book, which will have something to do with benevolent magic, and we'll build on all three of the *Shamanic Secret* books we've been giving so far. Perhaps we'll even call it *Shamanic Secrets for Benevolent Magic*.

Everything Is about Feeling

Reveals the Mysteries
April 10, 2003

I was intrigued last night by what Isis said in another context, that benevolent magic works here on Earth, but it's covered by this layer of ignorance. Is that
special about this planet, or can you use benevolent magic anywhere?

Benevolent Magic Is Integrated Everywhere

Benevolent magic is integrated everywhere, and everywhere includes
Earth. The only reason that it is not used or integrated by all cultures on
Earth—some of them use it now—is that we need to have a certain level of
ignorance here so that you can rediscover things. You understand all the
Explorer Race information, but there are some peoples who have managed
to retain a certain isolation over time who . . . not every member of the
peoples, but some members have been receiving this wisdom and know
how to use benevolent magic for their own—and of course, their own peoples'—best interests. Often it will be done in the form of living prayer [see
p. 245], sometimes there is this or that ceremony associated with it and
other times it is benevolent magic in a similar form as you know it. It
might have other appearance things associated with it, but that doesn't
alter the outcome or result.

Can you say that a rain dance is a form of benevolent magic?

No, I wouldn't call it that, no. That is a ceremony done to invite something that you wish. I am not an expert. My people did not do that.
Actually, I do not claim to be able to speak of these things. For me, I know

of only one way to invite the rain, and I believe that may be in the *Shamanic Secrets* books somewhere.

If it's what you taught Speaks of Many Truths.

Yes. And that works very effectively, but it does not incorporate . . . my job is shamanic and spiritual teachings, not explaining ceremonies that work for people in other ways. It is not my job, though I have seen such a dance. I am not the person to ask about this thing. If you wish to have someone come through who can speak of Native American ceremonies, that could happen at another time, but I am not that person.

Is this the first time that benevolent magic has been brought out and discussed with the general public?

I believe that Speaks of Many Truths and Zoosh began speaking about this several years ago in the *Sedona Journal of Emergence!*

I don't mean in the past few years. This has not been talked about in public before over the past thousand years, right?

As you say, in public, no. It has been discussed privately to certain initiates and so on, but the key is not how we say the words—the key is *understanding.*

The Flow of Life

In more traditional, sacred cultures, first you teach people about how all life cooperates with all other life, flowing—meaning they talk about the flow. When you think about the flow in a linear world, you tend to think of things flowing from upstream to downstream. But it's not a directional flow. The flow means that everything is in, say, suspension. The need might be over here in this suspension, and then that which can fulfill that need will migrate toward the need, possibly without even knowing who the person is who is needing it—or the object, place, thing—only that the need requires some cooperation by others. And others who can supply portions of the need and who enjoy supplying those portions because that is something they do and it is part of either their work or their life, flow over there because they're attracted to that need.

It's like you can do something and someone needs it, so you flow toward it, you can connect with it, you immediately provide the portion you can provide. Then others provide their portion and so on. So that's why sometimes if you do benevolent magic, in this case, the flow goes where there's a need, then the need is fulfilled in bits and pieces, although usually not immediately. Or it's fulfilled partially, and then other parts are fulfilled as other portions arrive and give what they do.

They're not giving something in a sacrificial way. They're not, say, cutting off their arm and saying, "Here, I can live without it." They are rather providing something on the energy level. In the case of a human being, you would essentially be doing something that you could do anyway and that is a pleasure for you to do, or it would turn out to be a pleasure. You can think of many things you might do for someone that you would actually enjoy doing. You might give somebody a ride because you enjoy his or her company. That person gets to where he or she needs to go and you enjoy his or her company on the way.

That would be a human example, but the portions that fulfill a need are bits and pieces of different things—all in suspension—and then simultaneously all kinds of other needs are going on, including that which is fulfilling the need of the first thing.

But you made an incredible comment. I hadn't related this to the basic fact of creation: There's a need and all needs are fulfilled.

So you see, that is what is usually taught initially in sacred cultures. And from there, using that as a base, in that sacred existence, there is all of this flowing about all the time—not flowing from here to there, but just in existence flowing toward something that has a need for which it can offer what it has to offer to fulfill that need because it has it. That's what it does! Equally everything is flowing toward each other to fulfill everybody else's needs because they do that. And if what you do hasn't been called for, you are simply in existence, intended to enjoy your existence. That is the foundation.

If you build from that point knowing that it is the foundation, then you don't have to explain magic as benevolent magic, because if you start with that fact of benevolence . . . meaning that if you try to do magic that forces someone or some thing to do something that it does not normally do or that it would rather not do, it will not work because it is not benevolent for everyone concerned. In benevolent magic, you might provide for someone's need because it's something that you do and enjoy doing. It's always intended that way. It's never intended that you make a sacrifice; it's something you enjoy doing.

Connect with Benevolent Feeling—Everything Is Feeling

How do you know, as a student of the sacred in that old method (that's not the method I use, but I'm using it because it's in practice in some other sacred cultures), that the magic you're trying to use is not benevolent? You will know because you've been exposed to that feeling. Your teacher doesn't just describe that this is what is—as I've described to you before—but the teacher immerses you and helps you to connect with it on a feeling level so that you can feel that benevolent feeling of that existence all around and about you. Once you can feel that feeling, then anything you say to fulfill your needs or the needs of others must be said . . . in every word you say or gesture you do or anything like that, the feeling must always be maintained.

It's not that you're superimposing the feeling over what you're saying, but rather that as you're saying something—you might think it first and then say it, you understand—if it's not compatible with that feeling, then you'll know you can't say that. Stop and wait a minute or two until that feeling subsides, and you can then reconnect with that benevolent feeling that I was speaking about and say something else. You keep doing that until what you say, with the gestures you're using, feels just right.

This is a way to learn that system, and the sacred cultures that are still using that system on Earth in your time that have been doing it for years and years—maybe thousands of years in some cases—all use variations on that system. That is why in recent years all of the channeling through Robert [the channel] has been stressing feeling. *Everything is about feeling.* Notice your feelings—*everything is feeling*—because if you don't use feelings and you don't understand how your body feels and how your body teaches you on the basis of feelings, you will constantly be making mistakes that might harm you or others.

We do not expect you to be shamans or people functioning in the world of magic while you're trying to be practical. We simply want you to learn how to do that in moments so that you can understand your own body's feelings, what they are telling you, so you can learn how to use the basic feelings of your body. You would not use them as you would use a hammer. You use a hammer or a saw, and it's a tool—you pick it up and you use it. This is different. This is something that your body has. The tool is there. You do not *use* the tool; you utilize the tool as it exists.

Say it is like a saw or something that only goes back and forth. You don't try and use that saw as a hammer—it doesn't work that way. No, you use that warm feeling that we're calling a love feeling—the love-heat/heart-warmth/physical-warmth [see Overview]—you use it as it exists. You start with that feeling and build on that feeling, learning how to do different things using that feeling. Once you have learned all of those things, then perhaps you learn how to use other feelings, but along the way, you learn to notice that if you get an uncomfortable feeling instead of that warm feeling . . . you understand, we're using the warm feeling instead of the feeling into the benevolent everything that the sacred cultures have been using.

So this warm feeling is easier to notice. You don't have to practice for years to feel that kind of thing, all right? You either feel the warmth in your body or you don't. So it's very simple. The warm feeling, if it goes away, then you know you have to change the words, you have to change what you're doing, you need to do something different because something you're saying isn't right. Of if you get an uncomfortable feeling in your body, again it's the same thing. Stop immediately, wait a couple of minutes, then try to generate the warm feeling again. And then go ahead and try to do and say what you are doing. You understand, the method I am using to teach and that Speaks of Many Truths and Zoosh and others are using to teach . . . this method is much quicker, much simpler, much more easily adapted to than the more ancient system of the sacred cultures.

And that has not been taught?

I'm not saying it hasn't been taught. What I am saying is that it is simply quicker. It's not better—it's quicker and it's almost as accurate. The reason I say "almost" is that sometimes people think they have the warm feeling when they really don't. They might just have a little bit of the warm feeling and they think that's enough. But it needs to be a significant feeling, the warmth. So it's not quite as accurate as feeling that benevolence all around you and staying focused in that feeling of what we were calling the flow before—staying in that feeling and knowing that everything you say and do must be in balance or cause your body to feel always that benevolent feeling.

That's why teachers from the past or the teachers from these sacred cultures not only exude this wonderful energy, but it's also why they must speak and do things in a very certain prescribed way, why you always see their hands moving in a certain way, why they will sit down in a very specific way, why they will simply do everything in a very certain prescribed way. Because that way, every single thing they are doing, *everything*—all the physical gestures, every single thing—allows them to feel connected to that flow of energy, and to an extent, it flows out from them . . . and others, especially if they are sensitive, will notice it.

This teaching is also something that takes a lot longer to learn and absolute dedication. You really can't do much else, which is why in these sacred cultures, as I'm referring to these cultures, not everyone in the culture does this. Only some people are taught it and do it, and when they learn things, they will do those things for themselves, their family, everyone in their culture. It will be their job, because the other people are out doing what must be done: they are hunting, gathering water and doing all of those things to keep life going on, building or whatever they do. Everybody does his or her own thing.

Now, I'm not saying that one way is right or wrong. In your life, in your complicated times of distraction of this and that and so on, it is too difficult for the average person, much less the person studying sacred or shamanic things, to get connected and to do as those sacred-culture teachers might do, because that requires 100 percent of your attention 100 percent of the time. You can't do that; you have to do other things. But you can do the warmth.

Feeling Your Path

When you were a teacher in your time, were you able to have the time to do this?

Yes, because having that taught to me, I had a lot of alone time. Plus, generally speaking, things were more benevolent and peaceful. Granted, there were animals running around, some who were dangerous to human beings, but human beings were not part of their food group, and we would know, by our own feelings, when we needed to stop and let them pass in front of us. Or if we were passing too close to their homes or their young, we would get a feeling. It wouldn't feel right to go in that direction.

You don't question. You don't say, "Why not?" You get the feeling, and you honor it. You go, you turn, even if you have to walk back on your path. You might even have to retrace your steps a little bit, but then you sort of walk around something. You don't ask why. Asking why is just saying, "Oh, yeah? Prove it." Of course, the people who came along later and didn't know how to do that, they might have said, "Oh, yeah? Prove it." They would either walk into trouble or have trouble themselves. Or sometimes if they brought a weapon and ran across trouble, whatever it was, they would shoot it and go on. But they'd still be on the wrong path for them physically.

So they wouldn't find something that was good just because there was a wild bear there in the way with her cubs. Bang, bang, bang—they would shoot the bear and her cubs, and think, "Well, okay. Now I can go on." But they'd still be on the wrong path, because if they would retrace their steps if they knew how to do that or had someone with them . . . very often in those days—not your current time—you would have a guide with you, and the guide would feel that and the guide would walk around and you'd follow the guide and you'd say, "Why aren't we going this way? Isn't it more direct?" And because the guide knew that you did not understand spiritual things in those times, say a hundred years ago, the guide would say, "This is a safer path and a better path." You would listen to your guide, go on that path, and you would not only wind up on a better, safer path for you as a person, but good things could happen. Maybe you would take a detour, and on the detour you would discover something you wouldn't have discovered otherwise that was to your great benefit.

In this way, the detour around the bear and her cubs is my example of feeling something and paying attention to your feelings and changing your course. Maybe the bear and her cubs were there because they needed to be there for their own reasons, or maybe they just stopped there knowing that they needed to be there for some reason and they were there and they waited, and it turned out that the reason was that you needed to deflect and go around the other way. Then you would go around the other way, and who knows what you would find? Maybe it would be something good, maybe something that would help you, maybe something that would help others whom you know. It could be anything.

What I'm saying is that the bear and her cubs in this example . . . maybe she was doing something for her cubs or maybe she was even doing something for you. So if you don't pay attention and you say, "Well, show me. It doesn't feel all right, but who cares? Bang, bang, bang!" . . . not good. It's not good for the bear and her cubs, and it's probably not good for you either.

You Are Utilizing Your Body to Feel

You were trained to feel into the flow, right?

When you're feeling that life around you, it's like you're walking through something that is stuff, all right? You can put your hands through the air . . . right now, put your hands through the air. You don't feel anything, but what you're really feeling is, you're feeling what you normally feel. It is something, and the way you can tell is if you whisk your hand quickly through the air, there is a sense of breeze. You could say, "Well, if I were in a vacuum, I could do that quickly and I still wouldn't feel anything." But because there is something there . . . do that. Do that with your hand quickly so you can actually feel something, yes? That's because there's something there and you know it.

Now, to feel it is different. That's a physical feeling, but to feel it, you are using your body's feelings—not what the mind says is emotion, but not unlike what the mind classifies as emotion. Emotions are physical feelings in the body, are they not? But they're also, by the mind's classification, difficult to define, whereas the body's classification is that a feeling is either a good feeling or a bad feeling: "Yes, this feels good; no, this doesn't feel good."

So you reach that energy where the bear and her cubs are down the path and you feel something that's uncomfortable, but before you got there, you'd been feeling this good feeling, relaxed. Suddenly it doesn't feel quite right, so you start turning around. You turn in various directions and eventually you find a direction that feels the best. Then you walk in that direction. If for some reason you can't, maybe because there's a cliff there, then you walk back the way you came and find an alternate route, all the while turning and noticing which way feels the best. How do you know which way's the best? Because that's the feeling you have when you're connected with all this wonderful everything around you. So you're utilizing your body as a means to know which way to go, and the ancient teachers would do everything on the basis of what feels good.

That's why you will see teachers even today from some ancient cultures who will simply do everything in a very similar way. If they do something that other human beings do, they will do it in a prescribed way, and it will look like everything they do is ceremonial. But if they've been taught in that fashion, it's not just ceremonial. They do it because it works and it allows them to maintain and feel that good feeling. Therefore, it works for them and that's why they do it, and you'll know that's why if you get a good feeling from it yourself radiated from them, because that benevolence that is there tends to be amplified and radiated to other human beings.

That way the human being feels it, and those who are sensitive in proximity to that human being who's feeling it may also feel it. This is because the human being is here to learn and the human being is here to help other human beings to learn. That's why the feeling is amplified to a human being and not to, say, a dog or a cat. Dogs aren't here to teach other dogs and cats aren't here to teach other cats like humans are here to teach other humans. Although a dog might teach a human and a cat might teach a human, dogs and cats don't have to amplify energy to that human because they will teach you as a dog or as a cat what they know according to their species wisdom or according to their individual wisdom within their species. But the human being amplifies the energy so that other human beings can feel it and notice that this isn't just words coming from this person—it's "I feel something and it's something that's a feeling and a triggering. It's a good feeling coming from them and it's triggering a good feeling in me."

This Needs to Be Practical for Your Time

You've never mentioned who taught you. Did you have a teacher?

Certainly. It goes back and back. That doesn't mean that the information gets better the farther you go back or gets better the farther you go forward. I know some people used to think, "Well, if we just go back farther and farther and farther, we will get the purest information," but that's not necessarily the case. When you go back farther and farther and farther, it's a way to trace the roots of something, but it isn't necessarily going to give you a broader picture. As a matter of fact, it's likely to give you a picture that applies less to your time because it will apply to those times in that place in those circumstances.

But don't you feel that when you and Speaks of Many Truths give your experiences from four hundred years ago, you try to give them now in a way that is applicable to our time?

This is why I gave the comparison between the way sacred cultures would learn and the way we have been teaching, which has to do with the warmth you can feel in your body. I'm not saying you ought to try to learn that system of feeling that energy around you, I'm not recommending that, because you can only really learn that and feel that and follow that if you are someplace where you do not have to do anything other than learn. I am comparing it. I'm saying this is *a* way, and what I'm teaching is another way.

Granted, the way I'm teaching may not be quite as accurate as the other way, but it is something that is practical and can be done by anyone, even if you are building brick walls or are a carpenter or a stockbroker—it doesn't make any difference. You can learn this warmth system, but you can't be a stockbroker or a carpenter and learn the other. So I'm making it practical for your time.

This Is Just a Continuation of My Work

Speaks of Many Truths talked about his fear of heights, which because of your ability to work with him ended up as the skill of long vision [see Shamanic Secrets for Physical Mastery, chapter 3]. Did you have something similar that your teacher worked with—a fear that you brought into this life which was transformed into a skill or a gift?

No, I didn't. Good question, though.

He tells how beautifully you worked with him, how slowly and gently so he felt safe. When you were alive, were you aware of your past lives and where you came from?

No. Sometimes if it was important, my teachers might bring it up if they knew, but my best guess is they would only know if they needed to know in order to support something I was learning. I remember them saying that once, that they could see in a vision that I had a past life in which I did such and such and that I would thus be able to do that in this life more easily, but it wasn't what I would call significant. That was really not something that was part of our culture—past lives and all that.

I am choosing to make myself available to people on Earth who wish to learn and apply the sacred teachings for the benefit of themselves and their people and others whom they wish to support.

Has that been ever since you left that life in the 1600s, or is that just recently?

Ever since I completed the physical life. It's just a continuation of my work. After all, I didn't keep my work exclusive to my own tribal peoples. I would travel around some and sometimes others would travel to our area, and if they needed something I could provide, I didn't keep it to myself. It was something I could do, so I would do it for them if they wished to have it done.

There again, this is another teaching, but it's like you're a bodhisattva, or you're saying, "I'm going to stay here until the rest of the humans . . ."

No, no, I'm not saying that. It sounds that way, but I'm not going to stay here for that reason. I'm not saying I'm going to stay here until everybody else is at a certain level. It's specifically what I said. I'm not drawing a line in the sand, saying, "And then I'm going to go on." I'm just saying that as long as people need that here and want to enjoy these teachings and get something out of them, I will be available. Should there come a day when that's no longer needed or required, then I will face that day and go on. But that day hasn't come yet, so there's no need to even think about it.

And going on involves another life in another system?

I haven't had any need to think about it, so why would I think about it now? Do you know what you're asking me to do? If you knew you were walking down a path and you might reach that place where the bear and her cubs were and then you would have to change your path and walk around that and then go on . . . what you're asking me is what will I do when I get to that place where the bear and her cubs are. But I don't have to think about that because when I get to that place and the feeling changes in my body, I will know what to do.

Feeling Lives Past the Physical Body

So the feeling works even on the level of . . . so you have the same feeling?

When the time comes that what I have to teach is no longer needed here, then I will just continue on using the feeling. Feeling lives past the physical body. And I will just go, just like other places, in my description of the need. Right now the need is Earth and her people, and I am providing what I can provide because it is my pleasure to do so. But should that go away at some point . . . this is a beautiful way because there is something you can do and you enjoy doing it, it gives you pleasure to do it and it helps others. And those others are the same way. They have something they can do—everybody has something they can do and that they enjoy doing. Helping others to do what they enjoy doing . . . it is a pleasure for everyone. That is why things work in a pleasurable fashion.

That's why in some sacred societies that people look into here: "How did they do that? How did they move that big stone?" and so on. Well, it was because the stone was happy to move using that energy. But first you had to check with the stone to see if that stone was compatible with that energy. If it was, then you asked the big pile of stones—there were all these stones—you asked for stones who would like to come and move to this place. Then only those stones who wanted to come, came. You didn't question how they came. You didn't say, "Come down this valley and turn right . . ." They came however they wished to come, and they were there. You didn't tell them how to go. They came the same way I went when I walked around the bear and her cubs—feelings. I use that as a humorous example.

Other Personalities in the Channeling Stream

I asked a question one night and you said, "That's why I did this ten years ago." And I said to you, "You went here ten years ago?" and you said, "Yes, I was cooperating." Can you explain this?

This is how it works: Sometimes different entities are present in combination through a channel like this who can channel multiple beings, and it would be as if the entity who is speaking is part of a stream, as if it were a stream of energy. And then if there is something missing in that stream . . . you ask a question, and only parts of the answer are available from that personality's stream. Then parts come in from other streams, other personalities, and they provide it. Sometimes the being will make a gesture so that you know that something is being added or it will look to the side—essentially it doesn't have to do that—and it is telegraphing you that it is getting advice or information or resources from some other place.

I never saw Zoosh do that.

No, Zoosh didn't want to do that. Still, it is typical; all beings are like that. Sometimes they simply do not have the experience, so a stream might come in then temporarily and, not replace the being who's talking, but simply combine in that moment so more than one personality is present for a moment. And then, in that moment, you might have a momentary doubt for a moment. You might say, "Gosh, this sounds like somebody else." And then that is no longer necessary and that stream of personality is not needed any longer because that question has been answered. It might stay for a moment as if to say, "Well, maybe she's going to ask something, a follow-up question on that." But if you don't, then away it goes.

So that's how you've heard from me before. Something was asked—I believe you were talking to Zoosh—that had to do with Earth experience as one might live on Earth and practice and do different things on Earth. And Zoosh, without missing a beat as Zoosh would say, simply allowed that—my personality, in this case—to come in and speak through the Zoosh personality. I was not kicking Zoosh out but just supporting Zoosh and being there, and then when that question was fulfilled, moving off. That's how you heard from me.

Now, this doesn't typically happen with channels who do not channel many, many beings, but what will occur in that case is that the being a channel is channeling will sometimes either go to another level to get that information it can acquire, or it simply will not be able to answer the question very well. This sometimes prompts the channel to search around and find other beings whom he or she might channel to get a deeper answer. But in the case of this channel, Robert, because he can channel so many beings and is familiar with so many beings and is at ease with so many beings, then that kind of connection can be made, at least on a temporal basis.

You would have felt a connection because Robert's past self was Bear Claw, and Speaks of Many Truths was Bear Claw's teacher, and you were Speaks of Many Truths' teacher—so you would have felt a connection ever since he started channeling, wouldn't you?

Yes, but it didn't require my personal attention very much, because after all, Bear Claw was the past life and spoke at length helping Robert to channel, to get going. And then eventually Speaks of Many Truths came in, and he's very capable, so it didn't really require my attention. I only came in much later when there was a search for further information—that's all.

I'm Just Here for Human Beings

Speaks of Many Truths is going to work with the Sirians at 3.0 Earth. Is that part of your commitment?

No. I'm just here for human beings.

But human beings are going to use you for quite a length into the future, aren't they?

That's up to them, eh? And of course, ideally they won't need me for quite a ways into the future because they'll be doing things for themselves and then I will go on. And they won't miss me because they'll be doing it themselves.

Right. And you're not going to sort of join up with the Explorer Race into becoming the Creator?

No.

Can you say if you have past lives on other planets that you remember?

Yes, but I very rarely make any connection with them because the experience on those planets does not relate to this planet and so there's nothing I can use from them other than the good feelings of warmth and family and culture. That's nice, but I had enough of that here on Earth so I don't have a need to relate or connect to those lives. It is simply something I notice and that's nice, but it doesn't have anything to do with my work here.

Did you come here because you felt the need for your skills and talents, that you could aid the Earth? Is that why you came?

I don't think any child comes here with that idea in mind. Rather, it was the next reasonable place to go, because once you acquire a certain amount of capability . . . and you understand, capability is a platform upon which, when you add other things, then follows talent and then follows capacity and then follows education and then follows application— like that. So with that level of capability from being on other planets, the next logical place to come—if I can use logic as a reason, even though that's not the reason—on the basis of flow, of the feeling of life around me, was here, and it was a good life.

So you only had one life here?

Remember what I said before. When I'm no longer needed here, I will go to where I'm needed. Perhaps I will be there in spirit form, perhaps I will be there in a life of that place. I came here the same way—not because I'm any greater being than you or anyone else who is here, but that is how it was. This was the next place to be in that energy, it was the next place that attracted me, and I was born here as a baby like everybody else.

But only in one life?

Yes.

One life and then you're out?

Oh, I'm not really out.

Right, you're still learning.

Well, I'm still available. I don't know that I'm learning so much. I'm here to provide; I'm not here to learn. One has a human life here on the planet to learn. I don't have to be here, if that's what you're asking. I could go elsewhere. But if you're asking me if I'm here to learn something, the answer is no.

You're not here to learn, but don't you occasionally pick up something?

I'm in spirit form. I talk to you often from my physical time, and that's why you sometimes might get the impression that I'm here to learn something. But I'm always in spirit form. I choose to speak to you from the time when I was physical so that I can cater what I say and how I say it to the physical needs of physical Earth human beings, speaking from that personality at that time while having access to the full spirit that I am. So in that sense, I'm not here to offer the services I'm offering. I'm not here to learn anything. If I happen to learn something, then okay, but that hasn't happened. That's why I've come to believe that I'm not here to learn anything but I'm here to provide a service, just as other beings come here to provide a service.

I've met many, many, many beings, thousands who are here to provide a service, and many of them have been animals who are very wise and who come here to provide a service but they're not here to learn anything—cats, dogs, horses, fish, snakes, birds and so on. Somehow they do something, interacting with humans, which causes the human being to learn something or to want to learn something and so on. It just might be a reaction the human being has, or it might be something the animal can clearly demonstrate. Sometimes they make an effort to communicate with you; usually a pet might make that effort. Other times it's just, "Oh, well. If they didn't get it from me, they'll get it from somebody else," and they go on with their lives, especially if you might represent a threat to them, in the case of animals.

It's Your Duty to Feel Better

Do you feel that Zoosh's timeline of five, maybe seven years ago, when he said we would be going out in space in twenty-five years, is accurate?

I'd say, don't ever be attached to any predicted timeline, because it's predicted from that moment into the future. Things have changed. You'd have to ask Zoosh, however. That is my answer. The trouble that you are really dealing with right now is that difficulty is creating this addiction based upon . . . you're trying to use time as a means to structure progress. Time equals progression. But the thing to do now is to learn how to use what's desired in your present and have markers to know when you're on the right path to accomplish what you want.

Then you're no longer using time and years to get to what you want, but rather, "This is what I want for the future. I want"—for example, a typical desire—"peace and happiness and for everybody to have enough to eat and all the shelter they need," that kind of stuff. And that is a goal and maybe many goals. Then we suggest to you, "This is what you ought to be feeling now," or "This is how you would feel if you had all those things," putting yourself into that future frame. And then if you could recognize that feeling in yourself, you would be able to regenerate that feeling in a moment and say, "Okay, this is how I'd feel."

You get yourself essentially connected to that future time when you have that: You have all that you need, you're happy, everything is good for you and everybody else. And so you connect with that physical feeling, the way you feel in your body. And you connect with that from time to time so that you can then notice how much of that feeling you have in the present.

Then you do the same thing that I might have done walking down the path, and if I felt the bear and her cubs there, I would have turned in the direction that felt better. See what I mean? This gives you a method other than time to know that you are on the path toward achieving that feeling or achieving that future, and it doesn't use years at all. I'm giving you an overview of that, but that's basically what you need to have now so that you're not stuck on timelines on the basis of years, which are very iffy and constantly change and are not at all accurate.

And that can also be used personally for any goal that we want?

Yes, absolutely.

There's conditioning, from religions and cultures, that actions that are selfish . . . how can I say this?

Let's say this: When you ask for something for yourself, you (being connected to all other life) are actually asking for something—if you're asking for something to improve the quality of your life—to feel safer, to feel better, to have what you need in order to feel safer, feel better and so on. You are simply doing your duty. To feel better is your duty, because if you do not feel good, you are radiating your discomfort all around and about you, because you are signaling to others who have what you require—you are signaling, you have a need—to those who can come and fulfill your needs so that you feel better. When you say something for yourself, you then, as in benevolent magic, say, "I need to feel better," and so on using the proper words [see *Secrets of Feminine Science: Benevolent Magic and Living Prayer*]. You then give permission for those beings or people, places, things to come to you, to find you, to help you to feel better.

If you don't do that, you are actually not doing your duty, because then you continue to exude that discomfort all around and about you, and it creates a general feeling of "ill at ease" in the energy of everything around and about you. You have a duty to all the energy you are in to feel as good as you possibly can all the time so that others, when they come across your path or they are in contact with you or you walk near them, do not pick up a discomfort from you. So doing something for yourself is actually your duty so that everyone will feel comfortable when they are in proximity to you.

That's a great answer for the work-ethic and the religious people who teach poverty and sacrifice.

I feel it is important to recognize that. I realize that many religions use external philosophy that was appropriate for the times to accomplish—in those times when that philosophy was created—the goals of those times. But philosophies need to cater themselves to the goals that need to be accomplished in their own times. Those religions do not need to be discarded; they simply need to serve the needs of the times that you are in, in which case they adapt. This is what I believe. If they do not adapt, then people will often find something else. And for those who are comforted by those religions as they are, then they are still good in service—providing something good for those who wish to have it. So I'm not saying to get rid of it; I'm just saying that this is my philosophy and it is what works for me. I am sharing it, but I am not saying it is the only truth.

Humans in the Natural World

Reveals the Mysteries
November 3, 2003

I asked about the fires in California that have occurred this fall, and Speaks of Many Truths said that this was a matter concerning Mother Earth and her need to keep the forests for the trees and animals. He said that this is an ongoing concern she has, and although she does not desire to harm humans, she does desire that humans honor the boundary of their world and other worlds she protects. She feels that she is protecting our world and providing for our needs. She wants us, meaning all humans, to learn from her example—to honor and protect our own and to honor and protect others.

Separations Are Intended to Show Who You Are

Mother Earth takes her work with you here very seriously. She feels that in order to accomplish her purpose with you here—a purpose that you yourselves have requested her to do—she must show you certain ways of being, and those ways of being do encourage certain separations. I know that the New Age community often talks about the breakdown of separations. But quite obviously, some separations are important, and that is constantly reinforced in your physical life every day. Parts of you would not do very well mingling with other parts of you. That's why your body has very specific component functions. Certainly you understand that the porcupine is not intended to marry the deer and other examples you can think of.

Separations are intended to show, not that everything is separated and must always remain so, but rather that in order to experience fully all that Mother Earth has to teach, one has to be clear, very clear, who you are. The animals are not here to learn; they are here to teach for you. It is quite well known throughout the universe that you are all here as volunteers, as the Explorer Race, to learn things that are not available to learn on a daily, moment-to-moment basis in other worlds. Therefore, you need teachers, and you need to live on a teacher, such as Mother Earth, and you need to live in a teacher, such as Mother Earth's physical self that you know as your physical body, and you need to bring your motivation in the form of your immortal personality, also known as your soul.

So this is not unlike the universe where, when one travels as the Explorer Race, one would find different planets where certain beings who are very compatible live together freely and comfortably . . . one would expect to find that. But one would not expect to find on other planets deer married to porcupines (I'm using that extreme example because it's something you can smile about but understand). So clearly Mother Earth shows you that there are different beings on this planet and that some beings are more compatible with others. You might like the porcupine at a distance, and I would say that with the porcupine that would be a good idea. You might enjoy seeing the deer occasionally—if you're fortunate, a little closer up. But you are quite clear who you will marry.

Mother Earth Teaches by the Natural Cycle

Mother Earth has other ways of showing you the natural world, and that's what I'm speaking about here—the natural world. In the natural world, everyone at least has some general idea, such as I've just spoken about, of who you are intended to be with, where you are intended to live and how. You are not rabbits or ants. You do not burrow into the ground and live there—although occasionally you have some subterranean dwellers, but that is not your current expression of community for most of you. You are not birds and you do not grow wings and fly about in the air. You are human beings. You are intended to embrace that and to embrace learning, some of which will not always be easy, but that is how one acquires knowledge and then wisdom.

Mother Earth chooses for you to do this mostly with each other, and she nurtures and encourages some animals and plants to be amongst you as examples—and in time, as you learn to communicate better, as teachers from whom you can understand in ways that *you* recognize as understanding. She does not, however, encourage you to live in an unnatural way. By "unnatural," I mean sprouting wings and flying about in the air. It is one thing to build airplanes and to fly about the air in those, and this is part of your current romance with technology. But Mother Earth does want you to recognize that there are certain necessary boundaries in the natural world so that all beings in this natural world will understand generally who they are, where they need to be, who they need to be with, how they will survive and how they will thrive.

Mother Earth has set up certain boundaries for that, you might say. She has provided you with what you need. You eat the animals, just as many of the animals eat the animals. You utilize parts of the animals you cannot eat in garments and in other ways. You grow crops and eat those. Yes, you understand all this, but you are not so clear on what do to, where all the people can live.

What to do? You have many, many people, and of course, in time you will migrate out to some of the other planets, most likely Mars for a starter. You will have to adapt Mars to your own needs, but you will be able to do that and it will be quite an adventure. And of course, in time you will develop philosophies, a global philosophy that allows your population to gradually shrink over time in a benevolent way. Obviously, this can be done by people marrying. Some of you will choose not to have children, and others will perhaps have one child, but I will not go into all of this because others have in your time and you can seek out such literature if you choose.

Now, what I'm trying to say to you is that Mother Earth teaches by the natural cycle and by the natural way of existence. She does not wish to encourage you to live in the animal world. She doesn't expect you to live in, you might say, the vegetable world or the tree world—we can say, "tree land." She does not expect you to live on top of every mountain where certain plants and animals have learned to adapt over many thousands of years to those conditions and can even thrive.

She's allowing, you might say—she's somewhat tolerant—for some high mountain people who have also adapted over years and learned to survive, if perhaps not quite thrive. As long as there are not too many people living in that world, she is tolerant. She does, however, require that you learn how to honor the other worlds where the natural beings are living in the natural world, living in their natural cycles, who are here to teach you. She requires that you honor their world and their space.

You Must Honor the Borders of the Plant and Animal Beings

Remember, the animals and plants—granted, they are not all here; some of them have moved on, or as you say, are now extinct—are all here to teach you. You are gradually learning how to communicate with them, and to receive their advice will perhaps take a little longer, but you are getting there.

If you expect that you will be able to get their advice in a way that will serve you—much less, you might say, interest you—it cannot be done by these wild animals if they are living in a zoo. They acquire their natural wisdom, which they can pass on to you, by living free. Freedom is a necessary ingredient to developing the knowledge and wisdom. It is not always easy or simple or comfortable, but it does always teach, and because you are out in the wilds, so to speak, as an animal, you are quite receptive to learn.

You human beings are now living in your cities essentially for safety reasons, though you don't think about cities as safe, most of you. Nevertheless, you live there so that you are safe from the wild animals. There are not many bears roaming around on city streets, not too many lions or elephants charging along. Most of you do not have to tolerate alligators and other hazardous creatures on your city streets. You understand why you are there.

What you must recognize is that if these animals and plants are to teach you, they must be free, they must be safe, and you must honor *their* borders. Mother Earth does not want to punish you, to deliver you some kind of severe abuse, but she does insist that you honor the borders of the beings who will in time, by your learning process, teach you how to live on Earth—not only in a graceful, gentle way, but also in a nurturing way in which you can thrive.

You know that some human beings in your societies and cultures thrive, whereas others struggle and some others suffer. The animals and plants know how it's possible to live, even amongst all other kinds of animals and plants, and not only survive but thrive—each and every one— so that no tribe or species has to die out. They know that everyone can get along, even with animals eating each other and with plants birthing and dying. It can be done. It requires balance. The animals can teach you that—not as a theory, not even as a philosophy or as a religion, but they can teach you that on a very practical, day-to-day level. They can essentially teach you how to live on Earth, enjoy the experience and be happy you came here.

Now, how many of you can really say that you have that now? Some of you, yes, but not all. So you need to honor boundaries so there are free animals developing this wisdom. You will learn to communicate with the animals first because you are attracted to them, many of them—dogs, cats, horses and even wild animals you find attractive, such as deer and so on. Plants will take longer, but you will do that. Many of you are attracted to the trees, especially some of the big or unusual ones. You will get there, and they will teach you also.

Mother Earth Has an Agenda for Your Education

So Mother Earth has in her consciousness an ongoing program (you might say, agenda) for your education. She cannot communicate with each and every one of you—except perhaps at the deep levels of your sleep as Creator and your angels, guides and teachers do—but she has others here who can pass on wisdom to you. That is why you must learn to recognize the borders of what I'm going to call "tree land"—you might call it the forest.

Granted, from time to time there will be fires as part of the natural cycle. But when you, very often from your own desires to live in more beautiful surroundings (I know all of the reasons), when you live in those surroundings . . . not gently on the land, such as, say, pitching a tent, living for a time and moving on nomadically as people were intended to do here. But when you cut down the trees, bring in heavy equipment that has to smash its way in . . . if there's no road, you have to cut down the trees, build a road, dig up the ground, run in pipes and so on. When you do that, you injure the forest, you injure tree land. And unintentionally, you destroy that which you came to experience.

When Mother Earth sees this going on repeatedly, it not only damages her agenda for your teaching so that you may learn and become happy and fulfilled by your experience on Earth, but it can even damage her own functions. You might wonder sometimes why there is drought, especially ongoing drought in a place. That is because you have not yet learned from the trees and some animals—the trees and plants know how to do this— how to welcome the rain while needing it as well.

When you need something, you're more inclined to be welcoming of it—you have not learned how to do that. That's why Mother Earth needs places on her Earth for herself, as well as for the animals, that can welcome the rain so that the rain comes, nurtures the ground and . . . those of you geology students or agronomy students can figure out and pass on to others the simple facts of water percolation and the water table and so on.

Natural versus Unnatural Trees

This has to be done now by trees. Look at your deserts—not the ones that appear to be natural, meaning that can be traced back by your scientists as having been there for thousands and thousands of years and beyond, but the deserts that are quite obviously more recent and can be traced to humankind's actions in the area. Look at your deserts and you will see that it doesn't rain there very much because there are no natural trees.

What's the difference between a natural tree and an unnatural one? Trees, of course, are not unnatural, unless they've been grafted onto something else, for instance. But a tree that has been welcomed by nature . . . the seed falls from one tree or perhaps from a fruit of the tree, rolls around, flies around, travels around the way seeds do and is welcomed—meaning it stops somewhere because it feels welcome. (Animals, plants and humans all have feelings, and those feelings function exactly the same for all of you.)

When the seed feels welcome, it stops somewhere. It not only has to feel welcome, but it has to feel physically that nurturing is available: water is there, soil is there and there is that which will encourage life. This is the same reason human beings know how to seek out life when they are knowledgeable. Where is a place you can thrive? There must be water. There must be other things that will support life—forests, for instance. You understand. The tree then grows there because it not only feels welcome but also has what it needs to survive and thrive, since the tree wishes to have further generations.

So these natural trees, welcomed and maintained in the natural cycle, tend to develop and build on their wisdom of what one needs to survive and thrive. That's a natural tree, whereas a tree perhaps grown in a nursery, as you call it, by humans to look a certain way or to be a certain way— or that is perhaps even altered to be miniaturized or turned into something unlike its normal self—then purchased by a human being who likes trees and who plants it in his or her yard . . . this tree is not natural. It is not welcomed into land that provides nurturance. It is not the natural cycle. Even though you might water the tree, even if you establish communication, it cannot give you wisdom, though it may be able to give you information. It has a personality, it has feelings, all of these things, but it has not been given the opportunity to develop its own wisdom based upon its desire to survive and thrive.

Now, when you go into the forest and destroy the very beings who will teach you how to survive and thrive, after a while Mother Earth says, "Well, if that's how you feel"—of course, she knows that this is not how you feel, but she gets annoyed sometimes—"then maybe I shouldn't protect these teachers so much, even though they are here entirely for you." So if there is a fire started, even though the trees are all asking for rain to come and put out the fire, maybe she is slow to bring that rain about. And maybe there are other factors that human beings have intentionally or otherwise caused that spread the fire.

How to Welcome the Rain

Now, understand that Mother Earth is not abandoning you. She is passing the stick, as we say in the shamanic world. She is passing the capability of creation onto you. She is saying, speaking to human beings, "I know you do not understand, at least those of you who are running things in your societies, or perhaps it is not your concern at this time, about what trees have to offer your own cultures and fulfillment. Still, I want them to be available for you when you do get to that point. Therefore"—Mother Earth is not thinking this; I'm interpreting her feelings—"it is my intention to call upon those human beings who know how to bring rain, who have been trained to welcome the rain, trained by their teachers, guides, angels, perhaps even Creator, but certainly trained by the trees themselves. There are people like that in your cultures. Usually they go unsung or unknown. Sometimes they are known for what they do, and sometimes they are known for other things, and very often they will pass on their skill and knowledge at some point in their lives to one or more."

And this is helpful, because Mother Earth says to you now, "It is up to you to put these fires out. I will have the rain somewhere nearby, but you must stand out in the forest, not just the ones who are fighting the fire. You must stand out somewhere in the forest, perhaps near where the fire is but safe." Stand on the ground, preferably in your bare feet or with perhaps some thin leather covering over the bottoms of your feet. But I recommend bare feet, since you do not know how, most of you, to acquire the hide in a benevolent spiritual way, to make the shoe yourself in a way so that the shoe itself accentuates your capabilities rather than restricts them. I will say more about that some other day.

Since you don't have that knowledge, then the best thing to do is to stand out on the land barefoot—and by the land, I do not mean the concrete. I mean stand on the dirt, because dirt in its own nature, especially if there are some plants around, has shown that it will welcome the rain because there are plants there. Stand out there and fill your heart and your feeling self as much as you can with the feeling of welcome. Try to do this at a distance from the ruckus going on to put out the fire so that you do not welcome the discomforts and fears of others. It can be at a significant distance—twenty miles away even.

Stand on the ground and fill your heart and body with the feeling of welcome. While you maintain that feeling, just remember—you have been out in the rain; you know what rain feels like—what it feels like to have rain falling on you, not blowing against your face uncomfortably, but gently, a pleasant rain. Maintain the feeling of welcome while you recall this in your mind, and try to recall it enough so that you can almost feel it on your body. Sometimes you might get the feeling of what it is like to be rained on while you're feeling welcome. You know you've felt welcome yourself by other people or even by places, or you have welcomed others who have acknowledged that they feel welcomed—not just saying, "Oh, thanks for welcoming me. I feel welcome" [said in a flat, unemotional tone], not that, but a genuine feeling of welcome.

This does not require you, the rain welcomer, to be a shamanic person, a mystical person or a medicine man or woman. They have been taught other ways to welcome the rain, and you can be assured that if they feel permission to do so from Mother Earth or their guides and teachers, they will be doing it. But in order to heighten the experience, to bring rain as soon as possible to areas that need it, then you do so. I assure you that anyone can do this. You just have to know how to feel the feeling—not of being welcomed, but the feeling of welcoming as in welcoming others. And you have to remember what it's like to be rained on physically. This doesn't work to stimulate it by shooting a hose up in the air and having rain fall on you. It's not just physical. It has to be actual natural rain that's falling out of the sky.

If enough of you do that, Mother Earth will consider that you are bringing the rain the way trees do, welcoming the rain, and she will speed the rain toward you much more quickly than it would have arrived. Or your weather people will say, "Well, we never expected that rain to come here. It looked like it was going somewhere else entirely." I cannot guarantee you that you'll hear that, but it could happen.

Know How to Work with Mother Earth

Now, that's your homework. This book is about homework, as you know, and it's also about helping you to understand who you are, why you are here, what you can do to improve the quality of life for all human beings, how you can learn these things and how you can recognize, appreciate and value the natural world so that you can be a part of the natural world and survive and thrive the way the natural world knows how to do, rather than to be apart from it. One can only be apart from the natural world for a short time, because the natural world chooses to welcome that which welcomes it.

This is not a threat. You have seen how Mother Earth from time to time seems to do things. These are what you call storms or sometimes disasters. It is not her threatening, "If you are not part of the natural world, we will summon the storms and Earth motions." No. It is rather that Mother Earth lays these challenges in front of you—the storms and Earth motions—and says, "Here: Learn how to interact and work with these storms that are part of my natural function and these Earth motions." Learn how to do this, and you can many times protect the people, the property and the land from such destruction. You have amongst you now many people who are learning how to do this in the natural way, meaning to work with Mother Earth utilizing *her* methods of moving storms about or encouraging slow and gradual motion of the Earth rather than sudden and violent motion.

These things must all be done utilizing the same means that Mother Earth uses in order for her to survive and thrive. Once one knows how to do that, you can encourage, say, an earthquake—which, as you know, happens over a few seconds—to happen over many years. Mother Earth is prepared, if you know how to work with her using her methods, to make that motion over a few years rather than suddenly. But you must have humans who learn how to do that. Why? Not because she does not know how, but because you are here to learn. You are creators-in-training. Creator allows you to come to this planet to learn these valuable lessons, and learn you shall, in time.

Nomadic Peoples: The Natural Way of Life on Earth

Speaks of Many Truths and Reveals the Mysteries
November 4, 2003

his is Speaks of Many Truths.

Life Is about Change

There are certain people on your planet that you as a society, an Earth society, cannot live without, such as—and this has been stated in the *Explorer Race* books—the gypsy people, the Bedouin and some Native American tribes, who are all nomads, nomadic peoples. You understand, they move from place to place according to the seasons or according to cultural necessities. Even in adapting to your modern civilizations and their needs, they are living the way it was originally intended for human beings to live on Earth—that is, as nomadic peoples, moving with the seasons and moving with the rhythms of the cycles of Earth.

One of the main reasons seasons exist on Earth at all is in order to create cycles. Your physical bodies have cycles. Your cycles are, of course, childhood, being a youngster, being more mature and eventually becoming old. This is the cycle of the physical self of the human. Animals and even plants have the same cycle, and this is all in reflection of Mother Earth's cycles.

Mother Earth is demonstrating cycles that are long and short. The Ice Age and other things like that are what you might call long cycles. Even the motion of Earth's surface—continental plates, as you call them—these are long cycles. And there are shorter cycles, such as the seasons—winter, spring, summer and fall, for example—but there are even shorter cycles than that, such as night and day, rain and sun. All of these things suggest that life is about change, transformation, adaptation and development, and on and on it goes.

This is important and is a foundational element in all life everywhere, even though on Earth there are things that are experienced here that are not typical to life in other places. Nevertheless, even in other places where life is more benevolent, cycles are a constant.

This is Reveals the Mysteries. I want to talk about the natural way of life intended for human beings on Earth.

Your Times Are Shaping You

This planet was always intended to be a school, and therefore, as a teacher or even an administrator of the school, you might say the intention would be to create the ideal circumstances for learning. I realize you could study the history you know, much less observe life around you, and say, "What's so ideal about this?"

Well, part of the difficulty is, of course, that life has changed, and the original setup for Earth was much less complicated and had many more opportunities for learning and was quite a bit more benevolent. A reasonable person might say, "Well, walking around with saber-toothed tigers and dinosaurs doesn't sound very benevolent," but that is only if you accept the idea—the contemporary idea, you might say—that the present human being relates directly to the human being who was intended to be the ideal student in the ideal school.

I'm not saying there's anything wrong with you in your time, but rather that the times are shaping you rather than the school shaping you, as was intended. Still, if you understand the ideal, you may be able to adapt at times to some portion of it that you can utilize in your time. So don't assume this is a lecture. I'm not here to chastise you for creating what you have created in your times. Rather, I want to explain what was intended.

The original intention of this school was that human beings would be nomadic, not only for reasons such as moving with the seasons in order to experience a more benevolent state of life—such as moving out of the cold into the warm, moving from perhaps a dry place to a wet place, moving to a place where there was food or good hunting and so on. There is this, of course, but there is more.

Since in the early days of the school here on Earth, it was possible for people to communicate with less language than as you know it today. In your times today, you have not only many languages that people speak, but also many dialects, and even within those languages you find many complications of the language—perhaps technical language or literary language or even what you might call slang or popular forms of language. So things are very complicated in your time.

Even in My Time, People Were Very Receptive

In the past, the situation was much different. There was more of the intuitive, as you would call it, or feeling, as I would call it—a knowingness. This is not something that is intended to be vague, but it is something that you can, in fact, incorporate in your own time along the lines of instinct, which I've talked about extensively or you may have heard about from my student, Speaks of Many Truths. Now, in days gone by, then, it would be possible to walk around a saber-toothed tiger or a dinosaur, although Earth was not set up for the Explorer Race just then. But it would have been theoretically possible, because there would have been an acknowledgment of the value of being in all parties. If the saber-toothed tiger needed some distance and space, then you would give it that distance. If the tiger was not hungry, then you might be able to be a little closer. If the tiger felt safe, then perhaps a little closer yet.

The whole point here is that this was a time in which it was possible for all life forms to be considerably more receptive to other life forms, and therefore, in my time, even if we didn't have to move, sometimes we would move about just to experience life in other places, acknowledging the value of all life as we went along—not just in ceremonial ways, which I believe is a misinterpretation in your contemporary times of what Native Americans and other native peoples do. It was not just ceremonial, but rather there would always be people such as myself who could communicate with the animals and the plants and even other human beings who may not speak our language, utilizing feeling.

The whole thing about sign language developed as a result of Native Americans and other native peoples—you can adapt this to your country—interacting with Europeans and others who did not have a basic feeling and awareness for the simple needs of an individual. People need food, they need shelter, they need clothing—you understand, the basics. So if one would meet with others, or in the case of our tribe moving about, if we would meet individuals, the first thing we would do was to offer food or water or, if they were obviously cold, something to warm them up, something to wrap around their shoulders, you understand. This was an offering, and perhaps they would have something to offer in return, but if not, then all right.

The main point, what I'm trying to say here, is not to tell you how to live. What I'm trying to say is that even in my time—which was much later than the early days I spoke about before, using the animals for an example so you could recognize a time period—people were still very receptive. I'm trying to make that point clear to you. You understand what it feels like to be receptive, and you also understand what it feels like to give to somebody else who is receptive. But it is much more complicated in your time, and most of you feel overwhelmed by your society most of the time because it's so complicated. Therefore, you generally do not feel safe to be receptive unless you are in special situations or if you are very strong and self-assured for other reasons.

Using the Receptivity of the Left Hand

So let me continue on: Since people were encouraged in the ideal level to be nomadic, the reason was not only to meet others and to expand your experience—to know and to feel what can be offered and what can be received by all life forms one meets, be they plant or animal or human or even elements of Earth—but it was also important to experience that which was safe. By being receptive, one could feel something miles and miles away.

You might reasonably ask, "If you were just walking around as a tribe to find some place benevolent to settle or even sending out individuals to explore, how would you or they know where to go?" Well, for one thing, water and animals and even vegetation that is safe to eat can be smelled. If you have an attuned sense of smell, which we had in our times—since our senses were not assaulted by chemical vapors and so on and we weren't used to having to pinch our nose off except occasionally for the same reasons that exist in your time—then we could smell things at quite a distance. But even that had its limits.

So by being receptive—which is one of the foundational elements of instinctiveness—we could literally feel at a distance what was ahead. We could feel for water. Sometimes I have referred to this when teaching Robert [the channel] things of the shamanic and mystical world, such as "long touch," but it is not exactly long touch. Long touch is actually a form of very gentle contact, usually to the auric field of that which is touched, so there is no sense of sudden invasion. This must all be done very gently and respectfully if it is to be done in the way I believe is benevolent—and the way of benevolence is *the* way, from my point of view.

How would we know, then? How would the explorer or mystical man or woman know where was water, where was food, where was also that which might enlighten us, where was that which might be interesting and safe? After all, one might want to experience something new and interesting, but safety is also important. No matter how adventurous you might feel, there are others to consider, young and old and so on, when moving about.

So we would initially use our left hand, hold out our left hand—that is the feminine receptive hand as we believed. You cannot see me doing this, but if I were to describe it, I would hold out my left hand with the fingers somewhat spread apart—not stretching them apart, but just relaxed and straight ahead. Occasionally my hand would be turned with the fingers a little bit more toward my body, and other times my hand would be bent at the wrist (keeping my arm straight but bending at the wrist), turning my hand so that a portion of the palm—not fully bent back, but just a little bit of the palm—might be exposed to what was in front of me, keeping the arm straight in front of me (but slightly bent at the elbow was also acceptable).

What was being felt here was not being felt on the hand. Rather it was being felt in and near one's heart center—because the heart and the solar plexus function in the company of each other to alert an individual who is not only instinctual but knows what feels good to him or her as to what is safe and also what is needed in any given direction that he or she points the arm. So we would walk generally in that direction. That's how we would be able to find things, even if we had to move into unknown territory.

So this was something that people in the distant past knew how to do. After all, once you practice this for a while, you do not have to point your arm out, although sometimes you do it, especially if you're in an area that is completely unknown to you. You understand, I'm not talking about receiving whatever energy, whatever feeling of whatever is in front of you, you understand? I'm not talking about receiving it and pulling it into your heart or solar plexus, but almost like . . . this would be an example, a comparison in touching something:

Say you were going to touch something and say you were very tentative. You would touch it very lightly, or you might even, if it were an animal or a pet or somebody else's pet, perhaps a friend's pet, not exactly touch the cat or dog or horse, but you would reach out in the general direction—you have all done this perhaps—allowing the animal to smell your hand. When you do that, of course, you usually do it with your palm facing down and your fingers relaxed. This is usually seen. But another way to do it is to have your palm up. When you have your palm up and your fingers stretched out, a dog might find that a little less threatening. A human would certainly find that less threatening, and so would a dog. That's just a little note for you.

When reaching toward something, or even when you are used to this system, just simply using your heart and solar plexus area, you do not pull it into your body. Rather you simply touch it very lightly or you come close to touching it. This is how you are using, you might say, your energy body, which you sometimes call your auric field. When you are no longer using your arm, you are really stretching out your auric field from your heart and solar plexus, and to lesser degrees, from other parts of your body. You literally stretch it out. Do you know, utilizing that method, that you can stretch in an infinite distance?

Homework: Reach for the Moon

For some of you who wish to experiment with this, I will give you some homework. I want you to use your arm stretched out. Don't try to reach with your heart or solar plexus. Remember, in this case, I don't want you to pull something into your body and I want you to be safe, so I'm going to give you a slightly different way to do it. I want you to use your right arm and, in this case, aim your palm downward toward the ground. I'd like you to reach toward something that you know you've never felt, I think it's safe to say, and that's the Moon.

Now, you don't have to wait for the Moon to be full. Just be sure you're reaching toward a portion of the Moon that is lit up, only because you will feel safer reaching toward something that is illuminated. I do not mean this symbolically—you will simply feel safer reaching toward something you can see rather than something you cannot see, and I want you to feel safe and I want the Moon to feel safe.

I know you cannot physically touch it, but I'd like you to imagine and utilize a form of long touch. I'll tell you how to practice it: If you have a dog or cat (or if you don't, then use a wall or a chair, but not another person, never that), what I want you to do is to reach toward that animal, a beloved animal. It has to be your friend, someone who lives with you, you understand? Or if you prefer—and it would be much more convenient perhaps—just reach toward any object in the room. I would recommend something on the ceiling so it will not disturb other people. That's something you can even do lying in bed. What you do is you make certain you cannot actually physically touch the ceiling, but reaching with your right arm, you explore the contours of the ceiling. Perhaps there's a fan up there or perhaps it's just a flat ceiling.

You can imagine what it might feel like, but don't make this a mental thing. I want you to reach with your right arm and hand, and if you can, find something on the ceiling, even a corner of the ceiling as it touches the wall. Try to move your hand along the contours of it and see if you can notice a change in the energy. The whole point is not to feel something that is not obviously physical, but to feel something at a distance that is physical. Practice with that, because you'll be able to get a sense . . . it won't be like touching something physically and getting the full effect of that, but it will be utilizing your imagination (as Zoosh likes to call it, the divine part of the mind) and utilizing the capacity of touch (you've all touched things, you know what touching feels like) and also utilizing the potential for touching something or exploring something—you might say reflectively, yes, but also respectfully, at a distance.

So experiment like that first, and then when you are ready, go outside. Or if you are indoors and have to stay indoors for any reason, open a window or a door so you can have a direct line of sight to the Moon. Try to make sure there are no wires, electrical or telephone, between your line of sight and the Moon—or if you cannot see out of your eyes, have somebody else arrange you so that you can do this. Reach toward the Moon and see if you can touch it at a distance.

This is not exactly what we do when we feel at a distance to know that something is safe, but it is homework toward that end, and if you are reading this book, I am taking it on some degree of assumption (not completely though; I'm using something else) to know that you have enough interest in it, if you should care to do the homework. Someday, perhaps in pages like these, I will give you more information or perhaps even find another way to teach you—if not directly, then perhaps you will find a way to learn on your own about all the things you can do or learn to improve your life, even improve the lives of others, by learning how to use your instincts by understanding and applying your physical body's full capacities. This is but one.

Humans Are Born with the Desire to Be Nomadic

So we would walk about and become nomadic. Now, why do I say that this is meant for all of you? By being nomadic and walking, you necessarily have to experience things in a completely different way, especially if you are some place other than your home territory. I know things are complicated in your time, and I do not realistically expect you to just go walking anywhere you wish to walk without regard for personal safety or the laws and rules and conventions of your time and place of culture. I don't expect you to do that. But I would like you to consider, even think about, the value of being nomadic sometimes.

Now, you can explore. In your time, it's very popular all over the world to travel and to visit new places and meet new people. So you can see that traveling is something that is built into you as a desire. There are, of course, companies that propose to you to travel and companies that serve your travel needs and all of this, but these companies do not inspire the desire and the receptivity on your part to travel and to move about from place to place. You are born with this.

Anyone who has been around babies knows this for certain. The first thing babies want to do when they can start moving—and you know, you've seen them—is to kick in the crib. And when you see a baby kicking lying on her back in the crib or wherever you have the baby, maybe on the bed, it is kind of fun and amusing. But you don't necessarily make the connection, unless you are a parent or a grandparent, that that kicking motion is a lot more understandable if you turned the baby over. Of course, I'm not suggesting you do this for a real young baby, but when the baby is able to turn herself over on her own, she will perform that same motion that you simply call crawling. Babies are born with the desire to travel.

Human beings are literally born with the desire to be nomadic. This tells you that Creator—your guides and angels, yes, but Creator—has designed a place for you to learn by being nomadic, by experiencing cycles of time and change. By experiencing these things, you learn. So what I am saying for you is, not only am I supporting travel, but I am encouraging you that when you do travel, try to walk about, try to touch what is safe to touch. And if it is not safe to touch, in the case of an animal or a building . . . or perhaps you're interested in a boat and you'd love to be on it, but for one reason or another, you can't. You can try long touch at a distance. But don't try to touch the boat itself; try to touch its auric field. You might perhaps be able to . . . how many times have you climbed up to the top of a hill and wished you could climb further up, even to the top of a mountain? If you can't do that, then maybe you can imagine being on that mountain.

Creator Does Not Directly Connect with Your Mind

People in your time do not fully grasp how important the imagination is. It is not just a mental link to all that you might wish to do; it is the inspiration connection between the mind and . . . what? You think I'm going to say Creator, but I'm not going to say it that way. It is the mental inspiration, yes, the mental connection between your mind and your body, and from there to Creator.

Creator does not connect directly with your mind. That is why many of you want Creator—or God or whatever you wish to say Creator is by name—to speak to you, but Creator does not speak to your mind. However, anytime you wish to feel Creator, you can feel Creator in your own body by doing that heart-warmth, the love-heat/heart-warmth/physical-warmth [see Overview]. The fact that you can feel that warmth in your heart or solar plexus as instructed in these books and in the pages of the *Sedona Journal of Emergence!*, then you will know that you are feeling something that Creator has purposefully provided for you so that you can experience the link between you and Creator. So the inspiration goes: imagination to your body to Creator, like that. That is the easy way to be in touch with Creator, and it is the way Creator wishes to be in touch with you— through your physical feelings.

You Cannot Live on Earth without Nomads Being Here Also

I'm going to gloss over that for a moment, because I don't want to get you too far advanced in your homework before you're ready. But I am going to say before I move on to other things that in the past, many of you have read in the *Explorer Race* books and other magazine articles or even in the *Shining the Light* series perhaps, various beings who speak through this channel just reminding you of something that may have seemed a little vague, and that's that you cannot live on Earth without there being some nomadic peoples here actually practicing that form of being.

You cannot live, you cannot be here, without that desire to move around, because the human being was designed by Creator to want to travel. This you know from babies, yes? They want to travel: "Put me on the floor. I want to go, go, go!" And you know this from your own desires to travel very often or the desire to be free to move about, just as a youngster might feel when he desires to move out of his parents' house and get out on his own. You can all identify with this.

And yet to be nomadic is something that many of you cannot do or do not do for your own reasons, though you might experience a sampling of it by traveling when you can. Still, there are people amongst you who are nomadic in your time. In your Western culture, one finds people who have trailers or what are sometimes called caravans. People who live in those or who use other forms of campers or even tents will move about for the sheer pleasure of being nomadic, all right? And of course, there are peoples whom you identify as being nomadic, even in your time. It has not been easy for them to maintain their culture to move about, but they've made the effort. Two of the more well-known groups like this who move about as a general rule, though sometimes they will settle in a place for a time, are the Bedouin and the people you call Gypsies, though they might refer to themselves as Romany.

So you literally cannot exist on Earth without fairly large groups of people moving about on a regular basis. This does not, however, refer to people moving for the purpose of conquering, so I'm not referring to armies invading other countries, whatever their justification. That's not being nomadic, although it certainly applies certain principles that I've spoken about. I'm talking about people moving about for the sheer pleasure of it, for the sake of discovery, and also moving about sometimes simply because it's cold and they need to be someplace where it's warm and where the water isn't frozen so they can be comfortable and live better.

I'm mentioning these things today for this chapter because it grows somewhat out of the previous chapter and also because I want you to realize that things you might take for granted—meaning babies crawl and then they walk, stumbling about for a bit, and so on—these kinds of things you take for granted and don't necessarily think about, are based upon very specific purposes Creator has for you to learn the lessons you need to learn and desire to learn as the Explorer Race living on Earth.

Using Receptivity in Your Everyday Life

How can we use this in our lives in a small way? Obviously, every human needs to walk more just for health, since evidently we were designed to do that, but how can we use that to make our lives better?

That's why I tried to give that homework, because it's small. You have to remember that these books are kind of a primer. We're not trying to do things that are too advanced here, and yet the books, even at this level, are still much more advanced than many other things, such as teaching long touch, which requires me to somewhat regulate who reads the book. We can't have people touching things at a distance that are not intended to be touched by human beings, you understand? So essentially there will be certain checks involved here, but the homework was given as a way to begin.

I understand your question. You're saying, "Well, how can we fit this into our daily lives in order that it might perform a function that is useful?"

Or, "How can we conform to a function that's part of our body that we're ignoring?"

You will use walking, most of you, as a means to get from one point to another, and sometimes if you are with a good friend or a lover, you might walk a little slower—but, of course, you are enchanted with each other and you're not really noticing your surroundings too much, most of you. What I'm going to suggest is, either with another person or on your own, that you walk. Now, I recognize that I sound like I'm excluding families with children, but parents out there, you know it's all you can do to take care of your children and it's a little difficult to be highly receptive to other things, so do the best you can when you can.

The moment you see something (ideally in nature, but if you don't live in nature, you'll have to do the best you can) that is out of the ordinary in the world in which you live—and by that I mean where you spend most of your time, including your time of sleeping—that is as natural as it can be from, say, the plant world (let's keep it to the plant world for now), stop and look at it. Perhaps it will be a rosebush. If you're careful, you might even be able to lean over and smell it, but don't get too close—you don't want to capture a bee or find a thorn. But here's what to do:

Say it is a rosebush in your neighbor's yard. Perhaps your neighbor's not home, and maybe the dog is scampering about and doesn't look entirely friendly. Then apply what you've learned in this chapter. Reach out with your right hand. If the dog gets excited, reach out with your left hand first and open your palm. Allow the dog to see it. You don't necessarily have to move your hand close so the dog can smell it. The dog can smell at quite a distance; it doesn't have to come right up to you.

So you can use either your right hand or your left hand for this, in terms of interacting with plants. If you want to try your left hand, you can, or you can use your right hand—either one. Keep your palm down and try to use your first two fingers (I'm calling the thumb, "the thumb" here, so the first two fingers would be the two long fingers). With your hand relaxed and your palm down, reach toward that flower and follow the contours of the flower as you can see it from a distance. You won't, of course, be able to touch the flower, but you will be able to follow its contours, kind of making a pattern with your fingers in the air as you move around the contours.

When you do this at first, exploring something at a distance—even, for instance, a tree at a distance that you can't touch for some reason—exploring the contours . . . when you do this at first, I'm not saying to try and be highly receptive and touch it. But if there aren't people around and you feel safe, then do that. Be receptive, focused entirely, putting all of your attention—if it's safe, of course—on that flower or on the tree, as in my examples here, feeling its contours at a distance. After you do this a few times, you might find that you'll even catch a vague sense of fragrance.

Now, you know that the human being in your time does not necessarily smell things at a distance, though it can be done if the smell is strong enough. What I'm suggesting here is that you use long touch like this in concordance with your ability to smell something. That's why I'm aiming you toward plants, because they often have a nice fragrance, even trees.

So try to feel the contours at a distance, and if you can't get a sense of what it smells like while you are tracing the contours or touching it at a distance, using that homework—this is after you have done your homework with the ceiling and after you've done your homework with the Moon, so you have a little experience—then try to imagine what it smells like. Perhaps you've smelled roses before, so try to recall what a rose smells like. You see, what I'm doing here is giving you some training so that in time, by reading the pages of this book and by practical experience (reading is not enough), you might be able to utilize some of these skills—not only to find water when you need it, but even to find food when you need it.

Finding Which Direction Is Safe

You've been to picnics and to restaurants, and you know how food smells carry, but say you're out in the middle of the countryside and you need to find water or you need to know which direction is safe for you to walk in—maybe your car broke down. Maybe it's best to stay by the car, but sometimes it might feel safe to go up to a certain farmhouse.

Then I'm going to suggest that you extend your left arm—this after you've done all the other homework—and point it straight ahead, standing off by the side of the road so you're completely safe. Look down to see where you're putting your feet, then point your left hand straight ahead with your palm down, again with your hand open but relaxed. You can take your hand right now and open it and have it relaxed, and have an idea of what that's like—pointing your two fingers straight ahead. Point straight ahead and say out loud, "Is this a safe direction for me to move toward?"

This is also built on the heart-warmth, the love-heat. If you get warmth, then just take note that that's a safe direction. Then moving counterclockwise—always move counterclockwise—move your body . . . figure that the direction you started with is 12:00, whichever direction that might be. Moving counterclockwise, the next thing you do is move to 11:00 and pause for a moment while you're aiming your hand there. Then say, "Is this a safe direction for me to move?" You can drop your arm between motions from 12:00 to 11:00 and so on.

Try to remember what's safe. If you need to, you can tell somebody else or just try to recall. If you're not sure, do it again. Gradually move around the clock in the counterclockwise direction. I realize this is a little early for this homework, but I want to give you some practical applications. Don't do this homework if it feels uncomfortable to you. Only do this if you want to move forward and have done the other work, plus perhaps read the other books in the *Shamanic Secrets* series, which would be nice.

Shamanic Secrets for Material Mastery *and* Shamanic Secrets for Physical Mastery?

Yes. So then if you get an idea what direction is safe or even have pointed at the farmhouse and asked, "Is this a safe place for me to go?" if you get strong heat in your body, you'll know that's safe. If you get an uncomfortable feeling, then you'll know that's not safe for some reason. Don't jump to conclusions why it may not be safe. Just know that it's not for you to go in that direction at that time.

If you get no response at all, then just know that you can ask that question at another time or perhaps you could rephrase it. But for right now, just assume that you'll try another direction. Go around the dial, so to speak, moving counterclockwise, until you finish at 1:00, and make note of which directions you had the most heat in your body for. These directions might be something to explore, to move in.

Now, I'm not saying, "Do this." This is very advanced for a lot of you, but at times it might be particularly valuable. It could even be used, if well practiced, in a survival situation. I do not claim to be giving you life-and-death survival information here, but it is what I used in my time, and I have given the training to Robert. When I have given this training to Robert, he has used it at times to protect his safety, meaning to know which direction to go in, and also to protect the safety of others whom he was with, and it has worked.

So I'm not campaigning for you to try it; I'm just suggesting to you that in circumstances you're unsure of—I'm not talking about a battle zone, but if you're unsure—it might be something to try. And if you get good at it, if you find yourself in a battle zone—hopefully, you will not, but some of you who are reading this might be soldiers or police officers or others in such an environment—then you will get some idea of what direction might be safe, understanding that it may not always be safe. You just get the heat. If you get the discomfort in your body, you'll know it's not safe in that moment. That doesn't mean it's permanently not safe, but just in that moment. If you get no feeling, then simply continue to move around the dial, so to speak, until you find a direction that is safe. If you get an uncomfortable feeling in all directions, then wait.

So I'm not trying to suggest that you do this; I'm saying it's something you can experiment with. Now, how would you experiment with it— meaning what would you do if you had a day off? You might drive out to the countryside, maybe with a friend. You could take a picnic and what-have-you. Try not to photograph this kind of thing, okay? I'd rather have you experience it, not see someone else's experience of it and not share your experience of it with illustrations, even with photographs, because sometimes it's better to demonstrate by showing someone how you did it or recommending for them how to do it. In short, there needs to be some sort of personal touch here.

Still, I know you live in times where you like to capture images, but it's important for you to know that a captured image will always feel captured— meaning that there's a residual imprint of whatever is photographed that does not feel comfortable with the capture in that moment. That's why sometimes, even with your modern technologies, things are not permanent. Maybe what was captured in that photograph would prefer to be released. I know that sounds a bit fanciful to some of you, but we can explore it in a later chapter since the capturing of images is a very contemporary factor in your time.

So try this homework sometime by just going out on your day off, maybe. Just stop any place that's convenient, even in a park, if there aren't many people there, but ideally someplace where there aren't people around. And when you're moving around the dial, as I'm calling it, make a note of what's off in the distance. If there are people or animals in the distance, then skip that spot on the dial and go around to another spot. Also, make every effort not to point at something man-made, especially electrical wires or telephone wires or things like that, because that can throw you off. Generally speaking, if you point your arm and feel in your body toward something like that, even a communications tower, it will feel very bad, so try to avoid that. Don't point at an airplane in the sky or anything like that.

This Is a Practical Application of Your Instinctual Capabilities

Remember, this is something you are very gently sensing at a distance using your physical body, training yourself to learn how to use the applied instinctual capabilities that Creator has literally built into your body so that you can function also from your instinct as well as from your mind, in order to learn how to live better, safer and hopefully even happier or more fulfilled. So I'm exposing you to a little bit of that here so you will understand the practical applications of the heart-warmth, which is a portion of the instinctual work that I'm teaching.

So when you're out there, then, knowing that, point to those various things until you feel a sense of warmth. And then if the area is safe, walk just even a few steps in that direction. The moment the warmth stops in your body, stop and do that again, going around the dial, so to speak, noting which directions are warm. Then walk in that direction, always being careful to note where you're putting your feet so you don't step in any animal burrows or anthills or anything, recognizing that the feeling you feel, even in the safest place, is always heightened by all beings who live there.

This training will be kind of fun because you will be completely excused from accomplishing anything. You don't have to walk from point A to point B. You are literally learning how to walk by feel. If some of you want to improve the experience, you can also walk by putting the front of your foot down first rather than your heel. You will find that this is very similar to reaching toward something with your fingers rather than touching it, say, with your arm or your wrist. The front of your foot, with your toes and so on, is very sensitive, not unlike your fingers, and you will actually generally feel safer walking that way, putting your, let's say, "foot fingers" down first. You don't have to do that, but you can practice that if you like.

Just do that for a few turns—walk this way, walk that way for a short time—and then stop. Now, I know you asked for some simple things you can do, but as you can see, this is not simple, because even though Creator made it, built it into the physical bodies of human beings, in your time because of all the complications of life and instructions and "do it this way" and "don't do it that way" and all that, it has to be specifically explained to you. I can't approach you as if you were an uncomplicated person living in an uncomplicated life. I have to be very specific—especially since I am not standing there with each and every reader showing you how to do it. So I'm trying to be as clear as possible, given the circumstances.

Try that a few times, and you'll feel a greater sense of knowing which direction is safe. Eventually you will be able to walk along directions or generally in directions. You may have to walk around things that aren't safe to walk through, such as water or a drop-off on the side of a hill or buildings and so on. But you may generally be able to learn how to walk along feeling the warmth in your body to know which is a safe way to go—and when you get good at it, to even drive along that way, but I don't want you to push that.

Take the steps slow but sure, as I've given them in this chapter. I know that for some of you this is pretty advanced and for others it will be more of a review, but that's all right. It's good to review, and sometimes when you review something, you get good at it, noticing things that you have forgotten, and it makes you a better teacher if you like these things and want to pass them on to others.

Remember, I'm not trying to replace the means by which you know something is safe. I'm not trying to eliminate maps. I'm not trying to eliminate knowledge or wisdom. I'm trying to say, relearn something—and I say re-learn it, because you all learned it and knew it as babies. Relearn something you forgot in your complicated world so that you can have that instinct available to you for its many and multifaceted applications, many of which I will expose you to in the pages of this book and others which you can try yourself.

Even a simple application is to go over to your closet in the morning—or if you pick your clothes out in the evening, do this then—and simply reach your hand toward a garment and notice whether your body feels warm. Where you get the most warmth, then that might be the thing to wear. I recommend that you do this just before you get dressed, so doing it before you go to work is best because your body doesn't interact that way except for that which you are doing right then. Your instinct is immediate. It isn't about what's best for you to wear next year. It's better to use this as it's intended.

So say you're doing this just before you're getting dressed to go to work or a party or out on a date or something. Point or even reach over and feel the fabric of one thing at a time and ask, "Is this what's best for me to wear now?" Do you understand? You can even do that with your accessories, ladies, or men with their ties and so on. You may not always get something matching. If you're not comfortable with it, then do what you like, but it might be interesting to go out wearing what feels good to you in that way that is instinctual, utilizing the method Creator has provided for the human being—and I might add, has provided for all plants and animals as well, but human beings are here to learn. Utilizing that method that Creator has provided might actually simplify your life, because sometimes what you wear can not only be comfortable to you, but it might cause an action or a reaction in someone else that's either good for you to know or might bring about some kind of benevolent occurrence.

So I'm giving you that as something to know. That is another way you can practically apply the elements of touch at a distance and even contact—meaning touch by contact—using the heart-warmth to know what is in your physical instinct, what is the best for you to do in that moment. Perhaps that's a more direct answer to your question.

Nomads and the First Alignment

Knowing as we do now about the First Alignment [see Shining the Light VII, *chapter 44] and how business is going to take over and boundaries will tentatively vanish, will we be able to maintain and sustain the level of nomads needed in the next fifty years?*

Yes, I think so. But part of the reason I am mentioning this about nomads, meaning people who are culturally nomadic, is that if those people who are culturally nomadic decide for one reason or another to settle down, then I'm encouraging those of you who may be able to be nomadic. Perhaps you are retired or independent. Don't let other people tell you, "You shouldn't do this," or "You should do that."

If you are able to get in your camper or trailer and travel around and explore new places and so on, please do so. It will be a form of carrying on, not only the tradition of being nomadic, but of supporting and maintaining the cycle on Earth of . . . how can we say? Earth has cycles, but this is a physical illustration. The necessary honoring of the cycles of life in a human being—you are a baby, you are a young person, you are a mature person, you are an old person—you will honor the cycles by moving about as it was intended for human beings to be able to do. You can't always do it in your time, but this way you can.

Isn't the multinational corporation itself actually encouraging this almost nomadic movement, where people are sent to this country, that country, this office, this place?

No. That's not being nomadic. Simply being sent somewhere isn't being nomadic. Being nomadic is choosing to move on your own or being prompted by what is nature, meaning from the natural world—it is cold, you must move someplace where it is warm, like that. Or conversely, for people who are equipped for the cold weather, it is getting too warm and now they want to move someplace where it is cooler. That is acceptable, so it's more like that.

Using Your Instinct to Make Decisions

I am trying to provide certain practical applications of what Speaks of Many Truths has referred to in the past as "instinctual body work" but which I would prefer to call "the instinct"—because human beings in your times and in your cultures often think of instinct as something animals do. Sometimes they are even made fun of by other human beings when they say they are using their own instinct, and yet people who develop and sharpen their own instincts and utilize the tools that Creator has provided and that I try to share in some way in these pages . . . it might be possible to make decisions that you have already perhaps considered mentally or to support your mental decision or vice versa, as you say. You might be able to make decisions that are better for you in your life, and you might even be able to make some decisions about a wide variety of topics. But I'm giving a little bit of homework about that so you can get an idea of how it can be used.

One of the best ways to utilize it in the beginning of this training is to use your right or left arm and to point toward something—and perhaps, if it is a physical thing, move your hand around to feel the contours, or even if it is something printed, move your hand back and forth across the print, touching it or not touching it. Move your hand above it, perhaps, or just touching it, or something like that. You may not want to do this with something on a computer screen. If it's on a computer screen, you may be able to point to it, but your physical instinct will probably interact with the entire machine, not just what's printed on there. Whereas with a book or a magazine or something on paper, the symbolism will be clear. Still, you can experiment with it on a computer. It might work.

Your physical body will in time understand that this is a communication and just feel, "Is this something good for me?" or "Is this application good for me?" Maybe you are pointing to a day in your calendar: "Would this be a good day to go out with my girlfriend?" or "Would this be a good day to take my husband to dinner for our anniversary?"—this kind of thing. Point to it, and if you feel a lot of heat, then that's a good day. If you feel discomfort, then that's not a good day. Anytime you feel discomfort, immediately let it go. Just relax and let it go. If you feel heat and you're enjoying that, you can feel it as long as you like. If there's no feeling at all, then you can rephrase the question or ask it again at another time or point to another day in the calendar book.

Using Your Instinct for Reassurance Concerning Your Loved Ones

Do you see a time in our future as the Explorer Race on this planet where we will basically get back to that natural rhythm, that natural way of life?

You might be shocked by my answer, but you will also be reassured. No, it will not happen naturally, but it can happen if people such as the readers of this book find by applying some of these things in their lives that it actually feels good and that their lives are improved by applying them. Then you can tell people about it. You don't have to just say, "Go buy the book." You can tell them or show them how to do it, and if they want to know more, they can read the book or you can loan them your copy.

The main thing is that people won't get back to it just by some magical happenstance. They'll have to want to do it. And as you know, in your time if something feels good and if something good is accomplished by it and you can point to it and say, "Look. It felt good and there it is. It's good. It's adding to my life benevolently" . . . if you can say that, then it's pretty safe to say that with that physical evidence you would get, you can then say, "Well, this is good. It works for me, so I recommend it for others." You would not just be talking about something you read about, but rather you would be talking about something that is your personal experience for which you've had physical evidence in your physical body that it's good—in short, applying it, doing it.

Don't recommend it just on the basis of thinking about it. I try to give little things that are not overwhelming and also other things that require more time and that are a bit more involved so that you can do different parts. You can do this a little bit or you can do more, and you can even imagine certain things that you might try. But when using long touch, don't reach out and touch another human being. That is not safe to do. It's not safe for that other person; it's not safe for you.

If, however, you are concerned about another human being or worried about someone—I know that many times every parent has had that experience and very often every youngster will have that experience about his or her parents or brothers or sisters or favorite animals and so on—if you are concerned, then first picture in your own mind what that loved one looks like. Then say, "I'd like to see this person's face, so I know that she's okay." That's all. It may give you a response in your mind's eye, so to speak.

But this may not work for many of you, so the other thing you can do is to just—and this is the easiest—picture that person for a moment, then relax the picture from your mind so you're not seeing anything. Then go into your body and see if you can generate or feel the warmth in your body. When you have the warmth as much as you can, then for a moment—not for a long time, just briefly—picture the one you care about. If at any time during that picturing of that person, the heat fades or goes away or you feel uncomfortable, immediately stop picturing her.

The whole point is not to send that person your heat. You don't send out your heat. It is rather a way of creating an acknowledgment of value that you feel that warmth for that person. It doesn't have to be sexual, you understand. It's affection. Also, if that person is concerned about you—perhaps you are relatives or lovers separated from a distance or something—then if your loved one does that, feeling that heat and then picturing you, there will be in that moment of picturing—and you can share this with that person if she wants to learn—not only a sense of warmth, but briefly . . . that's why

368 ❖ SHAMANIC SECRETS FOR SPIRITUAL MASTERY

you have to briefly picture that person's face. You have to briefly do it so that you can maintain feeling the heat, because doing two things at once like this can be a bit challenging.

If both of you have done it within the same twenty-four- to thirty-six-hour period, you will not only feel the warmth and briefly picture her face and so on, but when you do it, you will also feel reassured. The reassurance will allow you to know that she has similar feelings for you. Don't use this to know that someone loves you or wants to make love with you, in the case of desiring someone; use it only for someone who is a relative or a family member or someone whom you love, or even a favorite cat or dog or horse.

If you feel the reassurance, then it's working. If you don't feel the reassurance, it may also be working, because it's not intended to be something you send. The heat is something that you do for yourself because it feels good, it connects you with Creator and it is a foundation of the instinctual training. But this being more advanced, especially if you're worried about someone, maybe your relatives in the old country, it can allow them, even if they don't know how to do the heart-warmth, they might, if they picture you—say there was an earthquake or something—feel reassured.

You can't always keep your friends and relatives and loved ones safe, since this is a planet where people come to learn and they don't come to experience a life of a thousand or fifteen hundred years like you might have on some other benevolent planet where it's benevolent all the time. But given that you can't always protect people, still they sometimes can feel reassured by knowing that you love them or care about them in this way.

Don't pick up a picture and go into the heart-warmth and look at the picture while you're feeling the warmth. I don't recommend that, because that is a captured image (and I will say more about that later in the book). Also, very often there are other things in pictures—plants, dogs, cats, fences, houses, trees—and all that affects the feeling of the picture, okay? Try to picture the person. If you have a picture nearby, before you do the heart-warmth, you can pick up the picture and look at it for a moment if you need to picture that person that way. But if you do this, before you go into the heart-warmth and picture her face, turn the picture over so you cannot see it and your eyes do not happen to alight upon it.

It's Time to Use Your Gift from Creator

So anyone who wants to follow this kind of life will be able to do it, but they'll have to choose it, sort of separate from the mainstream of the way life is going on this planet?

That's right, you have to choose it, but the advantage of choosing it is that you will know this is something you want to do because it has proven itself to be of value to you. It isn't just that Reveals the Mysteries told you that it is of value to you. I don't want you to accept my word. I want you to try it, and if it works for you, then do it *because* it works for you. If it doesn't work for you, then let it go. Assume it is meant for other people and there is something else that is meant for you, even in some other part of this book or in other books. But don't say, "Oh, it's bad."

Very often in your society, if one gets a bad feeling about something, the assumption is that if it felt bad then, it will always feel bad. But because I like to teach you about your feelings and what they mean and how to interpret them, you now have some tools that you can use to know whether something is good or good for you, meaning whether there's warmth—meaning whether there's love for you, yes, where it's appropriate (you can figure out "appropriate" from your mind), but whether it's love for you to do in that moment by using the heat, instead of saying, "Well, it felt bad once." Perhaps you can identify with this, many of you.

Perhaps you will have eaten something or overeaten at a certain time. Or let's say you had a hamburger once and the meat wasn't quite right and it made you feel bad, and you've been shy about eating hamburgers ever since. Well, what you can do now that you have the heart-warmth—perhaps you've dressed differently by pointing your finger at something or touching something in your closet and felt warmth or not warmth—is you could perhaps point at a hamburger. Maybe you're at a cookout at the office picnic or with friends or family, and hamburgers are being prepared. You can discreetly—you do not have to walk right over and point two inches from the hamburger—point at a distance to where the hamburgers are being prepared and say quietly to yourself, "Is this something good for me to eat?" And if you feel warmth, then you'll know that that's all right or that, generally speaking, hamburgers are safe for you now and you can try again.

It's very easy to get caught up in behaviors in your complicated society that might keep you shy about interacting with something because at one time you had an unpleasant experience with it. But this way you can at least discover that something may be all right for you at this time, because not only is that product (in the case of the hamburger) or that situation (in another case) different for you now, but *you* are different as well. You have grown, you have learned, you have experienced life, and perhaps you are wiser. And so it's time to use not only your mind to know whether something is good and safe and proper and so on, but also to use your physical body, your instinct, your gift from Creator.

The Moon, the Sun and Other Planetary Bodies

Speaks of Many Truths and Reveals the Mysteries
November 6, 2003

his is Speaks of Many Truths.

Your Feelings Are Being Stimulated

It is not widely know that as the Moon builds in light, it amplifies the feelings that any human being already has. You may not be able to interpret that feeling that you might be having all the time, but as it gets amplified, you experience the physical feeling more. That's why it's important to look at how urgent that feeling is and see if you can find out what it means—try to interpret it—because not only is the Moon doing this to your people, Earth people, at this time, but also, the more population you have (the more human beings, you understand), the greater the feelings each and every individual has in terms of how you feel them. So given a population on Earth as it was in my time, even with a full moon, there might be a significant amount of feeling.

But in *your* time there is the same physical mass—the same size of Earth, the same size of the Moon—and the same amount of light is generated or reflected, as you say, by the Moon. The Moon is the feminine energy that nurtures and supports feelings, yes, but with all the people on Earth, human beings also create little moons in themselves, amplifying feelings. You know how another human being can stimulate your own feelings. Just think of how many human beings you have and you can imagine how much more your feelings are being stimulated. That is why there is so much education in your times now and why it tends to cycle with the cycles of the Moon.

This is Reveals the Mysteries.

The Rise of Feminine Energy on Earth

In your time there has been some consensus that the seeming agitation of people is brought about by a population, by the complexity of society, perhaps even by agitations stimulated in society, such as in the television world and news events and so on. But there is something else.

For many years now, different beings have been talking about the rise of feminine energy on your planet, and although this delivers nurturance and support, it also delivers more of a need for an interaction between people. Now, the man knows that he is attracted to the woman, not just for love and companionship, but also for sexuality. That is interaction in the physical sense—in the intimate sense, you understand—and yet underneath that it demonstrates a profound feminine trait, and that is attraction.

So what we have here now in your times is an increased attraction of people to each other—not just sexually, although the size of your population might suggest otherwise, but also an attraction of people to each other to perform other factors of the feminine being. By this I mean that the feminine is known for creating peace, harmony. Who is it that calms the kids down when they're tearing around the house? Dad just gets upset, yells and shouts, in your Western societies, all right? But Mom calms them down: "Let's do this. Let's do that. What's going on? Okay, you do this and you do that," and so on. So I'm not talking about discipline here, but I'm talking about a desire for people to interact, resolve their differences, discover what they have in common and be able to create together on the same team.

I'm trying to put this in your contemporary terms. So what is it, aside from the contemporary understanding of the feminine, that delivers such a sense of urgency? As you know, for those of you who've read these books for a time, each of you is made up of Mother Earth's body and your own immortal personality—provided by Creator and supported by Creator to maintain a recognizable personality from life to life—and yet there is more.

Planetary Disturbances Affect You

One has to consider not only Mother Earth's body, but one has to consider what Mother Earth considers her family on the physical planetary level. For you a family might be your mother, your father, your grandmother, your grandfather, your brothers, your sisters, your cousins, your aunts, your uncles and so on—you understand completely. Earth also has this. You must remember that you are here on Earth as the Explorer Race to learn the lessons of Earth and what you can learn about in physical experience in the world of time, cycles and seasons. Given that, it produces quite a bit of variety and opportunity.

So the fact that you have family as you understand it is something that is a given to you all. You understand that. Mother Earth—you being a reflection of her personality besides Creator—also has family. To Mother Earth, family is the solar system in the immediate sense: the Sun, the Moon and the other planets and moons in the solar system. In the order of which there is predominant influence outside of Mother Earth, there is the Sun and the Moon, but still, the other planets and their predominant moons are also influential. We will have much more to say about this from various beings and perhaps myself as well in the forthcoming *Explorer Race and Astrology*, which you can read about if you wish. You can read that book to support what is being said in the understanding of Earth and her influence upon you.

Now, Mother Earth also welcomes a certain amount of variety in her family. You notice I said that the Sun and the Moon were the predominant factors outside of Earth herself. So you might reasonably say, "Well, then I assume that the planets closer to Earth must also be influential." And I would say, "Yes, this is true, but you do not really feel it that way."

It's like this: You grow up in your families and you take certain things for granted. If you have a brother and a sister, if you have your mom and dad, if you have your grandma or grandpa or other relatives who are what you might call fixed individuals whom you see frequently or all the time in your family, you adjust to their energies. The planets are like this and even the predominant moons are like this, but interestingly enough, it is the energies of that which passes through your families that sometimes startle and create changes. Maybe you or one of your brothers or sisters has a friend over when you're young, and this friend makes a big impact on the family. Or perhaps a long-lost cousin comes over, maybe with a family, and these people have a big impact, or there is some other such event.

It is the same with Mother Earth. You have heard perhaps from time to time of so-called meteors coming in, banging into this planet or that planet. I'm not talking about Earth in the distant past—you don't have to go back too far to find something that smacked into one of the planets. Of course, most of the time these things just pass through your solar system without hitting anything. After all, the distance between the planets is great, and it's not difficult for something to pass right through your solar system and keep on going. Also, things are . . . you see this in the night sky wherever you are, that things approach your Earth and burn up in the atmosphere, and they are coming from a long way off.

In this case, it is like the analogy of the family. Someone comes from a long way off or someone unexpected comes, and it changes things. Everybody reacts differently. They change their energy, and maybe it has a big effect. Perhaps this unexpected person is just passing by, or maybe he or she stops for a time. So the big influences in terms of what make changes are these things that pass through the solar system or even occasionally burn up in your atmosphere—occasionally in terms of all that passes through your solar system.

So there is that—those things affect you. But after that effect, things calm back down, and just like in a normal family, you get used to your brothers and sisters and mom and dad and so on again. Now, you might know, depending upon how you were raised, that if one is raised in a small family—say mom and dad and one or two kids . . . you say "kids," yes? Do you still use that term?

Yes.

So you might say that this can be a certain way, you feel a certain way. Often people who are raised like this might react differently when in crowds, all right? They might like it, or they might feel uncomfortable. I'm not going to go into all of that. I'm sure your psychologists and sociologists have a thorough understanding of that, and I'm not trying to say that one thing is better than the other. I'm just trying to create an analogy here so you can understand how your physical bodies react to something in an intimate situation, meaning in a family.

Now, it is quite different for people raised in large families. They might be used to certain situations, meaning lots of people—"people in your hair all the time," as you say. This might cause other actions and reactions when encountering people when you grow up—not necessarily good, not necessarily bad. This is just part of your personality, you understand? So the reason I'm bringing this up, what I'm saying here, is that depending upon what you are exposed to, sometimes the greater number can have a greater impact on you, either causing you to feel this way or that way based on your personality.

Your Responsibility Level Has Been Changed

Now, what's going on for you these days is that exposure to many things is making your life seemingly more complicated. And as you know, in recent years you've been told that it is your job to take over many of the functions of what Mother Earth has done for herself. There has been some support by human beings for that, taking over this and taking over that. What you may not have understood and what I'm going to expand on here a little bit is that it is not only that you might need to take over certain things that Mother Earth has been doing for you in the past, but also that you may have to understand that Mother Earth is more than you thought she was.

I think you are clear who Mother Earth is: a planet and so on, with her atmosphere, her auric field and so forth. But what I've been saying here is that Mother Earth does not consider herself to be that only. She considers herself to be her family, meaning the Sun, the Moon, the planets, their predominant moons and so on. So your responsibility level has been changed. Now you are expected—and really this has been coming in for the past sixteen to seventeen years of your time—to also provide for each other some (not all, of course) of the energy that is provided by the Moon, in the case of our talk today.

Now, given that and given that you've been told that the feminine energy is rising for some time now, this tells you that many of you have incorporated certain functions of the Moon. This doesn't mean that you walk around and glow at night, but it does mean that the Moon—which heightens and supports certain feminine qualities and characteristics in all human beings, be they male or female—has been incorporated initially in your physical body as what science would call a latent characteristic. This is because your body is made up of Mother Earth, yes, but Mother Earth considers her body to also include her family. Therefore, you are beginning to demonstrate certain characteristics of Mother Earth's family.

You Have Been Living in a State of Partial Confusion

Now let's get back to Speaks of Many Truths' original comments at the beginning of this chapter. Given your population, how many billions . . . and every single one of you, not just people who read New Age material or who like channeling. These things take place almost as if Mother Earth says, "Now," and you go forward and you begin doing them.

As Mother Earth releases certain characteristics that she not only provides but that her family provides, then these characteristics are still needed—these demonstrations, these applications, these literal physical effects. These characteristics are still needed by you and others on the Earth, and you as the Explorer Race and creators-in-training literally take them over. You don't always consciously know about it, but one of the purposes of these books is to alert you to these things so that you can understand more—not only about the way Mother Earth and the solar system literally function for your benefit to learn your lessons here, but also so that you can understand why *you* as an individual or other individuals you know or come into contact with are different, are behaving differently and are acting differently.

Many of you can remember back to a time—how many times have you heard this, eh?—"when life was simpler." Or even for people living in complex societies, "When you knew who you were and what you were supposed to do, and everyone else was like that too." Now many of you have been in a state of at least partial confusion for some time, yes? So it's important to know that there is more than one factor involved here.

The factor I'm talking about today—and I think this will startle you, reader—is that right now every human being on Earth, including the very young and the very old and everyone in between, is currently demonstrating (meaning performing the function of, in terms of the Moon's actual qualities that she provides you with that you are demonstrating) 17 percent of those qualities themselves. If you factor in how many people are living on Earth right now, is it any wonder that your feelings are sometimes—how can we say?—as the kids say, "in your face"? So there you have the basic situation.

Use Rhythmic Motion to Calm Yourself

I want to give you something you can do to create a calmer situation for yourself. I'll give you a couple of variances. For those of you who are physically active, try to get a little more physically active—meaning that one of the best ways to calm yourself, if you are feeling your feelings more than is comfortable (meaning that you feel agitated), is to do something physical and rhythmic. I think that's why you find in recent years that running has become so popular as a sport or even walking—some people do a form of racing with walking.

But I'll tell you something: One of the things that's even better than running is swimming. For one thing, you are in water, and that's a feminine, nurturing substance—it flows, is adaptable and so on. Also it requires, as any swimmer knows, very precise functions—meaning that you are swimming and you have to raise your head to breathe in certain ways. For some people, this is not the best because they may not be coordinated in that way. But let's just say that one of the best ways to nurture and calm that excessive feeling in your body, which you are literally transmitting . . . this will calm the feeling, but how will it calm it? It will calm it because when you do something like this, this physical activity, the rhythmic part is what calms you, but the physical part, the exertion, allows that energy to flow out of you.

Now, not everybody can do that. Those who run, they also do the same thing. It may not be as ideal as swimming, but it is helpful. There are other activities that you can imagine, but it is important that they be rhythmic, meaning repetitious, and that they be physical. But for some of you, you cannot do that. Perhaps you are not as physically fit as you maybe once were, perhaps you've never really had that opportunity or perhaps you are limited in your range of motion for one reason or another.

Then the thing to do is to develop some kind of action where you can even, for those of you who cannot stand or walk, perhaps move your arms back and forth. I'm doing something here that you can't really see, but I'm going to try to demonstrate it: As one might sit, you could take your arm and bend it at the elbow and put your hand palm downward. Simply move your hand, not with violence, but with vigor out to the point where your elbow is straight.

The reason I suggest having your palm down is that this allows you to interact, for someone who's sitting, not only with your own physical body . . . because you get your palm up, your hand up, near your solar plexus but you don't actually touch your physical body, and by thrusting your hand out, you tend to encourage your physical energy to flow out. It's very important to remember while you thrust your hand out to the point where your elbow is straight or almost straight, that when you bring your hand back . . . it is vitally important to understand that you bring your hand back very slowly and gently so that your physical body does not react as if a blow is coming its way. But when you thrust your hand out, that is done quickly.

This is something even for people who are physically fit but are stuck behind a desk at work or something. You can do this with one arm even when you're on the phone with somebody and thinking. Sometimes it's a wonderful way to get rid of tension, the type of tension that might very easily develop in the workplace. Remember, you can do this with either hand, either arm, and it will let go of a lot of tension. But more importantly, don't forget to move your hand back toward your solar plexus very slowly and gently, and to send it out quickly—not quite as if you're going to hit something, but very quickly—and then stop it.

What this does is that it not only feels better doing that a few times . . . you don't have to do it fifty times and the next day sixty times. It's not exercise so much. What it does is that it tends to encourage that extra feeling that creates tension in your physical body—which will usually, initially, be felt in your solar plexus and in your lower chest, toward the middle there—it will encourage it to flow out. So it not only decreases your tension in that moment, but it will tend to encourage your energy to flow out. By your energy, I mean your excess energy that is building up in you because you are taking over some of the functions of the Moon.

Now, for the Moon . . . the Moon is reflective, and in that way, that's how the Moon can function and release—or you might say scientifically, reflect—that energy. But the Moon has her own characteristics, and they are designed to nurture and so on as I've discussed in this chapter. So for you, as a human being, you cannot perform like the Moon. You are not planetary bodies, so to speak, but you can learn how to allow that energy to flow out.

Once you do that . . . and from time to time, you can continue to do this thing with the arm. Obviously, for people who swim or run, that will happen naturally. But for people who don't, you can do this, and even if you're physically fit, you can do that thing I described sitting down or standing up, whatever you like. It will teach your physical body that it is all right for that excess energy that is built up in there and feels like tension, it is all right for that to flow out. So it's kind of a way of showing your physical body what it needs to do. It's something that sounds very simple, but for many of you, it will make a profound difference in letting go of that excess tension.

Since you are performing these functions of the Moon, you might say, "Well, if it's 17 percent now, is it going to get greater?" (I'm anticipating your questions.) And yes, it will. It will get to the point where it's about

20 to 22 percent, meaning it will increase, but it will not increase now. Now it is about as much as most people can handle, and that is why you need this information. I think I've described it pretty well.

Your Physical Body's Language Is Physicality

Can you use either hand in this exercise?

Either hand. Whatever feels good to you at that time.

But only one at a time.

That's right, and always moving gently back toward your body so your body doesn't react as if it's being attacked. When your body feels attacked, it tends to hold on, you see? We want this to perform the function of giving your body permission and to demonstrate a motion outward of energy that it would normally . . . your feeling energy would normally hold on to that for you in order for you to process it or for you to have extra energy. But if you only do this, you understand, if you're feeling extra energy, like a tension, which many of you feel, then when you do that, you will demonstrate physically to your body.

Remember, your physical body's language is physicality. You can't just talk and say, "Do this." You have to be physical. It will demonstrate physically to your physical body what is acceptable to do. So you're not exactly throwing the tension off with your arm. You're literally giving your physical body permission to release that tension, and you will know that the tension is beginning to release as it begins to calm in your body a bit.

For those of you who are in agitated situations at work, you may not be able to do this in front of other people, but you could perhaps excuse yourself on your break and maybe go outside or into the bathroom and do it a bit, and then you'll relax a bit, okay? Try it there, and also try it at home— there are plenty of tensions there. But it's not about tensions in your normal environment so much, all right? That's just when you become aware of it. It's more about this job you're taking over for the Moon.

You brought the hand back to the solar plexus. So do we assume that that excess energy is in the solar plexus?

It starts there. That's where you tend to take your world in, and that's the part of your body that alerts you that something needs to be done: you need to do something, you've reacted to something, you have a gut feeling. In short, I'm not talking about something that is deep inside your body, but rather it feels like it's on the surface, a tension right there in your solar plexus. You can almost feel it. It's like excessive.

How many people have felt that and said, "Something's going to happen," but then nothing apparently happens, but maybe something happened on the other side of the Earth that you didn't know about? But if that feeling is uncomfortable, this is what you can do. I'm not saying if the feeling is comfortable or you don't mind the feeling, do it. Only do it if it's uncomfortable and you need to let go of it. If you need to have a better sense of how many times to do it with your arm in that thrusting motion, I'd say surely no more than ten or twenty times for most people.

All of Mother Earth's Qualities and Abilities Are Latent within You

So is that energy flowing in from the Moon? Is the Moon radiating more energy?

No. Remember, if you are taking over the duties of the Moon, just like you're taking over some duties of the Earth, then it's not that the Moon is broadcasting more energy to you. It's that you are literally taking over some of the duties of the Moon. In this case, it's to nurture and support feelings, all right?

You said this was latent within us—so then is the energy coming from within us?

What's latent within you is every function of Mother Earth that has been spoken about before—all of her qualities and abilities. And what hasn't been spoken about so much is her family as she might consider it. Of course, to a planet, the whole universe is her family. But in terms of what affects you and why you are here in this physical location, it is to be on Mother Earth by what she can do for you and with you, and now to also begin to assimilate in your latent qualities, meaning your physical bodies made up of Mother Earth's body.

As far as Mother Earth is concerned, she is influenced by, supported by, nurtured by and interacts with her physical planetary family, which is the solar system as you know it. Therefore, if you are taking over some of the duties of Mother Earth, at least in a small way, you might reasonably be expected to take over some of the duties of her family members. So the Moon is not radiating any *more* to you. It's that you are taking over some of these qualities in order to learn your lessons as the Explorer Race and creators-in-training.

The reason there is an excess of tension is that there are so many of you living on Earth now. We received this training in my time, not because it was necessary, but simply because there were times we would work with people where the Moon energy, the feminine energy, would be helpful, and we therefore learned how to interact with the Moon, how to do much of what you're sort of finding yourself having to do in your time for beneficial reasons. It's latent within you now, you understand, because your body is made up of Mother Earth's body and these capacities are part of what Mother Earth might refer to as her family obligations.

Mother Earth interacts with her solar system, as you call it, she interacts with her family, just as you might interact with your own family. How many of you have had family obligations come up before? But now you are here to learn not only about interacting with your own families but going beyond that. That's why many of you . . . well, you have friends overseas and interact with them, maybe even go to visit with them. This was not typical in my time. And you might have other situations, like global trade, yes? You interact with others on another shore, even if you don't know them, because they provide a product or service that you use and so on—all businesses know about that. That wasn't the case in my time either.

The Moon Has Personality Characteristics

Could you say that we're generating this energy, then?

Let's just say that the energy exists, since you have cycles of the Sun and the Moon. That's very close, but I'm splitting the hair because I want to be as accurate as possible. I'd say that you have within you—and this might cause many of you to think considerably—all capacities of what Mother Earth can do and all capacities of what her family can do. I don't want to be unfair to your question. I'd say that at least partly what you said is true, and yet it can't be entirely true because you are not generating all functions of the Moon. You are just literally taking over some.

A little bit. Well, a lot of the energy the Moon radiates comes from the Sun that she reflects.

That is the scientific understanding. Just because it is the scientific understanding . . . I do not feel obliged to support science exclusively. Although science might say that this is the case, you can also understand in your own family, when your youngsters are outside or a beloved family member is with you or a friend, if the Sun is shining on that person, he or she might appear differently than at night when the Sun is not out, yes? But that does not mean that his or her personality does not exist, that he or she does not exist as a being, you understand? So science might say, "Well, the Moon shines because the Sun reflects . . ." and all of that stuff. I'm not saying that's untrue. What I'm saying is, yes, that's true, but that does not alter the Moon's personality.

So the Moon has a function and she has a personality, and she imparts nurturance and the characteristics I've discussed to some degree here. And the fact that your attention is drawn to the Moon is something that is provided by the Sun. After all, if the Moon, for one reason or another, did not reflect that light at night and did not emanate as a result of her characteristics in a more noticeable way, especially to draw your attention to look at the Moon—"Ah, beautiful Moon," and so on—then you may not perhaps be feeling as influenced by the Moon.

For example, for those of you who can feel energies, you probably know that if you look at the Moon—not stare at it, but if you look at it—and just breathe in and out a couple of times, you will very often feel calmer when she is showing light. I don't recommend doing this unless the Moon is at least, as you say, half full or greater. If the Moon is full or even a day or two before the full moon or a day or two after, I don't recommend taking in even a full breath looking at the Moon, because it will heighten the Moon characteristics in your own body, and you've already got that quite a bit. In our time we might do it differently, but I'm adapting this to your time.

So as I was saying, the Moon has personality characteristics, but the Sun provides a means of noticing them and perhaps creating greater attraction. You look at the Moon, and that makes a difference. I might add that a person can look at the Moon, even if he or she cannot see, and still have this experience, so I do not want to rule out those of you who cannot see or who perhaps cannot see well. You can still interact with the Moon. Someone might say, "Well, turn your head like this. Now your face is toward the Moon."

All This Will Help You Reintegrate into Your Complete Selves

So this sixteen or seventeen years that this has been happening coincides with everything pretty much that's happened concerning the discussion of the rise of the feminine energy?

That's right. And you know, it does, as the philosophy teachers say, beg the question. You might reasonably say or think out there, reader, "Well, if that's going on with the Moon, then are we going to take on the Sun's characteristics? Are we going to take on characteristics of the other planets?" Yes, in time. And all of these things will help you to become more balanced in your whole personality.

Many of you have said—and I can identify with this, having been human myself on Earth—how you would like to feel your complete being, not just be separated from your being. One of the simplest ways to do this, beyond the unconscious experience at the deep-sleep level, is to coordinate with certain instructions—such as I'm talking about with the arm motion and so on—and come to balance in the feelings in your body and in your senses. Certain senses will be heightened in the future . . . let's just say that certain senses will be heightened in more noticeable ways in the future that everyone will really comment on.

This will have a lot to do with you beginning to take over up to a point—or slowly taking over in some cases—the energies and so on provided by other parts of Mother Earth's family. All of these things will support you very gradually, in the physical state as the human-Earth physical family, in incorporating greater portions of your natural personality and capabilities that exist beyond this physical plane as you know it on Earth. But it will happen within the context of living on Earth, of being an Earth person, of having the experience of an Earth person on Earth in your time and also demonstrating the capacity and wisdom and necessity, of course, to live in time and distance, so to speak—to live in sequential moments with consequences.

So then what you are experiencing now, you might reasonably assume, is that you are being reintegrated into your complete selves while existing on Earth as you know it. Of course, this will happen over time, and this tells you that, of course, some of you will pass on during this time and you will not require the gradual reintegration. When you pass on, you will pass through what is sometimes referred to as the veils and so on, and you will simply be reintegrated with your normal, complete personality. But as new generations are born and as time goes on and so on, you as the Earth-human family—meaning one total group—will gradually begin to reintegrate consciously, as you exist on Earth, this form of your complete selves. I think that is good news, wouldn't you say?

That's wonderful. I've never heard it explained like that.

It's important to not interfere with what you, as the Explorer Race, are here to do, but at the same time, it's also important to say that you have done a lot of it and "Let's"—meaning everybody together—"use what we've learned"—speaking somewhat as the Earth-human family here— "and apply what we've learned to our reunification of our total personalities as we exist elsewhere and with other lives and other existences with Creator and so on. Let's use what we know and re-create that here in this environment. And while we do that, we will be able to discover not only what applies with wisdom and what works, but also we will be able to perhaps pass on what works in a larger sense to our total personalities that exist beyond this planet, as well as that part of our personalities that is here, thus bringing out within our total being a greater perspective applied in the practical testing ground of Earth as we know it."

Don't Send the Tension Out to Anyone

When you move the energy out because you have too much, what are the effects of that on other people?

The nice thing is that you feel it as tension, and that's because it's energy that needs to be elsewhere. When you thrust it out, never thrust it. When you're thrusting your arm out, try to make sure that your arm does not terminate—meaning at the end of the motion outward—pointing at someone, even an animal. That will be easy to do; that won't be hard. If you're in a crowded place, just have the thrust terminate upward. It doesn't have to be straight up, as in a salute, but upward to a degree so it would arc over the heads of the people, you understand?

The main thing is that the energy will not harm others; it will simply broadcast out of your body. After a while you'll discover that when this tension comes up, you will no longer have to do this motion with your arm because your body will have learned that the tension—meaning that excess of energy that is intended to be broadcast the way the Moon broadcasts it—will just automatically broadcast. So that will work. If there is ever that kind of tension again, you will know what to do because you can make those motions of your arm. And if you find in doing that that the tension does not broadcast, does not release, and you do not relax a little bit, then the tension is something for you personally—meaning you need to perform some action or activity in your own life to change, to do things differently than you are doing them and so on.

I'm not saying that this is the cause of all tension, but rather that for many people, it is the cause of excessive tension. Yet tension is also a function physically to support action of some sort or even a changing of the way you do things. You understand this because many of you have felt tension and then you perhaps began to do something differently and the tension went away. It's like, "Oh!" It was an "Oh!" experience, yes?

But still, as you move that energy out, does it have an effect on other people?

As I said, it does not do that because the energy needs to be elsewhere. It will find where it needs to be on its own. That's why the point is that we do not want to direct it toward anyone. It will simply go out and find its own place. So that is not something you need to worry about, nor is it good to send it to anyone. It will simply go out and find its own way.

Astrology Gives the Soul Physical Markers for Its Time on Earth

I think for the first time someone has explained how astrology works. If all the qualities of all of the planets are latent within us, then as the planets move and certain energies interact with us, it activates something within us, correct?

Let me just say this: Astrology, being a gift to humankind, helps you to know and understand your personality as you were born in order that you might serve the purpose for your soul having come here—which you might reasonably do throughout your life—and then just build on that. It's like your soul says, "Well, I'd like to do this and this and this, and that's life. I know I may not be able to do it all or complete it all, but I'd like at least to begin. And given that beginning, perhaps I can build on it as I experience other things, other places, other lives and so on." And so in order to do that in a physical world, you need to have, one might say, physical markers that will heighten the potential for learning, gaining, growing, applying and so on—all of those potential characteristics and possibilities. That is why a person might be born at a certain moment.

I might add as an aside here (and this is something that has puzzled midwives and doctors for years) why some women will give birth, go through labor, fairly quickly. I'm not just talking about a woman who's had a child before and in the births that come after that—especially if the mother does not wait too long—the labor is not quite as long. But why in other cases does that baby seem to hold on before he or she is born? The baby is a soul and has quite a bit of wisdom of the soul and connection to Creator and all wisdom before he or she is born. So the baby says, not as a thoughts but as a soul: "This is what I want to be and do in this life up to a point. I want to have these opportunities, and in order to do that, I need to be emerging from mother into the physical world at exactly this moment, because the physical expression of Mother Earth and her family at this moment will heighten my opportunities to have the experiences that will support my learning, growing, changing and so on in this life at that exact moment."

That is why sometimes labor lasts a little longer. I'm not talking about it lasting twenty-five hours instead of fourteen hours. I'm saying that it might last, say, an extra twenty to forty minutes. That's why sometimes doctors or midwives in the past—especially midwives, I think, know this better—and some of your physicians who've had maybe many, many births and perhaps have some "midwife" understanding, do not always say, "Push." You know, "push" isn't the answer to everything. Sometimes it's, "Well, wait."

A midwife will usually, especially if she's been doing it a long time and has been trained carefully, from my point of view, in this sacred matter—meaning understanding the energy of Earth, the energy of the human being, the energy of the moment and the energy of circumstance—be able to say, "Wait," and then pause until she, the midwife, feels that the moment is just right. Then she will say, "Push." I'm bringing this up now, not to wander too far from the topic, but to prompt doctors to consider that expediency, while it has its place in medicine, is not always the answer.

Family Is More Immediate on Earth

I have one more statement. You said that each person has his or her personality created by the Creator. I don't agree with that. Our immortal personalities existed before this Creator as discussed in the previous Explorer Race *books, correct?*

Yes, but I'm trying to talk within a specific context. You understand, the people who are reading the *Shamanic Secrets* books may not have read that other material. There's a tendency to assume that one reads the *Explorer Race* books and then one reads the *Shamanic Secrets* books. This kind of sequence is not necessarily true. Quite a few of the readers who find the *Shamanic Secrets* books appealing will not read the other *Explorer Race* books.

I know, but I feel I have to always build on what went before or I'm not doing my job.

You're right. So this is my answer to your question: My answer is that while what you are saying is true, Melody, it is my intention to explain life to the readers of this book within the context of Earth and this solar system, the energies that you yourself interact with, the creation of this universe by Creator and what you are doing here for your purposes here. But I do not disagree with what you are saying.

Okay, that's good. That will make it simple for the people who just read these books, but it will allow the others to feel like they're not being left out.

Not only that, I would recommend at this point that when you ask that question, you say, "This question is based upon previous *Explorer Race* books."

So just as we're doing this now for the Moon, latencies within us will connect with other planets in the solar system, and whatever their function to us is, we will help with some of that, right?

You've already begun to express some functions of other parts of Mother Earth's family beyond her physical self, but it is too soon to begin to discuss that because those functions are not affecting your daily lives. I will discuss only the Moon here for this book, because that is something you are all feeling now and it requires action so that you can feel better and so that you can in time begin to fulfill your capabilities of certain latent characteristics that you are born with, as Creator has placed you here on Earth to learn and to function and to ultimately feel more fulfilled. I will discuss these matters, however, as they become more of a noticeable daily event. That's why I gave a marker before in this chapter, so that you might notice when some of these things begin to happen, because you will notice it through physical things.

So I will finish up in some way. Now that you understand that the Moon and other planetary bodies are Mother Earth's family, you might consider what I've said in this chapter about the Moon and families in general in a different light. What I was talking about with the Moon and what you are doing with the Moon is real, and yet it might prompt you to take another look at your own family, to overlay your own family over the map of Mother Earth's welcoming of her family.

The fact that you have families, as you understand them, is a direct effect of you being here on Earth. When you were on other planets living there, family was important, but you were much clearer that your neighbors and even people on the other side of the planet where you were living were also family. But here family is more immediate because of time, space, touch and other qualities that you know and understand as being part of your Earth life.

The intention of this book is to help you to understand how to live more benevolently on Earth for the sake of yourselves, your family, your friends, and for Earth itself. It is also intended to help you to expand your context of family in a practical way that feels good to you and others. So while this chapter ought to be taken literally, I want you to also consider its symbolic meaning to you as well. Good life and good night.

Let Go of the Complexities of Your World

Grandmother
November 7, 2003

I am Grandmother. I am often involved in the teaching of shamanic peoples, especially women. That's who I am.

Reveals the Mysteries talked yesterday about humans taking on the functions of Mother Earth in relation to the Moon, and I thought it would be wonderful if you could comment on that from your point of view, since it was particularly the feminine energy that was being activated in all humans, male and female.

Females Will Feel the Body More

The noticeable point for women is that regardless of your culture and regardless of what information you take in or are exposed to, you will actually feel your body more. Not from the outside in, but your body will be more—how can we say?—not so much sensitive, but you will be more aware of your physical body. If you have discomforts, you might be aware of those, if there is something you can do about it. If it is a long-term discomfort and you can't do any more about it than you're already doing, then you won't notice it anymore. It is not a burden so much, but it is something that may require some action on a woman's part.

What I'm referring to for women are feelings; I'm not talking about disease or anything. What I'm talking about is that sometimes, because of the way a woman has been raised or treated, she may not feel that it is safe or that she has permission to say something or do something that would be feminine—nurturing, comforting, friendly, loving or whatever like that, according to the relationship you have with someone. If you have those feelings that you not only would like to do, but more to the point, if they are being prompted by others around you and you know that they want you to do this but for some reason either you are not doing it or they are of two minds—they want you to do it, but for some reason in their training or culture, they do and they don't—then you will have those feelings stronger.

Males Will Experience Contradictions with Their Wants and Needs

For the male, he will experience things that are personally contradictory—meaning that he will feel that he wants and needs. That's the number-one—just that he wants and needs. Whatever the male is normally receiving, he will want and need more of it, usually because the male is substituting something for what he really needs because of your Western cultures and some Eastern ones as well for the male.

Most males on Earth in your time now—not all, but most—are in a contradictory situation within themselves. They want and need various things, but the way they were raised, they do not feel they have permission or it is not safe, very much like the feminine. That's what I spoke of before with the feminine. This is where that comes in.

Feelings Allow You to Feel More of Your Natural Way of Life

So what's going on for both males and females now is that you are feeling your feelings more strongly, and it might seem to be difficult, but there is a reward available. If you act on these feelings in a way that is benevolent (meaning it does not harm you, does not harm others), if you act on feelings like that, you will feel not only a sense of relief for having done something that makes you feel better—done something for yourself or others that makes them or you feel better—but you will also have a sort of euphoric feeling, a feeling that would remind some people of wonderful feelings they have had before for various reasons.

This is not "greater feeling" or "lesser feeling" by whatever the act is. It might simply be getting someone a cup of tea, something that simple. Or it could be rescuing somebody from an emergency situation. But besides the release of tension, the way you feel the euphoric feeling will be the same. And every time you do something like this, it will tend to last longer so that the feeling of euphoria—not complete euphoria, not so much that you cannot do anything else, but this wonderful feeling—will tend to last longer, well past the experience. The more of these things you do, the more this euphoric feeling will tend to begin to permeate your life.

It will require, however, eventually that when you feel to do something for others, that it is all right to ask them if they want it, not to just do it—unless it's someone you've lived with for forty years and have that unspoken communication with. Then just go ahead and do it if you feel that person's permission. But in the case of someone you do not know so well, if you ask and you feel that this person is receptive, then in my example, bring him the cup of tea. It's not a duty, but it will cause you to begin to feel that euphoric feeling more often.

I'll tell you why: This is a way that most people—you would say, souls or personalities—on other planets or in more benevolent diversions of this planet where there is no school going on . . . this is how people feel there all the time. This is because they do not have the training—or as you say, conditioning—that prevents you from doing things that are natural and helpful and benevolent for yourself and for others. They do not have training against that, so when they feel that somebody wants something, they just naturally provide it if they can and if it is no harm to themselves or others. So this is what's going on now in feelings. It's a form of training to allow you to feel more of your natural way of life.

Talk to Your Physical Body to Discover What to Do

Now, some people in some situations, war zones or urgency—the feeling of "Gotta get there, rush, rush"—you may not understand the feelings. You'll feel them, but you may not understand them. I will tell you the number-one confusion you will have about these feelings, and that is that if you are feeling a sense of urgency to "Go here, go there, quick, quick, do this, do that," for whatever reason, the feelings I'm talking about could add to that. They could make you feel like you're not getting wherever you have to go fast enough, because the way these feelings can be felt, if you are confused about them, is that they will give you the false message—in your mind only, not in your body—of urgency.

So that's where you will need to use your mind. If you are doing something for whatever urgent reason and you feel a greater sense of urgency, it may not really be necessarily required. It might even be, when you get to where you're going and you can slow down . . . if you can, stop, pull over to the side of the road or sit down if you're home and go into that feeling that feels tense. You can even touch, if you want to, that part of your body gently with your fingertips if you like, instead of your palm.

If you put your fingertips on that part of your body where you feel the tension—either the left hand or the right hand or both, whatever feels better—it might be possible to get a picture. Ask for a picture in your mind's eye of, not a symbol, but of something that would be good to do, either for yourself or for others. Say it just like that. And you might get a picture. Sometimes if you are being trained—meaning if you are a shamanic spiritual person or something like that—you might get a picture of something symbolic to do, meaning to move something from one place to another place that may not seem to have much purpose: for example, move the teapot from the stove to the table or something like that. It may not mean much to the average person, but it might mean something to the spiritual trainee.

But on the other hand, if you are not a spiritual trainee in the full-time sense, perhaps you will receive a picture of something you could do. Don't feel that it is an order. If it is not convenient or not possible, this is what you can do: You can say, "When I get the opportunity, I will do this thing for this person if I have permission from him or her and if I feel welcome to do this." Just say that out loud. What you're saying, you're talking to your physical body, and it's not about harming anyone or being harmed. You talk to your physical body—most people feel the tension in their intestines or abdomen, but some people will feel it in their legs and so on—and you have your fingertips touching that area. And then if you get the picture, that's what you say.

If you don't get a picture or if you're not sure, then this is what you say: You say, talking to your physical body—if you can, look at your body when you do this—"I am unclear what you want me to do, so please in my dreams tonight or the next time I sleep or in my inspiration"—which may come from spirit in some benevolent form of Creator—"prompt me what to do, either physically or with a feeling of what to do. And when you do this, if I have permission and it is a good thing for me and others, I promise I will do it." That's the key. You have to say, "I promise I will do it," because your physical body is trying to give you a message to do something that is going to be good for you or others or both. When you do something for others, in the larger sense—and by the larger sense, I do not mean philosophically, I mean in the larger *physical* sense—that is a good thing for you and everyone else, and you will also feel the benefits.

You Have a Physical Connection to the People of Earth

Now, what do I mean by the larger physical sense? You have been told over the years by many beings that you are all one—meaning everyone on Earth is all one being—and that really sounds philosophical. This does not mean that you are all of one mind or all of one heart. Although it might mean that and can be interpreted that way, it is much more physical than that. You know that you have fingers, toes, arms and legs, and you can say when considering your thumb or your toe that, "Something's going on with my thumb or with my toe," and that's some portion of you. Yet you are quite clear mentally that your finger or toe is part of your body. So even if it's a finger or toe, an arm or a leg, you, your body, are all one.

It is the same for all physical bodies of all people on Earth. You have a physical connection to these people as well. That is why in more enlightened, I would say, societies—meaning not smarter but just having an awareness that is beyond only mental, an awareness that is physical— everyone understands that if even one person is not feeling well, then everyone is not feeling as well as they could be. So everyone is devoted to helping this one person to feel better, not only for that person's sake, which is certainly a big part of it, but also because everyone will feel better, even if it is not something obvious. It might take the form that your dreams will be better or that you will have more endurance or anything like that.

But in your world today, it is not fully understood that you are all one physically. If some people are suffering somewhere for whatever reason, it would be beneficial to everyone to relieve their suffering and to try to serve their needs in some way that does not harm you, does not harm anyone else and is beneficial to them. You live in complicated times because you have lost touch with that, but you can begin.

The way to begin is in situations that come to your attention. Perhaps you are in a meeting and someone needs something and it is not going to cause you any harm and you can provide it. Then you do so, and you go on. You feel better, they feel better, and it's good. The easy way to do it is sometimes like that. Sometimes it is difficult to change life in a family, but if you want to and if you can, then you can begin where you are with the people all the time. But I would suggest that you try to begin in situations where you are not with the people all the time. That way people tend to accept you for exactly what you seem to be in that moment rather than keeping you tied to a long-time experience with you, even though you may not be what you once were in the past—such as a family might do with you.

Enlightenment Cannot Be Forced

I can see how this is going to lead to peace on Earth, because if we're only at 17 percent of this usage of our capacity now, when we get to higher percentages, we're going to be forced to deal with war and violence and starvation because we will feel it so much more, right?

But not forced. You have to remember that Creator and creation and all that is physical in this school—which is every person—cannot be forced. Enlightenment cannot be forced. You know that knowledge and wisdom are sometimes forced because of circumstances, and I realize you are saying, "Because of circumstances, this knowledge and wisdom will have to come about." But it is not that way, because even though it seems to be that way, it will not just continue to evolve toward the previously mentioned number, 25 percent.

It will pause and wait for you to demonstrate a physical action of some sort to acknowledge what is going on and to essentially give permission to the greater physical to allow this to take place—meaning it is not that you are being enticed, but rather it is as if something is being offered, and if you do nothing, then it will continue to be offered. But if you do something to show that you accept the offer, then it will move forward. Until then, it will continue to be offered. That is why individuals will tend to move forward with this on an individual basis.

It will continue to be offered, and certain individuals will go ahead because some individuals will accept the offer by performing some physical act—they will be inspired, will eventually get someone a cup of tea, to use the example—and, in doing so, follow their own feelings that were prompting them to do so, which would be benevolent, yes? So that would be the offer accepted, and then that point inside of you will expand more. And when it expands to a certain point, then other capabilities within you may begin to demonstrate themselves. But we are talking about one thing, and I'm not going to go ahead of that.

So we're almost being counterconditioned to move beyond our conditioning?

Your conditioning in the detrimental sense that holds you back is being released by you being reminded of your true nature. As you go forward doing these things, as they feel benevolent to you, you will begin to do what is natural to your overall personality beyond Earth only, and the other will just fall away. And you will in time literally forget the other training and conditioning, and will identify such training and conditioning as involving other people perhaps, but you won't personally claim it for yourself—meaning that conditioning you had as a youngster, for instance. You won't identify with it as yourself because you will have already moved on to this other, which is more your true self.

Excessive Mental Is Not Benevolent

So that's one aspect—paying attention to the urges and the desires you have to be benevolent toward others. Are there other aspects of this?

That is what I wish to keep it to, because if we make it too complex . . . complexity is perhaps one of the worst things in your society today. Generally speaking, life on other planets—and life in more benevolent places as well—is simple. It is uncomplicated, and that is why your little joke you make sometimes, where you say you go on automatic . . . "going on automatic" is a light joke, meaning functioning without thought, right? That's what it really means. That condition of functioning without thought when done benevolently is your typical situation on other planets. *You don't just function however it feels.* You have that ongoing. When you feel euphoria here, that is the normal way of feeling in these other benevolent places. And it does not require thought.

Thought is a tool that you use here to attempt to make sense of that which doesn't! Very often it becomes what some people call rationale, but other times it can just as equally become justification. This is where your society, by being too complex . . . that forces too much thought, which will ultimately if not immediately cause you to trip over justification and reinforce judgment and essentially stop growth, limit opportunities, narrow your focus and so on. One thing leads to another.

So you see how important it is. It is now the whole thing of complexity. Although it can be mentally exciting . . . you know you can be mentally excited while you overlook things you must do. How many times has the average person, the reader . . . how many times have you suddenly noticed you had to rush to the bathroom because you were thinking about something or doing something mental and you forgot that you had to honor the physical, or forgot that you had to eat, or forgot what you do with family or children or pets and so on. Now, if you have pets or children, they will remind you! But when it comes to yourself, physically, your body will remind you. If you don't understand the reminder, it will become stronger. This is how people sometimes develop discomforts.

So excessive mental, especially stimulated by complexity, is not benevolent. We do not find it on other planets or societies where benevolence is the natural course of events. It does not exist. But you find it in this society in your time now . . . because it is what? A substitute for what you really want and need.

Now, that's something I brought up before about men. Men very often are utilizing something as a substitute for what they really want and need. Women are not immune to this. They do it too, but a woman's body tends to have more reminders than a man's body of the cycles of life, because of a woman's natural cycles. Therefore, a woman is reminded of this, but she is not immune to these frailties.

Begin with yourself, what feels good, but try to be clear whether something is a substitute for what you really want and need or whether it is what you really want or need. You will know. How can you know? By how it feels. You will know because after you do something that is a substitute, you don't have that feeling of being fulfilled. Your desire for something doesn't fall away. The desire is still there. For example, some people will eat something and they will feel better, but there's still an underlying tension and there's no feeling of euphoria or relief, you understand. And whatever you were doing, you still continue to do. That is probably a substitute.

But if you do something that fulfills what your body really needs, even if it is something that must be done more than once—as in changing one's habits in some way—then what could happen is that you will notice that your craving for the substitute, whatever it is (a behavior, an activity, a consumable), will simply wane. It will not instantaneously disappear, but it will be much less and will continue to be much less until it is not present anymore. Then you will know that the thing you were doing was a substitute and the thing you have begun to do is the actual thing that serves the purpose and satisfies your body's needs and your spiritual needs as well. It's good to have those physical markers, because without that, it's just a philosophical debate in your mind, yes?

Find Your Commonalities with Other Beings

You have considered now that feelings are opportunities. Sometimes they are opportunities unfulfilled, but then they will return to be fulfilled in some way. Try to be clear that you are serving the actual feeling if you have a tension in your body. Ideally you could talk to that part of your body directly and say, "What is this tension about? Can I help you?" But not many of you can do that, so the thing you can do, as I said, is to put your fingers on that part of your body and ask for an inspiration or a dream, to know what to do. But there is more.

Sometimes it is not clear what to do, especially in your complex world, and generally speaking, what I advise you to do . . . and of course, you won't always be able to do it because sometimes you'll be at work and so on or serving the immediate needs of others. But when you are on your own, what I generally urge you to do is to do less. Try to educate yourself less about the complexities of the world and rather try to educate yourself more about what you as a human being have in common with the animals or in common with the plants or in common with other human beings.

This will reassure you, not just mentally, but more importantly it will reassure your physical body that you are welcome here, that you are at a place that welcomes you physically as well as spiritually and mentally and on the feeling level. It will reassure you that you are literally in a safe place, a place where you are surrounded with beings who are like you in many ways, even if they don't look like you or even if they walk on four legs or if they have flowers. When you can do that rather than continuing to educate yourself about complexities and contradictions, when you can be more clear physically about what you have in common with other people, plants, animals, even parts of Earth, you will begin to feel, not only safe on Earth in your body, but welcome. Now, that gives you a little homework.

Homework: Honor Where You Are Hurting

People watch television too much or watch the news, and the news, while being informative and in its own way enlightening, is something that ought to be consumed of in small doses—meaning, say, in a magazine. This is not to read everything—for the average person, you understand— but to read only those parts that feel good to you, or in the case of the news, just to watch the parts that not only feel good to you but, if it is something that is complex or difficult, that you can do something about.

But when people continue to educate themselves in complexities for which they cannot do anything about or for which they feel powerless, you just make yourself feel worse. Compound that times every time you do that. That's why people feel so unsafe and frightened all the time—not so much because of circumstances that you feel instinctively with your body and feelings all around you, but rather because of the compounded fear, agitation and complexity, which confuses.

So do people need to stop reading newspapers every day and magazines all the way through? What if they're addicted to it?

What I will recommend is to read those magazines and newspapers as a feeling being, not just as a mental being. Do you know how to do that? When you are sitting somewhere, not particularly doing anything, put your right or left hand on your stomach and just leave it there very gently—not judgmentally, but as one might hold something precious. That's it. When you are reading, if your stomach at any point starts to get tense and upset, stop reading that thing and go on to the next thing. It will be a struggle because your mind will want to know, but you have to remember that your mind is not aware of the damage it can cause physically to yourself and others.

When you get conditioned to hurting yourself, then it's awfully easy for you or anyone to hurt others completely unconsciously and not know it, because your normal feedback—that which tells you that you are hurting somebody else—you will immediately feel it in your stomach or some part of your body. But if your stomach is used to being ignored even though it's giving you messages of something you're doing that's causing harm to you, then it will constantly feel bad and you will not be able to discern the difference when it's an instinct message, which means there's no love for you to do this—you understand, the love-heat/heart-warmth/physical-warmth [see Overview]. You won't be able to discern because you always feel that feeling of "no love to do this." So then you have to begin to honor your stomach. Your stomach is often trying to tell you something.

When you are just sitting and not reading and not watching TV, sometimes there is a fear of not continuing to stimulate. That's why you mentioned the term "addiction." You understand that with people addicted to drugs, the drugs essentially stimulate one thing or another. Even if they are stimulating a relaxed state, this is a stimulation that would not have happened otherwise. So if you are using the mind constantly . . . it's not just that you understand your world, but if you are never just sitting and being with yourself, your body resents you. If your body resents your personality, you're not going to have much fun and you're going to miss almost all the messages your body can give you.

So this is, you understand, an extension of what I was talking about before in terms of complexity. In this case, then, what I recommend is that before you read, say, a newspaper, which in the case of a newspaper . . . a newspaper is different than a magazine because you might have a page in front of you and there will be many stories, you understand? This is what I want you to do. Keep a hand on your stomach at all times—not as a task, but as a reassurance. It is a physical language. Then glance quickly over the page. Do you know how you might glance over a page and notice a heading of an article and be interested? If you feel a tension in your stomach, don't read it.

So what I'm saying is, start listening to your body. Don't ask your body to produce words—it won't happen. Just notice feelings—and I've given you a way to practice noticing feelings by looking at the newspaper and noticing. See, your body will not only give you tension about something that it doesn't want to know more about, but it will, on the opposite side, give you a good feeling about something it *does* want to know about. Maybe it's something you are also mentally interested in, or maybe it's something you would never think of reading in a million years. Maybe it's the funny pages or something like that.

You know, Robbie [the channel] has had some of this training in the past, and I will give you something he does as an example. Sometimes when he is changing channels on the television, in the past he has, when changing channels, come across a cartoon station aimed just for children—not just cartoons of people falling off cliffs, none of that stuff, but maybe a cartoon on a public broadcast station where it's very benign and nurturing. Although he may not have any interest in this mentally whatsoever, his body will suddenly react with a good feeling, so he will watch it for a time, even though mentally he might be bored. He will watch it because his body feels nurtured by it.

So you see, if your body is being nurtured by something, you know you need nurturing. Sometimes it's not clear what nurturing is. Sometimes what you think is nurturing is actually a substitute. The only way to know what is nurturing in that moment is what your body tells you, and it will tell you through physical feeling. So when you're looking through the newspaper or a magazine, if you suddenly get a warm feeling, then just point to different articles on that page, or you may have to turn a page back and point, if it's something you haven't read and if you get that feeling or a little more—you understand, some good feeling. Then read that, even if it might mentally bore you. It might, as I say, be something silly, but your body needs that to be nurtured in that moment.

The Mind Is Cut Off from How Your Body Feels

It's a little hard to understand the body being nurtured by something the mind doesn't like.

But you see, the mind may be bored by it, not because it doesn't actually like it, but because the mind will have been exposed to it before. Now, you understand, in this way the mind is very much like Creator, and that's why in your time there is the tendency to hold the mind up above all else. The mind has one of the same problems that Creator has, and that's that the mind is cut off from how your body feels.

That's how people can invent things that are only destructive—atomic bombs, germ warfare—because the solving of it, getting to the solution, is so mentally stimulating that it's wonderful. It's almost euphoric because it's so mentally stimulating, and yet it is quite clear to absolutely everybody else, "Why are you working on this? It can only harm people?" "Yes, but the problem solving is so exciting." Do you understand? The mind is cut off from the impact it's having on your body.

The mind of you and everybody else on Earth is cut off from the impact of what your mind does to your body. That's why the mind might look at a cartoon or the funnies or something like that and say, "I've seen those before"—meaning not necessarily those exact ones, but maybe when you were younger you saw cartoons or maybe at some point in your life you read the funny papers. And so the mind says, "Oh, I've done that before. That's boring."

But your body might feel differently: "Oh, I want to read that," or "Oh, that feels good." So your body might want to linger on that article. It might want you to watch children's cartoons on television—maybe not. But I'm trying to give you an example you can understand, not because you don't have the capacity, but because you're learning something new.

"What am I doing mentally that may be shutting out my physical instinct that is telling me, in every moment, what's right and benevolent for me and what isn't good for me and not benevolent?" Obviously I know that you want to know those things, but now you know that your mind, by being "addicted" to this knowledge . . . but from my point of view, I'm not going to say addicted. I'm going to say, being attached to being stimulated, regardless of how much that stimulation creates complexity and discomfort for your body. That is something you can become aware of only by being more aware of how your body feels.

Homework: Reassure the Physical Body

So how about some homework—something simple and easy? How about giving yourself some homework? Every day sit in a comfortable chair and put one hand or the other or both on your belly, just below your solar plexus or somewhere else if it feels better. But you want to keep your bellybutton open, exposed—not necessarily without clothes on, but to one side below your solar plexus just where your belly starts to curve out. Put one hand there and just leave it there gently.

This is very reassuring to the physical self, even if you are dressed. Just sit there for ten to fifteen minutes, and if you catch yourself thinking, just let it go. Just try to sit there without thinking. It will be boring mentally, but it will give your physical body a message that something may be changing. It's reassuring. You can't talk to your physical body. You can't do anything mental and expect your physical body to pay attention, because your physical body, although it accepts and loves your mind, does not assume in any way that your mind has mature capacities.

Remember, when Creator did this experiment, I feel that the mistake was because of too much suffering, you understand? And your mind does what it does, and because it's doing that, it turns, you might say, a blind eye to your body. So I won't give you too much. Just put your hand on your body with the intention of it being reassuring. Don't slap your body as if to say . . . you know, the way people hug each other and thump each other on the back? Never do that to anybody, and if people do it to you, just say, "I'd rather you didn't thump me. I don't like that." Tell them outright. They need to be educated. Sometimes it's the only way to get people to stop it.

So when you put your hand on your body, just put it on gently; don't rush at your body with it. Just slip your hand there and leave it there for ten to fifteen minutes. Do it with both hands, if you like—whatever feels good. Go with your feelings. Just do that for ten to fifteen minutes a day, and try not to think. It is important to do this because it has everything to do, not only with spiritual growth, which I know you want, but it also has to do with simplifying your life, which I know you want. And it has to do with allowing more of you to be present.

Sometimes you see old people sitting and staring off into space. Sometimes they are remembering things, and other times they are just sitting and being. When you get older, you're not so much attached to the complexities of the world. You have time to sit and be, but you do not have to wait for that. And while you're doing this homework, all you have to do is put one hand or the other on your stomach. If it happens to cover your bellybutton, that's okay, but I think it's good if you part your fingers so it's not covered. Keep your hand there for ten to fifteen minutes or longer and do as little as possible.

If you have a cat and the cat happens to jump up on your lap, the cat will settle down on your hand. Don't move your hand; let the cat settle on your hand. Cats might do that. A lot of times cats jump up on your lap because they're also trying to show you, "See? Touch your belly. Feels good." So if the cat jumps up on your lap and just plops down on your hand, leave your hand there. If you have both hands there, leave both hands there. If you have one hand free, you can pet the cat, but this has to do more with contact of your own body to your own body. Petting the cat is the cat's way of showing you what to do, and the cat knows that it is attractive to be touched—not attractive in the beauty sense, but attractive. So do this. I think you will find it very reassuring.

Why not cover the bellybutton?

Because if you cover the bellybutton in your body, it can decrease your awareness.

Captured Images and the Physical Objects in Your Life

Reveals the Mysteries
November 10, 2003

This is Reveals the Mysteries. Greetings.

Welcome.

The Feelings of the Artist Become Superimposed on Artwork

In this day and age in which you find yourselves, where images (to say nothing of image in general) are so important to people and the representation of oneself—philosophically, pictorially and in the perceptions of others—is so much a part of your culture, it is important to remind you of the unnatural association between what I call captured images, in the form of photographs, and a personal identity, a corporate identity and even a political identity. If you wish to present an image, as one might in the case of historical representations, one might reasonably, from my point of view, present an image in the form of a painting—which would be in a contemporary sense the best guess of the illustrator of a historical subject, one that perhaps would precede the time of photographic images. I find no fault with art, because something that is hand painted will often carry with it the feeling of the artist at the time.

This is why, at least in the past, when you would see an advertising image, even if it was ideal or beautiful or analyzed to be symbolically perfect for the audience whom you wished to purchase your product or service, it didn't always work, sometimes for what were termed intangible reasons. Sometimes the intangible reason would be simply that either the public or the people whom you wished to purchase your service had changed—their mood, their interests had moved on elsewhere. But from my perception, as I look at your cultural creations, it is most often the case that the artist who created the image was probably being driven on by a bosses or bosses, creating for the artist an uncomfortable mood.

Anyone who chooses the field of art knows that although passion in creation is the stimulus that supports a tangible creation, the reason artists are often dissatisfied when they stop the creation of any given object that they are working on is because of the feeling they had at the time of the duration of the creation—which might have ranged initially from passion and could have gone through anger, disappointment, discouragement, exultancy, happiness, joy. All this stuff is layered right in there with the pigment or with the blows striking an object, in the case of a sculpture, or the finger marks known only to the artist in other forms of creation— images or sculptures, statues and so on. And that is why, even though the artist may not see in her creation exactly what her heart or mind's eye saw at the beginning (and there may be some feeling of dissatisfaction there), the ultimate reason an artist feels dissatisfaction is that her feelings in all those layers are encased or superimposed on the artwork.

Now, there is a reason I'm using this explanation about artwork in comparison to captured images. There are also artists who are totally conscious that the image they wish to represent is filled with the feeling they want the viewer of that artwork to experience or take away as a result of contact with this art. Therefore, these artists make every effort to be filled with that feeling in the creation process to the best of their ability while they have to pay attention to what they are doing.

Such artists are often profoundly successful if they are reaching a group of people who are, for any reason at that time, influential and are particularly excited by or, in some cases, soothed by that feeling. Of course, that feeling may not be entirely imparted to the viewer of the art. It could, in that sense, trigger another feeling in the viewer due to the unique and individual nature of feeling creation and feeling reception in your society and in any society.

Photographic Images Hold the Feelings of Their Subjects

How does this relate to photographic images? Photography is an essentially scientific process that involves materials that have not volunteered to be photographs—but then one might easily say that the paint or canvas or wood or clay of any artist has not volunteered either. But as a result of the strong, passionate feeling of the artist—or even soothing, calm feelings, depending upon what the artist is doing—the materials themselves might become enthusiastically involved, since they have feelings themselves.

However, in the case of photography, in the sense of film, even the professional photographer knows that it is essential to pay attention to what he or she is doing. The photographer has to set this and set that and make sure about this and be careful of the light and so on. So the photographer has to remain somewhat distant from the subject because of the technique involved, even though he or she has the artist's eye and those feelings that any artist has in the creation of an image. But here, in the case of photography, one is essentially capturing an image that one could appreciate later or print in a certain way for the sake of effect.

Now, in your current time, you have the so-called digital or computer-composite photograph that interacts with various computer techniques. I do not have all the words for this, but I'm sure the reader understands what I'm talking about. In this situation, there is even less feeling involved. This is not to say that you wouldn't have feeling for the subject. Maybe you're taking pictures of your grandchildren or other people—perhaps beloved pets and so on—or you're in a place you love. Of course you have feelings for that. I'm talking about the casual photographer here in this sense.

But there is ultimately one fact that covers all of these things, even art, even painting, but most importantly and most specifically photography (since most people do not paint and most people do not sculpt, but many, many, many people in your time do take photographs in one style or another): The captured image will hold, in that moment of time, the picture, yes, but also the feelings present during the time of the photograph. In this case, this is not only the feelings of the photographer but also, most importantly, the feelings of the subject being photographed—and this is most important in how it differs from a painting or sculpture, for example.

The Feeling Moment Is Captured and Held in the Photograph

Think about your life. You will find that on any given day, to say nothing of in any given moment, you have a whole range of feelings running through you. You think this, you feel that, you feel this, you think that and so on. Most often, every single human being is in some form of conflict internally in your modern society on the basis of what you need to do versus what you haven't done, what would be nice to do, what isn't and so on. This is all kinds of things: what you would like to do, what you can't do and so on, plus what you have accomplished, the happiness of the moment, the disappointment, etc., etc., etc. You can imagine the full range of feelings and all of the descriptive words involved.

This moment—not just the photographic image, but this *feeling* moment—is captured and held in the photograph. This is why you might find very easily, when looking at other people's photographs—I don't mean being entertained by other people's trip photographs for hours and hours, but if you simply look at a person's photograph, especially look closely—that you will often pick up feelings. One normally picks up feelings, at least in the reaction you have to the photograph. But one normally picks up feelings from a photograph by looking at the eyes of the subject or the person or the animal, for that matter.

Feelings are directly viewable, especially with a close-up photograph. But I have to tell you that even if the subject of the photograph has his or her eyes closed or perhaps is wearing dark glasses, for example, the feelings of that person equally, along with the image, imprint on the photograph.

Relatives Tend to Relate to How You Used to Be

But, of course, there's more. All of you who come from family . . . you all have family of a sort, even if they are not blood relatives but people you were raised with. You know that when you see these people in later years, whether you see them all the time or perhaps, in the case of relatives at a distance, once in a while, regardless of how interested they are in what you are doing in the immediate moment, they still tend to relate to you in the moment as they knew you when they first met you or as you impacted them in one way or another as a personality when you were younger.

That's why meetings with family, even happy times, can be difficult, because uncle or auntie or even your cousin and so on treats you as what you were—not out of any sense of meanness, but simply because that's how your relatives relate to you. That's why sometimes when you go to family gatherings, it might feel a bit like an ordeal, at least with one person or another. And you find yourself wanting to say to uncle or auntie or grandma or grandpa, "You know, I've changed, Grandma. I'm really not like that anymore." [Laughs.]

I'm chuckling because I want you to understand that having lived life as a human being, I completely understand it and am compassionate about this. But it is a little funny, you know, most of the time, although I know sometimes it can be awkward. Still, the purpose of this chapter is to very gently—I'm not trying to wave a cudgel over your head—suggest that you not put so much energy into photographing your loved ones, things that you like, even a beautiful tree in the park.

New Photographic Techniques Are Possible

Right now—and this will change in the future—the way you are using science, your photography does not have the capacity to change the feeling imparted from the photograph to the viewer of the photograph that represents how that photographed subject *now* feels, as compared to how that subject felt when the photograph was taken. Now, you might say, "That's not possible." But, in fact, it not only *is* possible, but on other planets, when one does choose for whatever reason to show an image, the image always—as you would say, technically—updates to the current feeling and, as it would be called there, experiential level of the subject represented in the image.

Now, there's more than one reason why I'm suggesting this, you understand. There are people working who will read or hear about this field of photography who are advocating that such a technique is possible. And there are people working on the leading edge and really pushing beyond the leading edge who are advocating that it is possible to take a photograph (even at a distance) of a person, place or thing, and know—on the basis of the analysis of the photograph—what the subject was feeling . . . to not only be able to extrapolate psychologically what they may be feeling today, but to be able to incorporate into the mechanism of the photograph equipment itself and the image it produces of how that subject is now feeling in the current moment. I want to support that.

Part of the reason I'm talking about this subject is I want to support the development of those techniques. Because in coordination with other technology that is being developed—much of which you find in various forms benevolently, of course, on other planets—working in concordance with such techniques as I'm discussing and somewhat advocating, this will not only allow you to see the photograph but also to know and understand how that photograph is useful in the current, up-to-the-moment application.

Using the Love-Heat to Discern Feeling in Your Photos

As you know, your current state of photography available to the general public does not do that, so I'm not going to talk any more particularly about the future development of your photography as I've been discussing just now. I want to rather say that photographs taken some time ago are to be winnowed out a bit. Now, this is what I'm suggesting; I'm not commanding or demanding anything. But I'm suggesting that for those of you who keep photographs, that you pile them all up in front of you and that you pick them up and hold them for a moment.

You can do this one of two ways, okay? I'm going to give you homework. That's what this book and the *Shamanic Secrets* series are about: to improve the application of your spiritual techniques, to improve the quality of your life and, as a result, when applied in benevolent ways, to improve the quality of the lives of people around you and perhaps even your entire society. So carrying that through, you can winnow through the photographs with the idea of eliminating some on the following basis.

First, you can have the photographs face up so that you can see them, if you feel that you can make a choice based entirely on your feelings. But if these are photographs for which there is strong feeling, perhaps some tragedy (perhaps the person has passed away or something like that), or any strong feelings that you might have that would seem to overcome your capacity to make a decision based in feeling of what to keep and what to let go of, in that case, then turn the photograph over so that you cannot see the image on the surface. (This is, of course, for photographs that are prints.) Turn it over so you cannot see the surface—this technique can still work.

Pick the photograph up and hold it in front of your chest or solar plexus. For those of you who can feel heat, as we've discussed numerous times—the love-heat/heart-warmth/physical-warmth [see Overview]—notice if you feel warmth. (I will cover how to do this if you don't feel the heat, but I'm going to go through the heat part first.) If you feel warmth, then keep the photo. If you feel discomfort, then set that photo face-down in a pile to the side and relax for a moment until the discomfort goes away—it won't take long, just a few seconds. Then pick up the next photograph.

Before I rush on, there's another pile of photographs I want to talk about. There will be some photographs that you have no feeling about whatsoever: you don't feel the heat, you don't feel the discomfort. Put those in a pile of their own. You'll probably keep those for a time, but not indefinitely.

Now, when you go through all the photographs you're going to go through in that sitting, then what I recommend is that all the photographs you felt warm about, you're going to keep and put in a "keep box" or whatever storage you have. For those photographs you felt discomfort for in your body, seriously consider throwing those away or taking them away from your possession. You could, if you choose—in the case of family and friends—offer those photographs to your family or friends and say that you're winnowing out your photography collection or your photo collection. You'll have to decide whether that's right for you, whether it would feel good or safe doing that. But it's important that those photos leave your possession fairly soon, because they are not causing pleasantness.

What's happening, of course, is that you look at a photo, and even though you may not be consciously aware of it, it makes you feel uncomfortable, either on the basis of your reaction, or just as possible—even more possible, just not known in your time—on the basis of the feelings the subject had when the photo was taken. And the subject of the photo (a person, place or thing) has probably completely changed, is either in another form, or in the case of a person or an animal, has changed his or her mood completely, and this doesn't reflect his or her present mood. Or perhaps the subject has moved on, living life in another form in another place, or has gone on to be with Creator—however you choose to perceive it according to your feelings and beliefs.

Looking at Photos without the Love-Heat

So that's what I recommend in the case of feeling the heat. But a great many of you have not begun that process or are having some difficulty with it, so I want to give you another process. If you pick the photo up and you hold it in front of your body or look at it, I want you just to notice in your chest or solar plexus if you feel discomfort, an uncomfortable feeling—even if you don't feel the heat, you can do this. See, you can use that system. You will be able to notice an uncomfortable feeling.

If you feel the uncomfortable feeling by looking at the photo, put it in the pile of photos you are going to get rid of. That will work fine. If you don't notice any feeling, then you can keep those for a time; you'll probably at some point disperse them in some way. And if you have a good feeling—you may not be able to identify it as warmth—then you'll want to keep those. That's pretty straightforward. Remember, even if you don't feel the warmth, if you want to try the process of looking at the back of the photo—meaning you're holding the object up, you don't know what's on the front, and you get a bad feeling looking at the back of it—still put that photo aside to be released, discarded in some way or passed on to others, if you choose.

Always wait until that bad feeling passes. You can see that this is not going to be an exceedingly long process, because a bad feeling like that tends to go away almost instantaneously when you remove something from your immediate place of being—meaning your body when you hold the photograph up to you. You're going to be holding it, say, eight to ten inches away from your solar plexus or your chest or your tummy, as you call it. That lets you know almost immediately, since this is a space that is essentially an intimate part of the space that you feel and that you interact with in the world. So captured images, you understand now, are something that you need to interact with entirely differently.

Looking at Computerized Photos

For those of you taking photographs with your computer techniques, however, where you print some and not others, I'd like you to try something. You will be able to do this. People using film or even a printed photograph from their computer may not be able to, but you will be able to do this. Look at the photos you have on you computer. Try to put them up on the screen one at a time.

Now, this won't work quite as well because the computer itself is made up of materials that did not volunteer to become a computer; they are part of Mother Earth's body. And although it is possible to put that computer (or any man-made object) at ease, and remind it of who and what it is and was, and allow it to feel safe and comfortable, that is an entirely other process. I may have—or Speaks of Many Truths or others may have—given that process in the past. So, you see, if you are looking at the computer, you are already looking at something that is not comfortable in its own right because it is, as I say, a part of Mother Earth's body that has been used and existed elsewhere in some other form, and was comfortable being in that form and that place. So it may not work very well, but you can try.

This is what to do: First look at the blank computer screen and notice how you feel. Have nothing on there if you can, since you are looking at photographic images, or have as little on the screen as possible. Notice how you feel, because that is sort of your baseline to understand your own physical feelings. Then put an image up. Put up one at a time. Notice how you feel. Use the same technique: either the love-heat, if you know how to use that, or simply a physical feeling that corresponds with the way I described the other techniques. Perhaps this is something uncomfortable; you can make a note of that image as being one you are to let go of.

But in the case of a computer image, instead of simply discarding it, I want you to essentially set it aside—I don't know how you do things on the computer, but you'll know what to do. Put it in a separate place, a "folder" (I think that's what you call it). Then go through the ones you're going to go through in that sitting. Try to go through at least ten every sitting, no matter what technique you use. And then, in the case of this computer image, there is something I'd like you to do. After you've come up with maybe two or three that you've discarded—you might go through more photos than that—and you're quite sure that you're really not comfortable looking at them . . . you don't have to check them to make sure you're getting the uncomfortable feeling again.

It's always important to note what your first feeling is, because your first feeling will be clearer to you. It will be your physical body telling you, "This is how I feel"—"I" meaning not just your physical body, but the overall you. You understand, this technique also teaches your mind about physical creation, its impact, its application, its knowledge, its wisdom and essentially how to function in the physical world in order to experience happiness and fulfillment. That is the purpose of your physical body. Most people in your time are not fully aware of that.

So to continue on, what I'd like you to do when you get three or four photographs in your discard folder, is to simply pull one out, especially one that might have a close-up of someone's face, but it doesn't have to. It could be a photograph of a place. Don't question it. Just pull one out, and because this is the computer, I'd like you to manipulate the photo in some way using your computer techniques so that when you look at the photo again (not immediately, but when you look at it, say, the following day) . . . again, pay attention to what your first feeling is. See how you feel. You might get a feeling where there is no particular reaction. Put that in its own folder and process it. "Process" means continue on with the photographs. If you manipulate the photograph in some way and it still gives you an uncomfortable feeling, then just completely discard it.

Now, you recognize, some of you, what I am saying here. I want you to understand that it is possible to, even on a fictional level such as this, transform an image into something that you personally like or even find amusing; you can do something like that. It might be fun. It might be silly. It is perfectly all right to do that because it is a fictional creation— meaning no longer a photograph of what was actually present in the moment at the time the photograph was taken, but it has become something of an artwork, based upon your capacity to interact with the computer's techniques.

The underlying message here, what I'm trying to suggest, is that it is possible to notice your feelings and how you interact with something that is a captured image. It is possible to alter your feelings, not on the basis of something you personally generate to generate a feeling—to force, as you might say, a feeling—but to note how you feel in your first exposure to that image, at least of that day (or if you want to wait a week, that's all right too).

So if you've altered the image, then put it in a separate folder saying something, whatever is clear to you—that it is an altered discarded image—and wait. Wait three to five days or longer, and someday look at those images again. Remember, always pay attention to your first reaction. If that altered image still feels uncomfortable, then simply discard it. If, on the other hand, because of the changes you made to the photograph, whatever they might be, if it feels good or you don't get an uncomfortable feeling, you can keep it for a while, but keep it in that folder.

Captured Images Pull You into the Past

Remember, this is not so much about changing things to suit your purpose—it's not about manipulation. Rather, the real thing this is about, you understand, is paying attention to how you feel and understanding that the way you actually *feel* about something has everything to do with material mastery and everything to do with knowing what is for you, what is intended to be for you, or with you, or love for you, or benevolent for you, or associated with you in some way that is meant to be associated with you in that moment. In short, it is understanding the basic application of the method by which all beings everywhere in the universe know what is for them, as compared to what is meant for others.

In that sense, one does not condemn the photograph, in whatever technique you use, as being bad. The photograph is not bad. It is simply not meant for you in that moment on the basis of how you feel physically. So when that is thoroughly understood, then you simply, in the case of this learning, discard it. But when you discard it, know that you are not simply abandoning it to reach whatever conclusion it might reach in the form in which you are using it—you understand, as a photograph. But rather you are literally sending it on its way. In the case of some photographs, you might pass them on to friends or relatives who wish to have them— ideally in such a way that you will not see them again. Send them to Aunt Effie or whoever lives on the other side of the continent or something.

So what I would suggest is that you understand that a captured image can hold your reaction to somebody—a person or a place or a thing—in the past. It can pull you into that past when you look at it, so all the feelings of that moment in your life at that time come back to you, and it feels uncomfortable. It can hold the person, place or thing in that position, and it might cause him or her—not in the moment you look at the photograph, but in the moment you interact with that person after having looked at the photograph—not to be able to express how he or she is currently to you, because you are reacting in your mind's eye and recollection to the photograph just as much as you are reacting to that person in the present moment.

Know What Is for You and What Is for Others

I realize I am being very detailed here, but because we are talking about technology here, it is necessary to be fairly explicit. What I am talking about is you understanding your own feelings to know what is for you and what is for others. When you look at a menu in a restaurant, you order what you would like to eat; you don't order the other things, because those things are for others. This is no different.

We're not saying that the photograph you discarded is evil. We're not saying it is even bad. We're simply saying that it is not for you. It is either for others or it is meant to be released so that the captured images and feelings can move on. It is a way of releasing, letting go. You will be surprised when you winnow out your photographs like this, keeping only the ones that feel good, that when you look at your photographs again, it will be a much more pleasant experience, and you might even wish to do it more often.

Everything about You Is Constantly Being Radiated

I'd like to look at it from the other side. If someone takes a photo of you and captures your energy in that moment, is that like a Xerox copy of the energy, or is that actually taking energy away from you?

It is actually taking energy. You understand that as a living personality, you come here to Earth and you are given or loaned the materials of Mother Earth's body so that you might learn as much as you can—not only about what you want to learn when you come here, but in the way Mother Earth has to teach it. So you acquire something that is not possible to acquire somewhere else. You have to come to Earth to experience an Earth body, to learn what you wish to learn and other things that Mother Earth may wish you to know and understand, and to improve your overall quality of existence wherever you may go in life.

So as a result, you know that one of the things Mother Earth likes to demonstrate on a regular basis, no matter who you are, is the senses— smell, taste, touch (in other words, contact), what you see and, most importantly, what you feel . . . because you don't have to see, you don't have to touch, you don't essentially have to do anything if you can use your feelings. You can be somewhat out of touch with all of your senses, but you will always have your feelings. The other senses—sight, sound, all of that—are all meant to support your feelings. They are like the brothers and sisters that support your feelings.

So one of the most important things to understand about Earth is that she is always radiating her feelings. She doesn't send them out, but she, like you, feels her feelings and they naturally radiate out. What a photograph does is that it literally captures . . . someone stands in front of you and takes a photo, and you, as a living being in a Mother Earth body, are always feeling whatever you are feeling, and those feelings are radiating out in various forms, perhaps to acquire what you need—sending out, really, a signal in some form. It may not necessarily be the idealized form that you want, as you understand it to the best of your ability, but it will be a step toward reaching that or achieving that, in some cases, or even acquiring that. It will be something.

So it's like a signal that's going out. Or it might even be a signal that's being broadcast by you: that you are prepared to cooperate with others in what they wish to do or what they need. In short, everything about your life having to do with all that you do, even when you are asleep, is constantly being radiated so that other beings—human, animal, plant, parts of Mother Earth's body—can interact with you to provide for your needs in the very best way that can be done, given that everybody else is doing the same thing. So there is this mutually cooperative thing going on. Simply to have a person stand in front of you does not create a problem—or behind you or anything like that—because all of these people standing in front of you are parts of Mother Earth's body as well as souls. But to take a photograph captures a bit of that radiated signal.

Although this does not harm the subject of the photo in any significant way, what it can do is, it will delay the signal, either coming in or going out, because the photograph will be processed and looked at by someone else, taking the subject—at the moment only of looking at the photograph—out of the context of constant interaction with everyone (every person, place or thing) that is necessary in this creation school and generally around the universe. This interaction takes place between all beings to provide in the best way possible what all beings need, desire or even need to acquire—perhaps even temporarily—in order to understand, and once the understanding takes place, to be able to move on with that understanding and all kinds of other ramifications of life that many of you know and understand.

In Your Time People Constantly Take Photos

So the photographic image, when looked upon by another, tends to generate a—how can we say?—a nonsequenced moment for whoever is viewing the photograph. Now, this is not a major problem; if a single photograph is taken, it is nothing to be too concerned about. But think about it in your terms, in your society . . . and that's really why I'm bringing this up now.

Nowadays it is typical for people to take photographs constantly, and the technology even exists—not for the purpose of spying on you—where you might be walking about on the street and pictures are being taken all the time to preserve the public safety in some way. And of course, many people in your time have those "walk about" phones, some of which now have the capacity to take photos and so on. In other words, the whole idea of capturing images is becoming almost a function—albeit artificial—of life itself. Of course, the desire for this is to stop the world in this image, because your world is so complicated and overwhelming in many ways that the attraction of having a fixed image that you can look at in that moment, regardless of what it shows, is somehow calming.

But I am suggesting that if others take hundreds of pictures of you over the years, as long as they don't look at the pictures very much, it's not a problem. But if they look at them a lot, then it can be a little . . . not problematic, but you would have to make an effort to do something to encourage the release of being held by photographs. I'm going to give you something simple you can do.

Release the Energy of Captured Images

For some of you, just simply say out loud, once only:

> *Living Prayer*
>
> "I AM ASKING TO BE RELEASED FROM THE BOUNDARIES OF ANY AND ALL PHOTOGRAPHS TAKEN OF ME BOTH INTENTIONALLY OR SIMPLY BY MY APPEARING IN THE BACKGROUND. I AM ASKING THAT MY RELEASE OF BEING BOUND IN ANY WAY BY THESE PHOTOGRAPHS BE COMPLETE NOW AND ONGOING."

Just say that once out loud; don't whisper it [for more on living prayer, see p. 245]. If you can, just walk out on the land and say it. It's better to say it on the land, ideally barefoot. You don't have to yell it. Just say it out loud in a normal speaking voice, ideally with some kind of intention—meaning like you would say, for instance, "I'm going out now, and I'll be back later."

This is something you're saying and you mean to do it; it's an intention. Try to say it with that kind of energy, that kind of feeling. And that will release 95 percent of that energy. For those of you who wish to do something in other ways, feel free to do something ceremonial, if you are attracted to that. But regardless of what way you release the energy, I think you will find over the next few hours that you will feel a sense of relief. Something will just literally lift off of you, and you won't really know what it is.

Public Figures: Do the Love-Heat

Now, let me tell you that not only is this going to be helpful for people who have had photos taken of them and who may find that they have photographs taken in the future—which is something that some of you can't help in your now society—but it's particularly important for people who are in the public eye. Politicians, movie stars and so on, it's particularly important for you to say this, because even though you want people to view your image as something attractive and idealized, it can also tend to hold you in the same way. You can allow people to be attracted to your image in some way that does not require their permanent fixating of you in the past, meaning at the moment that the photo was taken.

So I would prefer, then, essentially here to give you the solution, which I feel will work for almost everyone and, as you can see, almost completely, in a way that is tangible and will probably be tangibly felt by most of you—that will work. You're not going to be able to stop the almost obsession with photographic techniques developing in your now present and immediate future. But it is my intention by speaking about these things at this time to try and place at least the advanced photographic techniques on a more flexible standing—to take a picture that can, in fact, represent the actual feelings of the person as he or she is in existence currently. Of course, the photograph itself may not be able to do that unless the materials it's made of are honored and appreciated and allowed to be themselves. Again, as in the case of the computer, we'll need to talk about that in the future.

What does this do to public personalities, such as movie stars or television stars or people who are on television almost every day on the news? Millions of people are looking at them. Are people taking something from that person by watching the movie or the television?

No. They cannot take from you what you do not give, what you do not send out. But what occurs for you on the Earth energetic level—meaning on the feeling level—is that if you do not make an effort to replenish your energy, you will gradually become more edgy, agitated more easily, even if your lifestyle is not overwhelming due to the demands of your profession.

I recommend doing the heart-warmth, the love-heat, as a way to regenerate your personality and to nurture yourself. Do that on a daily basis for at least two to three minutes. If you cannot do that, then do something physical that is clearly nurturing. For example, take either hand and simply put it on your chest—whichever feels comfortable and whatever place on your chest—or just below your throat. Just put it there for a few minutes in some place where you're quiet, where the phone will not ring to disturb you—turn the ringer off. Just sit there for a few minutes every day. That will be helpful.

Of course, the love-heat will be ten times as helpful, because putting your hand on your chest or on your stomach or some place like that—or both hands there like that—will feel protective and nurturing, and that will be helpful, but the warmth can actually regenerate your personality, your true nature, and your capacity to continue on in a benevolent way for yourself and others. Most importantly, you will feel it, though, as a gestalt of energies, in the case of this application of your question.

So it's possible, then, that the very act of having pictures or movies taken of you, if you're a movie or television star and you don't know about this . . . there's such a high incidence of drugs and alcohol and antidepressants and chaos in some of these people's lives, and this could contribute to that, right?

It could contribute to a degree, but I'd say that most of it has to do with what they see, what they feel, what they hear and the unrealistic demands upon them in their personal lives and so on. The warmth would be profoundly helpful to them and would also help them in time to be able to understand what gives them actual happiness. After all, when you choose a career like this, you believe in that moment that this will ultimately provide you with some kind of happiness or goal that you're striving for. But it's very easy to get caught up in the day-to-day interactions of whatever stage you are in along that career passage.

It's not only very easy to give up what you had before you went in, but it's very easy to get distracted. So you need to continue to generate the warmth and to go into the warmth and feel it more—to not only remind yourself of who you are in that moment, but to not lose yourself in the false personality that is created by being a public image. Politicians and movie stars understand this very clearly, even news broadcasters and baseball stars. Image is something they project in order to reach the people they are intending to convince of something, and it's very easy to get caught up in that image and lose yourself. It is this, as well as the overwhelming aspects of doing that, that can bring on depression and many of the other things you mentioned.

Using This Technique as a Walk-in

What about a walk-in who has pictures of the life of the previous soul who was in the body? Does that affect the walk-in?

Yes. I particularly recommend that walk-ins, as soon as they can . . . wait a couple of weeks after you come in, if you know when you came in, and go through all the photographs you've got. If there are family photographs, be sure and offer them to other family members who will probably want them. If you have very young children, you can put them aside, but put them in the attic someplace where you won't see them and separate yourself from those photographs.

When using that technique, I don't want you to make a mental decision. Use your physical body, because your physical body will tell you on the basis of how your body feels, even with you having just walked in, whether these photos are something that you want to keep around or not. If there is a mixed feeling or no apparent reaction, then just put those in a separate place and set them aside, and check them again some time in the future—you understand, if there is no feeling or you're not sure how you are feeling. Set those aside and wait three months, then check them again. If there's warmth or good feeling, then keep them, of course. I'm not going to go over that again; we've covered that, how to do that.

Work to Simplify Your Life

I think the point is that, in your times, there's so much of a desire to stop the moment . . . that is really what photographs are all about, not just remembrance. The original purpose of photographs, you understand, was to be a remembrance of a moment or a remembrance of an individual. But in your time, when society is quite a bit more complex, it is intended to stop the moment so that you can literally not only capture the feeling *you* had in that moment when you took the picture, but bring your complex world to a halt, so that when looking at this photo, you can literally recapture the moment. But this is not so good.

WALK-INS
Zoosh

"Walk-in" simply means the transfer of one soul out of the human body, followed by the welcoming of another soul to come into that physical body, which is meant for it. It is not random. It is not done without permission. Everything is done with sacredness and with permission.

Normally, of course, as you know, when a soul leaves the body, the normal process follows and the body dies a death. In the past, it was rare for a walk-in to occur, but now you're having something occur that is requiring more walk-ins. You are all quite well aware that the population on Earth is becoming, not exactly excessive, but it is reaching certain boundaries—given that you need to grow food and have fresh water and support to sustain all the human beings plus your animal population. So there are certain limits as to how many human beings can be here, and yet there are more souls who need to come to Earth than there are means for you to be born here. Therefore, the walk-in circumstance has been allowed by Creator to take place much more often.

You have billions and billions of souls who need to come here, some who do not need to be here very long but either need to create resolution from previous experiences or have a great deal to offer to the population on Earth. And because what they have to offer needs to come from an articulate adult rather than a dependent child, walk-ins occur most often in an adult situation. It is extremely rare and will continue to be rare for a walk-in to take place for a child. In your time now, walk-ins are something that can be expected for people who are seventeen years old or older because of what is needed and what needs to be resolved.

Also, you have to remember that if a soul has finished its life here . . . say you were born here and you went through the birth process and you grew up as a youngster and lived your life. Normally, if there isn't a walk-in, you simply have your natural death or your life ends in the way your soul expected it to given certain parameters. So normally your soul would go on, as you are immortal in your personality—your immortal personality, also known as the soul, goes on—but the body would die. But in this circumstance now, instead of the body dying, another soul that is attuned to that specific body that your soul is leaving will be welcomed by that body—*only* if it is that specific soul.

So this is not random in any way. That soul knows it's going into a certain body in a certain place, and your body knows that it's receiving that soul and that both will be compatible with each other. It's important to understand this, so you understand that this is really another form of birth. It just eliminates the long process of childhood.

I recommend that you set the long-range goal of simplifying your life, of trying to find things (like winnowing out your photographs) that allow you to simplify your life. You can even walk around your house, if you want to do this, once you've gone through your photos. You can walk around your house and pick up objects that can be picked up—not people

or animals. Pick up a cup or a saucer or something like that, a simple little object, and hold it in front of you and notice your feelings on that. If
you get a bad feeling, you might want to give that item away, or pass it on
to a friend or relative, or put it in the box for the church bazaar or whoever sells items to raise money for good causes.

By the way, if you pick something up and you're pulling it toward you and
you're feeling bad, don't continue to pull it toward you to get to that eight or
ten inches. You'll know, once you start feeling bad, that this is something you
need to let go of. I know that seems to be obvious, but I want to make certain you understand. I want you to understand that these things are meant to
be with others or they simply need to be discarded in some way.

Once you have done that with as many things as possible, you will discover that your life will feel better, that you will feel better. And you can
apply this technique to almost everything. As I say, it's a little soon for you
to be applying it to people, because people are constantly changing their
feelings and it's different. A photograph, a cup, a saucer, even a table, something like that, does not constantly change its feelings, but a human being,
an animal, even part of nature, is in constant change, in flux, so we don't
apply this technique directly to that. Perhaps someday in another book, I
will give more advanced techniques.

Almost All Objects Have a Physical Impact on Your Body

*Are you saying that if you live with many objects—art, books, CDs, DVDs, furniture,
plants, things—that that very complexity is a problem?*

Yes, because almost all objects, when your eye falls upon them, have a
physical impact on your body. Your mind, for most of you, does not have
the capacity to pull up the recollection of everything that was gong on in
your life when you acquired this object, whether you purchased it or
acquired it some way, or it was given to you. Your mind cannot do that,
but your body does. So everything you look at will often give you a feeling of what you had when that object first came into your life.

In the case of a book, for example . . . perhaps you acquired this book
with the intention of reading it. Say you happen to look at the book
some time later. Your physical body will relate to it according to your
original intention for acquiring it. If you haven't read it, you'll get a slightly
uncomfortable feeling.

Many people in your society, you understand, do not recognize what
they are feeling, and that is because there is such a state of discomfort for
you on a regular basis that you don't really realize that this is out of the
ordinary or not healthy for you. But if we put you out, say, in the woods,
for instance, where you know things are there for their own purpose and
you don't have to move them around and you don't really relate to them as
your personal possessions—trees, animals, wind, rain and all of that—you
tend to relax. This is not only because it's a natural environment and your

body relaxes in a natural environment (being made up of Mother Earth's body, which is natural here on Earth), but also you are removed from any responsibility or any recollection by your body of something you should do or might have done or could have done or were doing in the moment when that object first came into your possession or when you—in the case of, say, moving into another home or even visiting somebody else's home— became exposed to the object.

So if you want to discover how to feel a lot better, look around the house. Hold that book up in front of you. How does it feel? Do you feel uncomfortable? You have to ask yourself, "Is this because I want to read it?" Open the book and read the first couple of pages. If you get a good feeling in your body, that's why. If, on the other hand, you read a couple of pages and the uncomfortable feeling doesn't go away, let go of that book.

Pay Attention When You Acquire Objects

There are other things: picture frames, cups and saucers, furniture. In the case of furniture, one often finds, as with other objects, that these are things that other people have used at times. I don't mean simply that others come to your house and sit on your furniture, but I mean that often-times furniture is purchased used, usually because of how it looks and so on, or what it can do, how you need to use it. But, of course, it's most important for you when you acquire it to pay attention to how you are feeling and interacting with it. You can change the feeling a little bit. We'll simply give you the means to do that.

In the case of buying a used chair . . . let's call it a recliner chair. Although not everyone has those, many people do and many people wish to acquire them. If it is used or even new, before you get it home, you sit in the chair: "It is certainly comfortable." You lean it back: "Oh my, that's wonderful. Oh, I want to get that." And when you first sit in it, notice not only how it feels physically, but how do you feel? What are your feelings in interacting with it? If, when you first sit down, your feelings are, "This is good; this is okay," or "This is slightly uncomfortable," then it's still probably all right to purchase.

When you get it home . . . ideally, of course, if you can spend some time with the chair before you actually bring it home, then you could do this before you purchased it and know for certain whether it's safe to bring home, but that's not always possible. So let's say you bring it home. What you could do is perhaps put it outside under a porch. Some of you like to do ceremonial things such as smudging the chair—that's perfectly all right and something I support. I think that can be useful.

Relating to the Natural State of Objects

Also what I recommend, for those of you who are shamanic students— and perhaps you are if you are reading this book—is that you stand back from the chair for a moment and consider what it's made of. If it's leather, then it might be an animal. If it is fabric, try to make your best guess what the fabric is. You might be able to figure out or someone might tell you if it is an artificial fabric—in which case, just try to figure out, as I say, what that fabric was originally made of. Perhaps oil had something to do with it in its natural state. You don't have to figure out what it's made of in terms of the chemical and the chemistry; that's not it. I want you to figure out what natural products it's made of—what the product may have started out as.

Whether it's cotton or oil.

With the frame of the chair, you would know: "Well, this came from a tree somewhere," that's clear. And after looking at and considering the metal springs, you could say, "Well, this was at one time rock or stone, part of a mountain perhaps." Keep it simple, like that. You may not be able to figure out all of the materials, but probably you'll come up with—in the case of the chair—fabric (maybe cotton or something like that) and stone (in terms of the metal) and trees (in terms of the wood). In the case of plastic, then you can use oil. I believe oil is somehow associated with plastic in some application of it. You can consider that.

Then what I'd like you to do . . . you don't have to sit in the chair while you're doing this (perhaps it's not even good to do that), but stand or sit next to the chair and imagine being oil. Not the application of oil, such as gasoline or heating oil, but imagine being oil in the ground in Mother Earth's body. You don't have to think about what she uses it for. Just imagine, just picture yourself as oil—for those of you who are actors and actresses, this will be easy, but for those of you who are not, just imagine. Try to feel. Be yourself, but try to feel yourself as oil to the best of your ability. When you have the feeling captured or acquired in that moment— let's call it "acquired"; it's much easier to acquire it—then reach out with your right hand and touch the chair.

You do not have to touch it in the spot where the plastic is, in the case of the oil. Just touch any place on the chair. Wherever you touch on the chair, that feeling of oil will migrate to whatever oil is represented in the chair. Keep your hand touching the chair as long as it feels good. At some point, you're going to simply want to move your hand off the chair; it may be after a couple of minutes. This is where it's important to know how you feel in your body. Use your feelings in your body, your physical feelings, because all beings everywhere—including on Earth—utilize feelings as their primary means to function in their world.

So notice—for those of you who can do the love-heat—are you still feeling heat while touching the chair? When the heat fades, you can very gently remove your hand. If you get a slightly uncomfortable feeling in your body when you remove your hand, then put your hand back on the chair. For those of you who do not do the heat, if you get the same uncomfortable feeling in your body, put your hand back on the chair and keep it there until you can very gently and slowly remove it from the chair without having that uncomfortable feeling.

Do the same thing for trees, feeling yourself as a tree—go through the same process. And do the same thing for the metal, for which you would simply imagine yourself, feeling to the best of your ability . . . you can't just hold a picture of it, you have to *feel* yourself as a mountain. Then touch the chair and go through that process. In short, what will happen is that the chair, as you relate to it, will remember who it is, and by remembering who it is in that moment, it will feel much better. As you know, it is much more comfortable to interact with beings who feel good than to interact with beings who don't feel good. It's the same for the chair. Everything is alive.

Imprinting a Place with Your Presence

Is there some way you can do your whole house at one time?

No. But what you can do, if you wish to imprint the house with your presence, which is especially important if you just moved into a house . . . or let's say you're a traveler and you have to stay in motels or hotels or even guest rooms. The thing to do is to take your hands, curl the fingers slightly and sort of . . . this is a bit of what I call spider medicine. Take your fingers in your hand and sort of curl your fingers in and out a little bit—not completely, just a little bit.

Put your fingers on the wall and touch them . . . press your hand on the wall and sort of move your fingers around a bit. Or if you like, just curl your fingers a bit so that you can touch the wall with your thumb and fingers. Ideally use only your right hand—that is, your projector hand. And just go around very lightly touching the objects in the room. This imprints you physically on the place—the house, perhaps, or a hotel room—and allows that which is in that room to be more at ease with you, to ease its feelings a bit.

So you don't just barge into a room so that that which exists in that room, that which has feelings, does not know who and what you are and is tense. Many of you travelers know that sometimes you'll go into a room and it's tense; you don't relax right away. Either the room has not been arranged in such a way to help you relax, with the proper colors and so on, or perhaps the previous guest was tense and the room, being alive in its own existence—everything is alive—has remained tense. So go around very gently with the tips of your fingers and thumbs, and touch the walls and the objects. Don't rush it. Very gently take five to ten minutes to do this. If you're feeling tense and uncomfortable, don't use your left hand.

This is particularly important in the bathroom, where you're going to take a shower or a bath. One feels very vulnerable doing that, especially in a hotel room; one does not have garments on and so on. So gently just touch the wall with your hand that way, and touch the walls of the tub and the tub itself and even the fixtures—just lightly, don't linger. Then wait a minute or two, and it will feel safer, because that which you have touched has had a chance to get used to who you are, what you feel like. You will impart your feelings.

Try to be calm when you are doing this so that you are not running those agitated feelings into the walls. Then whatever tension is there, based upon its experience . . . remembering that it is not a wall but rather what it was before it was made into a wall—it may have that original tension. If this is a home, it would be good to do what I recommended with the chair. If this is, however, a hotel room, simple contact in this general way will allow it to react to who you are. So try to make the contact when you are feeling calm, so it can react and relax and know that it doesn't have to be tense; it has been touched. It knows who you are, and it will feel relatively safe.

That would be good for someone who is going into a new office too, taking a new job, right?

Yes. Ideally do so when other people aren't around or are not likely to see you—perhaps after hours—so that you can allow the objects and so on in the room to become as used to you and feel as safe with you as possible. In the case of an office where people come and go regularly, you might do this once a month. It won't take much more than five minutes tops to do the whole office. Again, just a gentle touch and move on.

If for some reason you've acquired knowing how to do the heart-warmth, the love-heat, and you feel a sudden burst of warmth when you touch something in the office, linger while the warmth is there. As the warmth fades, then lift your hand and move on. There may be a reason. You don't have to analyze the reason in your mind. Just notice it and move on.

Feelings Are Their Own Language

I have one more question about books. What if when you look at the books, you don't feel guilty because you didn't read them? Let's say you bought them as reference books.

What makes you think that the feeling I'm talking about is "guilty"?

You said one would feel discomfort if he or she had bought them to read and hadn't read them.

But why do you identify that as "guilty"? You don't have to answer that question, but many, many, many other readers will identify with the feeling I've been describing exactly the way you described it, meaning feeling guilty, so it's very important that you said that. I must tell you that it is essential, if you are going to work with these systems, to not ascribe a word to a feeling. Feelings are their own language. If you make the effort to say that this feeling—I'm not talking about early work that you might do when learning New Age and metaphysical things; I'm talking about this more advanced work—that this uncomfortable feeling is because "I'm feeling guilty that I didn't read the book," if you say that this feeling is "feeling guilty," you will miss the whole point.

The whole point is to learn how your body communicates. Your body does not communicate in complex ways; your body communicates in the function of this teaching that I'm giving you on this long-term basis. It's not about "guilty" or "I should do." It's not about anything. It's just discomfort, no reaction that you can feel or a good feeling, warmth. Let's not even call it "a good feeling"; it's warmth. You understand that it will feel good: "Feels good." It feels good, there's no apparent feeling or it feels uncomfortable—period. We don't want to ascribe the term "guilt" to it, even though mentally it seems to make complete sense.

You understand, I'm not saying you are bad or wrong for asking the question. I'm saying, let's not involve mental descriptions with physical feelings. The whole purpose of physical feelings in your body, regardless of your language—the word "guilt" wouldn't mean anything to you if you spoke another language—is to know discomfort. That means, "This is not for me; it is for someone else." No reaction means that, "I need to inquire further about this," asking the question or interacting with this in some other way in the future. Or in the case of visiting someone's home, it's not yours anyway, so it doesn't make a difference. Or in the case of feeling good: "This is for me; this is good for me to have here." Warmth, yes? Feeling good. The discomfort? Not feeling good. That's what it's about.

We need to keep it simple. The whole crux of simplifying your life is having things around that cause you to feel good or at least neutral, meaning no feeling, and allowing things to move out of your life to someone else's life or even to be discarded that don't feel good. It's that simple.

Extra-Credit Homework:
Acquiring Books with Feeling

Many, many readers will identify, quite reasonably, with the mental construct of, "I didn't read the book; I feel guilty." But that's not it. It's rather: "This was the physical feeling, not the thought, I had when I bought this book. This is the physical feeling I had when I bought this book." Consider the person who goes to a bookstore, perhaps a shamanic student or a New Age student. For the sake of fun—extra-credit homework for you out there—you go to the bookstore and you don't go to the section you normally go to. Do this on a day when you have some time. Just go to the bookstore and use the warmth. Allow yourself to walk around the bookstore and just stop in the places where you feel the most warmth.

Allow your eye to move along those places where you feel the most warmth, and just run your fingers very lightly near the books—I'd recommend not touching the books. Use your left hand with your fingers, if you can, pointing toward the books. Use the wand—some of you know what that is [see p. 6]. Make the victory sign or the peace sign with your hand and turn your palm down, then relax your hand so you still have the two fingers out. The wand, in a nutshell, is essentially an extension of your feelings, as in a receptive state with your left hand.

Point the wand toward the books, always from the right to the left, and notice where you get the most warmth. Then pull those books out. Try to pull them out so that the back is toward you, not the title, and the books that have the most heat . . . acquire those books if you can, one or more of them. Bring them home. Don't look at the titles. Put them face-down somewhere, wherever it feels good. Notice where it feels good to put them down—maybe near your bed.

Don't read the books if you can possibly help it. Just put them face-down and keep them around. When you want to have a good feeling, pick them up and hold them for a while. That warmth will come back to you. Or if you want to acquire some of the knowledge, don't look at the book, what it says, but put your left hand inside the book, on the pages. Feel around for the right spot, and put your hand in and leave it there for a moment, as long as the warmth is present. Then take your hand out.

Some of you might acquire knowledge and wisdom this way, suggesting for those of you of a more technical nature a long-range means of communication, which I won't go into in this book at this time. But that's something to do for an experiment—extra-credit homework. It's for you, gentle reader, to go out and do it. Keep those books around, not to read, okay? Don't read them. Keep them around as long as you feel the warmth the moment you pick them up.

Your World Has Everything to Do with Feeling

Why am I using books as an object? This could very well be dishes, silverware. It could be towels. It could be anything that you go to acquire purposely or something you buy when you're out shopping that you weren't seeking but that attracted you when you saw it. You keep it around for a very specific reason that relates directly to this chapter. Think of all the objects you've acquired in all these different ways.

Why not have something around that you can go to, pick up or even look at and always have a good feeling? Be sure you always have a good feeling, and have something to compare it with. You have that good feeling in your body, then sometime later you look at other things in your home. Notice what you are feeling then, and it will give you a baseline to know what is best to have around your home in terms of objects. Useful, eh?

It would drive a left-brain person crazy, though.

Well, it's important to know that your world has almost nothing to do with fact and everything to do with feeling. I'll put a percentage on it. Your world in which you are living—even if you lived in the 1800s or if you live now or, say, fifty years from now—your world has 99.98 percent to do with feeling. I realize that's a decimal, but I'm trying to be as accurate as possible. That's why I talk about feeling so much. Because if you want to be happy and you want to feel good at least 99.98 percent of the time, then you will try to have things around the house that feel good, whether they are towels, books, picture frames or art.

It's funny, you know: This can soothe your life. Do you know that being soothed and feeling nurtured and loved and dense (as a result of having this warm and wonderful feeling) is absolutely natural for all life? Why do you think you are born inside of mom in a liquid environment, where you are totally safe, where you are experiencing total femininity, even if you are a male? You are being nurtured. This is to give you the baseline of what natural life is about. And warmth—what we call the heart-warmth, our love-warmth, the love-heat—is all about remembering that to the best of your ability. Granted, you can't submerge yourself in water and breathe that way—meaning naturally, without technical means—but the heart-warmth will help. It's the baseline of how you interact with things.

Your home is intended to produce that effect within you, especially since many of you live complicated lives. But to use your mind to say, "I ought to do this; I should do that," or even, "This looks interesting; I want to pursue this," ignoring your feelings . . . then you bring that thing home, and because you are living in a 99.98 percent feeling world, you will be able to say, with almost absolute certainty, that whenever you look at or interact with that object, if you had an uncomfortable feeling when you bought it, you will have an uncomfortable feeling with it indefinitely. This doesn't make it bad; it just means it's meant for someone else and there is something else that will feel good to you. You want to have things like *that* around.

Use the Warmth to Welcome Yourself

So say you go to the bookstore after having done this homework, and you walk around the store and you know that there are certain things you love to read about, so you go to that section. If you do not feel comfort in that section that day—maybe it has to do with the people who are there, meaning perhaps you feel crowded or it's noisy or there's some distraction—then this is what to do: If you can do the heart-warmth, experience it for a moment or even at a distance.

Let's keep it simple. Say you are someplace where you can relax and feel the heart-warmth. Feel your warmth, and simply use your right arm, once you have the warmth in your body. Just aim your right arm out in front of you and ask that your warmth welcome you in the bookstore in the section where you wish to go so you will feel safe, calm and comfortable. And just hold your arm out for a moment. You can even exhale two or three times by blowing—not real strong, just so that you are aware of blowing out.

Because you're feeling the warmth and it is love, you're not going to harm anyone else in that bookstore. But your warmth will welcome you in that place in the bookstore. It will probably feel better, even if there is noise, or youngsters discovering books for the first time and enjoying them, or many people in the store, or perhaps even the owner or a clerk at the store is having a tough day—not unusual in any business—and that is radiating around the store a bit.

Still, you will walk into the store and perhaps feel comfortable with your own welcoming imaging, and walk around the store and look in various places as you like, and walk over to that section, and it will feel better than it might have otherwise. Then walk up to the books and use the warmth. Yes, first use the warmth and see if you can feel, without looking too closely at the titles, where you get the most warmth on that bookshelf. Then look at the titles, and even if you find books that are interesting or that you came to read—make sure you hold them up in front of you—if they feel uncomfortable, don't automatically assume that you're not supposed to read that material. Try a different copy of the same book. Everything is alive.

Hold the book up in front of you and see which copy feels best. In the case of a popular book, there might be five, six, ten, twelve, fifteen copies. Even a book that sells reasonably well, perhaps the book you're looking for, might have three or four copies. Try each copy, and see which one feels best. The one that feels best . . . if you want to, buy it; take it home and do what you did with the chair. Remember that the book, if it is a hardcover, that's fabric. It has paper, so you know in your world that that's trees. Be the tree.

Go through the whole thing and hold the book. The book ought to feel better. When you're done reading the book, hold it up in front of you. Notice how it feels. If it feels warm, you can keep the book. If there's no apparent feeling, hold it up in front of you again in a few weeks. Notice the feeling. And if there's even slight discomfort, well, you've read the book, you don't need to keep it. Give it away to somebody. Sell it. Pass it on. But make sure that it passes on, even if you sell it for just a little bit. Make sure it goes away, because it's meant for someone else, maybe many someone elses. That's the good thing about books. They can pass on from hand to hand, and that's a good thing.

Welcome Yourself Wherever You Go

So you can use this technique to welcome yourself in a doctor's office, a job interview, an airplane, anything, right?

Yes, you can. Remember, though, to always and only use it when you are feeling the warmth. Make sure you are feeling it pretty good. And you don't even have to picture where you are going. You can simply hold your right arm out, and while you are feeling the warmth, you can say, "Wherever I go," always maintaining the warmth. You can just say, "Wherever I go," hold your arm out and, maintaining the warmth, blow very gently. This, of course, will not alter other people. It cannot be used to persuade other people. Business people, don't assume . . . if someone wants your product or doesn't, it's not going to sway that person one way or the other. It is meant to welcome you in that place so that you will feel better, all right?

In the case of flying on a plane, it is meant to welcome you so that you will feel better, more relaxed on the plane. It's not meant to alter the lives of other people, and as long as you do it only with the warmth—if you lapse in your consciousness and do it sometime when you're not feeling good and blow that out in the direction of, say, the plane—it cannot, it simply will not harm anything. It will not change anything for the plane. It would be no different than emanating, just by being on the plane and feeling uncomfortable for whatever reason; it would simply feel like that for you, all right? But, in short, it wouldn't do you any good.

But if you are feeling the warmth and you send it out "for what I do today"—meaning the plane, the airport terminal, the check-in, the taxi ride or the drive to the airport—in general, it will welcome you to wherever you are by feeling that warmth. Even in various things you do that day, the warmth might come up for you, which means that your welcoming warmth happened to stick to that thing or that circumstance or your soul interacting in that moment to help to bring up something benevolent for you.

The point is, keep it only to the day, if you are a business traveler or even just interacting with your life. It's not a magic potion; it won't automatically make your day wonderful. But it ought to include things in some way. I recommend that you start with something simple: the department store, the supermarket, the bookstore. Do that. Start with something simple, and if it works for you in some way, use it for traveling or use it for your day.

But use it only, at this stage, for a day, and ideally when you begin, practice, practice, practice—first doing it just for a given place so that you can become certain . . . not in your mind, but so your body can become certain. By doing it, you have trusted that this system works, because you've done it many times and you know it works. And after all, if you do that, you're going to acquire it as wisdom. Wisdom is the knowledge you use in your life because it works for you. It may or may not work for somebody else, but if it works for you, then you use that wisdom.

We've talked about many things in this chapter and even gone off on a couple of short tangents to expose you to different idea or things to consider, and I dropped a few things into the suggestion box for those of you who are working on various forms of research. I will, from time to time, do that in these books if I want to support those avenues of research, because I feel that they ultimately or even on an immediate basis have some benevolent applications in life. I want you to know most importantly, though, that although the purpose of these *Shamanic Secrets* books has been stated, the overall purpose is intended to help you to feel safe and welcome on Earth in your physical body as it is now and as Earth is now. Welcome. I'm glad you came.

More on Captured Images

Reveals the Mysteries
November 11, 2003

You might wonder why I have so much knowledge about captured images. I want to tell you a story about that. In my time we also had captured images. You didn't know that, did you?

No.

Captured Images in My Time

We had that, and I'll tell you one of the ways in which those captured images were discovered to be not a good thing. When I was a young boy working with my teacher, we went for a walk in the woods as we often did so that life as it would take place around us could be taught about. During one particular walk, my teacher said, "Now, when you come across the first significant life form you see (meaning one I hadn't seen before), I want you to remember it in as much detail as possible." I was about, let's say, in terms of your measurement of time, about seven years old.

So my teacher and I went our separate ways. I think maybe he stayed a little closer to me so he could make sure I was safe, but I didn't see him— I'm just saying what I think he might have done. I was walking along and I saw butterflies, but I'd seen them before. I saw deer and I had seen them before. I even saw a bear cub at a distance, but I had seen a bear cub before. I walked on a bit farther and I saw my first elk. I hadn't seen an elk before—they're like big deer, you know.

When I saw the elk, I stopped; the elk was moving, not quickly. I walked carefully so as not to disturb the elk, though I'm sure the elk saw me, and

I made certain I kept my distance so that the elk would not feel that she had to lead me away from her family. Elk will do that. That's why they go off on their own. If they feel they're being hunted, they will lead you away from their young ones or from the herd so as to keep them safe. So I kept my distance, and I would, from time to time, show my hands, my palms, toward her so she could see that I carried no weapon.

When she looked at me, I did not engage her with the hunter's look and look at her eyes. If I had, she would have known I was hunting her or even scouting for the hunt. The moment she looked up at me, I immediately looked toward the ground so she would know I was not hunting or scouting but rather doing something of my own purpose. Then she relaxed. When she relaxed, she would, as all beings do when they relax, reveal more of her personality.

So after a while she trusted me, and we walked along—me at a bit of a distance and her doing what she was doing. She circled back a bit because I'm sure she was no longer concerned that I was a hunter or scouting for the hunt, so she went back for a drink of water. Then she raised her head, but she very carefully didn't look at me. She knew what I was doing and she had received my message. Without looking at me, she sort of moved her head in my direction and to catch my attention, because that's not a natural head and neck movement for the elk. When she did that, I looked in her direction, though she was not looking at me, and at that exact moment, she nodded. I knew she wasn't nodding at anyone else because I didn't see anyone else, plus it had been preceded by that unusual gesture. Then she just waited. She stood in one spot so that I could understand her and learn her as much as possible, and I did that.

Drawing the Elk in the Dirt

While I was doing that, since I was young and the young are liable to make mistakes in the process of learning, I took a stick and I drew in the dirt. Looking at her, I drew her there in the dirt—just a picture you might draw in the dirt with a stick. Then I felt maybe she would run off. You know, I was a youngster. I didn't fully realize she had completely engaged me and wouldn't run off, so I forgot. We walked on for a while, and I forgot I had drawn her picture in the dirt.

Well, my teacher found me and he thanked the elk from a distance, safely and comfortably. He showed me how to thank the elk, which I then did. What he showed me to do was to put my hands down at my sides and to have my palms facing the elk, and then to bow slightly and say, "Thank you and good life"—like that but in our language. Then the elk went away.

The teacher asked me to describe as much as I could remember about the elk. We were walking back, and as we were walking back, my teacher kept asking me, "Is there anything else you can tell me about the elk?" I described as much as I could, including her appearance and what she did and where she went and how I felt being in her presence and everything I had been taught up to that point. My teacher listened and listened, and then he said, "There's a lesson for you here, and I will bring you back to this place when the lesson can be completed." This is not something my teacher had ever said to me before that point, so I had no reason to think there was anything good or bad, but rather, "Oh, this is something new."

So time went on and I continued to work with my teacher. It was what you would call summertime, and in a measurement of about maybe twelve to fourteen days later, the hunting party came in and said, "Oh, a wonderful thing. We came across an elk and she was standing by this tree, and we couldn't get over the fact that she didn't move. We came up and she didn't move. We practically walked right up next to her and she didn't move. We noticed something funny after the kill, and that's that there was some kind of . . . almost like a picture in the dirt. It looked like someone had drawn something there, but we didn't know what that was. It was strange though."

We had to eat and there's nothing wrong with hunting at all, but it is important that I was clear who that elk was. And for the first time in my life—I was young, but for the first time in my life—I could not eat something. Even though we, my people, cooked the elk and ate hardy that night, and what was leftover was dried and saved for future times, preserved in case we needed it, and the hide was honored and used by some people, I couldn't eat that night. I felt funny. I wasn't sure whether my drawing in the dirt that I had forgotten had helped the hunting party or whether something wasn't quite right. I kept going over to my teacher, but he said, "We will work tomorrow and not tonight," so I was nervous as students often get with their teachers or when they don't understand their lessons.

My mother was worried about me since I wasn't eating, so she asked my father. My father asked my teacher, and my teacher said, "He will be all right. Let him sleep and give him something else to eat just for tonight, and tomorrow we will complete his lesson and then he will understand and he'll be all right then." So my father and mother took me back to our place and gave me a little something they had that was dried—not the elk though. So I ate and slept kind of fitfully that night. I kept waking up and sleeping and waking up.

The Elk's Personal Connection to Me

In the early morning, my teacher came to get me, and we walked out. My teacher said, "Do you remember the drawing in the dirt the hunting leader spoke of?" I said, "Yes," looking at the dirt, studying it as it were, and my teacher said, "Do you know how that drawing got there?" I said, "Yes. I forgot. I put it there." The teacher said, "Let's walk out to where that is." We were walking and I was nervous and upset because . . . in our time we didn't have pets, but if we made a special contact with a being unlike ourselves, an animal as you say, we would feel a special kindred spirit. And of course, being young I felt it even more so. So I was nervous going to the place where this special animal, this elk . . . I had never seen an elk before that day, and I was nervous to go to the spot where I knew she was killed. And also my drawing was there and I hadn't told my teacher.

My teacher felt my nervousness, and before we got to the spot, because I was getting upset, my teacher said, "No, no. Let's wait now." The spot was up on a hill, and we were at the bottom of the hill and my teacher could see I was very upset. I wasn't showing it very much, but he could tell. He said, "Let's sit down here for a minute." We sat down, and my teacher said, "I want you to understand something. You haven't done a bad thing, but you've had to learn a lesson the hard way. Sometimes it's very hard to learn a lesson when you do something, whether you didn't know or didn't understand out of ignorance, or whether you did something intentionally but you forget about it. It doesn't make any difference whether you did it intentionally or unintentionally, whether you understood it or didn't. It still has an effect. In this case, you were studying your new friend. I know that's how you felt about the elk because she made contact with you in some way, didn't she?"

I said, "Yes," and we discussed again the unusual way she had nodded at me. My teacher told me that it was very unusual for an elk to do that, and he felt that she had done so because I was a child and that, even though I was a child, I knew all the proper ways to honor her and to show respect for her, and she decided to show respect for me in a way I would understand and it was special. I was listening to that, and I felt like I wanted to cry but I didn't know what to do, so I sort of held it in. Then my teacher said, "So it was right around this time maybe that you made the picture in the dirt, wasn't it?"

And I said, "Yes," the way children respond in a kind of ashamed way, even though my teacher reassured me that I need not be ashamed, that this was part of my lesson. Still, you know how children are, and I was upset. So that's the way I responded.

My teacher said, "It was at that moment, you see, that the elk had made this personal connection with you, and because you were so happy about it, you drew this picture in the dirt so that you could admire your experience with her after the moment passed. But although it's all right sometimes when you are young to make pictures in the dirt, in this case, this was a spiritual lesson for you and you knew that, didn't you?"

"Yes," I said.

"And also you knew that something unusual was happening, didn't you?"

"Yes," I said.

"And it wasn't like a childish drawing. It wasn't an innocent drawing," my teacher said to reassure me that he wasn't treating me as if I had made a mistake.

"Yes," I said.

"So you made the drawing, you understand?"

"I made the drawing," I said.

"So this is what happened: Over the time the herd was nearby this area . . . that's why the elk walked around. She didn't take you to the herd, but she walked around to where they were and near where they were and made contact with you since you were clearly doing something from her point of view that had to do with learning about other beings. So because she made that contact with you, she decided that perhaps you two were going to be special friends, and when she could get away, she would get away from the herd and return to that spot. First she would come to the water, because that's where she was when she made that special gesture toward you. Isn't that right?" my teacher said.

"Yes," I said.

"And then after you didn't return, she walked over to the place on the hill, and when she saw the picture in the dirt, she thought perhaps it was a sign that you would return. When she could, she would come over to where that sign was, and that's where the hunting party found her. Now, you know we have to hunt in order to live. Hunting is not bad. Still, I understand why you didn't want to eat last night and why you won't eat the dried meat and why you won't be around or be comfortable being around the hide of the elk."

I didn't say anything, but my teacher could tell I was upset. "Still, I want you to know, for it is important, that capturing this image the way you did in that personal moment made a personal connection with this being. And even though our hunting party and all of our people were happy that we had something to eat and the kind of food we like also, still it wasn't her that the hunting party was intended to find. There were two other elk and they had actually gone out away from the herd to be found.

"But because she was standing on this hill, it caught the hunting party's attention, because it's not typical for elk to stand on hills overlooking hunting parties because it's easier when they're up in that area for them to be seen. So the hunting party was attracted to her instead of the two elk who came out to be found and to give their lives that we might live, which is a wonderful thing the elk do for us, and also keep the rest of the herd safe.

"So it went the other way. Those two elk returned to the herd and they felt a bit odd, and they will continue to feel a bit odd and they will continue to go out until the hunting party goes out and finds them and makes the kill and brings them back. I think when they do that, you will find that you'll be able to eat that meat and even use the elk hide once it's been honored and treated. You'll be all right with that. But for the rest of your life, even when you grow up and even when you become an old man, you will from time to time amongst our people have uncomfortable moments around an elk hide or even a piece of one. And when that happens, you will know who that elk hide was. This is going to be a bit difficult for you, but it won't be horrible. You'll get over it, you'll get over the pain, but you have to remember now that even at that time you could have made the image, but you would have had to rub it out immediately."

Of course, then I asked if I could I make pictures with the other youngsters and was it okay for the other children to make pictures near where our people were living or staying at that time, or should they always rub them out after they made them. My teacher said, "See, you are a good student. So you teach the other children when you are with them. You pass on lessons only to them that are meant for children. You understand?" my teacher said.

"Yes," I said, because my teacher wanted to make sure that I wasn't passing on lessons to little children who were not meant for that. Maybe they would be meant for other things to do with our people.

My teacher said, "But it's good for your young playmates to begin to see you for who you are becoming, so tell them gently, one by one or altogether, that it's fine for them to make pictures in the dirt, but when they're done that day or even done with the picture, that they must always rub the picture out. If they ask you why, you can tell them, 'Because the spirits might come and want to interact with those who are the spirits of those pictures.' The children might say, 'But they're just funny little shapes. They don't mean anything.' And you can tell them that all the shapes that they know, that they make, that they see and that they can imagine, all have a being somewhere near our world, meaning in that case where we live, that looked like that or at least part of them looked like that. 'Oh,' the children will say." And that's exactly what I said. And so that was my lesson about captured images.

How to Deal with Captured
Images in Your Time

Grandfather
December 6, 2003

This is Grandfather. I will speak a little bit about captured images.

Tracing Photographs for Remembrance

I recognize that in your time such things are often keepsakes—that's how this method started, to have a remembrance of a time or a place or, most often, a person. I recognize the value of that. I would like to support that a bit, meaning that the original purpose can be supported if one has a sentimental or loving connection to the image, even if you do not consider yourself to be an artist.

Have someone acquire for you or get yourself some thin paper, sometimes called tracing paper in schools. Place it over one of your photographs, and very lightly with a pencil, not pressing too hard, trace the photograph to the best of your ability. But before you put the pencil on the paper, look at the photograph and decide, does this photograph cause me to feel good? If it causes you to feel good, then you'll want to keep the tracing. If it causes you to feel bad or pain or sadness or unhappiness, then you will do something else with the tracing.

I'm not suggesting that you do anything with the photograph. But do the tracing as well as you can with as much detail as you can—just lines, not shading. If it makes you happy looking at the photograph, then put the tracing aside; keep it. Try to keep it in a place of its own, but mark it as to which photograph you traced. This will give you a sense of current and personal connection with this photo from the past.

If the photo makes you unhappy, sad or cry, for instance, then I recommend that when you finish the tracing, take it outside, fold it up or roll it up, either one, but don't crumple it. You can place it in a small box or sack, if you like. And simply take a small tool like one might use in a garden and dig into the ground a little bit—not too far, a few inches is fine. Place the tracing in the ground, cover it up with the soil you took out, pat it down and leave it there.

You will find that much of the unhappiness you have had in looking at this photo will disappear then. Give it a day or two, and the photo will not weigh so heavily on you. Possibly what it represents will not weigh so heavily on you either. Then you can decide what to do with the photo. Perhaps you will keep it, perhaps you will give it away or perhaps you will do something else. It's up to you.

I want to acknowledge that photographs, even in your time with your methods as compared to the early days of photographs, have a spiritual purpose. That's why I'm starting this way. You have had examples, of course, that suggest that captured images can be harmful or cause unhappiness, and I acknowledge that. But now you have something you can do about it.

Putting Good Feelings into a Photograph

I feel that there are too many captured images in your time. They tend to hold whatever was in the image in that time and moment the image was taken, either prompting in the viewer of that image various feelings that may have nothing to do in the immediate moment with the person, place or thing that was captured in the image, or it might pull the viewer into that moment and stimulate those feelings in him or her.

I would recommend for people who must use captured images or photographs, for whatever reason, to try to put the feeling of happiness into the image—and not just fake, not a fake smile. But if you must use the image for a business card or some other purpose, try to relax for a moment before image is taken. Remember something happy that makes you truly feel happy—don't pretend—and smile.

When you have a good feeling, smile. It doesn't have to be a big smile; it's better to have a good feeling that you are feeling than a big smile if that big smile is fake. So smile, as I say, and open your eyes. When you open your eyes, that is the cue, as you would say, to that person who holds the image taker, for him or her to take the image just then. The image taker can take one, maybe two or three photographs, but in no longer than the accumulated time of five seconds. That's about as long as you will be able to maintain that feeling with the distractions around you.

An image like this can be displayed for years and years to come, because it will prompt only a good feeling in those who see it, unless they have some personal problem around the situation. Maybe they know you and you have not settled a problem—something like that. But that would be rare. Most people will look at the image and feel good. This is what I recommend for people who must use photographs for whatever reason.

The Image Taker Is an Artist

As far as candid photos of various events (weddings, birthdays and things like that), try to take the photo, if you possibly can, when you as the image taker feel happy looking at the scene—not just because something is happening that is comical, but rather because there is a genuine feeling of happiness going on and you feel it. The image taker, then, is an artist, and not because of the way the photo looks in the moment of it being taken. I know this is accepted as artistry in your time, and there's something to that, but the image taker is an artist in her ability to recognize the feelings of the moment in what she is looking at through the image box and to recognize her own capacity to be sensitive and respond to that feeling in kind.

This way the image will have a benevolent effect, yes, but it will also prompt the viewer—say, of a wedding or birthday picture kind of thing—to be more than just a witness to an event that has gone by. It will draw that person into the happiness of the moment, even if he or she does not know the people, and to be more of a "witness present" than a "witness from afar."

This is what I recommend: I realize that it cannot happen in all cases; some professionals take pictures of things that are unhappy to inform the public of this or that event. But when taking pictures of happy things or perhaps of beloved people, pay attention to what they are feeling, not just what you are feeling. Both are important.

Photographs Can Initially Result in a Loss of Physical Energy

Is there any effect on the person whose picture is being taken when someone looks at it later? Does the viewer draw on that person's energy? Is there any negative effect to that person?

No, but when the image is taken, it does capture, however minutely, some energy of the person or people or place or what you might call "thing." It does capture some of their personal energy. This can be problematic for people of fame, movie stars, heads-of-state and people like that, because not just one camera is being activated—many, many are, sometimes hundreds. And that is why sometimes so many cameras capturing so much of an individual's personal energy can actually prompt that individual to feel tired, and not just from the flash of light. By the way, that flash is generally detrimental—even in a small way, for some people—in a way that can cause discomfort.

That's why it's important for famous people or people who gather attention to allow such picture taking only in brief moments. I know you've see those pictures of someone moving from a building to a vehicle that moves, yes? That person usually sits down in the vehicle and is like, "Ahh . . .", not just from going through the many picture takers, but there's also a loss of physical energy.

It is not permanent, meaning that for those who can have the photograph right away—you have that technique today where you take the picture and look at it immediately—that feeling from looking at that image . . . the photographer, especially if he or she is a sensitive person, can look at that image and get a certain feeling. But two, three, five minutes later, that feeling is not quite as present. That is because personal energy captured in images will gradually be recovered by the person whose image was taken, leaving behind the image but not the personal energy. It takes a few minutes.

So my recommendation to people of fame, whatever the reason: After having many people take your photograph, whether it's flashing or not, try to rest for a moment after this is done. Or if it is ongoing, then find some reason to excuse yourself for a moment. Go off somewhere quiet and rest—no lights, don't read, just quietly close your eyes and rest for a moment in some space, ideally space that is not illuminated artificially. If there is sunlight, that is all right. Then in even a few minutes, your energy will rebuild sufficiently.

I would like to recommend for official events where many people take photographs of those people present, that there be less image takers and that they share the images. So many image takers can drain energy personally for a time, can cause temporary discomfort in those being photographed. And I feel that over time this can create a strain in terms of needing to rebuild personal energy over and over. This can take a toll deeply in the person who is photographed in this way, by many, many picture takers. The toll is not something that is lethal, but it contributes to that in those who have been photographed much and have had to rebuild their personal energy.

If those people take the time to do this or have the opportunity or, better yet, are encouraged to take the opportunity in the way I recommended, they will be all right. But given your society, very often people will simply go from that experience and go on, do something else—meaning they are tired, but they push on. It can take a little more energy to rebuild your personal energy than is healthy when this is done repeatedly. The effect over time is, in some cases, enough to take a year or two off your life span. In some cases, it can cause the person to be distracted.

I strongly urge anyone photographed in this way to never drive after that experience, to never do anything that might be dangerous, such as prepare food with knives and so on. Don't do that right afterward, because it takes your body a few minutes in the ideal circumstance of sitting and relaxing and rebuilding to feel all right. Once you have done that, then you can drive or do things that might be a little dangerous, if you like—such as preparing food with knives, as I said.

Native Peoples' Reaction to Early Picture Takers

Some early tribes that were visited in the past century or maybe the past century and a half didn't want anthropologists to take their pictures, because they said it took part of their soul. Where did that idea come from?

It wasn't an idea. These people lived in harmony. It may not have seemed to be harmony to those from the outside, but when you live in harmony in your world, you are connected in yourself with your feelings to all others in your world through feelings. Everyone has feelings: the largest, the smallest, it doesn't matter. And so your feelings are greatly heightened, sensitized. When a picture taker comes and, *click*, snips a moment of feeling, it actually causes a feeling of discomfort in the person.

That is why that interpretation in your books was printed, because those who tried to communicate to the picture taker or the anthropologist explained it to him in the way the people felt this person could understand it, because these people felt, from their position of being, strong feelings, sensitive feelings. You have to have that when you live in nature that way to know what is safe, what is for you and what is for others—all of these things discussed in other places in these books. You have to know. And yet for those coming from another world where they were used to shielding their feelings, not feeling them if they could possibly help it . . . the people would have known that about the strangers who came in like that.

So to the best of their ability, those people would explain their objection to the experience in terms that those outsiders could understand. If they said, "Well, my feelings physically felt discomfort, pain," or even a term you call "nausea"—and I'm not talking about "feelings being hurt" in the contemporary term—then they would apply their wisdom to that experience the way they would apply it to any experience in their world. If they would feel that in relating to something else, they would know that that experience was not for them; perhaps it was for another. It was not their job to condemn it but to know that it was not for them. So that is why they explained it or it came to be interpreted in that way.

There Is No Interaction with the Person Who Was Photographed

So when someone takes a picture of a human, there is a bit of feeling taken into the picture that is taken from the person and from which he or she can recover. But then in the case of movie stars, sports stars, holy men, heads of state and others, as you said, millions of people look at that picture. Yet there's no further interaction back to the person who was photographed, right?

Correct.

Okay. But what about, for example, holy men who have their picture taken to be used almost as a connection to them? Do those holy men emit extra energy into the photograph or something?

If they have stated that this is the case. Most often this is not the case; most often this is a practice that is developed by those who admire that person. But most often such individuals would not say, "Use this photo-graph to connect to me." This is not likely. But if they do say that, then, well, they must be doing something to make that connection. Generally speaking, I think this would be a practice developed by those who admire this person.

What about the ultimate image—mummies from ancient Egypt and from other cultures who mummified the human body? Does that have an effect on the reincarnating soul later?

This is a different subject entirely. It is not . . . I will say that it does not apply to this situation. But it's a good question, and the simple answer is, no. But there is more to it. Ask it some other time.

I will.

Bury Photos That Make You Sad

Many, many people have photo albums, and they look back at the photos ten, twenty, thirty, forty years later. Are you saying that you don't recommend someone keeping photo albums if what was photographed was unhappy at the time?

Pay attention to how you feel when you look at the photograph. If it makes you sad every time but you want to keep the photograph, then make the tracing as I recommended. And after you follow that procedure, bury the tracing, if you can, if you are able. Sometimes a person gets older and cannot crawl about on the ground like that.

What about burning it?

No. I have given the method that I recommend. Let me go back a moment. If the person is old or unable to bury the tracing himself, then make sure the tracing is placed in a box. It does not have to be a wooden box; it can be a simple cardboard box with no lettering or numbers on it—just a plain box. And then ask somebody else to bury it respectfully in the ground for you.

This is how it is buried respectfully: It means that the person who is doing the burying pays total attention to what she is doing physically, meaning that she takes the box and does not think about the picture. Ideally, she has not seen the picture. And while she takes the box out to the yard or wherever she is (maybe she doesn't live near dirt, so she takes it someplace where there is dirt), while she is doing that, she is paying attention to what she is doing physically.

She walks to the dirt and picks up a little garden tool, and she is completely paying attention to what she is doing physically, looking at the shovel as she digs, noticing how it feels in her hand, all of that. She puts the box in the ground, covers it up and pats the dirt down—that's what she pays attention to. That is the easiest way to be respectful, rather than to try to say words or sing songs. It's much easier to be physical; it does not require any thought. If thought does come in, try to keep it about something neutral—for instance, a waterfall you have seen or a rainbow. Keep it to something neutral but natural in life.

Understand that the purpose of these books is to share points of view about shamanic and spiritual practices that will benefit those who do the practice and those who are either exposed to the practice or benefit from it. Therefore, even though your question is about others, it is important. For the person with the album and many photographs, it is possible that after the tracing is done and buried, the photograph will no longer prompt you to feel sad, in the case of sadness.

But it might also be that the photograph will have no meaning to you anymore. In such a case, the photograph can then either be disposed of or you could give it to a family member, if he or she wanted it. So the photograph album will not just be something to remind you of times, places and things, but you, by doing such a process as I've suggested, will become more respectful and honoring of the physical body that you occupy for your journey on Earth.

Your Physical Body Is Mother Earth's Body

The physical body is Mother Earth's body. Most often she reclaims these physical bodies from you souls here on Earth sooner rather than later. "Sooner" means that the physical body, even under ideal circumstances (healthy and so on), is reclaimed, generally speaking, at or before one hundred years of your time. But if there has been an effort made to honor the feelings in your physical body and not prompt unnecessary sadness or unhappiness or misery through recollection, the physical body, given ideal circumstance for the sake of this example, will usually last longer—maybe 120, even 140 years. This is without any other change—just being respectful.

Remember, the body as you experience it is part of Mother Earth's body. If you do not treat your body respectfully, if you abuse your body (you know about this; doctors will tell you), probably death will come earlier. If you do not treat your body in the way I am talking about here—this is not a threat, it's just reality from what I have noticed—Mother Earth will reclaim the body sooner, saying, "Well, I need to have that part of me back now, because that part of me is feeling uncomfortable with so much recalled stimulation of pain and unhappiness. I will take it back now and process it my own way, and soon it will be all right."

So I am talking about not only being kind to yourself but honoring Mother Earth in ways that you perhaps have not considered. I know that in your time captured images are very popular, and I do not expect you to change the world overnight or try to say that captured images are wrong or bad. Rather, move toward captured images that prompt in the viewer a good feeling. This honors your body, it honors Mother Earth and it honors life.

It's Not about the Captured Image—It's about You!

So that tracing process actually removes the emotional charge from the picture?

It actually removes that unhappy feeling in you, the viewer. This does not mean that . . . say you traced a photograph of the whole family, eh? If you give it to a family member, it doesn't mean that that person will not have that experience. It is not about the photograph, the captured image; it is about you. Always remember that. If it is about you, you can do something about it. If the picture itself has this image and is something that has that effect no matter what you do, then what is the point of this book, eh? [Chuckles.]

This book is to encourage you to practice things that are benevolent for you and maybe, when done in the best ways, benevolent for others. That is the intent. We would not discuss some object with you that you cannot change, even though sometimes you've become enamored with the idea of changing something to something else. Anybody who has been in a relationship for a long time knows that you cannot really change that apple into a banana, much as you try.

But you can learn to like apples [chuckles].

Yes

You Come from a World That Is Calm

Know that your embracing of images of the moment is completely understandable in a world and culture that is moving too fast for you. Even for the very young who like fast, the world is moving too fast for them. And they are the ones who are most enamored with the methods of captured images now in practice, because for them, in their hearts and souls, the world they are experiencing—even that which excites them—is moving too fast.

There will always be a desire by people to slow down their world. Before the image-taking machine, there were pictures painted by artists, and before that, there were temporary images, pictures in the sand, and pictures on walls of caves and so on. In all of these things, there was a desire to slow down the world in which people were living.

Know that this all relates back to the time in one's mother. When you come to this planet to be born through mother, you come from a world that is very calm—all of you. It can be as slow or seemingly as quick as you wish it to be, but in your heart and your soul, you are always very calm—maybe happy sometimes, but still calm. When you move from those worlds to Earth, you have to have a time of change—you say, transition—from calm to something else. That's why you spend such a long time in mother growing. With some animals, it's not so long, eh? Yet animals on Earth are here to teach, at least by example. But for the human, you are here to learn.

You are here to learn, so there needs to be a time when you can transition from the way that is your normal way on other worlds to the school now that is Earth. And that's why there is such slow time with your mother, and that's why in the past when mother was with child, she was helped, encouraged to relax, not encouraged to work too hard. If she had to do some hard work, others would do it—her sisters or her mother or her grandmother sometimes, though grandmother would need to rest too. Maybe the men would do it. In your time it is good to honor that as well so that mother can be calm, feel the process inside her, love the process and love the baby coming along to join your world.

You'll find that when people have a desire to capture images in whatever way, it is always the desire to slow down your world, to experience the nature that exists beyond all time and in time as well. Your true nature expresses itself most often as calm and happy. Embrace your true nature with these images and provide a means to remember who you are.

That's beautiful.

Take Public Transportation

Someone who hadn't driven a car for a year or so got in to drive to run an errand, but he stopped and got out. He was agitated, and he explained that with the calmness he had felt while not driving, the flowing more into the magnetic side of his being, the sudden need to think and act was like an electric shock almost. So how in these times in which we're living can we flow more to the loving, magnetic side of our nature when there are such demands on us, such as having to drive and work and be in society? We can't all retire to a cave, you know.

I will say that the long-range solution is automated transport. Think about it. The desire to be able to travel in a vehicle from one place to another or anywhere you wish to go feels, of course, in your time like freedom, but it has had an impact on your world. Many of the places you would like to go to have been changed, sometimes on a permanent basis, because of those who desire to go there, eh? Because of roads, parking lots and so on.

To answer your question in its precision, the long-range solution is less people driving—initially using professional drivers and eventually automated drivers so no humans need do this. In the short-range, I recommend this practical solution: If you can, don't drive; take transportation. I recognize that in some small towns, this is less likely, but speaking to those in big cities, transportation is often available, especially in modern cities. Try to do that more often. In some cities, this is very practical; there are many, many forms of transportation.

Use Fragrance to Feel Safe and Calm on Public Transport

When you can take these forms of transportation, it is easier on you. It is very important, though, that if you are taking transportation, I do not recommend you read. I understand why you do that; it takes you into your own world, and you do not have to interact with the crowd in the vehicle. But I recommend something different. It's a bit old-fashioned, but you can do it in your time. You can even do it in a similar fashion to the way it was done years ago, but for a different reason.

Years ago in your cultures, modern methods of moving sewage were not well in practice. Smells, then, in cities were quite awful. Ladies could be seen, and sometimes gentlemen, with a small container about the size of snuff box or smaller, which contained a little product and some perfume or some such thing. And people would hold this up to their noses. I know that might look odd in your time, but think about it.

For those of you who wish to try this, obtain a small container, perhaps even a little bottle—not one where liquid might spill out—that could emanate fragrance that is safe to touch and that is a fragrance you like and which maybe has a calming influence on you. It might be better to use oils that prompt certain feelings. I'm sure essential-oil experts can make a recommendation. I would say that rose fragrance will cause calm, perhaps happiness—such a thing like that. There are other fragrances that cause other things. Perhaps when you travel, you might also feel uncomfortable in a crowd. You might find that a fragrance will cause you to feel safe, calm, strong—maybe all three. Perhaps you have some physical discomfort; there might be a fragrance you can smell. Just hold it up near your nose and smell—that will ease your discomfort. Such things are available.

You can do these things because, for those who read, to just escape into your own world might cause you to feel safer, and I honor that as a need, but it might be better to honor who you are and where you are and with whom as well. Think of it this way: Not only can you prompt yourself to feel safe and calm using this fragrance as a stimulation, but when you are feeling safe and calm, you can observe your world more. You can look out the window of the transport at what is passing or perhaps glance around the vehicle to try to catch a friendly face or smile. And even if you are not looking into the eyes of people, you might also perform a valuable service.

All Feeling Will Radiate

If you are escaped into your world of reading, it is almost as if all of your energy is going in. And I understand why you do that. But if you are feeling safe and calm or happy or strong . . . those things that might be supported and nurtured by an essential oil or fragrance can and will emanate such energies out of you. You don't send them out, you understand? Just feel them for yourself, because *all feelings radiate all the time.*

So these feelings . . . think about it: crowded vehicle, people upset, it's uncomfortable. You can only do good by feeling your feelings that feel good. Don't send them out; they will go out of your body, and then you will have to stimulate them again. If you send them out consciously, meaning, "I'm going to send this good feeling I'm having to that person over there," if you send it out, that is a willful act. Even when meant well, this can interfere with what that other person is doing, cause him discomfort.

That person feels something, and he may not feel it as good in such a crowded environment; it might just feel like he has to protect himself more, you see? It's not ideal that way.

It's better to feel your own feelings, if they feel good like this. All feelings will radiate. And when you are feeling calm, strong, happy—whatever you are using to prompt this—you can only do good for those around you who are receptive. So you can serve yourself and serve others in this way. That's what I recommend for travel as homework for those who wish to try it.

Pay Attention When You Are Driving

I know this does not answer your full question, but it gives you somewhere to start. For those of you who drive—many, many of you do that—it is very important to be in your body. Be present in the moment, yes? I know that driving can be boring sometimes. When you are stuck in traffic and just creeping along, it is perfectly all right to listen to the radio and so on—quietly, not loud, because your attention first must be on what you are doing. But if you are moving along—even slowly, but moving along—I do not recommend such stimulation. It's very important to pay attention.

You may not realize this, but those who drive cars have the same responsibility as those who drive buses or even trains or planes. You must remain vigilant, alert, in order to maintain safety for yourself, your passengers and your fellow beings around you. I know you know these things, but my job is to encourage you to be physical, to be feeling, to be spiritual and to be thoughtful while you are being an Earth person now.

Receptivity Is Always Preceded by Feelings of Safety

Is the act of consciously being receptive equated to the magnetic side of the self? Or does it create that in you or connect you to it?

No. Being receptive is always in the most beneficial way, in the way that works the best. It is always preceded by feeling safe and confident. That is why there are so many misunderstandings. If people must be receptive, say, in business or in other circumstances, maybe relationships, but they do not feel safe, they will narrow the aperture of their receptivity. And all that is being projected by that, to which they are being receptive to at that moment, will be greatly filtered.

It is this filtering method that may protect, to a degree—by necessary barriers, felt for various reasons—whoever is being receptive in that moment, but it does not make for communication that is clear. So you see why I am encouraging that you support yourself with something that will work without requiring constant "every moment" mental discipline. That's why I'm encouraging things such as fragrance support.

Think about it: A salesperson—a salesperson on the telephone, a salesperson in person—could even have a ring, okay? Not just a little box with fragrance in it, but a ring that holds solid perfume or just a small drop of something. Such things exist. They might be hard to find, but perhaps these things can be found in an antique store.

I've seen one. Yes.

And it is also possible to have a ring that pops open on top, and then you can wear a fragrance-dispensing device. Think of it. You are on the telephone for six, eight hours a day taking orders, trying to sell things, and it's very difficult, not easy. But if you had fragrance you could smell, then you would not have to remain mentally disciplined—because you are not going to be able to do that all the time. You need something you can do, that you can use for yourself that allows your body to work. Your body is created to react to various things, not only to help you to discern, but to nurture and feed you. Do you know that it is possible when you are very hungry to be sustained for a time just by a good smell? Not just the smell of food, but even a smell that is nurturing, supportive and prompts a feeling of safety.

I recommend this for all people, and you will find that it does not require as much mental discipline to be happier, more successful and more nurtured in your world. Mental discipline can be good many times, but if you can begin to allow your physical body to show you what it can do—just by smelling something that smells good to you and has a benevolent effect— you might just begin to realize that your physical body is there to help you. And it's a real good way to feel good about your body, no matter how it looks. When your body can do this "magic" for you and change the way you feel just by what you smell . . . try it; it could be fun. It certainly can be nurturing and supportive, and there is nothing like discovering something your body can do for you to feel a lot happier about being in it and on Earth, even for the short time you are on Earth in this school.

I Am the Masculine Side of Benevolent Earth Energy

I've not had the pleasure of talking to you before. Can you tell me anything about yourself? Have you had a life on Earth?

I am the masculine side of benevolent Earth energy, like Grandmother is the feminine side. It is my job to support not only the masculine but the feminine side of Earth's natural spirit and all that is of Earth. I can relate to other planets and other places too, but that is my job, that is what I try to do.

I have been helpful in the past to many who are learning about Earth and how to be on Earth, just as Grandmother has. Sometimes I choose to feel my Earth connection in ways that might remind you of my personality by occupying briefly, say, a tree or a cloud. If I am focusing my attention in a cloud and you happen to be looking at it, you might see a face. If you are by a tree in which I am focusing my attention, you might feel my personality or you might find that your eye is caught briefly by the tree, and the tree definitely seems like someone—though all trees are someone, they are all individuals.

Mostly I am simply that part of Mother Earth's energy intended to relate to human beings about who and what you are here in the masculine sense—whether you are a feminine or a masculine being—and in any sense that is about Mother Earth and you, who are temporarily about Mother Earth while you occupy a portion of her body. Good night and good life.

Thank you very much.

We will speak again sometime.

Very good.

Benevolent Population Reduction on Planet Earth

Grandfather
May 23, 2005

his is Grandfather. Greetings.

So there are new energies coming in that are interfering with babies being born?

A Declining Birthrate Is Benevolent

I will comment on that specifically. You know—we have discussed this in the past and it has been printed, I believe—that there are many more people living on Earth right now than the planet can comfortably accommodate. This does not mean that this group or that group ought to go and live somewhere else, on some other planet. It means, rather, that it is important to stabilize—in a benevolent way—the population of Earth and gradually allow it to be reduced by the natural process of life, not by wars or famine or disease or other things like that.

Those things are not part of the natural process of life—*not*. Wars, famine and disease are not part of the natural process of life. So there needs to be something that can function benevolently that will allow all souls to be born, to live their lives, to enjoy them as much as possible, but not necessarily to be born on Earth. So I would like to comment on your question to say that yes, it is true that there is energy, but that energy is not malevolent. It is benevolent.

The birthrate that would have otherwise been at the current level for Earth will gradually reduce. It will not reduce by some disease factor being the cause; it will not reduce by some external component of violence. Rather, it will reduce simply by the benevolent energies and needs . . . the benevolent energies radiated by those needs from Mother Earth, on whom you live.

In order to provide the greatest benevolence for you as an environment to live in, Mother Earth needs to have less of you living here. So the easiest, most comfortable way for that to occur is for the birthrate to decline. This is what's going to happen. Those lives who would've been born here will still be born, just on other planets, so that those energies are not something that is causing harm.

You Need to Come to a Consensus

Now I will reiterate a bit for those who have not read all the *Explorer Race* material—which is in itself quite an undertaking [laughs]. Due to the nature of the experience of all human beings on Earth, you need to be able to interact with each other as much as possible, not only in order to come to your individual understandings of life, but in order to come to a consensus of how you're going to live your lives on Earth together as life goes on.

This has been happening for a time now in the most efficient way in the business community. The business community is not exactly taking over life on Earth, but it does appear to be that way at the moment. This is because the greatest form of consensus that is tangible in ways that can be not only felt but also noticed, observed and considered, is happening with the global business community. Alignments and realignments are taking place in order that business can operate as efficiently as possible, with plans to bring greater efficiency in the future.

This is not necessarily being done at the cost of human life, but there is no question that sometimes that is the unintended result. This is not a good thing, I assure you, but in time there will be greater benevolence because the business community, while not having as a global community a priority other than efficiency and profit, ultimately will begin to assume some of the responsibilities of otherwise inefficiently operating local governments. And the reason those governments are operating inefficiently is because the money they take in does not equal their expenses and they therefore have to struggle in order to do as good a job as they are doing.

So we have a situation, then, where somebody must say, "Well, how can we help?" Business will ultimately take over because right now, as a global business community, they are in a position to do so. Initially this will not feel very good to most members of the global human population, and their resistance to becoming part of a global business machine will ultimately prompt business to compromise the way they are doing things and allow for the fact that if they wish to make profits, they will have to please their customers—which is the entire community of human beings on Earth.

This does not mean that there will be a global order of life that requires you all to become numbers in some vast business computer, but rather it means that ultimately what you see happening around you now is a move toward compatibility. And right now the only thing the global community completely agrees on—even all of you reading this—is that products and services must be available to serve the needs of the people.

Think about it: No matter who you are or where you live, if there are not products and services available to you, it is extremely difficult for you to exist. In many cases, it would be impossible. Therefore, you have emerging on the surface of the planet a system that is more efficient than even the most benevolent local government, a system that realizes on a daily basis how interdependent it is with other forms of itself—and that's the global business community. If you can understand that and not resent it too much, you will be able to flow very easily into your short-term future.

The Global Business Community Will Unite and Humanize You

Your short-term future, from my point of view, is what will develop over the next thirty, thirty-five, forty years. In that future, you will find a dependability—meaning something you can count on—if you are aligned or, in that sense, working within some form of the business community. But we have to redefine what you understand as the business community. The business community will be not only what you now know as that community, but we have to incorporate all forms of service, including the most benevolent forms. Health services, social services, child-care, even healers—yes, channels—all of these forms of service, all of these things that you don't always think about or even classify as having anything to do with the business community, will be united into it. They will not be enslaved by it—I want you to be clear on that—but rather united into it.

How can you bring about in what seems to be a massive corporate structure the greatest humanity and the greatest humanitarian experience? You must include in that structure the needs of human beings, not only to be fed and clothed and sheltered (yes, those basic needs), but also to be loved and nurtured and supported so that they will produce, by the very nature of such care, the best that they can produce on the basis of their own unique and individual talents and abilities.

So what you see around you is not just a unification of the global business community but a humanizing and ultimately a more humanitarian business community, which then gradually evolves into a humanitarian community globally. I want you to understand this on the basis of its actual function and application in life. If you understand this, you will not be as alarmed as many of you are when you feel that the government is unable to serve your needs of the moment or that many of the services you used to count on or situations you used to know that you could depend on are not there.

Your Population on Earth Is Overwhelming

Much of this is because the population that you have on the Earth is overwhelming. What would be the most benevolent way to reduce that population? It's not benevolent for it to be reduced by war. It's certainly not benevolent for it to be reduced by famine—that's a terrible way for it to be reduced. And it is not acceptable either for it to be reduced by disease, all that suffering. How benevolent could that possibly be?

But what is benevolent is for the birthrate to reduce so that no matter how much loving couples are coming together to enjoy each other or even to try intentionally in that enjoyment to have children, no matter how much that is done, no matter how much effort is made by the medical community to bring about birth, there will be a decrease in the birthrate. Mother Earth has stated (though she does not talk, but to put it in terms that you can understand and identify with), "This many and no more," in terms of the guests—and you are guests—living on her body. And because she loves you and Creator loves you, and because all your souls and the souls of all beings are all part of one loving Creator, it is very clear that this simplest and most benevolent means to reduce the population is to reduce the birthrate.

So I'm not suggesting that while the birthrate is what it is that you immediately have as many children as possible [laughs]. What I am suggesting, rather, is that you know that this is the case and that if mothers or fathers or couples are having difficulty having children, don't assume there's anything wrong with you. Even though medical science will say, "It is this, it is that," they are not wrong, but the overall reason is entirely due to the fact that Mother Earth says, "This many people on me, not as many as there are." So over time, the population will stabilize by this means, since this is the most benevolent.

Businesses Have Already Taken Over Services from the Government

What do you see as the first services that business will take over from the government, and where are they getting the money for that?

Business has already taken over services from the government in the sense that many people who are employees in a business are much more likely to expect and anticipate that their corporation will provide services that their government has clearly indicated that it cannot or, for various reasons, will not provide. A perfect example of that is: In the United States and other places, you have something called social security. But in businesses that flourish and exist well into the future and that can be depended upon to exist, you have something called retirement that could be very dependable as long as the business is doing well.

There's also child-care. This is very often integrated into the business. You have your children and you want to keep them near—you can't leave them at home, they are too young—so you bring them to work with you. It's fun. It's a fun thing: "Let's go to work!" And the children are right there in the office somewhere or in the factory somewhere in their own safe place with people who work for the company but who are well-trained, loving individuals and look over and take care of the children while you're at work. Those are just two examples. These are services that many people were petitioning the government to do.

For example, with child-care there was a tremendous desire for the government to set up child-care centers all over, and some governments have attempted to do this, and some of them are actually doing it quite well. But in other places, governments have said, "It's too much—we can't do it." And so the employees, in the case of an employee in a corporation, said, "Well, what can *you* do?" And the corporation, because it cared about the employees and also because it wanted the employees to be able to devote their attention to their duties at work, felt (quite rightly) that if the employees knew their children were safe and well cared for and nearby if anything should happen, that, well, it was natural to have childcare right there.

It works. Then mother and father will feel good about it and on their lunch break go have lunch with the children. How wonderful! And then they will come back to work and devote their full attention to their duties at work and feel completely comfortable and safe that their children are well cared for and nearby. This is what I feel is a strong example of something that corporations are doing and will do more of in the future if word gradually gets out that this is something that works well. And there's more.

The functions of the police are gradually being taken over by corporations. Granted, some people are not comfortable with this, but they will find that even though business does not have all the details worked out, in time many corporate policing agencies will be quite benevolent. The whole point is not only to create security and a secure environment—as the employees will then feel much more relaxed and safe—but also to create examples of a lifestyle that can be looked up to, especially by youngsters. So there will be certain individuals who are expected to have a high standard to the best of their abilities while they are actually human beings [laughs].

So this will also be a role of the police, not unlike the role of the police in your community now. But working for corporations, they will be able to be paid better and have many services available to them that are otherwise very often not being provided to municipal police departments now, simply because the governments do not have the money to provide these services to them (though the police and fire department and so on deserve them). It's not because the governments don't want to give it to them—it's that they don't have the money. But one corporation might very well be able to do that, therefore having its own police department, and another corporation its own fire department—all of these services that right now are often provided by the government.

Governments at first will feel a bit truculent about embracing that, but after a while many governments will see quickly—others will see it later—that this can be a good thing, because this entire segment of the population is well cared for privately. Therefore, governments need only care for

450 of SHAMANIC SECRETS FOR SPIRITUAL MASTERY

this other segment of the population and can reduce their budget, reduce their expenses and at times reduce taxes. And this, of course, will be popular as well.

Housing and Education Will Also Be Connected to Corporations

Does this imply that all of the employees for a certain corporation will live in the same community?

Not necessarily, but in some cases they will, simply because there will be levels of support that will be present. There will also be . . . how can we say? It might be attractive to live in a community where, granted, the corporation may own the housing, but where people will, if they work for that corporation and work their way up in the corporation and so on, have a guaranteed housing situation. They may not, in that sense, necessarily own the property themselves, but they will have a nice housing situation for themselves and their families that they can count on. And there will be many other benefits someday.

With really massive profit-making corporations, they will have their own universities, which will make complete sense. What better education can be provided for students who actually want to work for that corporation than the one the corporation can provide itself? And there will be government influence there, saying, "Well, these subjects and this and this and this and this all need to be taken so that they can be good citizens"— much like what the government requires now of its educational branch. But that will happen.

And then the corporation will say, "Well, these people want to work for the corporation, so we can also teach them all of these skills that will put them in very good standing, completely prepared for working for the corporation so that when these people come into our fold as employees, we do not have to retrain them and they can just step right in, take over these jobs and be able to count on a dependable job where they can grow and raise families and enjoy their lives." This is happening to a limited degree already.

You Will Work with Mother Earth to Create Many of Your Energy Resources

I feel that it will evolve in greater ways, and over time as the population gradually reduces benevolently, the resources that are available to support life will have less demand on them, and this will be good for Mother Earth as well. Some things Mother Earth can produce herself to support and sustain you. But since you are all being trained now to learn how to create in more benevolent ways for yourselves and others, you and others will learn how to create or support Mother Earth to create many of these resources, which she will allow you to work with her to bring about in abundance.

Such as?

Oil. After all, it is quite obvious that at some point it's going to run out. And since you're burning it up—and you know, it has many other uses than being burned—it is really something that will need to be replenished at some point. Right now there are many people who are concerned: "When might this replenishment be needed?"

So at some point it will need to be replenished, and at some point you will be burning less of it and there will be other means to create the energy—the efficient means of transportation that will be enjoyable but may not be as dependent upon burning as much oil as you are burning now. A lot of this research is going on right now and will present itself in your world of the future.

What about the method Nikola Tesla invented to send electricity through the Earth, using the cavity of the Earth as a resonance?

The reason this was not adapted as a means by which electricity would be distributed around Earth was, in the larger sense, Mother Earth's choice. Mother Earth herself made it clear to Creator that she could not accept that. This is not to say that there have not been attempts for various reasons—experimentation over the years—to utilize this method. And it is also not to say that there isn't a certain amount of electricity floating around in the air. After all, electricity is Mother Earth's physical energy body. So given that, electricity is around about you in some form all the time. But the reason you are using the form of electrical distribution—and actually the form of electricity that you are using now—is because Mother Earth and Creator agreed on that.

Men and Women Will Be Allowed to Be Their Natural Selves

That is really interesting! If we use electricity as life force, then what is magnetic energy? Is it a spiritual life force?

Thank you. That's right. And magnetic energy, then, is also her feminine energy. Electricity is her masculine energy, but she doesn't think of it that way. Magnetic energy is her feminine, her loving, her receptive, her nurturing, her supportive energy. It's what brings things together that want to come together. It is the foundation for her physical energy, which is electricity, which helps to move things about and helps all life on her body to move.

You know that there is electrical energy in your body that helps things to move about in your body, and that happens because you are made up of Mother Earth and because you are living on Mother Earth as a human being. But you also have magnetic energy within you. You have love, you have nurturance, you have support, you have the feminine energy. And without the feminine energy, none of you would be here, since you are all born through women.

So there's going to be more feminine energy and less births?

It means that male beings will, as time goes on, be allowed to be their natural selves and not be forced into an artificial mold that does not allow them to be their natural selves. First, there is the feminine in worlds like this. *Then* there is the masculine. You know this because there has to be the feminine to give birth to the masculine. And it is the same in the creation of planets. There has to be the feminine, the receptive, to acquire the material for the planet, but we won't go into that right now. So I will say that when men are not being forced into an artificial image of what a man must be according to other men and, to a degree, according to other women, then the man, the young man, the boy, will be allowed to be his natural self, which is much more benign and benevolent.

Likewise, the woman, the young woman, the girl, will be allowed to be her natural self. She will be allowed to be her natural self and not forced into some artificial image of what other women think that this girl or young woman ought to be—and what men think as well. This way, not only will people be enjoying their uniqueness as individuals, but it will be quite clear to them as they grow up where their talents lie, who they are, what they can do more easily than other people and, therefore, what would be a good thing for them to do as an occupation. You can see that not only is this benevolent, but it is profoundly benevolent for the efficient running of the community that provides products and services, which you now refer to as business.

Children Will Be Treasured

Even now you can see that this pressure is present, even though you have lots of births going on, and that's in the form of cloning. Now, I'm glad that the desire in many corporate senses, as well as in humanitarian senses, is: "How can we create the most benevolent and helpful child so that people do not have to suffer with conditions that they are born to?" I understand that there is a lot of humanitarian feeling behind the idea of cloning, and I understand that there is also a lot of other feeling as well, not always so humanitarian. But even when you have cloning working efficiently, if Mother Earth still feels that there are too many people on Earth, the cloning will not take. So don't fight it. It's not going to be something terrible. It's not going to be suffering.

And ultimately, since the birthrate will drop, children will be treated, recognized and appreciated much more as the valuable treasures that they are when there are less of them. And there will even be, in many neighborhoods, a sense of sharing a child. Oh, it's not that the child goes from house to house necessarily, but everyone in the neighborhood . . . right now you might find that a typical neighborhood is, let's just say, one side of one block and the other side of one block, just one block. So you might find in a family community, let's say arbitrarily, twelve children—there might be more, there might be less. But in the future, when the birthrate drops, you might not have more than one or two children where you might have normally had many more.

Therefore, those children—wherever they are, born to whatever parents—will be considered neighborhood treasures. Everyone, including those who would've loved to have children themselves (and yes, they'll be sad that they don't have their own children), will follow the lives of these children. There will be people who put out newsletters who do not reveal the intimate secrets of the children but say, "Oh, Matilda got her first tooth today," or "Johnny had a wonderful game at his Little League"—things like that. Oh, there'll be talk—it'll be good to be a child. There'll be lots of presents [laughs].

In short, it will be a good time to be a child. And there will be a lot of protection and safety for children, because initially this will be felt and experienced by many people as a global crisis: "What's happening? Are we going to be able to continue our population?" and so on. But I assure you, you will be able to continue. It's just that through this natural process, people will continue to grow old and die as they do now at the same rate, but the birthrate will go down and you will have a very benevolent (as benevolent as possible) way of reducing your population.

Don't Withhold Pain Relief

I would like to add something here now, even though it's off the topic, and that is that I'd like to encourage governments, corporations and the global community at large that when people are getting older and they're suffering (or when people have a disease or an injury and they're suffering), please do not withhold pain-reducing medication. This is silly. Don't assume that something is a part of life. It's not intended to be.

The suffering that exists is allowed by Creator so that you can create and be creative, so that you can be encouraged and encourage others to find solutions to this suffering. That is clearly meant, not just as a challenge, but as a means to bring you together as a global community. Don't withhold pain medication relief, okay?

Walk-ins Will Increase

Now, if the birthrate is going to go down and all of these souls out there that haven't experienced Earth want to experience this school before it's over, then the percentage of walk-ins will increase—is that correct?

Yes, and that's been covered in another book entirely [see *The Explorer Race and Walk-ins*, coming 2006]. I will say that the walk-in process, as it has been referred to and defined by others, involves a soul in a given body, where instead of death occurring as you understand it—the person dies, the body returns to Earth and the soul goes on—the soul will simply exit the body gently, without any suffering. And the body will go on, but at the moment of exit, another soul will come in, in the most benevolent way and supported by Creator and all loving beings.

So instead of there being a birth as you know it, the souls who walk into those bodies already having been lived in by a previous soul . . . the souls that walk in, as you are calling it, to those bodies all desired to come to Earth to experience life on Earth, but none of those souls desired to go through the birthing process. They all wanted to come in with a body already in existence.

I will refer those of you who are interested in that process to the earlier sidebar [see p. 413]. For those of you who are more interested, there are other books available on the topic. This publisher will put out a book in 2006 that is meant to be a practical handbook for people who believe they may be walk-ins to live more comfortably on Earth and to live more comfortably with the people and the circumstances walk-ins find themselves in.

Two Living Prayers for Benevolent Population Reduction

The birthrate now versus five years from now—what kind of percentages?

No, I'm not going to do that. Why do you think I'm not going to do that? I do not wish to artificially excite people. I want you to think of this as something natural. You are the natural creation in your body of an Earth human being. You all know that there are cycles of existence on the Earth. One of the most basic cycles, of course, besides birth and death, is winter, spring, summer, fall. You are constantly exposed to the fact that there are cycles: night and day; you get hungry, you eat; you need to eliminate that leftover stuff in your body, you go to the bathroom. Cycles.

Earth is about cycles. There have been in the past on Earth other times when the birthrate dropped. Now, what you can do to support the most benevolent way for the population to drop on the Earth—if you'd like to support it, and I know many of you would—is to say the following living prayer, if you like.

If you like you can say this [for more on how to say living prayer, see p. 245]:

Living Prayer
"I AM ASKING THAT THE POPULATION OF HUMAN BEINGS ON EARTH BE REDUCED IN THE MOST BENEVOLENT WAY AND IN THE MOST LOVING WAY NOW."

It seems a bit redundant by saying "the most benevolent" and "the most loving," but it is an acceptable redundancy, because I want you to understand that the most loving and benevolent way is simply that people can still love each other. They can still have intimate relations and enjoy each other's company, but birth will be less likely as time goes on.

This will not be permanent, but it will be for a while in order for the population to decrease. It will stabilize at a certain point and maintain that stabilization, and when that occurs, sufficient time will have gone by so that people will be able to say, "This seems like a really good number of people to be on the Earth, given what Earth can do for us, given what we can do as creators-in-training, yes, but also as benevolent-beings-in-training, to support, nurture and maintain benevolence. Given all of these teachings that we have assimilated in our applying that are working, we can see and understand as a global population that this general number—a little bit more, a little bit less, but this general number—is a good number of people to have on Earth to do what we want to do here and also not to be overwhelmed with population."

See, you will come to that conclusion yourselves. Right now many of you—not all, but many of you—are living in circumstances that are entirely too crowded, and it is creating a lot of strife, which would not be created if you were not in a crowded situation. So we need to gradually decrease the population in the most benevolent way over many years, and this can easily be done in the natural cycle of life as I described in this chapter.

Now, we've talked today about some of the changes that are intended to take place. I know many of you are frightened and upset, and I understand. Sometimes these things are not happening in the most benevolent way. So for those of you who like to say these things, I would like to give you another living prayer that you can say to give you something you can do when you feel that things are just out of your control—as a feeling, you understand—and you're desperate to improve life for all beings. You will have this feeling come up from time to time when there's a disaster or some kind of catastrophe and for other reasons, perhaps.

This is what to say:

Living Prayer

"I AM ASKING THAT THE CHANGES IN THE HUMAN-EARTH COMMUNITY NOW OCCUR AND EVOLVE IN THE MOST BENEVOLENT WAY FOR ALL PEOPLE AND ALL BEINGS ON EARTH NOW."

This covers the present. It covers all people on Earth and all beings as well. And "now" is in the present moment and in all present moments—meaning in the present moment and into the future. If you feel energy when you say this or warmth or good feelings, just be in that energy and good feeling for a time. That will help to bring it about.

So rather than getting caught up in your upset about what's happening in some other part of the world or even in some other part of the neighborhood, say something like that. Because a living prayer can be said more than once. Don't say it over and over and over again repeatedly, as one might say something one is trying to learn or remember. But just say it when those feelings come up, because that's when the need will be the greatest for you in that moment. And when living prayers are said in conjunction with a strong feeling of need, they are more likely to be fulfilled in the most benevolent way possible.

I am thankful to you all for your interest, and I am hoping and requesting that you have the most benevolent lives that you can create and that you can be supported in having. Good life and good night.

Part 2:
The Language of Feeling

The following chapters were originally published in *Shining the Light VII*.

Masculine and Feminine
Components of the Feeling Body

Zoosh
March 3, 2001

Excerpt from a private session, with permission.

hen you say you understand the phrase "As you think, so you create" . . . that is a complete fallacy in your time. The mind has become almost godlike in the reverence people have for it. It is not godlike in its own right, but people consider it such a wonderful thing because they see the value of thought as a unifying force among people, helping to minimize conflict. I grant that, but "As you think, so you create"? No.

The Human Mind Inhibits Creation

The human mind stands outside of all creation on Earth. It can observe and instruct, but more often it controls. And it is the control aspect of the mind that actually inhibits creation. As a child is being raised, in whatever faith or philosophy, the basic conditioning conveyed is, "Don't," "Stop" and "No." Those words in any language, no matter how well intended, immediately or gradually cause the child to feel that his or her natural feelings cannot be trusted.

This is a complication on Earth, because the human mind judges feelings as being entirely in reaction. But, in fact, feelings have a masculine and a feminine component. Reaction is entirely the masculine component, but the feminine component of feelings is in creation. If you can understand that fine point, you will have some insight into how creation works. Creation is achieved by human beings in cooperation with all life. Human beings have some problem with this, not understanding it fully.

The assumption is that Creator is all life, meaning that the human being creates in cooperation with a creator, but that's not true. You create in cooperation with all life equally—the Creator, a plant, a mountain, a rainstorm, an animal or an atomic particle. Creator and all Its creations, including all human beings, are equal elements. Therefore, when you create, the feminine feeling process is in contact with that same feminine feeling process in all other beings in the universe. Creator would be the last being in the world, if I might use that colloquial phrase, to consider Itself separate. Creator is not separate and is not "greater than." Creator is absolutely equal to all Its creations. How could it be any other way? Therefore, all feeling on the feminine level is the means by which you create your reality.

When adults tell children, with the best of intentions, "Don't touch that," or "Stop doing that," it has no great effect unless spoken harshly. If spoken tenderly, it has no restrictive effect on the feminine creation ability along feeling lines. But if spoken harshly or even with a spanking (perhaps not to punish or hurt, but just to get his attention so baby does not stick his fingers in the light socket), this perfectly reasonable action produces an impact that the parents do not realize. The actual impact is that the baby, who is a being in much greater harmony than older humans, begins to distrust his feelings. And therein lies the problem.

The Feminine Feeling Self Connects You in Harmony with All Creation

The feeling ability of human beings—the feeling body—is unknown in your time, and it's something you need to know. Any human being can learn how to interact with the feeling body, to rebuild or, in most cases, to begin to develop a sense of understanding of how the feeling body works, that it has more than one component, that it is not strictly in reaction to anything. The reactive part, to remind you, is the masculine part. But the creation portion of the feeling body is what literally creates your world.

For example, people are always asking for things they need. Sometimes this is a genuine need; sometimes it's merely perceived. If you knew how to ask for that using your feminine feeling self, you would have a good chance of receiving it. Now, what if an individual were to ask for something that might harm somebody else, perhaps in a moment of anger? What if that person was to focus into those feminine feelings and ask for something harmful? It would not work, because in your feminine feeling self, you are connected in harmony with the feminine self of all creation. When you are connected that way, you are the divine creation portion of the human being, or the Explorer Race. This is the core, the root of your being, why you are here. It is, in short, what you are.

Now, even if you could manage to wish something harmful, when connected with that, it would never occur. You would be slightly distant from that feminine creation energy of all beings, not quite able to tap into it for a time until you learned that this is not acceptable. However, you probably would simply not be able to say it, because when you are connected to that feminine-creation-feeling portion of yourself, you are able to speak and desire only in terms of benevolence.

Homework: Differentiating the Masculine and Feminine Feeling Bodies

So I would like to give you a little homework to help you differentiate between the masculine side of the feeling body and the feminine side. It will not be difficult. The first stage is simply to notice the masculine side of the feeling body—don't try to control it, just notice it. Notice how you react in your feeling body to whatever is going on around you for the next few days. Just notice. You don't have to keep a record; you can if you want to, but don't make it so detailed that it interferes with your life. Notice that you saw something, heard something, felt uncomfortable. Or be more specific: "I felt uncomfortable in my chest or arm," something like that.

After that, wait a few days. Then experiment with the feminine portion of the feeling body. This begins with creating a feeling. So between the two assignments, you can make a list of feelings you would enjoy experiencing, anything you like: love, happiness, humor. Remember, some things that are considered to be experiences or actions are also associated with feelings, so explore that.

Now, after that, experiment a bit. Begin when you expect no interruptions, when it is calm and quiet. You can, if you like, use earplugs to eliminate sound, but allow sounds of nature to be present unless they are too distracting. Wear as little clothing as possible, very loose and comfortable. Now lie down or sit. If you sit, do not cross your arms or legs. Take off anything made of metal other than gold. Remove any other metal unless it is something that has been on your body for years.

Simply relax on the bed or in a comfortable chair, and pick an emotion or a feeling from your list. Recall when you had this feeling, unless there is a painful memory associated with it, or imagine it with some story you tell yourself. Rather than attempting to create something, I'd like you to stimulate it with your mind so that your mind feels part of the process. That's important because of the great authority your generation and generations before you have given to the mind. Your mind has been conditioned to believe it must be involved in everything. So we're going to use the divine part of the mind, which is the imagination.

Now, remember and try to bring up the memory, as an actor might do, to create that feeling in your body. Before you do this, you can, if you like, focus on creating heat in your chest or solar plexus, the love-heat/heart-warmth/physical-warmth [see Overview]. You can also create the heat at the end of the exercise. It is important for the mind to know that it is being consulted but it is not the authority. This way the mind will feel involved but not overwhelmed.

I want your mind to feel that it is not being shut out, but rather that it is being incorporated into the process as an equal participant. Go to a feeling and try to create it—maybe two or three feelings each time you do this. Between feelings, just relax for a few minutes to give your body time to adjust. Then go on to another feeling. Once you are into that feeling, try to stay in it as long as you can. Your mind is going to want to think about it, which will immediately prompt other experiences or reactions in your body by the masculine feeling self. Try to stay in the feminine feeling, the generated feeling.

End with the heat in your chest or solar plexus or wherever it shows up. Don't try to move it around. It might show up in one place one night and in one place another day. That's fine. When you end that way, the mind will recognize that it is participating equally in something, and over time it will begin to feel more relaxed in general.

Do this exercise for two to three consecutive days or nights, and then stop. Take a few days off, and then do it again, always ending and, if you choose, beginning with the love-heat feeling. You will find that in time you'll be able to differentiate the masculine feeling self from the feminine feeling self. This will give you a much greater understanding and possibly access to the creation abilities you actually have.

The Mind Is Overwhelmed

Most people's minds feel overwhelmed all the time because there is too much for them to do of which the mind is entirely incapable. That is why as you look around your world, you see the great benefits that science and technology have provided along with the horrible catastrophes they have created. That is because the mind does not have—nor is it naturally equipped to have—a set of morals associated with harmony. Only the feelings can do that. So you can get different thoughts that feel perfectly true to you individually, but when connected with feminine harmony, all beings feel exactly the same. That's the unifying element.

Many people's minds or mental selves are in total panic unless the mind is being used in a disciplined fashion. That's because their minds know that the mind itself is completely out of its depth when it comes to creation. This is why people are often nervous and agitated. That nervousness is a large part of why the human being does not live for 150 to 200 years, which is your natural life cycle in your present body. The mind is overwhelmed by a task that it was never intended to do and of which it is entirely incapable.

The creation-feeling feminine self is not able to feed and nurture the physical body because it has been short-circuited by well-intentioned conditioning within you. If the human being were able to feel this feminine feeling (love and so on) on a regular basis, the incorporation of that feeling would extend life. You might reasonably ask whether there is a feeling you could experience on a more frequent basis that would actually improve your quality of life and perhaps extend it. I cannot guarantee it, but the love-heat feeling was initiated by Speaks of Many Truths so that people would begin to connect with that feeling of access into the feminine feeling self and possibly enter into a harmonic creation ability that would connect them with all life.

Your Natural Creator Self

This work is not intended to give you something you don't already have but rather to show you something and present you with physical evidence of it, to acquaint you with the feelings you have in your physical body, to show you something that works in minute and detailed steps. People have asked me over the years why they have to learn these things in such minute, slow ways on Earth. These are creator lessons. You, the Explorer Race, are intended to become the Creator someday, but in order to do so, you must completely understand the consequences of creation. The only way to understand that is to experience it on a personal level. That's why you come here, why you learn things incrementally. That is why I'm reminding you of the existence of your natural creator self.

You don't have to learn how to become a creator. You're here to learn how to experience on a personal level the impact of your creation so that you do not frivolously or flippantly create something that could have a profound, hurtful impact on beings. As I stated in *Explorer Race: Techniques for Generating Safety*, that is simply because your Creator—not your original Creator, but the Creator of this universe where you have been for some time—does not personally understand the feeling of pain from Its own experience. It has been shown this feeling by another being, but It had to be taken out of this creation briefly to experience it. And the creation suffered a little bit for a time, but now it is all right again. This Creator has encouraged you, the Explorer Race, to take over for It eventually, and to do so, you have to be more finely tuned than this Creator. That's why you are going through these exhaustive steps, so that you will not make the same mistakes as this Creator has done, with the best of intentions, when you take over this creation.

One likes to think of the Creator as omnipotent, wonderful, without error. But, in fact, all creators need to learn. That's why they exist in the form that they do—because they are learning. And just as a parent feels toward a child, this Creator wants you, the Explorer Race, to be better than Itself. So you go through this long, exhaustive lesson for which there has been so much suffering. And now, through the re-exploration of the creation process, you are going to re-create benevolence here on Earth. This is the purpose of the homework I gave you, that you can as a human being, in your portion of Creator, come into that harmony and create. You'd be surprised how much good you can do and what a short time it will take once you learn how to do these things.

The questions you asked triggered this information because it was you who asked and at this time. Others have asked similar questions on previous occasions, but it was not the time and it was not you asking. I am not trying to say you are God or something like that; I am saying that certain souls (my perception of souls is immortal personalities) have gotten together before this experience on Earth and said, "Well, when the time is right, you ask me a question and I will deliver the information." How will we know the time is right? The time is right because human beings of many cultures on Earth—with their conditioning, awareness of the world and experience of being human—can personally grasp this knowledge. It is something that humanity needs and can experience in this moment. So my answer, while it might seem oblique, is in fact the direct answer to your questions.

It's the Feminine Feeling Self's Job to Instruct

I will tell you what you can do to make me happy: Embrace life as much as you can. Experience physicality in ways that please you and feel good to both your masculine and feminine feeling selves. Now that you have the homework, you can discern those things. Don't favor one over the other. It is not your job to discard the masculine feeling self but to instruct it.

The feminine feeling self's job is to instruct. Women know innately that it is their job to instruct men, even if they are not conditioned to believe that. Very often the woman has difficulty with this, or she could even get into trouble by telling the man too much. But the woman is born knowing that as a feminine being, it is her job to instruct. What she doesn't realize, because your society has not yet sufficiently evolved, is that she needs to be instructed in all the true harmonious feminine arts and abilities so that she can instruct in ways the masculine being can hear and embrace without feeling threatened, condemned or intimidated in any way.

Therefore, understand that your feminine feeling self is intended to instruct your masculine feeling self on which feelings are the best to experience, not only in terms of generating those feelings, but (and here is the crux of the matter) in experiencing, seeking, creating—in short, in living a life where those benevolent and wonderful feminine-inspired feelings will be felt in reaction to what you are doing. When the masculine feeling body has learned to distinguish which feelings are good and not so good, beneficial or not, in terms of your relationship with yourself and others, it will then seek out experiences with all life. It will react with those wonderful feelings the feminine feeling self has shown are intended to be felt in the harmonic feminine feeling selves of all other life.

Human beings do not always have access to these feelings because they are here to learn. After they have learned, they will choose to experience feelings prompted by the feminine creation feeling self, not only because of some statement by Grandfather or Uncle Zoosh, but because it feels good and has a benevolent effect on all other beings. That, my friend, is what you can do if you choose.

The Keys of Enoch

The major strength of the book *Keys of Enoch* lies in the illustrations and their effect when you touch them. To do that, lay either hand palm down on the illustration and see what happens (experiment with which works better for each illustration and at different times). Do this only two or three times a day, however, as the material is rooted in the past and is extremely potent. Therefore, I do not choose to support and sustain such books; I merely acknowledge that this material is true and worthy of doing.

Generally speaking, I do not support what I call the Jehovan past. Jehovah is a past incarnation—thinly but not directly connected to the Creator of this universe. In the past, I might have, for the sake of being polite and not wanting to shock people too much, indicated that Jehovah is somehow connected to the Creator of this universe. That is not a lie but rather a diplomatic statement, and at times I know how to be diplomatic. Therefore, I would say that work such as this *Keys of Enoch* book can root you to the Jehovan past and take you into a more challenging future. So, in short, I don't support it.

Grasp the Future Timeline!

I have informed people that if they continue to burn water—break it down into hydrogen and oxygen and use it for fuel, which is happening now—this planet will eventually look like Mars. Now, understand, you could see that along a Jehovan timeline, an experience line. It is intended that a different timeline be engaged, and one of the ways you can engage it is the method I have suggested—working with your feminine creation feeling.

Recognize that your vision is associated with what I would call the past timeline, not the future timeline, which in order to be activated, must be grasped by human beings in the present. And the more who grasp it, the more likely it will be engaged and the old timeline left behind. When you are in your feminine creative-feeling self, the idea of burning water will be unthinkable. But when you are engaged in the Jehovan timeline, which embraces science and technology with mind but without heart, then it seems perfectly acceptable to burn water, especially when you think you have an inexhaustible amount of it.

Of course, it's not only *not* inexhaustible, but the replenishment of pure water, rain, is life giving. That's why animals prefer it. Animals will drink water you put out for them, but they much prefer to drink life-giving water that comes in the form of rain or bubbles up from a spring. That gives life. So recognize that the consumption of water in the form of fuel could occur along the Jehovan timeline. But to grasp that future timeline, do the homework I've given you.

Societies have existed on other planets—Mars, for example. Mars looks like Earth in a lot of ways; however, the most striking thing about it is the absence of water-supported life. The water has been burned up. I have stated that it is essential not to use water as fuel. It is too easy, for one thing. An engine that runs on water was demonstrated a few years ago—not only is it too easy, but it poses a serious threat.

There are always stories of automobile companies purchasing and with-holding patents for certain products that increase fuel efficiency, resulting in better mileage. Well, sometimes corporations do good deeds—although they might be for self-serving purposes. One of these good deeds is the decision not to produce engines that run by breaking down water. A water-injection system for vehicles was tested awhile back that improves mileage but stimulates the same pattern or technological means. Observers and participants watched demonstrations in shock. It was dangerous, not just because it threatened various industries, but much more to the point, it threatened all life as you know it. So the corporations did you a service by blocking that device.

You have done well, my friend. You have learned how to be a human being. You have learned the valuable lessons that have taken you to this point where you can ask these questions in the right time and in the right way. It has produced this wisdom, this knowledge, this important aware-ness. It will help many people.

Steps toward
Unity of Consciousness

Reveals the Mysteries
May 5, 2002

This is Reveals the Mysteries.
Welcome.

Union in the Dream State

Let us first talk about dreams and dream phenomena. It's important to note that as your responsibility for the functioning of different aspects of this planet increases, so will you be expected to provide balance on the planet—first in your unconscious state, then in your dream state, then in your subconscious state and finally in your conscious state. You have been working as a people to provide balance on the planet in the unconscious state for some time. One of the results of that work is the general public's increased awareness of problems all around the world that need to be addressed in ways that do not simply involve control or order. They have to be resolved on a permanent basis that nurtures and feeds people, even if there seems to be no apparent way to do so.

Now you've added to that the dream state, which is the next level of your responsibility and which you've been working on for a time. But you are beginning to do more than simply share or complete each other's dreams and understand the uniform application of how such things work. You are learning now on the "lab basis," meaning applied challenges, to see what you can actually do as groups of shared dreamers.

Groups of shared dreamers always have to do with entities—individual personalities as you understand them on Earth—who have lived together before in other lives or will live together in the future and as a result have some sense of familiarity on the soul or immortal personality basis. There is at least enough familiarity that if you sample or complete the dream of one of the members of your group, it will not be so remote, strange or uncomfortable that it causes you to feel that it is foreign. Such a dream from some soul personality who is not this familiar might cause you to at least wake up suddenly or feel as if you had a nightmare, even though the dream itself, as you remember, it was not nightmarish in its quality.

With these new challenges, you are beginning to resolve the incompatibility that you often see from one group of individuals to another. Those you've shared lives with before or will share lives with in some way in the future—who make up a dreaming group like this on Earth now—are from all walks of life, all nationalities, religions, races. This shared commonality has nothing to do whatsoever with any kind of mutually shared interest, but is strictly a familiarity based on past, future or, even in some rare cases, other-dimensional interactivity. So these levels of responsibility you will feel more and more. Eventually, groups will expand to include those whom you might have some contact or slight contact with.

As a result, you will have a need for some greater capacities. You are working on these capacities now as you are finishing the dreams of your fellow compatriots or loved ones or friends from other lifetimes. Sometimes it is because the people have died suddenly while asleep; other times you do this because their dream cycle was interrupted while they were involved in a very important dream that needed to be finished. You will finish the dream for them. Don't be alarmed, then, if you have these dreams that seem to be in some way wholly foreign to your life. Don't assume there is a pattern to them that is unsettling, that they are necessarily visions. Unless they have a wide, sweeping panorama of global events or an intensely personal feeling, with the faces of people you know now and their body shapes—not just their faces superimposed on the dream images, but the genuine sensation of individuals you now know—unless that is present, you can be reasonably certain it is just an overlaying of familiar individuals onto the last vestiges of the dream as a result of your waking process . . . as you wake up.

Now, in order to recognize your responsibility, you need only to sleep when you sleep. You do not have to say, "I will finish the dreams of my fellows." You don't have to do that. It has begun. This is a part of your agreement, which you have arranged on the unconscious level. There are many more things that you have set up on the unconscious level, and these will filter into what you do over the next seven to eight or ten years, according to the sequence of timing that feels right to each and every one of you. They are based entirely on the shared, mutual feelings you experience—not only in dream circles, but also globally—as a result of sensations from people on the other side of the world or even the sense of awareness brought about by reading or viewing or hearing about the news of the day or speaking to friends or communicating with them in some way.

All these things and others might easily bring up a sense of shared, mutual feeling, which might—if you deem it is appropriate on the unconscious level (acting as the human race united), if you deem it is the timing that is intended and has been triggered—inaugurate or initiate another series or sequence of applications used to resolve such difficulties, challenges and problems that arise out of a need to create absolute union. Then you can all be united, not only on the unconscious level (as you all are right now according to your arrangement and according to the overall desire of the vision of the Explorer Race), but also according to simple practicality. This creates a world that works for such a vast population living on a fairly small planet, intermingled with animals, plants and other species. Such complexities require your attention. You might not have felt a need for such attention when your human population was smaller, but now that it is bigger, it requires this attention.

Union in the Subconscious State

As time goes on and you begin to develop the same sense of union that you have unconsciously developed in your dream state—and this will take awhile—you will then move on to the next level of union in the subconscious state (even though you've begun to touch into that level right now). Union in the subconscious state allows you to be vaguely aware on the conscious level, moment to moment, of the need to unify. When this begins to happen, you will see vast, sweeping changes on a physically perceptible level of groups of individuals, then whole populations and cultures, making radical change—not violent, but radical change—in perception, attitude and general homage paid to each other. This will occur not on a religious level, but on a level of politeness and caring that you have only hoped, wished and dreamed for in the past. Once that is established, you will then move on to the totally conscious level of union.

All these things will take time. But I bring to your attention today how much progress you have made. You are totally unified as a human population on the unconscious level. You are working toward union on the dream level. You have begun with union on the subconscious level. In short, you are making progress.

That's wonderful! What is the benefit or purpose of finishing the dream? What happens if it doesn't get finished?

It's not a problem if it doesn't get finished. Its benefit is that it is simply a vehicle that allows you to unify and become aware at least of the unsettledness of the lives of other human beings. In short, it is a means by which you can make a connection—a further connection, let's say—between your feeling self, filtered as it is and protected in the dream state, and the feeling self of other human beings living on Earth now.

You talked of a group of dreamers—what kind of group? Are there two? A thousand?

It could be anywhere from two or more. It might be that you are involved in more than one group. One does not arrange spiritual groups according to dozens.

You said that we have set up other things at an unconscious level to lead to unity. Are they too far in the future to talk about? Can you give us a hint?

You mean that which you have planned to initiate? I will not speak of those things now. If I speak of them, you will wait for them to happen, and you will wait indefinitely. In short, I do not wish to derail the process by making conscious something that is intended to function—how can we say?—on the analogy level. It functions the way your heart and breath work, without your thought. You don't think, "Okay. Now I'm beating my heart and beating my heart again."

These are the six billion humans on the planet? Or maybe this is also connecting to the other 94 percent of the Explorer Race?

It is unnecessary to connect to any being except to those on the planet now. Because you are here, you are functioning in the physical; you are not exclusively in spirit. If you are exclusively in spirit, there is no need or reason to apply physical lessons, experiences and so on.

So are the other 94 percent all on a spiritual level? They don't have lives waiting somewhere else?

They might. It is up to them. But waiting is not quite the same on the spiritual level as is, say, waiting for the bus.

To Share a Dream Is Intimate Indeed

Is there any scenario where you could finish someone's dream and cause a problem?

No, because you are asleep. If you were finishing it on the conscious level without all of the training and all of the steps I've mentioned in sequence . . . yes, you could. But you would not even be able to do so on the conscious level without all this training in unity. So that is theoretical.

So we're making progress.

It is important for you to understand that there is a reason when things happen. And that what appears to be unreasonable and outrageous might be just that, when seen as an individual event. But it is also important at times—maybe not every time, but at times—to pull back and look at it in the larger context, which is what I'm doing here. Meaning that, since the topic is dreams, if you usually have certain types of dreams and you suddenly have something completely unusual for yourself and it doesn't fall under the qualification I gave before as an exception, then you might consider that you are perhaps finishing or following up on a dream sequence that was left unfinished by someone else—not because the other would suffer a trauma from that, but because it allows you to experience a connection with another human being at a deeper level than simply, "Hey, how you doing?" or other things you say that are often intended to keep people away from you, not to draw them closer. This is much more intimate. To dream, to share a dream, is very intimate indeed.

Is there any learning a dreamer in such a case could use in his or her physical life?

Generally, in this case, no, because it is so far afield from your own life that there is no apparent connection or application. That's another way to know. You might not know immediately, but if you keep a dream journal or if you recall your dreams, within two or three days you might know if there has been no connection whatsoever. For one thing, you don't have to try to remember all of your dreams; you will know when you wake up. "That was really strange," you might say, or "I've never dreamt anything like that before," or "That was wild," or "That was wonderful." It's not just something frightening; very often it might be something wonderful that doesn't relate in any way that you can understand to anything you might normally dream—or, for that matter, in any way to your life.

Aboriginal Dreamtime

When one reads about the Australian Aborigines operating in Dreamtime . . . based on what you just said, does that mean they're totally unified on the unconscious level?

You are all totally unified on the unconscious level, but I think what you're trying to say is that they are totally unified on the dream level.

Well, where would you put the dream level? Is it another level between the conscious, the unconscious and the subconscious?

I didn't put it that way, because I don't want to unnecessarily complicate the process. But if you're changing the subject to ask about these individuals, then I will simply say that for them to function, it is not quite consciously. Rather, it is a bridge from the conscious self. It is a bridge from the spiritual conscious self into the dream state, to function on a unified level unconsciously, on the dream level subconsciously and consciously for a specific purpose. Those who can do this must do so benevolently. Oh, various war research individuals have tried to do so malevolently . . .

As a way to influence reality?

Yes. It has always been a catastrophic disaster—usually for those who are the researchers.

Would you say that what the Aborigines do, then, is a step up, a step on the path ahead of us?

Not necessarily. That is a shamanic act, done almost always with the intention of improving the quality of life for troubled individuals, groups or even vast populations. In short, it is like the doctor of the dream or a dream doctor; it is a shamanic function done to improve the quality of life. But you do not all have to become physicians or dentists, you know.

I didn't understand that it was a shamanic technique.

No, individuals do it. It is only . . . like in other groups of people, some individuals do this or that. Are you all in your culture bankers?

Life Extension Demands You Release the Attitude of "Suffering Makes One Stronger"

I want to talk briefly, not at length at this time, about the conditioning of the religions and, more importantly, the historical philosophies that have made up the means by which you have been able to justify your history of Manifest Destiny and other things in the United States to accomplish your goals and purposes as a society. Specifically, at this time I want to talk about why only a minority of people are given pain medications or, for that matter, the means to die—not just people specifically traumatized, but those who are suffering lingering deaths from diseases. Why isn't there a vast amount of research into these areas? Why isn't there a tremendous amount of application so that people can, as you like to say, die with dignity?

Now, it's perfectly all right for those whose bodies are changing in some uncomfortable way to accommodate for those changes in a hospital or hospice, with care by professionals and loving family members, but there needs to be a recognition that in order to improve the quality of life, simply extending life, or life extension, is insufficient. Speaking to the researchers here, before life extension can even be embraced by the physical body, for the physical body to embrace and allow and encourage and nurture such life extension, you must reassure scientifically and on the feeling level. The scientists must become more complete and apply their feelings in nurturing all human and animal subjects they are working with to want to live longer. And one of the vital and obvious means by which to accomplish this is to be able to mentally and on the feeling level— including touching—reassure all participants that whatever pain they experience, whether it has to do with their death or part of the process involved in extending life, that their pain will be completely dulled so they do not feel it and can experience life to the best of their ability, interacting with family, friends and loved ones.

It's vital that you do this—I'm speaking especially to life-extension advocates—if you expect to truly accomplish a life that goes on 150, 175 years, in which you feel vital. Of course, this will not happen immediately, overnight, but it cannot happen by transferring pig organs to the body of a human being. I grant that you are doing that on an experimental basis. I'm not going to comment here whether I think it is a good thing or a bad thing, but I am commenting that the obvious advantage is to have your own human organs last for 150, 175 years at fully 80 to 90 percent of their youthful capacity—even in the 170th year. This is what you want in life extension.

I want you to clearly recognize that there is a direct connection between the physical body's reassurance—physically, on the feeling level—between a confidence of no pain to suffer and the desire to live longer. As any physical person knows, when you get injured, when you get hurt, sometimes the pain is slight, sometimes it is great. There comes a point in time when the physical body cannot, nor will it (this is a matter of permission), give permission to go on beyond a certain point. When the pain gets to be too much, that's it. The physical body says, "Okay, I would much rather change my physical matter into something else in which I am more comfortable." And of course, your soul personality will also agree. "Oh yes, I'd much rather be elsewhere," says your soul personality. "I want to go and be with God or get on with my other lives," whatever your philosophical belief is. And your physical body says, "I'm in complete agreement. I'd rather be elsewhere, not experiencing this pain."

Life Extension and the Elimination of Pain

So in order to get what you want—a longer life, a happier life, more comfortable, more vital—you will literally need to change the means of your science, your medicine and your philosophy to embrace on the feeling, loving level. Not, "Oh, I love you, I love you"—those are words—but the literal feeling as a love-heat/heart-warmth/physical-warmth loving experience given many, many times in these books [see Overview]. I really want to encourage all of your scientists and life-extension advocates to experience that, to do it and to apply it in their work to the best of their ability while they are working with experimental subjects and volunteers.

And remember, the goal is to reassure the physical bodies of these beings—whether they be human or animal or plant—that your desire is to see them live longer, happier, more comfortably and without pain. This has to be a convincing situation that doesn't only function on the mental level, because on the mental level . . . that goes without saying. Everyone, for the most part, wants to live without pain. But to convince the physical bodies of all these beings, you must make reassurance and nurturing on the physical, loving basis a given, not an exception.

When it is a given, it is as with the animal; the animals naturally love, they love one another. This is a natural, a complete given with most animals whom you at least identify with. It is essential that you recognize that it is natural for human beings to do this too, but because of the complexities of your world and the challenges you experience in this growth school on Earth, it is sometimes something you forget to do. But for something that is such a common experience—all of you experience it, birth, death, *all* of you experience pain—you must do what you can about what you can influence.

You *can* influence the experience of pain, so kindly let go of this attitude—and it is purely and exclusively an attitude—that suffering pain makes you stronger. The reason that whole thing developed was to create a rationalization, to reassure people that once they got through their pain, they'd be stronger. And while that might be true sometimes, it is not a reassurance to the physical body to want to live longer. So understand that my conversation with you today is to draw a direct correlation between life extension and the elimination of pain as you know it.

Is it a religious issue? Why do we seem to suffer more in the United States than people do in Europe? They have painkillers that they give out liberally.

What I would say is that many times in other countries . . . other countries have absolutely no qualms about providing pain medication. But very often you will find that these other countries have had to face the fallacy of their religious beliefs or, in some cases, their philosophical beliefs because of the vast suffering brought on by war. In Europe and in other countries, Asian countries, who have experienced war and such phenomena of vast suffering, the idea of allowing such suffering without providing the pain medication that is available would be unthinkable. We use Europe as an example, because in many places in Europe there has been, out of necessity, a recognition of the shortcomings of religions, philosophies and other forms of conditioning that try to rationalize pain as something of value.

Pain-Free Existence Is Possible

Now, the origin of this idea is to explain why life is the way it is, which is ultimately the purpose of any philosophy or religion. And when people experience as a universal fact that certain things cause pain, such as things that are absolutely accepted as being part of life (birth and death), there needs to be an explanation. I will tell you that someday all birth will be pain-free. Not just from drugs . . . yes, drugs are good. Stop thinking of them as being bad. Granted, you have some uses of drugs now that are not so good, but in time you will find a resolution for that; it will not be as hard as you think. But recognize this and appreciate it: The purpose for which drugs exist at all is to relieve pain and improve the quality of life, whether a technique of application is taking place or whether a step toward greater length of life is being embraced.

It is not my intention today to take on the vast issue of birth and death and pain and all of that. But I do want to suggest to you this linkage between life extension—whether it be a few years, or vastly into the future, a huge length of life for a single individual in a single body—and the experience of pain and the embracing of life. The linkage is total and direct. So, life-extension researcher—and I know you are working on this all over the planet—recognize this and first put your efforts into the relief of pain, which is not that difficult with what you know now for all people.

It can be done fairly inexpensively, and then it will take several years for the individual's body to believe that pain-free existence is possible in extraordinary circumstances or even in expected circumstances such as a lingering death, as will be the case for many of you. Also, there will need to be global acceptance of the fact that no one has to suffer because it is so easy to do something, to switch the pain off for the purpose of being able to live comfortably or at least experience a comfortable death . . . so one could say goodbye, have a kiss, a touch, an embrace with loved ones and friends. Don't leave this research up to only the military, which will seek to do this for the sake of defense procedures with soldiers. Recognize that this is a reality. If physicians globally embrace this, it will be a gift to humanity and your lives will ultimately improve. How many of you would like to live to be 170, 175 years old if you would know that you're going to be vital and pain-free? Think about that.

Everybody. Thank you very much, Reveals the Mysteries.

Experience Creation in a New Way

Zoosh, Reveals the Mysteries and Miriam
September 2002

Zoosh: Understanding Attraction

hose of you who find that the coming year [2003] has distractions will also find that it has attractions. You will find a couple of things functioning here that will surprise you. For one, you will find that you are attracted to people in ways most of you have never been attracted before. By this I do not simply mean sexually, but rather that you will be attracted to people, wanting to make friends or do things together, even things you don't normally do with anybody other than the friends or family you now have—activities, picnics, sports, whatever. You will find that certain people look more appealing, even people you would not normally want to include. Don't be shy about that, especially if he or she is responsive. The unity of people is beginning. Don't feel so bad [chuckles].

Meet Unlikely People

Why do I put it this way? Those of you who feel that you are safer or more comfortable with one type of person might be a little unsettled by having these unfamiliar feelings frequently this year and, for some of you, well beyond this year. They will arise regardless of whether people are like you and your friends and family or not. Try to get over your feelings that it must be only the people you've always known, and reach out. Say, "Would you like to join us? We're having a meal," or "We're going to the movies. Would you like to join us?" If that person doesn't want to or if there's not a return smile, he or she doesn't make eye contact, then go on about your life. But perhaps you will have him or her sit down and enjoy tea with you in a restaurant or do some other casual human activity that does not make a big impact on your life. Just try it. Talk, even at the bus stop or around the water cooler, as you say.

Attraction is a funny thing. You will find that your feelings of attraction will be heightened in this coming year. You will find that the function of those feelings will be heightened as well—meaning the way you know physically in your body that you are attracted to someone or something. And you will find it much more difficult to ignore those feelings. This does not mean that you have license to become a pest [chuckles] about people who do not want your attention. Learn to work with these feelings. You might have made a mistake. Maybe it's not the person you thought; maybe it is someone who looks like that. Or maybe the person does not want your attention, you see, which might be the case. Maybe you are right; maybe you are attracted, maybe you do want to include him or her, but if he or she is not ready, give that person permission to say, "No," or "Not at this time." There will be others you will feel this attraction toward, many opportunities.

Develop Your Own Sensing System

Understand that the physical feeling of attraction within you is heightened in this coming year because it is time for you to begin to learn the feminine means of creation—and it is not sufficient for only women in your culture to learn this. Women know a great deal about the feminine means and qualities and functions of attraction. Men must feel it as well, not only to begin to resolve some of the more male-dominated problems— meaning wars, disputes and long-standing antagonisms—but also to find solutions that do not involve control, manipulation or force. How can we fit this into what works for us? Or, as feminine attraction qualities really work, what can we fit into what to accomplish our purpose?

It is as if you are developing your own sensing system—not a *mental* sixth sense, but a *feeling* sixth sense. That's why it has been difficult for you to mentally construe, create and theorize about how the so-called sixth sense works. I'm not just talking about precognition but about the means and the manner of knowing how to create in ways that are benevolent for all life around you. I'm talking about what is naturally attracted to what to produce the qualities, the goal, the purpose and the ideals of what it is we're actually trying to achieve or a step toward that. And as you know, the journey begins with steps. So I want you to be aware of that.

New Qualities of Attraction

It's my job to give you the mental overview, the concept, the understanding to know what is physically happening to you. Your powers of attraction—not just how others might be attracted to you, but more to the point, your function of physical attraction (how it feels to you, what you know in your body, how you feel in your body)—are being not only activated but heightened in this year and, for some of you, beyond. You can begin to understand creation from an attraction point of view rather than from a strictly control-and-manipulation creation point of view. It is not time to be learning how to hammer the nails, how to force these two boards together, but rather what kind of shelter naturally seems to attract one piece to another to form protection and nurturing for yourself and your loved ones. I grant, that's a ways off. You're not going to immediately learn which stone is attracted to another stone so it can make a structure that will remain standing for thousands of years, which will create seams and so on that will defy the stonecutter's current understanding of how to achieve it.

The more you learn about the actual qualities of attraction, the more you will discover that your capacities are much greater than you thought. Attraction is not just about, "Who do I want to go to the dance with?" [chuckles] or "Who will I go to the movies with this week?" Attraction goes right down to the very basic level, how the seed knows where to sprout, which sperm finds which egg to create the exact child the mother wants. Understanding attraction will allow you to experience creation in a new way. I wish you well in your pursuits of attraction, and I think you will enjoy it.

Reveals the Mysteries: Apply Benevolent Magic

In this coming year [2003], you will be called upon to perform tasks that you have never been called on to do before. The workings of your physical body will now begin to break through the chains of conditioning that you've experienced in this life. You have all been conditioned to believe that your power and influence are limited. Sometimes the conditioning was unintentional, and other times it was not only intentional but even subversive. This kind of subversion sometimes exists to sell you products or services, but other times it has the hidden agenda of making you subservient and receptive to whatever immediate stimulation can be activated in you. You know you've all responded to advertising or even made spontaneous purchases at the market or the auto store.

I want you to know that your physical body is not an accident or some scientific model. Nor is it an example of evolution—which, by the way, is a theory but not a natural fact, though those who believe in evolution try to persuade others that it is a natural fact. Your physical body is very carefully constructed by Creator—not only to activate the functions of life within you, but to be able to connect to Its overall Spirit as well as the soul personality you express in life. But there are other factors that sometimes show themselves in a given life in a spectacular fashion. You all have heard about the woman or boy who has executed some act of great strength in an unexpected fashion, lifted a car off of someone just like that; it makes the news. Scientists are, regardless of their theories, essentially baffled about how this is done.

This is an example of the capacity your body truly has, and your Bible as well as your other religious books have this correct: Your body is fashioned after the Creator's body, only in miniature. The Creator, while not having a physical body as you understand physicality, still has the capacity to create. You might say that the Creator is condensed creation, which would suggest that your physical body is also about creation. Because of this fact, you are being activated—not only on the physical level by the means I suggested in your conditioning, but more to the point, by Creator—to be creative in ways that imitate Creator's desires for your benevolent good.

Making Things Better

How might you see this begin to show itself this year? You will all begin to have desires that feel like they can go beyond wishes, hopes and dreams to be able to make things better. Whether this "making things better" is a desire or a need, a hope or something that seems to be impossible, you will have the desire. More to the point, you will have a feeling that it is possible; you need only to know how to do it. This is a huge step for you all, considering the lifetime of conditioning you've had. Think about it. Think about something you'd like to do that's benevolent. How many of you are ill or injured and would love to have certain capacities, or have fears you'd like to transform into strengths and so on? It's easy to think of something.

This coming year, through books such as the *Shamanic Secrets* series and teachings in the pages of the *Sedona Journal of Emergence!*, it will be my intention to instruct you on how to achieve those goals in a practical, physical sense through the further understanding and application of what your friend Zoosh has called "benevolent magic." Benevolent magic is just a fun way to refer to natural creation, which is possible by any being in the creation of this Creator. You are activated, yes; you've been activated before, in steps to prepare you. You've already been given instructions. But in these brief comments, I will give you a glimmer of what you might expect to be able to do, along with some homework.

Creativity—The Capital "C"

Once you've done the work, you will be able to begin working with something that is an actual substance. From a scientific point of view, it would seem to come out of thin air—meaning that what it produces is not quantifiable or measurable before the effects are noted. If you could measure this substance, you would call it creativity. In time you might come to refer to it simply as the capital letter "C." Some of you will refer to it using the capital "C" followed by the digit "2," meaning creative, meaning you as Creator's children are "2." Do you understand the digital reference?

Here's some homework for you in the next few months (especially during January, February and the first part of March) if you have a pain, an ache or a disability in your bodies. This is for you to practice on your own bodies—not on others, even though you love them and want the best for them. You learn what works on the basis of your own physical feelings. I might add that your physical feelings are the divine touch of Creator, Its touch from the inside out. You know that Creator loves you, and yet if you do not pay attention to these feelings, Creator will find a way to make them more obvious and hard to ignore [chuckles]. This is not because Creator wishes to punish you, but rather because Creator needs you to pay attention so that you will know the consequences of not doing so. This is not punishment but an effect. If you are going to learn how to create, you must begin experiencing creation that you prompt in your own physical body because, young or old, you've had a lifetime to learn how you personally, physically feel in your body—if you're old enough to understand this, that's the distance of your lifetime. You've had this understanding; now you're going to re-create it.

Healing with Love-Heat and Light

Here's your homework: For those of you who can do the love-heat/ heart-warmth/physical-warmth [see Overview]—let's not call it an exercise, it's an *experience*—for those of you who can do this experience, do it that way. For those of you who can visualize, visualize condensed white and gold light. White light alone will not work. Sometimes in your visual spectrum you might see light as white when it contains other colors. But if you see light as gold, it will be easier for you to assimilate all colors. This is something your science actually knows. So I recommend white and gold, but you can do just gold if you wish.

Put the warmth or the light in a place that is the exact point where you feel some pain, discomfort or need in your physical body, even if it's just a stomachache. If you've experienced a wound or an injury or were born without some part of your body that you'd like to have, address your pain first. If you don't have any pains, don't be too shy to put that warmth or that light in some area of your body where something is missing or where you'd like to be better in some way. But you can't fine-tune it at this point. You have to trust your body. If your body has pain at some given point, it will be receptive to this warmth or the light right in that spot, and your body will know what to do with that. These are lessons in creation.

What about those of you who do not know or have not learned how to do the love-heat? Feel love and experience the heat as often as you can.

Wherever it comes up, feel into it and go into it more, feel it more. I want you to actually move it to the spot where you have the pain, even though you might feel it in your chest or abdomen area. This is the next step. For those of you who do not do the love-heat, use gold light, use the visualization of gold light.

THE GOLD LIGHT EXERCISE
Isis

To do the gold light exercise, imagine a gold light in your solar plexus area. It's important to start it there—or if you prefer, you can start it behind your bellybutton. Consider it to be like a light bulb. Let the light gradually move into the rest of your body, and imagine that your body is glowing with the gold light.

Remember, let it start within you and radiate out. Some of you will be able to feel something benevolent. Many of you will feel like you are using your imagination, but since the imagination is the divine part of the mind, that is perfectly all right. Stay with that feeling for at least five minutes.

It's particularly helpful to do this before you go to sleep—either before you take a nap or before you go to sleep at night. It's perfectly all right to do it if there's somebody else in the bed, but not if you are entwined with that person. Try not to be touching anyone when you are doing it, but shortly after you do it, then you can touch someone if you like.

You may also do this in a chair sitting up if you like, but lying down is best. If you sleep with pets, it is all right if they are near. This will not harm them in any way; they might actually like it. But ideally you would do it on your own. This is a particularly good thing to do if you do not feel safe sleeping at night. Perhaps you feel that there are energies in your sleeping place that are uncomfortable—then this is something you might try.

Healing with Your Tone

What about those of you who do not do either? Are we going to leave you out? No! We're going to do something else. That's why you have abilities and senses that are born naturally with you. Feel where that pain is; if you have more than one pain, pick one place. If it turns out that it helps the other places, that's fine, but pick one place. Then make a sound. It's not a tone that you measure musically, saying, "This note, not that note." Rather, it is a sound that is the most comfortable sound you can make. Go up the scale [sings] and find in your body the exact musical tone that you can make that feels the most natural and easy for you to do. Make that tone, and while you're making it, if you can, lightly touch the spot where you have the pain. Or if the pain is too much, you can touch the air right above that spot, five or six inches away if you like, and make the tone. Just naturally breathe in, making the tone as you breathe out and so on. Do that for a few minutes. Do all of these things, whichever way you do it, just for a few minutes.

But what if you feel like doing something else with the tone? You might open your mouth and go a-a-a-h. Maybe you'll make the tone with your teeth clenched, not with your mouth opened [makes that sound]. That's fine. If you want to make the tone with your hand, one hand or the other or both, in some gesture in front of you, do that—whatever feels good to you physically. Don't make a gesture that has a meaning known and understood by your society, because that gesture will have been mentally conditioned into you to mean something else, even if you are using it for the first time. In short, it is to be a natural motion of your hands, however you feel it's best to place them. Experiment a little bit, those of you doing the tone.

Healing with Fragrance

Let's move on. What about those of you who can't easily do any of those things? Let's give you an option. Some of you are very good with smell, very attuned to fragrances. This is what I'd like you to do. I want you to obtain some cinnamon and smell it. Notice the fragrance. Try to get it from an herb store or even a cooking supply store, because it will come in some form where its odor will be more significant. You want something natural, with no preservatives. See if you can memorize that smell. Remember, this is about creation, which you do with your body, and it is intended to have an effect on your body. Why do you think you have pain in the first place? It is to perform creation, to resolve your own pain. I know, you would have liked to have known this a long time ago! But you know now, and you have the motivation to do something about it, don't you?

Now, this is what to do with the fragrance method. Smell cinnamon as much as you can over the course of a few days—not just when you have the time, but when you can be relaxed. You will be prepared to perform the creation work when you feel the pain, wherever you feel it. It could very well be temporary—a headache, a stomachache, some kind of thing that passes—or some other injury you might feel or long-term discomfort you try to ignore. If you don't feel the pain, don't do anything. Wait until you do. You're a human being—you'll feel one eventually! Those of you who use the fragrance method will have memorized the smell of cinnamon by that time.

Hold your hand or the fingertips of your right hand—if you want to try your left hand, you can—parallel to your body, not pointing at your body, but parallel to it, right over your body, maybe five or six inches above where you feel that discomfort. And remember, don't pull out the cinnamon at that point; you will have had to have smelled it enough that you memorized the smell. Remember the smell of cinnamon. Focus only on your body's recollection of the smell of cinnamon, and do that for a few minutes.

About Your Homework

That's what I'm going to recommend for your initial homework. You have something that works with physical feelings, you have something for visualization, you have a tone and you have a fragrance. That's four choices. Just do one, whichever one works best for you. I've offered you the fragrance method as an alternative. Some of you have that capacity, and it might be good for you to begin to use it. That's your homework in the coming months and perhaps years. We'll give you more homework that will work forward from this point, initially for your physical body and someday for the physical body of Earth. First you begin with your own body.

Those of you who are in the healing arts, whatever form that might take, might also get instructions to work on others and support them to work with their bodies. The rest of you can follow instructions if you like to support and work on with and for Mother Earth's body, that she might feel better. Don't use all the methods you have learned before, but use the material- and physical-mastery lessons you will receive, building on the *Shamanic Secrets* series that Speaks of Many Truths and myself have given. I wish you good life in these pursuits and good life in general.

Miriam: Touching Living Flowers

My name is Miriam. I am one of the essences of the natural world. I am associated with water and the more delicate essences of life around—fragrance, the energy bodies around flower petals and the means by which such physical membranes are attracted to all those who might need them. I will speak only at this time. In the year to come, flowers will become much more sensitized, especially through their petals—not de-sensitized, but sensitized—to the touch and even the near touch of the human being.

Change the Way You Touch Flowers

As you might already know, flower petals do not like to be physically touched by the human being because of skin oils. The way the human being touches the flower petal needs to change. When a flying creature lands on the flower, it is often something very feathery that actually touches it, like fine hairs. For those of you who are around flowers this year, try to touch them first with the hairs on the back of your hand or leg or another part of your body. For most of you, the hairs on your head have been desensitized, except for the ones on the back of your neck. You can have a friend touch you to the flower petals this way, but not if the flower has been moved—you will have to lean down to the flower.

This is the best way for human beings to touch flower petals. I'd recommend working this touch first with roses, dandelions, violets, peonies or apple or cherry blossoms. That's what I recommend. All of those flowers can only imbue the human being with nurturing love and support qualities.

Flowers Will Diminish Hunger

If you are hungry but cannot reach or obtain food or for some reason cannot eat at that moment, touch these flower petals with those hairs on your body and your hunger will either completely go away or greatly diminish. If you can allow the flowers to grow where they naturally grow, that is best. The touch will not work or the effect will be greatly diminished if the flower does not grow where it has naturally sprouted up. The next best place is in a garden where the flowers can grow undisturbed, where they are not disturbed much, rarely poked at, and where weeds are not constantly being dug out of the ground. Understand that what you call a weed is often a companion, especially for a flower that has been planted by a human being in a place where it would not naturally sprout up on its own. What you call a weed is actually a natural companion that the flower welcomes to remind itself of the natural world. Please do not pull up many of these weeds if you can possibly help it. Then lean down and, if you have hairs on your arm, touch the flower petals—the outer ones are best, meaning those that fold outward. Just touch. Your hunger will go away.

My job is to prepare flowers for this touching. People who work with herbs and plant essences have known for years and years that these things can be helpful to people. But what even some of them do not know is that contact with these flowers in the way I mentioned can also be very healing.

The Flower Should Be in Its Natural State

Now, if you were to cut the flower, bring it to your body and touch your body, the effect would be about 1 percent, almost nothing. So the flowers that grow where they are welcomed by nature, natural and wild, are best, but those in a garden are almost as good. In a greenhouse, shut off from the sun and only receiving the sun, the wind and the touch of the flying creatures by accident, the effect is about 70 percent. In your home, with windows open or at least partway open sometimes so there is an air exchange, it's about 60 to 55 percent. In a home where the windows are shut almost all the time, the effect is about 50 percent. In a home where the windows are shut all the time, it's about 40 percent. In an office where the windows are shut all the time, which is typical in offices these days, the effect is about 20 percent.

This gives you some idea of the effect of these things. It might interest you to know that this kind of contact with flowers is even more effective when the humidity is higher, because water in its gaseous form heightens the experience. This does not mean that in a dry climate the percentages are decreased, but rather that in a moist climate the percentages are heightened.

The Flying Beings Will Contact Flowers

So I'm going to recommend that as homework. Try to make this contact in the safest, most comfortable way for you, and try to take note of these flowers, how their amazing life-giving qualities are well known to the little beings who fly into them or contact them in some way. They do this not only to consume what the flowers offer in the way your observers have noted, but sometimes the flying beings need some support, some nurturance. They will contact the flower, not only in the place to which you know they are being attracted (the center, the blossom, and so on), but sometimes they will crawl about on the outer parts of the blossom. When they do this, very often they are obtaining the physical support they need for the quality of their own life. If they have been trained by their own cultures to bring the essence of that wondrous energy back to their own colonies and families, they will pass it on to those who were unable to fly to that flower, usually the young who are not mature enough to make that journey.

If those natural beings know this and do this, there is no reason that you as human beings, who are natural in your own way but come here to learn natural creation, cannot do so as well. I wish you well in your journey, and I recommend that you try this out if you can. I think you will find it very enjoyable and in the future will have a much greater appreciation for the effects living flowers and their blossoms—rather than those that have been severed from their bodies—can have on you.

The Language of Feeling

Isis
January 20, 2003

Generally speaking, the reason the New Age is popular at all is because it is all about heart and feelings and not particularly about dogma—although one needs only to look to the New Age and its pundits to find dogma: "This is what is so! And that is what is so!" But you understand that the purpose of dogma is to help people feel safe. It is no different with the Church's dogma, because it was developed over years—I might add, somewhat lovingly, not just manipulatively—to serve the needs of the people and to create the safest, most predictable society possible. This way society would not have to be constantly at the mercy of unexpected passionate outbursts that often led to fighting, battle, fear, war and so on. So the Church attempted to provide not only the beauty offered by Jesus, the special person, but also a practical philosophy.

Creation Is Not Intended to Be Known

This is oversimplified, but any time the Church ran across something they understood or believed they could understand and did not actually have a good way to explain its complexities to the people of the time—whom they did not feel could take in complexities very well—they said, "Well, it is one of the mysteries of God." If you look at the New Age philosophy, there is not that much difference. There are attempts to explain mysteries, attempts to give details about what the mysteries might mean, but ultimately the further you go, the more mysteries there are.

It is not intended that life be fully understood and fully explained, because it is in the nature of creation (as any artist knows who has ever painted a painting and stopped rather than said, "I am done"). Creation is always opening, like a forever-opening flower, with variegated patterns, beauties, fragrances and so on. Creation is not intended to be known, it is intended to be experienced—not only by creating, but also by experiencing the creation. It can best be experienced through the use of feelings.

In the old days, in the old churches—not just the Christian Church, but other more ancient religions as well—the attempt was made to create workable philosophies, to try to come up with something that would allow resolution between peoples, to say nothing of tribes or countries, that would not require war or battle—another way to keep the peace. In many ways they were successful, and in some ways not. One of the ways that worked for a while was to create support and maintain the value of working things out mentally and spiritually. But because feelings—especially passion, strong feelings, arguing and so on—had been the source of much of the difficulty in the first place, creating wars and battles, the tendency was to discourage much exploration into feelings because of its difficult side. But now, as you know, people are experiencing their feelings more and more.

Heart Can Be Integrated Now

It may be possible—by gently exploring feelings and by looking for common feelings in all people to discover a way using the mind, using the spirit and using the heart—to find out how we, the human race, can live together in a more benevolent way. The love-heat/heart-warmth/physical-warmth method [see Overview] says, "Here is something you can feel, and when you are feeling that love-heat, it is possible to speak, but it is not possible to maintain the love-heat and speak in complexities." This tells you that the mind can work with the heart and the heart can work with the mind as long as the mind remains simple and uncomplicated. Because if you're going to find common ground with other people, you need to start in the simple, uncomplicated areas. Keep it simple, keep it uncomplicated—not because other people don't have the capacity to understand complexities, but because you need to start with your common ground, and the best way to find your common ground is to speak in simple, uncomplicated terms.

The way to avoid arguments is to stay focused in that love-heat, which you may feel in your heart. Some people might feel it in their legs, some might feel it in their stomachs, but it is a physical warmth that can be felt. That warmth is the physical experience of loving yourself and of feeling God's love. So if you can maintain that, it allows you to include heart and not have to yell and scream and become overly aggressive. As a matter of fact, love-heat is not about aggression at all; it is a way to include heart that's safe. And after all, isn't that the ultimate intention of religion, to create safety for all people? So the point is, heart can be integrated now. There is no point in trying to yell louder in an argument with somebody. That doesn't work.

Calling it "heart-warmth" is a bit of a misnomer because one might feel it in some other part of one's body. So to feel that physical-warmth and talk at the same time, maintaining the warmth all of the time, requires concentration and effort, at least in the beginning. In order to do that, one cannot communicate in complexities, so one tends to use basic communication skills. This allows others to do the same, and by doing so, more than one being is experiencing that warmth, which is loving oneself and being loved by the greater being also known as God. Thus one can communicate in an entirely new way for the times. And that way is simple and uncomplicated, using words with feeling and with thought and with Spirit's guiding hand.

The Warmth Is Communication through Feeling

The Church is the beginning toward a practical world philosophy that intends to create a better life for all people. That means that it is the foundation of modern times, including other religions I see no problem with looking for God within. After all, if God has created the heaven and the Earth and all the people on it, it is safe to say that there is God inside the people. One just needs to know how to look, and that is why I am recommending that we look with physicality and that physical feeling. No matter who you are, whether you are young or old, you can find that warmth, and it gives you physical evidence that something is happening. As long as you stay focused on the warmth, meaning wherever it comes up, you maintain your awareness of it. Try and go into it and feel it more, and when you can feel it, then talk. You will find that you can't talk in too complicated a way at first, but there is more to it. Whatever you can say, you have to maintain the warmth, because the warmth is the communication, and that is what people feel!

People are now responding to what they feel, not what they hear. That is why there are so many misunderstandings all the time, because people are responding to what they feel. They get confused in their own selves that way, and the reason the New Age is so popular now is that people are trying to understand their own feelings so they can improve communications between one another and between all people. In short, you can't leave anybody out. You have to include and you have to be able to communicate with the most basic and most nurturing form of communication, which is feeling.

You were taught this when you were a very little child. Your parents, whoever raised you, loved you and you felt their love. It is not that they said, "I love you"; that doesn't mean anything. They might as well have said, "Bow-wow." But they felt love.

This is why the child tends to gravitate toward the mother in the beginning. The mother naturally feels love because she gave birth to the baby. It requires a great deal of commitment to do such a thing. If you find yourself in that situation—you are pregnant, you have to give birth—there is nothing like that feeling of being presented by the midwife or the nurse or the doctor with your baby after the baby has come out of your body; you have that love. Fathers might feel the love, but it is not the same. It's a good thing, but it takes time for a father to develop love, and it is never quite the same as a mother's. This does not mean that fathers are not worthy; it means that most children almost always remember their mothers more fondly than their fathers.

Feelings Are the Most Important Method of Communication

The point is, from the very beginning, at the earliest time of your life, you are taught that feelings are the most important method of communication. Now people need to move beyond words. Even the most helpful attempts at improving the spoken word run up against the complications of your time, and that not only includes different languages but different nuances within your own language. Look at your culture. Most of you speak English—not all, but those of you in the United States can speak a few words of English even if you are new to the country. But think of the nuances, the slang, the dialect within that language. No, you need more than clearly defined words, because not everyone is going to understand your idioms, to say nothing of understanding your nuances—that a word said this way means this, but when said that way means that. It is clear that there needs to be some kind of communication that feels safe.

In the past, it was touch: "If I touch you in this way, then you can be reassured; if I touch you in that way, then you might feel frightened." If you're touched gently, you might feel reassured, but it is not always safe or considered proper in your time. So the best way to touch is through the feelings that you pick up from others. Everybody is picking this up more and more these days, and the reason there is so much confusion is that people do not know what they are picking up, or they simply do not understand their own feelings.

This is why the New Age people, or people who are interested in New Age things, are looking inside for God, because they are trying to understand their own feelings so they can understand themselves better and then take the next step to communicate clearly with others so that others understand them. And this has to start with the language everybody knows, no matter what their native tongue is, and that is what you feel. You know what you feel when you are laughing—you feel joy. You know what you're feeling when you are angry, when you are upset. But you also need to find out what you're feeling when you are feeling love and nothing but, and so you start with that physical-warmth. It will be very nurturing, very comforting, and even though it might take some of you awhile to get there, you can do it, especially if others around you are doing it.

Those who are interested in the New Age are really people who are looking to broaden their philosophy. Most of them are not interested in ignoring or abandoning other valuable philosophies, but they are intrigued to see a broader view. As you know, in today's world, which appears very complex, a broader view can be very helpful in order to understand and appreciate other people's points of view. The New Age, with all of its various faces and reflections, is attempting to provide a means toward attaining that broader view, as well as to provide new insights into that view itself.

Living Prayer to Help World Peace

Reveals the Mysteries
March 18, 2003

Dear Friends of Light Technology Publications and the Sedona Journal of
Emergence!: *We feel that many of you, like ourselves, have strong needs to
DO SOMETHING about our present world situation and feel frustration about
what we can do to influence the world. Recently, Reveals the Mysteries, knowing of humanity's needs and frustrations, speaking through Robert Shapiro,
came through with a living prayer for each of us to say [for more on living
prayer, see p. 245].*

for more on living prayer, see p. 245

*We were told that all of us could create a beneficial result if just 10 percent
of us would actually say the words of one of these living prayers with feeling.
Perhaps you could share this with your friends.*

Here is a living prayer for the world situation now:

Living Prayer

"I AM ASKING THAT THE SOULS, WITH OUR INFINITE WISDOM
THROUGHOUT ALL TIMES AND MANY PLACES, OF THE EXPLORER RACE
IN OUR NOW GUISE AS EARTH HUMAN BEINGS, PULL TOGETHER OUR
FULL KNOWLEDGE AND WISDOM OF WHAT HAS GONE ON IN THE PAST
FOR US—OUR TRAIL OF EDUCATION TO THIS PLACE AND THIS POINT
IN TIME.

"I'M GOING TO ASK US NOW TO COME TOGETHER AS IF AS A SINGLE
BEING TO RESOLVE CONFLICTS, DIFFICULTIES, WORRIES AND CARES OF
THE HUMAN DEMONSTRATION OF LIFE AND TO RECOGNIZE THE VALUE
OF EACH AND EVERY HUMAN IN THE WORLD IN WHICH WE LIVE.

> "I KNOW WE CAN DO IT, AND I BELIEVE IN OUR CAPACITY AND DESIRE TO BRING IT ABOUT WHILE SUPPORTING EACH OTHER AND CREATING THE WORLD WE KNOW WE WANT TO LIVE IN. I AM ASKING THAT THIS BE SO NOW."

You can say this once or several times. This is especially for those who have read the *Explorer Race* books, but it can be said by anyone. Some of the language referring to the Explorer Race won't mean much to those of you who haven't read the books or the articles in the *Sedona Journal*, but it is not necessary to have read the books in order to say this prayer to bring about the most beneficial results that living prayer can do.

Sometimes it is difficult to know what to do and how to do it in the most supportive way for each other. That's the key. To bring about resolution for yourselves now, you can do a great deal for yourselves individually using living prayer and benevolent magic. But to do something that affects the global population, human beings, plants, animals, everyone, you need to work together, and this is a living prayer to help you to unite in a moment and also to support, encourage and nurture that unity by simply desiring that it be so.

The purpose of the living prayer, then, is to request—never demand—that this come about in the most benevolent way for all beings, and specifically to the point, for those beings who are in the guise now of human beings, your selves on Earth, the Explorer Race, which includes all humans. And as a result, I believe that this will help you not only to come together in a unified way but also will remind you gently, very gently, that your guise as human beings on Earth is only a guise. You are more than that.

You have many faces throughout the universe, many before you got here and you will have many more after you leave here. It is a gentle reminder, then, that you are of many cultural strains and of many cultural hearts, and yet you are ultimately one being. And this moment in time is to show a practical application of what you can do, no matter what guise you may be demonstrating yourself as at any moment.

For those who want something shorter and simpler, I offer the living peace prayer:

> *Living Prayer*
> "I AM ASKING THAT THE HEARTS OF ALL BEINGS COME TO LOVE PEACE, CHERISH IT AND INVOLVE THEMSELVES IN ITS CREATION."

"You say the living prayer because it is a creation 'device.' The prayer itself is not an 'Oh, please help me' prayer. It is a creation. Living prayer is a creation. 'I am asking' is a creation."

—Zoosh

Dreams and Visions: Are They Real or Are They an Illusion?

Speaks of Many Truths, Reveals the Mysteries and Isis
May 27, 2003

The following email to Robert Shapiro led to several channeled responses.

Email Dated May 25, 2003

Beloved Family/Friends:

At your convenience, I request your meditative insight into what is really being conveyed in this attached series of "earth changes" emails, only one of a variety of similar information coming across my desk on a fairly regular basis (yours too perhaps?).

For years it has been my sense that such predictions, no matter how real to the recipient, are either a movie planted in the impressionable mass subconscious or a brand-new projection designed by the media masters of the dark side. No illusions/visions, however immense or outrageous, are impossible to manufacture any longer—as witnessed in the stunning technology of recent films like The Matrix. And all the admission ticket one needs is to resonate in harmony with such a frequency to get to "see" the movie for free!

As so many more family members awaken, I ask you, are we not tipping the balance to becoming responsible for our actions and our lives in a variation of the beloved Charles Dickens summation for Scrooge when confronted at last by the Ghost of Christmas Yet to Come? As best I recall, Scrooge, trembling, says, "I am not the man I once was. I will not be the man I have been but for this intercourse. Why show me this if I am past all hope? Assure me that I may yet change these shadows you have shown me by an altered life. Tell me, spirit, are these the shadows of things which must come, or only the possibilities of what may yet come?"

—With love, (name withheld upon request)

Editor's note: We do not want to print people's dreams and visions without their permission, so we are listing websites where you may find that information if you are interested:
- http://www.syzygyjob.net
- http://www.zetatalk.com/info/
- http://www.angelfire.com/fl3/gammadim/
- http://www.dreamdoctor.com/dreamboard/dreamboard.html
- http://www.network54.com/hide/forum/106909

Robert Shapiro Answers

Dear Friend,

I cannot read other people's visions, of course. However, the guidance I have always received about upsetting visions is as follows: "This is Speaks of Many Truths. These upsetting visions, my friend, are always and only intended in your time to encourage you to change disasters to more benevolent scenarios."

And also the following: "This is Reveals the Mysteries. In my time such visions were meant to encourage movement of the peoples, a change in practice, something to do; in short, it was intended to require response on our part. It was simply spoken—a warning most often, other times simply a possibility. In your time, it is different. Your time involves the teaching and the practical application of transformation and its results, consequences and further transformation, which may be required. You are, as Zoosh likes to say, living in the time of experience, application, results. Therefore, if I were you, I would approach such predictions on that basis. Equally, for those who receive such visions and predictions, don't be shy. If you feel a strong urgency or any urgency to let people know about them—go ahead.

"Try to tell people whom you feel will not be too upset or too frightened or experience some unpleasant medical phenomenon as a result. And yet, if you are getting the vision, it is most likely intended for you to tell at least someone. So do that if you feel the need. If you don't, then see if you can experience the love-heat/heart-warmth/physical-warmth [see Overview] or other nurturance that you may need so you feel better. A hot bath might be good for those who do not know how to do the love-heat—or a comforting bath in some way that you have available.

"Understand that the purpose for these visions, if they are upsetting, is for you to change them in some more benevolent way. If they are not upsetting, their purpose is to give you knowledge and foresight. If they are predictive, check out the physical facts first before you jump or leap into something that may entirely be a fabric of possibility. Don't assume it is an absolute.

"Predictions and visions are always and only possibilities unless they are accompanied by physical feelings during the prediction. If this happens, then mention it to others, that you felt this way or felt that way during the prediction. Then you might find that it is essential to attempt to transform it in some way. The simplest and best way, if it is an upsetting vision, is to go into the love-heat if you know how to do that. If you don't know how to do that, then visualize something better happening, and send out the vision to those you feel can now visualize something better happening and ask them to visualize that. That's what I recommend in general."

Isis Elaborates

Isis, I'd like to get more into this issue that is so strange to everybody, about . . . well, on the one hand there is duty, discipline, commitment, keeping your word, getting things done, deadlines, all this stuff, and on the other hand is the self-destructive way some of that seems to be. Many people I've mentioned this to just look at me like I don't know what I'm talking about because it's so ingrained in our nature.

I'd like to talk about something similar but different. There is something that is going on for people now, and you can identify with it as well, and that's that . . . I'm going to entitle this "Dreams and Visions: Are They Real or Are They an Illusion?" Understand that you've always dreamt. That is really what allows your soul to be at peace in your body. But many, many of you these days are having vivid dreams that wake you up out of a sound sleep, and they're often very upsetting and too real, as you say. This has to do, these days, with something that might surprise you.

For most of your lives, unless you are very young, you've experienced on Earth a great deal of Mother Earth assimilating your overwhelming passions. By overwhelming, I mean that which you really cannot take—you get angry, you get upset, you want, you need. In short, there is so much desire or fear or upset within you, it's more than you can bear. In the past, Mother Earth has taken that on for you so you could live—have a life. But now many of you are unifying with other people. You cannot all be in unity with every single person on the planet all the time, but you can, as individuals, be in unity with some people on the planet—or even in a dream, with one or two people on the planet, and they will be dreaming too.

Experiencing Others' Experiences

What's happening is not what I'd call a complete linkup, but there is a sensitization process going on that will allow you all to experience things that others are experiencing or to experience the dreams of others who are overwhelmed by their own life experience. So you might find yourself in a dream doing something or participating in something that is entirely unlike you, entirely foreign to your personality, or is seemingly crazy, for lack of a better term. You might be involved in something that is, in the dream, violent; or is, in the dream, strange; or is, in the dream, bizarre. It is so extreme, you wake up and then you settle yourself for a few moments. If you are afraid you are going to have the dream again, even if you are alone, speak out loud a few words of what the dream was about. You don't have to record it—that's unnecessary. You don't have to write it down in your dream book, especially if it's in the middle of the night and you need to sleep. Just say out loud a few of the words that will prevent you from going back into the dream. Then you can fall asleep and rest.

What I'm saying is that there are, all over the world, people who are going through agitating, overwhelming things. You yourself, as individuals, may be going through that now, and instead of Mother Earth taking on that excess of feeling that she has in the past, other human beings are taking it on—not in their waking state, since that would be like taking on a lesson from somebody else or taking on someone else's physical energy, but in the dream state where you are largely protected and looked after by your guides and teachers and angels and others. And yet as the Explorer Race and as creators-in-training, it is natural to be in school, yes, all the time. And in the past, being in school all the time meant that in every waking moment it was possible and even likely that you would be working on a life lesson or an experience that needed to be worked out in some way.

Working on Life Lessons in the Dream State

But now you are working on things in the dream state as well. Many of you—not all of you, but those of you who have not had this experience— may have it at some point. When you take on someone else's overwhelming feeling in the dream state . . . in the dream state, in your case, being protected as you are, you only take on a little bit, but you might experience something that is a total reversal of what your natural personality would do. Don't assume that it is predictive about your life. Don't assume that it is something for which you must mourn the world. It is rather, in the dream situation, something that allows you to develop and understand and experience compassion for others who are going through this great terror or fear or even desire—in short, a feeling that is too overwhelming for them in that moment. You do not experience their terror, their fear, their desire that they experience in their lives in their waking moments, but you do experience something that they are dreaming. You become like a character in their dream and they become a character in your dream. This allows you to experience a level of lesson that is only possible for the Explorer Race here on Earth.

It is what I would call a lesson in teaching mastery, as well as some exposure to a dimensional-mastery teaching and even a little bit of quantum-mastery teaching—quantum mastery being the mastery of consequences. You do not become masters of that, but you are being exposed to the teaching, which is only possible here on Earth, in this experience of Earth. And it is essential to be exposed to this teaching in an applied physical way, to have physical experiences, at least in the dream state. It is necessary because in other places you could not have these experiences; you could not react to these dreams with feelings. You could not experience an awakening to what other people feel, why they do the things they do on other benevolent planets, because to dream like that on another benevolent planet is too violent, even in a dream, for those planets.

Learn about Compassion in the Dream State

Know that these experiences are going to be safe for you and yet you will touch on them so that you will have much greater compassion to understand—even as a dream recollection, which is often vague and not always available. Even as that dream recollection, you will know and understand a little more and certainly be a little more compassionate when you hear about things that seem unfathomable: "How could they do that? I can't imagine or even think of doing that." "What is wrong with her?" "What is wrong with him?" "Are they crazy?" So creators must be able to be compassionate at all times toward the beings they have helped to create. You are not creators yet in this place, but you need to develop your compassion further.

In your time, you have some support to develop compassion, not only from your physical life, your day-to-day experience, but also by the means of communication that are available—radio, television, computer and communication between peoples and things that happen in the neighborhood and in families or around the world. You have the opportunity to hear about things, but now the opportunity extends further into the dream state, and that is something I want you to know about.

Release Judgment, but Don't Release Discernment

These dreams are different than visions. These dreams are about the capabilities of compassion. Compassion's job is not to change things. Compassion's job is to know and understand and appreciate perhaps the motivations or experiences of others. Compassion's job is also to give permission for you to act on the basis of others' needs without judgment. Compassion at the dream level will allow you to release a great deal of judgment. It will not, however, force you to release any discernment. There's a big difference between discernment and judgment.

DISCERNMENT OR JUDGMENT?

Discernment: n. 1. a. Perception by the senses; distinguishing by sight, direct vision. b. The faculty of discerning; discrimination, judgment; keenness of intellectual perception; penetration, insight. 2. The act of distinguishing; a distinction [*Oxford English Dictionary*, 2nd ed.].

Judgment: n. 1. To pass judgment upon, to judge, to criticize (with an assumption of superiority) [*Oxford English Dictionary*, 2nd ed.]. 2. The act or process of judging, the formation of an opinion after consideration or deliberation. The capacity to assess situations or circumstances and draw sound conclusions; good sense. 3. An opinion or estimate formed after consideration or deliberation, especially a formal authoritative decision [*American Heritage Dictionary*, 4th ed.].

Discernment is what allows you to be street-smart as well as to know the difference between something that is good for you and something that is meant for others or something that is not good for you or others. Judgment tends to protect you, you might say, but it also tends to keep you from your opportunities. So, you see, judgment is not always so good. It can protect you, yes, but it is not a good time to be kept from your opportunities now because they will be increasing and increasing in an increasing way. Therefore, it is better to be discerning rather than judgmental.

Visions Are Different Than Dreams

Now I want to talk a bit about visions, since this is something that is profoundly the case, which is happening for many of you now. Visions are different. They will often happen in a slightly somnambular state. This means that you are not asleep, but you feel sort of relaxed. For those of you who meditate, it is similar to that. For those of you who do not do that, it is something that begins as something you see.

Sometimes there are words, but most often there are pictures, and the pictures are sometimes alarming—perhaps of disasters, perhaps of global problems, perhaps of threats to your country or your friends in your neighborhood or something like that. Usually a vision represents, in your time, a disaster—an earthquake, a flood, a fire, something like that. If you have physical phenomena when this is going on, it is important to tell others of this vision. If, on the other hand, it is strictly a vision and you feel calm during the whole experience, it is also important to pass that on to someone or to various individuals.

Now, visions are different than dreams because they usually happen in a waking or semiwaking state. Many, many of you are having these visions now. Know that they are intended to stimulate change. You're aware of Earth conditions. Volcanoes are erupting, but that's good; it creates land, it changes the face of the land, and as long as the people are evacuated, it does not represent catastrophe. It is only a catastrophe if people are killed or wounded. I grant that sounds a bit hard on my part, but volcanoes are Mother Earth's birthing technique. It is the easiest and most benevolent way for her to bring more land to the surface or to alter the face of the land for your ultimate good, and a lot of that is going on—it's much better than having earthquakes that upthrust the land, which can cause catastrophic damage.

So for those of you who are seeing or feeling catastrophic disasters coming, if you would, tell your friends who can visualize or do visualization. Tell them of your vision and ask them point-blank—whether it be in an Internet message or spoken word—say, "I've had this vision and I'm concerned. If you can visualize, please visualize benevolence in the areas where I've had the vision. Picture the people happy and calm and peaceful, and everything as safe." Ask your friends who can meditate or visualize to do this. For others, don't be shy. You'd be surprised how many people can bring about change, even if they do not know they can do that.

If you are getting visions of disasters, feel free to put them out verbatim, meaning describe what you saw. Don't get fictional. Don't say, "And then I saw this," if you didn't. Describe only what you saw. If you like, you can add that you are frightened or upset and that you hope that those who can will bring about change. This will allow people who are religious to pray, but it will also allow them to feel a sense of urgency to change it, and that will trigger within them their unconscious creator impulses to bring about benevolent change—that's what it does.

You Are Intended to Make Unconscious Changes

You are creators-in-training. You are not intended to make conscious changes. You are not yet ready to be conscious creators, but you are intended to make unconscious changes. This incorporates not only what you do energetically as a soul on Earth, but is now beginning to include what you do in your dreams and linking it to your conscious state by waking up from that which upsets you. Be aware that dreams and visions are linked, as is the spiritual nature of each and every one of you, though many of you will look at someone and say, "I don't see it." But I am seeing, in fact, the spiritual nature of each and every one of you rising, and that rising will take place first in something that you are not quite in touch with—that which is called the unconscious.

It is not mental, the unconscious; it is largely physical, it is spiritual and it is feeling. That's why when you have these dreams, as strong as they are, you wake up not just with pictures or images but with strong feelings. These feelings are a relief to others who are overwhelmed with those feelings, and if you just speak a few words when you wake up about the dream, then you won't go back into it. That's what's going on.

Your level of responsibility as creators-in-training has increased and has moved beyond the unconscious into the subconscious, which unites all of the physical parts of you, the spiritual parts of you and that which functions in a state of mental awareness that you cannot touch or know at this time. The subconscious unites all that with your feelings (I mean your physical feelings), and therefore, this subconscious is the vital part of you that is allowing you to literally change the creation of Earth.

As creators-in-training it is intended that you do so, and no amount of conditioning to bring about distraction by whatever forces—be they corruptive or political or even simply greed by those who wish to make money or manipulate you in some way—can change it. Know that greed is not only something that others have, but greed is something that is within each and every one of you. This does not make you bad; it just means that you have the capability to feel about this or that in your life—that you don't have enough and you want more than you'll ever need so you can be assured you will always have enough. It is not in its own right evil, but sometimes it results in an evil by the accumulation of more than you'll ever need, which means that others do not have what they need.

Your Dreams and Visions Are Uniting

So I am simply saying that it is not my intention to cure every situation today. Just know that your dreams and your visions are uniting, and as creators-in-training and apprentices along the soul path toward creation, you have taken a giant step forward. And remember, if these dreams upset you—and I cannot stress this enough, which is why I'm repeating it—when you come to that waking state, even if you're wide awake, don't just think about the dream. Say something about it out loud—you must say it out loud. Thinking about it won't help. Say something about it out loud, even if you have to whisper (perhaps others are present). Say something out loud, and you will not go back into the dream, all right? That includes people who have nightmares regularly, by the way. If you have nightmares a lot, always say something out loud about the nightmare when it wakes you up. That will help to prevent it in the future.

That's wonderful for mothers to tell their children. It's wonderful for them to go to their rooms and have the children talk about it.

And particularly helpful for people who have had great traumas that they continue to dream about in an intention for their physical and spiritual and feeling bodies to cleanse themselves of that terrible experience.

So to summarize a little: The dream that you dream for others . . . when you wake up, you actually release that energy for the other person. And the visions, by talking to other people about them, help to dissipate it, to prevent it from happening?

Yes. Good night.

What Happened? Why Did the Channeling Change?

Zoosh
August 31, 2004

It's important for you to know this, reader, because I'm giving you all homework. You know how I am [chuckles]. My whole point is, if you are really spiritual students like some of you say you are, it is time for you to show Uncle Zoosh what you can do, all right? This is the challenge. I can't tell you exactly when an event that is coming up in your future is going to happen because I don't want you to: (a) get terrified of it, (b) anticipate it or (c) tell others all about it and walk down the street saying, "The end is near."

But I will say, it is in your future. Don't yell at me; I know you are doing all you can, but I want you to do a little extra instead of proceeding generally along the line of "minimum effort." The extra effort, however, won't involve anything that you normally do. I want to explain: I'd like you to apply yourself. Some of you work in your dreams, set up your dreams, request to have dreams with insight, and I don't want to mess with that. But many of you just go to sleep at night, or perhaps you do your disentanglement [see p. xxxi], or you might say some prayer to ease you into your sleep.

Use the Power of Your Natural Self to Dream for Benevolence

Here is what I would like you to do . . . and it is up to you how many of you want to do it, but I think it is something that not only you readers will like to do, but it is something that can really nourish life all over. It's easy and it will involve your full capability—and by full capability, I mean more than you normally have spiritually and otherwise in your normal day. And it might just be something that other people who would like to have a more peaceful and benevolent world in general, regardless of their religion or philosophy or spiritual practices, might enjoy doing as well, because it doesn't add much strain to your life, but it does make a difference.

I will give you the homework first so you don't get nervous, and then later I am going to tell you about the moment that caused the reason for the homework and also the change in the focus of the channeling/teaching. This is the homework. Try to do it before you go to sleep. For those of you who have lovers and so on and go to bed for fun and then go to sleep, the best time to do it is when you are in bed after all is said and done. Or sometimes, if you are on your own, when you turn off the light after reading or something, simply say out loud:

> *Living Prayer*
> **"I AM ASKING THAT I DREAM WITH MY FULL SPIRITUAL CAPABILITY**
> **OF BENEVOLENCE IN MY PHYSICAL WORLD ON EARTH**
> **AND BEYOND WHEN I SLEEP TONIGHT."**

That's all [for more information on living prayer, see p. 245]. Now, for those of you who say other living prayers or other prayers before you go to sleep at night, wait at least a minute or two for the energy to calm between the prayers, or if you say this first, then wait a minute or two before you say your normal prayers, because you might feel a very benevolent energy during this living prayer—or even, if you say it every night for a while, prior to saying this living prayer, as well as during and even after. And you want that to pass a little bit, to calm. Don't shove it away; it's nourishing, nurturing. It's benevolent, and the energy will support your life and your experience of your world.

Now, why do we say the prayer in such a way that it is quite clear that you are saying "my world"? It honors the fact that you are a portion of creation. It also honors the fact that your first responsibility, to the best of your ability, is to create the most benevolent life for yourself that is possible. And for those of you who might feel that this sounds selfish, it isn't, because you have to factor into your life all others who are in it. If you have children, if you have extended family whom you live with, if you have friends, if you have animals and so on in your life whom you experience, the most benevolent life would be not only that you are happy and happy with your life, but that the people around you are happy and happy enough with their lives so they are not complaining to you or so you do not pick up with your sensitivity how they may be distressed.

In short, it builds from the center foundation, and you are all responsible for your own lives first, and then you are responsible, in the greater sense, for the happiness of all other beings. In this way, nobody gives up responsibility for his or her own creation while taking over responsibility for others' creations. Of course, you cannot run the lives of other people entirely on your own, even in a spiritual sense, but you can create your own life spiritually to the best of your ability, because your soul will know you best. It is that simple.

So this is what I recommend you do for homework. You can say it just once. Because you are incorporating your dream state, this does not really add to your daily duties. And because it will happen in your dreams—it is not going to impact your sleep; if anything, you are going to sleep deeper and longer, if you like—it will tend to support and nurture greater benevolence in your life and support and nurture greater benevolence in your extended life, meaning all of those people and animals and beings you might meet, including plants and so on. And it can only be a good thing.

What Happened? What Changed?

Now [pauses a moment] . . . I would like to tell you why I would like you to do this homework. The witness here, my associate, who has been prompted to ask this question [see p. 516], has been prompted to do so because she noticed a few years ago that everything seemed to change. At one moment it was one way, and then suddenly it changed. Now, this was something that many people who were spiritual or simply sensitive did notice, that there was suddenly sort of a radical change and a shift—not only in the way you perceived the world, but even in the way the world perceived you—and you weren't really sure what had happened. What happened? And some of you weren't quite aware of it until a little after the fact, but you came to become aware of it later.

Let me tell you what happened. I'm not going to give you an exact time, but I'm just going to say that something happened in your future that affected your past, your past from this point back. Now, this is what happened: There was a convergence of angry people with problems that couldn't seem to wait. Just on the basis of that, I want you to notice how in recent years, it has been more and more difficult for you to be patient about anything. I am not singling anyone out as being exclusively impatient; rather, this is what many people suddenly felt, as if it were underneath them, like a vibration or an energy (in waves, not always consistent) of urgency. This is global. It does not affect the animals. It affects to a small degree the plants, and it affects to a large degree human beings.

Urgency, Creator's Gift, Is Accelerated by Technology

The urgency is to support you coming into your total being spiritually, yes, but this sense of urgency has been amplified unintentionally by certain broadcast-media effects. I am not trying to single out any industry, but there are satellites that revolve around the Earth for various benevolent purposes, to improve communications from one continent to another and so on, and most of you benefit from this. But some of those satellites broadcast not just directly from one point to another on the Earth—or transfer signals, actually—but they interact with surface stations on the Earth, broadcasting and transmitting and transferring back and forth all the time, which prompts a greater degree of amplification than might otherwise be used in the transference of broadcast signals. This does not include the telephone or anything that transmits communication of some form from one human being to another, nor communication on the automated level from one machine to another.

These radiating devices have produced purely unintentionally—I am not blaming anyone—a signal that could be measured. If you went down into the Earth about six to twelve feet, especially around these broadcast and transfer stations, you would find a measurable signal, yes, but it's more of what I would call a harmonic. An example of a harmonic would be if a group of people sang or if a group of tones were made by a musical instrument—and you have all heard of someone hitting a high note and a glass breaking.

Now, it is not exactly that dramatic, but the harmonic that is created unintentionally has amplified that benevolent signal being put out by your total spiritual being, by Mother Earth and, of course, by Creator, direct from Creator, to support and urge you to "wake up," as people say. It's not really "waking you up"; it's more to support and urge you to remerge with your total spiritual being. This has had an unintentional side effect, and that is that it has amplified the impact on you all of urgency. Once this was understood—or shall we say, once this happened—Creator could not lower the signal in the Earth or ask Earth to lower it for you, because it is so supportive and nurturing of all of your hearts. But it has prompted this excessive feeling of urgency.

You Can Counterbalance the
Accelerated Urgency with Living Prayer

You can do something about this. That is why I have given you this homework, because I think you can do something much more easily in your sleep, when you have full access to all of your spiritual capabilities. Your body is still on Earth, yes, so you have some physical function. Your soul supports that physical function, and your soul is out and about when you're sleeping, with teachers, guides, angels, sometimes even Creator, discussing things and being loved and nurtured as is necessary for living on Earth. What occurs is that in various moments, usually at the deepest levels of sleep, you are in full contact with your full spiritual capabilities—not only as an individual of Earth, but as an immortal personality. So you might say that your soul is fully active. (I use the terms "soul" and "immortal personality" interchangeably.)

This is why at these deep levels of sleep you are more likely to be able to fulfill the intention of this living prayer or request, whichever you wish to call it, that I suggested at the beginning of this talk—because that full capacity will allow you to do things, to support things and, most importantly, to be supported by the other loving beings you interact with when you are at these deep levels. So you can not only act, you can not only create, but you can be supported in your action and your creation by all of the loving beings you interact with when you are in deep levels of sleep. I am not talking about dreams that are troublesome or even psychologically based where you are processing things. I am talking about the deepest levels of sleep where you don't normally remember any of that when you wake up. Occasionally, people do remember, but it is not typical for most people.

So what I am suggesting, then, is that something occurs in the future that has prompted something in the past, and as I said, the occurrence in the future is a convergence of people with feelings of great urgency. The reason it prompted it in the past is that the thing that happens in your future required a buildup of a countermeasure, meaning to balance something. When you put a heavy weight on one side of the scale, naturally the scale falls to that side. If you put a balancing weight on the other side, then you get scales that are evenly balanced. You have seen pictures of the scales with the two little plates that hold weights on either side.

Now, in order for that thing that happens in the future to be counterbalanced, all that really needs to take place is that those people meeting in that future time do not feel as much of a sense of urgency as they would have felt. And what will balance that urgency isn't you saying that you want everybody to be more patient, because sometimes a certain amount of urgency is necessary, as you have all experienced in your life when the signal light changes while you are crossing the street and you suddenly realize that you have to pick up your pace. So we don't want people to universally slow down too much for all situations. (I use that example humorously, because most of you have experienced this at one time or another.) And there are other situations where urgency is necessary—for example, when you run, your heart has to beat faster and you have to breathe faster. All urgency is not a bad thing. So let's not blanket things, saying "good" or "bad." Sometimes, in different situations, different things are called for.

World Health Group Feels Frenetic Urgency

So now we will talk a little bit about what happens. In the future, when these parties, these individuals, meet because they feel so profound a sense of urgency, they do something. They do something they think is going to support their cause, but they accidentally create something that is not obvious to them for quite some time, and by the time it becomes obvious to them, it is too late to do anything about it. And I might add that this sometimes occurs when diseases are accidentally released into the public. This has happened once or twice, and the disease lingers and everybody says afterward, "What were we thinking?" meaning something was tried just to make sure that everyone would be safe. There have been instances in the past where, with the best of intentions, some form of disease organism was released by well-intentioned individuals who said, "Look! See, it will moderate!" Or in the case of the security of nations, "How are we susceptible to chemical and biological warfare?" and so on. You can research this; some of it is available in print. But it will probably just upset you.

So let's just say this: These people get together. Some of them are scientifically oriented, many of them are well educated, but quite a few are just regular folks with no greater degree of education than anybody else. And they all say, "If we can just release this organism—it seems to be very mild—it will support a greater degree of intellectual capacity, and if everybody on Earth gets just a little smarter, then we will be able to rationalize and talk together and make a lot more sense to one another," believing, as they do, that greater mental capacity makes for peace. But as you have seen in your recent history, simply greater mental capacity does not always make for peace; as a matter of fact, greater mental capacity has often invented the tools of war.

Your Mind Is the Student, Your Feeling Body Is the Teacher

Your mind on this planet is here as a student to learn from your physical body and the way your physical body functions, to learn from your physical feelings and the general feelings of many others around you, to learn from your spiritual inspiration and from the thing that you have noticed in animals but don't really recognize in yourself all the time, and that's instinct. Your mind is here to study and learn about creation and how to differentiate between what's a benevolent creation by yourself and what's a creation that isn't benevolent, even though mentally it will seem to be perfectly all right.

And the way you know that—and the way that's been discussed in many of these books: the *Explorer Race* series, the *Shining the Light* series, certainly the *Shamanic Secrets* series, the new *Ancient Secrets of Feminine Science* series and other books you've read—the way you know something isn't good to create, is because of certain feelings you get. If you get an uncomfortable feeling, you know that it's not right for you to do that at this time. Maybe it's all right to do it at some future time. If you get a good feeling, a warm feeling, a safe feeling, a happy feeling, maybe it's a good thing to do. I'm being very general here, because there are principles you would apply to anything that you create or hope to create. But I do not wish to talk for hours and hours here.

So what happens is that these individuals in the future get what they feel is a wonderful idea. They say, "Well, everybody needs to get these vaccination shots to support their immunity for this disease." And I'm not going to say what disease it is; I'm only going to say that it's a disease that you don't have amongst you in a way that you're conscious of right now. But I will say one thing about it because you've seen glimmers of this: It's a disease in people.

Imprisoned Chickens' Desire to Die Gets Eaten and Absorbed by Humans

You've seen the beginnings of this, especially in some countries, that are very troubling because it's a poultry-based disease. I will be specific: Although it has to do with chickens mostly, it also affects turkeys, to a lesser degree, but it doesn't really affect ducks very much. And it doesn't affect any wild bird, meaning if you have chickens on your farm or in a small situation you have with a house and an acre or something like that, and the chickens are free ranging where they walk around all over the place—not just that they have a small pen they can move around in, but they walk around all over the place and scratch and peck at the dirt the way they do—they're going to be all right.

It's imprisoned chickens especially, and you've seen this or heard about it, where a chicken will live its whole life in a very tiny cage. That is really quite a horrible thing to do to any creature. These birds are experiencing and have been experiencing over time a personal depression within them that just prompts them all to want to die. They don't want to live. And when a being doesn't want to live, it cannot help it. When it produces eggs for human consumption or when it is killed and used for human consumption, there is no way to filter out from the eggs or the meat of the chicken itself that desire to die.

This is so much in conflict with the human desire to live and survive no matter what, and you've seen this many times (doctors, medical staff, nurses and so on are particularly aware of this), where somebody's very sick and is hanging on and hanging on. This desire to survive is built into you by Creator so that you will have the best opportunity to fulfill the spiritual desires that you as your soul before this life—with your teachers, with your angels, with Creator—chose to do in this life. Of course, eventually, at the end of your life, you just let go, and because your teachers or guides or angels come and . . . well, they're not seen by other physical people, but they come and they are there with you, and you know then that you can let go. It's not a mental decision you'll have to make; you can just let go because you feel it. That's how everybody on Earth transitions at the moment when it takes place.

Live or Die? The Ambivalence Created by Eating Imprisoned Chickens

So this desire to survive in the human being is very strong. And this desire in the chicken meat and chicken eggs and, to a lesser degree, in turkey meat and turkey eggs, as well as in the other birds I mentioned, is in direct conflict with the human desire to live. What occurs as a result is a kind of ambivalence in the human, a confusion about whether there is a desire to live or not.

This has already been seen, even though the disease has not yet been identified. But I'm trying to tip off you researchers out there too. What is occurring is that one of the manifestations of the disease itself is that there is somewhat of an ambivalence about life. For people who have other stresses in their lives, this makes their lives miserable or uncomfortable at certain times. And this happens, as you all know. There are certain times that you all go through, times that are difficult or seemingly impossible, and you struggle on through and then you live on, you live your life. This happens a lot for soldiers, of course, or for people in hazardous professions, or for people who are sick or injured. Yes, you know about this. But it also happens when people are ill-equipped to deal with such things, not as adults might be. So this happens then sometimes for children, for youngsters who are not sophisticated enough to know how and what to do, what to say, when to ask for help and who to ask it from, and so on. And that's why some countries have seen a troubling rise in youth suicide.

So I'd like to suggest that one of the things that isn't being looked for too much . . . although, of course, forensic and other specialists are looking for anything that connects. But here is one of the things I want you to look for, you forensic people, pathologists and anyone who may have an opportunity: Examine not just the body of the person who has passed away or committed suicide but also the lifestyle of the person; examine how much chicken the individual ate and for how long. Now, I grant that people who are strong, who are determined or who have a cause that they are determined to fulfill will be less affected by this ambivalence, this confusion about "live, don't live." But for others, especially if they're going through a rough patch, it can make for some confusion. And some civilizations might even give a—how can we say?—an almost imperceptible nod to allowing certain circumstances to support suicide. I'm not saying suicide pro or con here. What I am saying is that I want the researchers to start looking toward chickens.

And ultimately, of course, what I'm saying is that even though I know it would be very impractical and it would take very much land and so on for producers, farmers and ranchers who have animals they are raising, that if they have chickens . . . I know in the old days, they just took up a lot of space, and then eventually they developed chicken coops, and then when further things happened, other things were developed. I'm trying to let some of you off the hook, okay? I'm not trying to say that agribusinesses are the enemy, but I am trying to suggest that efficiency is not always the first choice for benevolence. Never forget that. I'm trying to suggest that sometimes you're going to need to use more land to let the chickens roam around, have space. Those chickens, their eggs, their meat, will be safe to eat.

Cruelty to All Animals Must Stop or They Will Leave Earth

So, psychologists, pay attention. I know that you're not going to have psychologists for chickens, and I am not saying that entirely as a joke, because there are people who can work with animals and impart the animal's feelings. They really interpret the feelings into words that human beings can understand. Animals do not think the same way you do, but their feelings can be interpreted, just as human feelings can be interpreted. This is going on quietly all over the Earth, and I might add that a lot of veterinarians have this skill, but they just don't talk about it—at least the really good ones don't. And you know who they are, those of you who are farmers and ranchers. Some veterinarians just seem to have that gift; they know what's going on with your animals, even though medical science doesn't always point to it.

And of course, simply people of good will and good heart would never expect an animal to live its entire life in that teensy little cage hardly bigger than its own body. If you want to eat chicken and eggs in the future, I'm going to recommend that you pay real close attention to where they came from, because this is not something that is going to go away. Neither the chicken nor the eggs can be treated in this way.

You really need to pay attention to how you're treating farm animals. Now, ranchers who have cattle, for instance, they are actually quite well aware of this. That is why many cattle will range all over open country, because the ranchers know it affects their temperament, and their temperament does affect the way they are eaten and experienced by those who consume them. This is something that is actually well known and understood by cattle ranchers, especially smaller ranchers who make certain that their cows can roam all over the place. Granted, you have to get government leases and so on, and it's expensive, but they know this.

Don't squeeze out these ranchers so that large businesses that are geared toward efficiency can raise all cows in some small box that they stand in for their whole life, which is already done now with some animals. I know that this has been said in these pages before, and I know it sounds like I'm preaching against certain things, and I admit it. I understand that you eat meat, okay? I'm not trying to say it's bad. That's why you have such strong teeth. But I do not think that it is acceptable to raise an animal in a small box just so you can serve it and its very tender meat called veal. I think that you can get along without it. That's all I'm going to say about that.

I will say that if this continues to go on—and cows know that this is going on with beings of their own kind—then cows will also get angry, upset and depressed. And people who have been in the ranching business for a long time know that aside from making it more difficult to deal with the cows, there is also a bad feeling about how that meat will eat. This knowledge is not just based upon their intuition, which is certainly true and valuable, but also upon stories they've heard from other generations, from their fathers, their grandfathers, their great-grandfathers; these stories have been passed down. They say that if you eat a cow who has been forced to live in a box or cage like this, you're not going to feel good. It might make you feel poorly, might make you susceptible to catching some disease. Why? Because the cow doesn't want to live; it's suffering. When you eat meat from an animal who doesn't want to live, who just wants to die, your body might be confused, even if you want to live. So, you see, I'm not talking about things that are entirely unknown here. I'm just correlating them.

Health Group's Decision Jeopardizes Humanity

So when those people meet in the future and they have this wonderful idea that they will include in this vaccine something that will support greater mental development, what it actually does is it just creates—how can we say?—it might actually stimulate greater mental development. But a side effect is that it will create a slightly more disenfranchised mind or mental self, and it will support in all people an analytical tendency to classify everything that is not understood—and I mean a broad range of subjects that are not understood, especially your own physical feelings and unspoken thoughts—which will create unintentionally . . . this partly has to do with the way this chemical is created, but it unintentionally creates greater alienation from your own physical, spiritual and feeling selves.

So once it is released, included with a perfectly valuable and helpful vaccine for something else, that's it. It would be amongst you indefinitely, and the only way I think it could ever be cured and eliminated is by some major action of Creator through the Earth. And those actions in the past have usually resulted in the elimination of civilization as you know it, with only a few surviving, usually underground somewhere, to reemerge on the surface many years later.

I'm not talking about a select few; I'm talking about civilizations and cultures who, on the basis of how they feel, on the basis of how their mystical people and shamanic people and sensitives know that something is coming, know that they need to move quickly, and that if they do it, they will be safe as a people. For those of you out there who research peoples and what they've left behind—cliff dwellings and so on—there's always the question of what happened to these people: "Why did they leave this stuff and just disappear?" I'll tell you why: Because the sensitives amongst them whom they trusted and their shamanic people and their mystical people all had this feeling—you might call it an uncomfortable feeling, a danger feeling. They said, "We have to go."

They packed up what they could, food and everything, and they left. They left physically from their place, and as they got a few miles away, all those sensitives and shamanic people and mystical people suddenly started to feel better because they encouraged the tribe to go in this direction, not that direction—they could feel which was the safe direction to go. They started to feel better: "Let's keep going." Some of the people said, "It's a hardship. We left behind so many things that we use." But they were reminded by the elders, "Now, we've always followed the guidance and advice of our sensitives, our mystical people, our shamanic people. That's why we're still here." That kept people going until they found the next place where they felt safe and comfortable and that would support their lives. They reestablished themselves there, sometimes joining other people who welcomed them, other times establishing a civilization and creating that civilization elsewhere. But many of your archaeologists and anthropologists have studied this matter, so I don't wish to go into it too much here; I'm just pointing it out to you.

The Moment: Incident in Future Changes Focus in Past

So I've covered a wide range of subjects today in talking about this "incident" that happens in your future that required you all to do something in the past. What did it require? It required—and this happened a few years ago; I'm not going to give you an exact target date, because some of you felt it at slightly different times—and built into you an urgency to find your true being. This means (and I know that you can all identify with this) that the question "Why am I here?" or "What am I supposed to be doing here?" suddenly came to the forefront of your thoughts, and many of you have attempted to fulfill it. And the "Why am I here?" and "What am I supposed to be doing here?" are questions entirely spiritually based. That is also why in recent years there has been an upsurge, an upswing, in religious pursuits and, I might add, also in things that are called metaphysical or New Age, and people have tried to discover why they're here. So that's what happened, and that's its effect.

Mistreated Animals Want to Leave Earth and Go Home

We can only talk for just a given amount of time, because the energy is a bit overwhelming. That's because there are a lot of beings in the room who want me to talk about this and that, and I talked a little bit about this and that as well as telling you about other things. There are a lot of animal spirits here in this room. The animal spirits feel such a tremendous urgency that they all want to go home when they or any of their number are being mistreated by human beings. They see that this might continue to perpetuate and perhaps get worse, and they want to go home. That's why so many animals on Earth have become, as you say, extinct. Of course, their energy is still here for the future, and should human beings start to treat one another and the animals—and the plants, I might add—better, then they might choose to reemerge on Earth. But for now, a lot of them want to go home. That means home to their home planets where their souls live and incarnate and appear the way they normally appear on their home planets—whereas out here, they volunteered to be here to support you, to help you learn, to help you remember who you are, to support your knowledge and wisdom, and particularly to support your own hearts so that you would feel and experience some kind of benevolent, safe love.

Sometimes, as you know, love between human beings doesn't feel safe all the time. So there's a benevolent, safe love that you can count on, meaning you might have a dog or a cat, or you might have a favorite horse, or you might enjoy seeing the animals free out in the countryside, the squirrels, the rabbits, the elk, the deer and so on, depending on where you live—maybe it's the giraffes. In short, the animals are here to support and nurture safe and benevolent love for human beings, and of course, some of them are simply here to look nice, not necessarily to be hugged by you or to hug you. I won't discuss all of this, but they are here. The animal spirits wanted me to bring this up.

Decisions Not Based on Feeling Can Lead to Disaster

What is the name of this disease that will require the universal vaccination?

No. If I say that, then many people might actually avoid the vaccination. I will say that it's for a disease you don't know about yet. That's what I'm going to say.

Is this meeting about the vaccine, when these beings who feel the accelerated sense of urgency decide to secretly add the brain enhancer to the vaccine, a national meeting or a global meeting?

It's more of an international meeting, and it's not something public, it's not corporate. They are well intended, that's the thing. They're not monsters; they honestly feel that this is going to be a great thing, a wonderful thing. They do it with the best of intentions. Now, you know how many times you can look back in your history and read the documents of the time if you have them available. How many times were things done with the best of intentions, but they turned out terribly? So these are not evil people, but they are people who have a strong sense of urgency.

I might add that one of the reasons they have a strong sense of urgency is that they feel that they are literally sick of human conflict and what happens in human conflict, such as the terrible things that have happened in Africa and other places—not just where there are wars, but where there's fighting between groups of people. Terrible things happen, and these people at the meeting are just disgusted with that. They feel, as many people have felt in the past, that if everyone could just think more clearly, everyone would see that violence and conflict don't make sense. But that's not what changes things, even though it might seem to and there's even some evidence to suggest that it would. What changes things is that people feel their own hearts and their own love, and they begin to identify that other people feel the same way as they do about the basic qualities of life. People want other people to be happy—not necessarily to have the same things they have, but to be happy and have what they need to have in order to enjoy the basic needs of life. And when you all feel that way about everybody else on the Earth, life is going to change here and you'll take a big step toward heaven on Earth.

Living Prayer Will Keep the Health Group from Adding Brain Enhancement to the Vaccine

So if many people do this nighttime prayer now and mitigate the sense of urgency that these scientists and others at the meeting will feel, then they won't add the brain enhancer to the vaccine and the danger of human extinction will no longer be an issue?

That's right. That's what it takes. It takes a decrease in the feeling of urgency, and then what will happen is that the substance that might stimulate an improvement in the mind will not be combined with this vaccination. It will still be made available to individuals. It will be very expensive, but it will be available to individuals who want to improve their minds and so on as it is supported. But the brain enhancer will not be combined with the vaccination and people won't get it without knowing that they are getting it. So it's not going to stop the development of that product, but it will not be combined with something else that people need.

How far in the future is this meeting? When will this meeting happen?

I will not say. I've already given you a clue. When you become aware of a new disease and it's defined and there is an urgent desire as there often is—the same urgent desire as there is with any other disease to find some cure, and scientists are supported and encouraged to find a cure—it will be like that, the same kind of process as always.

What is the name of the new disease?

Something you don't know about yet.

Is it related to poultry?

Of course. Why do you think I brought it up? Fortunately, you don't have to figure it out. I know that sounds like I'm brushing you off, but I'm really speaking to others here. I'm interested and I'm glad that you want to figure it out—and you are, of course, not only the person I interact with for these talks, but also the representative of humankind, so I'm glad that you have this curiosity. The people who really have to figure it out are the people in the research medical community who create . . . who are beginning to understand, for example, that all the research they've done on men does not necessarily mean that their products, as a result, will apply directly to women.

This is why, for those of you youngsters out there who are looking for a job in the medical field that will be guaranteed to be huge in the future, there's going to be huge amounts of research done on various . . . not just diseases, but various things with volunteers who are women. Vast amounts of research in the past were done—medically and psychologically and so on—on people who are men, and the assumption was, "Oh well, this also applies to women," but it doesn't. Sometimes it does, but most of the time it doesn't. That's why women have had certain lingering diseases that seem to defy cure. I'm not going to indict the medical profession; it has nothing to do with science. But it does have a lot to do with your coaches and your societies, with the way your coaches and conditioners put greater value on one gender over another. But you'll get over that.

I'm talking about a disease that human beings have. I'm not talking about a disease for animals. Animals aren't going to be injected with this so they become intellectually superior. It's something you don't know about. That's all I'm going to say.

And I feel like I haven't been unfair with those who raise chickens. I've just suggested that you need to raise them in another way, that's all. Get them out of their cages and let them run around on the ground. I know all the problems. You will be able to figure it out. It's not natural for a bird to be raised in a building; birds need to be outdoors. Okay, they need to have some place they can come indoors when it rains, but other than that, they need to be outdoors. You know—I'm not telling you anything you don't already know.

Creator Training Was Set Up in the Past, Which Was Then the Present, to Prepare You to Resolve a Crisis in the Future

So the illustration [Fig. 35–1] you drew in response to my question as to what happened, what changed a few years ago to cause a difference, not only in the way life felt, but also in the focus of the channeling through Robert—the channeling went from Explorer Race information to material-mastery teaching ("You are an apprentice creator; learn how to do living prayer and benevolent magic")—all relates to the incident in the future that you saw from that time a few years ago and for which you are giving us a living prayer to resolve the situation you are describing in these pages?

Creators-in-training—what do creators do? Do they work a shift and then sleep? Creators-in-training do things even when they're sleeping! Yes, it relates entirely. What I said, that's what happened. And we couldn't . . . there was an urgency, we had to do something, and you couldn't do it overnight. I couldn't say, "Okay, you are all now mystical people and shamanic people, and you're all assigned to do this." You needed to have training. Therefore, I asked my friends Reveals the Mysteries, Speaks of Many Truths and others to come and train those of you who wish to be trained, who would embrace this, who would like to invest in the idea of being creators-in-training and do the best you could. And then, hopefully, when you engaged this process, you would choose to share things with other people, your friends and others, when you felt that certain of your

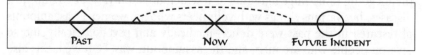

Fig. 35–1. In the nineties, the Explorer Race mentors saw the situation involving the vaccination scenario in the future and began training all humans to use their natural abilities as benevolent creators.

trainings were developed by you or by others that were benevolent for all. And many of you have done exactly that. Thank you very much.

Understand this, my friend—you are asking and I appreciate your clarity—I know that you're asking why the teaching, the channeling, changed. But for other people, they felt the change differently, as I described today. Most people do not have your experience talking to Uncle Zoosh, understand? So my answer applies to most people, not just those who are talking to me.

And along with the increase in the "creators-in-training" abilities in humans, the SSG, the sinister secret government, also seems to have increased its level of power in its efforts to control and manipulate the peoples and monies of this planet, right?

No, it's more their fear and their awareness that human beings globally are suddenly very interested in spiritual things and that this might lead to greater power and influence of individuals over their lives. And this also spreads, to a slight degree, to people's interest in religion, but it is not always the case with religion. Some religions are very benevolent; they support and nurture and urge their practitioners to be very humanitarian and so on. But other religions are very exclusive and talk about the enemy and the bad people, and how they should all feel guilty and ashamed for being alive. I do not really feel good about what they are teaching, but that's something that they are teaching at this time. They will change. Those religions that survive in the future will all change. And I'm not saying that they're all evil; they do many good things for their parishioners.

But you cannot teach that some groups of human beings are evil just because they are from another religion and hope to develop a more humanitarian Earth just as soon as everybody is of your own religion. If you do that, you're just asking to perpetuate and amplify conflict. I'm not trying to say that religions are evil. I'm just trying to say: Teach things that you can all agree on globally are benevolent human characteristics and qualities that you'd like to increase and support, as well as teach an understanding, from that religion's point of view, of who God is. God has many faces, maybe appearing in the belief forms of different religions in different ways.

The Good News: The Future Remains a Field of Infinite Possibility

The whole purpose of articles like this is to say, "Here's some information. Now you do what you wish with it." The whole purpose of anything channeled through this channel and others very often works to support and educate and—how can we say?—"to wise you up," to present you with something that you can do something with or not. It's up to you. It's our job not to tell you your future but to tell you more about yourselves so you know about your capabilities and to suggest at various times that different ones of these capabilities might be to your advantage to learn about, which is our way of telling you your future.

I want you to think about that. If we stress something suddenly, "out of the blue" as you were suggesting, then that's our way of telling you about your future: "Develop these capabilities, and you won't be sorry," like that. We can't tell you your future, but we can suggest, even with urgency, that it might be a good idea for you to learn how to do this, those of you who would like to. Now, as an example, for a person who's going to take a long ocean voyage in the future that he or she doesn't know about . . . maybe the parents decide it's time to move to this other continent: "Things aren't working well for us here, but we have a feeling that moving to this other continent, or even this other island . . . we're on an island and maybe we can move to another island, or maybe on a continent we're going to move sixty, eighty miles away to another continent." With boats and ships not necessarily being as safe as they are today, parents might urge their children to learn how to swim. They might not necessarily tell the kids why, but, "Oh, why don't you learn how to swim? It might be fun. You can swim with your friends, have time together and so on." The children all learn how to swim, and then the parents are relieved, thinking, "Well, if the boat isn't quite safe, then at least if they fall in the water, they'll be safe; they can swim."

I'm not trying to suggest anything about boats here; I'm just suggesting that sometimes someone who knows something about the future might suggest that you start doing things in a different way because of what could happen in the future, or even because of opportunities that you may have in the future, and if you have these skills and abilities, you can take advantage of these opportunities. If you don't, it might be more difficult. I'm just trying to cover your curiosities.

Now, I'd like to say to you all that these articles are not intended to be "gloom and doom." Rather, picture the future as a time of opportunities, not just as a time of impending challenges or "doom," as it were. And if there are opportunities, quite naturally you're going to want to have skills and abilities heightened—perhaps even things that are within you such as talents—and discover how you can do things in a way that will improve the quality of your life. You may even improve the lives of those around you, such as your love, your friends, your companions, animals perhaps or plants. And that's why I stressed the homework at the beginning of this article, so that you would know that there's something you can do that does not particularly weigh heavily on you as homework that you have to add to your life: "One more thing . . . oh no, Zoosh, not one more thing."

This is something that's designed to improve the quality of your life, to improve benevolence in general for all beings, and you don't have to really do a whole lot extra. Don't feel like you have to do it every night. Just say it when you think about it, before you go to sleep. It will have a cumulative impact. At some point, when you notice that your life is a lot more benevolent—which could happen, no guarantees—then you might feel that you have capabilities and capacities spiritually that you didn't know you had, and that maybe by improving your life and your experience of life—as being more benevolent—that that will spread around and others might feel their lives more benevolently too, especially if they are in any way associated with your life. This homework that I gave you at the beginning of the article is intended to, yes, improve your life, but ultimately as more people do it, it will improve the lives of all beings. Good night.

Part 3: The Beauty of Life

The following chapters were originally published in the *Sedona Journal of Emergence!* magazine.

Returning to the Heart through Scent and Song

Speaks of Many Truths
October 1997

Dear Speaks of Many Truths,
  I am having some God-awful dreams. They are so vivid. Many other people are having vivid, powerful dreams. Mine are so vivid, they are more real than my physical life.

—Name withheld

If you can obtain an aromatic dispenser—I think this is called essential oils, aromatherapy—that would be very helpful. Use lavender, perhaps, or something else that stimulates good dreams and benevolent sleep.

The Impact of Fragrance on the Sleep State

You would be surprised what the impact of fragrance is on the sleep state. At this time, as Zoosh has indicated, people are working things out that have been tumultuous on the planet. Also, individuals who are exposed to a dramatic work situation like hospitals or police work or the military, where there is regular intense interaction with other people, are doing more intense dreamings than others. I feel you can all benefit greatly from fragrance.

In my time, when people would have nightmares, that is what we would do. Sometimes herbs and dried flower petals would be simmered, and a person's dreams would become pleasant. You can try this for a few days—three or four nights, or maybe a week. You might like it. If so, do it as often as you want. But in the beginning, try it for that amount of time and then try a night without it.

Perhaps you have noticed when you have been around blooming flowers (especially when they are still alive, not cut), that they put out with great energy and gusto a fragrance that attracts the flying little ones. You will find that this will be very helpful. You can probably find a good diffuser in your own town. Keep it in the bedroom and use it at night. I think this will cure your problem. If not, ask me again soon and I will suggest something else.

The senses of the body do not travel with the spirit when it travels as the body sleeps. All the senses remain in the body and are active, even during sleep. That is why a sound will wake you up. You do not hear it when you are in some other planetary experience or excursion on another world with your teachers; your body hears it and calls itself together. This is what brings you back into your body.

If your dreams are unpleasant or too extreme, fragrance won't take those dreams away, but it ought to make them more pleasant. Use a fragrance of flowers that you like or one suggested by an aromatherapist who says, "Oh, this will improve your dreams." It will bring relaxation and comfort to the body. The body will feel, "Oh, this is beauty, this is wonderful," and all the senses will be calmed.

Sing from Your Heart

Humans are going through a tumultuous time right now. Is there any other guidance you have for the ups and downs? Everyone seems to have colds and viruses, but it's just the energy. Are there any other little shamanic tricks or tips that you can give them to deal with these energies?

One of the most valuable things you can do is sing. You do not have to have a wonderful voice. In your time people are told or reminded that they are a particular job: "Your job is to write," or "Your job is to read and compare," or "Your job is to drive a vehicle," or "Your job is to serve food," and so on. But because there is so much of this particular job description for people, a lot of people have forgotten the natural ways. Singing is one of the most comfortable and comforting things you can do for yourself and sometimes for others, especially in a family situation . . . and family is people, yes, but sometimes it is one person or animals when a person lives in the wild.

Even if it is just a little verse, your body gets used to singing. Don't worry if you carry the tune or not. Don't worry too much about anything but the words, which are the essential part. You will discover more in your time that the words of the song must be nurturing, uplifting, encouraging, enlightening, loving. It doesn't have to be all of those things, but positive, yes, because life is what comes from the heart. That which does not come from the heart we do not call life, but challenge to life.

The mind comes in to help determine what to do in the face of those challenges while staying in the heart. The moment you do something that takes you out of the heart, you step out of your path. You go onto a strange path that does not accommodate or understand your heart, so it cannot understand your needs. Your physical and your feeling needs—what you need to survive and also what you need to be and to feel good in your life—all of this is emanated from your heart. So be alert to the mind's way. The mind does not understand the heart completely, so it is the heart's job to remind the mind that one must stay on the heart's path.

If people are not feeling well, just remind them to sing a little bit. It will help you. Sing something pleasant. If they say, "Oh, I'm not feeling very pleasant," then have them look around for something beautiful or smell something pleasant.

For a lot of people, this will be flower odors; for others, it will be herbs. Some people like the smell of freshly cut hay or, in the city, cut grass. Other people like the smell of food cooking that reminds them of better times. Smells have a fabulous capacity to enrich and to create in your life a more benevolent and wonderful experience. Sometimes they can literally cure. But be alert to smells that cause you to feel uncomfortable, and avoid them.

Be very clear that songs come easily when you look at anything beautiful. In your time songs are sung about people, but because so many people have stepped off the heart path, the mind sings songs that might not serve the heart. But when you are on your heart path, all you have to do is look at a child, a flower, a tree, a mountain—anything beautiful—and the song will come easily. Make the words up. You will feel better, and your body will grow accustomed to the song.

Do you remember when you were young and your mother or father or your grandmother or grandfather sang to you? It was very nurturing coming from them. Now some of you have children of your own, and you sing to them. But for those of you who do not have children to sing to or who are not being sung to by others, know that the singer also benefits. Your physical body creates certain feelings. It moves inside when you sing. When you sing of beautiful things, you become more cheerful, and it creates for you the same condition that was created when you were a youngster.

The songs from your parents or grandparents supported your continuity. Certain songs could be heard regularly that were beautiful and encouraging. They gave the child—which is essential, you know—the beginnings of the knowledge that can be lived, which is wisdom. They gave the child the awareness that life can be beautiful and that he or she could count on hearing those songs. In your time, if songs are about sadness, then the child learns to expect sadness. It is very easy to overlook this.

So you can have that relationship with your own body. If you begin to sing things that are of greater beauty, your body will remember being sung to as a child (most of you have forgotten this), and it will relax. You will grow more physically comfortable. It will reassure you about life, reminding you that life can be good. And it can create an internal support for you.

This is something most easily understood by experiencing it, so the more you notice what you feel physically, the more you will find your good feelings. And when you have feelings that are not so good, do something to feel good. Sing. It is easy, something you can do yourself.

Cultivating Body-Centered Thought Processes

Speaks of Many Truths
November 20, 1997

In your time now you have almost completely finished the experience of the intellectual mind separated from the heart. As a result, to be able to read or even think about things that are not in alignment with your feelings is infinitely more difficult these days. This is why even if you have for years loved a certain type of reading, if it does not have direct, synchronistic alignment with your feelings of the moment, it is difficult to read.

For that matter, it is also difficult to do anything that is not associated with your feelings. You are being herded by Creator, your guides and your teachers into this position, not because it will be permanent, but because you have allowed the mind to become so separated from the heart and the feelings of benevolence in your body that your body often gets lonely and frightened because the mind does not have to live in the physical body to function. Since the mind's primary tool of expansion and exploration is imagination, when the mind reads and absorbs something, immediately there is often an imagination that frequently takes you out of your body to explore possibilities, theories, applications or even fantasies. This happens so much that no matter what is the stimulus for your mind—reading, moving pictures or television—there is a constant separation between thoughts, imaginations and the physical self.

As a result, Creator and your teachers have begun making a pressure cooker for you in which you do not feel comfortable. Even if you love your reading (or television or movies), you do not feel comfortable reading for very long. It feels as if you are distracted, and you feel or think there is something else you ought to be doing. It also tends to stimulate for you a strong sense of nervousness or give you nervous energy, which really means it is intended that you be more physical, come into your physical body, do physical things, even do emotional things within the physical self.

If you can begin doing more of these things, you will be able to read, but there will be a new way of reading. I'm going to give you some homework to make it easier for you to develop this new way of reading.

Homework: A New Way of Reading

The homework is simple. Most of you have done it before or have had it done for you. When you read out loud, even if you are reading to your cat or dog or bird or horse or children or grandfather, try to put some drama into it.

If you are reading a story, be the different characters. If you are reading the Bible, you can do the same thing. What is necessary is to put feeling into what you are reading. For some of you, it will even be necessary to stand up and walk around while you are reading. This is part of the reason it is now more appealing to you to listen to someone read to you. This is the reason for the great popularity of books that talk to you, because then someone is reading to you. To be read to while doing something physical such as driving your automobile or to read to someone else out loud are physical acts that necessarily bring you into your body.

In my time we didn't read from paper, but we told stories, not only to keep our wisdom alive, but also to entertain. And when we would tell stories, we would sometimes change our voices or move around and use gestures or even objects to explain things. Such storytelling practices are still in effect in your time. But in your time technology is so pervasive that you allow others to do things. This, then, is a static experience, meaning that if you're watching television or the movies, you are sitting still while others relate their stories in some entertaining way and they move things. It is not the same. When a human being talks to you and tells you stories, you are there and you get their feelings as well as your feelings, and it is an exciting part of physical life. But when you are simply reading (or watching), what happens is that you read a paragraph or two, and you want to participate. You want to experience.

What I am saying is that Creator is moving you to a position where what you think also needs to be what you experience. This means that there will be new levels of entertaining (as you understand it) coming to you. It means that dramas at home need not simply be arguments. They can be in the form of stories like the stories of old. If you can, make up a story. Take your favorite book and act it out with your family, or read something you are interested in to your cat or dog. It might seem strange, but it will bring you into your physical body.

In order to create the new way of communication, you will find that being in your physical body, using your feelings as well as words to speak, will produce much better and clearer communication. It seems to the mind that if we make new words, have these words be very precise in their meaning and then communicate these precise words to people, that will establish clarity. But it doesn't work that way because you are not only a mental being, but you are here to understand the physical plane. This means you must be physical and feeling, or what you call emotional, and you must be spiritual, have depth beyond your personal experience in this life. Of course, you must have instincts—your physical reaction to all that is going on around you—so that you can respond to it, whether it is something that is seen or smelled or felt or anything to do with instinct.

What is happening for you is that the way to clarify communication, to make it more easily understood, is to be more centered in your physical body. I'm going to give you homework, which I will do from time to time, because doing the homework—not just thinking about it, but actually *doing* it—will give you the feeling that you've been restlessly trying to capture lately, the feeling that has been missing from what you've been reading or watching, that restlessness that tells you that you need to be reading or communicating differently.

More Homework: Communicating Differently

Here is your homework: For those of you who know how to generate or be aware of the warmth in your heart, go ahead and do that [for more on the love-heat/heart-warmth/physical-warmth, see Overview]. But if you cannot easily do that, then this is what to do.

Take your fingers and put them over the part of your body where your heart is. Move your fingers gently, bringing your physical awareness down to that part of your body, and try to go inside where your heart is. This means you must picture and feel physically inside where your heart is. Speak while doing that.

The first thing you will notice is that you won't be able to use the vast vocabulary you normally use. Your vocabulary will immediately shrink. If it doesn't, it probably means that you're either very good at this exercise or, more likely, you're probably thinking more than you're physically feeling your heart.

Remember, you are to go into where your heart is. For those of you who can do the love-heat exercise, go where the heat is. Constantly focus on the heat, and while you're doing that, speak whatever you have to say, even if you are talking to your cat to say, "Hello, are you having a good day? Did you have fun while I was at work?"—anything simple—or having a simple conversation between couples or between a parent and a child.

Your conversation in this way will not sound like your normal conversation. If it's with a human being and you feel that he or she is conscious enough or knows you well enough, you can tell the person what you're doing. If it is with someone at work, then you don't have to tell that person. Do what you feel is best.

Then you will notice something: your vocabulary will greatly shrink. However, because you are in your heart space or in the heat space, which is the love space, people will most likely understand you better, even though you are using a more limited vocabulary than usual. That's your homework. Try it, and know that it is a step toward reinventing body-centered thought.

Healing Imbalances through the Five Senses

Speaks of Many Truths
December 28, 1997

ll right, this is Speaks of Many Truths.

Welcome. How do we make sense of all these sophisticated healing modalities? People are remembering things from Atlantis.

I would say this: In my experience (as far as the senses go), it is best to use therapies that stimulate or soothe or salve the senses. The senses are one of the best ways to communicate with the physical self and the emotional self, and by doing so, with the subconscious self. These areas will most often bring to the attention of the conscious self in some dramatic way a problem that exists within.

Using Smell for Healing

Aromatherapy, for example, is an excellent method. Basically, consider the senses: what you smell, what you taste, touch, see and hear. Generally speaking, anything that works with those senses is the best. I grant that you could say that everything does, but different things assist different people.

There are circumstances associated with disease that have certain smells. It is common knowledge amongst shamanic individuals that a certain disease has a particular smell. Then the proper medicines or medicinals, something that makes a smell or brings something into balance, are held up to the body in appropriate quantities—a little of this, a little of that, not enough, try some more, too much, a little less—experimenting until the natural odor of that person is exuded.

The combination of herbs and aromas combine with the disease aroma to make the natural aroma of that person. Someone who knows that person ought to be present, or perhaps the shaman knows that person's natural odor. This is particularly relevant to you right now because of the overwhelming diversity in potential diseases. This is largely due to the exposure to chemicals you have now that we did not have in our time, yet I feel that this method continues to work.

It is something that can be noticed by an observant person. If you put a dog or a cat (animals you are frequently exposed to) into a room with a sick person, it is not at all unusual for the dog or cat to go right to the spot that is injured, even if there is no surface anomaly the animal can see, sniffing that place. A dog might even try to lick it, which from its perception is to heal it, if the dog feels affection for the injured person. In the cat's case, the cat might lay its body on the wound in some way to heal it, which is one of the ways cats heal things.

Are you saying that each disease has a particular odor?

And that disease will be different in smell. It will have a general odor, but it will be slightly scented toward the person or place the person comes from, just like a food has a general odor yet would smell a little different according to how it is prepared.

So we need to know or have someone else who knows the natural odor of the sick person?

Yes, and this is usually a family member. You hold the herbs up to the person in the area where he or she is diseased and exuding that smell. I might say that the diseased area exuding this smell is not necessarily where there is a surface eruption but where the pain is the most significant. That is the place to smell. Then you hold the herbs, powders or whatever up to the diseased area. If the herbs or powders do not normally have a smell, which is so for some, they might need to be wet or burned so the person using smell can perceive the disease and find its treatment.

This is particularly helpful for a shaman or mystical or medicine person who is far from where he lives and who might be exposed to plants or herbs he is not familiar with. It is also helpful for individuals who find they have available herbs from other countries or places where they have never been. You can still use this smell, but to determine the proper treatment, you would have to experiment with doses. Start with a small amount, and experiment until the person's pain begins to recede. When that happens, that's the dose to give that person if the pain starts to come back. Then experiment with the dose again—you might have to give a little more or give it more frequently.

It requires experimentation; that's why medicine people are who they are. They discover these things and pass on the wisdom to others. In your time these medicines are written down and made a permanent record, but in my experience, different medicines affect different individuals in different ways, not only on the basis of the individual being, but different for the time of the day, the season, the circumstance (for instance, if a woman is pregnant) and the age or time of life. It can also be different according to different seasons, times or even locations. You have to experiment with it. It is a big project, but you have many people now and you can begin.

I think we need to review this further. You need someone who knows the natural odor to smell the odor of the person, and then you have to be able to smell the disease. Then when you smell your herbs, what are you trying to do? Get back to that natural odor?

Yes, you want to put enough herbs or powders—some of which might be mineral powders—near the diseased area, not to mask the odor of the disease, but to re-create the natural smell of that person. The combination of the disease and the herbs or minerals put in the same area then stimulates that person's natural smell. You might have to use larger or smaller quantities of whatever healing powder or herb you are using. You have to experiment. As you accumulate wisdom in these areas, you get better at it, and as others come to share with you what works for them, then you all share your knowledge together freely.

The idea is that whatever you put there that allows you to smell the person instead of the disease—that's the remedy?

Yes, of course. It's the remedy, from my perception. That's why it is important in your time to experiment with it very gently at first. In your time I understand you use what you call homeopathics, which is very minor amounts of the herb. Certainly in your time that would be a very safe way to begin the experimentation. But first you must hold the actual herb or mineral up to the person, because you cannot know what is exactly right for that person and what will cause that disease to recede completely without a person (usually a loved one) who can smell the natural smell of that person. It is important, this love; it can't be someone who just knows this smell and doesn't care. That person has to care. If the person cares, then he or she will be motivated to get it right.

Diagnosing and Healing with Sound

There are many techniques appropriate at different times. There are certain times in a person's life when music alone (a happy tune, perhaps people clapping and dancing nearby) is enough to transform a person's minor illness. Any parent knows that when a child hears someone having fun in the next room, that child will start to feel better and want to come in and join the party. This is not just jealousy or desire. It is real. In older people's lives, sometimes specific tones held for a long time or an instrument played repeatedly is more helpful.

When a person gets older, organs need to be attuned, not unlike the way a piano mechanic tunes a piano by using tools and listening to the strings. The older person can benefit mostly from a sound made by an instrument or an object, and that will work ten times better if the instrument is present in the room. It won't work so well if listened to on a tape recorder or earphones. It might be of some minor assistance, but it would be quite beneficial to hear specific tones.

There are people who can do something else that I will discuss. Not many are telling others they can do it, but I would like these people to become public. Some people can listen to a disease—put their ear up close, sometimes reach over with their hand or just lean over—and get the impression of a sound from a diseased or injured organ or part of a person's body. This works for animals as well; they can hear a tone from a diseased or injured animal. If you can make tones that will not drown out the sound you are hearing but still have this specific effect, it will be helpful.

There will be a tone that compensates for the tone of disease that comes from a portion of a body that is injured or diseased. You can make this tone with an instrument, with your voice or even with the voices of others if you cannot reach a higher or lower note and they can. This tone will not only cause the person to feel more relaxed but will also cause the disease organisms to retreat.

Disease organisms spring from places in your body that are in disharmony. Generally speaking, these places are very small, and if the organisms are not taken care of right away, they will continue to spread until they hear the tone that will cause them to retreat back where they came from.

If it is possible for your current science to chart this, I would say that it can be tested as follows: An organism diseased with cancer can be followed in its progression if you are a physician, but you can play tones that will cause the disease to retreat and you can see it retreat along the same path in which it came out. It won't just dissolve or resolve; it will retreat. Once it has fully retreated, you will see the exact spot where it originally emerged, telling you that this spot is susceptible to this disease. Any treatments you do in the future should be done on this spot first, regardless of where or how the disease may have spread, in case the patient has not come to you for a time.

Your sound, remember, is not intended to drown out the patient's sound that the sensitive individual hears from the disease. It is intended to act as a compensation. Sometimes it will be a sound that is quite opposite from the sound of the disease. Other times it will be a sound so close to the sound of the disease that it will be almost harmonic in nature, like the sound of a choir singing in different octaves. I would ask that people who can hear the sound of disease step forward. If these individuals can step forward to work with physicians, that is wonderful.

There is another application of this. There are also people who can hear sounds that precede natural disasters. This is better known, even documented, because of the reactions of animals before earthquakes. But there are other potential natural disasters, such as tornadoes. There are sounds not associated with the whirling of winds, actual sounds that precede the formation of a tornado (usually by an hour or an hour and half), even if it is a cloudless sky. I ask the individuals who have heard these sounds to make themselves known to broad-minded scientists, people in the weather-prediction community or even what you call New Age circles, because you might be able to help with a warning.

Remember, animals are hearing something. It is true that their range of hearing is broader than the conscious range of hearing of most human beings, but they are in fact hearing something. If you cannot hear it, then you might feel it. If you cannot feel it, then find someone who can hear or feel it. These capacities exist in human beings.

There are many children being born today who have these capacities, not on a latent level like many of you, but as a prominent experience. Parents, please be aware that your children may begin to demonstrate to you things they hear or see, things they smell or taste, things they sense in some way that may not be perceived by other individuals. Don't just say, "Oh, it is nothing." Ask them about it, but don't make too much of a fuss. We don't want the children to feel strange or odd, but just ask them. Make a note of it, write it down somewhere, and when the child brings it up again, write it down again.

Perhaps you will be able to encourage such perceptions in that child as she grows and changes and interacts with other children who might not have these skills and who might feel uncomfortable around the child. You can support your child and nurture her talents and abilities. As such talents and abilities become more widely known, people who were uncomfortable with them before will see their great value and the contribution that can be made to all beings. Your children will then be appreciated for what they can do, not just treated as if they are different.

You are saying that they can hear or sense something before an earthquake, tornado, volcano, flood—all these different things?

Yes, or a hurricane, or a typhoon, as it is called in some places—any natural disaster, including those you have little chance of experiencing. An asteroid hitting the Earth, for example. If you can find the crater where an asteroid has hit the Earth, you might be able to hear (if you can hear such things), smell or even taste (if you feel safe doing that) the surrounding stone. Or you might use your other senses to notice if there is something in sound, smell, taste or even sight that is distinctive to that experience.

Using the Senses to Know the Future

There are other possibilities. You have had ice ages before. Those of you who can do this can go up to where ice still is on the polar caps and smell, listen and taste the air near the ice or even the ice itself, if you feel safe doing that. If you use your perceptions, you can tell whether there will be an ice age or whether the ice is continuing to retreat. You can tell, and I will explain how. It is not a message so much from the ice but from the land that has once been covered in ice.

Go to the ice first and be around it. You can go to a glacier that has been there for a while and familiarize yourself with the smell, taste, sound, vision and so on, whatever senses are working for you in that avenue. Afterward, go to land that has, according to your science, previously been covered by the ice and see if you can smell, taste, hear or so on (whatever your skill is) that land. Again, smell a stone or taste it, because the stone is more likely to have been there during that experience.

If the perception is very slight, it is probably a memory the stone has. If it is very pronounced and strong, then it is not a memory but that stone preparing itself for the coming of the ice once again.

Are you saying that's a possibility in the near future?

I am not saying either way. I am calling to arms those who have these skills, because if it is a possibility, people will need to be warned. It will certainly not happen overnight, but it could happen. If it does, it will happen gradually, with plenty of time to make alternative plans, such as living underground for a time if necessary. But I do not think that will be necessary, nor do I think there will be an ice age in your time. It is just a good example of how these skills can be used.

In my time people would do such things to know if a storm was coming. They would listen to the rock. They might look at the rock, smell it, taste it, touch it—all these things. Different people have different skills. People are no different in your time, but the skills might not be present in most people's awareness. They are present in potential, and some people can do this now. With few exceptions, they just don't feel the permission to discuss it. It would be good for every neighborhood—not just every town or city—to have someone who can do this in his or her way. That way you can be warned.

The Memory in Stone

It is also possible to be warned of danger that might come from other human beings. If a rock in the area has been exposed to harmful acts by human beings against other human beings or animals, the rock would be sensitized to human violence, and if your senses register only faintly, you will be perceiving a memory. But if your perception is very striking, then it might be something that is going to happen in that area. You will have to experiment with it, but it would be worth it as an experiment.

I can tell you—as a matter of fact, I know—that many people who have had these skills or have trusted these skills in others have been able to survive circumstances others did not survive. They left the area, without any physical evidence readily apparent to the average person that they should leave, just because of their interaction with stone. Stone is one of the most perceptive elements on Earth. It has the longest memory of any being on

Earth I know of, and it is therefore very worthy of being asked (using your senses) what might or could happen.

Predicting Violence by Smell

You will have to experiment and keep notes, but in time, as you redevelop these skills, you might be able to avoid great disruption, not only in your neighborhood, but within your family. Do you know that an individual who is going to be violent, for whatever reason—even from external or justified causes—for fully three days before that violent act will exude something in his or her sweat that can be tasted, smelled or even felt by the sensitive person? A drop of sweat between the fingers of a sensitive person can tell him by feeling whether that person is going to commit a violent act. When I say violence, I do not mean something minor—I mean something murderous.

These are skills I will instruct you on at some point. I am just suggesting them to you now to remind you that such skills and abilities exist, and even though your modern science doesn't give credence to it, that attitude will change in time as anthropologists, archaeologists and social scientists come together to work. They will in time put out papers that will draw in the scientific community.

Many of you are looking for skills, abilities and potentials within yourself and other human beings to transform life in a way that will be more benevolent for yourselves, your family, your neighborhood, your community and all beings. You have within you these capacities. It is time to bring them to the surface once again.

Using Homeopathy

There is a flu, which some have suggested might escape Hong Kong and become pandemic. They call it the chicken flu, something that makes chickens sick but now has crossed to humans, which has never happened before. Some people feel it might go through the world, and there is no vaccination or antibiotic for it. What is your feeling about that?

I think you will find that homeopaths will work to keep the disease from you. With homeopathic medicine in your time, one does not necessarily have to be immunized from the disease; one can simply support and sustain the natural protective systems of the body. I recommend this, because when the disease is unknown and there is not enough time to establish the principles and to practice and study the smells and so on, it would be better to just become stronger. The best way to become stronger, to provide the maximum amount of medicine to as many people as possible, would be the homeopathic method, I believe.

It also would be supportive for many individuals with wasting diseases. Almost all severe wasting diseases that exist in your time happen not so much because the diseases are new, but because your immune systems are so marginal. If you can support and sustain your system of strength that you call immunity, this should prevent any major disease.

So we really have to work at it and pay attention to this?

I feel it is valid to pay attention, as you say. I do not think you can live in a sterile environment all your life, so I don't think it's realistic to tell people to do that. I also don't think it's realistic to take the universal anti-toxin [interferon] that exists, because it makes you dependent upon it. You must take it every day. The body does not produce it but reacts to it, meaning that if you take the universal antitoxin in existence now, you might have to depend on this drug indefinitely. Most people can't get it anyway, so as you say, what's the point?

Sounds Can Satisfy Disease Organisms

Of course, there are certain tones or combinations of tones that might help as well. You will have to experiment. They will be high tones, but they will all be natural tones—not from a mechanical instrument that makes a high tone, but rather a musical high tone or a sound made by a person. A woman can probably feed the disease organism so that it does not need to feed on human beings.

Do you know what diseased organisms need? Disease organisms are not just monsters; they are not unlike other beings who need to be fed. Most disease organisms are fed by sound. When you make the sounds, it feeds them, and then they do not need to feed off human beings or animals. Experiment with it. It is my intention these days to give you as many healing techniques as you can use, because these days the more you have, the better.

Say more about these tones—how will the very sensitive beings know?

Sensitive people who are exposed to such tones will feel a greater sense of strength and will feel an expansion physically—maybe not a large expansion, but they will feel themselves as if they are bigger then they are. This bigness is a sign of strength.

Would the revealing person need to know different tones for each type of disease?

Possibly, yes. With many people working on this all over the world, it would be something people can discover. Since you can record the sound, it can be recorded and then other people can imitate it. The recording itself will not feed the disease, however. You have to make the sound yourself or use a natural musical instrument, not an electrical one. Walk around outside in your neighborhood making your sound for a while. In my day they used to have what you could call "toners," people who would make the sounds. These sounds wouldn't frighten the diseases off; they would feed them.

If you frighten something off, that means you are saying to yourself that there are some forms of life that are not of God. If all has been created by Creator, then all must be equal in Creator's eyes. If there is some form of life doing harm to some other form of life, it needs something that it cannot get on its own and needs to have others give it what it can't get. Disease organisms will infect people if they are not fed proper sounds that will satisfy them. When they are fed these sounds, they do not have to strike animals or people.

So make the sounds from time to time. Once a month or so have different people learn the sounds for different diseases. Sometimes they will be inspired to make certain sounds. I generally find (this is in my time; it might be different in your time) that higher notes feed the disease, satisfying it so it does not need to make you sick. Lower notes sometimes take energy from the disease so it will need to be fed more. In my time this is the case; you can experiment in your time.

Do you think this would also work for what people call AIDS and cancer?

I think it is worth experimenting with. The tone does not have to be made by the person who has the discomfort or the disease. It can best be made by someone who can reach the upper register, the higher sounds— by a woman most likely, perhaps a younger woman. If the organism has already gone into the body but is not infectious, as in cancer, then the toner can get close (not unpleasantly close, but as close as is comfortable for the diseased person) and make the sounds. Do not touch the body, but make the sounds within four inches from it—no closer, though.

This might have some benefit, but it has to be done regularly. In the case of a person seriously ill, it would have to be done two or three times a day for at least five to ten minutes. Not everyone can do this. It might require a trained singer, but it is worth experimenting with. Then you can share your wisdom with each other. The more healing modalities in your time, the better.

I grant that there are some electrical fields and field effects that can support the physical body, but generally speaking, the amount of electricity would be exceedingly small and also the magnetism on any one part of the body. I will discuss that some other time. I feel stronger about using these natural methods that anyone can use without any money or access to exotic instruments.

These are things we have known in the past and have forgotten?

These are things that are known to some tribal peoples even today, but because their wisdom and culture has been largely unappreciated in the past, they have kept some of these things quiet. I feel that now you as a general population are prepared to experiment with these things. I am not saying to do these instead of the medical care you are doing, but to do them along with it and see if it helps.

Calling Star Lives to Gain Soul Skills

Speaks of Many Truths
March 19, 1998

I have heard about shamanistic healing techniques, but what about systems like acupuncture and acupressure? Did your people know about the meridian systems, and did they use them in healing?

I have heard of this now from others, but we did not do that. Our methods involved smoke and herbs and things I have discussed with you in *Shamanic Secrets for Material Mastery*. I am not familiar with this meridian part of the body, though I have been shown by some spirit persons what it means. I must say that I think it is a wonderful thing. Certainly, if we had known we would have used it, but it was not our way.

Were the chakras made known to you? Were you aware of them?

Not these Eastern things, no. I have had a spirit with a turban who came to me and spoke of things he said were the methods of the East. We talked at length, and I was very interested, though I had not heard of this before.

What about hands-on healing? Was there an attempt to transfer energy or to focus energy in the other person's body?

No, not hands on the body. But sometimes if the shaman had a special relationship with a tree or a mountain or a river, he might put a person between him and that object, then stand behind the person (usually) and pull the energy through him or her, while deflecting it from going into himself, the shamanic practitioner. So we were not involved so much with touch for person-to-person healing (except as I have described to you).

A person might be lost in the mind (and we had such things), meaning he had forgotten who he was—perhaps something had been a shock or had struck him on the head. Then we would usually expose him to familiar smells. If his family was still present, we would have them cook familiar foods or produce familiar odors (with herbs, for instance) that were what that person had been near before. We would take him to familiar places and let the land or the water touch him. If he could move about once a day, this would be done until he remembered. If after doing this for several cycles he still didn't remember, then we would just let him be who he was and start another life.

Star Lives Teach Unknown Skills

What about what's being taught now? It's called soul recovery. Did you do what they now call journeys to find people's souls or lost psyches?

I did not do this. I have heard of this from other tribal peoples. We did not do exactly this, but this is what we did: If a person had need of a skill for her family or herself, a shaman or a seer would see that she needed this skill and could not obtain it where she was. Then we would ask one of her star lives to emigrate to that person and live with her for a time and show her through feelings or experience how to do that talent. In this way, we would not interfere with her lives in the stars but would ask such a being, if one was available, to visit.

Sometimes the visit would be in spirit form, and the spirit would speak to the person in her dreams, or maybe in a vision. Other times it would be an intermediary life, between lives, but between star lives—on other planets. They would enter the person's body gently with those skills. The person would suddenly be able to do those things or be able to pick it up quickly. Other times a ship or even a light spirit would spend time with the individual and show her. They did this only if the skill was something totally unheard of by our people, unknown to people around us or those we knew who passed near us. That's the only time we would call on star lives.

Please give me an example of a skill.

The Boy Who Learned to Find Ice

There was a time when a young boy in the tribe, about seven years old, was told by one of our seers that he would need to learn how to find ice. Now, where we lived, it did not usually get cold, and if it did, we went south. Since ice was not something we normally had where we lived, none of my people knew how to find it. So no one had the knowledge to teach him how to find ice. Since it was not something we were around very much, no one had the smell of ice memorized so they could find it and then teach him the smell.

So we asked if one of his star lives would come. It was a between-life energy that came into his body, and one day he said to his mother, "Now I know where to go to find the ice." His mother said, "Make sure you take your uncle with you." So he went with his uncle, who was about twenty-seven, a fairly grown man. His uncle took enough food and water to last them three days. The boy said, "We don't need that much, but I think it's good to take a little extra." So they took their provisions and what they needed and left. They were back in about two days.

The uncle said, "Let me tell you what he did." So we gathered around the fire that night and the uncle told the story because the boy wanted him to tell it. He said that they went to a ravine not far from where my people lived and traveled far up that ravine. The boy stopped and said, "Here!" and pointed to a big rock. The uncle said, "I do not see any ice." But the boy said, "I know it's there."

So the two of them struggled and moved the rock, and behind the rock was an opening to a cave. The opening was big enough so that the boy and his uncle could crawl down into it. They found a place where there was ice, and the boy familiarized himself with its smell. They also found a place where the water was so fresh and clear with special minerals in it that when the boy and the uncle drank it, they were especially refreshed.

The uncle had a disease of the skin that no one had been able to help. Sometimes it itched and sometimes it bled; sometimes there were blisters and other times it was just red. It was very uncomfortable, and it sometimes made him grouchy, as it would anyone. About forty-five minutes after drinking the water, this rash went away. So they brought back as much of the water as they could carry and put the boulder back over the opening the way they found it. They came back, and other people with discomforts were also healed by the water.

The boy didn't know until he was thirteen years old why he needed to find ice. It turned out that an animal came to him in his visions regularly, and sometimes he would see the animal physically. I am not certain that this was a typical animal. It looked like a duck, but its feet were unusually big. I have not seen such a animal before or since. All I know is that it looked like a duck, but it had very big feet, and I have never seen another duck like this. This animal would tell the boy secrets—sometimes great wisdoms and philosophies, other times wisdom from the stars or secret things. I cannot even say today, they are so secret. He would tell us if he could, but sometimes the animal would say, "These are very important secrets. Use them only to heal others in their thoughts, dreams and bodies."

I am not sure whether this was a physical or a spirit animal. Maybe it was a spirit that could be physical, because we all saw it—not at the same time, but at different times, and everybody described it the same way. One day the animal came, and it was not well. It had something wrong with it, and it said it needed to be somewhere cold.

Did you still live at the same place?

Yes. And the boy said, "I will carry you." This time one of his brothers went with him, because the uncle was out hunting. He and his brother went to the cave and moved the boulder and took the animal down there where it was cold by the ice and drank the water. After about half a day, it was well. It thanked the boy and said it would teach him as much as it knew or could find out about healing, and the boy became the tribe's main healer. He was able to pass on some of the secrets, but not all. This animal said, "I tell only you these things."

I believe this person in our tribe has been reincarnated today and is now living in India. I do not think he knows who he was, but he is a spiritual man today as well. I have looked in on him from time to time.

That's beautiful. I love that. Do you have any more stories like that or where a starship or a being came?

The Three Who Visited a Planet to Learn about Plants

One time a being came to be with a young girl. The young girl had a great admirer. It was somebody four or five years older than she was, but he was going to wait for her to grow up. She found this young man personally attractive. He was good-looking, strong and would be a good provider, and she felt good that she would be with him someday. But they had nothing in common.

How old was she?

She was about eight years old, and he was about thirteen, twelve maybe, fourteen—I am not remembering clearly. He said, "I will wait." At different times, they would talk together with adults there. Sometimes grandmother would say this or grandfather would say that, trying to move the conversation in different directions to find out if there were some common interests, some threads, because a man and wife must have some common interests—though, of course, children would be that someday. The grandmothers and grandfathers felt that it would be good if they could start with some common interests, but no one could find anything. So one day her grandmother said, "I will ask to see if someone from somewhere can come and find common interests for you."

So she asked if her granddaughter had any star lives that could come to find common interests between her and her future husband. There was a time of waiting—not so long, about ten days. Then a being did come in a ship, not a big one, maybe about the size of one of your normal cars these days. The being said that if they liked, he would take both of them on a short journey and that the grandmother could come along to look after the needs of the child.

So they all went: The star life took everyone to a world where there were living plants. The plants are alive where we are here on Earth, but this other world they went to was a very special place. The plants were alive there too, but they could move about in much animation. They could speak in sounds you could hear in your head, any language. They could tell stories. They would sometimes ask you to lie down near them and talk to you in your dreams, and you would remember the dreams. Most important, these plants knew about the plants on this planet.

They told these people many stories, some in their dreams, some while they were awake, and they sang to them and helped them memorize certain songs. They said, "These songs and stories will support the plants on Earth, and when you sing these songs and tell them these stories, the plants will grow vigorous." Make sure you sing to the plants that grow fruit or berries—especially anything that has food—and there will be much that will come for the people.

So they memorized the songs and the stories, and on the way back home they thought of them and sang the songs. Then they had a mission together, something to do together, and from that day on they were very close—the grandmother too. The three of them would go out whenever anyone would find trees or bushes that had berries or fruit, and they would tell the stories to the bushes or the trees. They would sing the songs, and then the bushes and trees would grow abundantly, with enough fruit and berries for the people and the animals. The plants would be vigorous and strong.

This was something they did for the rest of their days. Sometimes they would go off for a few days to other tribal encampments and do the same thing for the plants and trees there. They became well-known for this. It gave them common ground, common interests, common stories, something fun to do together. They taught these things to their children as well. I think that some of this knowledge still exists, because some of it was shared through spirit stories as well—stories between tribes. I think that some of the songs are still alive in places like the tropics—Polynesia and places like that.

That is so beautiful. Do you know what planet they went to, what star system it was in?

I think it was Sirius. Sirius has, from what little I have seen, a fantastic amount of planets with animals, plants, water and waterfalls—it looks like the most beautiful place. I think I would like to visit there someday.

Well, you can do it if you want.

Yes.

That is just heartwarming. Wonderful.

I would say this too. Plants are very sensitive beings. They like music. They particularly like music you sing yourself. If it is a happy tune, that's the best, or a sacred song. But it is best for the song to make you happy or help you to feel love and joy and comfort—benevolence, as you say. Plants love this. It is much better to sing it or use your instruments to play songs yourself than to use a machine that reproduces sounds. Plants like this very much.

Think of a song you can sing to plants, thanking them for their beauty and the abundance they share with you. Thank the Sun and the water and the Earth for nurturing these plants so that they might nurture others. If you speak of these things in song, plants will grow big and strong for you and produce more than they might normally produce.

You all know that children like to be sung to. This is universal. You can sing to a butterfly, and it will stop what it is doing. If it is a song with pleasant words and you feel loving and joyful, it will stop to rest and listen to your song. Someday you will be able to hear the song it sings back to you—for it will do that.

Calling Star Lives with a Living Prayer

Calling in a star life . . . that fascinates me. Does the person who calls have to have a special connection to spirit?

No, not really. It's when you have a need like that. In our time, our people believed that if you had a need that could not be fulfilled any other way, you would either ask spirit or you would ask star lives. We would ask star lives because many times star people would come and visit us. We knew that we were from the stars—at some point it was in our culture, our stories—so it was only natural for us to ask the place where many of us were from.

We would just go out and look at the stars at night and speak to them out loud, asking what we needed to ask. In this request—we would call it a living prayer—you ask for what you want and need in a loving, generous and respectful way. Then you go on about your life—you let it go. You ask only once. Occasionally, you are guided or have the feeling to say the prayer twice, but practically never three times. Once you start saying it many times, it is less likely to happen, because if you have to say it many times, that means you don't believe it.

Good point. Is this ability to call in star lives unique to your people, or is this a common tribal point of view that just isn't talked about?

I have heard all of the tribal people (at a distance, when we speak of these things now in spirit) say that many tribal peoples have something they ask for like this.

When you told stories in your tribe, you would tell stories of the stars where you came from?

Not very often. These stories were usually told to youngsters when they were growing up by their grandparents or by the storytellers when they were young. We did not speak of it so much when we had grown up and become adults. Then we were living on the Earth and doing what we could here. We would speak of it only to the children so that they would know. The children would say, "Where am I from?" You had to tell them something that they could see. So you told the child, "Oh, we are from the stars," and they would go out at night to look, and they saw that they were beautiful. They could see where they were from.

So it is not such a mystery. It is very important for children to be able to see where they are from to be able to use their natural abilities. You can tell them stories, but they must have some evidence, something they can see now or touch. Many of you are from this country or that country, and you might bring something—photographs, maybe a piece of furniture—that the children or grandchildren can look at, can touch. There is something that they can understand.

When people grow up they can understand things in their minds and in their hearts. Children can do this too, but they need something they can touch or see or smell. That is why you see babies doing these things—they are tasting and smelling and touching. They want to know, and it is natural for all life to know by using the senses. When you grow up, you can think, you can imagine as children do also, but you also appreciate touching and having evidence. It doesn't mean that if you can't have evidence that something isn't, but having evidence makes you feel so much better about it. We would say, "We are from that star there," and point to the sky. The child would memorize that star. When they were out on the land someday, grown up, hunting or traveling, if they were ever sad or lonely, they could look at the star and say, "I am from there; my people are there. As long as the stars come out at night, I will never be lonely or alone."

That's beautiful, but you told me you were from the other side of the universe, so that's taking a little liberty with the truth, isn't it?

We did not feel it was necessary to be scientific with children—only in your time. You put more value on what you call truth than what is called heart. Heart is ultimately of the greatest value because it nurtures, it gives support, it feeds, but truth is different from person to person.

My First Memory of a Starship Visit

What was the first time you saw a starship come to your tribe? How old were you, what were your feelings and what was the situation?

I was very young, about three years old. I remember, because it is the kind of thing you don't forget. We were told that we were going to have a wonderful visitor. Apparently, the beings in the ship came regularly in those days. The visitors would bring wonderful things that we could play with, and we would sing songs, learn new songs and dance. We would have a wonderful time. You know, the adults spoke to us as the children we were—that's what we needed to hear. We would see wonderful sights. It would be much fun. Of course, all of us were excited, and we talked during the day, "Oh, when will it come? What will it be like?" as children do eternally.

And one day, the ship came. It looked like this in shape [draws Fig. 39-1]. This is a silhouette view, roughly. It sat on the ground. I think when it flew, it didn't have these little things that came down, that it sat on. It was gold in color, and when it landed, it had other colors: orange and white. The elders said, "Don't go near it right away; it's very hot." We said, "Oh." So we waited, and then gradually the colors went away. It was at night, and we couldn't see it so well. The Moon reflected off of it, but sometimes the Moon makes things look silvery or gray, so I wasn't sure what color it was.

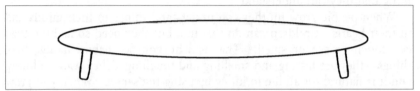

Fig. 39-1. A silhouette view of the spaceship that came to visit.

Then a door slid open, and I could see a light inside. The little beings (a little taller than us, but not as tall as the elders) got out, and they were flipping around in the air and tumbling, and all the children were laughing. The children were rolling on the ground and trying to jump up and down the way these beings were, and everybody in the tribe was laughing. The elder, the grandfather—the person who was not a chief but the elder of the tribe—came forward and greeted them, putting his arms out. The elder of the ship, who was a little taller than the others, got out and put his arms out.

Everybody came together and mingled with the littler beings on the ship. Some of them went back in and came out with little things they brought for the children. Some of them were shaped like triangles, some like balls and some like long squares—they were like toys, only they would float in the air. You could poke them, and they would float; then they would come back down. They would glow in different colors and then change colors. At other times, you could touch them together, and they would play little songs. It was wonderful. We had never seen anything like it, and it was fantastic.

They stayed throughout the night and left in the morning, just before first light. We had fun. We sang; we laughed. They brought out something not exactly like fruit and not exactly like candy. It was sweet, but it was sort of creamy. They would put their fingers in just a little bit and eat just a tiny bit, but they urged us to have all we wanted. It was wonderful! That is the first time I saw people from other places. The taller person on the ship talked to the elders, but I don't know what they said.

Do you know where they were from?

I was told that they were from a red planet far away. I think that nowadays, as I look back, they were from Zeta Reticuli. They were so much fun. They loved the children, and we loved them. It was always fantastic to see them.

I think by the time I got to be in my mid-twenties, they stopped coming as often. When I was younger, they would come at least once, sometimes twice a year and play with the children. When I got in my mid-twenties, they started coming about once every other year. They said there were things they had to do, but they would come back and check on us and make sure we were all right.

When you got old enough to listen to them talk to the elders, did they teach you things? What did they tell you?

They would talk about the future of this world. They would talk about the people coming who are you now. They would show us. They had a means to show a picture that floated in space, and they would show us the machines of your time and what they did. They showed us cars—that's when I saw cars for the first time—and trains. They showed us big ships with many people. They didn't show us unpleasant things. They said it would make them uncomfortable and us too. They just said that the people of this time—the time that you are in—would not have as much heart as we had, that they would have it but wouldn't know how to show it for themselves and others. For a time the human race would lose its way—that's how they put it.

So we listened and felt sad for the people of your time. Other times they would show us pictures of their planet and what they did and how they had visitors. Of course, we all wanted to go and visit, but they said it would take so long to get there and so long to get back. We asked them how long it took them. They said they didn't go home that often. They had a bigger ship out between our planet and their planet. They would go to that ship, and then they would go other places. They went many places in this area, but they didn't go home very often. That's one reason they liked to visit places like where we were. They visited other places too, other planets, and visited other peoples. They said it made them feel like home to see their old friends regularly.

Wonderful! So they visited other places on this planet too, other tribes?

They visited some people. They visited Maori people. They would sometimes visit the Australian native peoples. They would visit the peoples of the north country where there is the snow and ice.

Eskimos?

Yes. They would visit many different places. They said in the past, in years gone by, that they liked to visit people on the islands. They said that these people were particularly cheerful and that they had one time brought a tree that bore fruit and the people liked it very much. That was a long time ago. They said they thought that the tree had been here, but it hadn't survived well. So they brought a specimen they thought would live better.

They called it a tree or a bush (I am not sure which), but it was the pineapple. The people said, "Oh, this is wonderful."

Sometimes we would give them things, and they would take them back. If it worked for their people, then they would grow those things there too. They didn't need as much food as we needed, but they would always join us and eat just a little bit—I think partly because they were so very polite and partly for the pleasure of it. They liked the flavors of things. They particularly liked things that had very significant flavors. They would love the flavor but wouldn't need to eat so much to support them as we do.

Just for the sensation of it?

They loved unusual taste; they loved that. As far as I know, they still do.

The Building They Showed Us from 2150

They showed you pictures of our time of things that made you sad. Did they go beyond our time and imply that it would get better after the time of darkness?

They showed time in the future past this. They showed us once a place that was like either a small city or a university. The design reminded me of a picture I was shown by a spirit brother of Pueblo peoples [draws Fig. 39-2]. This is about 150 years from your time, in the future. It looked to me like a Pueblo building. These things here are like ledges where people walk along, and then they go in the building here. These things go all the way around. The building is square, but people walk all the way around. The people come out onto the ledges, and then they walk along them and go in and out the doors. So instead of there being what you have now—hallways in a building and doors—these are on the outside.

This way the people are encouraged to go out-of-doors, because in those times the people have so many things to do, so many fabulous games and employments to do. The elders there of the time—I think you would call them the government, but I would call them the elders, the wise ones— found ways to encourage people to go outside and breathe the fresh air and

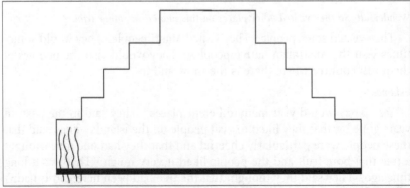

Fig. 39-2. A building from 2150 with ledges and energy moving up into the walls.

experience the Sun or the stars. Sometimes people would go out on the ledges at night and cook food, sing songs, look at the stars, tell stories and entertain each other. It is a place they gather at night out on the ledges, see? That is why it reminds me of the Pueblo peoples—sometimes they would do that too, I have been told by my spirit brother.

Are these great big skyscrapers or six-foot stories?

No, not so tall. Not much taller than big Pueblo buildings—maybe five, six stories. And in those times people don't have cars anymore. They have some kind of vehicle that flies around, but there are not so many of them. Each one of these buildings has everything that people need. If they need to go to the healer, there are healers there. If they need entertainment for their family, it's there—food, everything.

Going outdoors becomes more of a pleasure and a ceremony, rather than you have to go, so there doesn't need to be so many vehicles. The vehicles don't burn fuel. They have some kind of a clear thing that doesn't exactly look like a crystal but like a slightly foggy glass, and there is some kind of a small wafer inside that's dark. I think it's driven somehow by the Sun. The vehicle is clear. You can see in, and people can see out.

There is a lot of fun. The vehicles will land on the ledges, which are used for social things. The ledges are wide and accommodate people. It is a very social place, the ledges; that's where people meet each other and greet each other. They don't have as much socialization inside the building. They do more socializing on the ledges, and they feel safe there too.

Sometimes there are waters that come through there—now you call it floods. But it's not a problem because you can see that there is distance here. The first level is high, and with that distance there is room for the waters to go right through the villages where there are these buildings. Then the waters can flow through, and everybody watches them from the ledges and enjoys their beauty. Eventually, the waters settle down, and it is all right. In this way, if the Earth needs to flood, it floods, and everybody is fine. The buildings are okay, and the floodwaters will go right through town. It is not a problem; the waters go where they need to go.

The buildings aren't hurt by the waters because they grow into the ground. The building techniques in those days, I have been shown . . . the building is like a plant, like corn. It has roots, it grows into the minerals of the Earth, and then the minerals of the Earth feel that the building is natural, like a rock or a boulder. So the floodwaters don't shove it aside as an unnatural thing. Floodwaters are intended to move the unnatural, to clear the unnatural away from the natural bed of the stream, you see. When something is natural, the waters go around it. So the waters go around the buildings because the waters feel, "This is natural; Earth embraces it." It looks like a rock that grows out of the Earth for the foundation.

This is a technique that has been first mastered by farmers, then the farmers teach the engineers. It is a sacred way of communicating with the land, so when the foundation is laid, you don't dig anything. You just lay the blocks on the land, and then you go around and sing to them and hold your hands over the blocks. The minerals in the soil reach up and grab the rocks.

I will give you an example [draws Fig. 39-3]. This would be like a block. They are not exactly flat, not unlike an adobe block today. After the sacred engineers sing to the blocks and hold their hands over them, then the ground it is sitting on reaches up and grows into the block itself, like roots. It grows in and embraces it, and the land and the foundation stone become one. Then anything you build on that, the roots grow up a little farther, but not all the way into the building. See, it might go up that far [draws squiggly lines on Fig. 39-3].

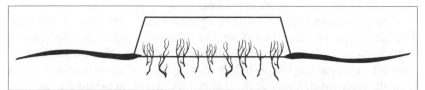

Fig. 39-3. Building blocks are placed on the Earth, then mineral energy grows up into the buildings.

This is totally new!

The building is interesting to you, eh? It speaks well for the future. When the building is like the Earth and the Earth is like the building, then it welcomes the building. There is no digging into the Earth, which disturbs it. When you disturb it, it can't wait to get rid of the building. It might invite floodwaters or storms and whatever it can to get rid of this thing. That is like a wound, but this is like a marriage. It becomes a sacred marriage. The building becomes sacred because it is embraced by the Earth, and the building and the Earth become married. It is a sacred marriage, because the building is welcomed by the Earth and is supported by its energies. Therefore, the building becomes essentially permanent. A building like that will stand there eight, nine, maybe ten thousand years easily and look good. It doesn't require much maintenance, because it will get energy flowing up from the Earth.

Visitors from the Pleiades

I didn't realize that ET visitation was a common or regular occurrence. Who are some of the other beings who would come to see you in ships?

I have heard from spirit brothers in South America that they came there very often to the high places. Once in a while the beings from the Pleiades would come. Then the children would have even more fun because the Pleiadian beings love children. They just love them so much, it is a wonder to see. They wanted the children to have fun, so they would take all of them up in the ships for rides. The grandfathers and the grandmothers, just about everybody, would go up at one time or another. They would never come for less than two or three days, and they would take people on rides to see the planet at a distance. It was wondrous, wondrous. They would not come very often, but when they did—oh, we would be telling stories for years afterward!

How old were you when you first saw the Pleiadians?

I first saw them when I was sixteen. I had been hearing the stories for many years, so by the time I saw them, I was so excited. They stayed for about two and a half days. We had a wonderful time. They eat like we do, though not exactly the same foods, so they would share their food and we would share our food. Oh, we loved to visit with them. They didn't come too often, about every fifteen or twenty years—just for fun, just to visit.

So they weren't here on any mission or for any purpose?

No, just for pleasure, for our pleasure and theirs. They are very special. I have a warm spot in my heart for them as I speak now about them. I am very fond of them even to this day. I have seen them now that I am in spirit form. Speaking to you as I am today, from spirit form now (though I speak to you also very often from the past), at this moment I can observe them. I see that they are a little troubled today—I think because their society is changing and they are uncertain how it will change. The teachers reassure them a lot. They need reassurance.

How is it changing?

They have been told that you will come there someday and that when you go, things will not be the same as they were. This can make you uncomfortable sometimes; other times you are excited, but sometimes it makes you uncomfortable.

So human beings will not go for another fifty or seventy-five years, but they are being prepared now?

Oh, certainly. Well, they live a long time; they live longer than people here. It will be in their lifetimes, most of them, so they will have lots of preparation before you actually get there. When you get there, they will have special people all picked out to meet you and pretty well trained so that you won't meet the whole population right away. They'll be cautious, which I understand [laughs].

Wild humans coming! [Laughs.]

Yes, they will be cautious, and perhaps that's just as well for the first few meetings.

When Grandfather Crossed Over

This idea of calling your star lives . . . is there another incident you could share with us, because this is totally new? The stories are so beautiful.

One time I remember my grandmother saying that she was a little sad because my grandfather was preparing to cross over (I like that term "cross over"; that is nice). Grandfather was lying down, and it was his time; he would pass over in a few days.

Where were you?

I was grown up. I was there with my wife, and we were consoling grand-mother and taking care of their needs so she could spend her time with grandfather. Grandmother would sometimes say . . . not unlike husbands and wives do, she would sometimes whisper to him, "I wish I could go with you." And then he would say, "No, no, you stay with the family, but I will come and get you when it is your time." They made this promise so she wouldn't feel so sad.

When it was his time, a star life came. It was a beautiful occasion. This star life said to grandfather, "I am your future life, and I want your wife to see me so she will know that this is how things will be in the future." The star life said, "You will be together and look like this." The being was gold. It was very thin and tall for people of our days. Nowadays you would say almost six feet tall, which is tall for us. The being didn't exactly look human but was almost like that. It had a body, arms, legs, but didn't actu-ally walk, sort of floated.

But you saw him?

I saw him, yes. We all saw him. He said to grandmother, "I wanted you to see this because someday you and this one (pointing to grandfather) will be like this together, and soon."

And so grandfather's spirit got up (we saw it) out of his body and took the hand of this beautiful gold being. They both waved, then grandfa-ther's spirit leaned over and kissed grandmother on her left cheek and the gold lightbeing leaned over and kissed her on her right cheek. She just had this good feeling (it was like tingles, you say), and then they went away into the sky. Grandmother cried, but they were tears of joy because she was shown that they would be together and she knew that grandfather would keep his word and come to get her. I was away when grandmother died, but I heard that they saw something like that. Grandfather came in a gold lightbody, and she knew him in that body. She stepped out and took his hand, and they waved to the family and went away.

What you said has so much heart energy!

It is good to know these things, because even though these are good stories, they are not rare experiences. I am able to know because of what I have been taught and because I am still on Earth and seeing things. I know you have many sad things in your time, but the beautiful beings still bring in the souls of the babies being born and they still escort the souls of those passing over. Some things don't change.

So you can all count on a beautiful experience when you pass over. You will let your Earth body go and thank it, and you will feel a little moment of sadness, but then almost immediately you will be so happy and you will feel wonderful and all will be well. You will know that all is well, and then you will be gone, wherever you go. I see this every day, spirits coming and going—animals too. Animals are happier because they know these things in their life, but we humans have to struggle sometimes, eh? When I was in my body (I talk to you from my body usually, but tonight I am speaking from spirit), I struggled plenty of times too. I know what it is like.

Well, we are only now becoming aware of what a glorious privilege it is, what a glorious purpose we have and how important what we do on this planet is!

It is very important, yes. It is worth all of the effort. Sometimes it seems like it isn't, but I can assure you, it is very much worth it.

One last thing: Many of you are now confused, your life is confusing. Some things that used to make you laugh now make you sad. Some things that used to make you sad now seem silly and you laugh. You are changing all the time now. Know that these changes are not so terrible, but they will be confusing. Sometimes you will feel as if you know yourself very well, that for the first time in your life you have a glimmer of your real self. Then the next moment it will be gone and you will say, "Oh no, that was so wonderful and now it's gone."

Know that these are little tastes of who you are, and it will come and go now. That's why sometimes you will change friends quickly or move about, or your family life will change. Right now you are in what I have heard called a "sifting time," meaning that the sieve you use to sift things and separate things is going on. It is not to separate but to put like with like. You are born to your family, and that is good, but sometimes you find that your friends are an even truer family. So for now, know that there will be changes, sometimes unexpected. But you will find friends sometimes in the most unlikely places and at the most unlikely times. These friends will feel so much like home to you, you will wonder how you could have ever gotten along without them.

Let me just say that this is all part of reuniting with your spirit families. Sometimes you will stay connected with these people; other times they will just flow into life for a moment and out again. It will be good. Know that this all has to do with rediscovering who you really are, and that's why there is so much confusion now.

Sometimes you might feel, "Oh, I need to do this work," and then say, "Oh well, that's gone, and now I think my regular job is good." At other times you might say, "Oh, I can't stay at this job anymore; I now know my work," and you go off and do it.

It will be sometimes unexpected and confusing, but ultimately, within not too many years, many things will make more sense. Many things will work a lot better than they are working now, and people will be able to see and feel and experience your common threads much more clearly.

Celebrate Dependence Day!

Speaks of Many Truths
April 24, 1998

I n your time great value is placed upon independence, being able to support yourself and have all that it takes so that life is safe and secure. Whole nations have been built on the concept of independence, and of course, in your country now, Independence Day is celebrated as a special event. People feel good about independence.

What I would like to talk about is something a little different than that, which I think it's easy to forget in your time. In my time we also like to have what we need, but we don't consider it independence to have it. We consider it dependence.

You Depend on the Earth and Each Other

In my time we depend on the Earth to support our feet. We depend on the rain to give us the water and feed the plants and the animals that also support us. We depend on each other because everyone does something a little different and together it creates our tribe, our people, our family, our neighbors: those who help each other and help all of us.

I don't think it is really so much different in your time. But the problems you have—neighbor to neighbor, person to person in your families, country to country, neighborhood to neighborhood and all other versions of that—are because people don't acknowledge the dependence you have on each other. If it were not for everyone doing their part, you would not be able to have and cherish what you call independence.

I am not judging you or making fun of you; I am just reminding you that if your neighbor is sometimes a little annoying, think about what she does. Maybe she is a little annoying sometimes, but normally she is pretty good. She has raised her children well, and the children are not annoying. If they were annoying, you would know, but they are not. They are children: They play, they sing, they laugh, they tease each other sometimes, but basically they are pretty good kids, which means that your neighbor is probably all right.

Maybe your neighbor does something in her work that you really don't think about: "Oh, I think she drives a truck," or "I think she is working at a farm somewhere," or "I think she's working at a factory." "I really don't know," you say, because maybe you don't really know your neighbor too well. But the people who drive trucks or work on farms or factories—all these people do things that serve the needs of others, just like the things you do serve the needs of others.

Dependence Is Benevolent

I want you to take some time and think about that. The next time you are craving some independence, just remember how valuable, how nurturing and supportive, and how ultimately benevolent it is to be dependent. You are born dependent. We are all born dependent. This tells you something. If humans beings were intended to be only independent, then you would be born in such a way that you would not require your mother or your father. You would hatch out, perhaps from an egg, and after you dried off, you would walk or fly away and begin your life.

Be aware that I know independence is cherished sometimes, and I understand it. Yet in my time I walk around from place to place. If people don't support what I do, even though my work supports what they do, I won't be able to go very far.

So just remember, it is all right to celebrate Independence Day, but maybe it wouldn't be a bad thing to have a Dependence Day and make it a neighborhood party. Find out what your neighbors do, even if it isn't something that interests you very much. After you go home or they go home (if it's at your house), think about it. Consider how what they do serves you or people in your family in some way. Really, you are much more dependent on each other than you realize.

People Are More Dependent in Your Time

I am trying to decide if that dependence is more now than in your time. You were a small tribe and had to look after each other, right?

I think people are more dependent on each other now than in my time. In your time the dependence factor is a moment-to-moment thing. We, after all, didn't have cars that we drove on roads. You have to trust, to depend on the other drivers to be good drivers. If they are not good drivers, it might harm you, your family, your neighbors or your friends. You have to depend on your neighbors to be honorable, at least most of the time. You have to depend on them to be polite, at least most of the time.

Perhaps, most importantly, you have to depend on your neighbors to look out for each other, which many neighbors do. You don't do it all the time, but sometimes you look out for each other. I would say that with as many people as you have living in your time, dependence is much, much more in your day-to-day life than in our time.

It really is. We have to depend that the food we buy is clean, that the airplanes are safe, that the cars are mechanically sound, that the schoolteachers are caring—on every level, that's right.

Yes. I think that this desire to be independent is really closer to a desire to be without cares, without worries. A lot of the things you might worry about, as we've discussed before, are things you really can't do any good worrying about. Nevertheless, dependence is good, I believe.

Make Your Dependence More Personal

The only thing is that in your time the dependence was so close and familiar, you knew the people intimately. Now it is so broad and impersonal.

Yes, you are right. How then can you make it more personal in your time? I believe the best way is to enjoy the simple things that people do all the time. That's true wherever you live. Have a potluck supper; even if you live in a big apartment building, have a potluck supper for everybody on your floor. If you live in the country, have a potluck supper at the grange or wherever you meet. Have something simple, where people are not required to be of this religion or of that employment but are just invited to come and bring something everybody can eat. Sit down and enjoy each other's company. Bring the children, bring the old people and get to know each other. You will like some of the people. You won't like all of them, but you might make some friends. You might get a little more personal. You might discover that you have made a new friend and start doing things together.

Since life is more complex in your time, the most important thing is, you have to make it happen. In my time, if there's an event to celebrate, we all know about it quickly. You're right, it's a small group. In your time, if you want to have a party or a potluck, you have to go around, invite the neighbors or slip little notes in their boxes: "Potluck Supper at Arthur's," or "Potluck Lunch at Betty's." You understand? "Everybody's invited, come and bring your family. Let's get to know each other." That's all. You have to make the effort.

Then neighborliness becomes something you want to do because you know the people, you know what you have in common, you know what you don't have in common. They become people with names and with children, pets, grandmothers or grandfathers. They become, most importantly, people with faces and names. You will want to look out for each other then.

That's a beautiful thought.

I just wanted to put that out, because in your time people need to make an effort to be dependent. You are dependent, as you say, but often unconsciously. You don't think about it. When you make the effort to be dependent, then you can appreciate the value of dependence and not get so caught up in the great value of independence.

It's dependence, but it's really the connection. Making an effort to connect with other humans is something we just don't do very much anymore.

No, but it can be done.

The Wisdom of Trees

Speaks of Many Truths
May 22, 1998

All right, this is Speaks of Many Truths. Tonight I'd like to talk for a little while about trees.

Trees Are the Philosophers of the Plant World

When people go out to the countryside, to public parks or to someplace where there are a lot of trees, they naturally feel better. Trees are the philosophers of the plant world. It is in their nature, once they are at least fifty or sixty years old, to begin discussing amongst each other. And trees have a good network, regardless of species. Trees have different ways of being and acting, different behaviors, even different ways of being for other species. That is why when people are near a very large old tree, most have a sense of peace and serenity, because this tree will have had many discussions with other trees and many observations of different forms of life. That is why in my time and before—and also in your time by some peoples—trees are referred to by the honorary title of "Grandmother" or "Grandfather." This respectful term denotes an acknowledgment of the tree's wisdom.

In my time if there were problems that could not be solved, such as an unexpected disease or injury or a child born who was different and no one could remember anything like that before, and if the mystical person or the grandmothers or grandfathers had no answer, then the sensitive or mystical person would be asked to find the answer on the land. Sometimes, if he had an affinity to speak with stone, he would speak with the stone people. But very often he would find an old tree and ask the tree, giving a picture in his mind's eye or drawing one on the ground in the dirt or just speaking and describing the situation. He would wait for the answer to come through in the feeling sense, not unlike we're doing now.

The Wisest Trees Have Been Welcomed by the Earth

I'd also like to say this about trees: The trees that have the greatest wisdom are the trees that have been grown out of their natural seeds in places where the land actually welcomed them. I'm bringing this up now because in your time you have much in the way of chaos. The unpredictable has formed a thorn in the sides of many peoples; therefore, the idea of controlling beauty and generating it with landscaping and so on is considered a valuable asset.

However, what often happens in such moments is that trees that are naturally growing in a spot where they've been welcomed by the Earth, nurtured by water and deposited by wind—what people of the outdoors sometimes call "volunteers"—are not often respected. The true outdoors person will respect such volunteers; there's a genuine respect and honor for such plants. It is plants such as these, which grow where they are invited and welcomed, that tend to become the wisest ones in their old age.

Think about it. A man or woman who becomes wise in his or her old age will often demonstrate and acquire that wisdom, because what that person is wise with has to do with experiences or times in which he or she was welcomed somewhere. This is not always the case, but many times it is. It may have been a welcoming to a place where it was hard to live and difficult to survive, but having succeeded in doing so, the person is wise and has much to offer the younger ones coming up.

Seek Wisdom from Your Elders

I'm doing this comparison tonight because your society is also suffering from a terrible malnutrition. That malnutrition is not only the people who do not have enough to eat; it is also the people of your time who do not know how to solve the unsolvable and who do not know where to look for the answers they need. Many times the answers are nearby, with the grandmothers and grandfathers who have much to offer. Sometimes you put these people in a building or a place that is intended to care for them. But while they may get what they need in terms of medical care and even food and shelter, what older people need more than anything else is to give back to life some of what life has given to them. They will flower when they are allowed to advise those who need their advice.

There is a well of information and help awaiting any youngster or young parent or middle-aged person. This well is in the form of the grandmothers and grandfathers and other older people who are waiting to give you knowledge and wisdom. Please seek them out in your community. Find out what they know about. And tell others if they have a problem in that area of their life: "Oh, go see Grandmother Nelson," or "Go see Grandfather Washington. He knows much about this and can help you." Find out what people know, and go to them. You will gain and they will gain, and it will become a custom after a while, something appreciated by all. Then when you get to be the age of grandmother or grandfather and have the need to do something, by that time people will be accustomed to seeking out you and other older people. It will give you something pleasurable to look forward to in your old age besides those all-too-infrequent visits with your grandchildren.

That's beautiful!

Asking Trees for Guidance

You talked before about walking up to a tree and offering something and asking for a picture. What you're saying here is that if people will do that, they can get guidance?

Some sensitive people can. I mention it this way because people do not always ask trees, since reasonably one would look at a tree and say, "Well, it may have a great deal of knowledge about trees and other things, but I'm not sure whether it can help me with my problems." And maybe it can't. It has to be old. I will give you a gauge to know.

With the exception of some trees such as Monterey pines, which can get to be old and still not be so big, the average tree will be old enough to give advice once it is one and a half to two feet thick at the trunk. If it is bigger, say a big old tree—ancient, as we say—it may have much to offer. But like other beings, sometimes trees are busy, in the middle perhaps of an important conversation, perhaps in a meditation, perhaps just enjoying the sun on its leaves or needles, or perhaps drinking in some water. If the tree does not give you a message right away, say, "Excuse me, Grandfather," or "Excuse me, Grandmother," whichever you feel is best, and step away and come back another day and ask. Or ask another tree. Trees, like people, sometimes are busy.

Will that tree have learned this information about people from direct interaction or from watching? Or if no people have ever been around, do the trees talk about people and their actions? Could it have learned this from another tree?

Trees, not unlike human beings, first acquire knowledge about their own species, then about other species of trees, then about other species of plants and then about other species of life. That is why I think of them as philosophers. When a human being has much knowledge about other kinds of human beings and other kinds of human activity, whether it be his or her own or not, one might say this is a philosopher. One might even grant these people a degree—a doctor of philosophy, as it was originally called. In the case of the tree, it is not much different.

As one has gleaned much knowledge and wisdom about one's own kind, one naturally begins to find out about others. If you are in a forest as a tree, animals will go by or fly by, depending on what kind they are. They might land on you or sleep in your shelter. If you have a part of you that you are no longer using—what you call a dead limb—maybe they will make a little nest there and you might enjoy their scurrying and scampering around on your body. It's kind of a pleasure sometimes.

So you will ask other trees first, "What do you know about these beings?" Trees, not unlike many life forms in what I call the natural world, are polite. They will ask other trees first before they ask the animal, because they won't assume that the animal knows how to communicate with them. If other trees say, "You can talk directly to them," then they will. But first they will be taking advice.

So they may be able to give you advice, even though they've never seen humans before, if they've heard it from other trees.

They may. If they have heard it from other trees and feel good about the being they've heard things from, not unlike human beings, then they may choose to advise you. If, on the other hand, they have heard things about human beings from other trees and are not sure that those other trees have enough wisdom, then it would simply be an opinion from another being, and they might not advise you. This does not mean they don't care for you. It means that they don't feel that they have anything to offer you that they are certain would be of assistance. As you know, person to person you might be certain that something is of assistance, but it may or may not be to others. Nevertheless, you want to be assured before you offer it.

How is the life force of trees structured? Is there a group soul for a species? They're not individually ensouled, are they?

Yes, they are.

Every little tree?

Every little tree, every big tree, has its own personality. When a tree is at the end of its cycle and no longer exists (either from a natural ending or an unexpected ending), its soul or personality will depart—first looking like its aged self, then looking more like its younger sprig self and then looking more like a spot of light moving on to its afterlife.

As trees, are they aware of their previous existences?

Trees are more beings of the moment. It is not common for a tree to examine its previous existence. The only time this will be done is if there is a need by that tree or by other trees that are consulting that tree. Then this would be done only if some particular wisdom was needed and was not available from live trees on the planet at that moment. Then there might be an attempt to examine previous incarnations or even to consult with advisers to trees.

That was my next question. Do they have teachers and guides as we do?

They don't have guides the way you do because they are not here to learn anything. They are here to teach by example, as the animals and the elements and other things are. School is in session for human beings, not other forms of life here. So they don't need guides, but they do have teachers or spirits who are available to them should they need them.

Trees and Life Forms on Other Planets

So where can we trace trees back to? Are there trees on most or some of the other planets in this creation?

As far as I know, there are trees on some of the other planets, especially Sirius, the place I have looked at with my long vision. Sirius, with its many water planets, is the place that has the most abundant variety of plant and animal life that I've ever seen. I really want to visit there someday! It's just wonderful—beautiful waters and huge trees, whose trunks measure in your measurements thirty, forty, fifty feet across, having lived for . . . it must be thousands of years. They must be very wise indeed.

And there are animals, some looking like the ones we have here and some looking very different, unlike what we have here. I have seen creatures who here would be land creatures, but there they are water creatures. And the opposite—I have seen creatures who look like they ought to be in a lake or sea, but they come out of the water and walk on the land as well. And I have seen flying beings who can also go underwater and swim—all manner of creatures. I think maybe it is that the animals picked to be on Earth might have existed there first and were adapted to Earth, because Earth has more land than many of those water planets in Sirius.

Ah, so we needed more land animals than water animals.

Perhaps.

You mean there are planets with life forms on them where there are no trees? This sounds horrible!

It sounds horrible because you are used to trees, and you love them. But there are many planets where there is nothing green at all. You would look at it and say, "How can people live like this?" You would look at the starkness of the surface of the planet and then wonder, "Say, where are the people?" When you had that question, someone would come up from below and say, "Why are you up here? We live down below." Then you would go down below and traverse in a cave, as I have done with my long experience (which is a little different than long vision), and then come into a beautiful place, looking very much like those places in Sirius, with underground lakes and seas with fish and animals. I do not know how they are illuminated, for there is no sun when I look up, but a glow seems to come from the water itself, and this illuminates the place, with birds and monkeys and all manner of creatures.

Trees?

Yes.

So they have trees inside particular planets?

I have seen this, yes. I cannot say it is that way all over. But in what I have seen, I have seen this. So sometimes the most stark-looking planet on the surface may still have wonderful life under the surface.

I think Zoosh at one time said that in the future of this planet, a lot of people will choose to live like that, underground.

I think this may be so. When the oceans heal themselves . . . I have heard, and perhaps you have too, that sometimes there are creatures in the sea that glow. I wonder if maybe it is some distant relative of this creature that causes that water to be illuminating on those other planets. Or maybe the creatures on this planet are *their* cousins!

I'm not clear on why beings would choose to live inside something rather than on the surface.

If the surface is not hospitable but the underground is, you also would choose to live underground. Though you may wish to come up and look at the stars or enjoy the surface, you might not live there if it were not attractive and supportive.

Could we ask someone to come in and talk a little bit about the illumination underground? Someone who knows about it?

I can ask now. [Pause.] They are showing me. If you look through one of your telescopic glasses—"microscope," you say—you can see little beings swimming around and little . . .

Like plankton or something?

Yes, there is a creature about that size—very small—that is in the water. When it feeds, when it is consuming food, it gives off light. And since there are many, many of them, there are always some of them feeding, and that's where the light comes from.

What about the areas underground that are not immediately adjacent to an ocean or sea? Where does the light come from then?

It is all adjacent to an ocean or a sea. There is more water than land, so there are more water creatures than land creatures, or the creatures there adapt to the water. For instance, looking with my long vision at a place now, I see monkeys. I have seen these with long vision on this planet too, but I see them in the trees, and they jump in the water and swim. I don't think monkeys swim so much here on Earth, but they can swim there and they like it.

I think that perhaps in more benevolent settings—not places where you have to struggle so much to survive—being around water is more common. For beings who have to breathe and eat, water is more common. Beings who do not need to breathe like us or eat or drink like us could live on the surface of a planet in an underground place like the one I'm looking at with water and animals. If you didn't need to eat or drink, you could live on what would seem to be an inhospitable surface because you could survive almost anywhere. So maybe these different types of places are meant for different types of beings, and that's why when human beings look at a place and say, "We could never live there," it would be as if somebody else said, "You don't have to; there is a better place for you to live. That place is meant for other types of beings who can live there and enjoy it just fine."

The planet you are looking at in long vision now, is it Sirius?

No, it is not in Sirius. It is something that begins with an A.

Andromeda?

No.

Aldebaran?

No.

Arcturus?

No. I can't make it out, but it begins with an A.

And it's around here somewhere?

Well, with long vision one cannot be certain. I think it is a ways off.

Well, we'll have lots of interesting places to look at when we start exploring.

So many that after a while you will just settle down and say, "This is enough. We'll stay here for a while."

That's great! This is beautiful, unexpected.

Trees Communicate with Feelings

What else about trees? Is there anything amongst the different species—do they specialize? Does a redwood tree know something different than a pine?

I think they do have species wisdom, but they are united all over the Earth. A Monterey pine will speak to an apple tree and have philosophical discussions, and the same communication will go on no matter what the distance between that apple tree and spruce tree, for example. There seems to be no limit to their capacity to communicate at a distance with other trees. I believe there is some limit to their capacity to speak with other beings. They might, for example, speak to a chipmunk on their own boughs but not speak with a chipmunk on the other side of the world the way they might speak to another tree—say, an olive tree—on the other side of the world.

Do they have something like your long vision, where they can see who they are communicating with?

I don't think they use sight as we know it. I think they use feelings. They can feel something so profoundly, it would be like this: We know that water does not see as we do, but water knows things by feeling the outside of those things as they are immersed in the water. Feelings are a lot like water. What they flow around, they feel, not only in the case of water from the outside in, but if that thing they are feeling also has feelings, they can feel it from the inside out as well. So a tree can know what something looks like as long as that something has some form it can feel from the outside in, and if it has feelings, also from the inside out.

So it's almost like the trees exist in this great body of air, which is similar to the water. Is that an analogy?

To them they would say they exist in the sea of feelings, though they have a different word for it. It would be their language. But in English it is like the sea of feelings or the ocean of feelings or even . . . it might be called the tide of feelings. It is like that. It has a relationship with the water.

And when you walk the planet as a human, do you have that ability as a shaman to feel those feelings in that sea or that tide?

Yes, because I have had many communions with trees, and as one gets to be friendly with a tree (not unlike when you are friendly with another human being), the longer you know each other, the more confidences you share. After a while the tree says, "This is how it is for me," and tells me. And then I say, "This is how it is for me," and I tell the tree. If the tree is interested, it passes it on to other trees. If it has heard it before, it says, "I have heard this before, and this is the way with you and your kind," or something polite like that.

So we can look forward in the near future, as we regain our own sense of feeling, to living in this sea of feeling?

In my experience, most beings in the natural world—and you might say, "in the benevolent world," such as other humans living on other planets where there is no struggle like what we have to live through here—all live in the sea of feelings. They do that now. And as long as the feelings are benevolent, they thrive. But if someone comes into their midst who is suffering, they all suffer, so they want to do what they can to help that person, not only from compassion and kindness, but because that person's suffering also affects them. It is the same here. It just is that in your time you have so many distractions and have grown so accustomed to your discomforts that sometimes you think those discomforts are your own, when they are really somebody else's.

And we all have our little bit of armor to survive, right?

You think you do, but you feel just the same. You think it is important to be strong and to tough it out, as you say. And there are times when that is important. But there are more times when it is important to note that there is nothing wrong with your legs, so how come they are hurting? Look around, see. Maybe there is somebody near you who has legs that are hurting. Go over and see if you can help. It will help them and you.

And that's how we will get this planet back to this state where everything is healed and healthy, and everyone is taken care of?

Yes, because you understand that indeed you are all one.

That's beautiful.

Cats as Our Teachers

Speaks of Many Truths
May 28, 1998

his is Speaks of Many Truths. I will speak a little bit about learning
from your cat or perhaps a cat friend you might visit or who might visit
you. Not all cats are prepared to teach at all times, but many of them will
or might. Some cats are inclined to be spiritual teachers for human beings,
and some have other things to do, not unlike people.

If you are living with a cat, you will probably have some idea whether
that cat is what might be called a spiritual cat or just a fun housemate or
companion. How do you know? If a cat exhibits unusual behavior,
sometimes called "cattitudes" (I like that one), it will sometimes look
suddenly around the room at things you do not see. Sometimes the cat is
hearing things you do not hear, or smelling things you do not smell, but
at least 20 percent of the time, the cat is seeing things you do not see.
The cat has an ability beyond instinct.

Experience What Your Cat Is Feeling Physically

If you can get to know your cat, if you are trusted by your cat, it is
helpful. Don't pick up your cat to do this. If your cat is in your lap,
fine, but more likely your cat will be looking at things somewhere
else. Before your cat does this, practice with it. How? I will tell you.
Say your cat is lying on the rug or sitting on the bed or sitting someplace where it is often happy to be. For those who are in spiritual practice, this will be easy. For those who are new to it all, you will have to
use your imagination. But for those in spiritual practice, do not go out

of your body but extend your sensing system within your body into your cat.

First you must make sure that you are calm, relaxed, not unhappy. So put yourself into a cheerful place whether you are a spiritual person or a person who has not been trained much in these things. Laugh about some things or relax. Then extend, or imagine yourself being in the body of your cat. Don't do this unless the cat lives with you. Otherwise, it can create discomfort for both you and the cat, and that would not be honorable.

If your cat wishes to have you present within its auric field or its energy inside and around and about its body, your cat will either look at you or continue what it is doing. I want you to practice with this before your cat does something unusual. Begin on a relaxed day. Try to make sure the phone will not distract you—turn the ringer off or something. If the cat suddenly gets up and walks away when you start doing this, then it is not acceptable to do this at this time. If you try two more times with the cat for a total of three times and every time it gets up and walks away, don't do it again with this cat. The cat might be sensitive to you; perhaps the cat is not comfortable with your energy at this time. Try a different cat.

But say the cat does accept your energy. Then try to remember what the cat is feeling—not emotionally (remember, the cat is thinking or seeing), but what the cat is feeling physically. What is under the cat's feet? Imagine your hands as the cat's feet with claws extending from the toes. Or imagine that the cat's tail is your own. It might be moving. If the cat knows what you are doing, it might do some things to support what you are doing. In other words, see if you can feel what the cat is feeling physically, as if the cat's body were your own.

If you have done this enough times, when the cat starts doing something interesting or provocative, seemingly looking at things, perhaps seeing something you do not see, perhaps hearing something you do not hear, even perhaps smelling something you do not know, you can extend into the cat if the cat is comfortable, and you may have done this a few times. If it allows you, you may (it is not a guarantee) be able to see, smell or hear what the cat is noticing. In this way, the cat will be sharing with you its abilities, but most importantly, the cat will be exposing you to abilities that you have.

This Is What the Sphinx Is All About

So in this sense, the cat is like the teacher. The cat shows you how to do it, and you continue as you feel connected to the cat teacher. To do these things, eventually you notice you can do these things without the assistance of the cat teacher.

And this is what they were trying to say when they built the Sphinx?

Yes. This is what the Sphinx is all about. And the Great Pyramid was really to just draw your attention to the Sphinx. [Chuckles.] It was look, see and say, "Look at this!" Because the pyramid is a shape, you can call it a word. It is a pyramid, an unusual one. What is it? You scratch your head and say, "I don't know." But when you look at this lion, you say, "Oh, we know what this is. We have little ones in our house." It makes the Sphinx much more easily understood by having something that is not easily understood near it.

Anything else you'd like to say?

That's all. I just wanted to comment on that exact thing, giving homework to budding shamanic and mystical readers out there. When you read the book that Zoosh and I cooperated in [*Shamanic Secrets for Material Mastery*], you'll have more of these activities, but it is a good beginning to do this with benevolent cat friends. (Don't worry, dog lovers, we will have things for you to do someday.)

The Wind Is a Messenger

Speaks of Many Truths
June 22, 1998

he wind is a messenger. It sometimes is the message, but usually it is a messenger. When the wind blows, particles of soil and dust are caught up in the wind, carried up, often quite far, and taken elsewhere. Is this just a happenstance? No. You must understand something: Anything that happens due to the natural resources or the natural life body of Mother Earth is not in any way accidental.

Nowadays, even in your time, there are still creatures who crawl about the Earth—ants, beetles, snakes and many others. There are also other creatures—squirrels, rabbits, mice, deer, elk, bear—and all of these creatures can be found in this area [in Northern Arizona]. However, these creatures cannot all be found everywhere. They are not found in the sea nor, more to the point, are they found in cities. One does not often see deer or elk in the cities, though occasionally one might see one or two in a zoo or some such place.

Carrying Energies Where Needed

The energies of these and many more animals I don't name who step on the soil (including human beings) are needed in places where the animals cannot go. Therefore, Mother Earth, knowing that this energy is needed and that it is difficult for spirit animals to go everywhere all the time, will take soil and dust that has been touched by these beings, blow it up in the air and carry it for miles and miles, then deposit it in cities or places that require the energy of those animals in a more physical form.

The spirit animal might be able to go there sometime, but sometimes the energy of something the animal touched is more important. Also, we know that soil and dust were once part of the bodies of animals, to say nothing of human beings. These energies might also be needed in the cities.

Bear energy is particularly needed, and lion energy is also very much needed in the cities, because bears and lions have a great deal to do with strength, survival, wisdom, insight and clarity—qualities that are often needed by citizens in big cities. Then there are also qualities associated with other animals (I am just naming some of their qualities): ants are very much involved with service, among other things; rabbits, thought; squirrels, cheerfulness and sociability; deer, love and wisdom; elk, wisdom and insight; and so on. All these qualities are often needed in cities, and this is a most important way for them to reach these places.

Also, sometimes they are needed in rivers, under the water or within it, or in oceans or on islands. The wind has the capacity to move some of these particles all the way around the Earth, because higher up in the atmosphere those winds blow pretty strong, as any pilot can tell you.

So what about the dust and soil in the cities? That also has requirements. The dust and soil in the cities will absorb a lot of anxiety and sadness, excitement and stimulation, nervousness and strength, and a vitality of the city that is completely different than the vitality of the country. Sometimes there is too much of it in the city. So when the wind blows, it will catch these particles, take them up high and either cleanse them in the waters if they need cleansing or, if city vitality or strength is needed elsewhere, it will be taken someplace else where it is needed.

These functions of the wind are vital. Therefore, when you are in a windy day, sometimes more than you would like—a "blustery day," as you say sometimes—this is a function of what I am talking about. There will be times when there will be many windy days and just a few calm days during the week. This tells you how much these qualities are needed. I might add that animals sometimes feel compelled, even if they don't need to travel here or there, to go out and walk on the land. Maybe they have enough to drink and eat right where they are, but they will walk on the land, knowing that the wind will be by at some point to pick up that dust. They will leave their qualities there.

Bears are particularly loyal to this. Many times bears will go places they don't really need to go because they know that their energy, which they can contribute easily by touching the soil (which does not tire them), can be utilized by others who desperately need it. There are places in the world where bears are unknown. Perhaps those people have seen pictures. People might have seen pictures of bears and heard about them, but they have never seen a bear. To have this energy available is most important. I speak of this because it is something so very real and not often understood.

This is a completely different function that Earth does? We've been told that our emotions cause the weather, but this is different, right?

This is different. The wind would be here even if there were no people on Earth because the wind is part of Mother Earth's nature. She would move her energies about. Maybe on one part of her body there is desert, in another place forest, in another place water. Even if there were no animals, she would swirl about with her wind and bring different portions of her body to different places.

Different Qualities of Water Vapor Carried by the Wind

You know that the seas and other bodies of water contribute water vapor into the sky, and it accumulates and flows over the land, enriching the soil and providing the animals and the people and the stone (which likes water) with life-giving water. Water is more life-giving having come from various sources, even different parts of the ocean. For those living on the seacoast where there aren't too many rivers or on islands where they are surrounded by the sea, where the ocean is close, the water has one type of quality; for those far away from the shore, it has a different quality. When the water is close to a populated shore, it is closer to people and land beings—animals and so on.

This water must be compatible enough, must be social enough, to accept an interaction with the animals, the people and the land. From the water's point of view, as it gets closer to the shore, the land comes up to the surface of the water, and the water touches the land in a more intimate way. The water is used to sitting on the land, as it does on the bottom of the ocean or a riverbed. But when it laps up against the shore, it is a secondary form of touch, where the land has the imprint of all those living upon it. Because of that, the water must be social and able to accept that imprint gladly.

Water farther out does not have to be so social with land beings. It can be comfortable with sea creatures or water beings and has to accept contact with human beings only when humans take their water ships and, for the most part, travel over the top of the water, with the occasional ship underwater. If a person is underwater in an underwater ship, the water has to give way for such a vehicle. Because those people do not usually touch the water physically, this water does not have to be so social.

There are different types of water. The water farther out to sea has strength, it has welcoming for the sea creatures, it has the union of the sea bottom and the skies, and it has endurance. The water closer to the shore is more sociable. It welcomes sea creatures, but it welcomes land creatures as well, so this water provides a greater sense of compatibility. When vapor evaporates from these places and drifts onto shore to form rain, the qualities of the water are imparted onto the land in order to feed land creatures, be they animal, human or stone, creatures from a part of Mother Earth's body. It will impart these qualities if the water comes from that source.

Now, if you happen to be living someplace where water vapor comes mostly as a result of an inland sea, its qualities will be different. Here is a body of water entirely surrounded by land; therefore, it must all be sociable. You might say, "Well, the ocean is touched by the land too." But an inland sea is entirely surrounded by the land, so it must be entirely sociable, accepting of water creatures, and must also have the quality of what I would call "bridging," the capacity of union. In this way, the inland sea unites the land through the water. When water evaporates from such a place, drifts on shore and rains or snows, those qualities and perhaps others will be imparted in that rain or snow to feed the land beings who may or may not have enough on their own.

Extreme Weather Allows Mother Earth to Cleanse and Transform Energies

I wanted to mention this because it is very easy to think about the weather as something pleasant or annoying, but it is important to consider that what is called the weather is a living, functioning being. It is as if people are living upon someone, and these qualities of that person—in this case, Mother Earth—are just as important as the qualities we have as people.

We breathe, we eat, we need all kinds of things—food and shelter and so on. We have blood that moves around in our bodies. We have many things that can be correlated to Mother Earth's qualities. This is natural because our bodies are made of Mother Earth, and she more easily contributes her physical parts to make bodies that have some connection to herself. That is why it is easy to say, "Oh, our bodies are very much like Mother Earth."

What about extreme cases like hurricanes or tornadoes? Is there an element of moving energy within them, even this is part of other cycles, other causes?

Sometimes. This is an expression of human beings' needs, but sometimes, especially with torrential rains that might cause floods, this is often a circumstance in which Mother Earth needs to wash some part of herself. She does not want to harm animals or people, but she needs to wash, just as you do sometimes, and she will use her water or wind to do that.

Most often you'll notice that she uses her wind. But sometimes she must use her water, and she will do so. Tornadoes are often brought about by unexpressed feelings in people, but another contributing factor also has to do with Mother Earth's need to make sudden changes. I am not talking about the damage that occurs to homes and peoples' lives, but within the whirlwind of a tornado, what always occurs is similar to atomic reactions where your machines bring things together that would not ordinarily come together. With her wind and the vacuum, an airless quality within the tornado, Mother Earth will create changes in that moment, not only in atmospheres, but in polarity—plus and minus.

Someday you will be able to predict the exact path of a tornado by studying the positive and negative charges produced within the tornado.

You will be able to do this electronically. In this way, you will be able to chart with 90-percent probability exactly where the tornado will go. I am saying this now to give a suggestion to meteorologists, but Mother Earth uses this to transform energies that can be transformed no other way.

Sometimes there will be energies not associated with personalities (as in spirits) that will be attracted to certain zones of the Earth. Often these zones are places where there are fault lines or deep cuts in the land, such as a river. These energies will flow to low spots. They are not negative, as you say; they are not unpleasant energies. They are just energies that are lost. When that occurs, sometimes they need to receive a positive or a negative charge, electrically speaking, so that they can act, not only as a conduit, but as a charged particle to influence other lost energies, to help them find an expression in physical matter.

I am being guided to say that in low-lying areas where these energies collect, the energies can be charged a certain way when the tornado passes. You know, tornados cover more open ground than just where human beings are. Those of you who have had this opportunity have experienced a feeling. There are not many of you, but some who have had the opportunity to be within the atmosphere (not so close as to be dangerous), to walk on the land where a tornado has just passed, have noticed that the air has a certain charged quality. It doesn't have to do with lightning associated with tornados but with the effect of the tornado itself.

Each particle that becomes so charged will then be able to perform its capacity a hundredfold. It will immediately gather to itself a hundred times its own mass (as scientists say) of energies that are lost and charge those energies. Once the energies have a charge of positive or negative—and neutral is not a charge—they can find their way into physical reality once more, becoming a plant or a particle of something that eventually will become water, a person, anything that could then be recycled as physical matter.

Asking the Wind for Wisdom

I seem to remember something you said about the wind also carrying messages another way besides dust and particles. Can you talk about that?

Sometimes the wind will carry wisdom many places all over the Earth. Animals and people need wisdom. In the case of animals, it is most often served by some energy connection within their species. Occasionally, the species will not have the wisdom an animal needs, but the animal does not pray for the wisdom. The animal needs the wisdom and the need is present and acknowledged, but unfulfilled. That gap is felt by Mother Earth.

Mother Earth is not comfortable with such gaps of need that are unfulfilled, so she will utilize her wisdom, incorporate it into the wind. Or perhaps if there is the wisdom the animal needs on some other part of the Earth, the wind will blow and the wisdom will come to the animal by the wind or through the animal's instinct. The wind will serve like that. It is not dissimilar for human beings, though for the human being most people do not have the knowledge to connect with a being or a sense of the unconscious wisdom that is available. People all over the Earth are praying for wisdom and inspiration for this or that, and the wind will blow, sometimes mightily, to bring you that wisdom.

Know this: If ancient peoples needed some wisdom for themselves or for their family or for their people, and it had not come to them, they used to climb to the high ground. They would ask on the high ground that this wisdom be granted to them and that they would use it to benefit all, meaning that even if it was wisdom they personally needed for themselves, they would not be selfish with it. If they came across someone else who needed that wisdom, once it had been given to them, they would give it freely.

Then, after they made their request and their oath, they would wait. The wind will blow in high places in ways that you do not normally feel in lower places—that is the original sacred reason for climbing to high places. So they would stay there. Some ancient peoples would stay there for two or three days feeling the wind, sleeping exposed, or if there was danger, perhaps in a tree or another way to protect themselves. If the person was shamanic, a medicine person, he or she might bring somebody for protection so that he or she could be exposed to the wind all day and all night.

After a prescribed amount of time, the ancient peoples would return, after offering some gifts to the high spot or the mountain. They always offered gifts to the wind, possibly in the form of something precious to them. Desert people might offer a little water; others might offer a little grain or some kind of food they had gathered.

In the case of the people of today, you might go up to some high spot for the day. Don't be saying what you want on the way up. Save it for the top or for as high as you can go. It you don't have the energy to get to the top, go as far as you can, then say what you want and promise to use that wisdom for yourself and give it freely to others in the most benevolent way you know how. Then make some offering of something in its most natural state. Water is a good offering, or some kind of food or grain or something that is meaningful to you—not just something you've plucked off of a box on your shelf, but something meaningful to you that if consumed by animals will not harm them.

Thank the wind, thank the mountain, and return whence you came, letting it go, even if the wisdom is not with you. Now that the wind has been informed of your need, it will search till the end of time to find that wisdom for you. It will be relieved from this service only if that wisdom is unavailable. Or if you come to the end of your natural cycle, then it will do other things.

So the wind is a devoted companion of human beings and animals, and a portion of Mother Earth's true self. It is a way you can relate to her, and wisdom will come when it can. So the next time you find yourself out in a blustery day and you have to hold onto your hat, don't curse the wind.

It's either searching for the wisdom that you or somebody else needs, or bringing wisdom where it's needed. So thank the wind and welcome it as an invigorated and invigorating traveler.

How the Wind Moves Wisdom

What are the dynamics of the communication? Does it come to you as inspiration or in a dream? How does the wind get it to you?

The wind will usually want to touch you. The wind might have gone someplace where that wisdom is known and plentiful, where a person who has that wisdom has walked through the wind, or in the case of an animal, an animal who knows that. The wind blows by and the animal or the person can spare some of that wisdom. It doesn't take it away from them, but it is in their auric field, as all your wisdom is. It will blow through there, sample that wisdom in your auric field and go on.

The moment it has gathered that wisdom for you, it will be eager to get back to you. It might take awhile, blowing along and around the Earth and through the canyons, but it will usually not take more than a month, something like that. It might take awhile to find the wisdom, but once it has obtained it, it won't take much more than thirty days to come to wherever you are.

If you are unable to get out into the wind, try to get some part of you out into the wind, even if you reach your hand out. Or open a window and let the wind blow in a little bit—you don't have to let it blow things apart in your house, but let it blow in a little bit. But the best thing to do is to go out in the wind. Go out—it doesn't have to be blowing fiercely or gusting; it can just be a breeze. At some point, it will come to you. Maybe it will come in a dream; maybe the wind will blow down your chimney and, because you are relaxed, the air current moving through your home will find you. Give it a chance, give it some time. And don't be afraid of the wind—it's working for you or others all the time.

What about areas where the wind seems to blow more constantly than other areas? Is there any significance in that, or is it just the topography of the land?

Some of it is the topography. You know, in open spaces at sea or where there are not many trees, the wind blows. But there are certainly other places where the wind is blowing very firmly. The people who settle in such places usually have something in them that likes the wind or there is some reason for them to be there. Very often they have wisdom. Sometimes they *need* wisdom, but fully 30 percent of the time the people who settle in windy areas have some wisdom that is needed elsewhere, so they will be unconsciously (perhaps some might know of such things) drawn to areas where wind is a regular citizen. Every time they go here and there, the wind will sample their wisdom and pick it up if anyone needs some—not taking it from them, but allowing them to share their wisdom with people they would probably never meet. They will be inspired with this wisdom that comes to them from some unknown person via this wonderful delivery known as the wind.

This area is one windy place. The wind here howls, it practically tears the shingles off, it breaks the windows—it's wild!

It's looking. The wind is seeking and it's finding always. Of course, if you had a vehicle powered by sails, you would say, "What a wonderful place!" If you were flying a kite as a child, you would say, "No better place to fly a kite!" If you were a bird flying up, wishing to soar to look and see: "It is a wonderful place to soar. You can hold your wings out in just the right way, and the wind will support you."

Jet Streams Go Where They Are Needed

We have never gotten this spiritual interpretation. High above this planet are very, very fast jet streams. What causes them, and why are they so fast? Tell me something about them from your point of view.

I did actually refer to that. This is, again, the high-altitude winds. It is these winds particularly that will take particles far, far around the Earth, across oceans. There are famous stories of people who work high up on tall buildings or who have the opportunity to be exposed to the air high up, who occasionally get struck by something: "Oh, what was that?" They think it was a flying creature, but it might be a particle of something. These stories usually refer to a particle of grain that has been picked up hundreds, if not thousands of miles away and is flying on the wind to some destination only the wind knows.

Are these jet streams regulated by the wind itself, by Mother Earth or what?

They are a part of Mother Earth's body. They are going where they are needed, when they are needed. The weather systems, your meteorologists say, are following the jet stream, but those jet streams are the mechanism by which those weather systems are taken to where they are needed the most.

They really change? There was a lot of publicity when the balloonists were trying to go around the Earth, and they had to go somewhere to catch the jet stream.

Yes. They were in residence in part of Mother Earth's mechanism for transfer. I will say one more thing. When you want to offer a prayer to people far away—maybe someone you know, maybe someone you've heard of, maybe many people—and you want it to get there so that people will feel it and know that someone cares about them, then go outside on a windy or blustery day and say the prayer out loud, facing away from the wind. In this way, the particles of the message will be picked up in the most gentle way for you, so you are not distracted by the wind, and taken with enthusiasm to those to whom you direct the prayer to serve.

Your Glasses Record Your Experience

Speaks of Many Truths
June 29, 1998

This is Speaks of Many Truths. Lenses that you put in front of your eyes are very receptive. It is true that rock crystal lenses are more receptive, but even plastic lenses are quite receptive, at least 50 percent as much as glass or, as it used to be, crystal. The lenses' job is to alter the way your eye sees so that you can see better. This is understood. Yet what lenses do, as is typical for all material, is so much more.

Your Lenses Retain All They See and Reflect Your Feelings

As you know, if you are in a relationship with somebody, that person sees you in a certain way, but over the years you reveal more and more of yourself and pretty soon he or she has a much broader image of who and what you truly are. It is the same for any material. The lenses in your glasses retain all that they see. This does not require the lenses to be on your face. Some of you take off your glasses at night and put them on the bedside table. If the lenses are present during some drama or even trauma, the lenses see it.

Let's say there is a sudden storm, thunder and lightning, and a bolt of lightning hits nearby and startles you. You wake up frightened; the noise and the children yelling are very frightening. Your lenses see all of this. You grab for your glasses and put them on, rush around and calm down the children, saying, "It's just a storm. Okay, come on in and sleep on a cot in Mommy's room," or what-have-you, finding a way to get everybody calmed down. You sing a song, tell a story, and maybe the storm goes by.

You take your glasses off, put them on the nightstand. Eventually, everybody goes to sleep.

You get up in the morning, put your lenses on, and you have a sudden feeling of agitation. You are not sure why. You think, "Are the children all right? Did my husband get off to work on time? Is the car okay?" But these thoughts are the reaction to your body's feeling response to the lenses' view of what happened in the middle of the night.

So the lenses not only retain that which they see, they also retain and constantly reflect back and forth. Lenses always reflect and refract to some extent the feelings that were profound in the room, especially on the nightstand table right next to your bed—the feelings that were powerfully yours. These lenses are used to being on your face, so they are going to be more responsive to *your* feelings.

Ask Your Angels and Guides to Cleanse Your Lenses

For those of you who believe in spiritual things, ask the angels or your guides or spirit doctors to come cleanse your lenses and your frames. Ask this every day or every other day, at least when you think of it, and they will come. They will be happy to come, but they need to be asked. They will cleanse the lenses and clear the frames. Then when you put on your glasses, you will have only your glasses on; you won't feel any agitation reflected or refracted from them.

Do you know that if you *don't* do this, as long as you own that pair of lenses they will remember through internal reflection everything they see and everything you feel while they are on your face or nearby? If you are watching television and there is upsetting news on and you become upset, the lenses will remember it all, just like a computer brain that retains everything. Plus, they will remember what you felt in reaction to it.

But do the lenses hold only unpleasant things? No. They are not what you would call biased. They will hold things that are pleasant as well. For example, let's say you live in pleasant surroundings or that you have become aware of this teaching and have asked spirit guides or angels to clear your lenses, and they are clear. Then you get up in the morning and have a wonderful experience. Maybe someone gives you a birthday party and all these good feelings are brought up in you, and your lenses see many wonderful, happy things. Then nothing perhaps happens that is uncomfortable during the day. The next morning you get up, having had a restful night, and put on your glasses. Immediately you feel up. [Laughs.] So it can work *for* you as well as in some complicated situations—as I said, television, life around you, people arguing nearby and so on. Your feelings and what the lenses see, as well as what you see, can complicate your life.

Interestingly enough, you do not always have to be looking in the direction of what is seen. You might be near something that is suddenly frightening or shocking—maybe a sudden loud noise that startles you. This happens while you are looking at something beautiful, perhaps a beautiful dress in the window of a store. You would like to get that dress, then suddenly—*smash!* There is a car crash behind you, or somebody drops a load of something on the sidewalk accidentally and it goes bang! It is such a shock to you. Temporarily, strong feelings, physical feelings, emotional feelings, will fill your lenses. Then it might be more difficult to buy that dress—or conversely, you may want to rush in and buy the dress without thinking about it.

If you have had a mixed day, as most people do, ask for the spirits, your spirit doctors or whomever you speak to about these things, to come clear your lenses of the discomforts they might have assimilated from what they have seen or from what you have felt—just like that, the *discomforts*. In this way, if there are comforts, if the spirits can (they may not always be able to), they will leave the comforts there to accumulate. That's what I recommend.

When Your Vision Softens, You Can See More

In my time, of course, there were no lenses. So after a time—not always, but sometimes—your vision would soften; you wouldn't see things so well. Usually about that time you were learning how to ask for help anyway, if you hadn't already learned, and you would have the increasing opportunity to ask for help from your friends, family or neighbors.

Also, it was about that time, if you were not specifically being trained for mystical or spiritual service, that you began to be more conscious of spiritual things. When your vision softens, it is easier to see things, and because your vision is softer, you use your other abilities. You listen more clearly. Your senses of smell, of taste and of sound

Lenses reflect and refract internally all that they see. When you touch them or hold them, you can take on some of what they have seen. That's why my people don't wear these "picture holders." Discomforting things, which the lenses are forever reflecting internally, can be taken on, but you won't know it mentally. So you are always trying to release pain that may not be yours (something on TV, perhaps) or that may be something you've already released.

It's in the nature of lenses to forever reflect and/or refract whatever they see. That's why your people use them for data storage. But they can store all they are exposed to, not only codes. The natural process of vision softening [aging or unfocusing] allows you to see things that are there.

become very important, and since your vision is softened, you might see auric fields. You might see lightbeings. You might see ships that fly in the night. Your other senses will hear, smell, sense, feel and so on to augment these soft visions.

The Synergy of the
Trees with the Birds

Speaks of Many Truths
August 13, 1998

One often hears with joy, perhaps even rapture, the sweet songs of birds in the trees. Of course, they speak to each other, and the musical variety of their speech fascinates and intrigues and gladdens the heart. Yet what do the trees receive from this? Do you know that most of the light-hearted joy that trees experience is the result of the songs of birds and insects that land on or move about in trees?

The tree emotion that is there most often is calm and insightful wisdom. For a young tree, of course, it is enthusiasm and even excitement. But as a tree gets older, there is a sense of self-evaluation: "Have I done all I came here to do?" At times when there is trauma, perhaps from lightning or the effects of human beings, that is when trees need birds more than ever.

Birds Help Trees That Are Being Cut Down

You might notice that when there is forest clearing going on—with human beings and their instruments to "harvest," as they say, trees—at first the birds will fly away. But then they will get a little closer or fly overhead and sing to the trees. Sometimes the song is one of mourning, sometimes it is one of encouragement, because as the tree gets chopped down, its spirit will replace it.

For those who are sensitive, it is true that from three to six hours after a tree is cut down, sometimes longer, you can see its gold lightbody shimmering, sometimes with white and—occasionally, if the tree was from far away—silver, metallic reflections. The tree is re-creating itself. It is reimaging what it once was in light, and in a way it is putting a stamp, a memory, on its total self so that when it chooses to re-create itself, it will have this memory of light to access in terms of how to grow, in what form.

Trees Use Gold Light and Bird Song to Re-create Themselves

One wonders—does one not?—when looking at a tree, how the branches know where to go. Why don't they go down, or up, or to this side, or to that side? They will go exactly as the tree has been before in its most benevolent and fulfilled state of being.

The gold light then creates a permanent memory image of what the soul of that tree, in the exact form, would wish to re-create in the hope that it can continue its natural cycle. The actual natural cycle for a tree is not to be cut down by humans, but to achieve the total intent of its physical appearance. Once it has done that—perhaps put out enough seed to re-create itself or foster new trees, as in the birthing process—it will gradually die off and eventually fall over to be utilized in other ways by animals and sometimes by humans.

And yet the song of the birds gives the tree so much vitality. Sometimes a tree will feel that it is at the end of its existence. Then a cheerful bird, perhaps a bird the tree has not heard before, will land on the tree with a song that is new and interesting and exciting, and so stimulate the tree with its song that the tree will feel it must reproduce that song in form. A tree, then, by the way its branches and leaves sprout, actually reproduces feelings and inspirations it has gathered from life around it, from other trees or from its teachers, in the art of beauty it demonstrates to the world by its physical form. In this way, trees are a living tribute to beauty while being beauty in their own right.

There are trees that are long-lived. These long lives are just as much a tribute to bird song as they are to the trees' enthusiasm for life. So when you see those insects crawling all over a tree and you worry, "Does the tree have this problem or that problem?" maybe the tree has invited those insects. Maybe even if those insects cause the destruction of the tree, this form of life will ultimately inspire the tree to reproduce itself in a way that will be impervious to such visitors. Or maybe, since the tree is cooperative and harmonious, it will become in its next life even more supportive of these creatures, so that these creatures, these insects, will be able to live better lives and be better supported in the food substances they need.

This is not self-sacrificing by the tree, but a way for the tree to say thank you for its life. Some pine trees will produce extra sap so that the insects can be supported. Some trees visited by woodpeckers—or even if their ancestors were visited by woodpeckers or previous incarnations of themselves were visited by woodpeckers—will re-create themselves in such a way that the insect beings the woodpecker is living off of will be more attracted to that tree so that the bird will be supported.

So, you see, the intention of the tree and the way the tree has of re-creating itself is largely a result of its own individual personality—not unlike human beings—or its wisdom and experience in life.

The Variety of Bird Songs Is Intentional

Do trees always reincarnate as the same kind of tree, or do they experience different species and shapes?

Sometimes they will try something different, but it is in a tree's nature to reincarnate along the lines of what it is. In that way, it can utilize fully the wisdom it has attained.

One might ask, "Why are there so many varieties of bird calls?" These varieties are intentional. Some song from birds is communication, granted, but some is just a melodious sound they make because they are celebrating life or because they are expressing a deep feeling. Some birds have sounds they make only for special occasions. Some do what trees like more than anything: the bird will express out loud a sound, as best the bird can make it, that represents the sound the tree would make if it *could* make a sound on its own.

Trees, as you know, make sounds as a result of wind and so on, but sometimes they have an urgent need to speak something with heart and sound. When this takes place, they attract a bird who can speak with heart and sound in a way that resembles closely the feeling the tree wishes to share, either with other trees or just for the sake of its own needs in that moment.

This Helps You to Understand the World

Is there any benefit for humans listening to songbirds?

It is important to involve human beings, as we do, but there are times when it's important for human beings to look at something that has nothing to do with them at all. In this way, you can understand the world, even if you are not personally involved. It is this skill that allows you to learn how to get along with people when you have absolutely no understanding of who or what they are. When you practice this study—of trees and birds interacting, in this case, or of other life forms interacting—you will learn a valuable lesson that cannot be learned any other way, and that is the lesson of humility. Humility allows you to approach an unknown situation without any need to be right.

The Stone Will Help You Create Balance on Earth

The Voice of the Stone and Speaks of Many Truths
September 29, 1998

On September 22 I was in my residence and heard, coming from the north to the south, this voice that didn't describe itself, but when I asked later who it was, it described itself as the Voice of the Stone. And this is what it said.

—Robert Shapiro

When the stone is rained on by natural rain, sand, having once been stone, will turn and invite the rain to come again. When the stone has not been rained on for a long time, it goes into the breath of aridness. It breathes differently during this cycle, and this type of breath does not invite the rain.

Breathe with the Stone to Invite the Rain

When rain comes, go outside near the natural stone of your village or town. Relax and notice the way you breathe on or right next to the stone. This works best with feminine rain, or a gentle rain, which is what a feminine rain is. Stay as long as you can and experience the rhythm of your breath. Do this enough so that when rain is needed, you can go out to that same stone and breathe in that same way.

When you do this enough, or there is more than one of you there who has learned to breathe with the rain and the stone this way, then the stone may begin to do the rain breath with you. You will know when that happens, because it will become easier to do the rain breath and you will feel stronger. This is also a sign that the surrounding stone might be joining you all in rain breath. This will help to bring the rain. Breathe with the stone several times a day to be sure the stone is still doing the rain breath.

The rain breath feels different at night when it's dark. It will be stronger; you will feel it. In order to recognize the difference between the rain breath and the Sun breath, breathe with the stone when the Sun comes out and the water is disappearing from it but it's still a little wet. Notice the rhythm of your breath. Notice how you feel. You will probably start to feel a little sleepy. This is when the stone is going to get its best rest. Sleep with it if you can.

Do the Sun Breath in Times of Flooding

The same is true if your people need the Sun and it's raining too much. When it has been sunny for a long time and you can find no wetness on the rock and perhaps rain would be welcome, go out and be on the rock or stand or sit near it. Try to touch it in some way. Breathe with it. Notice the way you breathe and how you feel. When there is too much rain and the people and animals (the free ones too) are suffering and there is flood with the rain, go out to the stone and do the Sun breath. Remember to feel as you did when the stone breathed with you and the Sun. Get into the rhythm and the feeling of the Sun breath. Notice when you start to feel stronger as the stone begins to breathe with you.

If the Sun comes to shine on you and the stone you are breathing with, thank the Sun and continue the Sun breath. When you continue, the Sun will know that you are asking for the Sun's presence for all the people and the animals. The Sun will appear for everyone as soon as the Sun can. Don't be concerned if the Sun goes away for a while. The Sun will return as soon as the Sun can. This is why the stone is so important around your town or village. Honor it with love and reverence, and the stone will come to love you and your people.

This is Speaks of Many Truths. I am glad the Voice of the Stone has spoken. Just a few years ago, Native American peoples and other religious leaders were going to begin to pass on their wisdom to the general public. However, for various reasons this event did not occur. So the stone, being patient, and the other parts of Mother Earth, being patient and respectful, waited a respectful time. Now the stone has begun to speak to those who can hear the wisdom that will help you learn how to create complete balance on Earth.

Mother Earth Must Be in Balance All the Time

It is in Mother Earth's nature to be in total balance all the time, but when you add even one person, one human being only (animals and plants are in balance with her), she must work very hard. *One!* She must work very hard to maintain her balance. At first when human beings arrived, she attempted to maintain her balance until she was advised by those who speak with her about these matters. They told her that it would be proper for her to speak to the human beings about how her body works. Those who could hear would tell the others and develop ways that were benevolent and beneficial, not only for her, but for them as her guests. And so she did this.

For quite a while, all was well. This worked in a satisfactory way until the beginnings of what you now know as technology, which really began some time ago. If you wish to track technology, the easiest way to do it is to study the history of war. War has prompted technology. This perhaps tells you a little something about the type of technology you are dealing with. Ultimately, the technology you will use when you are in balance and helping Mother Earth to be in balance will have no moving parts, and all portions of the technology will in its own right happily be doing what you would like it to do. And you, conversely, owing it honor and respect, will do what it likes to do.

You have thought, perhaps, you will be using crystals. Indeed you will, but you won't go and get them. You will go to where they are, or if they have all been moved, you will take them where they want to go, and when they are happily there, then they will be happy to help you as long as you allow them to stay where they want to be. They are no different than people. Think of them as crystal people, and you will be able to be at peace with that.

The stone has spoken to remind you of the way Earth works. Mother Earth cannot balance herself with so many human beings here now, so parts of herself are beginning to do again what she did so long ago—speaking to those first peoples and later to other tribes and clans of people who had a sacred connection with the Earth. Now, since these people do not receive respect, since those who have lived on from those days do not always receive the respect they once did, Mother Earth must speak to people of your time. This is what she is doing, and so the voice of the stone tells you. The stone, being Mother Earth's body, you see, tells you how to bring the Sun during the time of flood with rain—not the same way exactly when there is a flood, but flood with rain means too much—and how to bring or invite the rain when it is too dry. It is all done through connection in a sacred, benevolent way with Mother Earth's body.

Mother Earth Can Mediate Your Differences

You have wondered for a long time now, "How can we learn to get along with each other in these modern times with so many differences between us?" You have tried very hard, some of you, and others have just given up. I am not here to judge you. What I would say is this: It is much easier to learn how to get along with Mother Earth and let Mother Earth act as a counselor between you. In time, when the voice of the stone is speaking to many people, not just those who have the sacred connection to the Earth and know that everything and everyone is alive and desires the same rights, appreciation, honoring and loving that everyone else does . . . until that time, you will need someone to mediate your differences. Then what will occur will be this:

Say there is a man not from your tribe or clan, and his ways are so very different from your own, yet he can speak to the stone and hear the voice of the stone the same way you do. It may speak to him in a different language; it might respond to different questions than you would ask. But the personality of the stone is the same—benevolent, balanced, loving, nurturing, encouraging and, you might say today, empowering, because it teaches you how to do things in a way that has been taught throughout all time.

So you will then both go to the stone. Perhaps you will go to the stone near your village or his village, or maybe both places. You will both talk to the stone, and the stone will talk to both of you. Then afterward you will discuss what the stone said to you and what the stone said to him, and the stone will work out a good compromise you can both live with. The stone is, after all, Mother Earth's body.

Stone Is Your Physical Connection to Mother Earth's Heart

For some time I have been discouraging you from mining and taking pieces of Mother Earth's body out for this technology you are now utilizing, which is not the sacred technology. This is because the stone is vital to your understanding of how to live in a benevolent way where you will have everything you need, where all of your cares will be taken care of and you will not be hungry or thirsty. You will have shelter. People will be happy. In other words, life will be at peace and in balance.

This is all going to come initially from the stone, because native stone is still in more places on the Earth, at least on the surface, than where it is not. And if you are living somewhere near the ocean and there is not much stone, then conduct your talk with the sand—not the dirt—because the sand is pure stone in a pulverized form. The dirt might be made up of other things beside stone, and we want you to have the clearest connection possible.

Any particular kind of stone, or just whatever is outside your door?

Whatever is nearby. Ideally, you want to go where the stone is great, where there are mountains or where there are big rocks. In some places, there are not many mountains, but because ice has moved through years ago or because there has been Earth motion, there are big boulders. You can find those and talk to them. If you cannot hear in words you understand, then just talk out loud. Remember, thinking does not work. You must talk out loud to the stone. You do not have to speak loudly and disturb your neighbors, but you must speak at the very least in a whisper—not so quiet that you can't make out the words, but loud enough so that you can understand the words you are speaking. But it is better to speak in a voice out loud.

The stone, you see, is safe for you to communicate with. There are other forms of Mother Earth's energy that can be communicated with, but they are not always as safe. You cannot talk to water behind a dam, because the water is so unhappy that you will feel its unhappiness and it will make you feel uncomfortable, perhaps even ill. By the time you have made a connection with water that is moving rapidly in a creek, it may have already gone by. Water that is coming in from the ocean may be touched by so many human beings that you cannot make the best connection. But the stone is always there, waiting for you, watching you. Stone is even inside your body. So you know the stone for you is your physical connection to Mother Earth's heart.

If there is crystal actually in the ground close to you, is that better or is that just the same?

It is not better, no. It's all the same. Stone is the same. I suppose you could say that sandstone isn't always easy to communicate with—it is like compressed sand. But although sand or sandstone is not as easy to communicate with as more solid rock, you can still talk to it. You see, when you talk to sand, what will communicate back to you will be one particle of the sand as it came from one big rock or mountain. You won't be able to tell which particle it is, though the most sensitive will be able to find the general area or even that particle, but I do not think it is necessary.

Breathing with the Stone

For your own sake, it is best to sit on or lean against the stone. Sit down if you are not feeling too strong in the moment, and touch it. Breathe with it, perhaps when it is sunny, as the voice of the stone has suggested. If the stone has extra energy (which it does not always have these days because of Mother Earth's discomforts), it will share that with you gladly, just as you share food with your neighbors if they are hungry and have none. When you feel very vigorous and have more energy than you know what to do with, the stone might use it if it is tired. It won't take it without your permission, but if might absorb a little of your spare energy if you are breathing with the stone and touching it and have more energy than you know what to do with (as have some youngsters). But it won't take any energy that you need.

That's beautiful. How far away from civilization do you have to get? Do you need to go out in the country? Or if you live in a city and you have a rock there, would that do?

Ideally, the larger the rock, the better. If you live in a city, I realize it will be very difficult. You cannot do it with cement or brick because it has been touched so much by human hands and it has been forced unnaturally into shapes. It will not work with that.

What about big slabs of marble, like on a bank or a building?

Probably not, because it was taken without its permission and is upset. Stone does not get over things as quickly as a human being can, because when stone needs to alter some great discomfort, it will gradually erode, traveling gradually down to the sea where it will be washed by the saltwater. The rain is comforting to stone. Stone loves the rain, especially when the Sun comes out and shines on it afterward; then it rests. But if it is very discomforted, such as stone that has been exposed to human war, it will tend to erode and go to the sea where the saltwater is.

To clean itself?

Yes, because the saltwater can purify the stone; fresh water takes too long. It will also not work if you take buckets of water out and throw it on the stone and try that. The water has to fall naturally from the sky, natural rain. It won't even work if your machines have been up in the clouds throwing out particles to make the sky rain. That won't work either. It has to be natural rain, because you are learning a natural process.

Moving to Natural Technology

These things are known by sacred peoples of today, but it is time for them to be known by the average citizen so that you all have a chance to try it. Also, the world you are creating now is so involved in unnatural technology that many of you are disrupted in your natural flow of life. This technology compounds your disruption because it is unhappy.

Sometime in the future when you learn how crystals work (and they work very similarly to how you as a physical person work), you will be able to touch a crystal and see the wisdom of the universe printed in front of you—not on the computer screen, which is very limited, but floating in space. It will float closer to you if you wish. As it gets closer, you will hear its song and you might smell its fragrance, which will be beautiful if it is wisdom you desire to know and is beneficial and benevolent for all beings, which you want it to be. You want your neighbor to learn things that are beneficial and benevolent for all beings so that you will be supported by your neighbor, and your neighbor wishes this from you as well.

In this way, the words get closer. Eventually you reach out and touch the words. Then you absorb this knowledge without having to think about it. It goes into you, and you know it. It has a song, a flavor; perhaps it has a fragrance—any or all of those things. It might have pictures that suddenly come into your vision. It might have pictures or even voices of beloved ones who have passed over or maybe teachers you have not heard from for some time, perhaps from other lives. You will feel loving and benevolent as long as it is beneficial for you and your people and all beings. It will come to you this way. All this from natural technology.

At Home in the Night

Nightwalker and Speaks of Many Truths
February 1, 1999

I would speak of the night. It is the time of the test, when you all return to the womb where life began for you and you show what you have learned.

Being at Home in the Night

When you are in the womb, before you emerge into your world, you feel at peace most of the time. It is dark and safe and warm. Then you come out into the outer world, and you begin to believe after a time that the outer world is where you are safe. But when you are in your primal state and encouraged to be there, as for some of the sacred peoples who still live on the Earth (and others I am training), you begin to embrace the night. Because the night is the place of comfort and safety, you can be seen or not, you can be heard or not. You can be comforted by the strong shoulders of the night.

In my work as a living spirit, I teach people—sometimes mystical people, sometimes others—how to live in the night safely and comfortably, how to walk in the night, even how to sleep for moments in the night and how to be at home in the night. I have been told that there is a Daywalker, and I believe that that person might be available for you. But tonight I will speak at the behest of Speaks of Many Truths.

I have spoken to him many times on how to walk in the night, and as a result, he has chosen sometimes to do so. He walks like different animals. If there are carnivorous animals nearby who are not known to him and he not to them, then he walks like a bear or a powerful animal that will frighten the others away—not like a she-bear, because she might attract the male bear, and not like a savage bear, because the savage bear might challenge the male bear also, should there be one, but like a peaceful bear.

In this way, other creatures keep a respectful distance. They see not a bear; they see a man. But they see a man and feel the bear energy. They know that even if they were hungry enough to attack the man, the bear would be there at once to chase them off and perhaps harm them. So they hold off with respect. Once they get to know the man and make peace, then they attack him not. He is safe, and he comforts them. Perhaps he will sing them a song.

Animals like song, you see; they often make it. Sacred songs of the animals that are heard at night are legendary; the wolf, the coyote and many others make songs at night that they never make in the day. This is because they are speaking not only their individual truth, but also the memory of all their ancestors and relatives to come in the future. It is like marking the land, but in this case they mark the wind with their song, which welcomes future generations that will be born into that space who will be marked with that song. This way, when future generations are born, they feel that there is some part of them there to welcome them home.

When I work with human beings, I teach them how to move silently, quietly, and to be able to feel their way in pitch darkness, partly seeing but mostly feeling. The animal does the same thing. I know many of you think that the animal sees clearly in the darkness; this is not so true. They see partway but mostly feel. So I will teach the human how to heighten the sense of feeling, the instinct, so that she knows where it is safe, when, how to walk, with whom and so on. When you learn these things, from that day forth you will always feel as you did when you were in the womb, that the darkness is the safest place. The nighttime protects because you can be unseen. The daytime can do other things, but certainly you will be seen.

How to Walk in the Night

Most of us don't walk on land where there might be dangerous animals like bears; most of us walk in cities or small towns. Can you say something about that?

Yes. Begin by finding a place that is as dark as you can find it. For those of you in small towns, go out to the countryside to some place where you know it's safe but quite dark. It might be in a nearby pasture or field, or even on a road that is rarely covered with vehicles. Then walk for a ways. Try to make it as dark as possible. Feel your way.

Do not walk with heel, then toe; walk with the toes down first, the ball of the foot down first. When you do that, this part of your foot, with the toes touching and the ball of the foot touching, this part of your body senses. The heel supports but does not sense. The forefoot senses just as much as the eyes or the ears. This is body knowledge.

When you put that part of your foot down first, your body is immediately heightened and alerted so that it must range out farther energetically to feel what is around it. If you feel suddenly to stop, do so; wait until you feel to go ahead. If you don't have that feeling, turn around and return to your place of residence. You may never know why your body wanted you to stop. Maybe it is simple fear, but it might also be a warning. Perhaps there is something or someone ahead—or even an energy ahead—that is dangerous. Sometimes the feeling will pass; then you can continue. But in the beginning, honor this. It is practice, it is training. It will teach you how to feel safe at night.

Remember, those of you who do not have to worry about wild animals still have to worry many times about the most dangerous animal on Earth, the one who will sometimes kill without reason. You know who that is— the two-legged animal.

Night Spirits on the Planet

Can you say something about yourself? How long have you been doing this training?

I have inherited this training from others. I have been doing this for about 550 of your years. I inherited the job many years ago. I was once a man who walked the Earth in Canada (as you call it now). I was of a tribal peoples up there many years ago. I will not say which tribe, but we lived near the Cree nation and we got along pretty well with them most of the time.

I was trained by my grandfather to be the mystical man. Grandfather got a message one day, and he told me that after I died, I would have a great and important job to do on Earth that had been done and was being done by others, but those others could not come everywhere on the planet. There are those doing it on this island or that continent. We had different words for places, not the names you have now, but now I know the names: There is someone in Japan, someone in Eurasia and so on—different ones for different continents. My job would be to help the person—as spirit, you understand—who was assisting the human beings. In this way, my job would be to help in North America, and I would receive help. In time I would be taking care of only northern North America, and someone else would do southern North America. That time is near.

So all these years you have had Canada and North America.

Yes, but very soon—in terms of your years, in less than one year—they will have someone who will do southern North America.

Like you, it's someone who was a human who will continue in spirit, then?

Yes, a tribal person who has received throughout his life special trainings about the night. He will receive a little more soon after his physical death and then will begin teaching the people who must know these things when he is ready.

Nightwalker's Students

How many students do you have?

Right now, I have nine.

Do you count Speaks of Many Truths as one of them?

No. We finished our training many years ago.

When he was in his body?

Yes.

Oh, I see. So you work only with living humans?

Yes.

Do you contact them, or do they put out the desire for this training?

Either they will put out the desire, or their teachers might ask for the night spirit. Some people know me as Nightwalker, but others might ask for the night spirit.

Is this training in their dreams or in their full consciousness?

In their state of alteration, like a vision, not sleep. In sleep you are in a different world; you may not remember much of that. But when you are choosing a vision, then we can make contact. If we are very compatible, I might be able to speak to you during the night when you are not in the "altered" state. But if our compatibility is difficult, meaning not personally but energetically, I will then speak either to the person's physical teacher or to that person in his altered state.

So you teach people, as you said, how to walk where it's dangerous and how to use their body to sense. What else do you teach?

I teach them how to survive on the night air. The night air is usually more moist, even in the driest place. Say you are someplace where there is no water or food—a desert, perhaps—where you do not know the land well and you are not sure of what is safe to eat or drink. Then I will teach people how to live on the air, how to drink the air, how to consume the air. Two-legged humans must have water after two, three days maybe; most people die without it. But some teachings I give to certain students, and they can go five, six, even seven days without any water and two, three weeks without any food at all.

But it takes very slow and patient training, much discipline, in order to not only live on the night air, but to thrive. I do not mean simply curling up in a ball and living; I mean living in an invigorated fashion, feeling vital and full of strength.

And that takes years?

It takes as long as the student takes to learn it.

So in your 550 years, how many students have you had? I'm just looking to see how long you've spent with each one.

Perhaps less than three hundred.

And after they leave the planet, does that . . . oh, are you okay?

I am fine. The energy startled the cats earlier, when I was present; I came through the door. When I'm in a place of light, I appear as white light, but that is my electrical body being seen. At night I am unseen.

So you work with the students while they're on the Earth. Do they in turn teach their students too? Does this teaching spread?

No, they are sworn to secrecy. They are allowed to pass the teaching on only to their apprentice, if they are a mystical man or occasionally a mystical woman. They are allowed to pass it on to their one apprentice, a person to whom they teach everything. Mystical people might have many students to whom they teach different parts of their wisdom, but always only one they will teach everything to. This training is to be the last thing students are taught so that they will prove their worthiness before they receive it.

Are all your students from tribal or native groups?

All of mine are, but I have been guided that on other places, other peoples are taught, but always peoples who are mystical peoples by nature. The first choice is peoples who are tribal, meaning they can trace their ancestry back along the same cultural line for quite a ways. This creates the stable personality. But occasionally one finds the mystical person who cannot do that and yet he is the ideal student—it's not always one way only.

They use it for their own benefit and then pass it on to one person?

No, no. They do not use it for their own benefit. It can be used only for the benefit of all beings. If it is a case of survival for them, they are surviving because they are needed by other beings. But they cannot use it for their own purposes. If they do, they are warned what will happen.

So you're teaching things other than how to survive and how to walk in the night? There are many other teachings that you can't talk about?

No, this is what I do. I teach about the night.

But if you teach only one tribal person, I don't see how that person uses that for the good of all. Can you explain that?

Yes. What happens if the people in the tribe or clan are invaded? Many such occurrences happen at night because then people can be easily scattered or taken by surprise. But the sensitive one, the mystical person, maybe the medicine person, will know that it is happening and that people will have to leave in the night. The people do not know how to walk in the night to be unseen, to be invisible, so they must walk, one by one, in the footsteps of the one trained by Nightwalker. If they walk in Nightwalker's footsteps carefully, with the forefoot down first and focusing their eyes only straight ahead—everyone looking at the one who has been trained, or looking at the one in front of them who is looking ultimately at the one who has been trained—they walk quietly and disappear into the night, totally invisible to those who might be one, two, maybe even three feet from them. They will not hear them, will not see them, will not sense them, will not even know that they were ever there.

That's pretty powerful!

It is useful. It is to be used for such things as that—not to sneak up on an enemy and kill him. This is misuse. It has been done, this misuse, but it is always dealt with in the same way.

How?

I cannot say to you.

Do you plan to be here for quite a few more years?

It is not a plan. I will be here until I am asked to go elsewhere. I am happy to do this. It is a great honor, a service that I feel good about, and as long as I do it, it will be a gift for me. So I am pleased to do it as long as I am asked.

Do you have some of the mystical abilities, like long vision and long touch and some of these things?

Yes.

All over the world, or just in your area, in North America?

Not using it all over the world. To the extent I have some knowledge of what goes on in other places, it is because I have at times either used long vision or worked with others who have this ability, and they say things to me or I need to look other places to help them. I do not use it for my own curiosity.

Do you talk to your peers? Do you have long-vision readings with your peers?

No. I know what I need to know and how to teach and what to teach, but I have no need to talk to the others, nor have they ever demonstrated a need to talk to me.

Thriving in the Deep Night

How is this going to play out now as humans become more open to their heart energy and survival, and enemies become less and less? Will your teaching change?

No, because it will always be needed. I have been told that there will be those who will teach Earth space travelers, because space can often be very dark—perpetual night—and people will have to be taught. But we will have to wait until the sacred peoples or the tribal peoples or the mystical peoples are welcomed into space. Then I or another will teach them.

You'll teach them how to survive in the dark night, in the deep night?

I will teach them how not just to survive but to thrive.

That's the part I want to get to, that there's more to your teaching than just survival— that's what I was getting at.

Yes.

Say more about that. Are there some things you teach now that are more about thriving?

Yes. Perhaps as a mystical person, you might need to teach about the stars to your people, but you can only see the stars most easily at night. Therefore, you will go out at night and, by feeling, you will point to different stars. And when you point to the star that feels the best to you, this is where your people have come from, because you have come from a long line, you see? Tribal people, a distant culture.

So you point to the star and you breathe in the light that surrounds the star first. And you don't only breathe it in, but when you exhale [blows out to illustrate], you blow out a small portion of your energy—not your spirit, but your energy—so that the star can feel who you are and be reminded of your people and of what to teach you.

Then you breathe in the light of the star. You wait awhile, and you breathe in the light of the star. Then you will have visions: what to teach your people, things you never knew before, things you were never taught. You might teach them directly, or you might go and talk to your teacher or the grandfathers or the grandmothers or the elders, and they will pass on to the others what they feel is good for them to know. In this way, the people learn to do things that are beyond Earth knowledge, and they may need to use them sometime.

When you breathe in this starlight of the place where your people come from, you are filled with a tremendous sense of well-being. You feel wonderful! You feel enriched and nourished. Often you don't have to eat for days afterward because you are filled with the food of your everlasting heart and soul.

Beautiful! Is there other information like this that you can share?

[Pause.] You will have to ask other questions, I think.

What do you do in the daytime?

In the daytime, I will rest. I will sometimes go inside a tree, especially if it is a tree I have known for a time. Different ones will welcome me, and I will go and be in the taproot in the Earth and live there gently. Other times I might go into a cave and visit with the night animals. I have at times spoken with the night cats and other animals, and we have sung each other our different songs and told many stories. And when it is time to leave, we leave together and have an eternal kinship.

How do you move around? Can you just think and be somewhere, or do you actually move from one place to another to teach your students?

I oftentimes walk. If I have to cover great distances, as you know, if I have not met the student, I will feel him. Then I will feel his heart and allow him to feel my heart. If that student is not ready for that, he will have a teacher, and I will feel that teacher's heart and the teacher will feel my heart. The teacher will invite me when the time is right, and I will travel on the heart line to the teacher first. I will discuss what is right for the student first with the teacher and with the student only when the teacher says the student is ready. If it is somebody I know and have been working with and that person is at a distance, I have already made the heart link, so I will be able to move to him or her, covering great distances through the heart line.

That's beautiful.

How to Make the Night Your Friend

Let's go back again to where most of the people are on the planet. I know many people who are afraid to go out at night. Maybe they've had some experience that caused them to be afraid. What can you say to them?

You must learn how to make the night your friend. The thing to do is to begin in your bed. Often you will feel safe in your bed. You can begin as a child might. Perhaps you did this when you were a child: Put the covers over your head for a time. Leave just enough so that air can get in. If you want to bring a flashlight, you can do that—like a tent, you know? Then you will feel safer, more comfortable.

That's how to begin in the safest way. When you feel safe and comfortable, even with no light under the sheets and blankets, then be in your room where you spend most of your time and make the room as dark as possible. Try to plug your ears so you hear no noises; the less you hear, the better.

Begin like this, and then either drive or have a friend who does not need to talk very much take you out somewhere when it is night. But don't get out of the vehicle. Stay in the vehicle. If your friend can leave the vehicle, that is good.

I don't want you to drive out there, because if you do, you will be thinking about driving. I want your heart to be in the night. Drive out to someplace where you know what it looks like during the day but which is quiet at night. Do not go out of the vehicle yet. Drive out as many times as you want until you are ready to step out of the vehicle—but it must be dark, and your friend can say nothing to you. You can talk on the way back.

When you are ready, get out of the vehicle. Try to set the vehicle so lights do not go on when you get out. Then do not leave the vehicle; keep touching it. Hold a part of the vehicle, go nowhere and stand out in the night.

When you are ready, you can step away from the vehicle, but not very far—only far enough that you can still sense its presence. That is a beginning; I will give you more in time. You can begin with that.

You must remember to feel at ease with the night. You must treat the night as *someone*. The night is not an idea; the night is a living being. That is why you come into the world in the night, inside the womb where it is dark and safe. Before you live on this Earth the way it is now, you always think of the nighttime as the dark, safe, peaceful place, and you must be able to reacquaint yourself with that dark, safe, peaceful person of the night. So begin slowly, the way it is best to begin any friendship—slowly and gently, no rush. The best friendships begin that way, and then they last forever.

Advanced Teaching and the Moon

What about the energy of the Moon? We're just learning about the phases of the Moon. Can you teach that?

No.

Do you work with it in any way?

No. There is another who does that.

Who is that?

You will have to ask for her.

All right! So in your teaching, it doesn't matter whether it's the full moon or the dark of the moon?

No, but the advanced teaching takes place when there is a new moon—no Moon.

No moon?

No Moon, new moon. There is never no Moon, but sometimes I will call it the so-called new moon. I will call it no Moon because the Moon is facing another direction and shows you its back.

Well, there is one when it's really pitch-black. I think it's only one day, though. What about the beings you teach? Do they reincarnate back on Earth and remember this teaching, or do they go somewhere else and remember it? Does it stay with them?

I cannot say. Perhaps it will stay in their soul knowledge, their soul wisdom. It is not for me to say whether they bring it back to Earth, because as you know, Earth life is different than other planets.

Have you ever been on another planet that you know of?

I can recall one life on a planet. I was a sea person, a water person.

Do you know what planet it was?

All I know is that it was on the place Earth people call Sirius.

How wonderful! So you're dedicated to what you're doing? You have no interest in what you'll do after you leave here?

No.

Do you have a plan?

I do not need this. I have my work, and it is an honor, a privilege and a joy to do it.

Do you have teachers you can ask when something comes up that you need to know?

I have one, but I cannot say his name. He is a being of great love, insight and patience, and he will answer my questions if I need to ask them. I try not to ask him anything silly or things for my own curiosity. I know he is called on to help many, so I just ask when it is for others.

This Is a Type of Vision-Seeking

So if you have nine students right now, do you work with them, for instance, every ninth night? Do you focus on one, or do they call you, or . . . ?

There is no fixed relationship, but I can work with only one at a time. It will be this time with that one, that time with another one. But always at night. And I do not work with them at a distance, but either with them or nearby.

As you said, if we were in Canada, you can get anywhere you want by following what you said was the heart line.

Yes.

So is there a feeling of flying or a feeling of just instantaneously being there?

There is no feeling of flight. I just connect on the heart line, and there is a slight, briefest moment of very gentle, soft energy . . . then I'm there.

You could say they're in meditation—your words about a vision, like they're working in meditation? Is that how we can understand it?

I don't call it that. It is a type of vision-seeking, whatever way it is done for their people. It is not what you call prayer or meditation or repeating words. It is a feeling they are taught to achieve.

Is it what they call the vision quest? Or is it just that they really need to know something and they ask?

Occasionally, the first time might be a vision quest, but not so often. Not all peoples do this. They know what they need, they ask, and if it is the right time, I work with them. If the time is coming, I work with their teacher instead. But I don't always do it the same way—different ways, different beings.

But when you work with particular beings, you hear them when they ask, right?

Yes. Not always immediately, but when I have a moment, I hear. They might ask when I'm with another, and when I am teaching someone or working with them, that person has my total attention. So I won't hear it until I have a moment.

The Real, Natural World versus the Artificial World

You work with the students, but they're mystical and they don't have a lot of machinery or technology, right?

They might. Sometimes they do, but they know the difference between the natural world, the real world, and the artificial world. They have proven their worthiness before they work with me. And I know this; I can tell by the way their heart feels. I do not work with people just if they ask; they must know the difference between the real, the natural world and the artificial world. The world of machines is artificial because machines are not alive. That which makes up the machine is alive, but the machine itself is not a being. You must know this; otherwise we cannot work together.

So you think that theoretically you could have a computer programmer in the daytime if he's worthy. It's a heart quality, right? How do you decide when they're worthy?

I can feel it. The heart never lies. It has no capacity to lie. The mind can lie, but the heart does not know how, nor can it.

Is there more to worthiness than that feeling they have achieved, a level of shamanic training or something before you get them?

For the advanced training, it is helpful if they have proven their worthiness by learning things from their teacher or teachers. This way they will have shown that they are dedicated and that they are not slaves to the world of the artificial. In this way, they prove their worth. Yet if they live part of the time in the artificial world, that is acceptable as long as they are clear on the difference. They might need to live in the artificial world for people they help or work with or even say the occasional word or phrase to. But they will know the difference.

In the real world, everything is what it appears to be, though at deeper levels it may be more. In the artificial world, things are almost never what they seem to be.

Exchanging Wisdom

So basically, then, is it fair to say that most of your students have studied with a teacher before you work with them?

Most, but not all.

So you've had students whom you have felt to be worthy even though they haven't worked with a teacher? They have studied on their own or something?

Yes.

If you work with nine students now, have you worked with them a year, ten years, their whole life? How long do you work with individuals?

Different lengths of time for different people; there's no fixed number. Some people just for a few years (maybe a year and a half, two), others, maybe for their lifetime, and everything in between. But never after their life is over; only when they are here in the body.

Do you help them pass over or lead them?

No. Others do that.

Are you getting help now because there are more people to work with? Or will you be able to work with more in the upper part of the Northern Hemisphere?

There are more people now. It seems that there will be someone to do southern North America because there are more people—that's correct.

And will you train this being for a while as an apprentice?

No. This being will arrive fully trained. He will receive his training much the same way I did—in his life.

Did you do the training?

No, I did not.

Well, did someone on the planet train him?

He will have had his teaching somewhere on the planet, maybe not even on this continent. I do not know anything about it. If he was trained on another continent, maybe another Nightwalker worked with him. I do not know. All I know is that he will be male.

Do you find that when you have worked with so many different beings over these several hundred years, that you have learned from them sometimes?

Oh, often! I learn about their wisdom because I have to speak to them in the language and culture that is their own. This means that if my language is not understandable to them, then they will hear me in their language. But the words do not always translate directly, so we will have to talk and understand the nuances. We get to know each other, so I often learn about their culture. When I know more about them as people, I can work better with them and talk to them about things and circumstances. I can put the lessons into the form of life they live so they feel that they understand. It makes sense to them in their life.

I don't think you wanted to say what language you spoke, what tribe you were of originally, right?

I'd rather not say, only that my people lived near the Cree nation—a people I have a great deal of heart for, the Cree people.

Yes, I owe them something too.

The Herb That Bloomed Only at Night

Do you have a favorite story you would like to share about working with any of your students?

I can share only one story. I will tell you only part of it because so much of the training is secret. I will tell you a story about a child I worked with once. She was in training to be medicine woman and had Grandmother teaching her. But in their village, they needed to have a certain plant that bloomed only at night. It did not have much of a smell, and sometimes it would grow on this hill, sometimes on that one—they never knew where. And it was not always easy to find even in the daytime.

How to find this special plant? Grandmother spoke to the elders, and one of the neighbors knew about me, had been told. The elder said to Grandmother, "Ask for Nightwalker. He will teach you or the young one, whichever way you think is best. The decision will be yours." Grandmother thought about it for a time, then asked me to come and see her first. I did so. She was a wonderful person; she's still alive in spirit, but on another place now, another planet.

I came and spoke to Grandmother. Grandmother said, "The child is so young; can I be present when you do your teaching?" I said, "Of course." So Grandmother was always present when I taught the little one. She was, as you say, seven years old. I taught her until she was about nine and a half, almost ten. By then Grandmother was very old, almost too old to go find the plant on her own. So one night I came for the little one and said, "Are you ready to walk with me? We will find the plant, many of them, and they will offer their leaves." You see, the plant, could be found in the day, but when it flowered (it bloomed at night), the leaves would change their energy, their being, so that the leaves could be gathered only at night, not during the day.

And this was for a healing herb?

It was for an herb. I will tell you what it did in a short time. So we went. This was the first time the child had been alone with me, but by then we were like family. Grandmother was tired, and she kissed the child—not on the face, but on the back of her hand, as is the tradition with her peoples—and said, "I will wait for you." And we went and found the plant. She gathered the leaves in the sacred way, and we walked back together. I showed her exactly how to find the plant, how to honor it and how to speak to its night self. We walked back, and she had that wisdom.

The plant was for the treatment of sores that would erupt on the surface of the skin. Sometimes I think you call this cancer. But plant usage also must involve heart, spirit, wisdom—the time to apply it with the heart energy. And the person with the sores must be prepared also so that only a little bit of the plant is needed to do the greatest good for that person. This way the plant does not have to offer too much of itself, for it is small and has not so much to give.

When you walked with the girl and Grandmother, did they see you as a spirit or a person, or did they feel you?

For those who know me well, they see me like a silhouette form. If you do not know me well, then you feel me.

And would the silhouette be what we consider a Native American form?

That's what I am.

Feeling at Home in the Night

I have a sense of the feeling of how powerful this is. Because you can't talk about a lot of it, it's hard to get the depth of what you do across to the readers.

Let me say this to the reader, then: As you know, many times when you have learned how to do a challenging task and you have learned how to do it well and you feel good about it after having done it, this is a wondrous feeling. Although you can show others how to do the task, you cannot show them how it *feels*. They must find that out for themselves. That's what I'm talking about here.

This work is all about feeling and sensing. It is not very much about reading and studying. The reading and studying goes on in these pages to help you, to support you to have a simpler, more fulfilling life. But to know about the work, I can only tell you a little bit at a time. And I can promise you, as you do it slowly but surely, you will have that feeling. That's what the work is about: that feeling that feels as if nighttime anywhere is home. And in home, you are safe and surrounded by friends and loved ones.

When you learn how to walk in the night, you can be anywhere in the night—even in another country. Even if you don't know the creatures there and aren't familiar with the air there, you will have learned how to be at home in the night. The night will welcome you because your heart welcomes the night, and it will show you and ease your way to learn about night in that new place. And you will feel safe, welcome, secure and at home.

Perfect. That's very powerful. Thank you. We hope to talk to you again sometime. Good night.

Good night.

This is Speaks of Many Truths.

Oh, welcome!

That was my great friend and teacher, Nightwalker. He will speak again, I believe, and give more teachings in time, when he feels the readers are prepared. I just want to thank him in these pages, and to you right now: Thank you for welcoming Nightwalker, and I will thank your beloved four-legged cat friends for announcing Nightwalker's presence in this room. Good night.

Good night.

Compassion: The Key to Communicating with All Life

Speaks of Many Truths
April 9, 1999

Tonight I would like to talk about the method by which communication with all life is made possible: It is compassion. With compassion there is the heart connection. All these exercises about the love-heat/heart-warmth/physical-warmth are based on compassion [for more on the love-heat, see Overview]. It is not that you approach another being in a way that is psychological; it is rather that there is a warmth, a feeling, a sense of worth of all life. This feeling is compassion. Compassion is slightly misdefined in your dictionaries because it is too narrowly defined, so I'm broadening the definition a bit so that you can see how it functions in application.

Moving with Compassion

As you approach another living being, be it a plant or an animal—or even as you are simply walking and moving about with this heart feeling—you will find that something happens for you and with you that is different than, say, someone strolling through the woods whistling a happy tune. With this feeling of heart, of compassion, all life in the woods leans toward you. The trees move their limbs because they feel a like being in you; the animals move toward you. They don't rush up to you, but they lean toward you or else they do not run away, be they the very small or the very large.

With human beings it is different, because human beings do not always have this connection. We are born with it, yes, but it has to be taught and nurtured in the home and society to be maintained and developed. Even so, if there are very young people there, children, they might also be attracted, or the sensitive might be attracted. In some cases, the very old might also feel good. This is not to say that other human beings won't feel benevolently toward you, but with human beings, it is different. Let us say that you stop. You feel a great sense of warmth from a plant—maybe it is a vine. Or maybe, as you get closer, you notice it is not the plant at all, but a ladybug sitting on a leaf. And you reach toward it very gently, like this . . .

The left index finger and middle finger are pointed straight ahead and level, with the palm down.

You don't touch it; just point toward it. If the warmth in your chest or solar plexus area gets stronger while you are pointing toward the ladybug, then you will know it is the ladybug and not the plant so much. Then you stop, maybe kneel down a little bit, and there is this exchange of warmth between you. This is a combination of the responsibility of compassion and its rewards.

The Responsibility and Rewards of Compassion

The responsibility of compassion is that it is necessary to provide it. Just allow the heat to be within you, letting it naturally radiate. Don't do it if you feel exhausted. If you feel exhausted, then you are not doing it quite right. Most likely what you are doing (if you feel tired doing this) is consciously or even physically making an effort to project the heat outward. That will set up an opposition, because it is necessary to *allow* the heat, which is love incarnate. Love must be allowed to go where it feels to go. But if it is corralled and sent to a given place, then it creates a tension, and you, as the physical grounding for that, will feel tired. So take note of that.

The rewards of compassion are that other beings in the natural world (plants and animals) will naturally have a heightened sense of this heat and compassion near you, and this heat you both have feeds each other. The excess simply radiates on its own out to all life. I want you to understand how it works. If you can connect this heat with a word like "compassion," with the broader definition as given, it won't seem like a vague physical exercise.

How to Practice Compassion

I want to suggest to people who might be reading this that it would be a good time now to practice this thing, no matter where you live. If you are in a big city, you could go to a park, but if you go to a park, there might be many people. Try to find a place in the park where there are fewer people and where plants are growing wild. When plants grow where humans have placed them, they will often have less of the natural love energy because they were not welcomed specifically by the land on which they are growing. The most convenient plant to find in this case would be what is called a weed, because it grows where it has been welcomed.

If you can get out to the countryside or perhaps near a stream or a creek, finding wild plants will be much easier, and it also might be easier to find wildlife. Don't rule it out though, if you are in the city. Wildlife means simply any creature who does not owe its survival to a human being. This means it won't be a pet. This is not to say that you cannot feel the warmth with a beloved pet, but the idea is to practice with beings in the natural world who live their own way and survive as best they can.

It might be a small creature: a beetle or an ant. It might be a bird or a squirrel. If you are out near the country, it might be an eagle or a hawk, a deer or a jackrabbit. If you are living in a wilder country, it might even be a lion. For such creatures with whom you do not yet have a personal relationship (you have just met), it is better to keep your distance. Whether it be an ant or a lion makes no difference. Keeping your distance does not mean running away; it just means you don't run up too close to these beings, because they do not know you personally yet and you do not know them personally. You form a relationship the same way you do with a human being. After a time, should you get to know this ant or this lion, then you can go a little closer—or better yet, allow them to come a little closer, all the while feeling the heat of compassion. With this heat the animals will feel safe, and when animals feel safe, especially the bigger dangerous ones, the chance of them attacking you is almost nonexistent. This is important to know.

That's beautiful. That's in the forest.

I included the city because so many people live in the city and have gotten used to thinking of wild animals as something to deal with, like beetles or mice or rats. And I recognize that sometimes these creatures can be startling, but if you can recognize that they are doing the best they can, given that their natural way of living has had to adapt to living amongst human beings, then you can appreciate their flexibility. I'm not saying you have to pick them up and embrace them, for they would find that frightening, but rather recognize that a wild creature who adapts itself to a foreign environment and maintains its independence within its own family of creatures is a good being to acquaint yourself with.

In the coming years, as your world becomes more mingled and commingled with other societies and cultures, you will need to develop a quick, adaptable ability to fit into environments that may be unexpected, unpredictable or literally unknown. To make friends with wild animals who have learned how to adapt to a foreign surrounding, such as a big building, can be useful. Some of you will be able to communicate with words; others will simply have the heat feeling.

In the case of these city-adapted animals, don't walk up to them; let them come up to you. Don't be afraid. As long as you feel the heat—and it will probably be heightened more than you normally feel it—they will also be feeling it. They will be curious, and it will give them great hope to know that human beings are beginning to develop what they naturally do themselves.

Do you know that most animals who live with you in the city, maybe in your building—these beetles and little mice and so on—are not living in your building because they want to. It is not because they are living off of humankind living so much; it is because they have something to teach. And to the extent that you can have compassion with them, they will find some benevolent way to teach you what they came here to show you. If it is nothing other than flexibility, adaptability and kinship amongst one's fellows, then they will demonstrate that just by being themselves.

Begin with Animals and Plants

What about humans needing humans? How can humans be more compassionate to humans?

Begin with the animals and plants. When you get good at this with the animals and plants, with these teachers, then you will be able to practice these skills. After that you can begin very gently with babies whom you happen to see or who are in the family, perhaps. Or just allow the feeling of compassion, which you will feel as heat or sometimes as energy. Let it be in you and let it naturally radiate.

Some human beings will be attracted to this. They will make themselves known by approaching you in some benevolent way. Many human beings, though, will not acknowledge it. They will be shielding themselves because of their life or their experience. Don't try to change them or tell them what you are doing. Interact only with those who approach you. If they want to know what you are doing, why it feels good around you, show them how to do this thing. If, on the other hand, they are approaching you *with* that feeling, you will know it because the feeling in you will be heightened.

Looking Upon Others with
Compassion and Warmth

Speaks of Many Truths
April 9, 1999

f you stare at a cat or any wild creature, it will behave differently . . .

This is quite true. If you stare at animals without the feeling of compassion and warmth, they will immediately know it because they are attuned to their instinctual selves. The instinctual self is not involved with the mental self. Though the mind may have thoughts associated with these feelings, the mind is not the function of instinct. It is the philosopher, the analyst, but not the physical protector.

In order to have instinct, you must allow your feeling, your sense of community self, to radiate outward. If you are in a room with many people you like very much and they like you, you will feel a sense of community and will feel satisfied and comfortable and safe. When you feel this way, your energy radiates in many directions, having to do with this sense of safety. This is the community self, an example of the energy associated with instinct.

Encountering Animals in the Forest

Let's say you are walking in the forest thinking—not feeling compassion, but thinking—and you are walking quietly so as not to disturb others or attract attention. You come around a bend in the trail and ahead are three deer eating. You are not upwind of the deer, so they do not smell you, but you stare at them—not to be impolite, but because of their beauty. Suddenly they look up. They might look at you. If you are far enough away, they will not move away. But if you continue to walk even gently and quietly toward them, they will probably move away. If, on the other hand, you are feeling the compassion, the heat, the warmth, they might move away slowly [for more on feeling compassion, see chapter 48; for more on the love-heat/heart-warmth/physical-warmth, see Overview]. How do you moderate that so they move away as slowly as possible?

First, you try to give them as much space as they might need, as much space as you would want from a stranger approaching you who might walk a distance around you, not right up to you. Next, it is important to take note of how you walk. Don't put your heel down. A man or a woman who walks through the forest or anywhere putting the heel down first is walking willfully: "This is where I am going. Get out of my way!" [Laughs.] Even though you might not feel that way, it is felt that way by others. That's an important point.

But if you put down your toes and your forefoot first, this means: "I approach gently with respect." That is how it is felt by others. Remember, you are a feeling being whether you are aware of your feelings or not. This means you feel things around you, but you also project feeling, because in order for you to feel things around you, maybe other people, something has to happen for you to feel it.

You are not only a receiver, you are a projector. Human beings and all life project things to the extent they are respectful of all other life. As you walk through where these beings are, you feel good, you feel safe. But if plants were like humankind is sometimes, they would simply grow. A tree might say, "Wow, this is where I want to be," and instead of taking five, ten, fifteen years to grow up as a sapling, it punches through your house in a day or two, through the floor, through the ceiling, and says, "This is where I'm going to be. Get out of my way!"

Now, we know that trees don't do this. This is how the tree root works: The root, in the analogy, puts its forefoot down first, gently feeling the safest, most gentle way for it and the safest, most gentle way for life, for soil, for water, for the roots of other plants around it. Humankind can learn to live this way. Use this the next time you are in a crowded place, maybe a place where you are expected to meet people and are nervous: "What will they think of me? Will they like me?" Or maybe you are a big person or unusual-looking, and you don't want to frighten people. Or maybe you want to approach gently and quietly so that you can see but not be seen so much.

It does not make you invisible, but it makes you be felt less strongly if you put your forefoot down and your toes down first—not tiptoe, just walk naturally, but put your forefoot down first. (I think you call it the ball of the foot and the toes.) This is respectful, it is gentle, and when you do this with your body, your body knows that you are gently feeling your way. So the body is feeling for you; you have a heightened sense of feeling and you broadcast gentle respect. It is a way that you might wish to be felt by others. Remember this; it will serve you well.

Avoid Staring at People

Now, how does this affect human beings? Often you might see human beings, and because of their beauty or because they are unusual or because you are simply curious about them, you will stare. This is what is better to do, and you can practice this with plants and trees, if you like. Go someplace where there are plants and trees. If you are in a city, go someplace where there are weeds growing up through the sidewalk because they are wild and free and probably sturdy [laughs], meaning strong. Don't stare at them; glance quickly, and then stop. Make sure you have a place you can stop and think for a moment.

What did it look like? Remember it in the greatest detail possible. Then walk back and approach the same plant and look at it again. Is that what you remembered? If you did not remember it all, then say, "Thank you," and go on. Try it with a different plant until you can look at a plant or a tree (if you have that available) and remember it in great detail. But only give a quick glance; then stop and close your eyes. You have to do this right away; you can't wait for twenty minutes. Stop, think and remember as many details as possible, and then walk back to where you were. Approach the tree and look at it again. Did you remember all the details? Keep practicing this until you can remember so many details that when you examine the tree or the plant or the weed, you can say, "I have remembered this very accurately." When you have been able accomplish that, then you will be ready to look at people.

Remember, staring at people changes their behavior just like it does with animals. You might see someone beautiful or interesting and give a quick glance. Then if you are interested in the person, step outside the flow of human beings walking. Close your eyes and remember what the person looked like when you saw him or her. Because you have practiced with the plants and the trees, you will be able to remember very well.

This is the best way. That way you do not stare at the person. When you stare at people, they will feel it, even if you are not very conscious. You will feel uncomfortable if someone is staring at you, but you do not know why. Often when you feel uncomfortable like this, even if you are sitting or standing, doing something you enjoy doing, you will get the feeling to move. That is because your instinct tells you "someone is staring at me," and the instinct says that this is not safe. If someone looks at you with compassion, with that heat, the love and warmth that is unconditional, you do not have that uncomfortable feeling. When someone does this, they will usually know not to stare. A glance is sufficient.

Suppose you are talking with someone. Maybe you do not know this person, but you must speak to him. Perhaps you are purchasing something from him, or him from you. Again, glance; do not stare at him if you can help it. If he needs eye contact, look briefly at his eyes and look at what you are doing. But try not to stare unless you have the feeling of warmth and compassion in you. Then you can look at him eye to eye, and any discomfort he has will gradually melt because he will eventually feel safe.

Now, this is not absolute. With human beings there is always the unpredictable element. If you are feeling the warmth and compassion and are looking at someone, and the warmth and compassion begins to go away, then stop looking at her. Look at what you are selling her or what you are buying from her. Don't stare; just let it go. You do not have to know why. *Why* is less important than *what*. After all, to use your joke, if you are in a barrel in a stream approaching a waterfall, you do not need to know why the water falls; you just need to know what to do to get out of the barrel and away from the falls. [Laughter.] *What* is always more important than *why*.

Technological Surveillance and Photographs

What about technological things? Surveillance cameras? Satellites?

A good question. What about these things that are high in the sky and look at people? Oftentimes they are looking at buildings, but sometimes, without any particular need to do so, they are looking with a camera at people. What about cameras in general? A camera is being directed by a human being or by a being somewhere, so it is like staring. You might get this uncomfortable feeling, but you know that no one is staring at you. It could be a camera in the sky or even someone taking a photograph a long way from you, but the camera happens to be aimed at you. If the person were to develop the film and could make a bigger and bigger picture, you might show up on the picture eventually. He did not intend to take a picture of you; you were just downrange from the camera.

These things might also cause you to feel uncomfortable. The first thing to do is to allow your body to move. If you are sitting and your body wants to wiggle about, go ahead and wiggle about. Or do this [rocks forward from the waist].

Rock a little bit.

This allows the body to know that it has the capacity to jump up and move. If there is no harm in jumping up and moving, go ahead. It is always better to honor the body's need to do this. If for some reason you cannot do that or you would rather not, then move about. Maybe your hands will want to do this, as one might move his hands to shoo a fly away. If anybody is passing by, she will assume you are shooing a fly away, so don't worry about what people think. The eye in the sky might affect you, because a being (most likely a human being) is causing it to look at you. Motion can often make you feel better. If you cannot move, then allow the compassion, the heat, the warmth, and you will feel better.

I don't know if I should call it a tribal belief, but it seems that some native peoples have the belief that if you take their picture, you are stealing their soul.

This statement is a nontribal statement but is the best many people have been able to understand. Besides staring at the individual, the camera has a piece of stuff inside it that captures the energy. Everyone radiates energy. It captures the energy of the person permanently or until that photo and piece of material dissolves, is destroyed or returns to the Earth in some way. It does not capture your soul, but it captures a piece of energy that is meant to flow out into the world. This is why many people do not wish to have photos taken.

For example, some of you have gone to places on the land that are very sacred or where the energy feels good. Then many, many people come and take many, many photos. After a while you go there and even at a quiet time there is no energy in the land because the photos have captured so much of the energy radiation that the energy does not feel safe to radiate. The energy from the mountain, say, pulls back, just as you pull back your own energy if you feel someone is draining it. The mountain is no different than humans. It is the same exactly with radiating energy; you will always radiate energy, most of the time anyway. This is an example of something some of you have felt.

What about famous people? People in the news? Perhaps government people or movie stars?

These people—many, many photos all the time. People like this, if they are young, can tolerate it for a while. As they get older, such photo-flashing makes them disoriented, yes. But also, the more people who have photos of you, the less energy you have and the more you feel like withdrawing and the more likely you are to want to find ways where people don't take your photo (this is for the average person). If you make your living having your photo taken, there's not much you can do about that except to feel the compassion and the heat. Then this flows through you and replenishes you, fills you with your natural energy.

There is another thing: This capture of your energy can lead to being shy unless you are very vigorous physically. So my best recommendation for people in the public or people who have lots of pictures of themselves floating around somewhere is to do something that is physically vigorous—if not every day, then every two or three days, if you can. It can be exercise, but it is better if it is something you enjoy doing that happens to be exercise. For some it will be in the water, for others on the land, and for others it will simply be passion or compassion between adults. This will also help because this moves.

Being vigorous moves physical energy, which keeps the stream moving. If you exert yourself, then the energy radiating from all life around you flows through you because you need it and it replenishes you. If you are feeling compassion, the heat, the love, again it's the same thing: the energy flows through you, is transformed, even if it is uncomfortable energy. You do not have to transform it; it becomes transformed. But it is not for you to choose which energy. That which flows through you will choose itself.

That's still photos, but also moving pictures and television?

I have included that.

Your Responsibility for Materialization

Speaks of Many Truths
September 1, 1999

[From a public session in Hawaii.]

All right, this is Speaks of Many Truths. Tonight I want to talk a little bit about some of the agitations you might be feeling.

Mother Earth Can No Longer Resolve Dilemmas of Materialization

I realize that you are feeling these agitations on an unpredictable cycle. The typical cycle would have predictable highs and lows, but now you are feeling things that are curious, meaning you don't necessarily know what to expect when. This is because there are so many people on the Earth now that Mother Earth can no longer resolve even the most minor dilemma of materialization for groups of people.

For a long time, Mother Earth would provide what you needed as an individual or as a group simply on the basis of her own capacities to serve those upon her, just as she has served animals and plants and many beings who have gone before you here. But now you in your time are in finishing school. Some call it creator school, but I like to think of it as finishing school, because you have experienced before this life just about everything benevolent that this universe has to offer.

So when you came here, you had a pretty good idea of how people were supposed to live. But you didn't have too much experience (any of you here) in how people were supposed to live in an agitated society or in a society that was too focused on individuality to realize the bondedness between all beings. So Mother Earth has decided—she does not think but makes decisions on the basis of how she feels—that she will pay more attention to what she needs to do for herself, which I think many of you would feel good about because she needs to take care of herself now.

And because Mother Earth does not see in any way any difference between her physical body (her mountains, her rivers, her streams) and your physical bodies (the material of which she loans your souls to incarnate here), she has simply passed it on to you. This means that you have suddenly . . . within really the past few years, it has been creeping up on you, but suddenly in the past few weeks, you have actually had a dramatic increase in your responsibility for materialization.

It's Up to You to Materialize

Now, when I say "materialization," am I talking about going down to the store to get a loaf of bread and a quart of milk? No. I am talking about causing things to happen either on the basis of their necessity or because you may expect them to happen. This is why it is vital for you now to be jarred into a consciousness—meaning knowing, feeling and even thinking consciously of your expectations. Many of you who are all grown up will have had time to develop certain expectations. Much of this is based on conditioning, what you might expect on the basis of what has occurred since you were young.

But much of it is also based upon the conditioning of the spoken word, which has become more prevalent in your time because of mass communications. So now Mother Earth is doing something that I'm going to call "pulsing." This means that she is sending waves. Picture the waves originating in the center of her being, even though it is not quite at the very center. These waves will come out in a spherical pattern, and they will go through all human beings on the Earth. They will pass easily through animals and plants and so on, because those beings are not here to learn anything but are here to teach you.

But the waves will, when they pass through human beings . . . if human beings have no expectations, which occasionally occurs, especially with newborns, this will pass through those beings as well, just as if they were a plant. But for beings who have expectations (which is the mass of all people here), there will be something that will hit you in that moment like that [claps hands], meaning that you will be going along and maybe things have been fine for a week or so, and you say, "I'm glad that's going well." Then all of a sudden something hits you. It doesn't hit you like a ton of bricks, but it does hit you like maybe one brick.

It doesn't hit you in the head and knock you out, but you feel it. Maybe you have to sit down for a moment and rest and deal with the turmoil. This turmoil is precisely summed up in the word "expectations." It means that there is something within you that is a cynical expectation, which you must be made aware of because Mother Earth has passed on the reins of materialization to you and so it is up to you now to turn the horse to the left or to the right. Do you understand? It is up to you to materialize.

Materialization in this case means perhaps using a living prayer. Say there are people suffering on the other side of the Earth. In days gone by—let's say "years gone by" to give you some context—if people on the other side of the Earth were suffering, you could say a prayer, perhaps at church or some other place, and hope that the best would come of it, if you even knew about it. Or perhaps you might say or do something to contribute to a cause—send money to the Red Cross or something. But now it is required that you *do* something because people are becoming more and more one being as the days go by, becoming unified to the unity of all human beings.

You know that if you've got an itch, you've got to scratch it. If you've got a pain, you've got to do something about it or it might get worse. One being. If people on the other side of the planet—to say nothing of next door—are suffering, I don't care where you are living, you are going to feel it, and it will increase in feeling day by day.

Initiate True Magic: Living Prayer

This has been going on for a little while, but not so long. What can you do about it? Obviously, you cannot put yourself up on the cross and die for the sins of others, as the story goes about the famous magical being—who didn't, by the way, die on that cross, but that's another story. Now it will be necessary for you to initiate true magic. What is true magic? True magic in its most accessible sense is what I call the living prayer [see p. 245].

Let's say that you hear about this terrible earthquake over in Turkey. What can you do about it? Here is a living prayer. You might say out loud,

---
Living Prayer

"I WILL ASK THAT ALL BEINGS IN TURKEY WHO ARE SUFFERING BE ASSISTED BY THOSE WHO CAN HELP THEM THE MOST, THAT THEY BE HELPED TO FEEL NURTURED, SUPPORTED AND LOVED."

Like that—simple. Don't complicate it with details. Then let it go. This does not mean that you don't send money to the Red Cross. You can do that too, but let it go. Don't agonize about it. Don't worry about it, and don't say the prayer more than once. It is like a request.

For those of you who have had youngsters, you know that if a youngster says, "Mom, take me to the circus, please," then Mom might consider that and say, "Okay, honey, when is it coming?" The child says, "It will be here in two weeks," and then Mom says, "Okay, let's write it down on the calendar." But if that same youngster says five minutes later, "Mom, take me to the circus," the more the youngster says that, the less inclined Mom is going to be to enjoy taking her to the circus. Say it once and let it go.

So for the living prayer, say it once. If you want to optimize it, say it in your bare feet out on the land, but if you can't do that, then say it wherever you are. Once only. If you want to say something again, because perhaps you hear about someone at the bottom of a building in Turkey, that there is a tremendous rush to get to that person because people can still hear him or her . . . this person is still breathing and there is a big rescue effort. You can say something for that individual, if you wish:

> *Living Prayer*
> **"MAY THAT PERSON BE LOVED AND FEEL THE SENSE OF IMPORTANCE THAT HE OR SHE HAS IN THE LIVES OF OTHERS."**

You know, you could say, "May that person be rescued," but on the other hand, that may not always be the right thing to say—you have to go by your feelings. But say it once and let it go, because that is all you need to do.

Mother Earth will then be able to do what she does. The souls of all the individuals involved will be able to do what they do. In short, if you think of yourself as an antenna . . . antennae broadcast and receive. Every human being, then, is like an antenna, and you are all connected—now even more than you have been in the recent past, and this will continue to grow in its connection. If you say something like that, to the degree that other souls are willing to cooperate (even though they might not ever hear you or know you ever said it), this makes it more likely that it will happen, because you are all one.

Releasing Cynicism

So these sudden waves, shocks of agitation, are to knock out of your system or to bring to your attention that you are holding within you some cynical belief. And so when you feel that these days, look inside. If you don't find the belief, pay attention to your reaction to conversation, whether it is conversation with an individual, or whether you are listening to the radio or watching the television, anything. Pay attention to your reaction.

Do you have a cynical reaction? If you have a cynical reaction, such as, "Oh sure, they're going to do *that* again," then understand that you need to let that go, because anything you say in living prayer now will be affected by any cynicism you are holding. If you say living prayers for yourself or for your family, that will also be affected. And there is more.

Since all beings around you are learning their version of living prayer or coming more into their capacities for materialization, the energy of materialization is rising around you. As a result, anything you are holding onto . . . and you are holding onto cynicism, not just in your solar plexus, but in roughly the upper half of your solar plexus and about as much of your lower rib cage as your hand covers, right above the center of the solar plexus. You will hold cynicism there.

How will you know physically if you've got cynicism living there? Take your thumb and move your thumb down about one inch below the base of the bone here [at your rib cage] onto the soft tissue of your solar plexus and press in. If you press in about an inch and a half or so and you feel even slight discomfort, there is significant cynicism that needs to be released. If you press in, say, two inches, which is uncomfortable, and you feel some slight discomfort that you didn't feel at the inch-and-a-half level, then there is some subtle cynicism that needs to be released.

So if you press in, say, just a half inch or so and you feel some discomfort, then there is some significant cynicism that needs to be released. Don't beat yourself up about it. Just understand that there is an easy way to do it and there is a hard way. The hard way is to notice every time you say something cynical in reaction to something else or catch yourself thinking something cynical (meaning that the worst will happen)—that's the hard way. That's one way, and it is useful.

When you catch yourself, don't say, "Cancel that." Don't ever say that. Manifestation works on the basis of what goes forward, not on what goes backward. Just say something over again. If you catch yourself saying something cynical, just say, "Oh, but it could be different. Maybe something better could happen." Because you are going to catch yourself doing that, even if you use the easy way.

So what's the easy way? Now we come to the crux of the matter. The easy way is something that can be defined as very vigorous physical activity that you do by yourself—I think you know what I mean—such as running or really vigorous physical exercise or something that I'd like to call "constructive violence." Zoosh has called it this, and so I'm going to use that term.

Using Constructive Violence

What is constructive violence? This is violence that does not hurt you or anyone else, and yet it uses the actual physical actions of violence. I'm not talking about shooting a gun. That is externalized violence, meaning that you do some physical gesture and the violence goes out and happens away from yourself. I'm not talking about that.

Constructive violence always happens with yourself and in your immediate environment. Constructive violence is like this: You might have seen this if you've ever been in a gymnasium where fighters train. They have a heavy bag hanging, maybe someone will support it so that it doesn't swing too much, and the fighters will punch the bag. This is actually constructive violence. Of course, it's also training for the fighter.

Now, most of you can't do this because it's not convenient and you're also probably not in training for the next Welterweight championship. So what you might do is to strike something that is soft—not your companion [chuckles], but something that is soft and giving, and something that is reasonably resilient. So you might, for instance, get yourself set up in a position where you can strike some soft material such as the cushions of the couch stacked up, but get yourself in a position . . . ideally, you will be standing when you are doing this. If you have to, sit down, but it is better to stand because then you can put your legs and hips into the gesture.

You will sometimes see people doing karate exercises, for example, where they will start and then they will move forward, standing, and twist their arm coming out. If you know karate, you can do that, but most of you don't. So get something in front of you that is very soft—as I say, stack up soft objects such as pillows or something—and strike them as violently as you can without actually trying to penetrate the pillow into the wall, okay? No hurting yourself or anyone else.

Another option is to use a stick about fourteen to eighteen inches long and strike a padded couch, but it has to be done like this [makes a forceful movement], and I'd like you to be standing up. I realize that for many of you, this will feel very frightening, but you must be able to tell yourselves rationally—you can use your mind for this—that . . . you can know mentally that you are not hurting yourself and that the couch does not protest because it is not a couch after all (it is what it was originally made up from). And it is better to strike something rather than to do so in the air. You can do so in the air if necessary, but it is better to strike something that is soft.

I'll tell you something: People are actually born with constructive violence as part of their makeup. In my time and in the time of other tribal peoples—I live about 420 years ago from your time—people would dance. They would perhaps dance in some way having to do with before the hunt, but I am talking about children. Children would dance their names. Oh, it's true, a child might have gotten a temporary name that was used to describe him or her when that child was born, or the mystical man or woman of the tribe might have described that child by some temporary name. But once children started to toddle around, then they'd be around other people dancing for one reason or another for some ceremony, and the mystical man or woman would be taking his or her time and looking at the children who would be trying to dance as well.

This is actually a form of constructive violence. But in your time, because so many of you have been raised to feel shy about dancing in public, I have found that this kind of constructive violence I am talking about is better when it is done entirely alone with no one else around—you make sure no one else is around when you are doing it, or if you are outdoors, that nobody is there.

I have found that in your time of extreme individuality—that's the time you are living in—it's easier for you to do this when no one else can see you. But in my time the children would dance in some way. The toddlers, they'd fall down, of course, but that form of constructive violence wouldn't hurt them too much and they'd get back up and try to dance as best they could. Then the mystical man or woman would be able to understand the child's personality, and then he or she would give the child his or her real name. To some extent, even in your time, tribal peoples are still doing this. They might have a name they say—"What is your name?" "Oh, this is my name"—but they have a real name.

You Cannot Hold Cynical Beliefs Anymore

So I'm talking to you about this tonight because it is something that you need to take action on. You cannot hold cynical beliefs anymore. You might be able to indulge in them from time to time, and it will be just like an indulgence. Maybe you have an indulgence of chocolate sometimes or an indulgence in something that you know isn't good for you. Maybe you have an extra glass of wine after you've already had one—that's an indulgence.

Think of cynical beliefs also as an indulgence, albeit an unpleasant one, because this is something you can't do all the time. If you do, you will find that almost immediately after you're hit by that wave, the cynicism will manifest itself in your body in some fleeting way. It will be painful perhaps for a time: "Oh no, not that again," and then it will pass. But it will be there to get your attention, to say, "I can't be cynical anymore." Or in a true manifestation statement, you will say, "I must be more optimistic now."

Don't be afraid of being foolish. You might find yourself in a situation, maybe at the office, where someone else says something cynical. You don't believe it and you didn't say it, but you are within earshot. If you can humorously say, "It could work out better than that," and then just smile and go on, do so. If you cannot say that for one polite reason or another, then say it to yourself, because other people's cynicism can affect you also. So be alert to that, because cynicism in your time has come to be fashionable, and it is an indulgence that you can no longer afford.

You Are Reaching for the Future-Anchored Timeline

Would you talk a little bit about the void space? A lot of people seem to not know what their next step is and they haven't had clear guidance. They are asking for it, but they can't seem to make goals because it's just too hard.

Because it is unseen. Let's use the word "unseen," because you can all appreciate the unseen. Someone stands here and sees a flying saucer, and the other person (maybe even you) stands next to her and doesn't see it and feels kind of slighted. It was to that person the unseen in that moment, because that sight was for the other person next to him or her. Or perhaps your youngster looks up in the sky and says, "Look, a cloud shaped like a dolphin," and you're busy for a moment, but in what seems like two seconds later (which is actually ten seconds later), you look up and nothing, no dolphin. That was meant for your youngster.

The unseen is a practical fact of everyday life. The reason you are not being allowed literally to make fixed plans for the future is that most of you here tonight were born on the past timeline. None of you have been born on the future timeline. But there is an overlap—the past timeline and the future timeline seem to be intersected. This is because you are now shifting to the future timeline.

The reason you are not being allowed to build plans for the future is that your tendency will be—because you have been on this past-anchored timeline—to build those plans from the past, but in fact (since you said it so nicely), it is the void, meaning you cannot see the future. Of course, you can't see the future because you are still standing on the past timeline and you are reaching for the future-anchored timeline, which is much more benevolent and has to do with the true nature of your being. You cannot at this moment quite grasp it, but many people are reaching for it.

Make Plans Based More on Your Feelings

The future-anchored timeline has to do with your true nature. If you make rigid plans today for the future—a three-year plan, a five-year plan, a seven-year plan—you will simply be disappointed. That's all. It is better to make very flexible plans, meaning, "Well, I'll go here and maybe this will happen and maybe that will happen." In short, make your plans based more on your feelings, because your feelings are more likely to give you a connection to the future-anchored timeline than your thoughts.

In the past, in recent years (meaning for the past, say, 150 or 125 years), most people in North America or let's just say in the United States have been focusing on how to create on the basis of one step after another. You do this, and then you do that, and then you build on that, and then you go forward and build on that, and so on. That was all well and good then, but here you find yourself at a gateway. It is easy to think of a gateway as an optional thing, meaning that you can go through this gateway, or if you miss it for some reason, you can go through that other gateway or there will be another one. It is not that way. Now with so many people on the Earth, you need to be able to shift the way things are so that actions and reactions are less impactful in an unpleasant way.

Therefore, the future-anchored timeline, which is anchored in a benevolent future, is coming back—and a lot of you have known that a lot of your future lives are reaching back to help you now, but this is a little different. This is a whole existence that is much more akin to your natural existence and which is reaching back to you now—not to rescue you, but to bring you onto a connection of manifestation that is more benevolent for you. So don't feel funny if you can't stand here—wherever "here" might be for you—and look forward and get some idea of what's coming.

Generally speaking, that will not be possible for a time, even for the most sensitive. I know you are going to ask how long. I will give you some physical landmarks: as you begin to focus more on your physical feelings and what they mean to you individually, and in time, notice how similar physical feelings for other people also mean similar things but are not exactly the same (sometimes there will be complete discrepancies, but that's all right because you all don't have to be the same). You will know when that time occurs, when such note taking as it were, sharing of information, is occurring on an increasing basis, that you will be much more anchored on the future timeline.

But making plans on the future timeline—how do you do that? You don't. Now, on the past-anchored timeline, you've had to make plans because it was like you were walking on a tightrope, and if you didn't make plans, the chances of falling off into something entirely unknown and potentially frightening were very real. But with the future-anchored timeline, you go forward on the basis of your instinct, which is why I have been teaching for quite a while what I call "instinctual-body training," because you have your spiritual body, your mental body, your emotional body and your feeling body, and all these come together and make up your instinctual body.

This Is the Foundation of Instinctual-Body Work

The instinctual you is not rooted in the mind at all. The mind can think about it, but the instinctual you is entirely rooted in the physical self. The reason I have been focusing on teaching so many people for the past quite a few years now to focus on feeling the heat in your chest or in your solar plexus, a physical heat that you can feel, is because this is the foundation of instinctual-body work, as I've said before [for more on the love-heat/heart-warmth/physical-warmth, see Overview].

A deer in the forest maybe wanders into a new part of the forest because of changing weather conditions. Perhaps it has to move off the top of the mountain and come down into the valley, but because of the changing habits of human beings, it has to go into a different valley—there are too many people in the old valley. How do you as the deer find what you need? Food you find by your nose—you smell that. Water? Maybe you can smell it if it is nearby, but if it isn't nearby, then you have to trust in finding it. As a deer, do you simply ask, "Creator, lead me to the water"?

You don't think that way as a deer. You turn your body in different directions physically, and you notice where you have a stronger heat. You need water, so where you have the strongest heat, you walk in that direction carefully, paying attention to where you are going. Eventually you find that water. It works exactly the same for human beings. Human beings have to find water and food too. It can work that way for you. It can lead you to safety. It can lead you to all these things, but it can also lead you to your future.

As you practice this—and I'll teach you more about this as time goes on—you will be able to say it out loud. For instance, if you are a student going to college, you might say, "Would it be good for me to take pre-med, to be a physician?" Then you check in your body—nothing, no reaction. "Would it be good for me to take theater arts?" Nothing, no reaction. "Would it be good for me to study the law?" Ooh, heat. "Maybe I'm going to be an attorney or a judge someday." And that's what you do. This can be used for such decisions, and it can also be used to say, "Would it be good for me to see this movie or that move?" and so on. Simple mundane things: "Would it be good to eat a hamburger or a soy burger?" This might shock a few vegetarians [chuckles], so I'll skip lightly over it. It's a controversial issue.

A Living Prayer to Grab the Future Timeline

And so I say this: If you understand that this time, which could be on an individual basis . . . if you are reaching for that future timeline, it might take two or three months, or for some other individuals, it might be many years. If you can understand that this is the reason you are having trouble building plans based upon past steps, then you won't feel slighted by Creator. You won't feel as though promises were made and not kept. You'll understand that the future-anchored timeline is intended to cause your life to improve profoundly. When you know that, you will feel better.

So how do you grab the future-anchored timeline? I'm going to show you now. For those of you who know how to generate or feel the love-heat inside your chest . . . maybe I better show you. Put your hands together. Rub your fingertips a little bit—just a little bit so that it brings your physical attention to your fingertips. Now relax. Put the same physical attention anywhere inside your chest or your solar plexus area. See if you can generate or notice a physical heat that you can feel. Go ahead—if you like, you can do this. Move your hands around in front of you. Don't touch yourself; just move them around.

I know some of you have found it—go into it and feel it more. Now relax. For those of you who have not found this, don't feel bad. Go home and practice. See if you can do it. It might take some of you longer. Some of you got it right away, and some of you have had the training before.

This is what to do (this is advanced training for those of you who have gotten it): Put your right hand on your solar plexus, whether you are right- or left-handed, and then make this gesture. You'll be reaching out for the timeline like this [see Figs. 50-1 to 50-7]. You can have your left arm anywhere you want it—you can put it in your lap, you can put it on the arm of a chair, whatever feels good. If you put it on the arm of the chair, I do not recommend that you hang it over the arm. Just put it smack in the middle of the arm of the chair. Now reach out like this—not quite in front of you, but at an angle.

What you do is, you say the following once only. And you say this like you are reaching out to grab something:

Living Prayer
"I WILL ASK THAT I BE ANCHORED TO THE FUTURE TIMELINE."

Gradually close your hand and then move your hand slowly toward your body with the intention of getting your hand toward the center of your chest. Close your fist, and while having the heat, pull from there, okay? Pull as if you were making a physical motion. Pull in. Pull. When you have your hand there, then open it up and lay it lightly on

Fig. 50-1. Put your right hand on your solar plexus.

Fig. 50-2. Now reach out, as if to grab something. As you are doing this, say, "I will ask that I be anchored to the future timeline."

Fig. 50-3. Close your fist, and while feeling the heat, pull in from there.

Fig. 50-4. Pull in as if you were making a physical motion.

Fig. 50-5. Continue to pull in toward your body.

Fig. 50-6. Move your hand slowly, with the intention of getting your hand toward the center of your chest

Fig. 50-7. When your hand reaches your chest, open it up and lay it lightly on the center of your chest. Then slide it down so that it is over your solar plexus. Leave it there for five to ten minutes.

the center of your chest. Then slide your hand down so that it is over your solar plexus.

When you get your hand on your solar plexus with your palm toward your body, leave it on your solar plexus for a few minutes—even up to five or ten minutes is perfectly all right. To the best of your ability, do not think. You do not have to imagine what the future is like. If it is possible to stare at an image, say up at the ceiling or something that is completely blank, do that. That will help your mind to not think. If you catch yourself thinking, don't get angry, don't swear at yourself. Just say okay, and that's good; just stay with that. Some of you will feel an energy. If you feel an energy or if you have done the love-heat, the heart-love experience, then it's all right. Some of you may feel that heat, and that's very good. Just stay in the heat and be there. When you do that, you rarely have thoughts anyway. That's it; that's all there is to it. Doing it once is sufficient.

This will help you; it is a way to do it. You can only do the hand gesture that one time. So pick the time and try to pick it when you have really managed to develop doing the heat in the chest or solar plexus. Don't try to move the love-heat around. Wherever you notice it comes up that day, then that's where it is. When it is strong, then try to do this gesture, because doing two things at once is challenging. But you *can* do heat in the chest or solar plexus and pull on the future on the future-anchored timeline.

Don't do this every day. If you have done it, then don't do it again, perhaps, for another week or two weeks. And I tell you this too (this is very important to know): You can do it one time or ten times, but it won't have much more of an effect than the first time. Doing it ten or a hundred more times in only that other way—just pulling from the physical body, the abdomen—might add a teeny-weeny bit more effect. But do it those other times only if you want to in order to encourage yourself. That's all it is really for.

Now, what happens if you do the complete hand gesture again [Figs. 50-2 to 50-7]? Then the effect of what you did the first time will drop by about a third. Actual living prayer . . . why do I call it a living prayer? Because you are a living being. An actual living prayer is done only once. You are saying to all actual magical beings around you of which you are a portion that this is what you need, want or request. Once is enough. If you say it again, then beings around you—which includes every being on Earth connected in that way through here—would think (although it's not thought), "Oh, maybe this is like a prayer one says at a church, so we shouldn't manifest this." It's like that, see? So say it once. That's it.

What if it comes up again spontaneously?

If you do only the first gesture [Fig. 50-1], then there is no problem, but if you do the complete hand gesture [Figs. 50-2 to 50-7], it will drop by one-third.

Is it better to say the words out loud?

Always, because this is a physical world, and in a physical world, that which is done physically tends to be honored physically. Only say things silently, as I mentioned before for other things, such as, "Well, it could be better." You only say that to yourself quietly if it is necessary because of being polite—meaning that you cannot always say . . . sometimes it might be a quiet place and you might not be able to blurt something out loud.

You Must Live in the Present

What is the distinction between living in the future, living in the past and living in the present?

You must live in the present. You live right now in the present; you have no choice. You are not living in the past anyway—those days are gone. The past-anchored timeline is dissolving. That's part of the reason you have noticed that memory associated with the past is very unreliable these days. Either write it down or it is gone. Forgetting birthdays is a regular event, unfortunately. The past timeline is dissolving.

The difference is between a comfortable life, a natural life, which is your nature, and the attempt to control life. To control life is an illusion anyway. As anybody knows, if you have ever lived with someone who is controlling, you can only do so for so long. Often you will experience this as a youngster with well-intended parents or grandparents who will say, "Do this," or "Do that," and after a while, it feels like you've got a blanket over your head and you go through adolescence, which encourages you to develop your own personality so that you will do things your way, largely to get away from that.

The Heat Is Love for You

But I am not saying, "Do this or do that"—although it sounds like it, perhaps. What I am saying is that this is what I see from my perception. So the future-anchored timeline . . . I call it a timeline for the sake of intellectual understanding, but it is actually a heat line. What is heat anyway? It is love. When you do heat for yourself inside, it is you loving yourself physically. You are loved many times. You must learn to love yourself.

When you do this heat exercise in the solar plexus area . . . why here? Because this is the area of nurturing and creation. This is the area of physical manifestation or materialization and creation—that's why. That heat is love for you. It tends to create a better life, from my experience. When you connect with heat, it will be almost impossible not to connect to the future timeline. But say the living prayer out loud so that your mind feels better.

Heat line is love line. It is love for you. Eventually you can get good at this and you can get what is love for others, but work on yourself first. Don't send your heat to others—it doesn't work. They don't feel it that way. They might feel you radiating the heat, not because you are choosing to radiate it, but because love and heat naturally radiate. People who are close to you might say, "Wow, it feels good around you. What are you doing?" and you can tell them what you are doing. If they are very specific in their beliefs politically or religiously, put it in their tongue for their sake. If not and you want to say it your way, then say it your way—whatever is comfortable for you. Say, "It is something you can do for yourself. You might feel it radiating off of me, but I cannot give it to you. You get to give it to yourself."

This is empowering, yes, but it is also about teaching responsibility. In your society, with the best of intentions, almost all of you have been raised to believe that you have responsibilities outside of yourself that are much more important than the responsibility to you, but in fact, that has changed now quite a bit. This is not because you are intended to become self-indulgent or an egocentric individual, but rather because you build a more solid foundation on self-love than you do on externalized love only. How can you give real love to somebody else if you do not have self-love? You know this.

Fear Is Your Friend

As the onion is peeled and we unpeel layer after layer of junk, I personally have been experiencing fears that feel generational to me, almost racial, that predate my physical incarnation here, and this is very strong at times. I'm wondering if you have any insights as to how to get rid of that.

Don't. Fear is your friend, because it points to something that needs to be changed—not dumped, but just changed. If a man knows that he is going to war, if he is a wise man, he will learn how to conduct himself in battle. He won't learn the fine art of negotiation if he is going to be in a sword fight. It might be useful to be able to speak the other soldier's language, but first he must learn how to be a good swordsman.

Fear is your friend. In your time fear has become overly intellectualized, meaning that well-intentioned doctors say, "Let's talk about your fear. Let's talk about this, and let's understand it and confront it, and let's rationally explore it." This is all very useful, but it does not eliminate fear, which is good. We want people to get past fears that do not help them, but the best way to do this is with strength.

Remember instinct. A deer stands in the forest. It is thirsty. Where is water? It turns this way, turns that way. Where it feels the most heat, the deer goes toward the water. What about when the deer turns this way and feels really uncomfortable? You might say now, intellectually speaking, that this is a feeling of fear. But to the deer, it is not fear. To the deer, it simply means that it doesn't feel good that way, don't go that way.

In your time fear is misunderstood. Fear is always a message. If fear, as you say, is generational and has been put upon you or visited upon you by well-meaning elders or others, then you need to say to yourself rationally—you can do the rational process and that's good—things such as, "Well, what if something like that were to happen? What can I do to prepare myself?" So then you do a physical thing. You don't have to necessarily learn how to be a good shot, but some people might have to. A police officer has to learn that. A soldier has to learn that.

But for the average citizen? Maybe you learn about negotiation. Perhaps you learn about how to relate to those people who maybe seem to be a threat or where there are circumstances . . . let's make it simple.

Using Feeling Imagination to Become Big

Let's say, for example, that every day you have to drive back and forth to work, and you have to drive somewhere that is not safe. Perhaps you have to drive over a rickety old bridge or down a road where people are driving way too fast. You have that experience here on Earth very often, where the cars are whizzing past you. "Crazy driver!" you say.

Say you are surrounded by crazy drivers and you are doing the speed limit or less. You feel reasonably safe, but people are whizzing past you and sometimes getting too close to your car or, worse yet, to your bicycle or your motorcycle. You say, "Well, next time I drive on this road, I am going to do something different. People are going to see me." And this is what you do. Yes, you can all do this now—not right at this moment, but you can do this.

Practice this: Sit in a comfortable chair and imagine . . . because to imagine is feeling. You say to children, "It's just your imagination," but "imagine" is the foundation of feeling. Without imagination, love would be traumatic because you would have no foundation, no basis of connection to feeling. But I want you to imagine like the actor imagines when he is trying to convince the acting teacher that he's got it—you know, that he is the tree. Imagine that you are big. Don't see yourself as an elephant, because then you will imagine yourself as an elephant. That is not being big. Imagine yourself being big and expanding. Breathe in and out. Breathe one direction and then another, and get bigger. This is not a visualization; it is physical.

Go into your body and imagine yourself getting bigger and bigger and bigger. Try that two or three times, maybe all in the same night, and say, "Okay, tomorrow when I am driving on this crazy road with crazy drivers, I am going to try doing that—not all the time, because I have to pay attention and I've got to drive and I've got to be in my body." But this kind of "being big" thing can keep you more in your body and make you more alert.

So focus on being big: "I am big." It's not that your car is big, because if somebody hits your car, you will be annoyed and upset and maybe you will have to get it fixed, but so what? But if somebody hits your arm, then it is past annoyance. So it is *you* or *your family* you don't want them to hit in the car. Get big.

Now, what if you have to walk down the street with some people there? You don't like those people too much and they don't like you too much either. Of course, they don't know you and you don't know them. If you got to know them better, then this would probably not be such a problem, but a big city is challenging. So you've got to walk their way, and that's it.

Do the same thing. Big. You'll be surprised how that will help. It will not always help, but most people, believe it or not, are very sensitive.

This is also especially useful for women who walk alone at night to the parking lot. Maybe you sometimes practice being a tiger or a bear—it's much more effective to be big. Someone sees you and says, "Mmm, that purse looks good. I bet it's stuffed with money." Realistically, of course, it has $1.15 in it, you hope. You hope that you don't have to buy gas on the way home. But you are big, so someone looks at you and he or she feels uncomfortable, because even the purse snatcher is a sensitive person.

Purse snatchers, especially criminals who prey on other people, have to have street smarts or instinct to know whom they can grab the purse from and have the person just say, "Oh, dear! Oh, dear!" versus ending up with an eyeful of pepper spray. Maybe you carry pepper spray and it makes you feel better. But practice being big—it's very effective.

The Time of Magic Is Now

Once in a while, something will happen to some of you. You might have a profound experience. You might find when you are being big that suddenly you really *are* big. Maybe you are standing next to somebody and suddenly you see the top of that person's head. That's possible! Remember that the time of magic is now more than ever.

When you are living on other planets, when you are living at a higher spiritual vibration, which is your normal place to live, you have to stretch to come here. You don't have to stretch to go to a higher vibration—that's natural for you. When you are living in those circumstances, get big like that. Speaks of Many Truths says to you, "Okay, class, everybody get big," and everybody is suddenly big, their heads two or three floors up, looking down on top of the building: "Hey, we need more roof here." Just kidding.

But what is now different? The times are different. I share these magical things with you because I am not afraid of you being an ogre and going to school and being big and scaring the other youngsters. I'm not worried about you doing that, because remember, everybody is affected.

In my time we knew . . . and many tribal peoples in your time too and people who are living in a sacred manner, they know that when there is somebody in their midst who is not feeling good, everybody feels a little uncomfortable. Eventually someone says, "Who isn't feeling good?" Someone says, "I've got a headache." Someone else says, "That's all right. Hey you, help that person with a headache!" And someone says maybe, "Here, take aspirin," or something. "Feel better?" "Yeah, I'm better now." "Okay, we all feel better." This is the way it really is too for you now.

Now, simply in these times, becoming more aware of it cannot be denied, and so you must have the tools to know how to deal with it. "Deal with it" does not mean tough it out. "Deal with it" means to take benevolent action that works for you and harms no one. That's what "deal with it" really means.

People Born to the Future Timeline

For some of the souls that are incarnating now, are they in the future timeline?

I tell you that most everybody alive in this room now will in the next three or four years meet people who are born to the future timeline. Those people, they are in it. You could say, "Oh gee, I wish that was for me. That is easy, you know?" But I tell you something: After this life, you are all going to say to one another, "Oh, how did you do it?" "Well, I did it like this." This is more fun—it makes life much more fun.

Life here is very short on purpose because this school is a hard school, a very hard school here on Earth—and I don't mean the school where you go to learn mathematics and history, and learn how to be like everybody else. No, I am talking about Earth school—life. It is very difficult and very challenging. Creator does not allow you to live a normal life span here because it's too hard. A normal life span in other places is 1200, 2500 years, maybe more—that's normal. But here you live maybe a hundred years if you are, what? Lucky? Unlucky? It depends on your point of view.

Practice Being in the Body and Using Your Imagination to Feel

When you say "get big," it reminds me of something that happens to me occasionally when I meditate. I feel like the boundaries of my body drop away and I sort of feel like I'm as big as the room and then as big as the house, and I keep getting bigger and bigger. Is that the same thing you spoke about earlier, or is it a little bit different?

It is similar, but when you meditate, you are not in your body as much, do you understand? You are somewhat out of your body, and so it is a little different. When you are in your body . . . this is something you do in your body: When you are in your body, then you wiggle your feet around a little bit so that you stay in the body. So it is similar, a spiritual version of what I was talking about—meaning an etheric version in that sense.

It is like this: I am feeling big now, okay? I am putting my hands together like this—put them in a neutral position if you like. Breathe in and out of the solar plexus. You can breathe in and get bigger, or you can breathe out and get bigger, either way. Be in the body. If you think you are going out of your body, then wiggle your toes around a little bit and just imagine yourself being bigger. I'll give you an extra exercise on this, but first do this for a moment. Okay, relax.

Now for the extra exercise. Look up at the ceiling. It has contours and shape; it is not flat and smooth. You can see things that definitely would have a specific touch. Don't get up, but reach toward the ceiling and imagine what it would be like to touch some part of it. Run your imagination up your fingers and reach for it. Move your hand along what it is you are touching. Make sure that it is part of the ceiling and not another person's hand, okay? Do that for a bit.

This is like "let's pretend." What does it feel like? You can imagine what it feels like. You have touched things before and you have some idea of what it might feel like. But reach toward it and see if you can almost feel it on the basis of what you imagine it might feel like. Now rest and relax.

Now let's do the big exercise again. This time I want you to try and make yourself big going up vertically, and try to do the same thing. Try to touch the ceiling very gently with the top of your head. What you did with your finger, try to do it with the top of your head. Imagine what the ceiling feels like. Make yourself big. Breathe in and get big, or breathe out and get big—either way. Then gently explore the ceiling with the top of your head. Now relax.

Trying to Make Yourself More Visible

Now, some of you are getting good at this, and so let me say this: If you use this while driving somewhere and a car is speeding, as I said in the example, don't overdo it. Don't try to make yourself as big as the whole highway, because some sensitive people will see something in their paths. What you are trying to do is to make yourself more visible.

Why is that necessary? I'll explain. Because everyone is coming into a greater spiritual fact of life now, as compared to "toughing it out." So people are having unusual phenomena experiences—seeing things that are there but from other worlds, sometimes seeing through things that are there but in this world. Someone comes along and whizzes past your car; maybe a motorcycle or a car comes awfully close to you and maybe actually did not see your car. People crash into each other, and the policeman says afterward to the drivers, "What's the matter? It's pretty obvious that this car must have been there. You must have seen them, yes?" "No, officer, I didn't see that. I didn't see that. Really I didn't." He'll give you a ticket, but in fact, maybe you didn't see it.

So responsibility here appears to be with yourself, making yourself big, but responsibility is also about not making yourself so big that other sensitive people have to crash into a wall trying to avoid hitting the big blob in the middle of the highway that is taking up all the lanes. So try to make yourself no bigger than the car itself, or make yourself bigger maybe up and down, as long as you are not going through an underpass or overpass situation. Do that. It will make no difference if you are big like that—if on a concrete highway, suddenly someone sees a big blob moving above him or her. That is your head being big. They don't see it as a head probably, just a blob. They don't know what it is, or more likely, nobody sees anything, but people have a feeling of it.

Instinct Is about Feeling

Remember that instinct is about feeling. How many times have you had this? You suddenly feel something, meaning that maybe you are walking down a corridor and two corridors meet. You are going to turn right down the corridor, but you don't bump into the person who is coming around the corner because you suddenly get a feeling. You don't know what that feeling is, but you do know that you need to slow down. You slow down and get to the corner where you would turn to walk down the other corridor, and sure enough, if you had been going at the same speed, you would have been sprawled all over the ground with this other person, picking up bits and pieces.

It is instinct. Everybody is getting instinct messages all the time, so I gave you lots of shamanic exercises tonight, some before your time. But it is necessary to begin to give you some samples of these things so that you understand not only your own capacities but what is natural. When you are at a higher dimension in a normal state of being, you do these things without thinking. Here, you are still living in a world of thought. I speak to you in thought phrases.

I spoke to children whom I taught in my time a lot with touch and with my feeling. Then they knew what to do on the basis of feeling, instinct. This was not because we couldn't talk to each other; we had a level of language like you. But when teaching about things associated with feeling, if the person you are teaching is far enough down the road of learning, much can be done without words. You are coming into a time now, future time, the future timeline, where you will find that words only give permission or identify chair from rug, for example. But rationale, analysis, all these things will gradually become part of the past and then no longer what you do. It will be feeling.

Resolving the Unresolvable

This is essential so that you can resolve the unresolvable. For many of you, you have wondered and worried, perhaps, how to resolve the unresolvable. What about the purity of water? What about toxic waste or radioactive waste? These can only be resolved by understanding the way Mother Earth works, what I call shamanic principles or real magic. When you learn about these things, you can calm radiation.

When they dig for uranium, uranium is radioactive, but only so much radioactive. When it becomes plutonium, it is crazy radioactive—not natural radioactivity. It can be calmed by people knowing the proper magical means, but maybe such a person is not available. Then individuals must have the capacity to tap into the wisdom that is available somewhere else.

I give you lessons along these lines so that someday maybe you will know how to tap into wisdom, not only wisdom outside of yourself in spirit, but wisdom outside of yourself that another human being knows. Maybe you'll never even meet that human being, but you'll know how to do it and it will be there when you need it. Good night.

Your Choice: Grief Culture or Heart Culture

Speaks of Many Truths
September 18, 2000

hey said this is where Cook's crew came ashore [in Honolulu, Hawaii], and I figured maybe there had been violence here in the past.

There's no maybe about it. It is a sad thing in your American culture, but European culture is celebrated—even up to and including dramas and British-oriented programs—as if the British had a rich and advanced culture from the past. But if you examine the cultures that were in existence around, say, A.D. 1000 in the Gregorian calendar to 1200, 1300, you will not find in England a culture that anyone would really want to live in, even if you were royalty and rich. It wasn't much fun because they were so . . . regardless that they referred to themselves as being civilized, they were, in fact, so uncivilized. Whereas if you looked at cultures of the world around then, you would easily be able to find cultures much more advanced, much more "civilized"—even much more advanced on the creature-comforts level. It's one of those things.

Naturally, in the U.S. there is great interest in people who explore and find—although from the local population's point of view, Cook did not discover these islands but invaded them. Still, that's another point of view. One might say that from the German point of view, Hitler discovered France, but from France's point of view, you would definitely say that Hitler invaded France. That is well understood in your time, but in the dimmer past, it has become a little heavily romanticized, eh?

Now, one of the most pervasive and dominant day-to-day influences of your culture that is a huge burden to many of you from moment to moment is your personal judgment of your appearance. Do you know, this is another reason why it's good for people to be in Hawaii. You will often see something here in Hawaii that will astonish you. One of the reasons it's good for people to be here is to become more familiar over time with not only the Asian culture's values—and I do not mean scrimp and save and all the common ideas—but also, as a separate thing, Hawaiian values.

The Heart Culture of Hawaii

One of the most startling values one sees in Hawaii is how beloved it is considered, what a wonderful, joyous, heart-inspiring quality one finds in the admiration by many Hawaiian people of those who are big, immense. In popular culture, do you know that in the Japanese point of view, separate from Hawaiian culture, some of the most revered beings (not as gods, though there is some of that, but mostly in popular culture in Japan) are sumo wrestlers? It is considered profoundly attractive. It is not that they just happen to be big. If you are not big enough, as a sumo wrestler, you are considered "less than" in their culture.

But the Japanese culture has not affected the Hawaiian culture; Hawaiians have separately come to believe that the bigger people are often special. Very often Huna women and Kahuna women are big and beloved because of it, never in spite of it. It's a popular culture persona. There's a local TV show—it is a big advertisement, but charmingly done. It is on every day, it's so popular. It's not easy for them to assimilate enough material, since the entire program is based exclusively on restaurants and what they have to offer. It's essentially a big advertisement, but it is very charmingly presented by a brother and sister. The sister is no small person and the brother is gigantic, but he is one of the most locally beloved people—not because he is big and strange but because he is big and happy about it! He freely expresses his joy in food. The most popular and influential local chef is very big; recently he went on a diet to lose weight. His doctor said, "Lose weight now, Sam," and people said, "No, no! Don't lose too much! You lose too much, you won't be Sam Choy anymore!"

So it is a very interesting thing, culture. But the culture that those in the U.S. and other areas were brought up in is a grief-oriented culture. Did you know that? It has been your challenge, many of you, to be born to the grief culture, meaning that everything in that culture is tainted with shame or grief. People in the grief culture almost always feel guilty or frightened to be happy, because they think, "When is the other shoe going to fall?" You recognize that—that is grief culture. But here in Hawaii, native Hawaiian people don't think like that. Not grief culture, happy culture. Poor? Doesn't make any difference. Work hard? Have suffering? Still not grief culture. Big? Like food? Wonderful! Have more, eat more, get bigger! It's not always the healthiest thing, granted, but it's never shameful to be big.

To grief culture, friendship always means obligation. But to Hawaiian culture, friendship always means support and happiness. It's time for many of you to change, not only your mental thought of friendship, but your feeling associated with friendship. Look at your best friends. They are about support and happiness. But you were raised in grief culture, were taught that friendship means obligation (not *told* that friendship means obligation). "Taught" is different from "told"; "taught" means the facts, what happens.

So you know that grief culture is something you are trying to let go of. Disentanglement for you is largely the process of repairing and releasing grief culture from your body, "repairing" in the old meaning of the word. In your time now, repairing means fixing, but in the old meaning, it means releasing. We'll talk today about disentanglement and about grief culture. [For the disentanglement exercise, see p. xxxi.]

But why do you say "Hawaiian" so specifically? Is there any other term than "Hawaiian"? Grief culture is the United States—but is it Hawaiian and all native cultures? "Hawaiian" seems so localized, so narrow.

You wish to be accurate? I am saying this, not you; therefore, other people can say, "Oh well, there's this culture and there's that culture, and they're so happy and so wonderful." Contemporary society in the United States is predominantly affected by the manners and mores (or so scientists say) of those people who were kicked out of Europe—Calvinists and so on—but also by contemporary European culture. I grant that there are other cultures that at their roots are much happier—Cuban culture, much of South American and African culture, even places of the European culture that are better, New Zealand, Australia, all right? But I talk about the United States, and it is predominantly affected by those who were kicked out of some of the better countries in Europe (a famous play on the words of the line of the famous army movie [*Stripes*], the famous comedy; watch it, very funny), but also by European culture in general.

Now the European culture is predominant. Most European cultures, even if they are cheerful, wait for the other shoe to fall. Hawaiian culture does not have that at all; it allows for that, but it does not have it. It is not Pollyanna, always cheerful, but it is as close to that as it can be. Pollyanna is a Nordic kind of myth, but it is the wish, hope, dream of Nordic peoples, you understand, or ascribed to Nordic peoples.

But Hawaiian culture is fact. That's part of the reason why when Europeans invaded the Hawaii islands, they were—and there are no better words to describe it—enchanted with the local people, even though they were cruel to them. Is that not a paradox, that you could be enchanted with people and yet be cruel to them at the same time? Cruelty was cultured into the invaders; they came from a grief culture very powerfully influenced by the Church at its worst. The Church can also be at its best, but even at its best, in your time it has an underlying grief culture.

Grief Culture and the Church

It is not my intention, though, to say that it must be that way. If you want to find the best potential model for Christian religion in your time, go to a happily practiced Christian church entirely run by and completely focused in Hawaiian culture—not just Polynesian culture, but native Hawaiian culture and people here in Hawaii. If you can, just for fun, find something like that; it won't be easy. Very often there will be Christian guilt thrown in there.

What can you say about a religion that holds, as one of its role models, guilt, original sin, suffering for the benefit of all people—in short, grief. Grief culture is not only rooted in Christianity, but it is certainly one of its foundations. So Christianity needs to change in order to survive. I speak now only to Christian hierarchies: Do not be jealous of cheerful cultures. Look at them, not just for their value in business terms as you have done, but look at them as being genuinely valuable in terms of your own redemption. Jesus was almost always cheerful. Jesus did not encourage people to be serious. Your culture has brought out that he was serious. This is a complete falsehood. I am not blaming you contemporaries; it has been presented to you as a fact. But rarely are images of a happy Jesus shown to anyone but children, when in fact it was his nature to be happy, cheerful— to expect the best and with the best humor accept the worst and go on.

In short—speaking to contemporary cultures—looked at from my point of view, including that of my own people, the Hawaiian culture of native people is the most sterling example in your time of readily accessible cultures for you to emulate. There are other cultures that are cheerful, but not many. And they are not readily accessible, whereas Hawaiian peoples, even though they have much cause not to, are still welcoming with open hearts visitors from other places. Hawaiian culture has mastered feminine-warrior wisdom, which knows how to have an open heart and be vulnerable and be safe. I said a long time ago, and other beings through Robert also have said (but I started this for them), that the way to resolve inner strife and outer strife is through feminine-warrior wisdom. I say that, and then people say, "What is that?" I will say more about that later; I will say only a little bit now.

Hawaiian culture is very unappreciated in your time. Oh, on the surface it's appreciated: "Aren't they charming? Aren't they beautiful? Aren't they cheerful? But . . ." I speak to Christian leaders of your time and I include Jewish leaders and Islamic leaders. This is most important, because of all the religions of your time that are affecting your world, it is these three religions. Yes, Jewish people do not often think of themselves this way because they do not go up and say, "Join this religion." Islamic people don't think of themselves this way, but it is true for you a little bit too. Christian people, you know it's true about you [chuckles]. You want to bring Christianity to the world in a cheerful way, but you want to bring Christianity to the world in whatever way works. This is deep in Christian culture. Even contemporary Church leadership knows that terrible mistakes were made in the past about this and is trying to make up for it today. But it cannot make up for it without changing your own hearts.

Bring Your Open Heart to Hawaii

Feminine-warrior wisdom is epitomized by native Hawaiian culture—"culture of aloha," as it is called. Seek no further; don't try to study it under a magnifying glass. If you must, read a book about it, but don't read a book written by anyone other than a native Hawaiian person from this culture. If you try to read about it from other people writing it, it will be full of judgment. If you try to read about it even from a native Hawaiian culture person, there might be some well-intentioned finger-pointing, even from "feminine-warrior wisdom" people.

But if you come over, Christian leaders, don't bring all your trappings. You don't need anything fancy; just dress plain. Buy a Hawaiian shirt, maybe, or a dress. Don't insinuate yourself into the culture, but go to places where Hawaiian people might be—not just a cultural center, but also festivals, places where people gather. If a Hawaiian person says to you, "There's an event going on. Come to this. You will like it; be sure and come and see me too," do it. Don't just go with a notebook, a clipboard [chuckles], and make notes. Go with as much an open heart as you can assemble. If you are open to it, do disentanglement for at least three months first. If you are not open to disentanglement, bring as much of an open heart as you have and be prepared to do as much dancing as you can, dancing that is cheerful, all right?

Dancing a cheerful dance is the next best thing to preparations for disentanglement. It is not necessarily disentanglement itself, but if you are not open to disentanglement, do a happy dance. You will feel a little better. You don't have to be a Church leader to do this, but look at your religion; it might bring you joy. Look at your religious history honestly, not just written by Church members but by others. Don't dwell on it; just glance at it. If it is painful, just glance—don't dwell but take note of it. Because as you know, the roots of a culture not only speak of its image but provide the stories, which are then popularized, that create the values of contemporary culture, not only past values. Even those of you in what I call advanced Christianity or advanced contemporary religion who are trying to create benevolent Christianity, you do not have to discard Christianity but change the symbol.

I have seen the contemporary Christian symbol; try to make a better one than this. I realize that this contemporary symbol is an attempt to improve the Christian point of view—a heart with a cross in it. But I recommend that this be the contemporary Christian symbol: the heart. I do not expect you to embrace this in your lifetimes, but examine it and begin. I'm not saying I am the enemy of Christianity; it is because I am your friend that I want you to be happy and give the gift of the beauty of your religion to your children and to your children's children. There are stories about Jesus and his teachings that are of great beauty, if not in your own Bible exclusively, then in other books. You can find them if you look. Just remember, he was cheerful in his nature. If you want to study his actual nature, his actual day-to-day personality, don't bring a magnifying glass. Bring your open heart to Hawaii and try to make friends with the native Hawaiian peoples.

The Heart-Centered Energy of the Hawaiian Land

You said that heart culture was just Hawaiian, not Polynesian and all native cultures. Yet just a few hundred years ago, these islands were invaded by Polynesians who either killed or assimilated all the people who were here and settled here. Why are they now different here than their Polynesian ancestors and/or contemporaries?

The energy of the land here is very heart-centered.

So the Polynesians were transformed by coming here?

From where they came, yes, to come here. But as you say, what happened to those warriors who came and took over from those people who were here? They stayed, developed culture here. Some of them did, anyway—stayed and developed culture, brought their own people over. But they were tempered by the land. A local important goddess here creates land—the fire goddess, Pele. It is not a fire god; it is a fire *goddess*. This means that man can help to bring about birth, but woman always gives birth. If land is created here by the fire goddess—it must be a woman, it cannot be a man. No man of human Earth origin gives birth to a baby. This is a basic, obvious thing, but often in contemporary culture, the basic and obvious is obscure, and the more fine points, as you say . . . *that* is taught. The difficult analytical things . . . *that* is taught, often because these philosophies are from points of origin in Europe.

But look at native peoples all over the world. They will always have basic, obvious things at the roots of their culture, whether it is grief culture or joy culture or anything in between. They've managed to retain clarity, for the most part—very important in these times when one needs to discover, practice, appreciate and embrace common ground for the sake of necessary unity. In this time of terrible weapons, you must be able to look across the fences and borders of countries, yes, but even neighborhoods, even next door, and see what you have in common with your neighbors, whether your neighbors look like you or not. If you can see much in common, then you have a very solid foundation for friendship.

In short, business relationships and tolerance is not enough when terrible weapons exist. This is because human beings will get angry and upset sometimes. If the worst weapon is something that is not too awful, meaning a rock or a club . . . that can be terrible, but it will not wipe out life on Earth. But if guns, bullets, bombs, big bombs, chemical weapons and biological weapons exist, they can wipe out life as you know it. You must be able to see your neighbor, the person over the border, the person in another neighborhood, primarily for your common ground first. So solutions can come from feminine-warrior wisdom only.

Look to Feminine-Warrior Wisdom

Feminine-warrior wisdom at its root is knowledge and understanding of all practices of war so that war can be avoided. That's at its root of knowledge, meaning mental knowledge practiced through the physical, which makes it wisdom, but also strength and the core of feminine-warrior wisdom—heart, happiness.

Think how many times in your own life or the lives of others you have stubbed your toe or you have hurt yourself: "Ouch, it hurts!" Talk to ambulance people, doctors, nurses, therapists, New Age practitioners, healers, and there is one thread: They will all have stories about this; they've all met patients and people they work with who, in the face of the suffering these people had to deal with, could laugh and make a joke. That tells you something. You can stub your toe or hurt yourself—ouch! Shortly thereafter, if you make a joke or laugh if you can, even through tears or pain, then you feel better! There is great value in happiness. But in grief culture, it is analysis: "Why did this happen to me?" Obligation: "What do I have to do about it?" Blame: "Whose fault is it?" Action: "What can I do to get back at them?" That's grief culture.

This is important for many of you personally because of the challenge of being born to grief culture. I know, people can say to me, "Speaks of Many Truths, I was born into a wonderful, happy family. I've never known Christianity as anything other than joyful"—or Judaism or Islam, beautiful religions, all of them. I agree, they are. But they have a past. And even in contemporary times, there are people, because they were born to grief culture, who say, "My way is the right way." This is not only nationalistic but has roots in religion. Find feminine-warrior wisdom; it has roots in heart, and heart has roots in all life.

Hate has roots only in stories related to grief culture. You will find angry Hawaiian people, of course. But the basic Hawaiian culture is cheerful. You will find cheerful people from all cultures—Cuba, Italy, France, yes [chuckles], Norway, Scotland, yes, Russia, very much yes. Yes, poverty does not require misery. It can if the culture is grief culture, but it does not require it. You will not find that many native Hawaiian people are very rich; more often they are poor, as with other cultures. But land and feminine-warrior wisdom combine to create heart culture.

A Portal to a Project

Speaks of Many Truths
June 11, 2001

his is Speaks of Many Truths

The Portal Is Opening

There is a portal at this time, and in fact, the portal is opening. It is a portal that will allow certain souls incarnated on Earth now to exit before their time. Many have already done so. This does not mean that anyone should be alarmed that they are going to die unexpectedly, but if it happens, I will say this: It will be quick. It's not about a lingering death, it is sudden, and for the most part, you will not see it coming. But after it happens, you won't have to worry either that you will be stranded here in some spirit form.

Let me tell you what this is about: Before incarnation, for the last thirty to forty years, there has been available to some souls—not all—an opportunity to exit from the planet at a predetermined time, which is now . . . and for a while yet. I will say how long soon. This is the soul and the complete self, meaning that the walk-in situation, as it has been referred to before by the famous lady [Ruth Montgomery], is not the case here. This means that the body will not be left to have another soul walk into it and to continue life. [See *Walk-Ins and the Explorer Race*, available in 2006.]

Now, this opening is going to a specific place. There is a project—amongst many projects, yes?—that is requiring more souls of a certain nature. These souls do not always demonstrate these qualities in the personality, but sometimes they do. And you will be able to, as a surviving relative, should you read or hear about this, identify easily the qualities I mention in your loved ones. A moment.

Now, the most striking one of these qualities is a certain innocence. Innocence is expected in a child, so for those who are children, that quality will have been obvious. But it can also be seen sometimes in adults. Sometimes you will refer to it with the French term, naiveté, but it is other things. Sometimes it is expressed as a quality whereby one is open with the fact of being surprised, rather than trying to suppress it for any reason. There are other qualities, one of which is an overt heart-to-heart friendliness. And a third quality I will mention, though there are others, is that when there is anger in the individual, it is quickly expressed and then it is gone.

I am not saying that many people do not have these qualities; what I am saying is that these three qualities will have been in those souls and may or may not have been noticed by the family or loved ones. There were certain other qualities, in the case of those who have moved on, and of course, there are certain qualities in those who are still present. It is not a requirement, but for those of you interested in such statistics, there is about, at this moment, a 20 percent chance that this will happen to those souls who have included this as an option in their lives.

Now, this will expand. I don't want you to be frightened. Remember, when you move to the other side, it is a very benevolent place. Even though humankind has dreamed up, for various reasons—often many of them good reasons (although it may not have worked out to be good, they were often good reasons)—many philosophies about what's on the other side: terrible things and so on. But, in fact, it is all benevolent. It won't always feel benevolent, because of the nature of what will be discussed with you as a soul with your teachers and other beings, but there is no torture and suffering. These are themes that have been promoted by various religions, often for good reason. Sometimes the reason became political in the religion, but it started for a good reason.

Yet I am not here to rationalize the philosophies of man. Rather I would say that when these people move on, should some of them do so, that they will move on in a gradually increasing rate, because the portal is opening. Just now it is opening. It has been—how can we say?—in the early stages of opening for about the past six or seven months, and it will continue to open and reach its fullness of opening in about three-and-a-half years, after which time it will close more quickly than it took to open completely. After three-and-a-half years, it will close completely in about seven to eight months.

This Project Will Balance the Pain of Prejudice on Earth

Now, the project that these souls are working on when they go to the other side requires recent Earth experience. Working together with three and occasionally five teachers and evolved beings, these souls will form a certain harmony, which will balance—I realize I'm being vague here—certain difficulties on Earth. In time Zoosh may perhaps provide more details, but not at this time.

These difficulties are no more extreme than anything that has been around in the nature of humans for some time, but they will come to a head sometimes in inexplicable ways. The difficulties I will speak of, I will describe a little bit in detail so you can recognize this, and that is prejudice—prejudging, in this case, individuals because they are a portion of some racial or nationalistic or political group. There have been some shocking versions of this in the past—and in the present, I might add—but gradually people are beginning to realize now (and I hope religions will support this, as they sometimes have in the past) that if any of you are suffering anywhere on Earth, that it affects you all.

That is why sometimes—and many of you have noticed this, and that's another reason I'm bringing this up—you will wake up after an otherwise good sleep and feel uncomfortable for no apparent reason. Perhaps even you will wake up with a discomfort, maybe like a muscle pull or something like that, for no apparent reason. I grant that if your sleep were photographed, that perhaps an apparent strain on part of your body would have been obvious. But that's only part of the time. Most of the time, it won't be the least bit obvious and would be fairly baffling to any scientific observer. But it won't be any worse than any other discomfort you've ever had—after a few days, it will get better.

These things happen, not because you are being punished or singled out, but because you, as part of another group of souls, which is much more frequently found—70 to 80 percent of the human race at any given moment has this option in their soul existence—you will, if necessary, take on the pain of others, especially if it's too much for them to bear. You, of course, do not take that all on from one individual, but rather you take it on generally from the population at large. And you don't have to take on a lot; you just take on a little. When that happens, many, many thousands of others are also taking on a little, and it removes some of the burden of pain from others who have too much.

Now, I'm not talking about people in pain because of disease or even terminal disease or injuries such as accidents, but rather about people who are suffering because of being perceived as wrong or bad, just for existing. So you understand what I am saying is that fully 50 to 60 percent of this pain that you take on is the result of prejudice, although it may not seem to be such a terrible thing, to even be slightly prejudiced and to say certain people are like this or like that. One of the more common prejudices that comes in the form of jokes, for instance, that one finds pretty much globally, according to the structure of modern societies, is to put down, as you say, the tax people, with the casual overlooking of the fact of what the taxes support—not just government salaries, but most often government programs, and those programs are very often intended to help its citizens.

Even though it does not always work out that way, that's the intention.

I'm not here to say that this group is better than that group. What I'm here to do is to remind you how your activities, which are ingrained in you very often from childhood, will cause pain to others, and that pain will sometimes be felt by you or your loved ones. You know, it's an interesting thing, one might say, that this kind of pain is something you can tolerate—you can put up with it. As some might say, you can take it. But it's never intended for you to feel any pain at all, with the possible exception, in your current society, of the pain that you feel before death—but this pain actually escorts you, helps you to find your way out of the body. Pain is not the enemy; it is a teacher. I believe I have said something about this before, as have other beings through Robert as well and most likely many other beings in many other ways.

So the reason I am coming through to speak to you about this matter today is that this portal is opening, and I feel that the specific facts of it are good for you to know. It may not help you to feel any better at the loss of a loved one, or even at the loss of more than one loved one. But if you can understand the situation, sometimes it helps.

A Living Prayer for Taking on the Pain of Others

Now, how about some homework? Normally Zoosh does this, but I know that some of you might like it. If you ever wake up or suddenly, for no apparent reason, feel a pain and cannot think of any reason why that would happen, don't assume that it is only something that needs to be cared for by a physician. Yes, by all means seek out that treatment if you feel you want to or need to—this is not to discourage you from doing that or finding any therapeutic assistance. But when the pain first comes on, especially when it is slight—that's when to notice it, when it is not very strong and you're first noticing it—say these words, if you would, or something like it. But the reason I put these words in this form is that these words will help, if you are taking on the pain of others [for more on living prayer, see p. 245]. Please say,

> *Living Prayer*
> "MAY ALL THE BEINGS WHO NEED HELP RECEIVE
> THE HELP AND LOVE AND NURTURING THAT THEY NEED
> FROM ALL THE BEINGS WHO CAN HELP THEM."

That's it. Try to say that out loud—just that line. It is a prayer; it includes all beings, meaning spirit and form: human, plant, animal, all kinds of beings, regardless of whether they're the ones feeling the pain or the ones who can help. It's a living prayer; it is, as you like to say, nondenominational. But when you ask for that, it allows and supports much help to go to those who may not know how to pray.

You see, sometimes people will feel this pain or be suffering and not believe in God or religion anymore. Perhaps their life has become so miserable that they have given up on God or given up on Spirit, depending upon their training and conditioning as a youngster. And sometimes they just don't know about it. If you say this living prayer in this loving way, it can help them and support them, because you are doing what you can.

Don't say this as words that you mouth. I think that your religions of today have not stressed that point so much. When you say a prayer, you have to put your feeling behind it—not just your need, but also your good heart behind it. You know, if someone tells you . . . when you go somewhere, if someone says, "Welcome," with no meaning to it at all, just the word, "Welcome," you may not feel welcome, or maybe just a little bit. But if someone says, "Welcome!" [uses a very warm tone] with feeling, and you can feel that he or she means it, regardless of the way you respond to it, you can tell the difference.

It's the same thing with prayer. Say it with feeling and mean it, even just in that moment. And after you say it, let it go. For some of you, the pain will greatly decrease. For others, if the pain stays, then make sure you see someone to help you, if you feel that is needed.

You Can Change Your World!

I mention this now because it's important for you to know your abilities. These are not abilities that are new; these are old abilities. But because you are coming into a time—you're really in it now, in the early stages—of greater responsibility, greater trust and greater faith . . . it's not necessarily that you feel that right away, but Spirit, Creator and other beings are giving you more responsibility for your creations, your world, because you can, using methods like this, change them. You can change your world and make it better.

I will talk to you more about these matters from time to time as other things change and develop, such as portals and other things that are topical. But I speak to you of this matter now because I feel that you can change your world in ways that might surprise you and even improve the quality of life for you, your loved ones and also people and beings whom you may never meet. Isn't that wonderful? And that change can be good for you all.

One of the Most Important Tools You Have Is Pain

When people come here to Earth, one of the most important tools they have is, yes, pain. It is not a fun tool, but it does let you know that you're doing something that needs to be changed: to do it some other way, to ask someone for help or, in the case of extremes (meaning the pain one has before death), that you need to be elsewhere. And it takes that kind of pain, sometimes, to get you out of your body.

This is the pain that soldiers have on the battlefield and other places. That's why if you know any soldiers or if you've been one yourself, you've either experienced mystical things, things you've seen or felt, or you've heard about them from others. In your society, one does not always talk about such things openly. But many of you know, who have been in these military professions, what I'm talking about.

So you know that pain is normal, always—for the most part not necessarily welcome, but part of life. But if you can accept that and know that it's true, then I must tell you that those amongst you who are focused in their feelings, know them, work with them . . . people like this are sometimes called sensitives. But not all sensitives are conscious of being sensitive and are consciously working—doing, as it is sometimes called, their inner work, but also perhaps in application, doing other things with feelings.

How to Let Go of the Pain of Others

Sometimes you will look at people, places or things, and feel pain. If you can, immediately expel it from yourself and then say a prayer—a living prayer would be best. You can say a living prayer, such as the one I gave earlier:

Living Prayer

"MAY ALL BEINGS WHO NEED HELP RECEIVE HELP, LOVE AND NURTURING FROM ALL THOSE BEINGS WHO CAN HELP THEM."

Say that, and let it go. You don't necessarily have to look in the direction where you felt the pain; you don't have to think about it. Just say it, and let it go. Say it once only. Granted, you will be saying this prayer many times for different circumstances, but for each event or each time you notice it, say it once and let it go.

When you feel that pain in your body as a sensitive, that's what you need to do. But I recommend to try and blow the pain out first, meaning feel it and then [blows out through his mouth] blow out from that part of your body, as a yogic practitioner might do. You feel that part of your body, and you expel the breath from that part of your body. You can check this with practitioners; there are other more mystical aspects of yoga. Then say the prayer, and go on.

If you do not believe in such things, say any kind of prayer that you feel good about, and do try to remove the pain from your body in some way. Don't assume it's your own. If you keep taking in pain from other people—and that's the purpose of this little talk—you can acquire illnesses. That's why soldiers are trained to be steel-minded or steely-minded—but actually it's steel-hearted—so you don't take in other people's pain, which you are often inflicting yourself. That is very difficult, especially if one goes on with life, as many soldiers (to say nothing of soldiers' spouses) know about. These levels of pain are often processed in dreams, and sometimes it takes a long time to resolve it in that way. There are other quicker ways to resolve such things, and if any of you out there, readership, are soldiers or are living with or married to one or want to pass this on to military or former military, write a letter to the editor, and I will give an elaborate homework assignment for that.

Pain from Others, Anger and Pollution Can Result in Cancer

Now, one of the diseases that is most common as a result of taking in pain from others and not having a means to expel it . . . as you know, those of you who have been reading these books for a long time, disentanglement is my recommended way [see p. xxxi]. But one of the most important diseases of your time is cancer.

Cancer can be caused by many things—sometimes it is biological, but most of the time it has to do with misdirected anger. Anger is very misunderstood in your time. Sometimes it is caused by depression, which is also a form of misdirected anger, and other times it is caused by taking in the pain of others. Because there are so many people on your planet now, this is something that is almost hard to avoid, whether you're sensitive or not. And of course, another common way that cancer develops or is nurtured, let's say—if we can apply that term to cancer or disease—is through pollution. Those are the three major ways.

THE ANGER EXERCISE: A MODIFIED VERSION

Isis

A good modified form of the anger exercise would be to do something not unlike actors might do as training—meaning you have to feel it as much as possible. Imagine you are trying to convince a producer or a director who is checking you out for a performance that you can do it, because that person will have to be convinced that you mean it.

This is something you do entirely on your own without anybody else present. I do not recommend doing it if others are present unless they are doing it also at the same time, but I only recommend that in circumstances where you cannot get away from each other, such as in prison, and then only if the two of you desire to do this at the same time. For everyone else, try to do this on your own in your own space, or possibly out in the woods or someplace out in the open where you can do no harm to others and where no harm will befall you.

If you want to do this outside, bring along a friend who can stand off a hundred yards or so away to deflect people from coming your way. If you want to do it indoors, do it in a room where no one is likely to come into that room for at least an hour or two hours afterward. It would be better for there to be a six-hour gap. If it is a place where a dog or a cat must come in, I recommend that you do not do it there.

Now, the performance, or real thing you feel . . . I'd like you to get very angry. I know this is a contradictory thing for you. Most of you have been taught to control yourself at all costs or you might look foolish or some other thing, and although that might be appropriate in some societal situations, for the sake of this exercise, it is not appropriate—although you do not have to throw things, you do not have to break things. Imagine—some of you may have seen such a thing—a child having a temper tantrum. The child might yell and scream and jump up and down or lie down on the ground and hit her fists to the ground and so on. You don't have to do that either. You don't even have to get up if you are unable or have difficulty in moving.

The process is to shout, but you're going to whisper—you see? You put all of your effort and all of your feeling into shouting, but you whisper. This is why it's a mild form of the anger exercise. You whisper, but all the passion is there. Just think of something or someone you're mad at. The purpose of the exercise is to express the energy so you can release it and you do not bind it to you where it can give you constant discomfort.

Do this no more than three times a week—expressing your anger so you can say anything you want about the person as long as it is whispered and done with passion. You see, in order to truly express even this mild form of the anger exercise, you need to release; it's all about releasing physically. If you can get up and move around, then if you want to, jump up and down or wave your arms or legs—that's all right. If you can't get up for any reason, then move around as much as you can or shake your fist. But if other people might come into the room, then try to do it at a time when it's least likely that they would. Tell people that from time to time you may be doing the anger exercise, but it does not mean you are angry at them.

Remember, whisper. You can say anything you want about anyone as long as you whisper it passionately. You will know when you have let go of this energy that might harm you by holding anger because you will be able to say a person's name—or an event's name or a place or an object, anything—you will be able to say it and the energy, your physical feeling you had once, will either be greatly diminished or you will feel nothing. This will let you know that you have let go of that energy about that.

This is a well-established procedure. Psychologists often give an exercise like this, or more often counselors do. There are even instruments, objects, padded sticks that are sometimes available in sporting goods stores for the purpose of hitting someone or something without causing any harm. They're sometimes sold as toys. I do not know the name of these things, but some people might. If you know a counselor or someone like that, that person might know.

So to put it simply, this modified form of the anger exercise is designed to allow you to release energy that you are holding that might be causing you to feel uncomfortable or ill at ease and restricting your happiness in your life as you live in your world.

Anger, you know, has always been a way to transform such things. Zoosh talks about benevolent violence, meaning violence that does not harm anyone, including yourself. Zoosh talks about the anger exercise as this kind of thing. But what I'm going to suggest is dance.

Dance the Dance of Your Feelings

In your time dancing is very popular. Oh, granted, certain steps and certain music are usually traditional with it, but I think it would be better to dance the dance of your feelings, not in a self-destructive way, as Zoosh calls it, but rather if you can do a dance that is feeling-oriented—and as you know, "self-destructive" as Zoosh defines it is harming yourself or someone else, because you are all part of the same being, it's just not always obvious. You can have drums beating if you like, as some people did in my time. You could have a fire going, if you want to do that—some people in my time believed that this helped with transformation. You can do it at night—other people in my time believed that when the Moon was bright, you could do this, and the light of the Moon would help to transform your pain and inner feelings that were unsettled and needed physical transformation. And there are other ways.

I don't recommend using your music of your time, because it often has words that are either commercially oriented or are going to inflict certain feelings in you. And here's something that many of you may not know, but it is common: It doesn't matter what language the words are in; your feelings will understand what the words are about, or if not literally, what feeling is associated with those words. So be aware of that.

You might listen to music in a foreign tongue sometime and feel joyful, and then you might suddenly feel, for no reason that you can understand, sad or unhappy. That's because of the feeling stimulated in your body by the words or, to be more specific, because of your feelings reacting and creating physical feelings in your body in reaction to the words—otherwise known as feminine strength. Feminine strength has to do with perception and reaction; masculine has to do with vision and action. These are not the only qualities associated with feminine and masculine strength, but I'm just putting them in here so that you will know and think about it.

Now, I realize I'm covering a lot of things, and I know that the questioning process will bring out more clarity here. But I'm mentioning this now because I feel that cancer and other diseases that seem to be growing . . . sometimes the growths will seem to jump right out of your body. They don't always grow in—sometimes they emerge through the skin and grow out. You could ask, reasonably, why this is such a prevalent disease in your time. I feel it's important to discuss this. And why do these growths jump out of your body?

Even that is a message saying that when you do a dance based on your feelings . . . you might be jumping around and not necessarily following steps in a dance, a dance-hall dance. When you're jumping around, allowing your feelings to express themselves in a dance like this, a dance of the feelings, what happens is that the energy in your body associated with these feelings . . . not only associated with the present of these feelings, meaning what has stimulated these feelings in the present or most recently, but also with the past. If these feelings have any residuals, they settle into your muscles, and if there's a lot of it, it will settle into your *bone marrow*. Those of you who understand about cancer will know that that's an important clue. I've discussed it before, but I'm mentioning it again because in your time it is so very important.

The Easiest Means of Resolution Is Disentanglement

So to continue, the necessary means of resolution . . . I feel that the easiest means is disentanglement. Remember to ask the gold lightbeings to disentangle you. And please include in your asking of the gold lightbeings: "Also, please disentangle me from any pain I might be feeling that belongs to others and can be processed only by them." Say it exactly like that, verbatim. And it will help; it will remove a lot of pain that you cannot process.

I grant, earlier I talked about how you tend to, as the human race, process sometimes in small quantities the pain of others, but this is different. As you can see, a lot of this discussion of these two particular subjects is about pain. It's an important subject in your time, because there are so many people, and the more people you have in a given space, the more different types of pain you will feel. The more you understand pain and know how to work with it, the more easily you can accommodate its message. And that's what it is, a message, before it turns into something really uncomfortable.

The Purpose of Pain Is to Be Noticed and Acted Upon

Do you know that other than trauma-caused pain, which often leads to death, that the purpose of pain is to be noticed when it is very slight and to be acted upon then? It's not intended that you suffer miserably. That's knowledge and wisdom that has been misunderstood or lost in your time, and that's why I'm talking about it, because it's so important. If you can act on it with your feelings when you feel it, you can process a lot of stuff for yourself and improve the quality of your life. And as you learn how to work with pain in ways that support and nurture life in yourself, so in time will you be able to share this with others. So do work on it; don't worry if other people are teaching with it. You might be able to add something to the body of knowledge that will help, support and nurture all life. Won't that be wonderful?

Compatibility and Compassion

Speaks of Many Truths
June 12, 2001

ll right, this is Speaks of Many Truths.

Compassion Is Pointing the Way to Resolution

Now it's time to talk about empowerment once again. Many of your societies on Earth have attempted to avoid pitfalls—from their point of view, pitfalls of passion. Sex got caught up in this because of religions, because of the point of view of religion. But what they were really trying to avoid were passionate outbursts that lead to violence, as all religions and most philosophies know, to say nothing of the average person. And yet what happened, with the best of intentions, was that the empowerment of feelings was overlooked here.

Understand that the way Robert [the channel] is able to move storms when he desires to move them—and by that I mean deadly storms, hurricanes—is because in the moments he's detecting a storm on the television or computer screen, Robert is completely compatible with Earth and the storm's acceptance (as a portion of Mother Earth's body, which is the storm) to move in one direction or another. From Robert's point of view, this is hopefully away from land, where the storm is likely to inflict harm and damage. But the connection between Robert and Mother Earth in that moment is not only compatibility, it is also total and complete compassion for each other in that exact moment of detecting, followed by . . . if the storm is, for instance, accepting the motion—meaning Mother Earth accepts the motion away from land—the storm will then move away from land, according to the way Robert has been taught to do this.

Now, I want you to understand something: Such compatibility exists because compassion exists. Why do you think you have compassion for each other? And why do you think you are often learning how to have compassion for each other in new and different ways? Sometimes it is a simple thing that you understand, meaning something happens to somebody at work that has happened to you before, and you know exactly how that feels, and you tell your workmate: "Oh *yes*, I've been there before; here, let me help you. This is what I did to resolve it." Or perhaps you just make a joke about it, and the two of you have a little laugh and then go on and try to fix the problem. That happens all the time.

But more importantly, things happen in families and between couples and between friends that are always triggering compassion in one or the other parties. This is not only done to unite you and bring you closer; it is also done because it is pointing the way. You see, these moments are pointing the way to resolution. Resolution on a compassionate level—and on a compatibility level, all right, but on a compassionate level—is not always and only what *thinks* right in that moment. Sometimes it is what *feels* right in that moment.

Between people this is not always the case, because certain rules apply in society and between people, and sometimes, very often, these rules are a good thing, but not always. And history—not only of societies and the world, but also the history of families and your own history—tends to point that out. But what I'm talking about briefly today is the power of compassion as experienced in the moment of complete compatibility.

If Robert has the capacity to receive this training—which for him has taken many years but was and is possible—to actually physically cause a storm, which would otherwise hit land, to either move or in some cases occasionally dissipate . . . as time goes on, he's learning how to unwind the storm, as we call it, so that the rain still comes but the damaging winds don't, because sometimes you need that rain. As he learns this, I want you to understand that such compatibility can be used to resolve other things.

There are potentials in the resolution of certain illnesses, though more work will need to be done on that. There are also possibilities through feelings and applied feelings of resolution, compassion and compatibility, to change other circumstances, some of which are complete conundrums for you in your modern times. One of these is pollution; another is radiation.

In My Time Religion Was about Honoring

I'm not saying that this can all be accomplished by working with feelings. What I am saying is that sometimes the combination of feelings, living prayer [see p. 245], benevolent magic, compatibility and compassion can all lead toward resolution, even though that resolution may seem to be completely physically impossible. How many of you have heard about or experienced yourself something that came about as a result of prayer?

In your time your organized religions are often based upon what human beings have written down, to the best of their ability, in order to create a society that is more benevolent. Many of your religions are based on these writings and accumulations of wisdom from many years ago, sometimes thousands of years ago. Often these writings and these religions are very helpful; sometimes they're not as helpful as you'd like them to be. But many of you have heard about or experienced a prayer being answered, and some of you have experienced it and not known it, because some wider conflict or great disaster was avoided because a prayer was answered, be it a religious prayer or be it a living prayer.

We use the term "benevolent magic" because it incorporates benevolent, loving beings—not by will, but by requesting volunteers—to come and help resolve a situation that human beings cannot resolve. It creates union and unity between human beings and benevolent, loving beings who can do things you cannot. That's what we did in our time.

In our time we did not have religion as you know it today, but we did have a profound connection with Creator and all of creation. We observed, we reacted, and those who were given the ability—who were born to it, you understand—or the opportunity or both were encouraged to study nature, to study human behavior, and were given many prayers and living prayers to change things. We didn't do disentanglement the way you do it in your time, but we did something similar. We didn't even do living prayer the way you do it in your time, but we did something similar.

When settlers came over from Spain and Europe, and found native peoples in what came to be the United States—also known as North America and by other terms—they found what they thought, based upon their budding technological and intellectual society and religious society, were backward savages. But that was partly because they didn't understand that the people were paying homage to the land in every way—the way they were dressed, the way they were acting, the way they appeared, the way they walked, talked, slept, dreamed, everything. And when you pay homage to the land and your fellow beings, plants and animals, as well as elements of the land (lightning, rain, thunder, all of these things), it's not a religious homage where you pray to them. It's rather that you acknowledge that they exist, pay some attention to how and why, and attempt to interact with them for the benefit of all beings.

You Narrow Your Horizons When You Come to Earth

These talks I'm giving these days are designed to encourage and help you to realize what is possible in your time. The generations coming up now, the young people, will be more open to this, because they've had to broaden their horizons from youth. Older people may have some difficulty in that, but you can also just recognize that the horizons you normally have when you are not here on Earth are very broad indeed; you narrow them specifically when you come here and are incarnated.

You specifically narrow your horizons so you can work on one or maybe two things that your soul cannot resolve anywhere but Earth in these times. Probably this means that you need to have some method or means to quickly learn things, a quick learning of soul needs—meaning issues one has to learn and absorb in a new way so as to apply wisdom that is learned by you, because of what works in your life. These kind of lessons are speedily learned on Earth. It may not seem quick to you, but compared to the length of your life on another planet or someplace where things are benevolent all the time, you can, on Earth, learn something very quickly.

And during or after your Earth life, when you go elsewhere, you continue existing . . . because life goes on, and I might add, it goes on with the same core personality you have. You drop most of your pain and discomforts, but you don't drop all of your motivations when you move on to other lives. That kind of focus into resolution and sometimes application in Earth life is then applied to the broad spectrum of your other lives as time goes on. And it is very expanding.

Benevolent Magic, Living Prayer, Love-Heat and Disentanglement Help You to Resolve Problems on Earth

But you don't actually learn compatibility and compassion and all of that on Earth; you just remember it in these times, because now you are being presented—as a society as well as, as an individual—with problems that are frequently and seemingly impossible to resolve on your own, and sometimes impossible to resolve even in large groups or from society to society. That's when you need to use benevolent magic and living prayer, which invites loving beings of light creators and so on, as well as the Creator of this universe, to resolve it for you in very specific ways.

Prayer alone in the religious sense, although it helps, can be greatly amplified by learning forms of benevolent magic and living prayer. That's why Zoosh and Isis and myself and other beings through Robert have been talking to you about this for a long time, because those problems that you need to resolve will need to be resolved—if not completely, then at least you will need to *begin* to resolve them soon. I know you can do it, or I wouldn't be talking to you about this now. And Robert is willing . . . [chuckles] he is a little shy, but Robert is willing to expose a little more of what he can do these days to you so that you can appreciate what can be done.

That's why we've given homework in the past—the same homework we've given Robert before—the love-heat/heart-warmth/physical-warmth experience as we've come to call it, upon which a whole level of teaching is based, to encourage you to have more ways to make decisions using the feeling in your physical self in order to know what is best for you in that moment: who to go with, when to go, where to go, what to do, what to wear [for the love-heat exercise, see Overview]. This is not an authoritarian thing, though sometimes other people's opinions are very helpful. This, rather, is a means within you on the physical, feeling level, that warmth that you feel—sometimes on one side of your chest, sometimes on the other, sometimes in your solar plexus region or in your abdomen. This is a warmth that you feel to experience loving yourself.

When you love yourself, you are necessarily loving Creator. Creator and Mother Earth and all beings are completely united; they know that. But sometimes on Earth as a human being, it's easy to forget. Just know that all beings have feelings, and all beings everywhere have that feeling of warmth that you can trigger or find in yourself by using that love-heat exercise.

Now, you have also received instructions on disentanglement [see p. xxxi]. All of these things are intended to give you tools by which you can learn and be supported in learning so that you can do good for yourself and others. It is also a way to connect you, to give you a way to physically connect in a benevolent way for all beings with people all over the Earth, sometimes whom you meet and who will be trying to communicate with you. It can be used as a universal language; I will explain more on that some other time.

When You Meet ETs, You Can Greet Them with the Love-Heat

Most importantly, though, given the nature of space exploration—which many private companies, to say nothing of governments, are becoming more involved in these days—it's just a matter of time before the general public learns about contacts with extraterrestrials. And it would be really good, to say nothing of necessary [laughs], to have all astronauts know how to be able to do the love-heat, so that when you meet extraterrestrials, then that would be your greeting.

The ETs will know that greeting, and if you have the appropriate response from them . . . and the appropriate response would be this—we'll tell you exactly. The level of heat you normally feel as an individual, if that heat suddenly becomes much more so, then the extraterrestrial you are attempting to interact with will be feeling its own form of love-heat, and the two of you will feel more than each of you normally feels for yourself. And I might add that this greater love-heat will simply go out and be absorbed as nurturing, loving energy by any or all beings or existences that need it. So it works very well.

I haven't spoken in print about this before, but I'm putting it out now because there is a great deal of knowledge and wisdom I want to talk to you about, and this is part of it. I want you to understand it and appreciate its value, and to know that what we have taught Robert about this in the past as instinctual work is something I'm going to speak much more about. And I'm speaking about it now in the form of meeting an extraterrestrial.

So learn how to do the love-heat, if you can. It supports and nurtures you when you're doing that warmth; it tends to shove things out of your body that aren't you. Sometimes you take on other people's issues unconsciously, and then you don't realize it because it's a feeling and you try to process it. But since it is not yours, you can't really process it very well, and it just creates confusion. For those of you who feel confused a lot, this might be going on for you. So do the love-heat; it will tend to shove that right out of you and leave in you only what is nurturing, loving and helpful. I'm not claiming that this is a cure-all, but it can be very nurturing and very comforting.

This Is a New Way to Live

I'm going to finish with this: Many of you have been looking for a new way to live that allows you to do the greatest good for yourself and others, and also to do the greatest good for people and beings whom you may never even meet—which is often the case on the conscious level, but on the unconscious level, you meet these beings all the time. And very often it is exactly those meetings on this benevolent level (not just unconscious in the psychological sense, but on the soul level), it is your union with all beings (other human beings, yes, but animals, plants, planets, universes), it is that connection that will keep you going.

Very often at times when you thought you just couldn't do it anymore, after a good night's sleep or even a nap, because you feel that union, that bond, that love which is the foundation of all existence . . . the means to tap into that, to make it work for you and to help others in the process, is to know how to communicate with it using your feelings in benevolent ways. That's why we're trying to teach you exactly how to do that. I will say more soon in another article and give you more instruction on what you can do with instinct, if you know how to use it. It's all based on that love-heat, and it can support and help you to make decisions that are sometimes simple and day-to-day and other times more profound. I will be happy to do that.

But to give you a little sample, imagine . . . sometimes you want to wear a certain outfit, and other times you're just used to wearing the same thing. Maybe they're all the same color shirts, or maybe the same color pants or shoes. But do you know that they're all made up of living matter? And when you know how to point . . . there is a certain way to point, believe it or not, to certain shirts or certain garments or shoes. Then you will wear those garments or shoes, which are made up of living matter, living beings, that would be most happy to be on your body on that day and which feel most compatible with you in that moment.

This may seem like a small thing, but you'd be surprised how it all adds up to support a quality of life for you that most of you are striving for. That is a small example, but as you know, many greater things are built on little things, and that is how worlds, cultures, societies and universes are created. Good life.

Our Cultural Heritage from the Stars

Speaks of Many Truths
June 25, 2001

Does the growth of bone and calluses we see with corns represent the potential for or the latent suggestion of another toe or an appendage of some kind?

You are asking something important here, and I would say, oh yes!

A Sixth Appendage on the Foot

The human foot in my time is perhaps a little bit more natural—meaning to be seen in its natural state, since surgery as you know it in your time, having to do with cutting and removal, is not largely known. So what are called birth defects in your time are allowed to simply be seen and noticed. For myself in my lifetime, I saw quite a few of these. Usually I saw a sixth toe show itself just to the right of what you call the little toe. Most of the time it was small, but I have seen on occasion toes that were quite long, and on one occasion I heard about a toe to the right of that little toe that was about as long as, counting from the left over, the fourth toe. Corns are usually seen on one side or the other of the foot, but sometimes the left side also has an appendage. That was the one I was most interested in.

I did see an appendage that did not look like a toe but which looked like something . . . it was elongated, meaning that it was a corn. It came out, but it did not have the flexible aspects that one would associate with a toe: no means to grasp, no means to grip. But the bone appendage and the tissues callused around it gave the individual the potential of leaning forward in a different way.

This person went on in life—according to what I heard, since this person was in another village a few miles away at one point in my life—to be the hill climber, the one who could run up the side of the hill and look off into the distance. As his eyesight grew a little poor—he could see up close pretty well but not far away—he could still run up the hill on the basis of feeling, and he would usually carry one of the younger people on his shoulders up to the top of the hill who would observe quite striking distances. So they made a good team for a while—that's what I heard. They were impressive, what I think you call a lookout. I heard that the youngster who had unusually good vision could see details that one does not normally see with even the best vision that I have experienced or heard of.

This Is a Remnant of Our Extraterrestrial Origins

But not to wander too far from your question, one might reasonably wonder where this kind of thing occurs. Where do these other toes come from? Where does this appendage that grows out of what you call a corn come from? I believe, after talking it over with my fellow mystical men and women, and in discussing it with elders (not only of my people, but elders from other places), that it has to do with a remnant of our extraterrestrial origins. On two occasions, I have seen footprints of beings I knew were not human because the footprints were too big. A footprint in one circumstance clearly showed six toes, and on another occasion, the footprint clearly showed something that looked like that appendage I discussed before that came out of the side of the person's foot—like what you call a corn, but it came out farther than a corn.

I knew this footprint was not human because of the curious shape of the foot—there were six toelike marks. That was the footprint I saw, and it tends to support your idea of six toes as we discussed. Now, I'm pretty sure that that was the footprint of an extraterrestrial, because I noticed it . . . it was pointed out to me by a mystical woman in another encampment of people nearby—not my people, but people I had met many times (I have a student amongst them). They travel, but I see them maybe twice a year, occasionally three times, and the mystical woman whom I spoke to (who is not my student but who does advise my student) pointed this out to me and said that they had a vehicle from the sky land and these people got out.

This footprint, when I looked at it, was unusually small. At first I thought it was the footprint of a child, but the mystical woman assured me that the beings did not act like children. They were quite tall; they just had very small feet. If I had to say in terms of length, the footprint to me looked like the footprint of about a three-year-old child, but she seemed to feel that they were adults in their manner and composure, as well as in their wisdom. It was not unusual in my time for such vehicles to land and for the occupants to get out and talk with the people who were present—Earth dwellers such as myself. I had occasions like this at other times, and I believe I've discussed them.

But the thing I was the most interested in was the clear appearance of the foot and how it was designed for balance. When you consider that the beings were very tall and they had such small feet, you would have to say that the shape of the footprint would suggest that the toes were well arched—the marks from the toes would suggest that the toes were well arched. There was no direct line from the main body of the foot to the toe mark. I'd have to say that the foot seemed to be arranged—not having seen the foot myself, of course—in such a way as to create the best possible balance for someone tall, given the small size of the footprint.

We Come to Earth Handicapped

So my feeling is that even though this footprint does not remind me of a human footprint very much, it does suggest that there are beings living on other planets for whom six toes are normal. I'd often wondered, when looking at my own hand and the hands and feet of others, why we have only five toes. If you think about it, in order to have really good balance, one has to be especially well developed. Good balance physically does not come about naturally, which is why little children fall over so much. They have to learn how to walk, and developing some athleticism helps.

But imagine for a moment, if you would, with the human foot, another toe coming out to the left (in the case of the right foot) or to the right (in the case of the left foot) of the big toe. Think how much that would improve the balance. I have discussed this many times with other mystical people, and we all agree that it would improve the balance so much that a child could probably walk much more easily. And because it feels so natural to me, I find the appearance of what are called corns to be fascinating.

I have asked my guides and teachers many times where people come from who have these six-toed prints and if human beings in our form have ever had six toes, and all of my guides and teachers have always said that it is natural for the human shape, as we are now, to have six toes. So, of course, I would always say, "Why don't we?" And the answer was always something along these lines, and that's that if we had all of our normal abilities, we could survive much more easily on Earth, and Earth was always intended to be a challenge. If Earth was a challenge, which it is, as you know, we would be forced as individuals to reach beyond our normal capacities—meaning what we had learned in other lives—in order to survive here.

So it is as if everyone is born handicapped. That's why in your time when you call some people handicapped, it makes me smile a little bit—not because I think less of those who are handicapped, but because of the wisdom that has been shared with me that for a human being on Earth, being handicapped is normal. Some are handicapped more, and that is much more challenging. But all human beings are handicapped by not having their sixth toe.

Further, my teachers explained something that truly surprised me when I first heard it and then made complete sense (and I know you can identify with that feeling), and that's that the sixth toe also represents something more than improved physical balance. It is the portion of the physical self that supports and maintains spiritual and mental balance as well. Some of you do not know about the system in which fingers and toes and parts of the body—arms, legs and even different parts of different organs such as ears—represent or have attunements to other parts of the body. (I believe much of this has been explored by those who are involved in many of the physical healing skills associated with Ayurvedic medicine and other forms of doctoring that have been developed and practiced in the East.)

Yet if you think about it, certain things are missing—most importantly, this large appendage of the missing sixth toe. That level of balance, where we would not only be able to walk about easier . . . but if we had that level of balance stimulated mentally and spiritually, the chances are we would tend to perpetuate our natural order—meaning the balance that we achieve as extraterrestrial beings living and existing in harmony on other worlds. And while that is, of course, desirable and is our natural way, it is not, in fact, what is expected or required of us here.

As you all know, Earth is a school. We are expected to rise to the occasion of the challenge here; to reinvent potentials, possibilities and realities; to create new things; to adapt to necessary changes; and to develop skills and abilities sometimes forced upon us and other times sought out by us. As a result, in order to expedite and improve the search for such new skills and abilities, a certain level of transformation in the natural form of the human shape was adapted to Earth people, according to my teachers, so that we would necessarily and naturally gravitate toward solutions based upon the incompletion of our natural form.

Just as portions of our natural brain are not present and portions of our natural nervous system that exist in our human bodies on other planets are not present, so it is with this sixth toe that isn't present, even though the echo of its presence is sometimes seen, felt and heard by various members of Earth's human population and occasionally by those like myself who are fortunate enough to see the tracks of beings from other planets. That echo is a gentle reminder, when one sees a six-toed footprint, that the natural state of being is six toes.

Embrace Human Differences

So if we think about ourselves as being unusual and different in general from the humanoid population of planets, we might more easily be able to embrace the differences from group to group of human beings on Earth. Many times I have thought about those differences. It is like variety; to me it is a joyous variety. But in your time, because there are so many people and so many different philosophies that compete with one another, sometimes the different appearances of people and the different cultures and languages can be alarming and threatening.

But if you understand that all of these differences are designed to encourage us to re-create reality and to offer options to ourselves in other lives on other planets, as well as to other beings on other planets, then you will recognize that the true nature of the human being is to be an explorer. And the perhaps admirable trait of souls who accept and embrace birth on Mother Earth, allowing themselves to be born in these unusual adaptations of human bodies, is that they deserve and provide for one another what is needed—and that is that we need to honor each other and we need to honor other beings.

It is in our nature to adapt. I believe it is in our nature, because even within our mothers, as we are forming into Earth-human bodies, those Earth-human bodies are an adaptation from our natural state. I believe that this adaptation shows, from time to time, such anomalies as almost six toes and the occasional actual six toes to remind us of our cultural heritage from the stars.

Disentanglement and the Dance of Life

Speaks of Many Truths
July 30, 2001

All right, this is Speaks of Many Truths. Greetings.

As I do disentanglement, I've noticed that most of the people who have caused strong reactions in me are dead. How does that work? Do they hang the other end of the cord up on the veil when they go out? Can you talk about that? [For the disentanglement exercise, see p. xxxi.]

Don't Dissect Benevolent Magic to See How It Works

Explaining how it works will not help people with disentanglement; as a matter of fact, it might deter them. There are times when I don't explain things on purpose, because the more your mind becomes engaged with the process . . . if you think you know what the lightbeings are doing, you're going to try and follow them and watch them do what they're doing. But in the process of watching them to see what they're doing, to the extent that you can do that or that they allow you to do that, you are going to take in everything you watch—meaning that you're going to not only undo what they are doing as they are doing it, but you're going to create complications in their wake.

Say they're going in a specific direction and you're watching them and thinking about it—because you can't watch and not think about it. You will be thinking about it, and every time they do something, you're going to be thinking it. And even if you're thinking nothing . . . just anything, whatever you're thinking, when your thought process is working, the more your thought process is working, the more it complicates what they are doing. They can work through your thought process, but I think that the less you know, the better.

You understand, if you dissect magic—true magic, benevolent magic—if you take it apart and say, "This is how it works," step by step by step, it won't work anymore. Taking it apart and dissecting it is really the worst thing you can do.

You Have Lost Awareness of the Dance of Life

The point of disentanglement is not only to feel better and to be resolved, but to also understand how beings of their own nature, of their own existence, enjoy helping other beings. Your natural existence on Earth is artificial, yes, because the way you live, even in the very best way, means that you are still primarily experiencing individuality first—separation to a lesser degree, but that's there too. So as a result, when you experience those things, it necessarily divorces you on the mental level from how other beings are constantly helping you.

So the dance of life, where everything is intertwined, becomes less and less in your conscious awareness. It goes maybe into your unconscious or your subconscious, but you don't think about it consciously. And although that may be acceptable in some cases, in these times now especially, people need to be reminded of just how compatible all life can be and how when you are divorced from that compatibility in your conscious mind, you can very easily justify or authorize or command that you or others do things that are totally incompatible with the natural intertwining and flow of life.

You breathe oxygen, and trees exhale it—that's just a simple example. And yet if you look at trees as products, as forest products [chuckles]—that's just a way of making a tree a lesser being, to call it a product—it's as if you were literally taking the oxygen out of your own mouths or out of the mouths of your children. You say, "Well, look at all these trees! It can't hurt to take down one or two; we can use the wood." I'm not saying that you should do this or you should do that. What I am saying is that the less you are aware of the intertwining of life and how it naturally helps one and all, the less you help yourself.

You exhale carbon dioxide, and the tree breathes that in. It's a circle. The less you are aware of that on a moment-to-moment basis—not just intellectually aware, but actually aware of it as part of your life, the dance of life—the easier it is to either forget or to simply take action that you feel is a priority for whatever reason (whether it's justifiable or not) which is incompatible with that dance of life: "Oh, this animal is in the way; let's just get rid of it." You may not see how that animal helps you; it may not be direct in your mind. But there's no animal on Earth who doesn't help you in some way. I grant that you can give me an argument on that, but that's how I see it.

Disentanglement Reminds You of the Natural Rhythm of Life

So the ultimate point of disentanglement, from my perspective, is not just to help you to feel better, not just to disentangle you from discomforts and complications that you do not realize you are still reacting to . . . as in what you said before: long after the people are dead and gone, you're still interacting with their impact on you in your life. You're not interacting with their souls anymore, but the fact that you're still doing that is the reality. The more you understand how the gold lightbeings actually perform the disentanglement of every single thread, the more likely you are going to try to do it intellectually when it cannot be accomplished intellectually, or you're going to think about it while they're doing it, which will interfere.

You can think all day long or for the rest of your life about how you can perform the biological function of a tree, which serves human beings. It's not an accident that trees exhale oxygen; it's not capricious. It's something created by Creator: "How can we put these beings together who are completely compatible? Well, let's pick these beings and not these beings." It's not an accident that you don't have trees on this planet [chuckles] that exhale some toxic fume to you; it's all part of a plan. So from my point of view, the ultimate purpose of disentanglement right now is to remind people of the natural rhythm of life, which is essentially cooperative, one life form to another.

You Can't Disentangle a Past Life

Are unfulfilled or unresolved issues from past lives somehow affecting our present life? Are we releasing those cords also?

It is not a direct cord and it's not necessarily a past life. But you might have something that you didn't get in a past life or some other life, and your soul always needs to be in balance. So you didn't get something, you didn't resolve something, and you have an opportunity to resolve that in the life you now are in. And because you have that opportunity, then you might say that you will set up circumstances to create resolution of that thing that did not get resolved before.

But does the disentanglement create disentanglement for that past life? No. It will affect only this life. Each life is its own experience, and for you to say . . . it would be almost like you saying your request to gold lightbeings, but instead of saying, "Please disentangle me," it would be almost like you saying, "And please disentangle that person over there." [Chuckles.] You wouldn't do that. The gold lightbeings wouldn't do it, for starters, because the person isn't asking, and you wouldn't do that because that's not the way you're instructed. But saying that for a past life would be almost the same thing. So, no, they don't disentangle the past life.

Disentangle from Physical Objects

Is there anything more that you want to say about disentanglement to the people who read this and who are doing it?

When they go through their list of people and they have completed it—we've been putting this out long enough that some people will be close to completing if not have completed their list—then there is something you can go on to after that. This is a short-term homework assignment, but it's kind of interesting. What I'd recommend is that you ask that you be disentangled from all of the physical objects in the room in which you sleep. Take one object per night. Use the same testing methods you did with the people—meaning that after a few days of disentanglement, you say their name, and if you feel calm . . . if you say their name and you don't feel calm, then you need to continue saying their name in the disentanglement.

In the case of the object, say you looked around the room and said before you went to sleep, "Please disentangle me from this crystal or from this stove or from this bed"—in short, one or two things per night. Do that throughout your house, first starting with your bedroom where you sleep, and then do it with pets, for instance. I'm not going to cover pets and children, because that has come up previously in your disentanglement. But if it hasn't come up, then do it with pets or children or farm animals.

Remember, you're not disentangling from them because you don't love them, and you're not disentangling from them because you want to distance them in your life. You're disentangling from them because there may be stress between the two of you that you don't recognize anymore, because it's become part of the established feeling that you have with this person and you don't understand that it's based on an underlying stress. So if you haven't asked about family members or pets, do that. And as I say, do the objects—for example, the couch.

Do it on a progression. Start with your bedroom and pets and so on, and then do it with the other objects in your house. If you have books, you don't have to do one book at a time—just say, ". . . the books I have in this house," like that. But if it's a couch, you could say, ". . . the couch in the living room," for instance—you might have more than one couch. But it might be helpful, especially—this is vitally important—if you have used furniture, if other people had the furniture before you did or maybe you inherited it from friends or relatives.

Or bought it in an antique store or something?

That's right, perhaps it was an antique or something like that. That's especially important. So in those cases, do those things one at a time—meaning, don't say, ". . . all my couches," okay? And generally speaking, with an object that large, for which there are many parts that came from many places—there might be wood, there might be metal, there might be fabric; in short, lots of stuff from lots of places—you're going to do one couch per night.

Also do the walls of the home. In short, you could say, ". . . the building materials," but I don't recommend that. I recommend you say, for instance, ". . . the wood in my home or my apartment." Or you could say, ". . . the stone," meaning the masonry, or ". . . the metal," meaning the nails, for instance—like that. You don't have to say, ". . . the nails"; you can just say, ". . . the metal," or something like that. That will hold you for a while.

Now, you might reasonably ask, "Why?" It's because when you are disentangled and clear with all of the objects in your home, your stress level will drop another big chunk. Most people do not realize that their stress level is as high as it is because they are used to a certain level of discomfort in their lives that they don't recognize as discomfort anymore. But once you've cleared your environment and you've gone through all the objects in your home and cleared and disentangled from all of those, then from time to time, maybe once a week, after you've done all that, you can say in your disentanglement, "Please disentangle me from all the objects and pets and so on in my home." You can do it en masse once you've done it individually. That will hold you for a while.

That's enough for now, because for most people, that's quite a bit. For most people, that will take many months.

Disentangling Your Work Space

So we don't want to mention the office, then?

If you want to, after you've done all of that, which might take you quite a few months . . . we're talking about your home—think of all the objects you have in your home. There's a vast amount in most people's homes; it might take you a year. If your home is, perhaps, more simple or smaller and you don't have that many things, then you can start your disentanglement with the place where you work.

Perhaps you work at an office or a factory. Or perhaps you have your own business that causes you to travel around from place to place—then you can apply it that way. You can even, for instance, if you're on a plane, relax and close your eyes, put your hand over your mouth and quietly whisper to yourself (given the ambient noise on a plane, no one's likely to hear you) to be disentangled from the plane.

Now, the beings may not be able to disentangle you from every last aspect. You might say, "Please disentangle me from the plane and all the people on the plane"—that's two things. They may not be able to do all of that. But then you relax for a moment—twenty minutes, thirty minutes. You can relax while the beings are doing it. Do your basic disentanglement, and it should be all right. Make sure you do that after they've come around with the drink cart and all of that, and after you've said, "Hello," and "How are you?" to your neighbor. It's very easy to do this. I'm not saying you should do it; I'm saying you can if you want to, especially if you're a commercial traveler and you're always in planes, trains, cars or things like that.

But, yes, feel free to do it if you work in an office with your computer, your cubicle, your desk, your chair, and then other parts of the office. When you get this far, you'll have a pretty good idea what works for you. Some people will be able to say, ". . . all the desks in the office," other people will have to go one desk at a time, and there will be many variables in between. Try—you'll know how. You'll know whether you can say, ". . . my desk," or ". . . my workmate's desk next to me," and so on.

How will you know whether you can say one desk at a time or many desks or all the desks? How will you know? You will know on the basis of how you physically feel. Remember, in disentanglement you and your physical body are complete and total partners. You are anyway, but you are getting used to being a partner with your physical body when doing disentanglement. Yes, lightbeings are involved, but you're also learning how to interpret the signals from your physical body to know what works for you. So if you say, in this example here, ". . . all the desks of all my coworkers," and you get an uncomfortable feeling, then you can't say that. If, on the other hand, you say, ". . . my desk," and it feels okay, then fine. If you say, ". . . my desks and all the desks of the people in my unit," and it feels okay, fine.

If you say, ". . . my desk, all the desks of the people in my unit and all the rest of the people in my office"—maybe you're in a big office space; maybe you work for a newspaper or something—and you get an uncomfortable feeling, then you know you've taken it too far. Back off one. You might want to think it first, before you say it, because if you have to back off a notch from all the desks to just the desks of the people in the unit or ". . . my own desk," then you have to stop, wait a few moments—probably at least a minute—and say the whole thing over again, saying, "Pardon me," or "I need to say this over again." If you make mistakes with your disentanglement, you can't say, "Oh," and then just go and say, "Okay, just my desk." You can't do that. You have to go back to the beginning and say everything over again, but you have to wait for a time—a minute, two minutes—and then go back through it and say it all.

Disentangling from Previous Homes and Antiques

What about houses that you've lived in before? Let's say a child had a trauma or a woman got divorced. How do you go back to those houses?

You don't have to go back to the houses, but you do have to remember . . . obviously, you would have already done your people list, but you do remember the house. Try to remember the objects that were around. Maybe something will jump out in your mind, like the print on the fabric of the couch, for instance, which is sometimes retained in your memory. If you can't remember what the objects in the house looked like, then you can say, ". . . the objects in the room," or ". . . the furniture in the room where this unsettling thing happened," or "terrible thing happened," or whatever words you use to qualify it.

But if you can remember them, then do that thing where you say, ". . . the bed," ". . . the kitchen table," something like that—do that one thing at a time. And then also do the house the same way, but from a distance, because those objects might have some of your residual fear or terror or upset still in them, and it's not impossible—even for some of you who are well on in years—that even if that furniture isn't in that house anymore, that it's somewhere and somebody might be using it and some of your energy is attached to it. So it would be good to clear it, for your own sake as well as for the sake of whoever is using it.

So in the case of . . . let's say a person likes antiques. You're saying that she could be living in a house with energy that she doesn't even realize is disturbing her?

Yes, that's right. But you don't have to ask for spirit beings to come in and clear the objects. You can, of course, to the extent that you can do this with antiques—you might spray rose water in the general environment, but not on the antique. Some people like to do that. I think that's an old formula, a Cayce formula or something like that. You might smudge the objects, if you can do that. But, of course, you obviously can't do that with draperies or fabrics, for antiques and so on. But what you can do is . . . you don't necessarily have to disentangle those objects from whatever people did on them. Whether Ben Franklin signed the Constitution or the Declaration of Independence on that table, you don't necessarily have to eliminate Ben's energy. What you need to do is simply disentangle yourself from that object so that you do not have an engagement with that energy.

You might still, after that point, from time to time look at the table, for instance. Say the table was used for some coercive act; someone was threatened at the table or hurt or injured in some way. You look at the table, you feel uncomfortable, so you do your disentanglement on it that night, and you keep doing it every other night. You keep it in your disentanglement until you can look at the table and feel okay. Then maybe time goes on, your life goes on, and you still have the table around. One day you glance at the table and you feel kind of uncomfortable, so you put it back in your disentanglement for a time.

The More You Grow, the More Vast Disentanglement Becomes

After you've disentangled from the people, maybe after a time (a year or two goes by), you think of one of those people and something uncomfortable is there. You put that person back into your disentanglement for a while until that discomfort isn't there anymore, which tells you that something's happened. Most likely, especially if you're a conscious person doing things like this, you will have grown. But then at some point, you grow, and as you're growing, you're doing your disentanglement and you suddenly notice that with someone or something that used to feel okay, now you get a slightly uncomfortable feeling. It probably won't be profoundly uncomfortable, because you've already done your disentanglement. But you've grown; you're somewhere else on your chart of yourself.

Is it because you're more sensitive?

You may be more sensitive, but more likely it's not sensitivity at all. It's simply that when you grow . . . what happens? You get bigger, you expand, you cover more territory—and I'm not talking about physically—you access more. The tiny things in you, then, also expand; they become more. The teensy-weensy things that you didn't feel before, you now feel more—but that's good—so that you can then become aware of them and disentangle from them or do other things that you are doing and resolve them. So, in short, you do your disentanglement again, only this time, since you've grown, it's more vast, it covers more things, and on down the line. By the time your growth goes on, the arc of disentanglement is like this: you go on, it gets bigger; you go on, it gets *bigger*. So the more you grow and the more things like that that happen, your disentanglement becomes more vast, more effective, more thorough.

See, we're getting somewhere. We're doing it. [Chuckles.] It's not necessarily what you had in mind at first, but that's how the process works, eh? We go on, we do this, we do that. We chat, remind each other of our relationship, and then we get there.

Disentanglement Will Free You

Now that you've read these further details about disentanglement, I want you to understand that disentanglement is not a process designed to enslave you to a method or a dogma but rather to free you up. When you are more free of these things that are creating stress and conflict and, generally speaking, discomfort in your life, you will find that not only will you be able to do more things in a way that feels more compatible and comfortable for you, but more to the point, for those of you who have specific interests or are developing certain skills or are focused on certain ways of being, you will more comfortably, to yourself, be able to expand more, do more, act more, learn more, apply more—in short, be more with that activity than you have before. Not only will the stress level be greatly reduced or eliminated, but more of you will be present and available to act upon your goals, priorities and ultimate ideals.

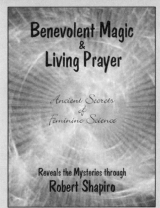
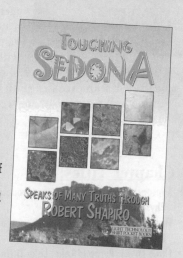
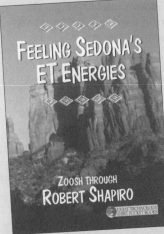

SHAMANIC SECRETS for PHYSICAL MASTERY

The purpose of this book is to allow you to understand the sacred nature of your own physical body and some of the magnificent gifts it offers you. When you work with your physical body in these new ways, you will discover not only its sacredness, but how it is compatible with Mother Earth, the animals, the plants, even the nearby planets, all of which you now recognize as being sacred in nature.

It is important to feel the value of yourself physically before you can have any lasting physical impact on the world. The less you think of yourself physically, the less likely your physical impact on the world will be sustained by Mother Earth. If a physical energy does not feel good about itself, it will usually be resolved; other physical or spiritual energies will dissolve it because it is unnatural. The better you feel about your physical self when you do the work in the previous book as well as in this one and the one to follow, the greater and more lasting will be the benevolent effect on your life, on the lives of those around you and ultimately on your planet and universe.

25^{00} SOFTCOVER 544 P.
ISBN 1-891824-29-5

Chapter Titles:

- Cellular Clearing of Traumas and Unresolved Events
- Feeling is Our Body's First and Primary Language
- The Resolution of Fear, Trauma and Hate
- Dealing with Fear, Pain and Addiction
- Shame, Arrogance, Safety and the Inability to Trust
- The Role of Trauma in Human Life
- Letting Go of Old Attitudes and Inviting New Energy
- The Waning of Individuality
- Clearing the Physical Body
- Using the Gestures to Protect, Clear and Charge
- The Flow of Energy
- Connecting with the Earth
- Communication of the Heart

- More Supportive Gestures
- Sleeping and Dreamtime
- Responsibility and Living prayer
- Communicating with the Natural World
- Life Lessons and the Vital Life Force
- The Sacrament of Food
- Working with the Elements
- Communication with Those Who Would Follow
- Elemental Connections
- Taking Responsibility
- Creating Personal Relationships

THE EXPLORER RACE SERIES

ZOOSH AND HIS FRIENDS THROUGH ROBERT SHAPIRO

THE SERIES: Humans—creators-in-training—have a purpose and destiny so heartwarmingly, profoundly glorious that it is almost unbelievable from our present dimensional perspective. Humans are great lightbeings from beyond this creation, gaining experience in dense physicality. This truth about the great human genetic experiment of the Explorer Race and the mechanics of creation is being revealed for the first time by Zoosh and his friends through superchannel Robert Shapiro. These books read like adventure stories as we follow the clues from this creation that we live in out to the Council of Creators and beyond.

❶ THE EXPLORER RACE

You individuals reading this are truly a result of the genetic experiment on Earth. You are beings who uphold the principles of the Explorer Race. The information in this book is designed to show you who you are and give you an evolutionary understanding of your past that will help you now. The key to empowerment in these days is to not know everything about your past, but to know what will help you now. Your number-one function right now is your status of Creator apprentice, which you have achieved through years and lifetimes of sweat. You are constantly being given responsibilities by the Creator that would normally be things that Creator would do. The responsibility and the destiny of the Explorer Race is not only to explore, but to create. 574 P. $25.00 ISBN 0-929385-38-1

❷ ETs and the EXPLORER RACE

In this book, Robert channels Joopah, a Zeta Reticulan now in the ninth dimension who continues the story of the great experiment—the Explorer Race—from the perspective of his civilization. The Zetas would have been humanity's future selves had not humanity re-created the past and changed the future. 237 P. $14.95 ISBN 0-929385-79-9

❸ EXPLORER RACE: ORIGINS and the NEXT 50 YEARS

This volume has so much information about who we are and where we came from—the source of male and female beings, the war of the sexes, the beginning of the linear mind, feelings, the origin of souls—it is a treasure trove. In addition, there is a section that relates to our near future—how the rise of global corporations and politics affects our future, how to use benevolent magic as a force of creation and how we will go out to the stars and affect other civilizations. Astounding information. 339 P. $14.95 ISBN 0-929385-95-0

❹ EXPLORER RACE: CREATORS and FRIENDS
The MECHANICS of CREATION

Now that you have a greater understanding of who you are in the larger sense, it is necessary to remind you of where you came from, the true magnificence of your being. You must understand that you are creators-in-training, and yet you were once a portion of Creator. One could certainly say, without being magnanimous, that you are still a portion of Creator, yet you are training for the individual responsibility of being a creator, to give your Creator a coffee break. This book will allow you to understand the vaster qualities and help you remember the nature of the desires that drive any creator, the responsibilities to which a creator must answer, the reaction a creator must have to consequences and the ultimate reward of any creator. 435 P. $19.95 ISBN 1-891824-01-5

❺ EXPLORER RACE: PARTICLE PERSONALITIES

All around you in every moment you are surrounded by the most magical and mystical beings. They are too small for you to see as single individuals, but in groups you know them as the physical matter of your daily life. Particles who might be considered either atoms or portions of atoms consciously view the vast spectrum of reality yet also have a sense of personal memory like your own linear memory. These particles remember where they have been and what they have done in their infinitely long lives. Some of the particles we hear from are Gold, Mountain Lion, Liquid Light, Uranium, the Great Pyramid's Capstone, This Orb's Boundary, Ice and Ninth-Dimensional Fire. 237 P. $14.95 ISBN 0-929385-97-7

❻ EXPLORER RACE and BEYOND

With a better idea of how creation works, we go back to the Creator's advisers and receive deeper and more profound explanations of the roots of the Explorer Race. The liquid Domain and the Double Diamond portal share lessons given to the roots on their way to meet the Creator of this universe, and finally the roots speak of their origins and their incomprehensibly long journey here. 360 P. $14.95 ISBN 1-891824-06-6

THE EXPLORER RACE SERIES

ZOOSH AND HIS FRIENDS THROUGH ROBERT SHAPIRO

❼ EXPLORER RACE: The COUNCIL of CREATORS

The thirteen core members of the Council of Creators discuss their adventures in coming to awareness of themselves and their journeys on the way to the Council on this level. They discuss the advice and oversight they offer to all creators, including the Creator of this local universe. These beings are wise, witty and joyous, and their stories of Love's Creation create an expansion of our concepts as we realize that we live in an expanded, multiple-level reality. 237 P. $14.95 ISBN 1-891824-13-9

❽ EXPLORER RACE and ISIS

This is an amazing book! It has priestess training, Shamanic training, Isis's adventures with Explorer Race beings—before Earth and on Earth—and an incredibly expanded explanation of the dynamics of the Explorer Race. Isis is the prototypal loving, nurturing, guiding feminine being, the focus of feminine energy. She has the ability to expand limited thinking without making people with limited beliefs feel uncomfortable. She is a fantastic storyteller, and all of her stories are teaching stories. If you care about who you are, why you are here, where you are going and what life is all about—pick up this book. You won't lay it down until you are through, and then you will want more. 317 P. $14.95 ISBN 1-891824-11-2

❾ EXPLORER RACE and JESUS

The core personality of that being known on the Earth as Jesus, along with his students and friends, describes with clarity and love his life and teaching two thousand years ago. He states that his teaching is for all people of all races in all countries. Jesus announces here for the first time that he and two others, Buddha and Mohammed, will return to Earth from their place of being in the near future, and a fourth being, a child already born now on Earth, will become a teacher and prepare humanity for their return. So heartwarming and interesting, you won't want to put it down. 354 P. $16.95 ISBN 1-891824-14-7

❿ EXPLORER RACE: Earth History and Lost Civilization

Speaks of Many Truths and Zoosh, through Robert Shapiro, explain that planet Earth, the only water planet in this solar system, is on loan from Sirius as a home and school for humanity, the Explorer Race. Earth's recorded history goes back only a few thousand years, its archaeological history a few thousand more. Now this book opens up as if a light was on in the darkness, and we see the incredible panorama of brave souls coming from other planets to settle on different parts of Earth. We watch the origins of tribal groups and the rise and fall of civilizations, and we can begin to understand the source of the wondrous diversity of plants, animals and humans that we enjoy here on beautiful Mother Earth. 310 P. $14.95 ISBN 1-891824-20-1

⓫ EXPLORER RACE: ET VISITORS SPEAK

Even as you are searching the sky for extraterrestrials and their spaceships, ETs are here on planet Earth—they are stranded, visiting, exploring, studying the culture, healing the Earth of trauma brought on by irresponsible mining or researching the history of Christianity over the past two thousand years. Some are in human guise, and some are in spirit form. Some look like what we call animals as they come from the species' home planet and interact with their fellow beings—those beings that we have labeled cats or cows or elephants. Some are brilliant cosmic mathematicians with a sense of humor; they are presently living here as penguins. Some are fledgling diplomats training for future postings on Earth when we have ET embassies here. In this book, these fascinating beings share their thoughts, origins and purposes for being here. 350 P. $14.95 ISBN 1-891824-28-7

⓬ EXPLORER RACE: Techniques for GENERATING SAFETY

Wouldn't you like to generate safety so you could go wherever you need to go and do whatever you need to do in a benevolent, safe and loving way for yourself? Learn safety as a radiated environment that will allow you to gently take the step into the new timeline, into a benevolent future and away from a negative past. 208 P. $9.95 ISBN 1-891824-26-0

Phone: 928-526-1345 or 1-800-450-0985 • Fax: 928-714-1132 or 1-800-393-7017
. . . or use our online bookstore at www.lighttechnology.com

SHINING THE LIGHT SERIES

ZOOSH AND OTHERS THROUGH ROBERT SHAPIRO

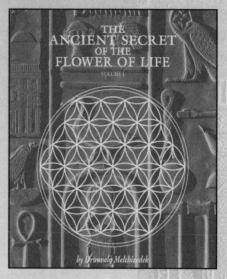
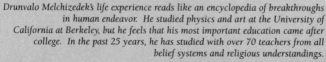

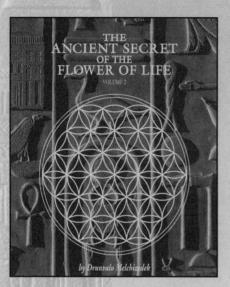

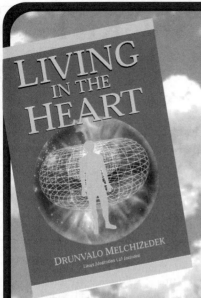

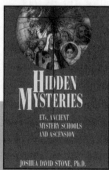
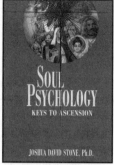
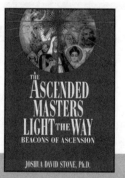

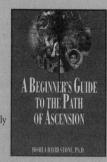

GOLDEN KEYS TO ASCENSION AND HEALING: REVELATIONS OF SAI BABA AND THE ASCENDED MASTERS

This book represents the wisdom of the ascended masters condensed into concise keys that serve as a spiritual guide. These 420 golden keys present the multitude of insights Dr. Stone has gleaned from his own background and his path to God realization.
ISBN 1-891824-03-1

MANUAL FOR PLANETARY LEADERSHIP

Here at last is an indispensible book that has been urgently needed in these uncertain times. It lays out the guidelines for leadership in the world and in one's life. It serves as a reference manual for moral and spiritual living.
ISBN 1-891824-05-8

YOUR ASCENSION MISSION: EMBRACING YOUR PUZZLE PIECE

This book shows how each person's puzzle piece is just as vital and necessary as any other. All aspects of living the fullest expression of your individuality.
ISBN 1-891824-09-0

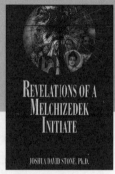

REVELATIONS OF A MELCHIZEDEK INITIATE

Dr. Stone's spiritual autobiography, beginning with his ascension initiation and progression into the 12th initiation. Filled with insight, tools and information.
ISBN 1-891824-10-4

HOW TO TEACH ASCENSION CLASSES

This book serves as an ideal foundation for teaching ascension classes and presenting workshops. It covers an entire one- to two-year program of classes.
ISBN 1-891824-15-5

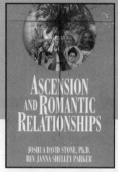

ASCENSION AND ROMANTIC RELATIONSHIPS

Dr. Stone has written a unique book about relationships from the perspective of the soul and monad rather than just the personality, presenting a broad picture of the common traps in romantic relationships and offering deep advice.
ISBN 1-891824-16-3

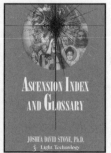

ASCENSION INDEX AND GLOSSARY

Ascension names and ascended master terms glossary plus a complete index of all thirteen books.
ISBN 0-891824-18-X

HOW TO BE FINANCIALLY SUCCESSFUL: A SPIRITUAL PERSPECTIVE

As one of the most successful businessmen of the New Age movement, Dr. Stone has written an easily digestible book full of tools and advice for achieving prosperity. This book conveys esoteric secrets of the universe that, if mastered, can lead to maximum manifestation results.
ISBN 1-891824-55-4

SPECIAL OFFER!
All 15 Books $179⁹⁵
plus shipping